What Others

M000280975

Bleating Hearts:
The Hidden World of Animal Suffering

A staggering investigation into the ethics of animal exploitation around the world, *Bleating Hearts* pulls no punches as it examines the many ways humans use and abuse our fellow creatures. Hawthorne artfully travels to the darkest corners of animal suffering, bringing to light not only the disturbing truth about people's mistreatment of nonhumans, but what we can do about it. Eloquently written and thoroughly researched, this doesn't just belong on every animal advocate's bookshelf—it deserves to be discussed and shared. This is a brilliant, powerfully persuasive book that will inspire you to make a difference.
Ric O'Barry, founder of The Dolphin Project

If there is a place in your heart for animals, this is an important book for you to read. But it is also more than that. If you want to lift the veil of denial, so that you can make your life an effective statement of compassion, you'll find this book to be nothing less than extraordinary.
John Robbins, author of *The Food Revolution* and *Diet for a New America* and co-founder of the Food Revolution Network (foodrevolution.org)

In the face of information that might render us speechless, Mark Hawthorne is thorough and articulate. *Bleating Hearts* empowers us with ways to challenge what has been both normal and hidden, making this book a remarkable achievement of vision and voice.
Carol J. Adams, author of *The Sexual Politics of Meat*

I can't think of any recent book that so comprehensively covers animal issues and gets it so consistently right. If everyone read it,

amount of suffering in the world would be reduced considerably, for it would be impossible to read *Bleating Hearts* and not be moved toward the vegan way of life. His facts are incontrovertible, his arguments are convincing, his detailed analyses are persuasive. This is a powerful and wonderful book that I cannot recommend enough.
Jeffrey Moussaieff Masson, author of *When Elephants Weep: The Emotional Lives of Animals* and *The Face on Your Plate: The Truth About Food*

Mark Hawthorne's *Bleating Hearts* is a rare accomplishment. Both encyclopedic and incisive, it should be required reading for every consumer with a conscience. His penetrating overview of our often unthinking and always multifaceted exploitation of nonhuman animals reminds us how deeply invested material culture is in horrors that, by design, we are not supposed to see. Hawthorne sheds an uncompromising light not just on our poor treatment of farmed animals, but of *all* animals, including those we abuse for fashion, entertainment, recreation, and even art. In allowing the reality of the human-animal relationship to speak for itself, *Bleating Hearts* will fundamentally change the way you look not just at animals, but at the world we share with them.
James McWilliams, author of *Just Food: Where Locavores Get It Wrong and How We Can Truly Eat Responsibly* and *The Politics of the Pasture: How Two Oxen Sparked a National Discussion about Eating Animals*

Bleating Hearts is gut-wrenching and heartbreaking. It's also a shining beacon of hope that simply must be read by anyone who envisions a compassionate world. By unveiling the hidden atrocities committed against animals, Mark Hawthorne arms us with the most powerful tool for change: awareness. Once we know, we can't but act.
Colleen Patrick-Goudreau, bestselling author and creator of The 30-Day Vegan Challenge

An important, timely addition to unmasking the myth of the

"humane treatment" of nonhuman animals. Hawthorne's searing indictment is must reading for both those new to the animal rights movement and for seasoned animal rights activists.
Tom Regan, author of *The Case for Animal Rights* and *Empty Cages: Facing the Challenge of Animal Rights*

This book deserves to be widely read. Well-researched and eloquently written, it is a most comprehensive overview of the cowardly and brutal way humans treat animals the world over. *Bleating Hearts* requires some courage as many chapters make for harrowing reading. Thankfully, this book also offers hope and features many organizations and individuals that will inspire readers to stand up for the animals we share the planet with.
Hans Kriek, executive director of SAFE New Zealand

Please don't read this book if you want a happy ending. Mark Hawthorne's depth and research surrounding the fragility and lives of our animal kin exposes too many "secret shames," sees an inevitable self-reflection, and should be mandatory reading for us all. A Chinese saying encapsulates perhaps something we can all do to create the kinder world that so many species deserve: "To close your eyes will not ease another's pain." Open your eyes, read, reflect, react, and be part of the dramatic change this book demands.
Jill Robinson, MBE, founder of Animals Asia Foundation

Mark Hawthorne speaks with a deep knowledge and passion. It's a heady mix that suffuses you with a desire to change the world. The shocking tales of animal cruelty are hard to comprehend, and *Bleating Hearts* may well make you angry and indeed could spark an eternal hunger for justice in your soul. The world needs us to use the facts so well laid out before us in this poignant book, to call for a revolution in society's institutionalized blindness in its treatment of animals. An excellent book that will sway hearts and minds forever.
Juliet Gellatley, founder and director of Viva!

In *Bleating Hearts: The Hidden World of Animal Suffering*, Mark Hawthorne shines a desperately needed and penetrating light on the underbelly of the human-nonhuman animal relationship. Hawthorne has written this book to speak for the billions of animals who have no voice. It has taken a great deal of courage to bear witness to and then put into words the mindboggling amount of animal suffering that most of humanity chooses not to see. This is not an easy read, but it is a must-read. And, once you read this book, you will no longer be able to say: "I didn't know what was going on." And, moreover, once you know, I hope, I pray that you will take action.

Joyce Tischler, founder of the Animal Legal Defense Fund

Bleating Hearts is a gracefully written, authoritative account of our mistreatment of our nonhuman neighbors. Exhaustively researched and meticulously sourced, it exposes the entire panoply of suffering that we inflict on animals—suffering that the animal exploitation industries keep carefully hidden from our view. Written in a clear, straightforward style with no sensationalism or deliberate attempts to shock, Hawthorne's descriptions of animal abuse throughout our society command our attention by their very judiciousness. *Bleating Hearts* is among the most important animal rights books of the 21st century.

Norm Phelps, author of *The Longest Struggle: Animal Advocacy from Pythagoras to PETA* and *Changing the Game: Why the Battle for Animal Liberation Is So Hard and How We Can Win It*

Much as you might spin a desk globe, this book allows you to stop and put your finger on any of the many issues concerning animals in the world and look at it up close, especially those the public almost never hears about. Stories and statistics provide the reader with a clear view of the sometimes surprising issues that involve animals, and while each chapter will leave you informed, often aghast, they will no doubt motivate many to absent themselves from inadvertent participation in cruelty and, instead, adopt animal-friendly choices. A useful, accessible, riveting read.

Ingrid Newkirk, president and co-founder of People for the Ethical Treatment of Animals

If you're looking for a hard-hitting, up-to-date, and well-researched indictment against the animal exploitation industries, this is your book.

Jonathan Balcombe, PhD, Animal Studies Department Chair, Humane Society University

Bleating Hearts is a must-read for anyone who cares about animals, humanity, or justice. Providing a no-holds-barred look at our complex and all too often cruel and exploitive relationship with other animals, this book will forever change the way you look at what you eat and wear and how you entertain yourself. You will come away informed, moved, outraged, and inspired to take action.

Nathan Runkle, executive director of Mercy For Animals

Bleating Hearts

The Hidden World
of Animal Suffering

Bleating Hearts

The Hidden World
of Animal Suffering

Mark Hawthorne

CHANGE
MAKERS
BOOKS

Winchester, UK
Washington, USA

First published by Changemakers Books, 2013
Changemakers Books is an imprint of John Hunt Publishing Ltd., Laurel House, Station Approach,
Alresford, Hants, SO24 9JH, UK
office1@jhpbooks.net
www.johnhuntpublishing.com
www.changemakers-books.com

For distributor details and how to order please visit the 'Ordering' section on our website.

Text copyright: Mark Hawthorne 2013

ISBN: 978 1 78099 851 0

A CIP catalogue record for this book is available from the British Library.

Design: Stuart Davies

Printed in the USA by Edwards Brothers Malloy

We operate a distinctive and ethical publishing philosophy in all
areas of our business, from our global network of authors to
production and worldwide distribution.

CONTENTS

Author's Note   xiv

Acknowledgements   xv

Introduction   1

Chapter 1 – Bleating Hearts: Animals Used for Food   5

Chapter 2 – Dressed to Kill: Animals Used for Fashion   68

Chapter 3 – Trials and Errors: Animal Testing   124

Chapter 4 – Poachers, Pills, and Politics: The Persecution
of Wild Animals   213

Chapter 5 – Ruthless Roundup: Animals Used in Sports   265

Chapter 6 – The Age of Aquariums: Animals in Entertainment   298

Chapter 7 – Animal Rites: Animals as Sacrificial Victims   359

Chapter 8 – Conceptual Cruelty: Animals Used in Art   398

Chapter 9 – The Horse Before the Cart: Working Animals   425

Chapter 10 – Secret Abuse: Sexual Assault on Animals   444

Chapter 11 – Achieving Moral Parity   471

Notes   500

Index   603

Also by Mark Hawthorne

Striking at the Roots: A Practical Guide to Animal Activism
(Changemakers Books)

For Nibbles and Sophie, my rabbit friends

Author's Note

Throughout this book, I include the remarks of people who regard animals as things, rather than conscious beings. This is exemplified by someone using the pronoun "it" or the possessive pronoun "its" when referring to a nonhuman animal, rather than using a personal pronoun such as "she" or "his." My usual inclination would be to follow the speaker's grammatical error with a parenthetical "sic," the standard literary practice to indicate someone has been quoted faithfully. But it soon became apparent that doing so made what follows too cumbersome, with so many "sics" filling a page. I have, therefore, simply left such speciesist errors as I heard or read them.

In addition, while I sometimes refer to people as "owners" of animals, I mean this strictly in the legal sense. Sadly, animals can be considered property, however much this may offend us. By identifying someone as an animal owner, I am emphasizing their role in exploiting another species.

Acknowledgements

Everyone interviewed for this book has my heartfelt gratitude. Special thanks to Carol Adams, Jonathan Balcombe, Marc Bekoff, Kate Fowler, Camilla Fox, Maneka Gandhi, Matthew Liebman, Lori Marino, Ingrid Newkirk, Ric O'Barry, Glenys Oogjes, Jill Robinson, Matt Rossell, and Kim Stallwood for patiently granting me so much of their valuable time. My thanks as well to Patti Breitman, Martin Rowe, and Erin Williams for helping me find the proper tone I needed to address the painful subject matter found in these pages. Of course, I can't forget Tim Ward, Elizabeth Radley, Stuart Davies, Nick Welch, Mollie Barker, and Trevor Greenfield of Changemakers Books. I must also credit Colleen Patrick-Goudreau of CompassionateCook.com, Jasmin Singer and Mariann Sullivan of OurHenHouse.org, and Ari Solomon, who is evidently everywhere; researching and writing *Bleating Hearts* was often an arduous journey, and their animal-friendly wit and wisdom helped keep me smiling and sane. Most importantly, I am forever grateful to my wife, Lauren Ornelas, who walks the social justice talk with more consistent strides than anyone I know, for her unwavering encouragement, her editorial guidance, and her insights as a longtime activist—and for being a constant source of joy, inspiration, and love. I cannot imagine how I got so lucky.

Introduction

Not long ago, my wife and I were visiting a wildlife sanctuary operated by the Performing Animal Welfare Society (PAWS) near our home in northern California. It was one of those warm fall days we're so fortunate to have in abundance, and I imagined the three African elephants we were observing from a few yards away were quite happy to feel the sunshine and have the freedom of their expansive habitat. Lulu, Maggie, and Mara are former zoo inmates, now closely bonded and cared for by PAWS. Beside Lauren and me stood an older man and woman. As we all watched the animals use their sensitive trunks to pick up hay and tuck it into their mouths, the woman asked her companion if he'd had the opportunity to ride an elephant during his recent visit to Thailand. "Oh yes," he replied, "I had the chance. But I didn't." "Really?" she said. "I would love to ride an elephant. Why didn't you?" There was a thoughtful pause, and then he answered, "I just didn't think it was right." Lauren and I were quick to voice our agreement with him, and the woman flashed us a look of annoyance.

This brief exchange illustrated to me just how deeply our world is consumed by animal exploitation. And yet, if you were to walk down the street of most major cities today, you'd be hard-pressed to identify more than a few examples of how humans use animals. You might see a pig's corpse hanging in the window of a butcher shop, or perhaps you'd peruse a menu outside a restaurant that serves meat. There may be a zoo nearby. If you live in New York City, you're likely aware of the horse-drawn carriages that ply the congested streets, and of course it's difficult to ignore the bullfighting arenas in Pamplona, Madrid, and other cities in Spain. But except for these and a handful of other obvious examples, our use of nonhuman animals is largely ignored.

What makes this especially surprising—and confounding—is that from that bygone moment when *Homo sapiens* began hunting animals for their flesh and skin, we've regarded the beings with whom we share this planet as a resource, whether for food, clothing, companionship, entertainment, or other ways to allegedly enhance the lives of human beings. At the same time, we've divorced ourselves from the means of producing violence: we know slaughterhouses and research labs exist, for instance, but they are hidden from view, and for that we are, regrettably, thankful. We warm to stories of whales and dolphins being freed from fishing nets, but when the narrative turns to fish being hauled from the oceans, our sympathy wanes. Kittens, puppies, and songbirds all earn our empathy. But what of animals confined in factory farms or those killed by the hundreds to test a new drug? This suffering is sanctioned by abstract injustice.

It has been argued that eating animals and wearing their skin enabled early humans to survive. Then, about 10,000 years ago, a shift occurred that would drastically alter our contact with nature. Over a period of about 5,000 years, hunter-gatherers planted crops and gradually tamed, bred, and herded animals, becoming farmers. They no longer had to search for food; it was right outside the front door. Domesticating animals, what historian Gerald Carson calls "man's oldest and most impressive accomplishment in experimental biology,"[1] marked the beginning of a new relationship between humans and other species. It has resulted in today's industrial-scale meat production, whose business is converting grain to flesh, and the industry makes no apology for viewing animals as insensate "things," rather than thinking, feeling beings with desires of their own. (Indeed, the food industry takes animal welfare seriously only when doing so reduces costs or improves taste.) As a result, meat, dairy, and egg defenders promote the moral fiction that eating animals and their secretions is not only good for us, but that it's perfectly ethical.

Like most people, I spent my childhood eating meat, wearing leather, and loving the cats, dogs, and mice I grew up with—and not once recognizing that I was treating some animals with respect and others as faceless commodities. I was well into adulthood before I understood that such an inconsistency is as ridiculous as it is unjust. The truth is, we have an impoverished understanding of the animals we share this planet with, and that has led to more than a little hubris on our part. Not so long ago, we believed humans were the only animals to use tools. Then we noticed apes, otters, and birds doing the same. We argued that it was just fine to kill animals because they had no sense of the future. Then we learned that chickens, the animals we eat more than any other, anticipate events and may even worry about them.[2] Researchers recently discovered that ravens use gestures, such as pointing with their wings, to communicate with their fellows—an attribute long held to be possessed only by primates.[3] We celebrated our status as the only animals able to experience joy. Yet, as we delve deeper into the emotional lives of other beings, we see that they too feel happiness, sadness, and other traits we previously regarded as distinctively human.

We used to maintain that humans are unique because we feel empathy. So we were surprised to observe elephants gently touching the skulls, tusks, and bones of their deceased kin, mourning the dead, and we've seen them come to the aid of sick members of their herd.[4] Same for dolphins, who seem to give emotional support to dying members of their pod and who apparently grieve afterward.[5] In 2011, scientists discovered that both rats[6] and chickens[7] feel empathy—a breakthrough that I hope will lead to a more charitable opinion of these animals, rather than thinking of them as "pests" or "just chickens." We regarded ourselves as separate from other species because only humans exhibit altruism or have the ability to perceive what is and isn't speech—two premises that had to be corrected when researchers noted chimpanzees displaying acts of spontaneous generosity,[8] while another chimp has shown an ability to interpret highly distorted speech sounds in a way similar to people.[9] We've claimed that humans are the only animals who kill themselves out of despair. But anecdotal evidence suggests that dolphins can and do take their own lives in captivity.[10] And although studies are still ongoing, recent research indicates that even bees may experience emotions[11] —a supposition that could augment the ethical stance against consuming honey.

Clearly there is much that we do not know about our nonhuman neighbors, and as I came to recognize the injustice of my own hubris, I embraced the vegan ethic and eventually produced a book on advocacy, *Striking at the Roots: A Practical Guide to Animal Activism*. The book's success taught me how deeply people care about animals and encouraged me to explore many of the routine abuses activists are campaigning to transform. Here, with *Bleating Hearts*, I examine animal exploitation that does not get enough (or any) attention. We hear and read a lot about animals raised for food, for example—and rightly so—but how often do you see a story about bear bile, the Taiji dolphin drives, or artificial insemination in the captivity industry? Yet once they learn of such inhumane treatment of animals, compassionate consumers are often eager to sound off against it.

I am reminded of Karen Davis, founder of United Poultry Concerns (UPC). In the course of researching material for Chapter 2, I discovered the nascent fashion trend of adorning one's hair with rooster feathers, and I tracked down one of the world's largest suppliers, a company that slaughters 1,500 birds a week to help satisfy demand. Once I shared the information with Karen, she quickly sent an action alert to UPC members asking that they speak out against this cruelty.

There are passages in *Bleating Hearts* that many people will find painful to read. Humanity's abuse of animals can be merciless in the extreme, and in trying to relate such cruelties faithfully, I have written about incidents and industry practices that may disgust you. But it is crucial that we see beyond the veil that hides this world of suffering from us. Equally important, we need to know that there is some optimism amid all the despair.

And so we begin with a story of hope.

Chapter 1

Bleating Hearts: Animals Used for Food

We are a business, not a humane society, and our job is to sell merchandise at a profit. It's no different from selling paper-clips or refrigerators.
—Henry Pace, owner of a livestock auction yard

Entering a shed where he worked in West Yorkshire, England, Brian Mallinson was startled to find a newborn lamb curled up with her mother. Mallinson felt a pang of compassion for the helpless animal, as did his co-workers, who were all charmed by the wobbly-legged arrival. Set anywhere else, the whole scenario could be a page from a children's story. Unfortunately, the shed where Mallinson and his colleagues found the lamb was in a slaughterhouse, and according to British disease control legislation, no nonhuman animal who enters a slaughterhouse, even a baby born there, can leave in one piece.

In an extraordinary display of empathy, the slaughterhouse workers declined to kill the lamb and her mother, even in the face of prosecution and threats of a £5,000 fine or six months in jail. "Both the lamb and ewe are fit and healthy," said the slaughterhouse's co-director, Richard Gawthorpe, who added, apparently with a straight face, "Everything has a right to live."[1] They appealed to the UK's Department for Environment, Food, and Rural Affairs to make an exception and hired an attorney to argue their case. Mallinson, manager of the slaughterhouse, had clearly grown attached to the lamb, telling the media, "It was so cute cuddled up to her mum. We thought it ridiculous that they had to be destroyed."[2] Luckily for the ewe and her lamb, whom the employees had named Larry before they knew he was a she, the government relented and granted the animals their lives.

Of course, the story of Larry the lamb isn't really about Larry. It's about the humans who made a personal connection with an animal they likely would have killed, along with her mum, under any other circumstances. Even Mallinson, a slaughterer for 40 years, no doubt missed the irony when he said, "To kill them would have been wrong and unnecessary"[3]—a comment that is, to be perfectly fair, outrageous coming from someone who probably murders hundreds of sheep a day.

Yet Mallinson and his fellow slaughterhouse workers experienced a moment of pure compassion; they recognized the cruelty inherent in taking an innocent life. If only they could see that behind the eyes of *every* sheep and every other animal who enters their invisible killing machine, there is a Larry. Such is the paradox that makes it difficult to reconcile how ordinary humans (people just like you and me) can be outwardly kind and hold ideas similar to our own, but engage in practices that would seem to be dramatically at odds with all they believe in. Animal exploitation is positively heaving with such contradictions, and they are never more evident than in the use of animals for food. There are no doubt numberless people like Mallinson—men and women in agribusiness who grapple with moral ambiguity—but the lucky Larrys are very, very few.

Like other compassionate consumers, I've learned a great deal about animal agriculture from reading bestselling books such as *Eating Animals* by Jonathan Safran Foer, *Animal Liberation* by Peter Singer, and *Fast Food Nation* by Eric Schlosser, as well as watching documentaries like *Food Inc.* and *Forks Over Knives*. Perhaps you have, too. Now the effects of humanity's hunger for animal products are becoming part of our social consciousness: that factory farming is a leading contributor to global warming,[4] that consuming animal flesh has a detrimental effect on human health, that most meat, egg, and dairy products come from facilities containing thousands of animals (often hundreds of thousands, in the case of the egg industry) who are made to endure such privations as restrictive indoor confinement and the denial of many of their natural behaviors.

What I did not know until I looked deeper into the animal-to-edible transformation is how horrifying some of the least-known practices can be. I expected death—I did *not* anticipate the extreme disregard for sentient life. As an animal activist explains in *Eating Animals*, "These factory farmers calculate how close to death they can keep the animals without killing them. That's the business model. How quickly can they be made to grow, how tightly can they be packed, how much or little can they eat, how sick can they get without dying."[5] In his book *Farm Sanctuary: Changing Hearts and Minds About Animals and Food*, longtime animal advocate Gene Baur gives readers a heartbreaking account of how the US egg industry disposes of hundreds of millions of unwanted male chicks every year, even grinding them up alive:

> I have watched unwanted chicks dumped onto an auger, a large screwlike device that is customarily used for processing grain or sand, then dropped through an opening in the side of a building into a manure spreader outside. I could hear faint chirping as live chicks, many of them horribly injured, were ground up and their feathers, flesh, and blood deposited on cropland as fertilizer. I later walked the field looking for survivors but found only mangled, lifeless bodies among the corn stubble. What stays with me most is the terrible irony of these newly hatched chicks, symbols of spring and rebirth, who'd been driven to fight their way out of their shell by the instinct to live that we all share, only to be ground up alive and turned into manure. And all because, in the industry's eyes, they have no value.[6]

While it's natural for people who learn of these abuses to ask how such things can happen, the reality is most of the cruelties perpetrated against animals raised for food are completely legal. In the United States, so-called Common Farming Exemptions state that as long as a corporation is treating their animals as other corporations do, their actions are generally considered standard within the industry and anti-cruelty laws do not apply. Practices such as confining animals in tiny cages or crates in which they can barely move, cutting off body parts without pain relief, and even dropping them fully conscious into a machine to be pulverized are all as lawful as they are merciless. But that doesn't mean animal exploiters want you to know about it. Indeed, the business of turning sentient beings into consumable products is the world's biggest covert operation, veiled behind walls of corporate greed and protected by special-interest resources. In praise of transparency, the late Supreme Court Justice Louis Brandeis observed that sunshine is the best disinfectant. Let's bring to light a few of animal agriculture's darkest secrets.

Live Fast, Die Young

Looking at the numbers, it's clear that chickens represent by far the most-abused species in the world. Of the estimated 65 billion animals killed in the world each year for food,[7] an astounding 73 percent—47 billion—are chickens.[8] If you find it difficult to wrap your head around that figure, consider it this way: In the time it takes you to read this sentence, more than 16,000 chickens have been slaughtered for food.[9] The percentage is even higher in the United States, where chickens represent about 8.5 billion of the 9 billion land animals slaughtered annually,[10] and not a single one of them is protected by the federal Humane Methods of Slaughter Act, which says that animals killed for food must be rendered insensible to pain, yet excludes poultry. At such high rates—thousands of animals per minute—agribusiness has devised a stunningly abusive system that emphasizes efficiency and speed, pushing cruelty to ever higher extremes. After being transported to a slaughterhouse on an overcrowded truck, chickens are hung upside down by their feet in metal shackles and then given a jolt of electricity so their heads will dangle long enough for a mechanical blade to slice their throats. The birds are likely still conscious as they bleed to death.

The industry has also developed a vertically integrated system in which everything involved in the farm-to-fork trade—raising animals, producing feed, transportation, and slaughter—is owned and operated by a single company. In addition to controlling costs, such integration has further removed chickens and other farmed animals from the public consciousness and reduced them to mere commodities. Animals who at one time were at least allowed to graze in a pasture, root in the dirt, or peck in a barnyard are today typically concentrated in small areas and often never feel the sunshine.

Chickens are perhaps the best example of this. Bred by the hundreds of thousands each day in huge hatcheries that rely on industrial automation in lieu of animal husbandry, chickens raised for meat—so-called "broilers"—are "grown" in massive sheds, while hens used in the egg industry end up crammed into wire cages to endure unrelieved confinement and deprivation. When considering the life of a chicken, it's important to remember that, contrary to what factory farmers would like you to believe, these are inquisitive, highly social animals who are at least as intelligent as dogs or cats. Chris Evans, director of the Centre for the Integrative Study of Animal Behaviour at Macquarie University in Australia, observes that chickens live in stable social groups, are good problem-solvers, and can recognize one another by their facial features. They use 24 distinct vocalizations to communicate an abundance of information to their flock mates, including alarm calls that change depending on whether a predator is traveling by land or by sea. "As a trick at conferences I sometimes list these attributes, without mentioning chickens, and people think I'm talking about monkeys," Evans says.[11]

As the world's taste for cheap meat has increased, so has the scale of chicken production. Throughout the 1950s, modest chicken coops that dotted the landscape were largely replaced by broiler houses measuring 28 by 200 feet (8.5 by 61 meters) and holding 8,000 birds.[12] Half a century later, chickens are raised in windowless sheds that vary in size by country. In the United States, a typical broiler shed is now 42 by 400 feet (12.8 by 122 meters)—100 feet longer than a football field—and holds approximately 24,000 chickens, with each bird allotted only about 0.7 square feet (0.065 square meters) of floor space.[13] The density is higher in Australia, where an average broiler shed is 15 by 150 meters (49.2 by 492 feet) and holds about 40,000 chickens, giving each bird approximately 0.6 square feet (0.056 meters) of space.[14] Higher still is the density in the European Union, where a 2010 law allows chicken producers to squeeze 21 birds into every square meter of a shed's floor space.[15]

Farmacology

In addition to packing in more birds per square area, the speed with which agribusiness raises chickens has doubled in recent decades. While US growers in the 1950s raised a chicken for meat in an average of 84 days, today's birds are slaughtered at about 40 days with a live weight of approximately 2 kilograms (4.4 pounds).[16] Their bodies are abnormally large, but they are still babies who chirp as they head to slaughter. Imagine a human baby growing to 350 pounds in eight weeks and you'll have an idea how fast and unnaturally these birds bulk up. The chickens' enormous growth is due in part to farmers supplementing feeds with antibiotics, which help prevent disease in filthy, cramped factory farm conditions and increase the efficiency with which animals convert feed to body mass. (Though scientists don't know exactly why this happens, one theory is that by changing the animals' gut microflora, antibiotics create an intestine dominated by colonies of microbes that are calorie-extraction experts. A 2011 study found these pharmaceuticals may have a similar effect on humans: people who consume antibiotic-fed animals may develop obesity.[17]) This practice of exposing birds, pigs, and cows to non-therapeutic dosages of drugs has become so routine that a whopping 80 percent of all antibiotics sold in the US—30 million pounds a year—are fed to perfectly healthy animals.[18] In contrast, the use of antibiotic growth promoters

BLEATING HEARTS: ANIMALS USED FOR FOOD

in the European Union was banned in 2006, and in 2011, the EU voted to end the prophylactic use of antibiotics in farmed animals as well.[19] Though groups including the World Health Organization and the American Medical Association have for years tried to ban the non-therapeutic use of these drugs in farmed animals in the US, their efforts continue to be thwarted by the two most powerful lobbies in Washington, DC: animal agribusiness and the pharmaceutical industry.

So, what's the harm in feeding antibiotics to animals or having them grow faster? For one thing, bacteria are smart. They mutate and develop a resistance to commonly used antimicrobials, which is why doctors are careful not to over-prescribe them to humans. The widespread misuse of these pharmaceuticals in agribusiness can easily lead to an increase in antibiotic-resistant bacteria, which can leap from animals to humans and make antibiotics less effective. This is exacerbated by antibiotics entering the food chain via farmed animals; in fact, such common bacteria as *Campylobacter*, *E. coli*, and *Salmonella* have become much more difficult to treat, and one germ, methicillin-resistant *Staphylococcus aureus* (better known as MRSA)—a so-called "superbug"—is now responsible for more deaths in the United States than AIDS.[20] A study published in 2011 found that nearly half the meat sold in the US was tainted with MRSA and that feeding antibiotics to animals is directly linked to the spread of this deadly organism.[21] Although Big Ag has vigorously denied that bacteria from humans can mutate in animals and spew back as a superbug—"Most informed scientists and public health professionals acknowledge that the problem of antibiotic resistance in humans is overwhelmingly an issue related to human antibiotic use," says the American Meat Institute[22]—researchers now have conclusive proof that this is indeed the case, and factory farmers can no longer hide behind their disingenuous rhetoric.[23] Overall, about 90,000 people in the United States die from antibiotic-resistant infections every year,[24] while the death rate in the European Union is 25,000.[25]

Does the US Food and Drug Administration (FDA) know that the non-therapeutic use of antibiotics for animals is a bad idea? Of course it does, and it's known that since at least 1972, when its own task force looked into the issue and recommended restrictions on the use of antibiotics. Five years later, the FDA pledged to withdraw approval for penicillin and tetracycline in animal feed, which would have been a start. But in December 2011, after decades of doing nothing about it, the agency reneged on its promise. The FDA said it hopes drug companies and the meat industry will reduce antibiotic use voluntarily.[26] Good luck with that.

Kellogg Schwab, director of the Johns Hopkins Global Water Program and a professor in the Environmental Health Sciences Department of the Johns Hopkins Bloomberg School of Public Health, is a second-generation microbiologist and just one of many experts deeply concerned about the spread of antibiotic-resistant bacteria. Schwab characterizes the current situation succinctly. You could not create a better incubator for resistant pathogens than a factory farm, he says. "It's not appreciated until it's your mother, or your son, or you trying to fight off an infection that will not go away because the last mechanism to fight it has been usurped by someone putting it into a pig or a chicken."[27] Prompted by statements from specialists like Schwab, and new, irrefutable evidence linking antibiotics to MRSAs, in 2012 the US government ordered the FDA to finish what the agency started in 1977 and ban Big Ag's non-therapeutic use of antibiotics. But don't think the industry will go down without a fight: farmers and ranchers now say the drugs are being used to prevent animal diseases, not to promote growth.[28]

Since the 1940s, chicken farmers have thrown another ingredient into the feed mix: arsenic. Like other pharmaceuticals, its use began as a way to combat disease—in this case, it helps control a parasitic ailment known as coccidiosis—but the ag industry soon learned that arsenic also promotes growth in animals. Oh, and it gives chicken flesh that rosy hue that consumers equate with quality meat. The industry notes that it only uses a form of arsenic that is chemically organic; that is, it contains carbon molecules. Trouble is, organic arsenic morphs into its highly toxic inorganic form all too easily, which is one reason the practice of lacing animal feed with arsenic was banned in the Europe Union in 1999. Reform elsewhere has been much slower. Not long ago, more than 2 million pounds of just one arsenic-based additive, Roxarsone, was being fed to chickens in the United States. But in 2011, after years of maintaining that arsenic-spiked chicken feed posed no danger to consumers, the FDA found inorganic arsenic—a known carcinogen—in chicken livers. This announcement prompted Pfizer, the nation's leading producer of Roxarsone, to suspend sales of the additive in the US. Does that mean the country's chicken-meat industry will no longer use arsenic? Not at all. Pfizer simply focused on selling another arsenic-infused drug.[29]

One of the reasons the FDA had thought arsenic was safe for humans is that animals excrete about 90 percent of antibiotics through their feces and urine. While this is true, guess where it all ends up: back in our waterways.[30] Between 2002 and 2004, Kellogg Schwab and his colleagues collected ground and surface water from a factory farm in a rural area of the mid-Atlantic United States. At the time of sampling, the facility held 3,000 pigs. In downgradient samples (that is, water coming from the direction of the pig facility), the researchers found 11 times as much *E. coli*, 17 times as much enterococci (pathogens responsible for serious infections), and 33 times as much fecal coliforms as water upgradient from the farm.[31]

But it's the animals who bear the real burden of pharmaceutical use in factory farms. In combination with selective breeding, chickens grow very rapidly on antibiotics, and this unnatural development and heavy body weight leads to a host of health problems. As one poultry industry text puts it, "The modern broiler has the genetic potential to grow at such a rapid rate that the bird will gain more body mass than its heart, lungs, or bones can support."[32] The result is a chicken who suffers from severe metabolic and skeletal disorders. Heart failure, sudden death syndrome (what the industry calls "flipover"), bone deformities, deadly infections, and an inability to walk are just a few of the fates frequently awaiting chickens raised for meat.[33]

One agribusiness solution is to feed the birds used for breeding in the chicken-meat industry (so-called "broiler breeders") less often, leaving them in a perpetual state of hunger. "When fed an unrestricted diet, fewer than half of broiler breeders survive more than a year, and most suffer from reproductive disorders," says Paul Shapiro, vice president of farmed animal protection at The Humane Society of the United States. "Given breeders' genetics, unlimited feeding can lead to broiler breeders suffering from obesity, leg-joint pain, and a host of other health-related issues. In other words, these animals have been bred to suffer. Because of the way we've relentlessly bred them for fast growth, the breeding animals suffer from chronic hunger, but if we feed them as much as they want, they endure severe discomfort and life-threatening illnesses. In this case, it's not a matter of trying to provide a good environment for the birds to ensure that they don't suffer; rather, these animals are prisoners in their own bodies and will suffer daily no matter what kind of environment they're in."[34]

"We've been bombarded with nauseating narratives about the evils of factory farming for over 40 years. The fact that we have not, as a collective gesture of consumer outrage, monkey wrenched these hellholes into oblivion speaks either to the human tendency to procrastinate or, worse, our pathological indifference."[35]
—James McWilliams

Nasal Implants

Restricting food intake to regulate weight gain and reduce aggression among confined roosters is a common practice throughout the poultry trade, but it becomes even more callous in the breeding of chickens for both the meat and egg industries. In addition to feeding birds on alternate days so they don't take on too much weight, many factory farmers have employed a small device driven through the nasal cartilage of a young "breeder" rooster's beak to prevent him from eating feed intended for hens and dominating access to the food. Called a Noz Bonz or Nozbonz, this 2.5-inch (6.4-cm) plastic rod is forced horizontally through the male's nasal septum when he is about five months old and his head is still small enough to fit between the narrowly partitioned rows of the hens' feeding troughs. (Males are supposed to eat from pan feeders that are suspended at a height the females cannot reach.[36])

A representative from Aviagen, which bills itself as the world's leading poultry breeding company, told me that "these devices will not affect male behavior in terms of feeding, mating activity, or other naturally expressed behaviors."[37] Yet he neglected to mention the injuries roosters suffer when they manage to get their heads into the hens' feeding system despite the Noz Bonz. "In my experience, Nozbonz are not effective for the purported objective (keeping male heads out of feeders) since the males are extremely food motivated and soon try their own experiments to access the female feeders," writes Suzanne Millman, associate professor of applied animal behavior and welfare at the University of Guelph in Canada. "Males will turn their heads to get into the grills and become vulnerable. If attacked by other birds, or frightened, they then often try to pull back and panic. They may injure or even kill themselves. They also sometimes rip the Nozbonz out in the struggle."[38]

Mutilation

Because most farmed animals are raised and confined in stressful, unnatural conditions, they frequently develop stereotypical behaviors—that is, repetitive actions with no obvious purpose—that would not occur in less-intensive environments. Pigs in crowded sheds will chew on other pigs' tails, for example, and hens stuffed into small battery cages will peck at each other. Agribusiness' solution for many of these injury-inducing behaviors is physical mutilation, cutting off sensitive body parts such as pigs' tails and hens' beaks without providing the animals any painkiller, which factory farmers consider too expensive.

Body parts are also amputated or mutilated as identification measures or allegedly in response to welfare concerns. Branding, castration, dehorning, ear notching, and mulesing (slicing chunks of flesh from a sheep's tail area) are but a few of the procedures animals suffer. The resulting pain may be acute, inflammatory, or neuropathic.[39] Male chickens raised to be breeders in the broiler industry undergo the amputation of one or more toes, and the mutilation—commonly referred to as detoeing—can lead to neuropathic pain should the damaged nerves develop into extensive neuromas.[40] Detoeing is performed because these industry-created roosters, with their very broad breasts, might otherwise severely injure the hens with their claws during mating. Carried out with a hot blade and without anesthesia or analgesics, the amputation is done soon after the young male chicks (cockerels) are hatched. Ian Duncan, chair of animal welfare in the Department of Animal and Poultry Science at the University of Guelph in Canada, explains that the inside toe and/or the backward-pointing toe on each cockerel's foot is removed at the last joint, which carries the claw. "It is, of course, a painful operation," he says. "It also means that the males have difficulty balancing throughout their lives."[41]

Unnatural Selection

Like their feathered cousins, turkeys are detoed shortly after hatching, but they endure several other abuses inside modern agribusiness. In consequence of the consumer demand for white meat, commercial turkeys have been genetically manipulated to grow abnormally large breasts; in fact, turkeys in factory farms now grow more than twice as fast as their wild ancestors.[42] The results of this exaggerated growth are similar to those experienced by chickens in factory farms: crippling leg and joint disorders, lameness, heart problems, and weakened immune systems.[43] Debeaked, detoed, and grossly overweight, these turkeys have trouble walking and eating. Producers also cut off the toms' snoods—the large flap of skin hanging over their beaks—giving other intensively confined turkeys one less thing to peck at. Needless to say, these birds cannot fly.

There's something else they cannot do, given their girth: mate naturally. Consequently, commercial turkey producers resort to removing semen from the toms and inseminating the hens—both done by force. Workers begin by grabbing a tom and restraining him on a workbench affixed with leg clamps. Generally, it takes just one worker to stimulate the turkey's reproductive organs by stroking the tail feathers, squeeze the vent (the orifice that encloses the genitals), and, in a procedure known in the industry as "milking," collect semen using a vacuum pump. To the semen is added "extenders" that include antibiotics and a saline solution, which give workers more control over the inseminating dose.[44] Breeding toms are milked up to three times a week[45] until they are about 16 months old and weigh up to 80 pounds (36 kilograms).[46]

Inseminating female turkeys with the collected semen is known as "breaking" the hens, and it is as violent as the term suggests. "Breaking hens was hard, fast, dirty work," activist Jim Mason writes of his one-day, undercover experience at a turkey breeding farm, where workers herded hens a hundred at a time into a pen and then drove five or six birds through a chute into a small pen. "I had to reach into the chute, grab a hen by the legs, and hold her, ankles crossed, in one hand. Then, as I held her on the edge of the pit, I wiped my other hand over her rear, which pushed up her tail feathers and exposed her vent opening. The birds weighed 20 to 30 lbs., were terrified, and beat their wings and struggled in panic."[47] With pressure applied to the hen's abdomen, her vent opens and a worker injects semen into her oviduct.[48]

According to Jim, workers inseminate one hen every 12 seconds, a pace that leaves little time for proper handling. Indeed, he writes,

"Having been through this week after week, the birds feared the chute and balked and huddled up. The drivers literally kicked them into the chute. The idea seemed to be to terrify at least one bird, who squawked, beat her wings in panic, and terrified the others in her group. In this way, the drivers created such pain and terror behind the birds that it forced them to plunge ahead to the pain and terror they knew to be in the chute and pit ahead."[49]

One of the consequences associated with the inhumane treatment of both the toms and hens is a condition known as deep pectoral myopathy. Common in factory-farmed birds, this pathology is caused by the exertion of the chest muscles beyond the lungs' ability to supply oxygen—due to the frantic wing flapping and struggling the turkeys exhibit during the artificial insemination process—killing the muscle tissue.[50]

No Sunny Side to Egg Production

Hold this book open wide. At roughly 93 square inches (600 square centimeters), the area you see spread before you is 26 square inches (167 square centimeters) more space than the average hen has to live on in any battery cage in the United States egg industry.[51] The European Union, which finally increased minimum-space allotments for battery-caged hens in 2012 to 116 square inches (750 square centimeters) per bird, currently offers the world's least-restrictive standard. Space allowances in Brazil, India, and Ukraine are among the worst, with each hen granted from 46.5 to 62 square inches (300 to 400 square centimeters).[52]

Whatever the allotted area, the floor that hens stand on is made of wire, and the birds are crammed wing-to-wing with six or seven others in an effort to keep industrial-scale egg production as profitable as inhumanly possible. Contrary to the bucolic images found on some retail egg cartons, no sunshine greets these animals in the morning, and they have no chance to enjoy many of their most important natural behaviors, such as nesting, perching, or dust bathing. They are confined 24/7 to cages, stacked one atop another in huge, gloomy sheds and are left unseen by any veterinarian should they become sick.

I witnessed such cruelty firsthand while taking part in a large-scale rescue of "spent" hens from battery cages in 2005. (Hens are considered spent, or of no use to the egg industry, after about 18 to 24 months.) The stench inside the shed was overwhelming, with ammonia vapors burning my eyes and lungs. How, I wondered, could an animal live in this hell for two years? Navigating my way past dense spider webs that dangled like diaphanous drapes from every surface, I opened tiny wire prisons to remove birds almost completely denuded of feathers. They seemed so incredibly fragile: all that remained of their wings were a few pitiful quills protruding from the bone. Instead of plumage, these White Leghorns were covered with swaths of red-raw skin. The combs that crowned their heads were flaccid and pale pink, rather than the brilliant rose hue they would regain, along with their feathers, after time in a loving home. The birds in the lower tiers of cages were in the most miserable condition, as they were caked with excrement from the hens in cages stacked above. The beak of every hen had been mutilated so that the upper mandible was transformed into a lumpy stub, frustrating their attempts to consume food pellets. Many suffered from untreated wounds, and I discovered the rotting corpses of a few hens who had been dead so long that their carcasses were a skull limply clinging to a bag of bones. Such gross negligence isn't necessarily a result of mean-spirited workers or lazy management, however; factory farms are inherently cruel by design, with battery-egg operations among the worst offenders. Here farmers use standard practices like stuffing cages with the most birds possible to yield paper-thin profits.

That's not to suggest that factory farmers are anything but fully complicit in their exploitation of animals. In the eyes of animal agribusiness, the laying hen's sole purpose is to churn out at least six eggs a week for human consumption, and the birds continue doing so until their bodies are exhausted and their egg production has declined. At this point, they're either slaughtered for low-grade chicken-meat products or simply killed and disposed of. I watched as farm workers entered the shed and began yanking terrified birds out by their legs so they could be replaced by younger ones. Because so much calcium goes into the formation of eggshells, factory-farmed hens' skeletons are chronically depleted and brittle. Yet spent hens are worth so little that the hasty "catchers" I observed were clearly ignoring the occasional snapping of leg and wing bones that got wedged in the wire of the narrow cage doors. I was told that the tens of thousands of hens we were unable to rescue would end up in dog food, so a few broken bones were of no consequence (except to the suffering hens, of course). Other methods for ridding the egg industry of spent hens include tossing live birds into wood chippers, gassing them with carbon dioxide, suffocating them beneath a blanket of firefighting foam, and burying them in landfills while they're still alive.[53] Such inhumane practices made headlines across the US in 2006, when two dozen dazed hens left for dead beneath a layer of earth crawled out and startled residents of Petaluma, California.[54]

And those are the birds who survive long enough to be abused for their eggs. As Gene Baur observes in *Farm Sanctuary*, every year millions of male chicks are ground up alive soon after hatching. The grinding machine egg factories use for this grisly purpose is called a macerator, and it's equipped with high-speed, rotating blades that shred the baby birds to pieces. Such a death is considered humane by many advocates of animal welfare, including the American Veterinary Medical Association, which cites agriculture organizations around the world as regarding the practice to be an acceptable means of euthanasia.[55]

But other welfare experts disagree. In 2009, the animal advocacy group Mercy For Animals (MFA) captured undercover video of day-old male chicks being dropped into a macerator at one large hatchery and shared the images with veterinarians and poultry specialists. Ned Buyukmihci, VMD, Emeritus Professor of Veterinary Medicine at the University of California–Davis, stated that the process of being shunted into the metal device is painful and extremely

Don't Buy the Humane Myth

Disgusted by factory farming practices, many people are turning to non-industrial sources for their meat, eggs, and dairy products. These alternatives typically come from small farms using such marketing labels as "free-range," "natural," or even "humane." It's a strategy meant to minimize the guilt of compassionate consumers, but the reality is even small systems unavoidably involve animal suffering.

Much of the cruelty has been built right into the animal: even chickens raised on pastures have been bred to grow at an abnormally fast rate, leading to crippling leg injuries and heart failure, and cows used in the organic dairy industry— just like those in large-scale farms—have been so relentlessly manipulated for maximum milk production that their udders become infected, yet cows on organic dairies may not receive antibiotics to ease their suffering. Moreover, these cows are still impregnated and their babies are taken away at birth.

Chickens in the egg industry, meanwhile, don't fare any better. "Cage-free" eggs, for example, usually come from thousands of hens who are crowded into large, filthy sheds with no access to sunshine or fresh air. And whatever the label, male chicks are deemed useless, so millions of them are ground up or otherwise disposed of like garbage every year.

No matter how they are raised, nearly all animals used for food end up transported in cramped trucks to exactly the same slaughterhouses used by factory farms, where they are hung upside down and their throats are cut, often while they are fully conscious and fighting to escape. All these animals want to live, and there is nothing humane about their deaths.

stressful for the chicks. Another expert, Karen Davis, founder of the advocacy organization United Poultry Concerns, said, "Given that the nervous system of a chicken originates during the 21st hour of incubation, and that a chick has a fully developed nervous system at the time of hatching, it is reasonable to conclude, as a fact of neurophysiology, that the chicks are suffering extreme pain as they are being cut up by macerator blades."[56]

"We knew that male chicks were being disposed of at an alarming rate, but there was very little documentation of that taking place within the animal-protection movement, and most of the documentation that did exist was years old," says Nathan Runkle, MFA's executive director. "The response we received to this investigation was really incredible. People have no idea about this ugly side of the industry. It forced people to talk about veganism as a solution to the issues facing farmed animals because buying cage-free or free-range eggs doesn't solve the problem of the disposal of male chicks."[57]

Shell Shock

Considered a delicacy in many parts of Asia, balut eggs are so full of misery that some enthusiasts recommend you eat your first balut in the dark or keep your eyes closed so you can savor the taste without being disgusted by the reality of what you're consuming. Because balut (pronounced "bah-LUHT") are fertilized duck eggs that have been incubated until the embryo is really neither egg nor flesh, what diners see upon cracking the shell is a duckling fetus—complete with head, bill, bones, and pinfeathers—who has been boiled alive. (When producers of the US reality show *Fear Factor* learned about balut, they made eating the eggs one of the gastronomic stunts contestants had to undergo.)

Balut eggs are immensely popular in the Philippines, where they are peddled by street vendors and purported to be a male aphrodisiac, further enhancing sales. Indeed, the city of Pateros, just outside Manila, is considered the balut capital of the world, and there the industry often relies on the old-school approach to creating

22

these culinary cruelties: non-ventilated rooms filled with light bulbs simmer at more than 100 degrees F (38 degrees C), allowing the duck embryos to develop inside their eggshells for 16 to 18 days (ducklings normally hatch at about 27 days). A small operation can produce 40,000 balut eggs a week.[58] Evidently this isn't enough to satisfy the Filipino demand, though, as balut eggs are now being imported from as far away as California.

Margaret Magat, who has devoted much of her writing to Filipino culture, did an extensive survey of balut aficionados and found that most of them season the yolk, embryo, and albumen with salt. She thinks this may have as much to do with a guilty conscience as taste, however. "Many of my informants expressed strong feelings of disgust at seeing the embryo or catching a glimpse of the developed little chick," Magat writes. "After studying the survey responses, I believe that the feelings of revulsion experienced by many at the sight of the fetus may be due to the idea of ingesting something that is clearly on the verge of being born."[59] She suggests that the salt may be used subconsciously as a kind of purifying agent, "to cleanse the balut eater from the impure action of eating and therefore ending the life of the baby chick. I speculate that if this is the case, the sprinkling of salt may be for the balut eater a way of atoning for the 'sin' of ending another's life for the sake of continuing his/her own. The notion that a life must be ended to ensure that others may live could be applied here, with salt acting as an offering to the sacrificed life."[60]

Yanking the Food Chain

With hundreds of thousands of animals confined in a relatively small area, a single factory farm can create as much fecal waste as a city. In the United States, industrial livestock operations produce somewhere between 500 million and 1 billion US tons (about 454 to 907 million metric tonnes) of manure annually, compared to 18 million tons generated by the country's human inhabitants.[61] While most people would consider animal excrement to be fertilizer at best—and indeed much of this antibiotic-laden dung gets sprayed on cropland, leading to a host of environmental damages—factory farmers have an additional use for it: food for cows. Each year, US ranchers happily feed their bovines as much as 2 million US tons (about 1.81 million metric tonnes) of "poultry litter," which consists primarily of chicken and turkey droppings scooped up from the floors of massive buildings where the animals are confined. (And let's not forget that chicken feces may contain highly toxic arsenic compounds.) Farmers say it's both a cheap source of protein and a way to dispose of the mounds of feces that continually accumulate inside industrial poultry farms.

As disgusting as it sounds to feed this mess to cows, it gets much worse. Because it's collected from the bottom of sheds that house chickens and turkeys, poultry litter may include not only bird poop, but a variety of other waste substances, such as bedding material, feathers, dead rodents, rocks, glass, nails, and spilled feed.[62] The inclusion of spilled bird feed has many animal advocates and food and consumer groups especially concerned. A routine industry practice is to add flesh and bone meal from ruminants such as cows and sheep to poultry feed; when this feed is in turn given to cows as a component of poultry litter, it turns these natural herbivores into cannibals and increases their risk of becoming infected with bovine spongiform encephalopathy (BSE). Even birdseed that has passed through a bird's digestive tract carries traces of cow flesh.

Also known as mad cow disease, BSE popped up on the world's radar in November 1986, when scientists noted a newly-recognized form of brain-wasting disease among bovines in the United Kingdom.[63] Infected animals suffer a variety of symptoms— abnormal posture, lack of coordination, aggressive behavior, weight loss despite a healthy appetite, nervous temperament, progressive inability to stand or walk—until their debilitating condition becomes inexorably fatal and, in the absence of humane euthanasia, they succumb to what must certainly be a painful death. Since 1989, BSE cases have been reported around the globe, and a human form of the disease, called new variant Creutzfeldt-Jakob disease, has been traced to eating BSE-infected animals.[64]

As Michael Greger, MD, observes, mad cow disease is not the only cause for alarm in poultry feed. "There's also disease-causing bacteria, antibiotics, and arsenic compounds, which are not supposed to be fed to cattle," he says. In fact, says Dr. Greger, who devotes much of his energy to food safety issues as director of public health and animal agriculture at Humane Society International, the danger of cows contracting BSE may not be as high as we once feared. "The risk is low just because the incidence is very low in the US, though we don't have adequate testing. It may be on the order of a hundred mad cows a year in the US beef supply. One of those hundred would have to be rendered down and fed to other cattle. But it's such a widespread practice, I can certainly see it happening. But we slaughter 30 or so million cattle a year and we have 100 million at any one time, so the numbers make the risk very small."[65]

Steve Roach, public health program director with Food Animal Concerns Trust (FACT), isn't taking any chances. "It takes a very small quantity of ruminant protein, even just one milligram, to cause an infection," he says.[66] "If a feed manufacturer made feed, or even a feed store held feed under conditions that led to contamination by meat and bone meal or veterinary drugs likely to be found in poultry litter, they would be shut down. This unregulated use of substances normally prohibited in cattle feed creates risk to human and animal health through the spread of mad cow disease and antimicrobial-resistant bacteria along with the potential for toxic residues in meat from animals fed the litter."[67] In 2009, FACT was part of a coalition that called on the FDA to ban the use of chicken feces and other poultry farm waste as animal feed. In response, the FDA sent FACT a letter explaining that the issue of feeding excrement to cows was so complicated that the agency needs to study it further. Perhaps they could take a cue from countries such as Australia, Canada, New Zealand, and nations of the European Union, which have already prohibited the use of poultry litter as feed for ruminant animals due to food safety and other health concerns.[68] FACT continues its campaign, including asking individual ag interests to voluntarily stop using chicken litter as a feed ingredient.[69]

Not surprisingly, US agribusiness defends the practice as perfectly safe. "Science does not justify the ban, and the FDA has looked at this now many times," says Elizabeth Parker, chief veterinarian for the National Cattlemen's Beef Association. "We have tested 800,000 cattle in recent years and have not found any evidence of BSE circulating in the herd."[70] Eight hundred thousand sounds like a big number, but US slaughterhouses kill about 35 million cows every year and the US only tests 1 percent of these animals. Rather than playing Russian roulette with consumers, why doesn't the USDA follow Japan's lead and test *every* cow destined for human consumption? I'll tell you why: Because doing so would be costly and thus raise the price of meat.

At least one beef producer is willing to foot the bill for testing every cow who comes through their plant. Hoping to attract buyers from BSE-wary Japan and South Korea, Kansas-based Creekstone Farms Premium Beef was all set for comprehensive testing of mad cow disease when the USDA stepped in and stopped them. The agency expressed concern that a false positive from Creekstone could result in frightened consumers boycotting beef altogether. Creekstone responded by filing a lawsuit against the USDA.[71] Other meatpackers, meanwhile, worried that Creekstone would be setting a precedent that they'd all be forced to follow, adding a few pennies to each pound of animal flesh.[72] Not that the company is immune from food-safety issues: in 2011, Creekstone recalled more than 14,000 pounds of *E. coli*-tainted ground beef in 10 states.[73] (*E. coli* are potentially life-threatening bacteria that live in the intestinal tracts of many cows, pigs, and sheep, sometimes contaminating meat during the slaughter process as feces comes into contact with animal flesh.[74])

It is easy to understand why Big Ag likes to fatten herds with chicken feces. Moving poultry litter from the broiler shed to the feedlot is a win-win for farmers, who pay a mere US$20 per ton for the litter, versus US$160 per ton for corn.[75] This miserly practice wrings from the industrial food system the cheapest factory flesh possible, ultimately creating meat that is inexpensive, while still generating a tidy profit. But it may also prove to be deadly. "No one knows how safe American beef is," says Dr. Greger. "The problem is that by the time we do know, it may be too late. The incubation period of the human equivalent of mad cow disease can be decades, so for that and many other reasons, I encourage people to go vegan. Better safe than sorry."[76]

More Manure Madness

Speaking of manure, its impact even reaches from factory farms to the deep blue sea, where deadly algal blooms have become an increasing problem as nutrient pollution, fueled by animal waste, takes hold of coastal waterways. Two of the most harmful types of blooms are the so-called "red tide" and its eviler twin, *Pfiesteria piscicida*. Both red tides and *Pfiesteria* are dinoflagellates—microscopic organisms that can kill marine life. But *Pfiesteria* is particularly insidious, releasing a toxin that paralyzes fish and then cuts into their flesh, allowing the one-celled alga to dine on them. Unique among any other species on Earth, *Pfiesteria* is a shape-shifter that can morph into an entire alphabet soup of life-cycle stages, from amoeba to zoospore, and accommodate its appetite to feast on anything from plants to prey. This killer instinct has led some biologists to characterize *Pfiesteria* as the Tyrannosaurus Rex of dinoflagellates.

Actually, it's more like Godzilla or Mothra—a mutant born from the toxic sludge of modern civilization to wreak havoc on the environment. Found around the world, *Pfiesteria* multiplies 500 fold and becomes toxic when exposed to manure, feeding on the nitrogen and phosphorus before moving on to sentient meals. "That vampire organism is responsible for the largest fish kill that ever took place on any river in America," says Rick Dove of the nonprofit Waterkeeper Alliance. "It happened on the Neuse River in 1991. We lost a billion fish in a matter of days. We lost 200 million more in 1995. All because of *Pfiesteria*."[77]

Aquatic botanist JoAnn Burkholder, who co-identified the previously dormant cell in 1988, describes unearthing *Pfiesteria* as "the discovery of an organism no one wanted to hear about." She was the first to raise the alarm about its outbreak in the Chesapeake Bay and other contaminated estuaries, and she quickly became a target for commercial interests. "The tourism industry hated it, the coastal developers hated it, and it was bad news for agriculture," she says. "Various political interests and agencies like Sea Grant, which was heavily affiliated with the fishing industry, tried to discredit the issue." Dr. Burkholder says Hurricane Floyd and a few tropical storms flushed *Pfiesteria* out of the coastal waters—and therefore away from factory farm runoff—in 1999. "It will take a couple of hurricane-free decades before *Pfiesteria* populations will rebuild here."[78] But there are other ecosystems polluted with manure throughout the world where *Pfiesteria* can thrive, she says, particularly in Asia, where it's already been found.

The End of the Line

In "Consider the Lobster," a 6,000-word article for *Gourmet* magazine, novelist David Foster Wallace visits the Maine Lobster Festival and blindsides readers of this quintessential foodie publication with a meditation on the bioethics of boiling live crustaceans. Wallace, an avowed meat-eater, writes that he had to explore and question the morality of placing a living lobster into a kettle of 212 degrees F (100 degrees C) water, the animal clearly in distress as he clings to the sides of the pot or hooks his claws over the kettle's rim "like a person trying to keep from going over the edge of a roof." The cruelty of such a culinary endeavor is apparent to Wallace, who imagines what the lobster must be experiencing: "Even if you cover the kettle and turn away, you can usually hear the cover rattling and clanking as the lobster tries to push it off. Or the creature's claws scraping the sides of the kettle as it thrashes around. The lobster, in other words, behaves very much as you or I would behave if we were plunged into boiling water (with the obvious exception of screaming)."

In one of the article's most insightful and philosophical passages, Wallace writes, "Standing at the stove, it is hard to deny in any meaningful way that this is a living creature experiencing pain and wishing to avoid/escape the painful experience. To my lay mind, the lobster's behavior in the kettle appears to be the expression of a *preference*; and it may well be that an ability to form preferences is the decisive criterion for real suffering."

To those who would accuse the author of anthropomorphism, Wallace debunks the common view—cited by lobster-boiling apologists—that the animals have no cerebral cortex and therefore feel no pain. Indeed, he advances the theory that "lobsters are maybe even *more* vulnerable to pain, since they lack mammalian nervous systems' built-in analgesia."[79] It's an absolutely inspired piece, at turns funny and tragic, and anyone who reads it would need a pretty cold heart not to think twice about dining on these animals, who can live to be 100 years old and only want to be left on the ocean floor in peace.[80]

What makes Wallace's article so special is that we generally give little thought to the lives of lobsters and other creatures moving about beneath the waves. Even books and other sources arguing against cruelty to animals commonly overlook how fish, crustaceans, marine mammals, and other fresh- or saltwater beings are impacted by the world's hunger for animal protein. Humans raid the oceans for so much "seafood" that we don't even count the number of animals killed; we tally consumption by weight, as if these animals were sacks of grain.[81] They're certainly treated no better. Activist Dawn Carr, who sailed the Arctic aboard a commercial fishing boat as part of a documentary exploring PETA's anti-fishing campaign, describes fish taken from a net and tossed into a metal bin. "The violence used was shocking. Their delicate fins and gills twisted and tore as they were roughly ripped from the tangle of the net by hand. Some were still thrashing, while others were too tired to move," she says. "Many of the fish were vomiting up their guts, and their eyes bulged from the pressure changes. Some of these fish may have been struggling in the nets for as long as 24 hours. A few minutes later, their gill arches were slit and they were thrown into the next metal bin, where they twitched and gasped, slowly bleeding and suffocating to death. All piled on top of one another. Later, the fish were gutted and beheaded."[82] Up until the very end, these animals were fully conscious.

So too were the animals at the center of an investigation conducted by Mercy For Animals. Activists with the nonprofit visited a fish slaughter facility in Mesquite, Texas, where they witnessed appalling cruelty to catfish being killed for food and captured much of the abuse with a hidden camera. The disturbing video shows workers using pliers to rip the skin off of live fish, skinned animals still moving and gasping on the cutting table, and clearly suffering animals sliced in half. Yet even in the face of such graphic evidence, the Dallas County district attorney's office refused to bring animal cruelty charges against the workers.

Aquaculture

By nature bottom feeders, the catfish featured in the MFA video came not from the deep waters off the coast of Texas but from the state's vast fish-farming industry. Fish farming, or aquaculture, is essentially factory farming with a liquid coating, and it is has become one of the go-to solutions in the worldwide debate about the long-term viability and sustainability of food-production systems. Industrial-scale fish farms use huge inland tanks or offshore enclosures (such as nets) to raise the animals in what proponents allege are controlled conditions.[83] Though such a claim is in line with what meat, dairy, and egg producers would also like *their* customers to believe, the conditions in fish factories are far from controlled: they generate tons of excrement and are swirling with toxic chemicals and metals that damage the environment. Beneath the acres of fish-farming nets tethered in the ocean is a destructive blanket of fecal contaminants and uneaten feed producing bacteria that devour oxygen critical to shellfish and other bottom-dwelling sea creatures. (A fish farm with 200,000 salmon releases about the same amount of fecal matter as the raw sewage from 20,000 to 60,000 people.[84] Meanwhile, the waste from a farm in Lake Nicaragua raising tilapia—the most popular farmed fish in the US—has been compared to the impact of 3.7 million chickens defecating in the water.[85])

The farmed-fish industry—the so-called "Blue Revolution"—can't even ensure that the fish in these aquatic feedlots do not slip through containment nets and into the open water. While this might sound like a victory for the animals, domesticated fish can cause severe harm to fish in native habitats. Successive commercial breeding of Atlantic salmon, for example, has selected for large, quickly maturing, and aggressive fish who can out-compete with wild salmon for food, habitat, and mates.[86] They bring with them a host of diseases and pathogens that can infect and ultimately kill fish who have not been dosed with pharmaceuticals.[87] Moreover, the progeny of farmed salmon who breed with native salmon are genetically inferior, which scientists fear could lead to extinction for wild populations.[88] Just how serious is the potential for compromised survival? The World Wildlife Fund estimates that 2 million Atlantic salmon escape from fish farms every year—an amount equal to one-half the total population of wild salmon.[89] Farmed fish may also pass along their genes via fertilized eggs that drift from inside the net, through the mesh, and out to sea.

One of the most serious issues regarding aquaculture is sea lice—parasites that breed in the fish cages and ambush wild salmon, sea trout, and other fish as they migrate near salmon farms. Sea lice feed on the mucus, tissue, and blood of their hosts, literally eating fish alive. Historically, sea lice posed little threat to native fish, but with the expansion of aquaculture since the 1980s has come an outbreak of sea lice infestations on salmon in Canada, Ireland, Norway, and Scotland.[90] Fish-farming companies employ a variety of measures to combat the lice, including highly toxic chemicals.

Inviting readers to consider the environmental consequences of fish farming worldwide, Theresa Bert of the Florida Fish and Wildlife Conservation Commission writes that: "Overall, perhaps the most worrisome aspect of aquaculture effects is that they typically cannot be predicted until they occur; and that they can be extensive, complex, and irreversible." These effects include non-native aquatic species escaping into the environment, disrupting and altering ecosystems and the genetic diversity of wild populations; diseases being transferred to humans and other animals; and environmental damage caused by contamination.[91]

The ecological devastation caused by aquafarms is indefensible, distressing, and worthy of attention, but the industry's effect on the animals themselves is largely ignored by scientists and the mainstream media. Like its land-based model, aquaculture regards animals as commodities, an exploitable resource to be treated in whatever way generates the biggest financial return. Rather than indulging in their natural behaviors, or even being able to swim per the dictates of their instincts, the marine and freshwater organisms are crowded fin to fin in their artificial habitats, existing, as author Jeffrey Masson observes, "like bored zoo inhabitants."[92] To combat diseases that flourish amid overstocked tanks and nets, the fish are given antibiotics, and cheap feed is provided in the form of pellets that contain the blood and bones of cows, sheep, and pigs, feathers from the billions of chickens slaughtered each year, as well as fish meal and fish oil.[93] And the faster they grow the better.

Reproduction in fish farms is often performed the way factory farmers handle it—literally. In a process called "strip spawning," a hatchery worker pulls the female fish out of the water and uses his hand to express her eggs by applying pressure along the fish's

32

abdomen, essentially squeezing the eggs out, like toothpaste from a tube, through the vent near her posterior and into a bucket or plastic bag. Fertilized eggs are later transferred to an incubator for hatching.[94] Throughout the strip-spawning process, of course, the fish is being manipulated and restrained, experiencing the trauma of suffocation before being plopped back into the water.

At least fish subjected to strip spawning generally survive the ordeal. Farmed mollusks such as oysters, on the other hand, experience a more destructive torment: their tight-fitting protective shells are broken open with a knife while they're still alive. Sperm from the males and eggs from the females are removed, mixed in a beaker, and monitored for fertilization.[95]

Fish farming is expanding rapidly, exceeding even the growth of factory farming, which has become the dominant form of food production. Aquaculture accounted for 12 percent of the world's consumption of fish in 1992.[96] Ten years later, it was 30 percent.[97] As of 2013, the industry, having accounted for 47 percent of the 85 million metric tonnes (93.7 US tons) of "food fish" eaten in 2009, represented more than half of the fish consumed by the human population worldwide.[98] It is not unreasonable to speculate that in the absence of a drastic change in consumer behavior, before long the vast majority of fish eaten by humans will come from aquaculture, and this will stimulate a niche market for "humane seafood," similar to our current "humane meat" movement. A "humanely raised" salmon or crab will cost several times as much as a factory-farmed fish or crustacean—and will die in exactly the same, inhumane way.

For salmon and most other finfish, death comes after their gills are slit open, sometimes following a blow to the head. Trout and Atlantic halibut, on the other hand, are killed by packing the animals on ice and letting them slowly suffocate, a technique meant to extend their shelf life.[99] Adding to the fishes' misery is the routine practice of starving them for up to 10 days before they're sent to slaughter in an effort to reduce fecal contamination in the water during transport.[100] Imagine 50,000 stressed and famished carnivores confined in high density and it's pretty easy to do the math. The Humane Society of the United States reports that because farmed fish become habituated to specific feeding regimens, food deprivation or other diet changes may lead to a variety of welfare problems, including "cannibalistic behaviors that can cause eye damage and increased fin erosion."[101] The cruelest fate, poignantly described by Wallace, is dealt to lobsters (as well as crabs, crawfish, and oysters), who are kept alive until just before they're to be eaten, at which point most are boiled on stovetops. Whether they're a shellfish or finfish, these animals all experience frightening, lingering, and excruciating deaths that have prompted many animal advocates to wonder at what point the moral compass of the human race got crushed beneath the weight of humanity's arrogance.

Among the most controversial elements of aquaculture is feeding the captive fish, most of whom are carnivorous. Although defenders say aquaculture reduces the fishing pressure on natural resources, fish farmers are actually contributing to the problem since they are using wild-caught fish such as Pacific cod, Atlantic herring, jack mackerel, and blue mackerel to feed their fish.[102] This makes about as much sense as watering your lawn with Evian to lower your monthly water bill. Moreover, fish doomed to be turned into feed for other fish are taken from the sea using the very same industrial-fishing practices that are pillaging the world's oceans. Almost one-sixth of the entire catch hauled in by commercial fishing vessels goes to feed farmed fish.[103] It's an incredibly inefficient model that wastes the lives of countless smaller, open-ocean fish. According to John Volpe, an assistant professor of marine systems conservation at the University of Victoria in British Columbia, approximately 3 kilograms of forage fish go to produce 1 kilogram of farmed salmon, the ratio for cod is 5 to 1, and for tuna, the ratio is a staggering 20 to 1.[104] Some critics of aquaculture argue that the so-called feed-to-flesh ratio is actually worse than these numbers suggest. Montreal-based food writer Taras Grescoe, author of *Bottomfeeder: How to Eat Ethically in a World of Vanishing Seafood*, notes that in the case of salmon, the ratio is closer to 3.9 to 1.[105] That's almost 4 pounds of smaller fish—the Peruvian anchoveta, for instance, or sardines, herring, and krill—to produce a single pound of salmon flesh.

While this practice (another one in step with land-based ag models) has been the subject of some debate, almost no notice has been given to the chemical components used in fish feed. In addition to cancer-causing dioxins and polychlorinated biphenyls (better known as PCBs),[106] manufactured salmon feed commonly contains two pigments made from petrochemicals—astaxanthin and its cousin, canthaxanthin—to add a rosy hue to the fish. This process of dyeing farmed salmon flesh pink, sometimes referred to as "color finishing," enhances the meat's visual appeal, since consumers have learned to equate reddish salmon fillets with quality, and the flesh of salmon raised in farms is actually a dull gray. (In the wild, salmon acquire their pink tint by consuming krill, shrimp, and other crustaceans rich in carotenoids.)[107]

No matter what the fish look like on the inside, natural predators such as seals will make a meal of them if they can. This poses a problem for aquaculture businesses, since seals tear nets and literally gobble up profits. Marine Harvest, which bills itself as the world's largest producer of farmed salmon, claims they take a "humane approach" to hungry seals. According to their website, "The company policy is to discourage predators by employing a range of accepted and approved preventative measures, such as nets, which achieve a high rate of success while minimizing damage to wildlife."[108] But the company has had to admit that their employees have killed seals who get too close to their fish farms.[109] The issue has become a hot topic in Scotland, where Marine Harvest has operations and where animal rights groups say some 5,000 seals are killed every year by fish farmers. (Seals are a protected species in Scotland, but they can be shot to protect fish farms.) "At the moment, salmon farmers can, so long as they use the correct caliber of rifle and have the freely given variation to their firearms license to permit them to shoot seals, shoot and kill seals 365 days a year without need of any special license," says John Robins of the Scotland-based nonprofit Animal Concern.[110]

Although its exploitive endeavors are extensive, the fishing industry has yet to successfully farm one of the largest and most prized species, which is why tuna "ranching" is the latest aquaculture trend. Ranching bluefin tuna, the icon of the insatiable sushi market, involves capturing young wild fish in huge nets, then transporting them to offshore pens.[111] Here the fish gorge for months on sardines and can grow to be more than 1,000 pounds (450 kilograms) before they are slaughtered and exported, mainly to Japan. In Tokyo, a single bluefin tuna can routinely sell for as much as US$100,000, making this fish one of the most expensive meals anywhere. Indeed, a wild, 489-pound (222-kilogram) bluefin tuna caught off the northeastern coast of Japan sold for a breathtaking US$1.76 million in 2013—a record certain to be broken by the time the ink on this page is dry.[112]

But the nascent tuna-ranching industry may not last long. As conservationists fret over the future of bluefin tuna populations, warning of "overfishing," "unsustainability," and "stock collapse" (language, incidentally, that reinforces the notion of animals as commodities), scientists are busy trying to override the biological imperatives that prevent commercial breeding of the fish. Not only do these tuna take up to 12 years to reach sexual maturity, but they are not inclined to reproduce outside their natural habitat. That's about to change. Researchers in Australia have successfully tested hormone injections (delivered with a speargun) that essentially force bluefin tuna to spawn in captivity, thus creating a closed-lifecycle farming process—and another subjugated species.

Menhaden Reduction

With the increase in the world's appetite for fish and their touted health benefits—especially the omega-3 fatty acids found in fish oil, valued for lowering blood pressure and increasing mental capacity—

comes the commercial fishing industry's growth to satisfy it. This has become a major threat to what many biologists and environmentalists consider the most important species in the sea: a silver, foot-long fish called the menhaden. A voracious herbivore, the little menhaden are prized for their prolific ability to convert algae into omega-3s and other important proteins and oils. They swim in large schools with their mouths open, consuming phytoplankton (algae and other tiny plants) and, in the process, filtering up to 4 gallons (15 liters) of water a minute. Though bluefish, striped bass, redfish, bluefin tuna, and other fish are indeed high in omega-3s, they get these fatty acids by eating menhaden.

Because humans do not dine on menhaden directly, almost no one ever hears about what is happening to this keystone species, an animal crucial to the survival of marine ecosystems. Not only are they prey for countless other fish, but by eating enormous amounts of algae, menhaden clarify murky coastal waters, allowing sunlight to penetrate to greater depths. This in turn promotes the growth of plants that release dissolved oxygen as they photosynthesize. Menhaden also control the growth and spread of toxic algal blooms—the chief cause of underwater dead zones—that burst forth in part from manure runoff created by agribusiness;[113] the blooms block sunlight, suck up oxygen, and kill fish.

During the 19th century, menhaden were prized as a source of fertilizer and America's main source of industrial oil—whales having been hunted to near extinction by the 1850s.[114]

Fishing for menhaden became increasingly competitive and efficient with ensuing decades and the wars that helped shape new technologies. By the 1990s, what had become known as the menhaden reduction industry was essentially controlled by a single company: Houston-based Omega Protein. For more than a decade, Omega has been netting 90 percent of the menhaden caught in US waters, specifically the Atlantic and Gulf coasts.[115] The company uses every part of the fish, "reducing" their remains for use in a wide variety of products, including margarine, pet food, lipstick, linoleum, and omega-3 nutritional supplements. Though each of these products can be manufactured using more environmentally friendly ingredients, menhaden continue to be used because they can be caught and processed cheaply.

To satisfy demand, Omega catches billions of menhaden a year with the aid of spotter planes and a fleet of factory ships canvassing huge areas of ocean. Once a pilot locates a large school of menhaden from the air, he guides a nearby ship whose 170-foot hull can hold more than a million of the fish. The factory ship launches a pair of 40-foot boats, which spread a net nearly one-third of a mile long to corral and scoop up the entire school—tens of thousands of menhaden. As hydraulic equipment tightens the net, the fish thrash in panic, trying to escape. The factory ship then inserts a large vacuum tube into the churning biomass of menhaden, sucking them up and into the ship's refrigerated hold, where they will slowly die of suffocation.[116]

Though the menhaden population has declined by about 50 percent in recent years, H. Bruce Franklin, a professor of American studies at Rutgers University and author of the book *The Most Important Fish in the Sea: Menhaden and America*, believes their numbers could come back if we'd just leave them alone. "The fish is so fecund," he says. "If we give them a chance they'll recover."[117]

Shark Finning

When it comes to the widespread, commercial abuse of oceanic creatures, it would be hard to find a more abhorrent practice than shark finning. This involves catching a shark, slicing off his dorsal and pectoral fins, and dumping his body back into the water, where, now unable to swim, he will either suffocate because of his inability to move, bleed to death, or be attacked and gradually eaten by other predators.

Like any institutionalized cruelty, the finning of sharks is driven by demand, and the biggest market for shark fins is China. Shark fin soup has been a Chinese delicacy since at least the 14th century, when it was served exclusively to emperors of the Ming Dynasty and their guests. Such a noble beast as the shark, they reasoned, was only fit for a royal banquet table. Now an established tradition throughout China, shark fin soup is eaten at wedding celebrations, birthday dinners, and other special events. Demand for the dish has skyrocketed in the last two decades as China's growing middle class, estimated to be about 300 million consumers, embraces the kind of nouveau riche lifestyle their ancestors were denied.

In China's upscale restaurants, a bowl of shark fin soup can cost US$100 or more.[118] Though restaurateurs justify the expense by noting the high demand and invoking the food's imperial lineage, much of the cost for this culinary extravagance is likely due to how much preparation goes into making a virtually tasteless protein palatable. The shark fin is kept dry for three days before it is boiled for eight hours, the decayed flesh is removed, and then it is rinsed in cold water. Even then the gelatinous meat must be heavily flavored with spices and mixed with other bits of cooked flesh.[119] All this for a food with no nutritional value; indeed, a shark's fin is actually considered a health hazard. Because sharks are at the top of the food chain, they consume countless marine animals who are polluted with mercury, turning the shark's body into a highly toxic organism. Eating mercury-tainted shark flesh, say researchers, can harm the central nervous system and produce brain, lung, and kidney diseases. It may also render men sterile—an ironic consequence considering shark fin is purported to be an aphrodisiac.[120]

With their fins used in menus and as an ingredient in traditional Asian medicines, sharks are now the most hunted animals in history. "One hundred and four million sharks are killed each year, and 78 million of these are killed only for their fins," says activist and author Erik Brush, whose book *The Sixth Extinction* examines the connection between shark fin soup and the decimation of shark populations. "Of the 440 species of sharks worldwide, 242 are threatened and 52 species are either endangered or critically endangered."[121] Brush and other advocates argue that the unabated hunting could very well wipe out sharks entirely.

"There are estimates that shark populations are down 90 percent," says marine biologist Randall Arauz. "In some areas it's worse, like in the Gulf of Mexico and in the North Atlantic, where it's estimated at around 95 or even 98 percent."[122] Randall founded the Costa Rican nonprofit Pretoma (*Programa Restauración de Tortugas Marinas,* or the Association for the Restoration of Sea Turtles) in 1997 to protect turtles, who were (and are) being caught up in long, baited fishing lines. As Randall and his team discovered, the Taiwanese fleets off Costa Rica were after sharks and their fins, not the sea turtles also being hooked. Such species caught unintentionally while fishing for other marine life are known as "bycatch," and ecologically speaking, it's the offshore equivalent of clear-cutting a rainforest. Conservative figures suggest that unintended victims of the fishing industry represent at least 40 percent (38 million tonnes) of annual global marine catch.[123]

Not that such statistics deter many shark finners. "It is a very attractive business for fishermen," says Randall, who explains why the sharks are cast back after their fins are removed. "Basically, five percent of the shark is fins. If you catch a 50-kilo [110-pound] shark, that would be two and a half kilos of fins. You're going to get 70 or 80 dollars for a kilo of fins, but you're only going to get one dollar per kilo for the meat, so it doesn't make sense to waste all this space in your hold with this low-value meat. You might as well just chop off the fins and not bring the whole shark onto the boat."[124] Determined to see an end to the finning trade, Randall and his colleagues have turned Costa Rica into a model of shark conservation. In 2004, the country was the world's third largest exporter of shark products. By the following year, a Pretoma campaign had helped usher in a Costa Rican ban on shark finning, and Randall is now working to make the law international.

Because shark finning occurs at sea, far from public view, it is not on many people's radar. As it stands now, shark finning is illegal in 22 countries, including the United States, England, Australia, South

Africa, Canada, Brazil, Costa Rica, and Israel, as well as all the countries of the European Union.[125] Yet with an enormous financial incentive and vast oceans to plunder, traders still manage to traffic fins in these nations' waters. The European Union, for example, is the largest supplier of shark fins to China.[126] The good news is attitudes may be changing. A survey published in 2011 found that nearly 80 percent of people in Hong Kong believe it's no longer important to serve shark fin soup at wedding banquets, traditionally the most popular occasions for the dish.[127] Other countries are waking up to the devastation, too. At the 2013 summit on the Convention on International Trade in Endangered Species, the 178-nation body voted to grant trade protection to five shark species—a landmark decision that requires anyone fishing for these sharks to obtain strictly controlled permits to export the fins.[128]

Dolphin Deaths

For decades, dolphins have been collateral damage in humanity's fondness for tuna, captured as bycatch within huge nets because they school with yellowfin tuna in the eastern Pacific Ocean. In the 1950s, California tuna hunters became the first to exploit this relationship on a large scale using speedboats and high-tech purse-seine nets (which close at the top) to corral abundant schools of their targeted fish, along with the spinner and spotted dolphins who swim above them near the surface in pods of a thousand or more.[129] The technique was a boon to the tuna trade, and "dolphin fishing," as the industry calls it, resulted in enormous catches, ample profits, and the deaths of millions of cetaceans.

Dolphin mortality became a public-relations curse for canned-tuna companies, which were demonized for murdering Flipper and his kin. (Perhaps consumers would have been equally dismayed about the countless fish being killed if a tuna had starred in a popular movie or television show.) Many people boycotted canned tuna in the 1980s, and under additional pressure from environmental groups, the companies behind well-known brands like

StarKist and Chicken of the Sea eventually agreed to buy only "dolphin safe" tuna from fishing operations. Although it sounds terrific, at least for dolphins, this label only means that dolphins were not *intentionally* chased or netted during a fishing excursion, and it only applies to the US tuna industry: fleets from Colombia, El Salvador, Mexico, and Venezuela still net tuna and dolphins. Moreover, it's nearly impossible to prove that a company adheres to the dolphin-safe standard. As the Consumers Union of the United States put it, "Some tuna-fishing methods can injure or kill dolphins. The 'dolphin safe' logo indicates that those methods weren't used or that dolphins weren't harmed in the process. However, because independent verification of such claims—by observers who board fishing boats or make surprise visits to canneries to inspect captain's logs—is not universal, the logo is not an ironclad guarantee that the tuna in any given can was caught according to the standard."[130]

Bycatch is unavoidable in commercial fishing, and even if a dolphin is not accidentally killed, "safe" methods used in the pursuit of tuna may inadvertently kill other victims, including sharks, sea turtles, and non-target fish.

Because humans generally accord dolphins a high degree of respect, celebrate their intelligence, and go to some trouble to protect their dwindling populations,[131] it is alarming to see these gentle mammals, members of the whale family, chased and butchered for food throughout the six-month hunt that takes place each year in Japan. If you have occasion to see it, that is. Japanese fishermen and other locals go to a lot of trouble to keep their nation's "proud legacy"[132] of dolphin slaughtering hidden from public view. This is especially true in the village of Taiji, where fishermen locate pods of migrating dolphins out at sea and herd them into Hatagiri Bay with boats, nets, and long metal rods that crew members dip below the surface and pound to create an acoustical wall that disorients the dolphins' sonar.[133] The fishermen leave the animals overnight in a narrow cove and return at dawn armed with the knives and spears that will gradually turn the blue tide scarlet.

Town officials and bullies who support Taiji's Isana Fishery Union stalk, intimidate, and harass photographers, reporters, and anyone else who tries to record the killing; nevertheless, an account sometimes makes it to the press. Japan-based photojournalist Boyd Harnell managed to evade his minders long enough to witness one of the morning massacres and publish his observations in *The Japan Times*, an English-language daily. "Skiffs [small boats] manned by fishermen armed with long knives motored into the cove," he writes. "Using sweep nets, they forced the dolphins from the capture cove into the neighboring killing cove. Some dolphins tried frantically to resist. Others that became caught in the nets were hauled into skiffs. They were taken offshore and loaded onto longboats. I could see the longboats clearly through my telephoto lens. Some crew members had long knives. Others held hoses. The men with knives made repeated stabbing motions. The dolphins' dorsal fins and tail flukes were moving wildly. The stabbing continued until the dolphins became motionless. Several of the crew hosed down blood. A man tossed entrails and blubber overboard." Harnell calls Japan's annual slaughter an "ethnic cleansing of a species."[134]

To create the 2009 award-winning documentary exposing this atrocity, *The Cove*, director Louie Psihoyos and his team resorted to some serious stealth, both to elude police tails and to secure the incriminating footage that depicts the carnage in Taiji.[135] Among the tools the filmmakers used were camouflage clothing, face paint, tiny cameras tucked into headgear, military-style thermal cameras, aerial drones, cameras hidden on the ocean floor, and a remote-controlled helicopter. They even enlisted the special-effects wizards at George Lucas' Industrial Light & Magic to help them create "rock cams"—realistic-looking foam rocks that concealed high-definition cameras and microphones, which were secretly installed around the secluded cove's perimeter.[136] "They really outdid themselves," says Psihoyos. "[The rocks] looked really real. When we went back with a flashlight to find them, we had to pick up the rocks to tell."[137]

All these cloak-and-dagger measures helped reveal a practice that gets almost no media attention in its own backyard. As a result, although fishermen are chasing and killing about 23,000 dolphins a year, the Japanese themselves are generally unaware of it, says Richard "Ric" O'Barry, the marine-mammal specialist who is the emotional core of *The Cove*. He explains that the Japanese government suppresses news of the dolphin hunts. "A real democracy has a party in power and has an opposition party," he says. "They don't have that. They have one party, a right-wing party that controls the media and they make sure that the Japanese people don't know the truth."[138]

Passionate and outspoken, Ric has been at the center of the campaign against Japan's dirty little secret since 1980. That year, environmental filmmaker Hardy Jones captured images of the bloody dolphin massacre at Katsumoto, a village on Iki Island, unveiling Japan's government-subsidized disgrace to a worldwide audience. Consumption of cetacean flesh is not only considered taboo in the West, but tormenting the frantic dolphins for hours before slaying them in a cascade of blades and gore is a horrifying end. People were outraged, yet news outlets soon moved on to other disturbing stories, and in the pre-Internet era, an incident not being chronicled in the press was easily forgotten. Ric and the animal advocacy group Sea Shepherd stepped in, along with a coalition of other pro-dolphin activists, and together they have been putting pressure on Japan to end the cetacean tragedy. Ric rejects Japan's argument that dolphin hunting is a cultural practice that should be tolerated—even revered—because it is a 400-year-old tradition. "It used to be the culture and tradition of the Aztecs to take somebody's heart out while it's still beating, but that doesn't mean it's right," he says.[139]

In addition to being butchered and served as food, dolphins are also rounded up and sold to marine parks and zoos. This is especially painful to Ric, who blames himself for helping to fuel the captive-dolphin trade after his years working on the 1960s TV series

Flipper, which secured the dolphin's place in pop culture and perpetuated the notion that these self-aware creatures should be confined in pools for human amusement.[140] It was after a stint as a Navy diver that Ric was employed by the Miami Seaquarium, where he captured dolphins for display. He was so good at it and has such an abiding connection with the animals that when *Flipper* came along, the show's producers asked Ric to capture and train the five bottlenose dolphins who collectively played the title character. But he later recognized and regretted the suffering he'd had a major role in, and for four decades he has been on a mission to end the global capture and exploitation of dolphins in aquatic parks like Florida's Marineland and SeaWorld (an injustice we'll explore in Chapter 6). When he learned about the rarely-seen dolphin slaughter in Japan, Ric began visiting the country, now often in disguise to thwart his detractors, and makes appearances throughout the world, speaking about the violence to anyone who will listen. In addition to condemning the process of chasing and killing dolphins, Ric warns

---

The Return of Horse Meat

In 2011, after a five-year hiatus, slaughtering horses for human consumption became legal again in the US. But according to Lester Friedlander, a veterinarian and former chief USDA inspector, it is all but impossible to kill a horse in line with the federal Humane Methods of Slaughter Act. Slaughterhouses, you see, are not designed for horses: their heads, narrower than a cow's, are not secured in the "knock box," where a worker is supposed to stun the horse into insensibility with a single shot from a captive bolt gun. "The captive bolt is not a proper instrument for the slaughter of equids," says Dr. Friedlander. "These animals regain consciousness 30 seconds after being struck; they are fully aware they are being vivisected."[141]

---

of the meat's health risks: like sharks, dolphins are top predators who ingest some of the ocean's worst heavy-metal pollution, leaving their bodies laden with high levels of mercury.

Psihoyos hopes *The Cove* will help sound the death knell for Japan's dolphin slaughter. "What I set out to do was not so much make a movie as to create a movement," he says. "This movie is a tool to shut this thing down and end the barbarism we saw back there in that cove."[142]

Illegal Slaughter

It would be difficult to imagine a more nightmarish end to any life than what is doled out to animals in slaughterhouses: the smell of death; the sense of impending violence; the unrelenting speed with which workers must stun, kill, and transform one animal after another into products. Even the most graphic video scenes captured by undercover activists are generally recorded within slaughter-houses that are licensed by the government and subject to some form of oversight requiring that animals be killed humanely.[143] And while "killed humanely" may be the biggest oxymoron since "civil war," at least the executioners in regulated packing plants are answerable to agencies such as the United States Department of Agriculture; the UK's Department of Environment, Food, and Rural Affairs; and the Canadian Food Inspection Agency. These organizations inspect slaughterhouses and are authorized to revoke a business license if certain hygiene, workers' safety, and animal welfare standards are not met.[144]

Behind tall fences and walls throughout the world, however, are countless illegal slaughter enterprises operating outside the purview of official agencies. Here animals are lucky if they meet their end with a properly aimed bullet. But because guns and ammunition cost money and might startle neighbors, an animal's final moments in an unregulated slaughterhouse are more likely to be spent in agony hanging by the neck, bleeding out from a wound delivered with a dirty screwdriver, or, as was the case at one illicit butcher shop in

China, dying of disease or freezing to death.[145] Unencumbered by government policies, many of these operations have live animals on the premises and feed them garbage. Cows, sheep, and goats may also be fed ruminant-derived food, which, as we've seen, increases the risk of mad cow disease.

Many illegal slaughter facilities have no running water for sanitation or refrigeration to keep meat from spoiling. In England, undercover investigators from Hillside Animal Sanctuary visited an unlicensed slaughterhouse near Ilkley and recorded the throats of sheep being slit with a blunt knife. A subsequent raid by police revealed one sheep with a maggot-infested foot, another with a scrotum hernia, and a third with pneumonia and chronic mastitis, a painful infection of the udder. They also found a chopping block covered in bird droppings, maggots in meat, rusty carcass hooks, and an open sewer running through the slaughterhouse with human feces flowing from a toilet. The father and son who owned and operated this little slice of hell received three months in prison.[146]

In the United States, the slaughter and sale of an animal without a license is a misdemeanor and may be coupled with other charges, including animal cruelty, improper disposal of an animal, and creating a sanitary nuisance. This doesn't dissuade the owners of backyard butcher shops, though, especially in lucrative markets like Florida's Miami-Dade County. Because Congress has withheld funding for USDA inspections that would be required for horses to be killed and their flesh sold for human consumption, no slaughter-houses can operate for this purpose—at least not legally.[147] In fact, of all the meat coming from unlicensed slaughter businesses in Florida, horse meat is the most profitable product, selling for as much as US$40 a pound. If purveyors don't have access to a horse from typical sources—such as an auction or even a trainer willing to sell a losing racehorse cheap, no questions asked—they've been known to kill an animal in her stall on private property.

Beginning a few years ago, reports of pet horses being butchered by the side of Florida roads or in rural barns indicated an upsetting trend, and authorities speculated that the crimes were connected to the local demand for horse meat. The last plants in the US authorized to slaughter horses for human consumption closed in 2007, which not only buoyed the black-market trade but inspired violent attacks on companion horses. Describing the killings, Richard Couto, who is leading an aggressive campaign against illegal slaughter in Miami-Dade County, says the perpetrators literally cut and run. "There's a particular way you have to cut the throat of an animal for it to be humane, and these people are not doing it; they're cutting right into the windpipe of the horses, which means they are suffering a monstrously cruel death. They are choking on their own blood. It takes a horse 15 minutes to die from something like that." Trespassing on someone's property, the killers don't wait for suffering animals to die of their injuries. "They want to harvest the meat and get away as quickly as possible," says Richard, "so once the animal hits the ground, they start carving."

A former investigator with South Florida's Society for the Prevention of Cruelty to Animals, Richard has since founded the nonprofit Animal Recovery Mission to combat illegal slaughter. He's seen plenty of abuse, but nothing like what is happening to horses in his state. The killing of a mare named Bonita, he says, was particularly vicious. Four men broke into her stall one night and slashed her throat, but she didn't go down, perhaps because she was standing beside her young foal. Anxious to begin removing flesh, the men used a metal pipe to break the horse's legs, and she slumped to the ground. But Bonita was a fighter, and she struggled. To keep her immobile, one man sat on her head while another sat on her neck. The other two men sank their knives into Bonita, who was fully conscious as they hacked off slabs of muscle. When the foal cried out for her mother, the men taped her mouth shut. They left with Bonita's hind legs and 80 percent of her flesh; they later admitted to Miami-Dade police that while they were leaving, the mare was struggling to call for her foal. "When I got there the next morning, the foal was trying to nurse off the mare's carcass," adds Richard. "That is what is going on here, and that's why I'm not backing down."[148]

> "Bearing witness to the inherent cruelty inflicted upon the innocent victims of our appetites can be very painful, and I encourage people to know themselves well enough to know how much they can handle. The idea is to be an effective advocate who can speak to the truth—not endure self-inflicted abuse for its own sake. The effect of bearing witness can be traumatic, but that's not always a bad thing."[149]
> —Colleen Patrick-Goudreau

They Shoot Horses, Don't They?

Equally determined is Amanda Sorvino, a longtime animal rescuer who is campaigning to end the sale of "retired" racehorses to Canada and Mexico, where, after enduring crowded transport on trucks without food or water, the animals are killed with a bullet to the head or several knife thrusts to the neck.[150] Their flesh is then shipped to Belgium, China, France, Italy, Japan, and other countries where eating horse meat is considered as acceptable as dining on the remains of fish, chickens, or pigs.[151] Amanda and her father, actor Paul Sorvino, were featured in a 2008 segment of the television show *Inside Edition* to expose this practice. "If a horse can't run fast enough on the track, he goes to slaughter," said Paul in the program. "So he is literally running for his life." The reporter in the segment claimed that all the horse slaughterhouses in the United States had been closed. But at least one viewer knew that wasn't so.

"A woman named Ellen-Cathryn Nash contacted me and said the *Inside Edition* show was not factual," says Amanda. "She said, 'All three horse slaughterhouses were *not* shut down, as they said on the show. There is still a horse slaughterhouse in America, and it's called Bravo Packing.'" New Jersey-based Bravo Packing is a supplier of meat for "exotic carnivores," such as pet snakes and big cats in zoos;

indeed, the company eagerly promotes the fact that it sells horse meat to zoos. What Bravo Packing does not promote is how it procures, abuses, and eventually slaughters the ill-fated equines who end up there.

"The horses are killed in front of each other, outside in the kill pen, where they live," says Amanda. She and Nash, also a devoted horse rehabilitator, used a variety of ruses and a hidden camera to collect evidence against Bravo and its owners, the Merola family. Son Monty, says Amanda, was particularly cruel. "He would come out, sit on the fence, and shoot at horses with a rifle. They were target-practiced to death. He loved doing that; he thought it was fun." Foul-tempered and prone to violence (he had served time in prison for rape), Monty would shoot horses when he got angry and often start butchering them before they had died. "He admitted to me that they're still flinching while he's chain-sawing their legs off." Occasionally, he didn't even try to kill them. "If the horses were weak enough and wouldn't present a problem," says Amanda, "Monty would just take them into the slaughterhouse and cut off their limbs while they were alive."

Bravo Packing eventually lost contracts with several zoo officials, who suspected the Merolas were selling them "4-D meat"—flesh from diseased, disabled, dying, or dead animals (who died before reaching the slaughterhouse). Though 4-D meat has long been used legally as a cheap ingredient for pet food, it can carry remnants of diseases that killed the animals, and it may be filled with the residue of pharmaceuticals used to treat them, including penicillin, procaine, and trimethoprim. It is its sales to zoos that keeps Bravo in the horse-killing business, and Monty wasn't about to give up his fun. He even had a "lean meat program" that was an excuse to torture horses. Because lean meat is lower in saturated fats and preferred by many zoos, it sells for a higher price; Monty would simply let horses go hungry. Some horses starved to death, their bony bodies collapsing into the blood-soaked dirt of the kill pen.[152]

I write about Monty Merola's activities in the past tense not because he is serving jail time for his crimes, but because he died at age 49 before he could face legal consequences. New Jersey authorities did charge him with two counts of felony animal cruelty; however, Merola was diagnosed with throat cancer in 2008 and slowly withered away, much like the "lean meat" horses he refused to feed, succumbing to the disease in October 2009. Monty's father Joe, owner of Bravo Packing, now kills and slaughters the horses. The company continues to sell meat to zoos.

The Trouble with Tipples

First the good news: there's no shortage of vegan drinks out there. Now the bad news: animals are used to create certain alcoholic beverages. While this may be obvious with drinks like Irish cream or honey porter, animal-derived ingredients are often hidden in other beverages. Brewmasters, winemakers, and distillers might include animal contents for color or flavor, but the main use is during the fining process, when alcohol is filtered for leftover yeast and contaminants. Companies use a variety of animal ingredients to grab onto impurities and make it easier to catch them in filters. Following is a partial list of the animal exploitation often found in alcohol.

- Gelatin – a collagen made from bones, skin, and hooves. Gelatin is commonly used to attract tannins and reduce bitterness in wine during the fining process.
- Isinglass – a form of gelatin made from the swim bladders of fish. Many ales are cleared of impurities using isinglass.
- Egg whites. Used in the fining process for wine.
- Chitin – a compound found in the shells of lobsters, crab, and shrimp. Another material used in the fining process for wine.
- Cochineal beetles. Carmine and cochineal are pigments

---

produced from pregnant scale insects of the species *Dactilopius coccus* and used as a colorant in drinks such as wine and the aperitif Campari. Sometimes identified as "Natural Red #4" on ingredient labels.

For some adult-beverage companies, animal exploitation has become a marketing ploy, such as mescal and its worm or the latest insect-in-spirits craze: scorpion-infused vodka. There's even a brewer in Scotland that sold beer in bottles stuffed inside the taxidermied carcasses of squirrels, weasels, and a rabbit. Fortunately, alternatives exist for these animal-based ingredients, so finding vegan alcohol is not difficult. For a frequently updated list of beers, wines, and liquors free of animal suffering, visit www.barnivore.com.

Live Export

Australia, home to the world's largest wool industry, is also the largest exporter of live animals, driven primarily by the desire to squeeze one last bit of profit from "spent" sheep who are nearing the end of their useful wool-producing lives.[153] Like milk-producing cows and egg-laying hens, sheep are thanked for their service to humanity by being crowded together and sent to slaughter. In the case of sheep, however, the transport often isn't to the nearest slaughterhouse, but to a port thousands of miles away. Each year, Australia exports more than 6 million sheep, most destined for markets in the Middle East, where they are ritually killed for both religious sacrifice and food.

Although shipping live farmed animals from one country to another is nothing new, the suffering of the animals has increased as the distances they are transported have grown. This became tragically clear in the summer of 2003, when the MV *Cormo Express*, an 11-deck converted ferry, departed Fremantle, Australia, with 57,937 sheep bound for Saudi Arabia. After 16 days at sea, the ship arrived in Jeddah, where Saudi veterinary inspectors rejected the sheep, saying 6 percent of the flock was infected with scabby mouth, a highly contagious viral disease. The animals languished in the vessel under grueling temperatures for eight more weeks as Australian authorities scrambled to find a port that would accept the sheep, who were rapidly dying from heat exhaustion, infections, and stress-induced loss of appetite in the cramped *Cormo*. Australia eventually paid AU$1 million to the government of Eritrea to accept the animals, and by the time the crew unloaded the ship, 5,692 sheep had perished.[154]

During the ordeal, a worker onboard the *Cormo* told an Australian television reporter that they were dropping dead sheep down a long chute leading to a macerator, which grinds them up and "squirts them out the side into the water." The worker added that in many cases sheep were still alive when they hit the spinning blades. These are just the sheep the crew could see, he admitted: after nearly three months, fecal waste in the sheep pens was piled a foot high and covered the bodies of the dead and dying.[155]

The *Cormo Express* ordeal captured the world's attention, and there was a public outcry to reform live export. In addition to Australia temporarily suspending the shipment of live animals to Saudi Arabia, the disaster resulted in the federal minister for agriculture appointing a committee to review the livestock-export industry. The committee found that the animals' deaths were directly caused by the stressful conditions of long-distance transport, and they proposed new national standards for the export of live animals.[156] Instead of following this recommendation, the government established an industry-dominated panel to develop the Australian Standards for the Export of Livestock (ASEL).[157]

Not surprisingly, there are a host of problems with the resulting standards. To begin with, they are riddled with loopholes that exclude some animals. ASEL are also impossible to enforce and fail to require transparency or feedback in the export process. The little reporting that is done is handled by veterinarians accredited by the

Australian Quarantine and Inspection Service (AQIS); these vets are employed and directed by the live exporters. "Even when there are shipments that clearly breach the standards, AQIS merely requires they do better next time," says Glenys Oogjes, executive director of Animals Australia. "I mean by this that they add a condition to their license, often to reduce the stocking density on the next few shipments. In all the years since 2004, only once did an exporter have his license to export suspended for a couple of months—after hundreds of cattle had died." But the biggest problem with ASEL, says Glenys, is that they do nothing to relieve suffering. "No standards can change the very nature of the handling, journey, further handling, and slaughter in countries in the Middle East, which do not have animal welfare laws or humane slaughter practices. Still, we have around 40,000 sheep die on ships each year, and the live export industry proponents characterize this as 99 percent of animals arriving healthy at the other end."[158]

Animals Australia has documented countless abuses of Australian animals exported to the Middle East, where sheep coming off a boat are routinely purchased for home slaughter, trussed with rope, and tossed into a car trunk in 104° F (40° C) heat. After a grueling car ride, the animals will have their throats cut while fully conscious.

Youth Programs

As part of a never-ending effort to attract new generations of cattle ranchers and industrial farmers, agribusiness depends on one of nature's most reliable tenets: children adore animals. In fact, they love almost anything to do with animals, from teddy bears and cartoon rabbits to petting zoos and pony rides. Many families live with companion animals, and playing with Buddy and Daisy makes many kids just as happy as eating a Happy Meal. But the important connection between McDonald's and Old MacDonald's factory farm comes much later, and for children, the reality that animals are killed to make hamburgers, hot dogs, nuggets, and other meat products can be even more troubling than learning the truth about Santa Claus.

To help overcome the child's natural fondness for animals, those involved in the meat trade indoctrinate some children early, gradually desensitizing them to the pain and violence behind the gate-to-plate business. In ag-oriented youth programs such as FFA and 4-H, students drawn to farming because of their affection for animals can get hands-on experience with cows, pigs, chickens, goats—essentially any creature who might end up as breakfast, lunch, or dinner. After bonding with these animals comes a profound betrayal: the child is forced to part with someone she has groomed, fed, and loved so the animal can be sent to slaughter. To FFA and 4-H club leaders, these animals are simply "projects" who will be "harvested" or "processed," indoctrinating kids into the agriculture system; to young people, the experience can be devastating.

In an op-ed published in the *Chicago Tribune*, PETA's Jennifer O'Connor writes about her stepdaughter Bonnie, who joined a 4-H club because, says the nine-year-old, "cows are cool." Agribusiness doesn't care that cows are cool or sensitive or that they feel fear and pain. These animals are artificially inseminated on what the dairy industry calls a "rape rack," then later have their calves taken from them hours after giving birth—an indefensibly cruel practice for both mother and calf—so the lactating cows will "give" milk for human consumption. Bonnie was heartbroken to learn that the ultimate fate of all cows used in the dairy industry is slaughter, even one of her beloved bovine friends. "To see such a deep bond so ruthlessly broken was a painful and eye-opening lesson for Bonnie," writes Jennifer. "Her club leader was genuinely puzzled and irked by Bonnie's tears, dismissing her as 'sentimental.'"[159] Today, Bonnie is a vegetarian.

As a former 4-H student, Erin Williams understands that losing a farmed animal can be just as emotionally devastating as losing a companion animal. "Rabbits, chickens, ducks, sheep, and dairy cows were my 'projects' in elementary school and junior high," she says. "We had all manner of animals on my family's dairy farm in northern Illinois. I refused to sell them at the end of the season, so they stayed on the farm or we found homes for them with people we knew. However, my cow Zelda, who was a beautiful, affectionate, and rambunctious Brown Swiss, was killed because she couldn't conceive and therefore was unable to lactate. I didn't know that she had been slaughtered until about a week later, and I remember going to a fast food restaurant soon after. I sat down to eat my hamburger and couldn't take a bite of it, thinking about her and all the other animals just like her who were ground up in those burgers."[160] Erin has since devoted her life to animal advocacy and co-authored the book *Why Animals Matter: The Case for Animal Protection.*

Classroom Cruelty

Ag programs are also taught in schools (sometimes affiliated with FFA), where animals may be slaughtered in front of—or even by—young students. A lesson involving 16 chickens and the 31 eighth-graders who raised them illustrates the suffering animals endure and the conflict children face in these programs. Students at The Community School, a private school in Sun Valley, Idaho, were provided with a breed of chicks typically raised for meat. After seven weeks spent raising the birds, during which time many of the kids formed emotional bonds with the animals, students stuffed the chickens upside down into metal killing cones and cut their throats. Teachers Naomi Goldberg and Scott Runkel claim it took each bird about 20 seconds to die. A number of the children had misgivings about how the project ended, and 14-year-old Arielle Rawlings unknowingly characterized how ag programs like this desensitize kids. Referring to the chickens fellow students killed, she said, "Now that they're gone, I kind of miss them. But I'm trying to make myself understand that they were there for meat."[161]

In a lengthy letter to the editor of Sun Valley's local newspaper, Karen Davis of United Poultry Concerns strenuously objected to The

Community School's chicken project, observing that: "This classroom chicken-killing exercise is not only animal abuse but child abuse. Students were encouraged by their teachers to betray the birds who trusted them." Karen wrote that in using killing cones, which prevent the chickens from thrashing as they normally would when being slaughtered, students could not fully recognize the suffering the birds experienced. She also pointed out that although the children were told the chickens' deaths would be "humane," there is nothing humane about how they were killed. "Throat-cutting is extremely painful. Chickens have the same neurophysiological pain receptors in the neck and throat as humans do. They have the same panic responses, so forget 'humane.'... Twenty seconds is an eternity dying in agony, but it takes a chicken longer than 20 seconds to die by the knife, even when the killer knows what he or she is doing."[162]

Goldberg and Runkel defended the project in a written statement for the media that not only ignored the concerns Karen expressed, but seemed to suggest that a plant-based diet is somehow unpatriotic. "It is highly unrealistic for us to expect our students, or our fellow Americans, to all become vegans," they wrote. "What we tried to show the students was that if they are going to eat meat, it is possible to mitigate some of the more awful effects of factory farming by choosing to eat meat that has been raised and slaughtered in the most humane way possible."[163]

Karen had the final word in her organization's newsletter: "Thus far, not a single substantive issue raised by United Poultry Concerns has been addressed by The Community School—including the fact that the chickens they killed and consumed came from the very same factory-farm conditions the teachers piously claimed to oppose."[164]

No school, however, has received the kind of public drubbing that was dished out to Green Mountain College (GMC), a four-year liberal arts college in Vermont. Located in Poultney, a town perhaps best known for predating the American Revolution, GMC became the flashpoint for animal lovers everywhere when it announced in October 2012 that its "teaching farm" would be slaughtering two oxen, Bill and Lou, and serving their remains in the dining hall at the end of the month. The bovine best friends had pulled a plow for the college's ag program for so many years that they became veritable school mascots, known for their big, brown eyes and gentle demeanors. Their faces were even used as the program's Facebook profile—that is, until Lou hurt his leg and the school declared the mascots would be slaughtered and fed to the students.[165] Online petitions appealing to GMC to spare the pair quickly gathered signatures from around the world. Authors and advocates such as Marc Bekoff, Karen Davis, and Pattrice Jones joined the chorus of voices urging the college to reconsider. Pattrice lobbied especially hard for GMC to allow the animals to "retire" at the Vermont sanctuary she cofounded, VINE. Sadly, the college was unmoved. They announced on November 11 that they had euthanized Lou and buried him in an undisclosed location. (They said Bill would remain in their care.) In the end, perhaps we can't be too surprised by this, coming from an ag program whose idea of modern sustainability is so firmly rooted in antiquated practices like yoking animals. As historian James McWilliams put it, "Bill and Lou have been generating electricity and plowing fields for ten years on the bucolic Green Mountain campus, a campus from where students will graduate with a skill set enabling them to conquer the 18th century."[166]

Tragically, farmed animals kept on school grounds are not even safe from the general public. Just about anyone determined to injure or kill animals raised as "projects" for ag-education programs can force their way into a school farm, and such crimes occur all-too frequently—among the more repugnant examples: 35 pigs sponsored by FFA viciously stabbed and beaten by five junior high school students in Washington State;[167] 15 animals, including chickens and turkeys, beaten to death with a steel rake and a metal pole at a high school in Australia;[168] two FFA lambs killed with a hacksaw and chisel in California;[169] two chickens beaten to death with a tennis racket at a primary school in England;[170] and several FFA pigs bludgeoned with a shovel and then run over by a truck in Texas.[171] In nearly every instance of school-related animal abuse I researched, the alleged perpetrators turned out to be male teenagers; however, one incident in 2010 involved two 11-year-old boys who broke into a primary school in Sheffield, England, and murdered a hen.[172] The hen reportedly loved to follow students around and was probably killed thinking the boys were there to play with her. Emphasizing the property status of animals, the media reporting on these crimes generally refer to the abusers as "vandals," and they quote sources who invariably note how much the animals would have sold for at auction.

If teachers and ag-group leaders genuinely wanted to expose young people to the realities of modern animal agriculture, they would take them on a behind-the-scenes tour of a factory farm. Here, where animals are afforded almost no protection, students would bear witness to the intensive confinement, the physical mutilations, the absence of medical care, and the other abuse that animal interests fight to keep hidden at all costs.

Calf Induction

It's easy to see the influence of the dairy industry in New Zealand. Stroll through any town and it seems that on every major street corner you'll find a little grocery store that calls itself a "dairy," though you won't find any cows here. A century ago, these neighborhood markets were the only shops in the country allowed to sell cows' milk, cheese, and butter—products they still offer, alongside bread, candy, soft drinks, and other consumer goods. For Kiwis, the name for an industry that impregnates cows and steals their babies on a massive scale to earn a profit has become synonymous with the modest, mostly family-run businesses that provide communities with a shopping convenience.

In 2010, New Zealand's dairy customers—both kinds—were shocked by a television exposé on milk production. The news report featured graphic images of dead and dying infant calves whose mothers had been forced to give birth prematurely in order to align all the cows into a dairy's herd management table. By inducing (or, in many cases, aborting) the births of calves, the farmer is able to get as many animals as possible milking early in the season. Currently, half the calves in New Zealand's dairy industry are born in August, about 20 percent are born in July, another 20 percent are born in September, and the rest are born in October. Such a schedule is a financial concern for farmers, who want their cash cows grazing on the spring pasture growth at the same time. (Few New Zealand dairy farmers feed their cows grain.)

The practice of calf induction began quietly in the 1970s and now involves close to 200,000 calves a year. It starts with a veterinarian injecting the mother with dexamethasone ester, a drug that induces labor and causes the calf to be born before the complete nine-month gestation period. "The calves are either born dead or are so weak they will die after birth," says Hans Kriek, executive director of the New Zealand-based nonprofit Save Animals From Exploitation (SAFE). "The ones who do not die are usually killed by the farmer. They are either shot or bashed to death. Giving birth to a dead or dying baby is also highly stressful for the cow. Cows are often seen trying to help their dying calf in vain and their distress is very obvious." Hans adds that mother cows are at great risk of retained fetal membrane syndrome, where the placenta remains in the cow's body. This can lead to severe infection and death.[173]

Although large-scale calf induction seems to be restricted to New Zealand's dairy industry (at least for now), the country is the world's largest producer of internationally traded dairy products; indeed, 95 percent of New Zealand's milk is turned into products that are exported to 140 countries. In other words, the industry's homegrown cruelty is being exported around the planet.[174] The good news is that this practice has become so controversial that many veterinarians are calling for an end to it.[175]

Pigs as Presents

The concept sounds wonderful to many people: Help end hunger by providing a farmed animal to an impoverished family. Every November, just in time for the holidays, the mailboxes of compassionate people in developed nations become stuffed with glossy pleas from a seemingly endless procession of give-a-cow nonprofits, some endorsed by celebrities and all asking you to donate funds that will supply animals to the poor. For US$75, World Vision will send a needy family a goat, or a donation of US$30 will buy them five ducks. Harvest of Hope, meanwhile, offers a bull, plow, and seeds for a Ghanaian farmer for US$850, and US$45 will buy a pig whose "offspring are raised and sold for a profit, giving a family a steady source of income," reads the catalog. A Heifer International catalog encourages grandparents to donate the cost of rabbits (US$60) in honor of their granddaughter's first Christmas. "What better way to share the joy you see in the eyes of such a healthy, happy little girl than to make a gift in her name that can help provide a trio of bunny rabbits ... that helps impoverished families increase their protein intake and income." I wonder how the little granddaughter would feel seeing these precious animals slaughtered.

Most would agree that helping struggling rural families along the road to self-reliance is a laudable goal. Yet, apart from perpetuating what amounts to a nonhuman slave trade, giving to programs that exploit animals makes no economic or environmental sense. Consider the family that is provided with a cow or goat from whom they can take milk for nourishment and a little income. Ignoring the consequences of giving gastrointestinal complications to the 90 percent of African and Asian adults and older children who are lactose intolerant[176]—does a hungry child really need diarrhea to add to his misery?—animals require proper food, large quantities of water, shelter, and care, including occasional medical treatment. Just how is a disadvantaged family supposed to provide for one or more animals when feeding *themselves* is a challenge?

Journalist Palagummi Sainath describes a thoroughly misguided program that gave thousands of cows and buffaloes to many of the poorest farmers in India. The "livestock disaster," as Sainath describes it, was sponsored by the government and placed animals in locations where there is very little water and no fodder for feed. "Much of what the farmers have got is inadequate, inedible, and the animals won't have it," he writes. Sainath interviewed a number of disgruntled farmers who got stuck with animals they neither asked for nor could afford to keep. "They landed up at my house and made me take this cow," protested one farmer. "I said we don't want this. We have never kept cattle and don't know how to. Give one of us a job, any work. Instead, my son is full time in service of this cow. Were he not tied down by it, he would earn Rs.50 a day [about US$1.00] as a laborer. This brute eats more than all us in this house put together."[177]

Among the most outspoken critics of these programs is Andrew Tyler, director of Animal Aid, which encourages ethical shoppers to support charities that assist families without victimizing animals. "Meat and milk can be afforded only by communities with surplus wealth," Andrew says. "The average British dairy farmer, for instance, receives a very generous £32,000 annual payment from the European taxpayer. A 'gift' of animals to destitute communities, where no such support is available, will simply impoverish them further. It is far more rational to support such people in growing food that they can eat directly." By consuming plant-based foods themselves, rather than first feeding the nutrients to animals, he says, impoverished families conserve agricultural resources such as land and water. The response by some aid agencies forced to cope with the inefficiencies, expense, and environmental destruction of animal farming has been to established so-called "zero grazing" regimes in which animals are permanently confined in sheds. "But they still need water and food," says Andrew, "and, in such cruel and deprived environments, can suffer high levels of disease, early infertility, and premature death."[178]

Campaigning on this issue from an environmental perspective is the conservation group World Land Trust (WLT). They argue that giving cows, goats, and other grazing animals to people in arid environments, notably parts of Africa, adds to the problems of drought and desertification. "It doesn't look as if [aid agencies] have thought this scheme through properly," says John Burton, chief executive of WLT. "It seems as if they don't understand the connection between habitat degradation and poverty."[179] John later added, "They seem to be doing this just to make money at Christmas. It's a gimmick."[180]

"Ultimately, my objection is to the commercial forces that are seeking to persuade people of the poor world that their best nutritional interests are served by buying into modern, high-throughput farmed animal production processes," says Andrew Tyler. "With that comes an addiction to high-capital input systems, additional stresses on precious water supplies, environmental destruction, a loss of control over the means of production, bad health, a nightmare animal welfare scenario, and more human poverty and malnourishment."[181]

What You Can Do

Obviously, the first and easiest step any compassionate person can take to help farmed animals is to stop eating them. Becoming a vegan is the clear moral baseline if we wish to relieve the suffering of chickens, pigs, cows, sheep, other beings raised to become food. By not consuming meat, eggs, and dairy products, we pull support away from the companies that profit from animal exploitation. Visit chooseveg.com, compassionatecook.com, foodispower.org, goveg.com, vegnews.com, vegansociety.com, or viva.org.uk to learn more. In addition, there's a new vegan resource called Bleat you might like to explore: http://ble.at/.

I also encourage you to speak up about the cruelties perpetuated against animals. Talk to family, friends, and co-workers; tell them why these abuses concern you. Like most people, they're probably unaware of the privations and abuse animals endure to produce foods humans don't really need.

Become active for animals. Join or support an animal rights group or volunteer at a sanctuary for farmed animals. It need not take a lot of your time. These sanctuaries include:

Cedar Row Farm Sanctuary (Canada)
http://cedarrow.org

Edgar's Mission (Australia)
www.edgarsmission.org.au

Farm Sanctuary (US)
www.farmsanctuary.org

Hillside Animal Sanctuary (UK)
www.hillside.org.uk

Peaceful Prairie (US)
www.peacefulprairie.org

United Poultry Concerns (US)
www.upc-online.org

VINE Sanctuary (US)
http://bravebirds.org

Woodstock Farm Animal Sanctuary (US)
http://woodstocksanctuary.org

Other ways to help:

Shark Finning

The largest use of shark fins is shark fin soup, and even if you never eat this delicacy of despair, you can help by asking restaurants that serve it to stop. You can also lend your support to a nonprofit such as Food Empowerment Project (www.foodispower.org), Humane Society International (www.hsi.org), Pretoma (www.pretoma.org), or Sea Shepherd (www.seashepherd.org), all of which campaign against shark finning.

Dolphins

Though word is slowly spreading, relatively few people know about the slaughter of dolphins for human consumption. Perhaps the best action you can take is to educate yourself and share your knowledge with others. Purchase or rent *The Cove*—which, notwithstanding its conclusion, is an entertaining and engrossing film—and hold a screening at home, for example. Visit SaveJapanDolphins.org, the site for Ric O'Barry's organization, for more information.

Illegal Slaughter

Horse racing remains one of the main sources of flesh for the horse-meat industry. By refusing to support activities involving animals, we can help reduce the demand for and abuse of the countless horses, dogs, bulls, and other animals who are used and discarded in the name of "sport." (See Chapter 5 for more information.)

Consider donating to nonprofits that assist former racehorses, including:

Animal Recovery Mission (US)
www.animalrecoverymission.org

CANTER (US)
www.canterusa.org

Gray Dapple Thoroughbred Assistance Program (US)
www.graydapple.org

Horse Rescue Australia
www.horserescue.com.au

Manes and Tails Organization (US)
www.manesandtailsorganization.org

No Day Off Equine Rescue (US)
http://nodayoffequinerescue.webs.com/

Racehorse Rescue Centre (UK)
www.racehorserescue.org.uk

ReRun, Inc. (US)
www.rerun.org

New Stride Thoroughbred Adoption Society (Canada)
http://newstride.com/

Thoroughbred Adoption Network (US)
www.thoroughbredadoption.com

Live Export
In addition to not eating lamb and "mutton," you can reduce the
exploitation of sheep by not wearing wool. (See Chapter 2 for more
information on the wool industry.)

Youth Programs
There are many youth-oriented programs that do not involve cruelty.
If you know of a 4-H, FFA, or other ag club that is going to slaughter
animals, ask them if they will allow the animals to live. Many
students have been able to place farmed animals in sanctuaries such
as Animal Place, Farm Sanctuary, and many others. In fact, Animal
Place (animalplace.org) has a campaign called About Building
Compassion, which promotes kindness and compassion in our
schools, and PETA has developed its TeachKind program
(teachkind.org) to provide educators with free lesson plans and
materials that nurture the students' empathy while empowering

them to take compassionate action for animals.

Animal-Friendly Nonprofits

Rather than donating to aid organizations that exploit animals, such as Heifer and Oxfam, consider these humane alternatives that help relieve human suffering in developing countries:

Feed More International
http://awellfedworld.org/feedmore

Food for Life Global
www.ffl.org

Fruit Tree Planting Foundation
www.ftpf.org

HIPPO (Help International Plant Protein)
www.hippocharity.org.uk

Sustainable Harvest International
www.sustainableharvest.org

Vegfam
www.vegfamcharity.org.uk

In addition, Animal Rahat (relief) is a nonprofit organization created to make a difference in the lives of working bullocks, donkeys, ponies, and horses in India. You'll find them online at http://animal-rahat.com.

Finally, you can brush up on your vocabulary and help feed the world at FreeRice.com, which asks users to define words and then donates rice to the UN's World Food Program with each correct answer.

Chapter 2

Dressed to Kill: Animals Used for Fashion

To turn an animal into a fur coat is to ennoble it. As a fashion item, an animal acquires significance far beyond its own natural existence.
—Brendan O'Neill, *The Guardian*

If there's one thing Johnny Weir is as famous for as his figure skating, it's his wardrobe. Actually, Weir, who finished sixth at the 2010 Winter Olympics, may be better known for the latter. A few weeks before competing in Vancouver, Weir became the poster boy for fashion cruelty when he took to the ice at the US Figure Skating Championships donning a costume trimmed in fox fur. In response to a barrage of criticism from animal advocates, Weir had his outfit for the Olympics altered to use faux fur. But the future Ice Capades star has vowed to continue wearing genuine fur. "I totally get the dirtiness of the fur industry and how terrible it is to animals," he says. "But it's not something that's the No. 1 priority in my life."[1]

In fact, it doesn't even seem to be anywhere on his list. Some months after the Olympics, the unrepentant Weir told *New York Magazine*, "I know everything there is to know about the fur industry and I choose to wear fur."[2] Assuming that statement is true, and not just media posturing, one has to wonder if there is *any* abuse this guy wouldn't tolerate. Based on his comment, Weir must have watched undercover video taken inside fur farms, where the severe stress from being confined in tiny cages leads to a variety of psychotic behaviors, such as frantically pacing, chewing their limbs down to the bone, or infanticide. Surely he's seen how the foxes he so loves to wear are commonly killed: a clip is attached to an ear or a metal conductor is put in the victim's mouth, an electrode is inserted into his rectum, and he is jolted with 240 volts of electric current for 30 seconds or more, during which time the fox (or other furbearing animal) experiences the full force of a massive heart attack.[3] Weir must be aware of other execution methods, including neck-breaking, which often doesn't kill the animal but only paralyzes her. He certainly has learned that some fur-farm operators grind up the corpses of skinned animals and feed them to live ones to save on food costs.[4] And he has no doubt seen the harried fur-farm worker, too rushed to ensure his victim is dead, skin a fully conscious animal and discard him into a pile, his eyes still blinking.

Fur Shame

As shameful as it is, Weir's coldhearted attitude about the fur industry has helped bring attention to fashion cruelties and illuminate the dark world of animal-based apparel. It's a world long targeted by animal and environmental advocates for its trivial infliction of torment on fur-farmed animals and endangered wildlife. By focusing on the consumer, activists have convinced countless potential customers that fur is a vanity product driven by pain and suffering. "Fur is dead," as the slogan says. For decades, the message worked well: sales slumped and fur companies went out of business.[5] Twenty years on, PETA's controversial series of "I'd Rather Go Naked Than Wear Fur" ads and posters, featuring famous bodies in the buff, is still one of the most recognized campaigns in the animal rights movement.

After building up so much momentum in the 1970s and '80s, the anti-fur coalition should be celebrating the virtual demise of fur today; instead, fur seems to be enjoying a surge in popularity. Although fur sales took a precipitous dive in the '90s, the industry came back strong in the 21st century, according to the International Fur Trade Commission. Fur will probably never enjoy the success it did in the 1940s and '50s—when a sable or mink coat epitomized affluence and luxury—but the industry's recovery is troubling to say the least. The revival is partly the result of a well-funded, decade-long effort by fur concerns such as North American Fur Auctions and the Saga Design Center, a Denmark-based marketing group, to encourage up-and-coming fashion designers to include fur in their collections.[6] Young designers are treated to expensive trips, plied with champagne, and given free fur.[7] The initiative has worked so well that for the first time in 20 years, more designers are using fur than not.[8] They're moving away from traditional coats and jackets and adding fur to vests, purses, boots, and belts. Meanwhile, new markets in rapidly developing economies have given sales a boost, particularly in China and Russia, where fur has a long tradition.[9]

But Dan Mathews, PETA's senior vice president and the architect of the "I'd Rather Go Naked" campaign, believes any talk of a comeback is just that—talk. "What's popular in the press and popular among people are two different things," he says. "Fur is all over the runways, but it doesn't really make it to the streets. Almost every mass-market retail chain bans it, like Gap, J.Crew, Forever 21, and H&M, plus fashion lines like Ralph Lauren, Calvin Klein, Tommy Hilfiger, all Liz Claiborne's dozens of brands, and more. Tim Gunn, America's number-one fashion guru, helps PETA bring this issue to others in the trade and hosted a video showing not just the cruelty, but the progress being made."[10]

Whether the industry is in the midst of a bona fide renaissance or is attempting its own artificial resuscitation, the fact remains that tens of millions of animals are skinned every year, and fur peddlers use an assortment of unthinkably cruel means to produce their "merchandise."

Fur Farms

It is impossible to know precisely how many animals the global fur trade exploits, though it could be more than 50 million a year.[11] What *is* known is that about 85 percent of these minks, foxes, rabbits, sables, raccoons, chinchillas, and other furbearers are raised and killed in fur farms, sometimes called fur ranches.[12] Both are euphemisms. Animal rights philosopher Tom Regan argues that a more appropriate term for these operations is fur mills, since they crank out animals the way steel mills produce girders.[13] Not unlike the animal factories used for meat, egg, and dairy production, fur farms operate on paper-thin margins and intensively confine animals until the moment comes to kill them. A typical fur mill is comprised of long rows of wire cages covered by a roof and surrounded by a fence. There might be as few as 100 or as many as 100,000 animals imprisoned within.[14]

It is important to note that animals have only been farmed for their fur for a little more than 100 years; consequently, they remain genetically identical to their feral cousins. Held captive inside small wire boxes in fur farms, these otherwise wild animals—for whom freedom is a powerful biological imperative—literally go crazy. They routinely react by engaging in abnormal behaviors such as head weaving, pacing back and forth, twirling, and self-mutilation.[15] They may even kill their own offspring.[16]

Because the fur-farm operator's goal is to produce an unblemished pelt, animals are slaughtered using methods that preserve their coat while ignoring basic humane practices. Working undercover at a chinchilla farm, PETA activists watched the farm operator as he reached into a cage and yanked out a frantic animal. The chinchilla squealed as the man seized his head and jaw, arched his little head backward, and pulled sharply on his tail, breaking his neck. "He tossed the jerking chinchilla to the floor, where the animal writhed in continuous spasms. We asked if he was ever bothered by the killings. 'I don't feel anything,' he replied, and moments later added, 'I could do this all day.'"[17] Mental health professionals have a term to describe this kind of person: sociopath.

It is clear that the fur trade attracts the morally bankrupt, but torture has no limits in China, where an utter lack of welfare regulations means operators have the legal right to breed, raise, house, and skin animals however they choose. Assisting with a documentary and report on the trade, undercover investigators working on behalf of Care for the Wild, East International, and Swiss Animal Protection toured several fur farms in China's Hebei Province. The cruelty they witnessed and recorded is unconscionable. Workers begin by bludgeoning animals or slamming them to the ground to immobilize them. Not everyone succumbs to this abuse, however, and many are still piteously writhing and kicking as workers flip the animals onto their backs or hang them by the legs or tail to skin them. Once the fur has been peeled off the tissue and over the animals' heads, their bodies are flung into a bloody heap. Some survivors, who may live another 10 minutes, gasp for breath, and continue to blink. One skinned dog the investigators saw had the strength to lift his head and stare into their camera.[18]

China is a major force in the fur trade. It is now both the largest exporter of fur clothing and the biggest fur trade production and processing center in the world. The country's abundant surplus of cheap labor means they're also able to give manufacturers an economic advantage, while a growing number of international traders and processors have shifted their business to China.[19] Although many fur products carry the "Made in China" label, raw pelts from Chinese fur farms are primarily sold through international auction houses in Copenhagen, Helsinki, St. Petersburg, Seattle, and Toronto before being assembled in other countries. So there's an excellent chance that even a garment with the label "Made in France," "Made in Russia," or "Made in the USA" was created with animal skins from China's fur mills, where victims suffer the most obscene deaths imaginable.

Citing the extreme cruelty involved, the UK and Austria have banned fur farming, while the Netherlands has phased out chinchilla and fox farming. After animal abuse was revealed in Norwegian fur farms, fur was banned from the runways during Oslo Fashion Week in 2011—the first time that any city that hosts a global fashion week has taken such a stand against fur. In the US, where fur farming still flourishes, the number of mink farms has plummeted from 1,027 in 1988 to fewer than 300 today.[20] Activist Peter Young explored more than 200 fur farms as part of an extensive investigation of the industry in 2009. Says Peter: "Every farm I have visited is the same: mink in small cages enveloped in filth or foxes and their young spending their lives in wire boxes. The animals live in stress and fear, many driven mad through the conditions. Anyone who visits a fur farm will find animals spinning neurotically for their entire lives, having broken down psychologically from the stress of life on a fur farm. Anyone who visits a fur farm will smell it long before they see it. Fur farms victimize every one of the animals' senses, making their lives an insufferable nightmare from which relief comes only in death."[21]

Trapping

Once the fur-industry standard, trapping is now a distant second to raising and slaughtering animals in fur mills. But there are plenty of traps out there, especially in the US, where trappers kill about 3 to 5 million animals a year for the fur trade—more than any other country.[22] These numbers do not count non-target animals, including dogs, cats, and endangered species, who happen to fall victim to traps; to use the fur industry's parlance, such animals are "trash." The principal styles used to catch furbearers are the leghold trap, the body-grip trap, and the wire snare. Each comes with its own brand of misery.

Steel-jaw leghold traps have earned their reputation as one of the most merciless devices in the hunting-and-trapping trade. The trap consists of a foot pad and a pair of curved, spring-loaded bars that snap shut when an animal steps on or disturbs the baited pad. Staked to the ground or anchored to a tree with a short chain, the trap keeps the victim in place until the trapper comes back—often days later. If the animal has not died from dehydration, starvation, blood loss, hypothermia, or a predator attack, the trapper kills him by stomping on his chest, shooting him in the head, or crushing his skull.

It is not hard to imagine what an animal experiences in the jaws of a trap. With a nervous system that responds to pain stimuli the way humans do, animals endure swelling, hemorrhaging, lacerations, joint dislocation, and bone fractures, all exacerbated when they naturally struggle for their freedom.[23] But wild animals suffer an additional torment, as being restrained in a steel trap is extremely frightening. Animal behaviorist Desmond Morris says the shock trapped animals experience "is difficult for us to conceive because it is a shock of total lack of understanding of what has happened to them. They are held, they cannot escape, their response very often is to bite at the metal with their teeth, break their teeth in the process, and sometimes even chew through the leg that is being held in the trap."[24] Notoriously indiscriminate, leghold traps result in the deaths of about twice as many animals as trappers were intending to catch. Appearing before Congress, former trapper Dick Randall testified, "Even though I was an experienced, professional trapper, my trap victims included non-target species such as bald eagles and golden eagles, a variety of hawks and other birds, rabbits, sage grouse, pet dogs, deer, antelope, porcupines, sheep, and calves. The leghold trap is inherently non-selective. It is probably the most cruel device ever invented by man. My trapping records show that for each target animal I trapped, about two unwanted individuals were caught. Because of trap injuries, these non-target species had to be destroyed."[25]

Ninety countries now prohibit leghold traps, though Australia, Canada, Russia, South Africa, and the US are among the nations that still allow them. Indeed, these devices are so prevalent in Canada, Russia, and the United States that their governments threatened to lodge a complaint with the World Trade Organization against the European Union in the 1990s when the EU banned leghold traps and sought to forbid the importation of fur from countries that used them. The EU relented, figuring they'd lose that trade war.[26]

Body-gripping traps are intended to kill the animal quickly, by snapping her neck or back. They are constructed of two square, rectangular, or circular metal jaws hinged at both sides and powered by one or two high-tension springs. The trap is activated by a wire trigger fastened at the top and hanging into the center of the open jaws. When an animal passes through the jaws, he moves the trigger and the trap slams closed in a scissors-like action, crushing his neck or chest. Though these traps (sometimes referred to by the trade name Conibear) are meant to deliver an instant death, a lingering strangulation is often the result. In some cases, animals suffer even longer. This has been especially true with dogs who come across a trap on public property.

Bella, for example, a 20-month-old beagle, was out with her guardian on a piece of public land in Kansas when she stuck her head into a plastic bucket meant to entice the curiosity of a raccoon, coyote, or bobcat. A Conibear trap hidden within the bucket snapped down, crushing Bella's skull. Death was not immediate, however, and her guardian struggled to remove the trap as Bella whimpered in a haze of agony. She grew weaker from the extreme pressure, lost consciousness, and died several minutes later.[27] The story was front-page news in the local paper, which printed a photo of Bella's limp body, the trap's steel jaws still wrapped around her head. The graphic image shocked readers, but the story inspired a public discussion about the ethics of body-gripping traps. Trappers continue to defend the Conibear, which is really no surprise from an industry without regard for anyone else. Describing his trade, one Canadian fur trapper says, "I refer to it as murdering cute, furry little animals for some rich bitch in New York City."[28]

Like body-gripping and leghold traps, snares come with myriad welfare issues. A snare is a simple device: a length of heavy wire with a loop at one end and the other end fastened to a tree or anchored to the ground. In use well before steel traps, snares were once constructed from vines or a braided cord made of hair, plant fibers, or other natural material.[29] Today's trappers use a flexible braided steel cable to create either a leg snare or the more lethal neck or body snare. A leg snare is placed horizontally and activated by a small pan, similar to the leghold trap; it is designed to restrain the animal. A neck/body snare has a noose that is set vertically off the ground to catch an animal as he moves past; the cable tightens as he frantically struggles to get away, eventually strangling him or crushing his internal organs. Leg snares, while they don't kill their victims immediately, can tear through hair and skin and cut down to the bone.[30] Snares are as inherently indiscriminate and inhumane as other traps used in the fur trade; they expose the snared animal—who may be a targeted furbearer or a dog, cat, or other "trash" species—to psychological trauma as well as potential death from dehydration, starvation, hypothermia, and predation.

Dogs and Cats

They may be considered trash by some trappers, but an estimated 2 million dogs and cats a year still end up being turned into coats, hats, gloves, stuffed toys, fur trim, and other products. Most of these animals are bred and raised under the same miserable conditions as animals in other fur mills. To help meet demand, workers supplement these with dogs and cats taken from streets—sometimes as part of programs to eradicate homeless animals—or even stolen pets. In China, men peddle dogs at markets that deal with restaurants, which later sell the skins to the fur industry.

Investigations by The Humane Society of the United States (HSUS), Humane Society International (HSI), and PETA have revealed facilities throughout China, Southeast Asia, and Eastern Europe in which dogs and cats are skinned alive. An undercover investigator with HSUS/HSI watched as dogs in China were removed from a sack and methodically butchered. The first dog pulled from the sack reacted as many dogs would: he wagged his tail. The report describes the unfolding scene:

> The wagging stopped when the butcher tied the dog up short with a metal wire so the dog could hardly move. The dog began to panic and tried to escape. But the butcher lifted the dog's left hind leg and stabbed him in the groin area. Blood began to pour. The dog howled in pain and struggled more. With every move, the wire cut into the dog's neck. After a couple of minutes, the butcher began to skin the dog. As horrifying as this scene was, it

got worse. An investigator reported that he saw dogs being butchered who were still conscious as the skinning began, and investigators videotaped a German shepherd blinking his eye as he was being skinned.[31]

At an animal market in southern China, PETA investigators discovered dogs and cats destined for the fur trade. The animals were crowded so tightly into wire cages that they could not move. By stacking these densely packed cages one atop another, workers were able to load 8,000 dogs and cats onto each truck. After transporting animals in this deplorable state, workers threw the cages onto the ground, sometimes from as high as 10 feet (3 meters), shattering the animals' bones. Many of these dogs and cats still wore the collars affixed by a guardian.[32]

Once the flesh has been removed, dog and cat skins are stitched together into large, uniform sheets. They are separated by color, texture, pattern, and the length of the fur. Often they are sheared or dyed to make them more fashionable. To circumvent laws or appease a consumer's conscience, dog and cat fur often carries a label such as "mink" or "rabbit." Once fur is mislabeled, it is nearly impossible to identify the species because of the tanning, dyeing, and shearing processes.[33]

Although morally indistinguishable from other skin trades, the use of dogs and cats for fur is nonetheless an entry point for many consumers who might not otherwise think about the issue. In some countries with a long tradition of bonding with canines and felines—including Australia, Great Britain, and the US—the manufacture and sale of fur products made from these animals have been banned. Nevertheless, dog and cat fur is still sold in these countries. HSUS has found garments in which dog fur was being passed off as faux fur. And these weren't found on the racks of a discount store or piled in a box at a weekend flea market. In 2010, luxury retailer Neiman Marcus settled a lawsuit with HSUS for selling garments labeled "faux fur" that were in fact made from raccoon dog, a species native to Asia.[34] Macy's and Saks, Inc. were found to be doing the same thing.

Seals

Humans have been wearing animal fur for millennia, but the skins of seals were the first to be considered so beautiful that they should adorn the outside of the garment. Coats showing off seal fur thus began a European trend in 1840, and by the mid-19th century the fashion had spread throughout the Western world.[35] Seals have been slaughtered en masse ever since. Some countries seem more enlightened about "sealing" than others—Russia, a major fur market, surprised many when it banned the commercial killing of seals in 2009. Of the seal killings that continue today, Canada's and Namibia's are the largest and most notorious.

Canada's commercial seal "hunt"[36] takes place between November 15 and June 14 on ice floes in two regions: about a third of the seals are slaughtered off the country's east coast in the Gulf of St. Lawrence, and the rest are killed east of Newfoundland, in an area known as "the Front." These are traditional breeding and birthing grounds, to which harp and hooded seals migrate by the millions after a summer of feeding in the Arctic. Feeling safe on the frozen sanctuary, seals give birth, and the pups drink mama's high-fat milk for two weeks to put on weight quickly.[37] Into this pastoral tableau enter hundreds of off-season fishermen, who shoot or bludgeon helpless baby seals, transforming the placid ice into a crimson slush. Sealers in the Gulf prefer to beat seals with wooden clubs and hakapiks (large clubs fitted with a sharp spike, used to drag seals by the head across the ice), while most sealers in the Front opt for firearms, often taking aim at their victims from rocking boats.

Whatever weapon they choose, sealers are supposed to ensure seals are dead or irreversibly unconscious before flaying them. A three-point process, recently introduced to mollify critics of the carnage, mandates that after shooting or striking a seal in the head, the sealer must crush both the left and right halves of the cranium and then bleed the seal for at least one minute. But sealers are paid by the skin, so there is incentive for them to move as quickly as possible, rather than take these extra steps. Indeed, onlookers continue to describe sealers flouting the mandate. Says one witness to the slaughter: "As we hover over them in helicopters, it is plain to see that the sealers down below are not observing any three-point system. Instead they run chaotically across the ice. The seals raise their heads as the men approach, which means there is no way there can be a clear blow to the top of the head, as is required."[38]

The chief targets of the hunt are "beaters"—so named because these harp seals, between 25 days and a year old, beat the surface of the water with their flippers as they learn to swim. "Beaters more than a month old are mostly hunted in open water and are seldom fat enough to float," writes Farley Mowat in *Sea of Slaughter*. "The current recovery rate by hunters using modern rifles is probably no more than one of every six or seven hit."[39] Those who drown or die from their wounds in the water are not counted as part of the quota set by the Canadian government each year.

Fashion photographer Nigel Barker, best known as a judge on *America's Next Top Model*, wanted to use his lens and fame to expose the truth behind seal slaughter. At his own expense, Nigel set off with a film crew in 2008 and made two trips to the ice floes in the Gulf of St. Lawrence, once to film the birth of the harp seal pups, and again, 12 days later, to document the massacre. "I wanted to be there directly at the birth of the seals," he says, "which is the most extraordinary thing you've ever seen. It's the largest mammalian migration on Earth—greater than the wildebeests crossing the Serengeti. You have 4 million seals coming down from Greenland to this one area because they think it's safe." Nigel filmed hundreds, if not thousands, of seals being killed. "With clubs. Over the head. Skin being pulled off. Seals moving—*without... their... fur*," he says, noting that the men doing the clubbing are in too much of a hurry to ensure the animals are dead before removing their skin. "They're supposed to do a three-point check. Do they do it? No. I was there for days, and I did not see it—not one time." Though he's no fur apologist, Barker doesn't demonize the sealers, most of whom are in their early 20s. "These men need an alternative," he says. "They need a better way of life."[40] The product of Nigel's efforts is *A Sealed Fate?*, a 45-minute documentary that has been exhibited around the world.

Public opinion runs strongly against the seal slaughter, even in Canada.[41] Indeed, the country has been the focus of so much criticism for its inhumane treatment of seals that it is frankly astounding the government continues to defend it. Surely this must be hubris: Ottawa is simply supporting an unpopular practice because it feels it's being bullied by foreign interests, including the European Union, which voted in 2009 to ban the importation of all seal products in response to the cruel tactics used to kill seals. Canada's reaction to the ban has been nationalistic in the extreme. One of the Canadian Parliament's responses was to mandate that its Olympic athletes wear seal skin on their uniforms at the 2010 Winter Games. But the most bizarre display of defiance was when Michaëlle Jean, the representative of Canada's head of state, Queen Elizabeth II, ate a chunk of raw seal heart cut freshly from a victim of the slaughter. She swallowed the piece whole, as if to say, "In your face, EU!"[42]

Like its Canadian counterpart, the massacre of seals in Namibia—a small country bookended by Angola and South Africa—takes place on a cold stretch of remote Atlantic coastline, where men armed with clubs and knives approach a breeding colony of adult Cape fur seals and their pups. The nursing young are the sealers' main target; their prized, supple pelts will bring the best price from furriers. As the bludgeoning begins, pups try to hide behind their equally defenseless mothers. Some of the babies are so terrified that they vomit their mother's milk before, during, and after the skull-crushing blows. Soon hundreds of animals lie dead and dying. The Namibian killing of seals expands every year to higher quotas and could very well surpass the Canadian slaughter to become the deadliest.[43] The government has granted the sealing industry rights to kill 1 million seals until 2019.

Also known as South African fur seals, Cape fur seals are actually a species of sea lion, and the animals are protected under Appendix II of the United Nations Convention on International Trade in Endangered Species of Wild Fauna and Flora (CITES).[44] Nevertheless, from July 1 to November 15, commercial hunters in Namibia hire more than 100 unskilled workers to enter the breeding colonies, round up seal pups (most between 7 and 11 months old), beat them in the head with heavy clubs, and stab them in the heart. Inspectors are supposed to ensure the seals are dead before sealers remove their pelts, but in the rush to skin tens of thousands of animals, this imperative is often overlooked. The men also take aim at the adult male seals (bulls), shooting them and removing their genitals, which are sold to buyers in Asia as a virility booster. Six hundred pups are killed each day for 139 days until the quota is filled or the season ends, and 200 bull seals are shot each day until the allotted 6,000 penises have been collected.

In their careful study of the Namibian seal slaughter, zoologists Stephen Kirkman and David Lavigne conclude that the killings are inherently inhumane, and they express doubt that it will ever be possible to minimize the pain and suffering Cape fur seals experience as a result.[45] To justify the bloodshed, the Namibian government offers the same pretext that the seal killers in Canada use: they claim the seals' natural predation of fish depletes stocks and competes with their fishing industry.[46] "Hogwash," says anti-sealing activist François Hugo. "Namibia was once one of the most productive fisheries in the world, with seals and fish sharing a unique natural balance that had existed for 5 million years. In the late 1960s commercial fisheries caught 1.5 million tons. Almost all of it went to fishmeal for pet food and livestock feed, which is an unnatural protein diet for these animals. The government did not then consider to cull pets or livestock—so why now seals?"[47]

François, a former Navy diver, has been on a one-man crusade to end Namibia's seal pup genocide since 1999, shortly after he rescued a 10-month-old seal whose flippers had been severed by a fishing line. The organization he founded in his native Cape Town, Seal Alert South Africa, has no staff, no mailing lists, no office, and no fundraising efforts. Well, there was one effort. In 2009, François was close to shutting down the Namibian sealing industry with a US$14-million payment to the sole remaining buyer of Cape fur seal skins.[48] If he could come up with the money, he would take control of the sealing business and shut it down. With no database of supporters to appeal to, François reached out to the media to promote his effort and ask for donations. The transaction ultimately fell through amid accusations and recriminations from both sides, yet he remains determined to see an end to the massive annual slaughter. He has already succeeded in convincing Germany and the Netherlands—Namibia's two largest tourism partners—to join the US and South Africa in banning Cape fur seal products, and he secured a similar ban in the EU (though Namibia has since turned to Asia and Turkey as its main markets).

Even before the clubbing begins each July, the seal pups face long survival odds. Since Namibia's independence from South Africa in 1990, the country has doubled its annual fishing quota. That has left fewer fish for mother seals (cows) to feed on, pushing their hunting area farther away from the breeding colony along the edge of the coastal desert, where they must leave their pups behind. The longer the cows are absent, the more desperate their offspring become. "Starvation forces these hungry pups to attempt to find their mothers, and it is not uncommon to see 200 pups go off into the desert to die a horrible and slow death," François says. "Some pups grow so weak seagulls notice their state and start pecking out their eyes."[49]

Ironically, seals are among Namibia's biggest tourist draws, earning the economy nearly N$10 million a year (about US$1,125,300, or €853,000) through boat tours and seal viewing, while sales of seal fur and genitalia bring in less than N$100,000 (about US$11,253, or €8,534).[50] The last thing Namibian officials want is for visitors to discover the secret slaughter, so they engage in some careful sleight of hand. Sealers are let into the breeding colony at 5:00 a.m. They spend several hours bashing the heads of baby seals, load the dead pups in trucks, and disappear with their bloody booty by 9:00 a.m. "The government then opens the colony at 10:00 a.m. to paying tourists," says François. "There are warning signs that read, 'Do not disturb the seal colony and help us to protect this unique seal colony.' Clearly the government is hiding its seal-culling activities. Not a single travel website mentions the seal cull. Blood on the beach or dead pups is blamed on jackals."[51] Police have been known to arrest intrepid sightseers who take photos of the killing, and in 2009, British journalist Jim Wickens and South African filmmaker Bart Smithers were attacked by club-wielding sealers and later convicted of trespassing after they filmed some of the carnage.[52] Their video footage was eventually smuggled out of the country and provides a horrific view of one of the world's lesser-known cruelties.

Because of the cruelty inherent in seal killing, Russia ended its commercial slaughter of harp seals in the White Sea in February 2009 and banned the killing of all seals under the age of 1 year the following month.[53]

Lambs

Former Soviet leaders Leonid Brezhnev and Mikhail Gorbachev famously donned it on their heads. That's how Afghan president Hamid Karzai wears it today. Pop singer Madonna wore it as a coat—until her friend Stella McCartney shamed her for it. Apparently, the Material Girl didn't know she was draped in the skins of lamb fetuses. Not many people do when they buy the fur, which is marketed as broadtail (and sometimes karakultcha), one of the rarest furs in the world. When the skin has been peeled from the bodies of newborn lambs, it is known by other names—astrakhan, Persian lamb, and swakara among them.

Whatever it's called, the fur comes from the karakul breed of sheep, prized for the quality of their coat because it does not appear to be fur. Its very look and feel is the result of skinning the lambs before their coats become coarse and wooly. Until then—for about three days after birth—their coats are glossy, soft, and tightly curled; the pelt is often described as having the feel of suede. As many as 30 tiny lambs are killed to produce a single, full-length karakul coat.[54] These were babies who, like the offspring of dairy cows and so many other farmed animals, were taken from loving mothers whose natural instinct is to nurture and protect their young. Sheep form strong bonds with one another, and the practice of separating lambs from their mothers, who are otherwise inseparable, adds a layer of psychological cruelty to an already heartless trade.

Indigenous to Central Asia, karakul lambs are now bred primarily in Afghanistan and Namibia, though the traditional producer of the fur, Uzbekistan, is still a major exporter. It was there that Rick Swain, former chief investigator for HSUS, documented the common practice of slaughtering a pregnant ewe so the fetus she was carrying could be turned into haute couture. The fur trade claims that such skin only comes from still-born lambs;[55] after all, industry spokespeople assert, killing an adult breeding animal to produce a single pelt doesn't make good business sense. But Rick explains that after a karakul ewe has been artificially inseminated and given birth to four or five lambs, her body is nearly exhausted; she is forced to carry one more baby, who will be cut from the mother's womb. Rick's report graphically details the killing of a pregnant ewe 30 days before she would have given birth:

> There is no stunning, no attempt to use any "humane slaughter" techniques. The ewe is flopped onto the floor and held down on her back. She kicks with her legs in a vain attempt to flee. One worker controls the lower half of her body by stepping on it with his foot. The butcher makes a pass at her throat with a long knife. Her legs continue to kick as she struggles. The butcher slashes her throat once again, this time deeper. A fountain of blood gushes

onto the floor around her. The butcher then twists her head all the way around, until it comes off in his hands.[56]

He goes on to describe the next steps, which his team has captured on video:

Approximately two minutes after the sheep's throat was cut, the workers picked up the now headless body by the legs and placed it on a wooden cradle-like structure... [V]igorous movement in the dead sheep's abdomen, evidently the unborn lamb kicking, is visible in the videotape... Workers pushed on the sheep's abdomen several times. There was no further visible movement. About thirty seconds after the movement in the sheep's abdomen stopped (or was no longer visible), the workers shackled and hoisted the sheep's body and started skinning it... After the skin was removed... another worker tore open the uterus and pulled out the lamb, holding it up for us to see. The worker then tossed the lamb [fetus] onto the floor and we left the kill area.[57]

"I don't believe that any consumer with any bit of humanity or conscience could know how this product is made and then wear it," says Rick.[58]

Greenwashing Fur

In their effort to divert consumer attention away from animal cruelty, the industry now touts fur as the ultimate "eco fashion" in glossy ads and other promotional rhetoric. Arguing that fur is "a renewable resource," the Fur Council of Canada (FCC) says, "At a time when we are all trying to be conscious of how our lifestyles affect nature, fur is an excellent choice."[59] One of their efforts to fool the green cognoscenti is a print ad featuring a model decked out in fur beneath the headline "Environmental Activist." The ad copy explains that "wearing fur also helps protect nature, by supporting people who live on the land." By "people" they mean trappers, who "depend on nature for their livelihoods." Absent from the ad is any mention of the millions of "trash" animals trappers routinely kill while they are being "stewards of Earth." Indeed, the FCC would have us believe that fur garments and accessories only come from animals caught in the wild. "In nature, each plant and animal species generally produces more offspring than the land can support to maturity," reads the council's website. "Like other species, we live by making use of part of this surplus that nature creates."[60] This is a preposterous lie, as far as the fur industry is concerned, because the majority of fur used in the trade is produced in farms from animals specifically bred for this purpose, and they know it. (Canada's market for fur-farmed animals is three times the size of its wild-fur market.[61]) A 2011 study on the environmental effects of mink-fur production found that it takes 11 animals to produce 1 kilogram of fur, and that the industry has a higher impact than other textiles in 17 of 18 measurement categories, including global warming and toxic emissions.[62]

Those who do trap animals, say fur supporters, play a fundamental role in wildlife management by keeping animal populations stable.[63] Actually, trapping seems to have the opposite effect, with trappers historically depleting habitats of many species and destroying ecosystems by killing predators who help preserve the balance of nature. Falkland Island foxes, the only land mammals native to the Falkland Islands, and sea minks, who flourished in coastal habitats from Massachusetts north to Newfoundland, are but two examples of animals now lost forever because of fur trapping.[64] Conservation work has helped other species, such as swift and kit foxes, who were once abundant in North America's prairies and deserts but are now imperiled, thanks to a variety of human causes. In areas where trapping the animals is now restricted, however, their numbers are gradually returning.[65]

The FCC's transparent "fur is green" marketing ploy would be laughable if the reality were not deadly serious. Not only are animals tormented and murdered to create vanity products, but the industry contributes to a host of environmental and human-health concerns, including pollution, energy consumption, and the spread of toxins and carcinogens. Like factory farming, fur mills generate vast amounts of animal waste, which in turn produces nitrogen and phosphorus that can easily contaminate water systems, either by leaching into groundwater or as runoff skimming into rivers and lakes.[66] Meanwhile, in order to prevent natural decomposition, pelts (animal skins with the hair attached) undergo a variety of very unnatural processing and dyeing treatments as they are turned into fur garments. In addition to being serious environmental contaminants, many of the chemicals used are either toxic, known to cause cancer, or both: aluminum, ammonia, chlorine, chlorobenzene, chromium, copper, ethylene glycol, formaldehyde, lead, methanol, naphthalene, sulfuric acid, toluene, and zinc are all considered to be health hazards.[67]

Finally, the fur industry squanders fossil fuels. From the gas-guzzling trucks, snowmobiles, and boats used to constantly set and check trap lines to the wide range of power requirements for its breeding, feeding, and slaughtering operations, the fur trade sucks energy at every stage of production. Moreover, furriers recommend that the coat be stored in a temperature-controlled vault during the summer months, further expanding fur's carbon footprint. For those who yearn for fur, there are plenty of ethical choices that don't involve animals. This is not to say that the production of fake-fur garments is entirely eco-friendly, either; it still burdens resources and the environment. It's just that, even setting aside the issue of cruelty for a moment, real fur does more harm. Estimates vary on just how much more energy it takes to make a fur coat from animal skins as from synthetic fibers. A figure often cited in animal rights literature comes from a study commissioned by The Fund for Animals and carried out by Gregory H. Smith, a research engineer with the Ford Motor Company's Scientific Research Laboratory, in 1979. Smith concluded that it takes 15 times more energy to produce a real fur coat using farmed animals as to make a fake-fur coat.

Factored into his calculation is the amount of energy needed for food, cages, skinning, pelt drying, processing, and transportation. He found that a coat made from the fur of trapped animals, although less carbon intensive, still requires 3.5 times the energy of its faux counterpart.[68] Unfortunately, no one has done a recent study taking into account technological advances in apparel-making: some manufacturers are creating faux fur with biodegradable synthetics or from hemp and cotton rather than acrylic polymers derived from petrochemicals.

Fortunately, the greenwashing of fur is beginning to come apart at the seams. A print campaign sponsored by the European Fur Breeders' Association, for example, was banned in the UK after the country's Advertising Standards Authority (ASA) dismissed assertions that choosing fur is good because it "lasts a lifetime" and "helps conservation." According to the ASA's 2012 ruling, "Although we noted that the ad included information setting out the environmental benefits of wearing fur… we concluded that the ad was likely to mislead."[69]

The Byproduct Myth

Rabbit fur may not have the cachet of sable and mink, but it's become the fastest-growing segment of the industry.[70] Unlike most other animals used for fur, however, rabbits have a special place in the minds (if not the hearts) of many people, especially in Australia, North America, and the UK. Frustrated purveyors of rabbit meat call it "Easter Bunny Syndrome": consumers are not inclined to eat an animal regarded more as a holiday ambassador or companion than a meal.[71] While chefs and butchers struggle to overcome the public's aversion to eating bunnies, those in the fur business tell customers and critics that rabbit fur is simply a byproduct of the rabbit-meat industry.[72]

Let's consider the two trades. In the meat industry, rabbits are slaughtered at between 10 and 12 weeks.[73] At this age, although their flesh is considered tender, rabbits have not fully developed and still have their infant coat. The most popular rabbits for meat are breeds that grow large, especially the New Zealand white and the Californian. Rabbits bred and raised for their fur, on the other hand, are killed at between 4 and 6 months old, when their coats have grown dense and plush.[74] The Rex is the most popular breed for fur, while angoras, with their long hair, are repeatedly shorn or plucked to create rabbit wool. Confined to bare wire cages inside large buildings, rabbits bred and raised for fur suffer many of the same privations and attendant stereotypical behaviors (cage-biting, self-mutilation, etc.) as other animals used in the trade, as well as some that are particular to their species. Hopping, for example, is among the activities they are denied, and without the ability to exercise this natural instinct, rabbits may suffer bone disorders.[75]

Perhaps the best unbiased source for this discussion is the United Nations' Food and Agriculture Organization (FAO), which studies the food system and its byproducts around the world. In their report on rabbit husbandry, health, and production, the FAO acknowledges that the rabbit-meat and -fur industries are not compatible. Most of the pelts removed from rabbits used for meat, they say, are thin and unsuitable for fur garments. "Few skins are now retrieved from slaughterhouses: they are simply thrown away."[76]

Died in the Wool

For many consumers ahead of the ethical fashion curve, avoiding fur is just common sense. But wool is another matter. It seems like such a benign product and the perfect antidote for winter. Chilly day? Toss a woolen scarf around your neck. Chilly night? Throw a woolen blanket on the bed. Most people don't give wool much thought; after all, it's just the shorn hair of sheep and the sheep aren't killed, right? Unfortunately for those sheep, the issue is far more sinister than a haircut.

To explore the underbelly of wool we turn to Australia, responsible for about 25 percent of the world's production, making it the largest supplier of wool. The country's sheep and lamb population fluctuates, but it is currently estimated to be 68 million.[77] Each year, 6 million sheep who have neared the end of their "profitability cycle," their bodies exhausted after years of exploitation, are loaded onto huge ships for a grueling, weeks-long journey to the meat markets of the Middle East. This practice, called live export, is addressed in the previous chapter, and it's probably the most infamous of Australia's wool-related cruelties. Less well-known is that while shearing is supposed to be done in the spring as the weather warms, some ranchers with large flocks begin the process too early in the season, leaving sheep without the insulation they need to survive cold temperatures. Some 1 million prematurely-shorn sheep die from exposure in Australia every year.[78]

Incidentally, it's because of humans that domesticated sheep need regular shearing. Farmers had been raising sheep for meat and wearing their skins thousands of years ago, but it wasn't until they crossbred sheep with the longest hairs that they essentially created, over innumerable generations, an animal who consistently provided a thick fleece that could be spun into textiles.[79] Australian sheep ranchers took this one step further: after years of intensive selective breeding, they produced a sheep that has folded skin. With their wrinkled epidermis, Australia's Merino sheep have more surface area on which to grow wool. That means more profits for ranchers.

But like battery cages for hens used in the egg industry and other "advances" in animal exploitation, wrinkled skin comes with a serious drawback. The folded skin on the sheep's backside collects feces and urine, creating an ideal environment for the blowfly to deposit eggs. (This is called myiasis, but sheep ranchers have another name for it: flystrike.) The eggs hatch into swarming maggots, which eat into flesh and can kill the animal within days.[80]

Australia's wool industry has a solution, however, and it's not pretty. In a procedure called mulesing, ranchers use shears to cut two large swaths of wrinkled, wool-bearing skin from beneath the sheep's tail.[81] To save the industry money, anesthesia and painkillers are almost never used. The open wound eventually scars, becomes smoother, and is less susceptible to flystrike. The mutilation takes about a month to heal; in the meantime, the wound itself is an inviting place for blowflies to lay their eggs.[82]

Australian veterinarians studying the physiological effects of mulesing have measured the total cortisol concentrations in the plasma of sheep who have undergone the mutilation. (Cortisol is known as "the stress hormone" because stress activates its secretion.) They found that after mulesing, plasma total cortisol concentration increased immediately and rapidly and remained high for at least 48 hours. The mutilated sheep also experienced changes in their posture indicating discomfort, and, not surprisingly, they formed a lasting aversion to the person who restrained them during the procedure.[83] Another team of veterinarians tested the reaction of month-old lambs using an electroencephalogram (EEG), a tool that measures electrical activity in the brain. They discovered that the EEG patterns of sheep during mulesing were characteristic of someone experiencing acute pain.[84]

Ingrid Newkirk doesn't need scientific data to know these animals are suffering. The president of PETA, she has witnessed mulesing firsthand. "The pain and trauma of mulesing are so horrifying—having two huge circles of flesh cut from your living body with a pair of gardening shears could be nothing less—that these once-frolicking, joyful lambs, then oblivious to what men have in store for them, can no longer walk," she says. "Sometimes they lie, bleating, for days; then slowly, painfully, they rise and move slowly across the field, their world view changed forever."[85] In July 2010, Ingrid sent a letter to Australia's Prime Minister Julia Gillard asking that the country end mulesing. "I have seen dead mulesed sheep with my own eyes," she writes, "and everyone knows that there are humane options that should replace this barbaric act."[86]

The humane option PETA and others have proposed is that ranchers selectively breed sheep whose anatomy is not susceptible to flystrike.[87] Initially, leaders in the wool industry balked at the idea, arguing the mulesing was itself a humane alternative to maggots eating away at sheep. But PETA held its ground and in 2004 launched an international boycott against Australian wool companies that perform the mutilation and participate in live export. As major clothing retailers like Nordstrom and Gap signed on, wool trade groups in Australia got nervous. They agreed to end mulesing by 2010, but not before one group, Australian Wool Innovation— which is also a research and marketing body—filed an unsuccessful lawsuit against PETA, acknowledging that their campaign was hurting the wool business. Wool producers eventually reneged on their promised 2010 deadline, but are still considering a plan to phase out mulesing.

As for live export, they have no plans to stop. "In fact, quite the opposite," says Glenys Oogjes, president of Animals Australia. "They are determined to continue and sadly have both sides of our political parties supporting live export."[88] A number of organizations are maintaining campaigns against the practice, but it is no longer paired with mulesing in negotiations with the sheep industry.

Shahtoosh

The high, dry plateaus of Tibet and Ladakh would seem about as remote a location as one could expect to find on Earth. At 16,400 feet (5,000 meters), the environment is exceptionally challenging. Yet even here, in the rarefied air of the Himalayas, humans victimize animals. Poachers target the chiru, a breed of antelope able to thrive in the lofty altitude thanks to a double-layered coat that protects against buffeting winds and temperatures that can drop to -40 degrees F (-40 degrees C). While the top layer is coarse, the chiru's underfleece is soft and dense. It is this wool, called *shahtoosh*, that for centuries has been woven into diaphanous shawls and scarves and sold throughout northern India, Pakistan, and Nepal. So prized is shahtoosh (literally, "king of wool") that the shawl is a traditional wedding gift among those who could afford it. One shawl can fetch as much as US$20,000[89]—and cost the lives of five chiru.[90] Gathering in herds of up to a thousand, the animals are easy targets for poachers, who cut them down with machine guns, skin them, and leave their remains.[91]

As soon as the whims of fashion elevated the shahtoosh from a dowry treasure to a must-have accessory worn by consumers everywhere, trade in the chiru's precious wool ramped up considerably. In the 1950s, 20 to 30 kilograms (44 to 66 pounds) of shahtoosh were being processed annually; four decades later the figure had jumped to 3,000 kilograms (6,600 pounds), representing the deaths of more than 23,000 chiru a year.[92] The animals are killed in both Chinese-occupied Tibet and in Ladakh, which is part of the Indian state of Jammu and Kashmir; the raw wool is brought to the state's capital, Srinagar, where shahtoosh shawls and scarves are woven for domestic sales and illegal export. The incredibly light shahtoosh products are smuggled out of India in personal luggage, and overseas dealers negotiate to sell them in boutiques throughout Europe and the United States.

By the 1970s, efforts to protect the chiru included adding them to Appendix I of CITES, banning all trade in chiru parts and derivatives. Illegal hunting only seemed to get worse, however, and gangs of poachers outfitted with off-road vehicles, automatic weapons, and enough food supplies for a month became increasingly efficient.[93] Biologist George Schaller, who has been studying the chiru since 1985, speculates that their population declined from about 1 million in 1900 to possibly fewer than 100,000 in 1990.[94] (Actually, no comprehensive survey of the chiru population has ever been done—nor is one likely, due to the terrain and high altitude of the animals' habitat.[95]) Schaller was instrumental in dispelling the biggest myth about shahtoosh: that it is benignly collected after the chiru shed their wool on rocks and bushes.

Beginning in the late 1990s, Chinese authorities stepped up anti-poaching patrols and have made saving the chiru a priority. How effective conservation efforts have been remains debatable. The nonprofit WildAid declares that chiru poaching has increased dramatically in recent years,[96] while Schaller believes their population is making a comeback, although he agrees poaching is still a problem. "Some Tibetans even use motorcycles to chase chiru until they collapse, exhausted, and can easily be slaughtered," he says.[97]

Feathery Fashion

Like wool, down is prized for its thermal properties. Lighter than feathers, down is the undercoating of soft plumage on all waterfowl. What makes down special is that, unlike feathers, it plumps up—a property known as "loft." Because of its loft, down traps air and forms a protective layer of insulation to help ducks, geese, and other aquatic birds maintain their body temperature in frigid water and inclement weather.[98] It's an ideal blanket of warmth for these birds, so it's not terribly surprising that humans would discover a way to exploit it. In addition to jackets, down is used to insulate gloves, hats, comforters, quilts, pillows, and sleeping bags. Feathers, meanwhile, have long been a favorite item to decorate clothing,[99] and they're used on arrows and fishing lures. They are commonly combined with down as an insulation filler.

Most down and feathers are taken from geese and ducks slaughtered for their flesh; indeed, the down and feather industry says that sales of this byproduct help reduce the price of goose and duck meat.[100] In their investigation of duck farms throughout the United States, the nonprofit Viva! USA found ducks raised principally for meat kept in typical factory farm conditions: thousands of animals in dimly lit sheds, cramped confinement, filthy surroundings, and often no access to the outdoors. Investigators came across dead, diseased, and injured birds, and some were lying on their backs unable to stand.

Mutilation is a common answer to the overcrowding in animal factories, and many ducks suffer this, too. Because they have sharp beaks and tend to peck at other birds and fight under the stressful conditions they're forced to live in, factory-farmed Muscovy ducks routinely undergo debeaking: the tips of the birds' upper bills are sliced off without the aid of any painkiller. Just like the debeaking endured by female chicks in the egg industry, the debeaking of ducklings is traumatic and extremely painful to the birds, whose beaks are richly endowed with nerves and sensory receptors.[101] Although agribusiness claims this procedure is akin to getting your fingernails cut, in reality it's more like having the end of your nose cut—or seared—off. (Thanks to a campaign by Viva!, debeaking is no longer practiced on ducks in the UK.)

A further cruelty on duck farms concerns the absence of open water. Water is an essential biological requirement of aquatic birds like ducks, who spend about 80 percent of their time swimming, cleaning themselves, and preening their feathers in ponds, lakes, canals, and streams. Without access to open water, ducks can suffer heat stroke, their eyes and nostrils become dirty, and they exhibit a variety of abnormal behaviors, including head-shaking.[102] Water plays such an important role in hygiene that ducks can go blind if prevented from rinsing their eyes. Yet duck farms in the US and the UK regularly deny these animals this basic welfare need; drip dispensers are usually the only water they have contact with.[103] The problem, according to animal agriculture, is that water spreads disease. It becomes contaminated quickly, they say, with ducks evacuating into the water, and other ducks drinking from it results in serious health issues.[104] Animal advocates take issue with that argument, however. "I find it laughable that the industry claims ducks could get diseases from water," says Lauren Ornelas, who investigated duck farms during her tenure as Viva! USA's executive director. "If they could, we'd see ducks dying in ponds and lakes. Factory farms simply do not provide these animals with enough water."[105]

Live Plucking

Although much less common, another method for collecting plumage is to yank feathers and down from live geese and ducks. Those who profit from this form of animal cruelty reason that it's more cost effective to rip the feathers from the birds, let them grow back, then rip them out again (and again and again) before finally killing the ducks and geese for their flesh. Live plucking, as it's called, is practiced primarily in China, Hungary, and Poland.[106] These three countries are currently the largest exporters of down and feathers, with China responsible for 80 percent of the world's supply.[107] The US is the biggest customer, importing some 19,200 tons of down and feathers a year.[108]

Estimates vary widely on just how much plumage is obtained from live plucking. The industry claims it's only about 1 or 2 percent.[109] But in 2009, the Swedish television news series *Kalla Fakta* ("Cold Facts") reported that 90 percent of the 39 producers contacted in China, Hungary, and Poland answered that they use live geese, and the two-part program concluded that 50 to 80 percent of down and feathers come from animals who are live-plucked. Even more shocking is the undercover video footage taken by investigators in some of these goose farms. The video shows screaming geese bound and held between the knees of pluckers while their feathers are rapidly ripped out. Workers later use needle and thread to sew up gaping wounds in the skin of injured birds—without any painkiller. Later we see these traumatized geese lying on the ground in shock.[110]

At the request of the European Union, the European Food Safety Authority explored the issue of live plucking and in 2010 published their scientific opinion, which found that the practice of collecting feathers from live geese results in unavoidable pain and injuries that can lead to infection and even death.[111] Veterinarian and bird expert Laurie Siperstein-Cook likens live plucking to torture. "It's just like pulling a clump of our hair," she says.[112] Research conducted in the UK verified that pain receptors are present in the skin of ducks, geese, and chickens. Moreover, researchers found that the follicular wall of the feather is filled with sensory fibers, and nerves are present in the papilla, pulp, and feather muscles, with the feather firmly held in the follicle. In announcing their findings in 1991, the biologists referred to M. Zimmerman's often-cited definition of pain in animals as "an aversive sensory experience caused by actual or potential injury that elicits progressive motor and vegetative reactions, results in learned avoidance behavior and may modify species specific behavior, including social behavior."[113] They found that "[f]eather removal results in tissue injury which gives rise to motor behaviour and cardiovascular changes which, when repeated, results in stress-induced immobility and thus satisfies most of the criteria in this definition of pain."[114] (Unfortunately, the researchers tortured birds to demonstrate this.)

Ironically, many retailers—including DeWoolfson Down, HungarianGooseDown.com, WhiteGooseDownComforters.com, and AbsoluteComfortOnSale.com—actually tout the fact that their products come from birds who are "live harvested" and not killed, suggesting that live plucking is a more compassionate alternative. Other retailers have stopped carrying merchandise that exploits these animals. After a campaign led by Viva! USA, for example, Pier 1 Imports halted its sales of pillows, cushions, and other products that contain feathers.

The New Plume Boom

As a fashion statement, feathers were all the rage in the late 19th and early 20th centuries, when a lady's hat was not considered complete without some avian adornment. Plumaged headpieces ranged from a simple gull feather stuck into a bonnet or fascinator to an entire nest—complete with a stuffed bird—mounted on a wide-brimmed chapeau.[115] To meet the market demand, the feather industry killed millions of wild birds, and many species—such as the Carolina parakeet and the New Zealand huia—would never be seen again.[116] Rightly alarmed by the senseless carnage, animal advocates and conservationists in the United Kingdom and the United States encouraged women to boycott feathered hats. Sales finally plummeted in the 1920s, just as shorter hairstyles, which could not support lavish headwear, became more popular, and hatmakers turned to other materials.

A century later, feathered fashion is making a comeback. This time, however, consumers are bypassing hats and affixing feathers directly to their hair. These aren't just any feathers, however; these are the tail feathers of roosters who have been specially bred to produce brightly colored plumage. Known as saddles, the 12- to 14-inch (30.5- to 35.6-cm) feathers have traditionally been used in fly-fishing: crafted into lures that mask a sharp hook, the feathers mimic the appearance of an insect standing on the water's surface. (Fly fishers also use plumes from the rooster's neck, known as hackle feathers.) Today, saddle feathers are being worn by everyone from teens to celebrities. Indeed, the fad got a big boost in 2011 when Aerosmith frontman Steven Tyler sported feather extensions when he was a judge on the popular television show *American Idol*. Stylists generally affix four to eight saddle feathers to a patron's hair, sometimes charging hundreds of dollars for the service.

What remains hidden is the enormous cost to the roosters. One of the world's largest suppliers of hackle and saddle feathers is Colorado-based Whiting Farms, which kills about 1,500 roosters a week.[117] "They're not good for anything else," says company founder Thomas Whiting.[118] Because of the animals' tendency to fight, roosters are kept in individual cages for up to a year.[119] A photo depicting a row of barren cages at Whiting Farms shows roosters standing on wire, confined to a space barely larger than their bodies.[120] Whiting himself reveals the suffering the birds endure, as well as his own callousness, writing that "every hackle rooster seems to realize who exactly is responsible for sentencing him to a solitary cage for the last 6 months, with nothing to look at or listen to other than lots of other confined roosters. And he also realizes he probably has only one good chance to hammer the living hell out of you… My particular favorite is when they claw climb up your face, and then launch themselves from atop your head. And then you have to go catch the son of a bitch as he eludes you then ambushes you from under the cages. Your sentiments can quickly shift from wanting to evaluate their necks to wringing [t]hem. Some of my most sheepish moments in life have been after hurling an especially bad rooster across the barn in utter frustration..."[121]

Once the rooster's feathers reach the desired length, he is asphyxiated with carbon dioxide (a death that leaves his plumage unblemished), he is skinned, his feathers are prepared for sale, and his body is tossed into a compost heap.[122] Though there is some market for hen feathers, most of the female chickens born at Whiting Farms and other businesses like it are killed right after they are hatched—just as male chicks are killed in the egg industry.

Skin Trade

Of all the animal-based products we wear, leather is the most ubiquitous. You'll find leather in footwear, belts, suspenders, jackets, pants, swimwear, vests, dresses, skirts, hats, and gloves. It trims collars and adorns buttons. There's even leather underwear. It's also used for such accessories as purses, watchbands, wallets, barrettes, and bags, as well as luxury items like briefcases, luggage, and car interiors. Airlines promote leather seats as a reason to fly with them. Leather-bound books are sold as special editions. From dog collars and leashes to horse saddles and stirrups, leather is affixed to animals we love—while it can be used to whip and beat others.

Leather products are so varied in part because they involve the skin of so many species. Cows are a major source of leather, but so are pigs, alligators, goats, sheep, elk, deer, and horses. Other animals commonly skinned include sharks, stingrays, snakes, elephants, buffaloes, and ostriches. For every animal with skin, someone's invented a use for it. The industry produces about 18 billion square feet of leather a year, representing some US$40 billion in sales.[123]

Most consumers assume that leather is just a byproduct of the slaughterhouse: kill a cow for her flesh, and then take her skin so it's not wasted. One need only consider calfskin, which is prized as one of the most luxurious and expensive leathers and comes from the skin of newborn calves, to see that this valuable trade is hardly a byproduct. Indeed, the meat trade could hardly exist were it not for the sales of animal skin. Estimates vary on just how much leather is worth relative to the rest of the animal. One industry expert, Severin Johnson, value-added agriculture specialist at Iowa State University, says a cow's skin accounts for as much as two-thirds of what an operator will earn from the non-flesh products.[124] In South Africa, home to a well-developed ostrich market, the bird's skin earns farmers as much as 80 percent of their revenue; ostrich feathers and meat are byproducts.[125]

In an industry that views other beings as "resources" to be "harvested," squeezing the last penny out of an animal becomes standard practice, whether that animal is a spent hen from a battery-egg shed or a worn-out "dairy" cow who has suffered five years of repeated forced pregnancies, only to have her calf taken away; the privations of intensive confinement, which is physically and psychologically cruel; and abusive dairy workers, who have been documented kicking, stomping, and punching cows and calves.[126] A co-product of the meat industry, leather subsidizes factory farms while giving exploiters an economic incentive to kill more animals for their skin.

Like fur, leather wreaks havoc on Mother Nature. Turning decomposing animal skins into a non-decaying product like leather—through a process called tanning—requires a toxic stew of chemicals that includes formaldehyde, alum, trivalent chromium, glutaraldehyde, and calcium hydroxide.[127] Taking on the bulk of the devastation caused by tanning are developing countries, particularly those in Asia, where cheap labor and lax environmental regulations attract major polluters like the skin trade. Tannery effluent, which gets dumped into nearby waterways, is contaminated with carcinogens, lime sludge, sulfides, and acids.

The Indian Connection

China is the world's leading supplier of leather, but India is also a chief producer. That India—where cows have traditionally been revered—is a major player in the leather trade should tell you something about the greed behind animal exploitation. It's a mistake to say Hindus worship the cow. Although they hold an unmistakably special place in Indian culture, cows have always been prized as a source of meat, milk, dung, and skin.[128] Even imagining that cows enjoy a high degree of welfare is an exaggeration, though they are treated better in some areas of the country than in others. In rural communities, I have encountered robust cows living practically as members of Buddhist households, while in predominantly-Hindu New Delhi I have seen emaciated bovines lying in busy streets.

Cow slaughter is allowed in only a few Indian states, which means cows used for the leather and meat trades often endure a grueling march across state lines or even into other countries, where they can be legally killed. Those who fall behind or collapse on the way have their eyes smeared with hot chili peppers and tobacco by cattle traffickers to keep them moving. Others are crammed onto overcrowded trucks or trains. "The law says you cannot transport more than four per truck but they are putting in up to 70," says activist Maneka Gandhi of India-based People for Animals. "When they go by train, each wagon is supposed to hold 80 to 100, but they cram in up to 900. I've seen 900 cows coming out of the wagon of a train, and 400 to 500 of them came out dead."[129] In one case, 11 animals, most discovered with multiple limb fractures, were rescued after they endured a 473-mile (761-kilometer) ride from the state of Gujarat, where cow slaughter is prohibited, to the city of Mumbai. The cows had been tied together and forced to sit for 30 hours concealed behind heavy sacks of goods.[130]

Bribes help get an estimated 1.5 million cows a year smuggled past the porous border India shares with Muslim Bangladesh, where each cow is worth about US$350. With such a lucrative trade—not to mention religious tensions—at risk, most people seem content to look the other way. "It's too political," says Sreeradha Datta, an analyst with the Institute for Defense Studies and Analyses in New Delhi. "And every pocket is being lined, with a trade of this magnitude."[131]

Where are the cows coming from? Throughout the subcontinent, traders scour the countryside for cows who can no longer be milked. They buy the animals from farmers, who are complicit in the pain and misery their once-valued cows will be forced to suffer. Other farmers give their old cows to Hindu temples, but the temple leaders are too busy to care for them so they sell the cows in the local market.[132] Surely these devout Hindus must know where the cows end up.

"At the slaughterhouse, cows are bound by all four feet and tossed on their sides onto the filthy, blood-covered floor. Their throats are cut with dull knives, and other cows look helplessly on as their companions slowly bleed to death," says former PETA staff member Bruce Friedrich, who counts his visit to a Calcutta train station as among the most shocking experiences in his years working on behalf of animals. "[T]here were thousands of emaciated former dairy cattle, not good for meat, all being used for leather exclusively," he explains. "Many had collapsed from the heat, some mothers had given birth there in the barren lot; one newly born baby looked at me, pleading for help, as a vulture pecked out his eye. Our PETA India Director and I watched helplessly as a small truck was packed so tightly with cattle that some of their necks were sure to break en route to their final destination, hundreds of miles away in Bangladesh. All of these animals were being used exclusively for leather."[133]

Kangaroo Skins

One animal especially threatened by the skin trade is the kangaroo. Native to Australia, the kangaroo is the country's most famous symbol; the animal's likeness graces everything from guidebooks and currency to airplanes and the national coat of arms. Unfortunately, there are Aussies who regard this icon of their culture as an agricultural pest competing with farmed animals—primarily sheep—for forage and water, leading to kangaroo "culling" programs throughout the country aimed at "managing" populations.[134] But kangaroos eat grass, which sheep generally do not, and they have lower water needs than sheep, who will drink 10 liters (2.64 gallons) daily under average conditions (twice that amount in the hottest weather); a Red kangaroo, meanwhile, drinks an average of 1 liter (.264 gallons) a day and a Grey kangaroo 1.75 liters (.462 gallons).[135] Although kangaroos might occasionally destroy a crop in a localized area, there is no convincing evidence of substantial damage to rangelands and pastures.[136]

More recently, kangaroos have become viewed as a natural resource, resulting in hunts for commercial purposes. While kangaroo meat is a growing trade (mostly for pet food[137]), clothing manufacturers produce hats, boots, belts, gloves, jackets, shoes, and other apparel from kangaroo skin. According to a policy outlined in Australia's Codes of Practice for both the commercial hunt and "pest" control, the adult kangaroo is to be killed with a single shot to the brain, and any joeys (young kangaroos) found on or near the mother are to be killed as well, usually by smashing their skulls. Every year, this policy results in as many as 1 million joeys being pulled from pouches or discovered at their mothers' feet, and hunters bludgeoning, shooting, or decapitating the youngsters.[138] Such methods are inhumane, yet hunters are known to use even crueler means, including stomping joeys to death, slamming their heads against tow bars, or just leaving them to die from starvation, exposure, or predator attack.[139] Because females nearly always have an infant joey in their pouch and/or an older one at their feet, hunters are not only decimating kangaroo populations, but they are wiping out multiple generations.

Quotas set for each state dictate how many of the four main kangaroo species—the common wallaroo (also called the Euro), the

Eastern Grey, the Red, and the Western Grey—may be killed during the year; the total quota for all species in 2012 was 5.2 million, or more than 10 percent of the population.[140] Those figures, by the way, only reflect adult kangaroos; quotas do not include baby kangaroos. According to the Australia Department of Environment, Water, Heritage, and the Arts, two species of kangaroos are not allowed to be hunted for commercial purposes in certain states. Eastern Greys can be hunted in New South Wales and Queensland, but not in South Australia, and Western Grey kangaroos can be hunted in New South Wales and South Australia, but not in Queensland. Trouble is, kangaroos easily migrate between states, they are hunted at night, and it is very difficult to distinguish one species from another.

Kangaroos have been hunted to such critical levels that the common wallaroo/Euro, the Eastern Grey, the Red, and the Western Grey are now considered quasi-extinct with population densities of less than five individuals per square kilometer.[141] (For more details concerning the exploitation of kangaroos for their skin, see Chapter 4.)

Skin in the Game

Despite the myth, US footballs are made from the skins of cows, not pigs. According to sporting goods manufacturer Wilson, official supplier to the National Football League (NFL), NFL teams across the country use about 700,000 footballs a year. With the skin of one cow making 20 footballs, this equates to roughly 35,000 dead cows. Cow leather is also used to manufacture basketballs, volleyballs, soccer balls, and baseballs—the latter of which were made from horsehide until 1974.

Ivory Fever

There was a time when African elephants roamed the continent by the millions from the Mediterranean coast to the Cape of Good Hope. Neolithic rock paintings even depict elephants in the region of the Sahara, before it became Earth's largest desert.[142] Asian elephants, whose ancestors originated in Africa some 55 million years ago, once inhabited scrub forests from modern Iraq and Syria to the Yellow River in China.[143] All that has changed, of course, thanks in large part to greed. Besieged for their massive tusks, these once-abundant elephant populations have been reduced to groups in scattered areas of sub-Saharan Africa and in isolated patches in India, Sri Lanka, Southeast Asia, and China's Yunnan Province.

Ivory, which is another name for the teeth or tusks of many mammals, has been coveted for adornment and décor for thousands of years, but the world's lust for ivory—especially from elephants— experienced a dramatic surge beginning in the 1970s, as newly affluent consumers in China and Japan propelled an unprecedented demand. Trade in ivory had remained stable throughout the 1960s, then the price steadily climbed from US$5.50 per kilo in 1969 to an astounding US$300 just 20 years later.[144] Even elephants in national parks were no longer safe from the onslaught of poachers, smugglers, corrupt officials, and dealers who conspired to exploit these noble pachyderms for easy money. Armed with the readily available assault rifles that had become the symbol of Africa's civil wars, gangs of hunters began methodically gunning down elephants and hacking the tusks out of their faces with machetes. So-called "ivory fever" was in full bloom.

In 1989, CITES voted to list the African elephant on Appendix I, thereby declaring the species endangered. The price paid for ivory quickly plunged to US$1.36 per pound. By this time, however, vast herds of elephants had been slaughtered throughout the continent. In the decade preceding the CITES listing, Tanzania and Zambia lost more than 80 percent of their elephants, for example, while Uganda lost 73 percent.[145] In Kenya, 5,000 elephants were killed every year between 1975 and 1990.[146] In just 10 years, Africa lost more than half its entire elephant population, which fell from 1.3 million in 1979 to

625,000 in 1989.[147]

The CITES ban did reduce the carnage—for a time. But in 1997, CITES allowed several African nations to sell stockpiled ivory to buyers in China and Japan. Additional sales of seized ivory or ivory from culled elephants have been authorized; the last one, in 2008, put 108 metric tonnes of ivory from Botswana, Namibia, South Africa, and Zimbabwe into the international market. Enabled by these one-off sales, elephant poaching is approaching levels not seen since the pre-ban days of the '80s: current estimates are that as many as 35,000 African elephants are killed every year—nearly 100 a day.[148] The slaughter is now closely associated with ongoing conflicts in Africa, as well-organized dealers use ivory to purchase weapons and supplies.[149]

In Kenya, where killing an elephant for any reason is forbidden, poachers are financed by dealers in neighboring Somalia, who pay them as much as US$300 a month—twice what a Kenyan park ranger earns, says Ken Bernhard, a Connecticut attorney working closely with the Kenyan government. Bernhard's efforts to end the slaughter of the world's largest land mammals have placed him into the thieves' den itself, posing as an ivory buyer in Africa to help apprehend traffickers. Ivory smuggling is an incredibly lucrative business, he says. "A kilogram of raw ivory that is worth US$40 in Kenya sells for US$200 in Mogadishu."[150] By the time it reaches China, that kilogram of ivory sells for more than US$2,600.[151]

In fact, it's this kind of inflated markup that is fueling elephant poaching in Asia, where buyers hope to avoid the high costs associated with imported ivory. "Most of our small pieces are locally sourced," says a shop owner in Vietnam who specializes in ivory carvings. "Our prices are already too high, so we don't want to pay off more customs to bring it in from Laos or Cambodia."[152]

But of the estimated 45,000 to 50,000 Asian elephants who remain in 13 countries, fewer and fewer are seen with tusks, thanks to centuries of poaching, say researchers.[153] The tusk-free gene, which was traditionally found in between 2 and 5 percent of male Asian elephants, has increased to between 5 percent and 10 percent in elephants in China, according to Zhang Li, an associate professor of zoology at Beijing Normal University. (Female Asian elephants almost never grow tusks.[154]) "The larger the tusks the male elephant has, the more likely it will be shot by poachers," says Zhang, a member of the World Conservation Union's Asian elephant specialist group. "Therefore, the ones without tusks survive, preserving the tuskless gene in the species."[155] Zhang and his team have studied elephants in the southwest province of Yunnan, where two-thirds of China's Asian elephants live, since 1999, and they released their findings in 2005. The decline in elephants being born who will not develop tusks is *not* the result of natural evolution, says Zhang. "Rather, it is a reluctant choice made in the face of a gun."[156]

Around the world, the chronic stress from decades of poaching, habit loss, and wildlife management "culls" has resulted in a kind of species-wide trauma among elephants, and now they seem to be telling us they've had enough. Farmers and ranchers throughout Africa and Asia are faced with wild herds or individual elephants who raid crops and rampage through villages, sometimes leaving trampled bodies behind. It's the kind of thing that keeps Gay Bradshaw awake at night. Bradshaw, whose work focuses on trans-species psychology, is a specialist in the field of elephant behavior. "Elephants are experiencing genocide," she says. "For 500 years, their society has been under siege. Through mass killings, habitat degradation and appropriation we've been gradually snipping away at this vast civilization. What we're seeing now is the elephants' psychological, neurological, and biological implosion. They have sustained iterative waves of genocide, and now they have limited space and no buffer for recuperation." Dr. Bradshaw believes elephants are behaving the way humans do when being attacked, and is it really so surprising? Remember, these are sensitive, self-aware animals with long memories, and they feel the loss of every member of their herd intensely. "These elephants are in survival mode. They are all living on the edge."[157]

Other Ivory

A similar ivory fever narrative can be told about walrus herds, which occupy Atlantic and Pacific regions of Arctic latitudes. Calculating walrus numbers is more difficult, since they spend so much time underwater and tend to pile on top of one another when they gather on land or ice floes, but most conservationists believe the walrus is imperiled, if for no other reason than the animals' preferred habitat is melting away.[158] One estimate reckons the walrus population has dropped from 250,000 in the 1980s to 190,000 today.[159]

These large marine mammals use tusks both for defense and to heave themselves out of water onto the slippery ice. Though much smaller than those on elephants, walrus tusks were once the focus of commercial hunting, a practice that is banned under Appendix I of CITES and is now legal only for certain Alaska natives (Indians, Aleuts, and Eskimos), provided the walrus is not killed solely for ivory.[160] Walrus poaching is an ongoing problem, however, and even indigenous peoples can face stiff punishment. In 2005, Alaska native Herman A. Oyagak was sentenced to seven years in federal prison for killing six walruses, removing their heads to sell the ivory, and then sinking their bodies.[161]

Although historically less popular among consumers than elephant tusks, hippopotamus teeth have nonetheless been in demand for centuries for use in buttons, inlays, and other flat accessories. That demand increased when the trade in elephant ivory was banned in 1989. In 1988, the entire continent of Africa exported about 5,600 pounds (2,545 kilograms) of hippo ivory; by 1991— just two years after the CITES ban in elephant tusks—exports increased by more than 500 percent to nearly 30,000 pounds (13,636 kilograms).[162] As a consequence, populations of the common hippo have been decimated throughout sub-Saharan Africa, the species' native habitat. The number of hippos in Virunga National Park in the Democratic Republic of Congo, for example, fell precipitously from 20,000 hippos in 1990 to about 1,300 in 2003.[163] There are now just 753 individuals left in Virunga, says Emmanuel de Mérode, the park's director. "Poaching for bushmeat by armed groups from the early 1990s was the main cause of collapse," he says. "At the moment the population is making a cautious recovery."[164]

Despite their dwindling numbers, the hippopotamus is not considered endangered and remains virtually unprotected. The International Union for Conservation of Nature (IUCN) has even downgraded the hippo's status from "threatened" to "vulnerable" on its Red List of Threatened Species.[165] The Wildlife Conservation Society estimates the current population of common hippos at 125,000 to 150,000.[166]

Arguably the most elusive animal hunted for his tusk is the narwhal, a cetacean species inhabiting the frigid oceans of the northern latitudes. With a long, spiraling tusk that protrudes from their upper jaw nearly 10 feet (about 3 meters),[167] male narwhals have been called "unicorns of the sea."[168] Indeed, medieval traders passed the tusks off as unicorn horns and endowed them with magical lore, transforming the "horns" into collectibles coveted by merchants and monarchs alike. Queen Elizabeth I was so delighted with the narwhal tusk she received that she used it as her royal scepter in the 16th century.[169] Far more than just an overgrown tooth, the narwhal's tusk is a highly sensitive organ capable of detecting subtle changes of water salinity, barometric pressure, and temperature.[170] Unfortunately, their legendary appendage has made these whales targets for hunters eager to capitalize on what has become a scarce commodity.

Found predominantly in the Arctic waters of Canada, Greenland, and Russia, narwhals are not considered endangered—the Arctic Institute of North America puts their world population at 60,000[171]—but they are included in Appendix II of CITES, thus monitoring and controlling trade in narwhal parts so the species is not at risk of extinction. Hunting narwhal for their ivory is a major source of income for the Inuit, whose annual spring slaughter finds hunters lined up along contours of ice armed with high-powered rifles and grappling hooks. Gunfire fills the air as the migrating narwhals break the surface of the water, but many of these animals are left to die. "For even the best hunters, killing and retrieving a narwhal at the ice edge is a formidable challenge, one that requires near-perfect aim and timing," writes wildlife biologist and nature photographer Paul Nicklen, who grew up in an Inuit settlement in Canada. "The whale must be shot in the spine or brain (an organ the size of a cantaloupe) the instant it fills its lungs with air. Kill it at the wrong moment, and it will sink. Wound it, and it will swim away and possibly die later—though many narwhals apparently survive. I've seen more than a few bearing multiple bullet wounds. Even whales killed with a perfect shot often float beyond reach of the hunter's hook and sink. So much ivory rests on the seafloor, said one hunter, that a salvager could make a fortune."[172] In 2006, a single narwhal tusk sold at auction for more than US$16,000.[173]

"Ethical" Ivory

Killing an animal for his tusks is an indefensible act that leads many consumers to avoid ivory products. But what if you could obtain ivory from a source that does not require poaching—a species long since extinct? Such is the question surrounding mammoth ivory, which has become a burgeoning industry in Russia. Faced with international restrictions on the trade in elephant tusks, enterprising entrepreneurs are digging beneath the Siberian tundra to unearth the bodies of prehistoric pachyderms.

These ancient ancestors of modern elephants evolved 3 million years ago and eventually roamed the Asian, African, European, and North American continents.[174] They subsisted on vegetation and lived well in Siberia, but probably died out there about 10,000 BCE,[175] no doubt pushed to extinction in part by human hunters.[176] It's believed that as many as 150 million of these creatures lie frozen in Russia. Global warming has made their bodies easier to uncover, and every summer finds hundreds of Russians searching the melting permafrost for tusks (foreigners are not granted collection permits[177]). Some tusks are easily spotted on riverbanks, while others are recovered on the flatlands. Once the tusks are gathered in one place by truck, boat, or helicopter, traders send planes to pick them up and bring them to Moscow, where the highest-quality tusks fetch US$500 per kilogram.[178] Each year 60 tonnes of these tusks are exported to neighboring China, the world's largest ivory market.[179]

Though the practice of exhuming ivory from icy mammoth graveyards is thousands of years old,[180] the CITES ban on elephant ivory created a scramble for buried tusks, and the concern today is how the trade could affect poaching. A 2010 study by conservationists Esmond and Chryssee Martin concluded that so-called "mammoth mining" is most likely not having a negative impact on elephants in Africa or Asia. "There is no evidence of mammoth ivory traders colluding with African elephant ivory traders," the authors contend. "Nor are there confiscations of African elephant tusks that are being mislabeled as mammoth tusks. There would be no point in trying to carry out this deception because mammoth tusks are easy to identify."[181]

But Mark Jones, programs director at Care for the Wild, the nonprofit that commissioned the Martins' report, cautions that the world's demand for *any* ivory could be a danger to elephants. "Wild elephant populations were decimated by the ivory trade," he says. "By the time the 1989 CITES ban came into force, Africa's elephants had been reduced by more than 50 percent. Poaching continues to threaten wild elephants. Anything that encourages the continued demand for ivory products, whether mammoth ivory or elephant ivory, could potentially exacerbate this threat."[182]

Conservationists may tout ivory obtained from an extinct species as ethical, but it begs the question: at what point is it morally acceptable to use the body part of an animal? Regardless of how the animal died, benefitting from his or her remains is a form of exploitation. Consider, too, the consumer who covets a bit of mammoth ivory but can't afford the hefty price tag. To such a consumer, any ivory may become appealing, thus subsidizing the poaching of elephants for their tusks. Moving consumers away from ivory—decreasing demand altogether—will do more to ensure the long-term survival of elephants and other animals killed for their tusks than excavating ivory from the permafrost of Russia.

Beads of Abuse

Lustrous little spheres produced within the soft mantle tissue of a living shelled mollusk, pearls are composed of calcium carbonate in a crystalline form called nacre, deposited in layers to create their round shape. Pearls were among the first gems to adorn crowns, enliven dresses, drape around necks, and fill treasure chests. In their 1908 tome *The Book of the Pearl: Its History, Art, Science and Industry*, George Frederick Kunz and Charles Hugh Stevenson are downright rhapsodic, referring to the pearl as a "symbol of purity and chastity."[183]

A popular theory regarding the formation of natural pearls is that they are created as a defense mechanism: if a foreign object, such as a grain of sand, works its way into an oyster, clam, or mussel and the irritant cannot be expelled or digested, the animal coats it with layer upon layer of nacre, which is the same material as the shell lining, eventually forming a sizable bead.[184] (Other evidence suggests that pearls are produced when the tissue of the animal's mantle is injured. Wounds to the mantle sometimes heal with a cyst or pocket, into which the mantle secretes calcium carbonate.[185])

By the early 20th century, a technique for mass producing pearls was perfected in Japan.[186] With so-called cultured pearls, the industry no longer relied on the whims of nature to generate a pearl within a mollusk; in a startling precursor to the mutilations commonly practiced in modern factory farming, they manipulated the animal's anatomy to create a desired result. Making cultured (or farmed) pearls involves a bead—usually a piece of shell from a freshwater bivalve such as a mussel—and a graft, which is a small slice of mantle tissue from another oyster. In her book *Jewels: A Secret History*, Victoria Finlay explains the procedure:

Professional pearl-grafters relax the two-year-old oysters by placing them in a warm bath. When the shells open they insert a thin, sharp instrument, developed for the purpose by dentists, and use it to make a small cut in the animal's sexual organs. This forms a little pocket into which the graft and the bead are placed. It takes only a few seconds but the oysters need at least three months to recover from the trauma. Many die. No wonder vegetarian organizations around the world recommend that their members not buy pearls.[187]

Finlay writes: "It is ironic that to create the jewel that symbolizes purity you have to commit what might be labeled surgical rape in a more sophisticated organism."[188]

However pearls are ultimately created, the mollusk who hosts the gem generally dies after the pearl has been removed. This process involves prying open the animal's shell, "harvesting" the pearl, and discarding the dying shellfish. The question of what constitutes mollusk cruelty is often muddled in discourse concerning pain. Because oysters, clams, and mussels do not have a brain, some experts argue that they cannot be conscious of pain. But not having a brain doesn't necessarily mean the animals are neurologically challenged. "Bivalves and other mollusks have fairly sophisticated nervous systems, and they certainly react strongly to physical and chemical stimuli," says marine biologist Paula Mikkelsen of Cornell University. "However, whether this can be categorized as pain as humans understand it can be debated."[189]

Ethicist Peter Singer says that while doubts about the mollusks' capacity for pain are considerable, he leaves open the possibility that these animals do in fact suffer, and with a better-safe-than-sorry approach, he suggests that the best ethical choice is to leave them alone.[190] But Singer's position merely addresses one aspect of the debate, for implicit in any discussion of another being's life is the life itself. Even if oysters do not experience pain, humans impose their own will on them by using the oysters for financial gain. More importantly, animals have an interest in whether or not they exist, and humans have no moral justification for subjecting them to exploitation and then ending their lives.

Exploiting Insects

Fashion victims come in all shapes, sizes, and species. Consumers who like their decorative accessories with six legs—all still kicking—have turned to live insects: beetles and cockroaches covered in gems, crystals, and precious metals and attached to clothing with pins. Though the idea is centuries old, fashion designer Jared Gold is credited with (or blamed for) fueling a short-lived trend in the 21st century. Gold's "roach brooch"—a jewel-encrusted Madagascar cockroach—was prominently featured on *America's Next Top Model*, and soon he had tapped into a way to trivialize animal life for profit. The designer, who has since moved on to other creations, glued brightly colored crystals to the insect's outer shell and added a silver chain so the roach could explore an area of the wearer's sweater or blouse.

The bug bling craze has been around for hundreds of years in Mexico, however, where it's said the ancient Mayans started the tradition.[191] There the arthropod of choice is the maquech (or makech), a variety of beetle from the Yucatán peninsula. For each maquech brooch, a live beetle is adorned with tiny gemstones or bits of colored glass and a leash of thin silver chain with a safety pin on the other end.[192] The brooches are especially popular in the city of Mérida, where they are sold to tourists shopping at the Mercado de Artesanias.

It seems easy for some to disregard the life of a beetle or a cockroach. Designers may even think they're doing the insect a favor by enlivening their "ugly" exteriors with jewels, and consumers may consider themselves art patrons and believe they are making the life of a "pest" meaningful. But let's be honest: most probably just think it is avant-garde to wear a piece of living jewelry. For still other people, there's a certain ick factor associated with these and other crawling creatures; they'll abuse such beings sight unseen, thank you very much. And when it comes to abusing insects for fashion, none are as exploited as the silkworm.

Sheer Cruelty

Silk has been a status-symbol fabric since silkworms were first culti-vated in China some 6,000 years ago.[193] Sericulture—the commercial farming of silkworms—took hold throughout Asia and eventually reached other parts of the world, although China is still the leading manufacturer of silk, producing more than three times as much fabric as its nearest competitor, India.[194]

Silk production begins with the eggs of the silkworm. Soon after the eggs hatch, the larvae weave a protective cocoon by secreting a fibroin protein from their salivary glands, and this protein hardens into a gossamer-thin strand of filament when it comes into contact with air. It takes the silkworm two to three days to spin the cocoon, which is constructed of a single thread about a mile (1.6 kilometers) long. This process is a natural step toward metamorphosing into a moth. In nature, the silk moth will break through the cocoon toward freedom in order to mate and continue the life cycle. But in sericulture, the cocoon is prized for its continuous silk thread, so the silkworm is killed with heat—boiled, baked, or steamed right in the cocoon.

To what extent the silkworm suffers during this procedure we can't be certain. Some animal advocates have pointed out that worms secrete endorphins, the natural opiates that help control the neuron-chemical activity we call pain, and therefore silkworms are sensate creatures.[195] Trouble is, silkworms are not actually worms but the caterpillars (larvae) of silk moths. So, what do these insects feel, if anything? I put the question to Thomas Miller, an entomol-ogist at the University of California–Riverside, who says that silkworms have a central nervous system, but that they lack struc-tures equivalent to vertebrate pain receptors. "Bottom line," he says, "there is no evidence they experience what you call pain."[196] I remain skeptical of Dr. Miller's assertion, if for no other reason than science has a long history of explaining what animals are incapable of—that they cannot feel emotions, experience a sense of the future, or use moral codes of conduct, and so on, while recent studies have revealed the opposite to be true. It was not that long ago, in fact, that doctors performed surgeries on newborn humans without anesthesia, believing that infants did not feel pain.[197]

Whether or not they suffer pain, or at least feel stress, there is no question that with 3,000 cocoons required to produce 1 pound (453 grams) of silk,[198] and with more than 400,000 metric tons of fabric being churned out of the world's silk factories annually,[199] nearly 1 billion silkworms are exploited every year to make saris, neckties, shirts, suits, and other clothing and fashion accessories.

If you are disinclined to care about an insect, consider the human toll. Using underage labor is common in Uzbekistan, where children in this former Soviet republic work long days nurturing silkworm eggs into cocoons.[200] India's silk industry, meanwhile, exploits hundreds of thousands of children, many as young as 5, who have essentially been sold into slavery by their parents. "Contagious diseases, especially tuberculosis and digestive disorders, spread easily in the crowded rooms," reads a 2003 report by the nonprofit Human Rights Watch. "Poor lighting and constant visual strain damages the eyesight. The fine silk threads cut the fingers, and the cuts are difficult to heal properly. Children complained that employers beat them and abused them verbally."[201] Among the tasks they are forced to perform is reaching their hands into scalding water to check the cocoons that have been boiled.

What You Can Do

Fur

Please don't buy fur or products made with fur, such as cat toys. If you already own a garment made with genuine animal fur, please consider donating the item to a wildlife rescue organization. The fur can be used as bedding or nesting material and serve as a surrogate mother to orphaned or injured animals, reducing their stress and providing comfort. The donation is also tax deductible.

Traps

Throughout the US and in many parts of the world it is against the law to tamper with a trap—gingerly setting it off with a long stick, for example, before an animal is caught in it—but naturalist Jim Stapleton has a completely legal alternative. In *Sanctuary Almanac: State of Nature, State of Mind*, he writes: "[W]hen I am out in the woods and find a leg-hold trap, I carefully urinate in a yard-wide circle around it. Urine is a universal boundary signal among mammals, and many will not cross a closed circle of it. This works; I've tested it."[202] Another good reason to carry plenty of water when hiking.

See the following links for more information about fur:

www.harpseals.org

www.humanesociety.org/issues/campaigns/fur_free

www.rabbitfur.org

www.sealaction.org

Wool

There are so many outstanding alternatives for wool now that there is no reason to support this shear torture. Polartec Wind Pro, for instance, is touted by its manufacturer as providing four times the wind resistance of wool and is made primarily from recycled plastic bottles. Other cruelty-free options with good thermal efficiency include cotton flannel, synthetic shearling, and a wide variety of fleece clothing made from polyester.

You can also support retailers that have pledged not to sell Australian Merino wool products until mulesing and live exports have ended, including Abercrombie & Fitch, Aéropostale, American Eagle Outfitters, Limited Brands, Marks & Spencer, Talbots, and Timberland. When you buy from these companies, be sure to tell them it's their position on animal cruelty that gave them your business!

For more information on this issue, please visit www.save thesheep.com.

Shahtoosh

Efforts to save the chiru have been bolstered since the selling or owning of shahtoosh was made illegal in all countries that signed the Convention on International Trade in Endangered Species. Demand still exists for this wool, however, and poaching of chiru continues. The India-based nonprofit People for Animals asks that if you see shahtoosh being worn or sold in India, please report it:

WWF India Secretariat
172-B Lodi Estate
New Delhi 110 003
Telephone: 469 8578
Email: trfindia@del3.vsnl.net.in
For more information, please visit
www.peopleforanimalsindia.org.

Karakul

Ask designers who use karakul and the retailers who sell it to stop. Explain the cruelty behind this fur, which can end up in coats, skirts, vests, linings, accessories, and trim. Designers who use or have used karakul include:

Gucci
Via de Tornabuoni, 73
50123 Florence, Italy
Phone: +39 055 2645432

Dolce & Gabbana
Via Goldoni, 10
20129 Milan, Italy
Phone: +39 02 774271

Dolce & Gabbana
148 Lafayette Street
New York, NY 10013
Phone: 1-212-750-0055

Karl Lagerfeld
12 Rue Vivienne
75002 Paris, France
Phone: +33 1 44 50 22 22

Christian Dior
30 Avenue Montaigne
75008 Paris, France
Phone: +33 1 40 73 54 44

Miuccia Prada
Via Andrea Maffei, 2
20135 Milan, Italy
Phone: +39 02 54 67 01

Valentino
8 Place Vendôme
75001 Paris, France
Phone: +33 01 53299400

Givenchy
3 Avenue George V
Paris, France 75008
Phone: +33 1 44 31 50 00

Retailers that sell or have sold this fur include:
Saks Fifth Avenue
12 East 49th Street
New York, NY 10164-2114

Phone: 1-212-940-4048

Customer Service: 1-877-551-7257

Neiman Marcus

1618 Main Street

Dallas, TX 75201

Phone: 1-800-937-9146

Customer Service: 1-888-888-4757

Email: neimanmarcus@customercare.neimanmarcus.com

Barneys

660 Madison Avenue

New York, NY 10021-8448

Phone: 1-888-222-7639

Bergdorf Goodman

754 Fifth Avenue

New York, NY 10019

Phone: 1-888-774-2424

Email: bergdorfgoodman@customercare.bergdorfgoodman.com

Henri Bendel

712 Fifth Avenue

New York, NY 10019

Customer Service: 1-800-423-6335

Phone: 1-212-884-3000

Email: customerservice@henribendel.com

Devi Kroell

55 Fifth Avenue

New York, NY 10003

Phone: 1-212-228-3201

Email: customercare@devikroell.com

Down

Fortunately for ethical consumers, there is no shortage of down alternatives available. A new synthetic product called MicroMax reportedly gives comforters and pillows the loft of down without the animal cruelty. Other alternatives include PrimaLoft, a highly compressible synthetic fiber that—unlike down—is still effective when wet, and Ingeo, a corn-based fiber. You might also look for Polarguard®, Thinsulate™, or Quallofil®, to name just a few brands of polyester fleece available in many stores.

Leather

Many vegan retailers offer fashionable alternatives to leather, including footwear, belts, jackets, wallets, and bags. These websites will get you started:

www.alternativeoutfitters.com
www.beyondskin.co.uk
www.herbivoreclothing.com
www.mooshoes.com
www.thevegancollection.com
www.thevegetariansite.com
www.splaff.com
www.veganessentials.com
www.veganstore.co.uk
www.veganwares.com
www.vegetarian-shoes.co.uk
https://wickedhemp.com

Note: Some leather alternatives are made from vinyl or polyvinyl chloride (PVC), which are chemically produced materials that use significant amounts of fossil fuels and energy to manufacture. Even creating the popular synthetic product called pleather (short for "plastic leather") requires petroleum. Instead, consider clothing, shoes, and accessories made from hemp, cotton, jute, and even bamboo.

Kangaroos

Please ask clothing manufacturers that use kangaroo skin to stop. For more information on the kangaroo issue, please visit www. savethekangaroo.com.

Ivory

The ivory trade exists because of consumer demand, so please do not purchase any product made from ivory. Also be wary of bracelets that could be made from elephant hair, anything that looks like bone, and of "traditional" medicines that could contain elephant and other animal ingredients.

In addition, contact the countries in Africa that continue to "cull" elephants and lobby to sell ivory:

Botswana – email: info@botswana.com; phone: +45 5903 3939

Namibia – email: info@namibia.com; phone: +33 392 93920

South Africa – email: info@southafrica.net; phone: +2711 895 3000

Zimbabwe – email: info@zimbabwe.com; phone: +20 404 00302

Tell them that you will not visit their countries until they change their policies on this issue.

For more information about elephant poaching, please visit:

www.bloodyivory.org

www.elefantasia.org

www.elephantvoices.org

www.savetheelephants.org

www.tusk.org

Pearls

If you simply must have a string of pearls or pearl earrings, please buy something made of glass or plastic beads. Beware of some imitation pearls that are made from mother of pearl, an iridescent material found on the shells of mollusks such as oyster or abalone.

Silk

Much has been said in recent years about a silk product made from the cocoons of moths who have been allowed to naturally emerge, fly away, and complete their life cycle. So-called "peace silk" has been touted as cruelty-free and an ethical alternative to traditional silk. But the moths raised for peace silk (sometimes called Ahimsa silk) are still farmed and exploited. With so many luxurious fabrics to choose from that don't cause harm to insects or animals, why bother with silk at all?

Chapter 3

Trials and Errors: Animal Testing

Anything we could do to the animals we could do to each other: we practiced on them first.
—Margaret Atwood

Britches wasn't born blind. But his life began at a primate breeding colony at the University of California–Riverside (UCR), where baby monkeys like Britches were taken from their mothers immediately after birth and used as test subjects. Here, as part of an experiment to study blindness, the eyelids of the three-week-old stump-tail macaque monkey had been sewn shut with heavy black sutures. Strapped to his head was a green plastic box that emitted a high-pitched screech every few minutes. Researchers had placed in Britches' cage a padded post with two fake nipples affixed; apparently intended as a surrogate for the infant's mother, it was his sole comfort, and he clung to it constantly.[1] (We know from the notorious maternal-deprivation/torture experiments carried out by the late Harry Harlow in the 1950s and '60s that a frightened baby monkey will cling to an artificial mother at all costs—even when that cloth surrogate has been rigged by researchers to virtually blow the baby's skin off with high-pressure compressed air.[2])

Had all gone as planned, Britches would have suffered for six months in this condition, then researchers would have killed him and examined his brain, all to help them develop a travel aid for blind humans. Instead, animal activists intervened. Acting on a tip, they broke into the university lab one evening and rescued him, along with hundreds of other animals. Veterinarians examined Britches. Removing bandages that covered his head, they found cotton pads over his eyes that were filthy and soaked with moisture. Many of the coarse sutures beneath the pads had torn through the lid tissue and rubbed the eyeballs. It appeared, said one of the vets, as if the sutures had been applied "by an unqualified or incompetent person and that the infant was not receiving proper ongoing medical care."[3]

Britches opened his eyes after weeks of dark isolation in the lab, but he had a long recovery ahead of him. The torture he had suffered at UCR left him with a number of neurotic behaviors, including body spasms and shrieking. "If you touched him, he would just, he'd go into this seizure thing and clutch at his own body," says an activist who helped liberate him. "The way he kept clutching, it was like he was desperate to touch someone or something. The cage he'd been in was just metal, nothing soft on the bottom, and he was all raw and bleeding on his haunches from being in the cage. He was in such bad shape."[4]

Meanwhile, news of the UCR experiment reached organizations for the blind, and their leaders responded. Condemning the treatment of Britches and the waste of research funds, Dr. Grant Mack, president of the American Council of the Blind, said the experiment was "one of the most repugnant and ill-conceived boondoggles that I've heard about for a long time. Spending US$275,000 to artificially blind monkeys and study those animals in a very inhumane way in hopes that they will learn something that will help human beings is reaching quite far. I would think that their purposes would be served a good deal better if they would use the same amount of research to find out about blindness from blind people."[5]

With time and compassion, Britches slowly recovered from his physical and psychological wounds. Perhaps the most rewarding phase of his rehabilitation came when Britches was five months old and he was transferred from the attention of his human caregivers to a refuge in Mexico, where he was adopted by a female macaque who had already adopted several orphans.[6] His spasms all but abated, Britches at last could enjoy some semblance of the life he had been denied in the name of science.

Whether it's called animal testing, animal research, animal studies, animal experimentation, or vivisection, the exploitation of animals like Britches occurs throughout the world over three broad categories.

In *biomedical research*, by far the largest use, animals are used as models of people to study human health, disease, and injury. Examples of study targets include clues to the mechanisms of heart conditions and potential drugs to treat illness. This category also includes testing drugs to determine their toxicity (how poisonous they are). Research is generally a precursor to clinical trials using humans.

In *product testing*, scientists conduct toxicity tests on animals to discover how cleansers, food additives, pesticides, cosmetics, tobacco, and a broad assortment of industrial and consumer goods might affect human beings and the environment. For example, typical tests measure the level of skin irritancy and eye tissue damage a substance causes.

In *education*, animals are used in training medical, veterinary, and other health professionals or in teaching basic biology, such as anatomy. Dissecting frogs in high school is a common example most of us are probably familiar with.

Supporting these categories is an international industry of unsavory and generally out-of-sight "services," including breeding, cage manufacture, trapping, and a practice known as bunching. Before we explore vivisection's basic elements, let's consider an important factor that is often overlooked by ethicists and scientists alike when they debate the moral gravity that keeps animal research in orbit around our consciousness.

The Anatomy of Despair

The psychological abuse of many animals in labs begins shortly after birth, when a gloved hand takes them away from their mother and places them inside individual metal cages. Here they might remain for months or perhaps years, with the unremitting loneliness of solitary confinement broken only by the pain and terror of the experiments they're subjected to. For monkeys, dogs, and other beings who thrive on interaction with family and friends, prolonged seclusion is tantamount to torture, just as it is for another social animal: humans. A study of former prisoners of war (POW) returned to the US from Vietnam, where long periods of solitary confinement were common,[7] reported that they found isolation to be as torturous and agonizing as any physical abuse they suffered.[8] It is so well-known as a form of torture that the Geneva Conventions, which outline the humanitarian treatment of POWs, forbid the isolation of prisoners of war, unless they have broken a law.

Animals confined by themselves in cages for long periods develop a variety of abnormal behaviors, including pacing, rocking back and forth, head swaying, and constant rubbing against cage bars even as the flesh becomes bleeding and raw. Whether such stereotypical acts are a coping mechanism or an attempt to adapt to the environment remains unknown. What is clear is that these repetitive movements are a result of enormous stress.[9] At the University of Wisconsin–Madison, researcher Harry Harlow found that a perfectly happy baby monkey left alone in a stainless-steel isolation chamber became hopelessly depressed after just a few days, which is why Harlow nicknamed his device "the pit of despair" and "the hell of loneliness."[10] Monkeys placed inside other cages by themselves became profoundly psychologically disturbed. They would sit and rock, stare blankly into space, or repeatedly circle their cages.[11] And it's not only primates who can suffer from prolonged loneliness. A study conducted on mice concluded that four weeks of isolation so stressed the animals that they would react with violence when reintroduced to other mice.[12] These results came at the expense of many lives and needless suffering.

The legacy of Harlow's profoundly cruel maternal-deprivation research still haunts UW–Madison, which is why I was stunned to discover the university has rebooted these studies in terror. Someone who managed to tour the research facility told me that infant rhesus monkeys are separated from their mothers, held in isolation for six weeks, and then all the babies are thrown together to see how they respond.

For insights into the effects of institutionalized isolation on animals, I turned to activist Matt Rossell, who spent two years working undercover as a laboratory technician inside the federally funded Oregon Health & Science University's (OHSU) National Primate Research Center in Portland, Oregon. "What the industry does not want to face is that almost all the monkeys in research labs are suffering even before any protocol is ever assigned to them," he says. "Even if they are never used in a study, just the fact that they are stuck alone in a cage that's two feet by two feet, and that they can live like that for 25 years, causes a tremendous amount of suffering for them."[13]

Matt witnessed extreme reactions in which animals passing their lives in seclusion become so stressed that they mutilate themselves. "Some of them bite their arms, shoulders, and legs, and there's a varying degree of how much damage they do, from no damage to such severe damage that they have to be humanely euthanized," he says. "In the worst cases I saw, the veterinarians were continuously bandaging the injuries and covering them with duct tape because the monkeys were so determined to injure themselves they would tear bandages off immediately and continue to bite at themselves. I got to know this one capuchin who would just lick herself, one spot on her body, over and over and over again until it opened up an injury, and she would keep licking as it became a really deep wound that was pretty severe. When that would get bandaged up she would go right to the edge of the bandage and start licking there."

Although most animals can suffer from the effects of solitary confinement, the isolation of female monkeys is particularly harsh. To breed monkeys, says Matt, technicians put females in separate cages and watch their menstrual cycles for the few days when they're ovulating and then introduce a male. "If the female gets pregnant, she stays in the cage, gives birth, and the baby is taken away at six months of age. In the wild, female monkeys stay together for life—the mothers, daughters, and grandmothers *never* leave each other; they form family bonds that last a lifetime."

Vivisection apologists often defend the efficacy of animal research by arguing that the animals used are so similar to humans. This is certainly true of our collective reaction to social isolation, which taps into some of our darkest fears: being left alone on a desert island, trapped in an elevator, buried alive—all without the hope of escape. We can imagine the misery of being locked away in solitary confinement with every comfort taken from us. For millions of animals every year, such privations are coupled with a brand of torture we humans can only recoil at the thought of. Whatever moral calculus one might use to rationalize animal testing, the psychological torment of animals in labs cannot be ignored.

Bunny in a Bottle

Nalgene, famous for its line of popular plastic water bottles, got its start making equipment for animal testing in the 1940s. The company continues to capitalize on cruelty by manufacturing a variety of small cages and restraining devices made of polycarbonate and polypropylene and used by animal researchers around the globe. Fortunately, compassionate consumers now have so many choices in water bottles that there is no need to buy from Nalgene.

Biomedical Research

Using animals in biomedical research dates to at least the 5th century BCE, when the Greek scientist Alcmaeon of Crotona dissected the eyes of live dogs to explore the optic nerve.[14] Human cadavers were also used, but by the time of Galen, the physician who attended to the gladiators of Rome in the 2nd century CE, an edict from the Church prohibited autopsies, so Galen acquired goats, pigs, and monkeys from North Africa to experiment on, thus securing a sorry distinction as the father of vivisection.[15] Galen's influence was felt throughout medieval Europe as scientists regarded the Roman physician's conclusions—including critical errors about the heart and blood vessels—as sacrosanct. Indeed, Galen could equally be considered the father of medical malpractice, thanks to his reliance on animal research rather than human models.

In the 17th century, biomedical research took an especially ugly turn as the doctrines of French philosopher René Descartes were embraced by vivisectors. Descartes' philosophy, known as Cartesianism, says in part that animals are not conscious beings and therefore have no interests. Animals, according to Descartes, are soulless, unthinking machines, entirely different from human beings.[16] (Of course, animals were held to be enough like humans when it suited the scientist's purpose—the central contradiction of vivisection even today.) Some Cartesians went so far as to claim that animals felt no pain.[17] Consequently, researchers armed with the view that their living, breathing test subjects were no morally different than a telescope or a pocket watch carried out the most callous invasive practices imaginable, untroubled by even the slightest ethical obligation.[18] In a typical experiment, performed before the Royal Society of London in 1667, Robert Hooke opened a dog's chest by cutting away the ribs and diaphragm, exposing the lungs and heart. He then severed the windpipe and attached it to the nose of a bellows pump, with which he forced air into the dog's lungs. To disprove the belief that the lungs produced blood circulation, Hooke poked the animal's lungs full of holes with a penknife and noted how air flowed through the punctures. The experiment went on for an hour, with Hooke even cutting out a chunk of one of the live dog's lungs.[19] (This was, incidentally, nearly 200 years before anesthesia.[20] Even if a researcher believed animals could feel, there was nothing to relieve their pain in the 17th century.) Hooke noted that when he ceased to pump the bellows, "the Dog would immediately fall into Dying convulsive fits" but could be revived again with "a blast of fresh Air."[21]

An observer, depicting the general treatment of dogs undergoing vivisection, described the scientists' lack of concern:

> The (Cartesian) scientists administered beatings to dogs with perfect indifference, and made fun of those who pitied the creatures as if they felt pain. They said the animals were clocks; that the cries they emitted when struck were only the noise of a little spring that had been touched, but the whole body was without feeling. They nailed poor animals up on boards by their four paws to vivisect them and see the circulation of the blood which was a great subject of controversy.[22]

Given the moral paradigm shared by most Cartesians, a backlash was inevitable, and it is not surprising that the anti-vivisection movement traces its birth to the 17th century. In 1655, Irish physician Edmund O'Meara began vigorously articulating his objection to the cruelty, arguing that an animal's suffering could affect the accuracy of research results.[23] Meanwhile, O'Meara's contemporaries Robert Boyle and Richard Lower, both experimental physiologists in England, voiced concern for the welfare of their subjects. Boyle famously used an air pump to demonstrate on animals the effects of being placed in a vacuum and slowly deprived of oxygen. He spoke of excluding a kitten who had survived one experiment from further trials because "… it was too severe to make him undergo the same measure again."[24] Even Hooke expressed regret over the suffering he inflicted on dogs with his bellows experiments—though such remorse didn't prevent him from relying on animals in his research.[25]

Sadly, the centuries-old ethical arguments against scientific torture have had little real impact on the research community, which has declared unconditional entitlement to abuse animals however it wishes. Though laws now protect some test subjects in some countries (which we'll explore later in this chapter), the life and fate of animals in labs have changed little. Animals today are beaten, burned, and blinded. They are nailed down, tied up, and sliced open. They are starved, suffocated, shaken, and shot. Their organs are pulverized, their limbs are severed, their bodies are irradiated, and their spirits are broken. They are forced to drink alcohol, inhale tobacco smoke, and consume a variety of highly dangerous narcotics, including heroin. Name a modern disease, and they've been infected with it. Imagine a torment, and they've suffered it.

Even escape from the torture brings little relief for animals used as test subjects. I am reminded of a chimpanzee named Jeannie, who was a prisoner in three different labs before living her final days in a primate sanctuary. Jeannie spent nine years at the Laboratory for Experimental Medicine and Surgery in Primates (LEMSIP) in New York, where she was used for intensive and invasive research, including repeated vaginal washes; multiple cervical, liver punch, wedge, and lymph node biopsies; and infection with HIV, hepatitis NANB, and hepatitis C virus. She was also used in rhinovirus vaccine studies and was subjected to more than 200 "knockdowns" — anesthesia by dart gun. In 1995, after seven years of suffering, Jeannie had what LEMSIP personnel documented as "a nervous breakdown" characterized by serious emotional and behavioral problems. She spent the next two years heavily medicated for anxiety, but this did not prevent her from having episodes during which she screamed, tore out her fingernails, experienced seizures, slammed her body against her cage, and lashed out at anyone who came near her. She was "retired" when LEMSIP closed in 1998 and was taken in by the Fauna Foundation. Though Jeannie was cared for with patience and love, her screaming continued, as did her unpredictable aggressive behavior and self-mutilation: she sometimes attacked her hand or foot as if it did not belong to her. She would often wake up startled, perhaps unsure of where she was. Jeannie's nightmares finally ended when she died on January 1, 2007.[26]

The Global Use of Animals

The study of human health, disease, and injury today involves many millions of animals. Yet determining exactly how many animals are used worldwide is extremely challenging if not impossible. The most often cited figure is 115.3 million animals a year, based on calculations by the British Union for the Abolition of Vivisection and the Dr. Hadwen Trust for Humane Research.[27] Having a reliable figure is an essential step toward public accountability and an informed debate, as well as being important for effective policymaking and regulation. Unfortunately, this estimate very likely underestimates the number of animals who suffer each year.

Drug Testing

One hundred and thirty miles west of New Orleans, deep within the New Iberia Research Center (NIRC) on a decommissioned naval base, a technician slips a needle and syringe through the wire mesh of a cage and sedates a chimpanzee named Simba. The chimp, also known at the center as "ID XO19," was an infant when he was taken from his mother in the wild in 1967—well before the 1975 ban on capturing free-living chimpanzees in Africa—and he's one of thousands of nonhuman primates at NIRC who are routinely poked, prodded, and poisoned in an effort to study the effects of drugs. Under sedation, Simba is lifted onto a stretcher, where he defecates on himself before being transferred to a gurney. Another technician quickly shaves the chimp's forearms, armpits, and groin, after which yet another technician applies electrodes to his body. Blood is drawn from the left femoral vein near his groin. One of the technicians tries to introduce a catheter into Simba's penis to collect a urine sample, but it's taking too long, so she inserts a long needle directly into his lower abdomen and extracts 3 milliliters of the pale yellow fluid.

After checking his heart and blood pressure, technicians wheel Simba away and place him in a wire cage measuring 6.5 feet (2 meters) long by 5 feet (1.5 meters) wide by just over 7 feet (2.2 meters) tall. Simba is then injected with an experimental drug, and at regular intervals over the next 72 hours, his blood will be drawn and his urine collected from a pan beneath the cage. This is no ordinary enclosure, however: if Simba refuses to comply with requests to present his arm for blood withdrawal, noisy drills will slowly compress the cage and immobilize him between its walls—a practice that NIRC staff calls "squeezing up."[28]

Simba's suffering is hardly unique. There are roughly 1,000 chimps now housed in research facilities in the United States, one of only two countries in the world that still conduct invasive experiments on chimpanzees. (The other is the central African nation of Gabon.) Because all apes (chimpanzees, bonobos, gibbons, gorillas, and orangutans) are listed as endangered, chimps used for research have been bred and born in captivity, yet the babies are still torn from their mothers soon after birth so that they may serve as test subjects. For these animals, many kept in isolation, life is passed in long stretches of boredom punctuated by moments of terror. Not surprisingly, this exacts a heavy psychological toll. Video footage taken by an undercover investigator with The Humane Society of the United States in 2009 shows Simba swaying his head from side to side and repeatedly beating the concrete walls of his enclosure— clear signs of prolonged emotional trauma.[29]

Other animals suffer in the name of drug testing, too. Indeed, mice and rats account for most of the species used, but rabbits, hamsters, birds, cats, dogs, guinea pigs, sheep, goats, and even fish and horses are routinely dosed with the latest pharmaceutical concoctions in order to conduct ADMET screenings. These studies measure how the drug is *absorbed* into the body, how it is *distributed* to the tissues, how the body *metabolizes* it, how the body *eliminates* it, and the drug's *toxic* effects.

Pharmaceutical companies and the research industry alike love drug testing. For these vivisection advocates, drug testing offers a simple justification for keeping live animals enslaved in labs. Countless medicines, they argue, owe their existence to animal testing. Put another way, countless human lives have been saved, they say, because drugs are developed and tested using nonhuman animals. (And with the average drug taking as much as US$800 million and 15 years to develop, the stakes are huge.[30]) The research community typically touts the safety of children's medications, yet more than 500,000 outpatient children suffer adverse side effects from routinely prescribed medications every year, with kids under the age of 5 the most common victims.[31]

Unfortunately, testing drugs on animals isn't just a profitable practice—in many countries, it is the law. It was codified in the United States with the 1938 Food, Drug, and Cosmetic Act, which says that certain drugs have to be tested for safety on animals. The law traces its roots to a 1937 tragedy. In the 1930s, the wonder drug was sulfa, the first medicine that could effectively treat a wide range of bacterial infections, including many childhood ailments. Sulfa-based antibiotics are still around, but in the years before penicillin, sulfa truly was miraculous—hailed as a remedy for everything from venereal disease to leprosy—and one of its forms, sulfanilamide, was an immensely popular cure. But sulfanilamide was only sold as a bitter tablet or powder, and parents wanted a medicine their kids could easily swallow. In response, one enterprising pharmaceutical manufacturer, SE Massengill Company, introduced a product called Elixir Sulfanilamide, a sweet-tasting liquid with the curative properties of sulfa. It seemed the ideal treatment for sore throats and ear infections. The only problem was that the sulfanilamide was dissolved in diethylene glycol, a highly toxic chemical. Massengill should have recognized the compound's lethal properties, not only because diethylene glycol is used as an antifreeze, but because the FDA had advised against using glycol solvents in foods, the chief manufacturer of diethylene glycol had warned not to use it in foods and drugs, and medical journals had been reporting that consuming diethylene glycol was fatal.[32]

Despite the red flags, Massengill shipped Elixir Sulfanilamide to drugstores from coast to coast, pharmacists dispensed it liberally, and 107 people—most of them children—died.[33] Researchers administered Elixir Sulfanilamide to animals and they also died. That a chemical like diethylene glycol would kill both human and nonhuman animals was a coincidence; nevertheless, the mass poisoning was such a notorious event that drug testing was swiftly mandated, and the public breathed a collective sigh of relief.

Trouble is, testing on animals is far from a guarantee that a drug will be safe for humans, and history is rife with disastrous consequences of believing otherwise. To arthritis sufferers in the early 2000s, Vioxx seemed like an answer to their prayers: an anti-inflammatory medication without the gastrointestinal side effects often associated with over-the-counter painkillers. The drug had gone through the requisite battery of animal testing, which showed that it even had a heart-protective effect in mice and rats, and the FDA approved Vioxx in 1999. But rodent physiology is vastly different from human physiology, and Merck & Co., the drug's manufacturer, ignored the fact that heart attacks are virtually unheard of in mice and rats. Five years and 80 million prescriptions later, Vioxx had killed as many as 139,000 people worldwide from heart attacks and other adverse cardiovascular events.[34] Merck took Vioxx off the market in 2004, just as the personal-injury and wrongful-death lawsuits were pouring in.

Even nonhuman primates, who share roughly 96 percent of their DNA sequence with us, are not reliable predictors. Take AIDS research, for instance. Despite decades of infecting monkeys (and, in the 1980s, chimpanzees) with Human Immunodeficiency Virus—the virus that causes AIDS—researchers are no closer to creating a truly effective HIV vaccine using these animals. That's because monkeys and chimps can express symptoms of AIDS, but they don't die of it, while humans do. As one leading AIDS researcher put it, "What good does it do you to test something in a monkey? You find five or

Great Apes Gain Respect

Reflecting the growing awareness that experimenting on chimpanzees is unethical, many governments have prohibited the use of great apes (chimpanzees, bonobos, gibbons, gorillas, and orangutans) in animal testing. The UK prohibited such tests in 1997, and nine other nations— including Australia, Belgium, and New Zealand—either declared outright bans or introduced strict limitations over the next decade. In 2007, the Balearic Islands, one of the Autonomous Communities of Spain, even granted great apes legal rights. The European Union outlawed great-ape experimentation in 2010, and the next year, policymakers in the United States introduced the Great Ape Protection and Cost Savings Act. Now in Congress, the Act would end the use of chimpanzees in invasive biomedical research and retire all federally-owned chimpanzees to permanent sanctuary. In the meantime, the US remains the only large-scale user of chimpanzees for research.

six years from now that it works in the monkey, and then you test it in humans and you realize that humans behave totally differently from monkeys, so you've wasted five years."[35]

Other drugs, such as the arthritis medications Flosint and Opren, have tested well on monkeys yet went on to kill humans. Indeed, according to the FDA, 92 percent of the drugs that prove safe and therapeutically effective in animals fail in clinical trials using humans.[36] Of the 8 percent of drugs that do pass clinical trials, more than half are found to have toxic or fatal effects that were not predicted by animal experiments.[37] Perhaps it's no shock that poisoning from prescription drugs is now the second leading cause of unintentional injury death in the US.[38] Ray Greek, MD, and Jean Swingle Greek, DVM, write that animal testing persists "because it provides a sanctuary for pharmaceutical companies. In fact, it is itself fundamentally malpractice. There is *always* less than a fifty-fifty chance that a medication tested on animals will provide the same results in humans... usually much less. This is not science. It is expensive and dangerous gambling."[39]

Replace, Reduce, Refine

The research industry professes its commitment to a principle known as the Three Rs (sometimes abbreviated as "the 3Rs"), which aims to *replace* animal use with non-animal methods where possible, *reduce* the number of animals used, and *refine* the procedures as much as possible to minimize animals' pain and distress.[40] Implicit in this principle is an understanding that using live animals as test subjects is unethical and that researchers have an obligation to only use animals when no other option is available and to cause the least amount of suffering. Clearly, the Three Rs are a compromise between research interests and animal welfare advocates; in contrast, anyone with a strict view of animal rights would argue that *any* use of animals, regardless of the reason and no matter how humane, is exploitive and unacceptable.

The Three R approach was first proposed in 1957 at a Universities Federation for Animal Welfare symposium by zoologist WMS Russell and microbiologist Rex Burch and articulated publicly in their 1959 book *The Principles of Humane Experimental Technique*.[41] It was not until the mid-'80s, however, that the Three Rs began gaining traction and influencing national and international legislation governing animal research, including the Animal Welfare Act. But not everyone in the scientific community agrees with the principle. As Stuart Derbyshire put it in *The Scientist*, "Those of us who research on animals or support that research have made a moral choice to put humans first." Derbyshire writes:

Ultimately, we cannot have it both ways. It is not possible to advocate animal welfare and at the same time give animals untested drugs or diseases, or slice them open to test a new surgical procedure. The three Rs encourage a focus on animal welfare that is both unrealistic and dishonest. Regardless of any beliefs about the value of animals, if you engage in activities that are invasive or lethal to animals or if you control their reproduction, their living space and their habits, you are expressing a de facto belief that animals are sufficiently different from humans to make such activities justifiable. Scientists are keen to defend themselves against accusations of cruelty by promoting their allegiance to the three Rs but forget that the real reason for animal experimentation is to advance the welfare and understanding of humanity. Advancing human understanding requires the freedom to do more animal research, and often with higher species, and is incompatible with continued support for the three Rs.[42]

For those on either side of the research debate, replacing live animals with alternative models seems to be an ideal solution: the public gets the benefit of medical advancements and no animals are harmed. Some of the more promising replacement techniques include:

- *In vitro* ("in glass") studies on human cells and tissues. Researchers can examine human cells or tissues in test tubes or Petri dishes to study disease, test drugs, and manufacture vaccines. Because most illnesses impact the body at a microscopic level, these experiments are ideal for studying the course of human disease. Every human cell type can now be studied *in vitro*.
- Computer modeling. Because computers are able to simulate human body parts, scientists can use this technology to model diseases and help explain how various substances can treat them. The models are based on existing data and can be used to screen potential drugs at an early stage of their development.

- Clinical research. This entails observing and analyzing illnesses in human patients. Because it involves a shift away from lab work, scientists refer to this as "moving research from the bench to the bedside."

- Epidemiological studies. Also known as population studies, these examine the cause-and-effect relationship between lifestyle (such as diet, occupation, and habits) and disease. While animal testing concluded that tobacco, alcohol, and asbestos, for example, are safe for people to ingest, epidemiological research has proved all of them to be hazardous to humans.

- Autopsies. Postmortem studies of human bodies yield clues about diseases and their causes. Autopsies have aided research on diabetes, congenital heart disease, typhoid fever, and many other ailments. Unfortunately, autopsies are expensive and, as a result, not conducted as often as they once were.

- In the search for an HIV/AIDS vaccine, one of the most exciting technologies is a system called the Modular Immune In vitro Construct (MIMIC), which uses human cells to create a surrogate human immune system. Developed by Florida-based VaxDesign, MIMIC enables researchers to test the efficacy of new vaccines and drugs on hundreds of different tissue samples from a diverse genetic pool of donors— something that would be impossible using nonhuman animals.

Despite these and many other humane options, the research community has been resistant to using non-animal tests for some experiments, although at least one type of testing traditionally based on animals may be on its way out. Toxicity testing, which is supposed to determine the safety of products containing potentially harmful compounds, got a well-funded push from the US National Resource Council in 2007, and progress is being made to replace these painful studies with cruelty-free alternatives, such as cell cultures, tissue cultures, and computer models. The technology is now so advanced that a robot called Tox21—developed in collaboration with the National Institute of Environmental Health Sciences, the FDA, and other agencies—can screen 10,000 chemicals a week for toxicity to humans.[43] Tox21 analyzes substances and predicts toxicity more accurately than animal tests and is much more cost effective: a single animal-based reproductive toxicity study requires a minimum of two years, US$380,000, and 2,600 animals.[44] Tox21 could do the same test in a matter of weeks, making animal tests for chemical toxicity obsolete. (Case in point: In 2012, Covance, the world's largest contract testing laboratory, announced it was closing its massive animal lab in Chandler, Arizona, due to lack of demand.[45])

IACUCs

In the United States, all facilities that use animals for research, testing, or education and receive federal funding are required to appoint an Institutional Animal Care and Use Committee (IACUC), an internal review board that approves applications for the use of animals in research activities—known as "protocols." Introduced in 1985 in response to the Three R principle, this monitoring at the institutional level was also a way of avoiding regulation by an external agency and keeping animal welfare agitators off the backs of researchers.[46] The IACUC must have a minimum of five members, including one veterinarian with expertise in the species used by the institution, one practicing scientist experienced in animal research, one non-scientist, and an individual who has no other affiliation with the institution other than his or her membership in the IACUC. Such committees are often the only means of ensuring that animals used in research receive even the barest minimum standards of care. At least that's the promise. In reality, IACUCs create an illusion of protection, lack rigorous authority, and facilities are routinely found to be neglecting animals and inflicting suffering that even a researcher would deem inhumane, such as denying proper veterinary care and not giving an animal pain relief.[47]

The Achilles heel of any IACUC is found within its membership, which is composed mainly of employees of the lab, all chosen by the facility's chief executive officer. At least one IACUC board member not affiliated with the institution is supposed to ensure that the welfare of animals is not compromised by decisions made by researchers, yet such members are a minority voice on the board, and they are offered almost no guidance on how to fulfill their important role. We can infer that their membership often calls on them to express an opposing view in a roomful of financially motivated scientists—not a pleasant prospect, to say the least. When he served on an IACUC, Ned Buyukmihci—a veterinarian who's also an ethical vegan—was very careful not to simply vote *no* on every protocol; if he did, no one would listen to him. "I viewed my position on the committee as being an advocate for the animals," he says. "I don't believe that there was another person on the committee who had the views that I had." Dr. Buyukmihci reserved his *no* vote for situations he thought were particularly egregious, such as when a university researcher wanted to feed the mosquitoes in a study by letting them feast on the blood of a mouse, who would be restrained in a tube filled with holes and suspended in the middle of a mosquito cage. "The mouse could not turn around, could not scratch, could not in any way defend herself or himself, and was going to be allowed to feed the mosquitoes all night long," says Dr. Buyukmihci. "I objected strenuously to this. I thought this was one of the most inhumane things that they were trying to do in the campus. I pleaded with my fellow committee members to not allow this at all, because there were alternatives." In fact, a researcher conducting a similar study at a nearby university was using the blood from student volunteers to feed the insects. "Ultimately, the majority voted yes, but with a reduced exposure time down to two hours, which to me made no sense. Two hours to the mouse was a lifetime."[48]

Another serious flaw is that the board is predisposed to

approving proposals that are in the interests of that facility. Social psychologists Harold Herzog and Scott Plous upset many researchers with a 2001 study published in the journal *Science* that demonstrates this point. Funded by the National Science Foundation, a US government agency, they studied 50 randomly selected academic IACUCs with a total of almost 500 individual members. Each IACUC submitted its three most recent protocols and the committee's decision on whether to approve or reject them. Herzog and Plous then removed all identifying information and sent the protocols to other IACUCs for unofficial review and judgment. While review committees might tout their protocol decisions as being impartial, the study yielded vastly inconsistent levels of approval: 85 percent of proposals that had been approved by a local IACUC were rejected by an outside committee. Moreover, only three of the 150 animal research proposals had been rejected by a local IACUC.[49] In other words, scientists enjoy a clear advantage in their own backyards.

"Obviously there is a conflict of interest issue with paid employees of an organization in charge of reviewing the ethics of research projects that very likely already have federal backing and are awaiting approval," says Matt Rossell, who served as the alternate technician on the IACUC board at OHSU and was able to see firsthand how the review meetings operate. "In many respects I saw them as a rubber stamp. I felt there was a very strong, unspoken compulsion for those protocols to get approved. I never saw one that didn't. Members of the committee might have suggestions to tweak the project, but I never heard a discussion about whether or not the research might just not be necessary at all, and in the end, all that I saw come across the table were eventually approved." Even the merciless experiments conducted by Eliot Spindel, who collected millions of dollars in funding from the National Institutes of Health between 1992 and 2012, seemed above reproach, says Matt. "Spindel made a career out of injecting mother monkeys with nicotine and then, at the time, he was taking the babies prenatally via caesarean section, to then dissect the babies' lungs. His next protocol being reviewed was then going to use the same procedure and let the babies go full term and euthanize at a specific number of months and look at their lung development. This was approved unanimously without discussion. No discussion about whether animals should continue to be used for nicotine experiments after so many decades of human cancer patients have given us a wealth of clinical information. Do we really need to try to make cigarette smoking safer for pregnant women by torturing monkeys, or should we use those dollars for smoking-cessation resources and education to help pregnant women quit?"[50]

Of course, the IACUC's answer would be to continue funneling money into animal research. These committees do not view the purpose of the research through any lens that considers the harm inflicted on the animals; they simply presume a proposed animal experiment is necessary and move forward.[51] As a result of the failings of IACUCs, many more animals are being used for experiments, and oversight in experiments takes a backseat to the interests of an institution. Some countries, such as Australia and Sweden, require committees that review animal research protocols to include members who represent the animal welfare interests, too. In Germany, one-third of its 12-member committee must be experts from national animal welfare organizations.[52]

Good Science—or Propaganda?

Putting the ethical concerns about testing on animals aside for a moment, let's consider another important question: Does treating animals as mere biofactories achieve benefits for humans? The animal experimentation lobby will say yes, of course it does. They argue that modern medicine would be nowhere without animal-based models. But what does the science say? As we've seen, nonhuman animals may be complex biological systems, but they are inappropriate laboratory surrogates for human beings; they simply are not reliable predictors of how people will respond to a drug or treatment.

This was demonstrated in a 2013 study so startling that many peer-reviewed journals balked at publishing it. For 10 years, researchers examined the results of nearly 150 drugs that had tested well in mice but failed in patients with sepsis—a potentially deadly reaction that occurs as the body tries to fight an infection; it is the leading cause of death in intensive-care units. One clue to why mice don't mimic humans in drug testing has long been overlooked: it takes a million times more bacteria to kill a mouse. The study's authors recognized how unreliable mice are in sepsis research—and how important it is to use humans rather than nonhuman animals to test medications—yet so revered is the mouse model that scientific journals at first refused to publish their findings, believing the study had to be wrong.[53] (It finally appeared in *Proceedings of the National Academy of Sciences*.) Hundreds of millions of mice lost their lives for useless drugs.

Every species is different, and the same can be said of disease. Cancer is another example. A histiocytoma tumor can be a death sentence for a human, but in a dog, it is usually benign and goes away on its own. Meanwhile, scientists have devoted decades to inducing and suppressing cancer in rodents, and the results are not terribly surprising. "We cure cancer in mice and rats... we do it all the time," says Dr. Patric Schiltz, a cancer researcher. "But these animal models are not human beings. Human beings are much more complex."[54] Indeed, the scientific literature is filled with cancer treatments—such as taxol, interleukin, and interferon—that worked wonders in nonhuman animals, only to prove disappointing in people. On the other hand, when an experimental drug fails to successfully treat an animal, researchers simply throw the drug away and start over. We can only lament the loss of cancer cures that have been discarded because they were considered ineffective or unsafe during animal testing.

For their book *Sacred Cows and Golden Geese: The Human Cost of Experiments on Animals*, Ray Greek and Jean Swingle Greek explored the medical advancements gained through vivisection. The Greeks began by asking physicians how animal research had benefited their field. Surgeons denied knowing about any specific contribution, but they referred them to pediatricians. Pediatricians could offer no significant examples of animal testing benefitting pediatrics, but they suggested they speak with psychiatrists. Psychiatrists noted the problems with studying psychosis in mice and referred them to internists. And so on. "Each specialist, though unaware of true animal-model successes in his own field, was convinced that other specialists were reliant on this protocol," report the Greeks. "They too had bought what was fast appearing to us as a bill of goods."[55]

That bill of goods is largely crafted by the biomedical publicity machine, which churns out "news" that is often both unsubstantiated and dangerously misleading, especially when it refers to results based on animal testing. A study in the journal *Annals of Internal Medicine* found that academic medical centers routinely exaggerate findings from animal experiments and "often promote research that has uncertain relevance to human health and do not provide key facts or acknowledge important limitations." Most of the press releases promoting animal research explicitly claimed relevance to human health, yet 90 percent of these lacked warnings about extrapolating results to people.[56]

Upon searching the scientific literature, the Greeks discovered that the majority of recent medical breakthroughs were due not to animal experimentation, but to clinical observations by doctors and nurses on their human patients. "The animal-model community then tries to take credit for that," says Ray Greek, a physician who has spent the last two decades studying the differences among species in response to drugs and disease. "For example, there is a blood-pressure drug called an ACE inhibitor. The guys who invented it sketched it out with a pencil, literally drawing the drug's elements on paper, and then put it together in a chemistry lab. At some point along the way, the drug was tested on animals, which is required by law, and therefore the animal experimentation community says ACE inhibitors wouldn't be here today if it weren't for animal testing."[57]

Wasted Research

After being diagnosed with cancer in 2011, Helen Marston was shocked to learn that the drugs involved in the chemotherapy phase of her treatment were all discovered more than 40 years ago. "Considering how long these drugs have been around, I really started questioning what all the years of research and funding since that time have been used for, as clearly we have not yet found a cure for cancer—at least in humans." Helen, chief executive of Humane Research Australia, credits her longtime vegan diet with helping her get through treatments with very few side effects. "I regularly asked the medical experts what I should or should not be eating, and I was only ever told to 'Just keep eating a healthy diet.' There was never any mention of giving up meat or dairy, and yet they were surprised at how well I was coping."[58]

Why is the animal research lobby so concerned with who gets credit? In a word, money. "Grant money is the mainstay of research university budgets, so there is a huge financial incentive to conduct federally funded research on animals, since the university gets a big cut of the money from all grants awarded to its faculty members," says Lawrence Hansen, MD, a professor of neuroscience and pathology at the University of California–San Diego, and one of the medical community's most outspoken critics of vivisection.[59]

Institutions in the US that use animals rely heavily on funding from the National Institutes of Health (NIH), an agency of the United States Department of Health and Human Services. In other words, experiments subsidized by the NIH are underwritten by taxpayer dollars. Every year, thousands of researchers in the US and abroad compete for NIH grants, which many universities rely on to pay the salaries of their faculty. Animal torturers are moneymakers for universities because the majority of NIH grants go to animal-based research, not clinical research (that is, human trials). With an annual budget in excess of US$31 billion,[60] the NIH has been able to bankroll an assortment of cruel and ill-conceived experiments, including nicotine tests on pregnant monkeys meant to show that smoking cigarettes harms the fetus[61] (thanks, but we've known that for decades), force-feeding alcohol to newborn rats to see if it alters their sleeping patterns[62] (as if babies normally enjoy a few cocktails before naptime), and tearing infant rhesus monkeys away from their mothers to see if it traumatizes them[63] (do we really need more proof of this?).

"If I get a million-dollar grant to study osteoporosis in elderly women, the university where I'm employed will get none of that money," explains Dr. Greek. "But if I get a million-dollar grant to study osteoporosis in mice, the university gets roughly fifty percent of that. So there's no real mystery here about what the motivating factor is from the university's perspective. The University of California–San Francisco and Johns Hopkins University get over a hundred million dollars a year from NIH just from doing animal-based research." One such grant recipient at Johns Hopkins is neurologist George Ricaurte. The NIH gives Ricaurte about US$1 million a year to test the effects of recreational drugs on animals. For one experiment, Ricaurte thought he was injecting 10 baboons and squirrel monkeys with the euphoria-inducing drug Ecstasy, and then he published a scientific paper claiming it produced Parkinson's disease. What he had actually done was mistakenly administer overdoses of a methamphetamine that killed two of the animals and caused two others to collapse from heatstroke.[64]

Ego also plays a role in pushing animal testing, says Dr. Greek. "A lot of these guys who do animal-based research have hundreds of papers published in scientific journals. Their entire life—their entire self image—revolves around the research that they've done with animals. And if they don't publish a certain number of papers, they're fired, or at least not promoted. A professor's rank is based almost entirely on how many papers they get published in the scientific literature." Because they have PhDs and not MDs, says Dr. Greek, they cannot perform similar experiments using humans. "The MDs who do conduct animal research, at least the ones I've spoken with, say they do it just to bring money into the university where they work."

Another major source of financial support for universities is private industry, which relies more and more on academic institutions for their research capabilities. Studies suggest that about 25 percent of academic biomedical researchers receive industry funding, while about one-third of academic researchers and 60 percent of medical school department chairs have personal financial ties with industry.[65] And while it may make us feel good to donate to health charities, some of these organizations use your support to fund research using animals. The American Cancer Society, the British Heart Foundation, the American Heart Association, Cancer Research UK, and the Multiple Sclerosis Society of Great Britain are but a few of the nonprofits that provide grants to animal experimenters. In one of the most odious tests funded by the March of Dimes, a charity dedicated to fighting human birth defects, researchers sewed the eyes of kittens shut. The experiment was not only cruel, but it yielded no insights that would benefit anyone.[66]

Product Testing

Unlike drug testing, analyzing the toxicity of household products like cosmetics and detergents on animals is not legally required.[67] Nevertheless, agencies in Europe, the UK, and the US encourage manufacturers to conduct whatever toxicological tests they believe are appropriate to substantiate the safety of their products. Thus, in an effort to cover their assets in the event of a lawsuit, companies subject conscious animals to an extensive range of painful "safety tests" in which corrosive chemicals are dripped into their eyes, toxic compounds already known to be fatal to humans are pumped into their stomachs, caustic irritants are rubbed into their skin, or an assortment of other unspeakable tortures that result in a painful death. (As of March 2013, the import and sale of cosmetic products and ingredients tested on animals has been banned in the UK and all other member states of the European Union. This follows a similar ban in Israel.)

Product testing on animals is not new, but manufacturers came under intense scrutiny in the first half of the 20th century, when businesses had few restrictions on the ingredients of their products. We might shudder at the thought of cocaine in a soft drink or heroin in a cough suppressant, but back in the day, companies like Coca-Cola and Bayer used these and other dangerous substances to boost sales, if not get consumers hooked on their brand.[68] This laissez-faire business model led to a notorious case—and a new paradigm for testing products on nonhuman animals in the United States.

It began innocently enough: a mascara known as Lash Lure was marketed as a simple way for women to darken their lashes. Missing from the 1933 ad campaign for this "eyelash beautifier" was any mention that the product was derived in part from coal tar, which is not only toxic but flammable. It can also lead to severe corneal damage and blindness, and 15 women lost their eyesight after using the product. For one woman, applying Lash Lure even proved to be fatal when an ulcer caused by the product became infected.[69] Soon manufacturers turned to animal testing as a standard business practice, sentencing millions of helpless victims to horrific deaths.

Decades after the Lash Lure tragedy, the most common product-related animal tests measure the harmful effects, or toxicity, of a given substance and are administered on nonhuman animals in a variety of ways. The tested substance is generally considered poisonous—pesticides, weed killers, cleansers, solvents, etc.—but they can also be painkillers and therapeutic drugs. Make no mistake: these can be extremely painful, lingering deaths during which the animal may suffer for days or even weeks. Richard Ryder, who used animals while working at Cambridge and Columbia Universities, observes that testing the toxicity of some products can result in an especially dreadful demise:

> Because most cosmetic products are not especially poisonous, it necessarily follows that if a rat or a dog has to be killed this way, then very great quantities of cosmetic must be forced into their stomachs, blocking or breaking internal organs, or killing the animal by some other physical action, rather than by any specific chemical effect. Of course the procedure of force-feeding—even with healthy food—is itself a notoriously unpleasant procedure, as suffragettes and other prisoners on hunger-strike have testified. When the substance forced into the stomach is not food at all, but large quantities of face powder, makeup or liquid hair dye, then no doubt the suffering is very much greater indeed. If, for the bureaucratic correctness of the test, quantities great enough to kill are involved, then clearly the process of dying itself must often be prolonged and agonizing.[70]

Testing toxic agents is carried out in a number of ways, but the LD50 test, the Draize Eye Irritancy Test, and the Draize Skin Irritancy Test have received the widest condemnation, for reasons that will become clear.

The LD50 Test

Specifically intended to kill, the Lethal Dose 50 Percent test, or LD50, measures how much of a tested chemical it takes to wipe out half the animals it's administered to within a specified time period, although the objective is to set safe toxicity levels for human consumers. Products tested using LD50 range from pesticides and shampoos to drugs and cosmetics. The victims of LD50 testing are typically dogs and rats, but they might also be mice, rabbits, monkeys, guinea pigs, fish, and birds.[71] Incremental doses of a substance, measured in milligrams per kilogram of body weight, are injected, applied to the skin or eyes, introduced into the lungs, or force-fed into a group of subjects until 50 percent of the animals are dead. The median lethal dose becomes that chemical's LD50. For example, an "LD50 oral" of 4.5 in dogs means that 50 of 100 dogs died after being fed 4.5 grams of a tested substance per kilogram of body weight. The lower the LD50 rating, the more toxic the substance. (Not all substances tested are toxic, however. In a blatantly gratuitous infliction of pain, two scientists even measured the LD50 of distilled water, determining the dose that caused waterlogged organs to burst.[72])

The LD50 test was developed by JW Trevan, a British pharmacologist, in 1927 as a quality control for medications and has since become an international standard measurement of acute toxicity.[73] Tests may last anywhere from 14 days to six months, depending on the substance being measured and the species used. Before a blighted animal dies, she or he may experience, among other symptoms, abdominal pain, internal bleeding, paralysis, convulsions, or bleeding from the nose, mouth, eyes, or rectum. A particularly gruesome demise awaits animals used to test the popular anti-wrinkle treatment Botox. In these LD50 tests, researchers inject the drug's active ingredient—a highly potent neurotoxin known as botulinum—into groups of mice. Botulinum toxin is the most poisonous known substance, often used as a biological weapon, and even a minuscule amount can kill a human. In the laboratory, mice suffer a slow and excruciating death by suffocation as their respiratory muscles become paralyzed.[74] All for a product that temporarily removes frown lines.

Animal advocates and scientists alike have criticized LD50 as cruel, outdated, and ineffective. LD50 tests offer no information that would help treat poisoning in humans (animal testing does not make toxic chemicals less deadly), nor do they address toxicity to organs.[75] One of the principal problems with LD50 is that it's a statistical expression of a substance's toxicity under *controlled conditions*—in other words, the tests cannot reliably predict risk because they cannot account for a wide variety of other factors, such as the environment or even the method of testing used (it is not uncommon for a force-fed chemical to result in disease, whereas injection of the same chemical does not). Moreover, there is no agreement on how to extrapolate animal test results to humans. Exacerbating this challenge is the fact that animal species respond to poison in different ways. For instance, rats and rabbits cannot vomit and thereby eliminate toxins from their bodies, while such a reaction is normal for people. In his critique of LD50, the Swiss toxicologist Gerhard Zbinden described the tests as little more than "a ritual mass execution of animals."[76] One of product testing's most vocal opponents was the late Henry Spira, who framed his initiative against LD50 this way: "The test defies common sense. Does one really need to know how many bars of pure Ivory soap it takes to kill a dog?"[77] Fortunately, as high-tech alternatives, such as *in vitro* testing, become more accepted, LD50 testing should gradually disappear.

Selective Science

Animal welfare expert Bernard Rollin tells of a debate he once had with a physiologist who claimed that since electro-chemical activity in the cerebral cortex of dogs is different from that of humans, dogs do not feel pain as we do. "I pointed out that he does pain research on dogs and extrapolates the results to people, and rested my case."[78]

The Draize Tests

Of the photographs that come from the underworld of animal testing, few are as heartrending as those depicting rabbits immobilized in restraining stocks, only their white heads and pink eyes visible, often side by side in a long row inside a sterile laboratory. There's a visceral quality in these images—something that speaks to us on a subconscious level. The extreme vulnerability of the rabbits reveals volumes to us. Even those who know nothing about product testing intuit the despair and pain these animals are forced to endure. Perhaps that's why the image of rabbits undergoing this procedure—known as the Draize test—is often a powerful ingredient in anti-vivisection campaigns.

Developed in 1944 by FDA toxicologist John H. Draize and his colleagues, the Draize test attempts to evaluate the risks of exposure to cosmetics, cleansers, and other products. There are actually two types of Draize tests, the Draize Eye Irritancy Test and the Draize Skin Irritancy Test, both of which cause tremendous suffering to the animals used, generally rabbits. In the Draize test for eye irritancy, a liquid, granule, flake, or powdered substance is applied to one eye of a rabbit. (Rabbits are considered ideal subjects for this test because of the way they produce tears, making it harder to dilute or eliminate the substance, though this fact alone would seem to put the test's applicability to humans in question.) If you've ever had a grain of sand or other foreign object in your eye—let alone a caustic chemical—you can imagine the misery the rabbit is made to suffer. Describing a common reaction before test subjects were held motionless in stocks, one researcher observed: "Animal holds eye shut urgently. May squeal, claw at eye, jump and try to escape."[79] Now during most of these procedures, which may last several days or even weeks, the rabbit's eyes are held open with clips.[80] Researchers then measure the level of tissue damage. In addition to causing intense pain, the tested compounds often leave the animals' eyes ulcerated, infected, swollen, and bleeding.[81] Whatever the results, the rabbit is killed once the test is complete.

In the Draize Skin Irritancy Test, technicians shave a section of the animal's fur (again, usually a rabbit, although guinea pigs, mice, rats, dogs, and cats are also used in this test) and abrade her skin by repeatedly applying and ripping off adhesive tape. A test substance is applied to the skin and the area is covered with a gauze pad and wrapped in plastic sheeting or rubber. The animal is then immobilized and the skin reaction is checked and given a score on the Draize scale after four, 24, and 72 hours.[82] An animal may be used up to six times for these tests before he is killed, and several victims are used simultaneously for each test.

Both Draize tests have been condemned as much for their accuracy as for their cruelty, even by the scientific community. A study comparing the use of rabbits and humans as subjects in eye irritancy tests found that the two species respond very differently to substances, concluding that using animals overestimates how the human eye will respond.[83] One researcher hired to experiment on animals, meanwhile, admitted the eye irritancy test is callous and pointless. "I felt numb—no, guilty," she said about applying a common toothpaste ingredient to the eye of a terrified rabbit. "It isn't as if the end justified the means. We weren't researching some cancer cure here. We were testing a well-known chemical that has been used in household products for more than 100 years."[84] Meanwhile, a humane alternative for predicting how human skin will react to toxins uses human volunteers, and studies show this method—known as the four-hour (or 4-h) patch test—is more reliable than using nonhuman animals. One study reports: "The human 4-h patch test has been developed to meet the needs of identifying chemical skin irritation potential, providing data which is inherently superior to that given by a surrogate model, such as the rabbit."[85] As long as such advances continue to develop, the days of Draize testing on animals are numbered.

Callous and Careless

Sadly, the abuse of animals in the name of product safety goes well beyond the substances being tested. The same kind of frustration we see among factory farm and slaughterhouse workers—who often react to the extreme stress of their jobs by lashing out at animals—is evident among lab technicians, who may be entirely desensitized to the pain and distress of animal victims. These test lab workers have been known to beat animals, who are routinely left to languish in filthy cages between experiments and denied even the slightest kindness.

During nine months working undercover at Professional Laboratory Research Services (PLRS) in rural North Carolina, an investigator with People for the Ethical Treatment of Animals video-taped workers hoisting rabbits by their sensitive ears, slamming cats into cages, screaming obscenities and death wishes at the imprisoned animals, spraying bleach on them with hoses, and kicking, throwing, and dragging frightened dogs. Workers were instructed to clean rabbit cages by shaking them up and down—with the rabbits still inside. PETA's investigator was told that this practice had caused the feet of at least two rabbits to be completely severed. When she asked her supervisor if the employee was disciplined for maiming a rabbit, the investigator was told, "No, but don't clock in late, then you will get in trouble."[86]

Animals at PLRS suffered with bloody diarrhea, worm infestations, oozing sores, abscessed teeth, skin conditions, and pus- and blood-filled infections on ears, all of which either went untreated or were ineffectively handled by employees who had no veterinary training or credentials. One supervisor, after administering an expired anesthetic, pulled out a dog's tooth with pliers, the animal quaking in obvious pain.

While the research industry might claim that such cases are isolated incidents, the reality is this behavior is not only common, but worse than you might imagine. Whether callous or careless, lab workers cause so many animal deaths that a full accounting of them goes beyond the scope of this chapter; however, examples include monkeys and rabbits scalded to death when their cages are sent through blistering-hot, high-pressure washing machines—and the animals are left inside;[87] gerbils who die of dehydration when their water was just out of reach;[88] and nearly 100 cats, rabbits, and dogs killed at PLRS because the company had decided that the animals' six daily cups of food were too expensive. Among the other causes of death by design or neglect are botched surgeries, inadequate veterinary care, starvation, and being mistakenly placed in carcass freezers. Perhaps the most notorious case of laboratory negligence involves 32 monkeys who were essentially baked alive at Charles River Laboratories in 2008 when someone left the heater on in the primate room. The dead and dying animals were not discovered until the next day.[89]

Incidentally, PLRS, which tested chemicals used in flea and tick products for such companies as Bayer, Eli Lilly, Novartis, and Sergeant's, was shut down a week after PETA released its investigation. A North Carolina grand jury followed up by indicting four individuals who worked at PLRS, including a supervisor, on 14 counts of felony cruelty to animals—the first time in US history that workers have faced felony cruelty charges for their abuse and neglect of animals in a lab.[90]

Pet Food

There's something especially repugnant, even twisted, about the cruelty behind many brands of pet food. The pet food industry is fiercely competitive, and creating a successful product takes a lot of trial and error. Though most consumers have never heard of the practice, some manufacturers of foods for dogs, cats, and other companion animals engage in animal testing. And while that may sound reasonable—after all, who better to decide if a new formula of kitty kibble or doggie biscuits tastes good?—no animal should be forced to live in a lab facility, and indeed some of these dogs and cats, known as colony animals, never leave.

Moreover, the tests that pet food companies conduct on animals while formulating new products are often invasive, and animals in nutrition feeding studies are routinely killed once the tests are complete—or even before the tests are carried out. One research team killed six healthy Great Dane puppies and then minced their bodies, freeze-dried the remains, and ground them up to conduct a "total body analysis."[91] Their findings were presented at a symposium on pet nutrition and health. Another team, studying the role of dietary beta-carotene on the reproductive system of female dogs, removed the ovaries and uteruses of 56 adult beagles.[92] Yet another group of researchers chemically damaged the kidneys of 18 beagle puppies, fed them experimental diets, inserted tubes into their penises, and then killed them.[93]

A rare government rebuke of pet food testing came in 2006, when the US Department of Agriculture investigated a complaint by PETA that a lab contracted by Procter & Gamble (P&G) to test its Iams brand was subjecting animals to extreme abuse. An undercover investigator documented lab workers cutting out large chunks of muscle from dogs' legs and leaving them to suffer for days on a filthy floor. Other dogs were left to languish in barren steel cages and cement cells, while sick dogs and cats were denied veterinary care. The USDA cited the lab for more than 40 violations of the Animal Welfare Act. Across the ocean, a similar investigation carried out by the UK nonprofit Uncaged showed that experiments on 460 dogs and cats used to test pet foods from Iams and Eukanuba (another P&G brand) had caused kidney failure, liver damage, skin wounds, and other painful illnesses.[94]

Although all four of the major pet food companies—Colgate-Palmolive, Mars, Nestlé, and P&G—claim they no longer conduct invasive tests on animals, none of them has earned an endorsement from any of the animal protection groups working on this issue. For one thing, all these companies are actively involved in animal testing of other consumer products. Moreover, they may still use animals for other pet food tests. P&G's Iams keeps up to 700 dogs and cats in its laboratory in Ohio for nutritional trials, claiming that some studies are too complex for in-home programs.[95] They keep another 30 cats and 30 dogs at its research center in Nebraska. P&G breeds some of the animals it uses and buys others from commercial breeders.[96]

Further perpetuating the cruelty is the chance that victims of animal testing may themselves end up as a pet food ingredient. Although no university or research facility is going to admit it, countless animals from their labs are picked up by contracted dead stock removal companies, shipped to brokers, and sold to rendering plants. Here animals are dumped into large vats and cooked at temperatures in excess of 265 degrees F (129 degrees C). The lumpy soup that emerges from the cooker is spun at high speed in a centrifuge, and fat rises to the top as the heavier flesh and bone sink to the bottom. (In addition to being used in pet foods, the fatty material finds its way into a wide variety of products, including cosmetics, polishes, lubricants, soaps, and even dynamite.)[97] The resulting "meat" is then sold to pet food companies, ranchers, factory farmers, and the aquaculture industry. Of course, it's not just animals from labs who end up rendered: those killed by vehicles, zoo animals, and even euthanized cats and dogs from shelters and vet clinics—often along with their tags and flea collars—are thrown into the vats. Anything from a slaughterhouse considered unfit for human consumption is also sold to rendering plants. This includes so-called "4-D" meat: flesh from disabled, diseased, dying, or dead animals (who died in transit to the slaughterhouse) may not be allowed on the butcher's counter, but it's perfectly acceptable in your best friend's bowl. In the US alone, slaughterhouses produce about 47 billion pounds (more than 21 billion metric tons) of tissues and other animal "waste" each year, about a quarter of which goes into pet foods.[98]

Incidentally, the drug commonly used to euthanize animals, sodium pentobarbital, is impervious to the heat of rendering machines, which means countless companion animals are consuming small amounts of this lethal injection.[99] Unfortunately, we don't know what long-term effects trace amounts of the drug could have on animals.

Alternatives for Product Testing

In addition to the human 4-h patch test already mentioned, a number of cruelty-free methods for product testing are available, and more continue to be developed. These include:

- Non-animal toxicity tests. Rather than testing compounds on live animals, researchers can use something called high-throughput screening, in which hundreds of human cells grown in a lab are inserted into each of 1,536 wells, which are just a fraction of a millimeter across, housed on a single 3-by-5-inch glass tray. A robotic arm then drips a chemical sample into each tiny well, and a machine later determines how many cells remain while a computer analyzes the toxicity of each compound.

- *In vitro* human corneal tissue. Derived from human cells, products like EpiOcular™ and SkinEthic provide three-dimensional models on which researchers can humanely perform eye irritancy tests.

- Artificial human skin. EpiDerm™, Episkin™, Phenion®, and SkinEthic are just a few of the human skin equivalents that have been accepted and validated around the world for predicting skin sensitivity and irritation. These methods consist of normal, human-derived skin cells, which have been cultured to form a multi-layered model of human skin. They provide a humane and more accurate assessment of the potential damage a substance poses to human skin. Another product, Corrositex®, uses a protein membrane instead of skin, while DakDak, a gene-based laboratory testing platform, enables researchers to determine whether cosmetics and sunscreens may be effective in preventing skin damage caused by sunlight.

- In-home nutrition studies for pet foods. Feeding trials with companion animals who live with their families in homes is a much more humane approach than invasive studies in which animals are confined and later killed. These studies have been shown to work and have strong scientific support.

Education

Using animals as teaching aids has a long and ignoble history, especially the practice of dissection, which entails methodically cutting up and observing organisms. Some of the earliest animal dissections were conducted not in laboratories but in theater settings as a means of learning anatomy and biology. It was understood that animals were a substitute for humans, and the vivisectors of ancient Greece—and their audience—assumed that the organs of, say, a dog were analogous to the physiology of a man or woman.[100] This tradition continues today, though with a twist: now it's the high school, undergraduate, graduate, veterinary, and medical students who do the dissecting, not the instructors.

Classroom Dissection

For the last several generations, science classrooms have been where people generally have their first direct exposure to animal research. It is here that many students—armed with a scalpel, forceps, scissors, and probes—have been expected to pin down and slice open the remains of an animal or insect and explore his or her anatomy. It's a hands-on experience that leads to the death of millions of animals every year and leaves countless pupils either traumatized or desensitized (or both).

Campuses across the United States began embracing dissection in the 1920s, but it was pretty much limited to college-level courses. That all changed in the 1950s and '60s with the Cold War. The Soviet Union launched the world's first satellite into space in 1957 and, feeling their education system was lacking the scientific rigor of other countries, the US responded by infusing schools with new curricula emphasizing technology and biology. A federal grant from the National Science Foundation in 1958 led to an initiative called Biological Sciences Curriculum Study (BSCS), which made animal dissection much more widespread in secondary education. Soon high school biology classrooms were filled with frogs, cats, earthworms, rats, fetal pigs, starfish, turtles, sharks, and grasshoppers.[101] Not all these animals were dead when they arrived at the student's table. A major component of BSCS was frog pithing, which required the student to destroy the living animal's brain by inserting a sharp probe into the base of the skull. This doesn't necessarily lead to immediate death, but supposedly renders the animal insensible to pain.[102] In other words, a pithed frog may be completely aware of everything going on throughout a dissection. One former biology student recalls being surprised that a pithed frog survived for several days, his beating heart clearly visible through his open chest cavity.[103] Frog pithing is still practiced in classrooms around the world.

Biologist Jonathan Balcombe estimates that the educational toll on animals in the United States is probably close to 10 million vertebrates (frogs, cats, etc.) and more than 10 million invertebrates (insects) a year.[104] Although there has been a shift toward using more non-animal tools in the US, the majority of biology teachers still include dissection as part of their coursework.[105]

Classroom dissection is also waning in Great Britain, where school administrators are abandoning the practice out of respect for students' ethical concerns—and fears that they could injure each other with their scalpels.[106] Once a mainstay of British education, dissection is now being gradually replaced by plastic replicas or computer animation in many institutions. "Ten or 15 years ago, there was a steady stream of complaints from parents whose kids were asked to dissect," says Kate Fowler, head of campaigns for the UK-based nonprofit Animal Aid. "We know it goes on, and we still get a few calls, but we feel that dissection is less common now."[107]

Dissection is not simply a US or European exercise, of course. It is mandatory in biology classes throughout Hong Kong, for example, as it is in much of the rest of Asia. Other education systems, such as Australia and South Africa, have not made dissection compulsory, but leave it to the teacher's discretion. As a result, virtually all science teachers in Australia include dissection in their biology classes, and in South Africa, a survey of 242 prospective biology teachers at a South African university revealed that 71 percent would expect students to conduct a dissection in their classrooms.[108]

Fortunately, some academic institutions, such as those in the UK, have been open to criticism and have reexamined the value of requiring students to slice up animals. In their inquiry into the practice of dissection in the 21st century, Rian De Villiers and Martin Monk found that animal protection organizations have been especially important in this debate; activist groups are framing the argument that dissection is unethical, emotionally painful for students, and a poor use of school funds (non-animal teaching tools, such as computer simulations and three-dimensional models, are more economical). According to De Villiers and Monk, "the increasing public visibility of animal-rights campaigners in Northern and Western society at large has influenced opinion in the academy among both teachers and learners. There has been a reduction in the number of animal dissections, and even complete abolition in some countries."[109] One of those countries is India, where education officials have heard the concerns of animal advocates and are now phasing out dissection in undergraduate and postgraduate laboratories. It's estimated that replacing dissection in Indian universities with humane alternatives will save 19 million animals and insects a year.[110] Argentina, Israel, the Netherlands, and Switzerland are among the nations where you will not find animal dissection in primary and secondary schools.

Numerous studies show that dissection exercises can cause students to experience stress and trauma.[111] Reactions to this range from impaired cognitive abilities (resulting in less learning) to a numbing of the student's emotional and ethical integrity.[112] This numbing often heralds a gradual transition in which the student goes from being reluctant about dissection to entirely desensitized about the procedure—even regarding the animal's remains as garbage.

One study examining the behavior of sixth-graders in two classes encountering their first animal dissection revealed that virtually all of the students had some pangs of apprehension or felt at least somewhat conflicted about the prospect of dissecting fetal pigs.[113] During the weeks that the exercise progressed, many students appeared to harden, describing themselves as becoming "adapted" or even "immune" to the situation. According to the study's authors, this transformation was encouraged by the cultural perception of pigs as "unappealing," thus facilitating their use as "specimens." But such a callous perspective, however unjust, would not apply to other animals used for dissection, such as cats and rabbits, and so additional factors aid the students in psychologically distancing themselves.

A disturbing yet cardinal element in the students becoming morally ambivalent was their de-animalizing of the pigs: inherent in dissection is the act of eliminating the image of the animal as a being, thus relieving the pupils' remorse about cutting up some*one*, rather than some*thing*. As students removed organs and body parts, the pigs became objects devoid of sentience. This phenomenon is exemplified in a study of high-school biology students, who also dissected fetal pigs. One student said, "Every time we've worked on it [the pig] the face was covered. I couldn't cut the face. I could watch, and once the face was cut it didn't look like a pig anymore, and I could deal with that because it looked like—you know—a scientific experiment to me."[114]

The sixth-grade teachers further enabled the desensitization process by hiding the truth about the fetal pigs' death. Although many students in the study voiced concern about the origin of their pigs—often expressing fear that they might have been killed specifically for classroom use—when questioned, teachers offered such responses as "it came out of the mother dead," "they were runts... they died before they were born," they "died for a reason," or even that the mother pig "died of natural causes" while she was pregnant. Actually, fetal pigs are a byproduct of the meat industry: fetuses discovered in pregnant sows during the slaughtering process are sold to biological supply houses that in turn prepare and sell them for dissection.

An exercise that began with most of the class exhibiting anxiety about animal dissection ended with many students mutilating the pigs' remains—plunging dissection tools into pigs' heads and bodies—or enacting macabre scenes, such as decapitating the animals and proudly parading their heads around the classroom. One boy whistled a death march as he carried his pig to a trash can, and a girl brought pig brains out into the hall to upset the two students who had conscientiously objected to dissection. The study's authors argue that this transformation serves as a rite of passage into the scientific community, and other researchers agree. In their book *The Sacrifice: How Scientific Experiments Transform Animals and People*, Lynda Birke, Arnold Arluke, and Mike Michael address the moral hurdles students must navigate when faced with dissecting animals: "Whether or not the student goes on to a career in biomedicine, he or she must distance him- or herself to carry out what is a kind of moral 'dirty work'; coming to some kind of uneasy terms with such procedures thus becomes a crucial stage in the process of becoming a scientist. As the student progresses, that kind of psychological distancing becomes ingrained."[115]

George Russell is among the many testaments to that observation. Now a professor of biology at Adelphi University in New York, Russell recalls that pithing and dissecting many frogs as a biology undergraduate in the 1950s left him inured to the pain and suffering of these animals. "Frogs, for me, had been quite special creatures in my youth, and I had spent an inordinate amount of time seeking them out in their natural habitat, watching tadpoles metamorphose into adults, and pursuing as best I could an amateur's interest and love for the frog's natural history. Later, however, whatever initial misgivings I may have had regarding our laboratory studies gradually diminished, and the frog became a sort of object to be manipulated, a thing rather than a living organism."[116] Dr. Russell managed to regain some of his earlier feelings about frogs, but only after years of quiet nature study. Today he is a pioneer in the use of humane alternatives to dissection. "My unwillingness to use invasive animal study with college students is founded on a concern for the well-being of animals and equally a concern for the emotional and psychological health of young people. We choose to ignore the latter at our own peril."[117]

"Frog Girl"

If you're a high school student in the United States, and your school allows you to opt out of dissecting an animal in biology class, you can thank Jenifer Graham. In 1987, Jenifer was a 15-year-old vegetarian who did not wear leather or use products tested on animals. When she received a low grade for refusing to dissect a frog, Jenifer—with support from her family and animal protection organizations—took the school board to court. The ensuing four-year legal battle brought class dissection and students' rights to the public discourse, and Jenifer's story inspired a made-for-TV movie, *The Frog Girl: The Jenifer Graham Story*. Her case led to the 1988 California Students' Rights Law, which upholds the right of a student under the age of 18 to conscientious objection to dissection; where possible, the teacher must work with the student to develop an adequate alternative. Though Jenifer wasn't the first student to refuse to participate in class dissection on moral grounds, her court case and the national attention it received resulted in states across the US enacting laws protecting a student's right to refuse to dissect an animal.

Medical Schools

First, some good news: More than 95 percent of the medical schools in the United States and Canada have eliminated using live animal laboratories to demonstrate basic physiology and pharmacology. That is a dramatic improvement over recent years as institutions continue to see the value of lifelike human patient simulators and other humane, cost-effective methods for preparing the next generation of medical professionals. In 1992, only 12 medical schools in the US did not include laboratory animal exercises in their curricula for medical students.[118] Today, 173 of 180 medical schools in the US and Canada do not use animals for any educational purposes in their curricula. This represents a remarkable shift in attitude—not to mention hard work from activists and advocacy groups like the nonprofit Physicians Committee for Responsible Medicine (PCRM), which encourages higher standards for ethics in research and promotes alternatives to using animals.

The bad news is, of course, that some institutions persist in using live animals to practice emergency medical procedures, and although dissection is now used less to teach manual dexterity, it continues to be justified as a way to teach anatomical structure. The position of pro-vivisection groups is that studying living systems is essential to learning about the structure of the body. According to one such group, the American Physiological Society, "well-designed animal laboratories provide vivid, exciting opportunities for the direct study of how living systems work. Not only do these lessons foster active learning and the development of critical thinking skills in students, but they provide a unique opportunity for students to develop a lasting appreciation of the complexity of living systems and an abiding respect for living organisms."[119]

But does a student really need to kill her first patient to respect him? Indeed, at least one study suggests that rather than nurturing respect for animal victims, the medical school environment encourages students to cope with killing by denying any moral responsibility—in essence desensitizing future physicians to the sanctity of life. Before the study's 41 first-year med students conducted their terminal procedures on live dogs, they demonstrated widespread anxiety about having to kill the animals. They were able to neutralize feelings of guilt by displacing the blame onto others and pardoning themselves for any wrongdoing. This happened, the authors of the study argue, because medical school culture provided absolutions to students that appeased their moral apprehension about the dog lab and replaced it with a sense of fascination and awe. Not only had the stigma of killing the dogs vanished, but the absolutions morally elevated the behavior, "making it an honor or privilege to perform while leaving one's moral self completely unscathed if not somewhat 'enhanced.'"[120]

As for the argument that there is no substitute for the educational experience of seeing and touching living tissue, exercises using live animals have shown no measurable advantage over modern teaching alternatives, such as computer training programs. Moreover, most surgery residents develop their technical skills not by operating on animals, but by performing procedures on human patients while under the supervision of experienced practitioners.[121] Students at New York Medical College, for example, now study heart function using echocardiograms on fellow students rather than using dog labs, and they will "become just as good doctors without it," says Dr. Francis Belloni, a dean at the school.[122]

Veterinary Schools

Perhaps it makes sense that students learning to practice veterinary medicine would hone their skills and knowledge using animals. But because the veterinary field is a natural choice for science-inclined individuals who genuinely care about the welfare of animals, many vet students experience a deeply troubling conflict. Consider that the student may be required to participate in so-called "dog labs" in which animals are subjected to repeated surgical procedures, including practice in sewing up incisions, slicing into skin to study wounds, and the removal of vital organs. These are "terminal surgeries," meaning the animals are euthanized afterward, though they may be used in multiple procedures.[123]

Andrew Knight knows this conflict well. In 1997, Andrew, a longtime animal advocate, was a first-year veterinary student at Murdoch University in Western Australia. Murdoch is a highly ranked college with a sprawling campus in Perth named in honor of the Scottish essayist and scholar Sir Walter Murdoch (1874–1970). Like its namesake, Murdoch University is a no-nonsense institution, and in the 1990s, its school of veterinary medicine required all students to actively participate in animal dissections. But Murdoch the man also possessed an abiding sense of right and wrong, coming of age during a time of great social upheaval. With his sympathy for the underdog and willingness to champion lost causes, Murdoch doubtless would have been impressed with Andrew Knight.

"In the introductory biology units we dissected cockroaches, snails, worms, fish, rats, and body parts from abattoirs," Andrew recalls. "I tried not to think too much about where all these bodies had come from."[124] But when live rats were killed right in front of the students, Andrew voiced his objection. The academics in charge brushed him off, warning Andrew that seeing rats die was nothing compared to what was to come in later vet courses: students themselves would be required to kill not only rats, but toads, guinea pigs, and sheep. They suggested he rethink his career options.

Undaunted, Andrew began researching alternatives to using animals, and he embarked on his second year primed for a fight. He refused to take part in the labs, and found another conscientious student, Michael Taylor, to join his boycott. But the rest of the students were unmoved by Andrew's plea. "It's regrettable they weren't sufficiently motivated by the knowledge that, for the animals, entire lives were at stake," he says. "There was—and is—a better way to learn, and they could easily have seen that, if only they'd had the courage to look. Unfortunately, however, the overwhelming majority were cowards. Some were even nasty cowards, expressing their hostility with words and deeds to those few of us campaigning for the right to use humane teaching methods. Others were more sympathetic, on rare occasion offering support, although they very rarely had the courage to do so in public."[125]

Throughout the academic year, Andrew educated his instructors about available alternatives. They not only didn't budge, but they lowered his grades and those of Michael on the basis that they were not fully participating. Finally, Andrew reached out to Western

Australia's Equal Opportunity Commission (EOC), which investigates and fights discrimination in schools and other areas of public life in the state. They agreed that Andrew's stance as an ethical vegan constituted a religious belief and that his complaint against the university was a case of religious discrimination. Soon after the EOC began negotiating with Murdoch, instructors reinstated Andrew's and Michael's good grades and then, in November 1998, the academic council announced it was formally allowing students to conscientiously object to animal experimentation or other areas of their coursework. Andrew graduated in 2001 and is currently the director of Animal Consultants International, a group of experts providing assistance to animal protection campaigns worldwide.

Like Murdoch University, veterinary colleges around the globe are restructuring their student training programs by replacing labs that harm animals with progressive substitutes. Of the 28 schools in the United States accredited by the American Veterinary Medical Association, 25 allow the use of humane methods.[126] Among the alternatives gaining traction are Shelter Medicine programs, which bring third- and fourth-year vet students into animal shelters and humane societies to participate in surgery rotations. By assisting in and performing spay and neuter procedures, students enhance their instrument-handling skills, practice anesthesia monitoring, and observe the post-operative recovery of their patients, who are now more likely to be adopted.[127] These programs have been a boon to shelters, which are notoriously hampered by limited resources and stressful conditions, and they've provided countless vet students with real-world clinical experience. Indeed, a study by faculty at the Tufts University Cummings School of Veterinary Medicine in Massachusetts revealed that students who performed repeat spay and neuter surgeries at a local shelter outperformed students who learned surgical skills in the traditional terminal dog lab.[128]

With any luck, terminal labs are on their way out. In his book *Learning without Killing: A Guide to Conscientious Objection*, Andrew Knight cites a 1999 study of first-year students at the University of

Illinois College of Veterinary Medicine who were surveyed to determine what benefit, if any, came from terminal physiology labs in which more than a hundred dogs, rabbits, pigs, and rats were killed. Of the 370 students surveyed, only 20 percent felt they derived "great benefit" in their understanding of physiology from the laboratories. Most of the students had comments, some of which are illuminating, to say the least:

"It was difficult to get any great understanding of physiology because we worried most of the time about not having our dog bleed to death or die of anesthetic overdose before the experiment was over. In the end, what I learned about physiology (cardiology and respiratory physiology) I taught myself from the notes."

"Nothing that was covered in those labs could not have been learned from a demo, or a video. The guilt I felt for participating outweighed all beneficial aspects of the experience."

"The stress of the whole ordeal was worth nothing in the end. I studied from these books not from my lab experience."

"During one lab, my group accidentally killed our dog with anesthesia overdose because of lack of experience and the impatient ill-given advice of a professor. The experience overshadowed the benefit gained by the first lab."[129]

In 2000, all terminal physiology laboratories were removed from the University of Illinois curriculum.

Alternatives for Education

Faced with participating in dissection as a course assignment, most students keep any distress about it to themselves. This is especially true in high school, where peer pressure is a powerful incentive to remain silent, as is fear of getting a bad grade if you don't participate. College students may worry that a career in science is not for them. But those students who do not wish to compromise their ethics should feel no qualms about conscientiously objecting to animal dissection. As animal law experts Gary Francione and Anna Charlton remind us, "Whether a student has a right to refuse to participate in the use of nonhuman animals as part of a course requirement is, strictly speaking, a *civil rights* issue and not an *animal rights* issue."[130]

Fortunately, the alternatives to dissection are both plentiful and effective, and the market for them is now so great that Apple even offers a frog dissection application for iPads. Created by Emantras Interactive Technologies, Frog Dissection gives students a hands-on experience, allowing them to manipulate the organs of a virtual amphibian in 3D. Non-Mac users can check out products like Digital Frog and V-Frog, and students not wanting to dissect fetal pigs can investigate the software programs offered by ScienceWorks (see their DissectionWorks series) and Tangent Scientific (look for DryLabPlus®), to name just a few examples.

Many of the same software programs used in secondary schools have found their way into higher education systems. DryLab® offers a suite of simulations allowing students to "dissect" frogs, birds, cats, fetal pigs, earthworms, rats, and more. Undergraduate biology courses can also employ this same technology to teach human anatomy and physiology. With programs like VH Dissector CD-ROM, which combines virtual reality with cadaver dissection, students get a human exhibit featuring more than 2,000 anatomic structures.

Perhaps most significantly, medical and veterinary schools are now embracing training methods that don't require live animals, including interactive computer simulations, sophisticated mannequins, canine and feline models, digital surgery programs, and interactive virtual computer training programs that combine three-dimensional control with realistic images of organs. Schools are also obtaining the bodies of companion animals from ethical sources, such as Educational Memorial Programs and Willed Body Donation programs.

Many studies have shown that using alternatives to animal models in undergraduate, veterinary, and medical school yields educational results that are equal to—and sometimes superior to—using live animals. In a study of 305 high school biology students, 175 pupils who were taught frog structure, function, and adaptation by lecture performed better on a posttest than did the 175 students who were taught by doing a frog dissection. A study of 2,913 biology undergrads showed that the examination results of 308 students who studied model rats were the same as those of 2,605 students who performed dissections on rats. When the abilities of 12 veterinarians who had participated in alternative medical and surgical courses were compared with the abilities of 36 of their counterparts four years after graduation, no significant differences between them were found. And a study of 252 medical and graduate students showed that those who had used computer simulation achieved a significantly higher grade in the cardiovascular section of the final exam than their classmates who had participated in live dog labs.[131]

Humane alternatives are not only an equally effective learning tool, but they beat traditional animal labs on another bottom line: economic cost. In their comparison of dissection versus non-animal teaching methods, PCRM found that using animals is considerably more expensive than purchasing a variety of reusable alternative materials.[132] Although the initial set-up costs may be greater with a computer-based model, institutions ultimately see financial benefits since multiple groups of students can use these same programs for years to come.

In addition to the ethical, educational, and cost advantages to non-animal models, students report that they enjoy using these alternatives more.[133] They can perform lessons at their own pace, more easily make up missed classes, and repeatedly review programs until they have learned the material.

Where Do the Animals Come From?

The animals used in research, testing, and education come from a variety of sources, and a cottage industry has built up around ensuring that US vivisectors have plenty to choose from. The two main sources are Class A and Class B dealers; both are licensed by the USDA, which oversees the Animal Welfare Act. Most animals are either "purpose bred" specifically for research by Class A breeders, or bred and raised in research colonies. When they buy from Class A dealers, institutions have some assurance that they are buying dogs and other animals bred specifically for research.

Scientists prefer Class A dealers because they breed animals in closed colonies and offer "high-quality" research victims. One such Class A dealer is Charles River Laboratories (CRL). The world's largest commercial breeder of animals for sale to laboratories, CRL controls 50 percent of the market.[134] The company produces highly defined purpose-bred laboratory animals in 14 countries, including the United States, Canada, Japan, and throughout Europe, and it specializes in providing rats, guinea pigs, gerbils, rabbits, hamsters, mice, and primates. CRL has earned a reputation as a serial abuser of animals and has amassed the Animal Welfare Act violations to prove it: as mentioned earlier in this chapter, for example, it was at a CRL facility that 32 monkeys were carelessly baked alive in 2008.

Another Class A dealer representative of the industry is Carolina Biological Supply Company (CBSC), the oldest and one of the largest suppliers of laboratory specimens for classroom dissection in the United States. CBSC, like other animal enterprises, has a strict policy of secrecy, but activists have been able to gain access to the company and document its business practices. In their undercover investigation of the biological supply giant, PETA witnessed cats (some wearing collars) arriving at the facility in crowded cages, being poked with metal hooks, and finally being sent into gas chambers. Many animals survived the killing process, however, and one investigator saw a cat giving birth while inside a gas chamber, cats meowing after being gassed, and the movements of unborn kittens visible in the bellies of pregnant cats following gassing. Investigators also witnessed a number of animals alive and struggling as they were being embalmed with formaldehyde, including a rabbit, a rat, cats, crabs, and frogs. Particularly insidious were the actions of some

CBSC employees: one bludgeoned a cat to death for biting him, another laughed as a cat convulsed after being hooked up to an embalming machine, and yet another employee prolonged the drowning death of a rabbit by repeatedly pulling him from the water just before he succumbed. Other employees played catch with a rat before drowning him. The USDA charged the lab with multiple violations of the Animal Welfare Act, and CBSC paid a fine of US$2,500.[135]

Class B dealers trade in "random source" animals, so called because they come from almost anywhere, including an animal shelter, a dog track, an owner surrender, a hoarding situation, or a dog-fighting ring. Any adult with US$10 can apply for a USDA Class B dealer license. Animals from a Class B dealer cost less, but these traders in torture make up for that in volume with the aid of "bunchers": people who collect a bunch of dogs and cats and then sell these animals to a Class B dealer. Bunchers troll newspapers and online listings for ads reading "free to good home." They may even steal an animal from someone's yard, a practice that's been occurring for 150 years.[136] The USDA has broad authority to stop these thefts and inspect and monitor kennels to ensure that the animals have been legally acquired, but, as one agency official put it, "We can't be at every facility every day to make sure they are adhering to the regulations."[137]

Pound Seizure

In much of the United States, taxpayer-funded animal shelters are required by law to release "surplus" dogs and cats to Class B dealers or directly to research institutions after those animals have been held for five days (or whatever the mandatory waiting period may be). It's also happening in cities around the world. Legislation allowing pound seizures in the US began in the 1940s as an effort to reduce the expanding population of homeless companion animals while also supplying research institutions with test subjects.[138] Because the term "dog pound" is sometimes used when referring to an animal shelter, the act of turning sheltered animals over for research is known as "pound seizure." It's a practice animal shelters do not discuss with their communities.

Animal advocate Allie Phillips was shocked to learn about pound seizures when she began volunteering at a Michigan shelter in 2000. Equally appalling was the callous attitude of the shelter's director and staff, who seemed more interested in selling cats and dogs to Class B dealers than adopting them to guardians. Fortunately for the animals there and at shelters across the country, Allie had a day job: she was a prosecuting attorney who knew how to ask questions, gather evidence, and get results. "I had no idea that my dollars were funding a shelter that could engage in such a secretive barbaric practice and that our county government allowed it," says Allie, who currently serves as director of the nonprofit National Center for Prosecution of Animal Abuse. "I could not comprehend how the practice of pound seizure could exist in secrecy as it had been for decades." She quickly went head-to-head with the shelter, filed Freedom of Information requests for documentation on what was happening with cats and dogs under the shelter's care, and worked to get the animals out. As important as this was, Allie recognized it was vital that the community know what was going on. "When we began our public advocacy to the local government and sharing information with the community, I sensed retaliation by the shelter for our actions, including selling a cat named Karyn to a Class B dealer after we had been denied the opportunity to rescue her."[139] She and her fellow volunteers were able to end pound seizure in their county in 2003, and Allie chronicled her experience in her 2010 book, *How Shelter Pets are Brokered for Experimentation: Understanding Pound Seizure*.

Some shelter officials feel that if a cat or dog is slated to be euthanized anyway, at least that animal's death can serve some purpose and benefit science. But pound seizure undermines efforts of shelters to rescue and adopt animals. In his book *Empty Cages: Facing the Challenge of Animal Rights*, Tom Regan observes that the dogs a Class

B dealer will seek in a shelter to sell for research—friendly, socialized, docile—are the very same animals who stand the best chance of being adopted into loving homes. "They have learned to trust human beings, something dealers and researchers can use to their advantage. No fighting. No biting. Just calm, confident behavior, complete with a friendly wag of the tail, or, in the case of cats, a gentle arching of the back. Forgive me if I seem overly cynical when I ask: Is there no limit to the depth of betrayal to which humans can sink?"[140]

Thankfully, many states in the US now prohibit pound seizure.

Wildlife

One of the lesser-known practices in an already covert industry is the use of animals snatched from the wild, and it is legal—well, *mostly* legal. Frogs, turtles, and other animals are taken from their native habitats and sold with impunity throughout the world. In fact, frogs comprise half the vertebrates used for dissection, and though some are bred for scientific use, most are plucked directly from their wetland homes, disrupting ecosystems and contributing to the global decline of frog populations. Some experts estimate that as much as 90 percent of the animals used for dissection are wild-caught.[141] With amphibian extinctions progressing at an alarming rate, taking frogs from the wild only compounds the problem.[142]

Not that those who profit from animal research care much about such issues as extinction. Just as young monkeys are captured in Africa and shipped overseas to occupy zoos, roadside attractions, and even the homes of people looking for an exotic "pet," so are they exported for use in biomedical research. Indeed, poachers and traffickers have transformed the quest for research victims into a lucrative business, jeopardizing the future of threatened species around the world. Among the many failings of the 1973 United Nations Convention on International Trade in Endangered Species of Wild Fauna and Flora (CITES) is that animals listed under Appendix II of the treaty—species not immediately threatened with extinction but could become so—continue to be traded. CITES even allows animals to be sold for vivisection. As a result, thousands of wild and sometimes endangered animals end up in research facilities because they receive no real protection.[143]

The long-tailed macaque, for example, is listed under Appendix II, yet each year, thousands of these monkeys are carried away from their homes. Currently the most popular primate species used in biomedical research,[144] long-tailed macaques favor mangrove forests, riverbanks, and swamp forests.[145] They are native to the islands of Southeast Asia and parts of mainland Asia, but are also found as far away as Mauritius, off the coast of Africa, where they were introduced by either Portuguese or Dutch explorers in the 16th or 17th century.[146] Whoever left them on the tropical island nation, long-tailed macaques flourished in such abundance that they are now considered "pests" on Mauritius and a profitable industry centers around their capture and trade. An undercover investigation by the British Union for the Abolition of Vivisection (BUAV) found that macaques on Mauritius are torn from family groups using traps baited with sugar cane and bananas. Many sustain broken limbs as they are roughly handled by trappers, who routinely swing the animals by their tails.[147]

In a traumatizing transport, the animals are confined in small cages, trucked to an airport, moved to quarantine cages, and transferred to an airline holding cage before being packed into wooden crates and shipped as cargo, mostly on passenger flights, on extremely arduous journeys to research laboratories around the world. Throughout this ordeal, animals are subjected to loud noise, poor ventilation, temperature fluctuations, and long delays. According to one report, this grueling process can take up to three days.[148]

A key element of their suffering is that macaques live in closely-knit, structured societies. Males stay in their family groups until at least four years of age, but females remain for their entire lives, weaning offspring at about 14 months and continuing to have intimate contact with them. In the biomedical industry's hunt for new research subjects, however, infant macaques as young as eight months old are snatched from their mothers.[149] Yet being forcibly separated is just the beginning of their misery.

Macaques not sent off for research end up in breeding farms overseas. On one such farm, Xaysavang in Laos, filmmaker and activist Karol Orzechowski found macaques having to compete with one another for the bits of monkey chow workers scattered into the barren cages. "The manager of the farm told us that he didn't have enough money to feed the animals properly, so they were essentially feeding them only when they had to," he says. "I should note that I was told this during a lunch meeting at one of the most expensive restaurants in Laos." Some of the monkeys had deep, fresh wounds and were clearly starving to death. In fact, when Karol returned two days later, two of these macaques were lying dead. "One monkey crouched near one of the corpses and stared at it," he says. "Minutes passed, and he barely moved except to scratch at his dead cage-mate's fur. He paused and looked up at me and my colleagues, and there was a palpable look of pain—and perhaps hunger—on his face."[150]

Consider too the plight of baboons and vervet monkeys in South Africa. Deep within the country's woodlands, savannahs, and forests, these primates are being snatched from their troops and sold to animal researchers. They are also wandering onto farmland and into urban areas, pushed out of their natural habitats by deforestation and development. "These animals are practically considered vermin," says Michelè Pickover, author of *Animal Rights in South Africa*.[151] Indeed, baboons and vervet monkeys are so prolific in South Africa that they have been labeled "problem animals," giving farmers the freedom to shoot, poison, or trap them—even though they are listed under Appendix II of CITES.

Capturing these persecuted primates for use in research labs has become a lucrative business, with customers in the United States paying up to US$1,500 for a baboon.[152] Trappers use baited crates to lure the baboons, who may be trapped for days without food or water. Once the trappers return, baboons who are old, pregnant, or too thin are killed, since they do not meet the requirements for research laboratories. The remaining animals are held in holding stations before being shipped overseas or even sold to a lab in South Africa. The big males are especially sought after by research laboratories, and their removal from social groups results in chaos and disorder within troops.[153]

A final example—though hardly the last word on animals taken from the wild for research—is the night monkey (sometimes called the owl monkey). These small, saucer-eyed primates live in the trees of South American rainforests, where they sleep in tangles of vines during the day and forage for fruit, seeds, and insects after dark. Since the 1980s, night monkeys have been the principal preoccupation of Dr. Manuel Elkin Patarroyo, who believes the animals are crucial to his development of a malaria vaccine, which is considered by many scientists to be the Holy Grail of pharmaceutical research. From his lab in Colombia, Patarroyo claims that the little primate's immune system is nearly identical to ours, making them ideal models for experimentation. Breeding programs have met with little success, so Patarroyo relies on poachers to fill his cages. As documented by the nonprofit Animal Defenders International (ADI), trappers prowl the rainforest in darkness, searching for night monkeys. "When they are found, the trees are netted, the monkeys are torn terrified from their homes, and they're placed in sacks," explains ADI's Angie Greenaway.[154]

Although night monkeys are listed under Appendix II of CITES, the Colombian government has long turned a blind eye as members of a local tribe capture up to 1,600 of the animals a year and sell them to Patarroyo for US$50 apiece.[155] That finally changed in 2012, when Patarroyo's monkey-capture permits were revoked, but traders in neighboring Brazil and Peru have also been supplying him with night monkeys—a direct violation of international trade regulations.[156] Inside Patarroyo's lab, investigators have documented monkeys confined in dreadful conditions: some were dead in their cages, while others, having lost all their hair, were barely able to stand up.[157]

After more than 30 years of research, and the lives of countless night monkeys, Patarroyo has yet to produce a viable vaccine against malaria.

Vivisection as Sacrifice

From its methods to its moral ambiguity, vivisection resembles nothing so much as ritual animal sacrifice. We'll explore the sacrifice of animals in depth in Chapter 7, but it's important to mention here the transformation of one form of abuse into another. Just as astronomy grew from astrology and modern chemistry has roots in the ancient practice of alchemy, animal testing is associated with religious customs that date back centuries. The university system, where animal experimentation found its largest and most devoted patron, is closely tied to the religious orders of medieval Europe, with monks being the earliest faculty; indeed, ordination in the Church of England required a university degree—a prerequisite that continues today in most Judeo-Christian traditions.

Copernicus, Descartes, Newton, and other early men of science came from this system and were influenced by its association with religion and doctrines from the Old Testament, including the use of animal sacrifice to gain God's favor. Francis Bacon (1561–1626), a philosopher best known for establishing the scientific method of inquiry based on experimentation, believed that vivisection was an essential key not just for unlocking empirical knowledge, but for restoring man's control of nature, lost when humanity fell from grace after Adam and Eve sampled fruit from the forbidden tree. "For man by the fall fell at the same time from his state of innocency and from his dominion over creation," Bacon wrote. "Both of these losses however can even in this life be in some part repaired; the former by religion and faith, the latter by arts and sciences."[158]

While sacrificing animals in the name of religion was (and to a degree still is) a rite of atonement or appeasement, vivisection is practiced for physical salvation. Ironically, discussion about the link between animal research and animal sacrifice likely began with a vivisector. In 1825, English physician James Blundell, who performed blood-transfusion experiments on dogs, delivered a lecture on physiology at Guy's Hospital Medical School in London, saying, "When animals are sacrificed on the altar of science that Nature may reveal her secrets, the means are consecrated by the end for which alone experiments are instituted by the votaries of knowledge and the friends of the human race."[159] It's impossible to ignore the religious undertones in Blundell's language, and he would return to it again and again, going so far as to call the scientific sacrifice of animals "a sacred duty."[160] Six decades later, the English novelist Ouida (Maria Louise Ramé), remembered perhaps as much for her love of animals as her literary works, referred to vivisection as "the gigantic system of animal sacrifice," observing that the superstitious awe of religion has been replaced by the superstitious awe of science.[161] More recently, the correlation between the two forms of exploitation has been examined by such animal advocates as Joan Dunayer (*Animal Equality*) and Norm Phelps (*The Dominion of Love*).

In his book *Brutal: Manhood and the Exploitation of Animals*, Brian Luke offers ten features of religious blood rituals that also apply to the sacrifice of animals in vivisection:

1   Sacrifice is the rule-bound manipulation of an animal's body.
2   The rules governing the process must be followed precisely.
3   Sacrificial animals are specially selected for the rite.
4   Sacrifice can only occur at specially designated sites.
5   Sacrifice can only be performed by credentialed officials.
6   Regulations govern who, if anyone, may eat the flesh of the sacrificed animal.
7   Though the animal is destroyed, this is held to be incidental to, rather than the real purpose of, the sacrifice.

8   Sacrifice is men's work.

9   Sacrifice is claimed to be necessary for achieving some socially significant end.

10 Sacrifice establishes paternity.[162]

Of course, we can find additional parallels: the modern scientist's white lab coat, for instance, can easily represent the ancient priest's robe, the research table echoes the sacrificial altar, and both forms of exploitation are a demonstration of power over the masses. But the most obvious similarity is the researcher's use of "sacrifice" to indicate the killing of an animal. Joan Dunayer notes that "the word *sacrifice* is apt insofar as it suggests vivisection's futility, primitive irrationality, and selfish desperation. Vivisection's victims literally are a blood sacrifice, killed for professional and financial gain and always-hypothetical public benefit. More a religion than a science, vivisection consists of ritual torture, animal sacrifice, and self-worship."[163] Cognizant of the word's religious significance—and perhaps the criticism of animal advocates—some researchers have begun avoiding the use of "sacrifice" in scientific journals, preferring the less ambiguous "euthanize" or the more accurate word "kill."

Change of Heart

From Richard Ryder to Ray Greek, the medical community is filled with former animal researchers who came to recognize the errors inherent in their work. Cardiologist John Pippin is another example. After he received his MD from the University of Massachusetts Medical School, Dr. Pippin started building a successful career as a heart specialist. But it wasn't long before he was questioning the ethical implications and scientific value of experimenting on animals. "When I was awarded a five-year American Heart Association award in 1986 to do dog heart experiments that I designed," he says, "I firmly believed that my work, and similar work by others, was important to advance the detection and treatment of human heart disease. I learned by doing this research, and by studying the research of others, that my belief was false.

"We were all advancing our own careers, and we were discovering interesting things about artificially induced heart disease in animals, but we were doing little or nothing for human health. What we learned by using animals did not reliably predict what we would later see in humans, where the findings would have to be duplicated anyway.

"Simultaneously, I gained a better understanding of the cruelty and inhumanity of animal experimentation. I had dogs who were my family, yet I went to my lab and killed other dogs. The only difference was that my dogs got lucky, and that seemed to me a horrible excuse for loving some and killing others. The cognitive dissonance was enough to make my head explode. Our lab was certainly better than most in our treatment of dogs, yet the animals' suffering was unavoidable. This is when I concluded that if you perform or support animal experimentation, you can't hide behind claims of humane treatment. There is no such thing as humane animal experimentation.

"So I stopped doing this for both ethical and scientific reasons, converted my AHA grant to heart studies in human patients, and vowed to expose the fraud of animal experimentation whenever I had the opportunity. There have been costs from that decision, but it is likely the single most ethical and heartfelt professional decision I have ever made."[164]

John Pippin, MD, FACC, is now director of academic affairs for the Washington, DC-based Physicians Committee for Responsible Medicine, where he works to replace the use of animals in medical and drug research, medical education, and the training of physicians, nurses, and other medical professionals.

Messing with Nature

Remember Dolly the sheep? Dolly gained international fame as the first mammal to be cloned from an adult cell, rather than an

embryonic cell. She was born in Scotland in 1996 and was euthanized six years later—half a sheep's life expectancy—after developing a progressive lung disease commonly found in older sheep. A
genetic carbon copy of her "donor mother," Dolly was the product
of reproductive engineering. Scientists have since done the same
with other mammals, including goats, pigs, rats, monkeys, mice,
rabbits, cats, dogs, horses, and mules, but the big push now is on
cloning cows. Farmers believe this technology will help create herds
of extra-large animals capable of producing vast quantities of meat
and milk. But welfare issues are dramatically compounded, with
high levels of miscarriage, organ failure, and gigantism among
newborn clones.

Cloning itself is an invasive process in which the egg "donors"
and surrogate mothers endure grueling and distressing hormone
treatments to manipulate their reproductive cycles. These animals
are also subjected to invasive procedures to harvest eggs or implant
embryos, and surrogate mothers must then undergo an additional
surgery to deliver their babies, only 5 percent of whom survive.[165]
(Because of the supersized nature of cloned calves, deliveries are
often through caesarean sections.[166])

While some researchers tinker with animal cells and embryos to
boost the production of frankenfoods, others are toying with an
equally distressing abuse of nature.

Xenotransplantation

In 1984, a new brand of animal exploitation hit the public
consciousness. That's the year that, on the morning of October 26,
surgeons placed the heart of a baboon named Goobers into the chest
of Stephanie Fae Beauclair, then known in the media only as "Baby
Fae," a 14-day-old infant with a fatal heart defect. It's no exaggeration to say it was a monumental event, and xenotransplantation—
removing tissues or organs from animals and transplanting them
into humans—was hailed as a medical miracle. That Baby Fae
survived only 21 days before her body rejected the heart didn't

dampen the enthusiasm of xenotransplantation proponents, who claim this technology is required in a world where the demand for human organs far exceeds the supply.

Baby Fae and Goobers were part of science's learning curve, and since then researchers have developed a preference for pig organs, which they claim are a better fit for humans than even body parts from other primates, with whom we share so much of our DNA.[167] Yet the organs used for xenotransplantation (sometimes called xenografting) are not the byproduct of slaughterhouses but are from animals who are purpose-bred using genetic engineering, reproductive manipulations, and cloning technology. One of the chief reasons for all this scientific modification is that nonhuman organs are simply not intended to be grafted onto human tissue. Most xenotransplantations fail because a body's immune system is designed to destroy entities it regards as foreign. Moreover, organs taken from animals bring with them the potential for humans to become infected with both recognized and unrecognized infectious agents and for cross-species infection by retroviruses, which may be latent and lead to disease years after infection. To combat these risks, researchers—backed by biotech and pharmaceutical companies—are creating transgenic (genetically engineered) animals and antirejection drugs.

Researchers have been using genetically engineered animals for decades to model specific diseases—altering and breeding mice, for instance, who are predisposed to develop cancer.[168] In engineering the genetic makeup of animals, however, science continues to subject them to cruel procedures that result in severe health problems. One of the most commonly cited examples is the group of transgenic animals who came to be known as "the Beltsville pigs." Created by the USDA at its Beltsville, Maryland, research center, these animals ended up hideously deformed, unable to walk properly, and suffering from damaged vision, arthritis, diarrhea, and males with mammary glands.[169]

In the UK, an ill-fated xenografting program using genetically modified animals was brought to light by the group Uncaged, which obtained documents never meant for the public to see. Carried out by Huntingdon Life Sciences on behalf of the biotech company Imutran Ltd., the experiments involved removing the transgenic organs of pigs and placing them into the bodies of wild-caught baboons and cynomolgus monkeys. The documents and study reports leaked from the program reveal a catalog of suffering: highly social animals stolen from their natural habitats and families, baboons in metal cages being electrocuted by lightning, monkeys so stressed and sick that they can't move, pig hearts grafted onto the necks of baboons, death from accidental overdose. All told, at least 473 nonhuman primates and thousands of pigs were killed, along with an unknown number of animals through collaboration with researchers in Canada, Italy, the Netherlands, Spain, and the US—and practically no progress was made in overcoming the vast immunological obstacles to xenotransplantation.[170]

Military Research

Testing military weapons on animals has a long tradition, but such experiments entered the modern age in World War II. Among the boldest schemes of the day was for the US government to transform bats into weapons of mass destruction. Considerable time and money went into a plan to arm more than a million of these animals with tiny incendiary bombs and release them from planes above the industrial cities surrounding Japan's Osaka Bay. The objective was that as the bats roosted beneath the eaves of wood-and-paper houses, the bombs would ignite and reduce the landscape to ashes, "yet with small loss of life."[171] Well, except for the million bats, who would be burned alive. Indeed, thousands of bats perished as the idea was developed. During a test at the Auxiliary Army Air Base at Carlsbad, New Mexico, in 1943, the bat-bombs ended up destroying a hangar and a general's car. The plan was cancelled soon afterward.[172]

The United States continued using animals for weapons development after the war. In 1946, the military detonated a nuclear device in the sky near Bikini Atoll in the South Pacific. To discover the bomb's effects, they positioned 3,030 rats, 176 goats, 147 pigs, 109 mice, and 57 guinea pigs in a 22-ship flotilla beneath the explosion. Some of the pigs—used because their skin approximates that of a human's—were dressed in navy uniforms to see how the fabric would respond. Other animals were shaved and slathered in a variety of lotions to determine if they provided any protection from radiation burns. Officially, the test was known as "Operation Crossroads." But the military had another name for it: they dubbed it "The Atomic Ark." Most of the animals who did not immediately die from fire, radiation, drowning, or the blast succumbed shortly thereafter from their injuries, while the others were killed for further study.[173]

Today, the US military is one of the biggest abusers of animals, inflicting death and painful injuries on more than 300,000 dogs, cats, goats, pigs, mice, fish, sheep, birds, rabbits, rats, and nonhuman primates every year.[174] Animals are burned, shot, maimed, scalded, poisoned, gassed, and blown up. Among the most controversial examples is a program in which researchers outfitted live pigs in body armor and strapped them into Humvee simulators that were then hit with explosives to study how roadside bombs result in traumatic brain injuries. Other pigs got the full force of the blasts without the benefit of any protective armor.[175] In 2010, Britain's Ministry of Defence admitted it has conducted similar tests at Porton Down, one of the country's most secretive government facilities for military research, blowing up 119 live pigs between 2006 and 2009. Prior to blowing up the pigs, researchers inserted wires and tubes into their blood vessels so they would be torn open by the blast. Porton Down said the objective was to determine how much blood a soldier could lose before dying.[176]

Chemical and Biological Warfare

Long before chemical agents became one of the most horrific features of human conflict, researchers were dosing animals with them. Probably the most dreaded chemical weapon to come out of the 19th century was mustard gas (dichlorethylsulphide), later employed by French, German, and US forces in World War I. The effects of the poison—debilitating chemical burns, blindness, bleeding and blistering in the lungs, and death from pneumonia—were known as early as 1886, when mustard gas was tested on rabbits.[177] Of course, the horses and mules used in battle a century ago suffered right along with the soldiers in the trenches anytime they were attacked with a chemical weapon.

And animals continue to suffer. Whether it's to determine how an organism will respond or to establish the viability of using a certain species as a warning mechanism in the event of attack (think of the unfortunate canary in the coal mine), military researchers persist in testing chemical compounds on animals. Chlorine gas, phosgene, lewisite, and sarin are just a few of the toxic agents animals are subjected to, with the effects ranging from diarrhea, skin lesions, or irritation in the nasal passages to seizures, asphyxiation, or cardiac arrest. Death from lewisite exposure is particularly agonizing; dogs forced to inhale this blistering agent lingered for 10 minutes as the chemical ate away at their throats.[178]

Such tests can be misleading, however, as the results may not always apply to humans. During a US military test of cyanide poisoning, for example, researchers simultaneously exposed a man and a dog to hydrogen cyanide gas in the same airtight chamber. The dog cried out and experienced convulsions before becoming unconscious within 90 seconds, at which point the man simply walked out of the chamber with no symptoms.[179] Government scientists in the UK are well aware that chemical weapons tested on animals are not predictive of how they will affect humans—so between 1945 and 1989 they exposed more than 3,400 humans to deadly nerve gases such as sarin.[180]

No less gruesome than chemical weapons are the effects of biological warfare agents, which the United States and other governments invest heavily into researching. Funding for such research increased dramatically after September 11, 2001, when countries suddenly felt more vulnerable to attack than ever before. In an instant, the threat of someone using weaponized infectious agents like bacteria and viruses on people, animals, and crops was seen as too great to ignore.

The US and the UK now operate significant biological weapons programs, even though they are among more than 160 nations—including Australia, Canada, China, India, New Zealand, Russia, and South Africa—that are parties to the Biological Weapons Convention (BWC), a multilateral disarmament treaty. How can they do this? Because the BWC allows the development and testing of biological weapons for defense against acts of bioterrorism.[181] As a result, scientists ostensibly creating antidotes for incurable viruses—so-called "biodefense vaccines"—work within the US Army Medical Research Institute of Infectious Diseases (USAMRIID), located at Fort Detrick, Maryland. Here they infect thousands of animals each year with a wide variety of lethal pathogens, including anthrax, Ebola, dengue fever, tick-borne encephalitis, Crimean-Congo hemorrhagic fever, yellow fever, hantavirus, and Rift Valley fever. The typical reactions of animal victims after being exposed to these disease agents include internal hemorrhaging, paralysis, bleeding from their eyeballs and nipples, vomiting black fluid, psychosis, terminal shock, and, of course, death. Within 24 hours after the demise of one particular animal at USAMRIID, his body's organs, bones, and flesh had melted, reduced to the consistency of soup.[182]

USAMRIID will soon have some competition. The Department of Homeland Security is currently developing an enormous biological animal research center in Kansas. Known officially as the National Bio and Agro-Defense Facility (NBAF), the laboratory will expose farmed animals to the latest in bio-weapons technology—and undoubtedly achieve new levels of torture along the way. The site is necessary, says the government, because some biological agents can be used to specifically target animal agriculture and thus threaten the US food supply. NBAF will replace the aging Plum Island Animal Disease Center off Long Island, New York.

The US has no monopoly on testing chemical and biological contaminants on animals; in fact, it's safe to assume that virtually any government that possesses these agents—including China, Israel, and Russia—has evaluated their effectiveness on nonhumans. Across the Atlantic, researchers inside England's Porton Down labs have tested everything from mustard gas to anthrax and nerve agents since the top-secret center was built in 1916.[183] In the 1980s and 1990s, the South African Defence Force ran a covert chemical and biological weapons program. Research was carried out by contract labs such as Delta G Scientific, which produced chemical warfare substances, and Roodeplaat Research Laboratories (RRL), which produced biological agents such as anthrax, botulinum toxin, and cholera bacterium—and tested them on animals. One of the more unusual plans RRL developed was to use snake venom as an assassination weapon. The toxin from a black mamba would be extracted and injected into someone perceived to be a State enemy. The snake would then be killed and his fangs pressed into the flesh of the dead man, making it appear that he died from a snakebite. RRL researchers knew how much venom to use because they had tested their strategy on baboons.[184] Many of the primates used at RRL were captured in South Africa's Kruger National Park, where they were shot with poison darts in plain view of tourists.[185]

Wound Labs

The military's war on animals also includes the teaching of combat casualty care, which involves inflicting gunshot wounds, amputations, burns, lacerations, and other painful, life-threatening injuries. To simulate damage from a land mine, instructors will either strap an explosive device to an animal's limb, attach a detonation cord and blasting cap to his lower extremity, or simply blow a leg off with a shotgun fired at point-blank range. These "wound labs"—currently used by the militaries of six NATO countries: Canada, Denmark,

Norway, Poland, the United Kingdom, and the United States—are meant to train personnel in life-saving skills, with goats and pigs substituting for human beings.[186] In decades past, the US military's victims of choice were dogs, who were purchased from Class A dealers, supposedly anesthetized, and hung in mesh slings before being shot with high-velocity guns—a practice that ended in the 1980s following an outcry from animal advocates.

Although today's military may be more guarded about its training, much of which is considered top secret, it's clear that animal abuse is standard operating procedure. The military says that animals used in wound labs are anesthetized, but a video leaked to PETA by a whistleblower in 2012 shows goats moaning loudly and kicking as instructors from Tier 1 Group, a government contractor, saw off their limbs with tree trimmers, slice open their abdomens, and pull out their organs. The whistleblower said that the goats were later shot in the face and hacked apart with an ax while they were still alive.[187] Following complaints filed by PETA, the USDA cited Tier 1 for animal abuse, though this didn't deter the Navy from awarding them a taxpayer-funded contract to conduct 24 trauma training exercises using live pigs a few days later.

Former Navy SEAL Don Mann provides another glimpse of such merciless disregard for animals in his memoir *Inside SEAL Team Six: My Life and Missions with America's Elite Warriors*. Mann recalls his training at the Special Forces (SF) medical lab in Fort Bragg, North Carolina—called the Goat Lab:

"Day one, each one of us was given a patient in the form of a diseased goat... Mine was a big fellow with a long red beard so we named him Barbarosa, after the character Willie Nelson played in the movie of the same name.

"I've always loved animals and don't hunt. But now, after two other SF guys strapped Barbarosa down, I had to shoot him in the leg with a thirty-aught-six. *Bam!*

"For the rest of the Goat Lab it was my job to keep Barbarosa alive."

Mann does keep Barbarosa alive, and he grows fond of him. Then comes the last class session.

"Our final test day, called trauma day, was intense. I waited with my medical bag as Barbarosa was led around a corner by two SF guys. Minutes later I heard a loud boom followed by the SF guys screaming, 'Medic! Medic!'

"I tore around the corner to see Barbarosa on the ground. He was a bloody, smoldering mess. His face had been set on fire. One of his eyes had been pulled out, his right leg had been amputated, and he had two sticks impaled in his chest. In addition, he had suffered two slash wounds that weren't obvious at first."

Despite these horrific injuries, Mann manages to save Barbarosa's life again.

"The vet said, 'OK, you passed. Now throw him in the incinerator.'"[188]

As heartless as that sounds, Mann's experience is typical. Petty Officer Third Class Dustin Kirby, a Navy corpsman, remembers the pig he was given to look after during the advanced trauma treatment program he had attended before deploying to Iraq as a combat medic. "They shot him twice in the face with a 9-millimeter pistol, and then six times with an AK-47 and then twice with a 12-gauge shotgun. And then he was set on fire," he says. "I kept him alive for 15 hours."[189]

Fortunately, the US Department of Defense is finally being forced to account for the animals it kills for combat trauma training and replace these with human-based methods by 2018.

Regulations

Laws protecting animals used in research vary around the world. Truth be told, they are all but meaningless, as these regulations do little to actually protect animals. But some of these are worth noting as a reflection of society's efforts to codify vivisection practices. We'll begin with the country where more animals suffer in the name of science than any other.[190]

United States

It would not be until the 1960s that attempts to regulate the trade of animals used for research in the US would succeed on a national level. Previously, efforts to impose legally mandated guidelines on the treatment of animals used in labs or on how these animals were obtained by dealers had always run up against opposition from the powerful pro-research lobby. The American Medical Association, for example, claimed that such regulation was "likely to cause serious interference with, and irreparable harm to, the conduct of highly important research."[191] Vivisectors argued that measures such as the Animal Care Panel, formed in 1950, and the American Association for Accreditation of Laboratory Animal Care, created in 1965, ensured the humane treatment of animals.[192] Moreover, just like the claim from industrial agribusiness today that animals are well treated in order for meat, dairy, and egg producers to deliver a safe, quality product, the research community of the mid-20th century objected to any attempts by lawmakers to regulate their industry on the grounds that good science already demanded that animals used for research be well cared for.[193] Such claims, however, would prove just as false for vivisectors as recent investigations have demonstrated they are for operators of factory farms.

The tide began to turn in favor of regulation in the summer of 1965, when a Dalmatian named Pepper disappeared from the Pennsylvania farm she shared with her human companions, the Lakavage family. The Lakavages dearly loved Pepper, and when she went missing, they began a frantic search that would lead them to stumble upon the little-known practice of stealing animals for research. Pepper, they discovered, had been taken from their property and sold to a dealer and finally—after enduring a 170-mile truck ride crammed inside a small enclosure with other animals in "asphalt-softening, brain-fogging heat"—to a hospital in the Bronx.[194] As they tried to track down their beloved dog, the family learned that Pepper had died after an operation to test an experimental pacemaker.

The tragedy of Pepper's death became a media sensation and was covered in, of all places, *Sports Illustrated*, which soberly informed its readers that "1) many pet dogs are being stolen from the front lawns and sidewalks of this country, and 2) the thefts in large part are motivated by science's constant and growing need for laboratory animals."[195] Even before the story was national news, a Congressman from New York State named Joseph Resnick had introduced House Bill 9743, which would require that dog and cat dealers, and the laboratories that purchased animals from them, be licensed and inspected by the USDA.

The bill faced the usual hostility from medical interests, however, and was still struggling in February of 1966 when *Life* magazine put a face on the debate—or several faces, to be precise. In an eight-page article titled "Concentration Camps for Dogs," the influential weekly news publication exposed the growing demand for dogs in medical research. The story documented a police raid on a dog dealer's facility in Maryland and, accompanied by graphic photos of dead and dying canines, the conditions the animals were kept in. Readers were shocked to learn that: "50 percent of all missing pets have been stolen by 'dognappers,' who in turn sell them to the dealers. Some dealers keep big inventories of dogs in unspeakably filthy compounds that seem scarcely less appalling than the concentration camps of World War II."[196] It was a heart-wrenching piece of photojournalism, and it galvanized a nation of dog lovers, who inundated Congress with tens of thousands of letters demanding that lawmakers do something.[197] The public outrage was so vociferous that six months later President Lyndon Johnson signed a more ambitious law than the one Resnick had proposed: the 1966 Laboratory Animal Welfare Act, now known as the Animal Welfare Act (AWA).[198] Falling under the jurisdiction of the US Department of Agriculture, this was the first piece of federal legislation in the United States that established minimum standards for the care, transport, and acquisition of animals used in laboratories, and it also required the regulation of dealers who sold animals to research institutions. Any research institution that receives money from the federal government must adhere to the rules outlined under the AWA.

Unfortunately, the scope of the Animal Welfare Act is limited, applying only to the type of care an animal receives before and after a study—such as food, water, and housing—not during. Indeed, to help absolve animal researchers of the tortures they inflict, the AWA specifies that: "Nothing in these rules, regulations, or standards shall affect or interfere with the design, outline, or performance of actual research or experimentation by a research facility as determined by such research facility."[199]

Reflecting the public's growing concern about the treatment of animals, the Act has been amended many times, first in 1970, when it officially became the Animal Welfare Act. It was that year that amendments broadened the definition of "animal" to include any warm-blooded animal, not just dogs, cats, rabbits, hamsters, guinea pigs, and nonhuman primates, as well as making exhibitors of animals—such as circuses, zoos, and carnivals—answerable to the AWA. Regrettably, the amendments excluded horses not used in research and animals used in food and fiber research, retail pet stores, state and county fairs, rodeos, purebred dog and cat shows, and agricultural exhibitions.[200] Six years later, an amendment was added that outlawed the interstate or foreign transport of animals used in fighting ventures. Subsequent amendments to the AWA have increased penalties, introduced restrictions on where research facilities could obtain their animals from, and required that animal shelters hold dogs and cats for at least five days before selling them to a dealer so that owners have more time to recover their lost pets.

A 1985 amendment to the Act requires labs to appoint an IACUC, the internal review board we examined earlier. This amendment was in response to two major scandals within the research industry: the 1981 Silver Spring monkeys case, an undercover investigation that led to the first conviction of a researcher on animal cruelty charges and launched PETA as a leading pressure group, and the 1984 Head

Trauma case at the University of Pennsylvania, in which the Animal Liberation Front removed videotapes from the facility that showed researchers laughing as they used a hydraulic device to inflict brain damage on baboons. In 1989, changes to the law meant that colleges and universities came under the purview of the Act, but as of today, the AWA, as well as state laws, specifically exempt all elementary and secondary schools from any of their requirements pertaining to the use of animals.

For years, animal advocates have been urging the US Department of Agriculture to include rats, mice, and birds in the AWA. In 1989, the Animal Legal Defense Fund and The Humane Society of the United States filed a joint petition with the USDA, and later sued them, but their efforts came to naught. A decade later, an affiliate of the American Anti-Vivisection Society filed a suit against the USDA, which finally agreed to begin drafting rules that would extend AWA protection to rats, mice, and birds. Perhaps the government had seen the writing on the wall—or at least the magazine: in 1999, Harold Herzog and Scott Plous made a splash in the industry publication *Lab Animal* with the results of their study in which the majority of individual animal researchers favored the inclusion of rats, mice, and birds under the AWA.[201]

But often all it takes to derail compassionate reform is a fierce lobbying effort, and while animal advocates were celebrating their impending victory, some in Congress had sharpened their knives and were carving a bold plan to outmaneuver their opponents. First, Senator Thad Cochran from Mississippi introduced an amendment to an appropriations bill that immediately prohibited the USDA from implementing new rules for a year. This bought the special interests on Capitol Hill a little time. Then, North Carolina Senator Jesse Helms, who had close ties with agribusiness, added an amendment to the AWA that actually changed the definition of the word "animal" to exclude rats, mice, and birds. In a Senate floor speech that would strike animal welfare proponents as being somewhere between hallucinatory and obscene, Helms said, "A rodent could do a lot worse than live out its life span in research facilities."[202] President George W. Bush signed the amendment in 2002.

The exclusion of rats, mice, and birds—as well as fish—represents perhaps the biggest weakness of the Animal Welfare Act, since these animals account for some 85 percent of those used in experimentation. Reflecting a disparity that borders on the Orwellian, this is similar to the loophole in the federal Humane Methods of Slaughter Act, which stipulates that an animal must be rendered insensible to pain before being killed; that 1958 law specifically excludes birds, yet more than 90 percent of the 9 billion land animals killed for food each year in the US are chickens.[203]

United Kingdom

Nearly a century before the US codified its animal research, the British Parliament passed the Cruelty to Animals Act 1876, which the National Anti-Vivisection Society, founded the year prior, calls "infamous, but well named."[204] The Act was a licensing system requiring researchers to submit an application to the Home Secretary. If granted, the license permitted experiments on living vertebrates (the only animals covered) under anesthesia and only in registered facilities. Researchers were subject to scrutiny by inspectors appointed by the Home Secretary. Despite these rules, the Act was widely criticized as an ineffective tool to protect animals in labs. By the 1970s, there were 18,000 scientists licensed to perform experiments on animals and just four Home Office inspectors to supervise them.[205] Perhaps that's why only three researchers were ever prosecuted under the 1876 Act.[206] (Likely the most famous transgression of the 1876 Act came to light during the Brown Dog Affair, named for a dog who was the victim of two experiments, one in 1902 and another in 1903, at the University of London. Although the Act specified an animal could only be used once for vivisection, none of the researchers involved in the second experiment were prosecuted.[207])

After decades of welfare reform in such areas as homeless dogs and cats, animals used for entertainment, and the increasing number of birds found covered in oil along the country's shores, the hidden cruelties endured by all-but-forgotten animals—especially those confined in factory farms and research labs—began to be more vigorously challenged. In the 1970s, anti-vivisectionists used a variety of tools to bring awareness to the plight of animals in labs, and the media was happy to turn their powerful spotlight on the subject. The turning point came in 1975, when three major events in the UK catapulted animal testing into the public discourse. First was a January exposé in Britain's *Sunday People* on the use of beagles in tobacco research. Written by a reporter who worked undercover at Imperial Chemical Industries (ICI), the country's largest company at the time, the article described in detail how dogs are restrained and forced to inhale the smoke of up to 30 cigarettes a day. Then they are killed and their organs examined for traces of disease. The story was accompanied by photographs of dogs clamped into small boxes with muzzles and hoses strapped to their faces; it led to a massive public outcry.[208] Two weeks after the smoking beagles story broke came the publication of *Victims of Science* by Dr. Richard Ryder—a former animal experimenter who went on to work with the Royal Society for the Prevention of Cruelty to Animals (RSPCA) and coined the term "speciesism"—arguing against the use of animals in labs. The book received widespread media coverage and was even reviewed in scientific journals, though not favorably (*New Scientist* called Dr. Ryder's arguments "vacuous").[209] Finally, in June, activist Mike Huskisson of the Animal Liberation Front (then known as the Band of Mercy) broke into ICI and rescued two of the chain-smoking beagles. Although Mike was arrested for the action and charged with burglary, he was acquitted, and the publicity surrounding the case generated another wave of support in the fight against animal research.[210]

During Britain's 1979 general election campaign, the incoming Conservatives pledged to update the legislation on experiments on live animals. Public sentiment and a change in the political tide were all favoring reform, but advancements on behalf of animals can be like changing a tire in the dark—astonishingly difficult and apt to bloody your knuckles. Momentum was on the side of the animal movement, however, and among the groups working for reform was the RSPCA, which had long claimed that kindness toward animals was a native English trait.[211] In a 1983 report, the Society told the British government that animal suffering was the paramount issue in the debate on vivisection, citing as examples experiments in which animals poisoned in military research took several weeks to die, monkeys dosed with weed killer died after a number of days, and irradiated mice lingered in agony for six months before finally succumbing.[212]

The 1876 Act was at last replaced by the Animals (Scientific Procedures) Act 1986 (ASPA), which at the time was seen as demonstrating Britain's position at the vanguard of animal protection.[213] The 1986 Act covered any scientific procedures carried out on an animal that may have the effect of causing the animal pain, suffering, distress, or lasting harm. It included all vertebrate animals (mammals, fish, reptiles, birds, and amphibians), as well as one species of octopus. Like its predecessor, the ASPA was a licensing system administered by the Home Office, but this Act provided regulation on three levels, all of which were required: the facility where research is carried out (called the "Certificate of Designation"), the programs of work that may be undertaken (called the "Project License"), and the people who are permitted to carry out those projects (called the "Personal License"). These extra measures were in contrast to the 1876 Act, which had only required that researchers license the technique to be used. Many reformers regarded the ASPA as being the most advanced legislation of its kind, requiring applicants to sign a declaration that no non-animal alternatives will achieve the objectives of their project and to justify the severity of their proposed procedures. Dr. Ryder believes ASPA was a distinct improvement, citing the reduction in LD50 testing.

"The 1986 Act was, in my opinion, a huge advance on the 1876 Act, and it has inspired legislation throughout the EU and elsewhere," he says.[214] Yet the revised Act was still grounded in the utilitarian principle of weighing the suffering of animals against the benefits such suffering might provide to humans. In other words, the end justifies the means.

An amendment to ASPA comes by way of a set of requirements adopted on January 1, 2013, by all 27 members of the European Union. Known in the EU as Directive 2010/63, the legislation has been transposed into UK law as the Animals (Scientific Procedures) Act 1986 Amendment Regulations 2012. The Directive enhances animal welfare in many member states (enshrining into law the 3R principle of replacement, reduction, and refinement throughout Europe), but in the UK, it is business as usual, with controls and restrictions on the use of animals in labs being neither increased nor relaxed.

Australia

Each of Australia's six states and two territories has adopted require-ments that animal research and teaching comply with animal welfare laws based on the Code of Practice for the Care and Use of Animals for Scientific Purposes. The Code of Practice is sponsored by the National Health and Medical Research Council, which provides guidance on ethical issues and funds research using animals. The Code of Practice encompasses all aspects of the care and use of, or interaction with, animals for scientific purposes in medicine, biology, agriculture, veterinary and other animal sciences, industry, and teaching. It includes their use in research, teaching, field trials, product testing, diagnosis, the production of biological products, and environmental studies.

The Australian system relies heavily on the consideration of animal research and teaching proposals by Animal Ethics Committees (AECs), which are appointed by the institutions. The effectiveness of AECs varies, particularly as they assess the justification of a given research protocol and the procedures permitted on animals. The nonprofit Animals Australia has successfully lobbied for independent third-party reviews of AECs, and most state and territory governments are moving to implement an outside assessment at least once every three years.

More than 7 million animals are used in research and teaching in Australia every year.

Canada

The Canadian Council on Animal Care (CCAC) provides voluntary *guidelines*, not laws, for using animals in research. Created in 1968 to oversee the ethical use of animals in science in Canada, the CCAC was incorporated as a nonprofit and independent body in 1982. It is primarily financed by the Canadian Institutes of Health Research and the Natural Sciences and Engineering Research Council of Canada—which would seem to be the very definition of "conflict of interest." Moreover, the CCAC is comprised of 22 permanent member organizations, only one of which—the Canadian Federation of Humane Societies—is an animal welfare group. Most of the other members either actively promote animal-based research or they benefit from it, including the Canadian Association for Laboratory Animal Science, Agriculture and Agri-Food Canada, the Canadian Cancer Society Research Institute, and the Heart and Stroke Foundation of Canada.

The CCAC establishes local Animal Care Committees (ACC) that conduct assessments of research institutions to determine if those facilities comply with CCAC guidelines; however, these assessments are not made available to the public. Indeed, the assessments are deemed confidential, as is the composition of the ACCs. Members of the ACC are forbidden to reveal information about their local committee's activities.

Adding insult to injury, the CCAC claims it is exempt from public disclosure laws such as the Access to Information Act. In short, there is effectively no public oversight of animal research in Canada, which means taxpayers have no way of knowing if an institution using animals has violated animal care standards.

New Zealand

Overseeing the welfare of the some 250,000 animals used for research in New Zealand every year[215] is the National Animal Ethics Advisory Committee (NAEAC), a government-appointed body established under the Animal Welfare Act of 1999. NAEAC's main function is to give the government advice on ethical and animal welfare issues relating to the use of animals in research, testing, and teaching (known collectively in New Zealand as RTT). It also works with the Australian and New Zealand Council for the Care of Animals in Research and Teaching (ANZCCART), organizations engaged in RTT, and the local animal ethics committees (AECs) that oversee such activities.

NAEAC consists of not more than 10 members, who are appointed by the Minister of Agriculture, for terms not exceeding three years. Typical recent members have included a professor of ethics (the token welfare consultant), a biology teacher, a professor of pathology, a professor of surgery and anesthesia, and a veterinarian on the payroll of Auckland Meat Processors. Not exactly a cheerleading squad for the rights of animals.

The use of animals in RTT is regulated through Part 6 of the Animal Welfare Act. The Act requires that any person using animals in RTT holds an approved code of ethical conduct, works for a person who holds an approved code, or has an arrangement to use another person's approved code. The Act also makes the philosophy of the Three Rs a statute, supposedly requiring that those who test on animals give due consideration to reducing, refining, and replacing when possible. How effectively this bit of legislation is enforced is anyone's guess, since much of what goes on with New Zealand's RTT is carried out in secret.

South Africa

Although it is difficult to pinpoint exactly when animal research began in South Africa, historians believe it commenced shortly after the country's first university-based medical schools were established in the 1930s.[216] Today, regulations for animal testing officially fall under South Africa's Department of Agriculture, specifically the Registrar of Livestock Improvement. But in reality, says South African activist Michelè Pickover, the country has no regulations where animal research is concerned. "That's why there are quite a lot of independent contract research laboratories that we don't even know about. There's an Animal Protection Act, but it excludes animals in laboratories."[217]

The country's animal researchers do have a national code of ethics, which is referred to by animal advocates in South Africa as the "vivisectors' charter" because it is biased, voluntary, and allows researchers to police themselves. The code is not enforceable by law, and indeed exempts animal experimenters from any accountability and transparency, doing nothing for the animals beyond specifying the minimum size of the cages they'll be confined in.[218]

Michelè sums up how the system has failed animals in her book *Animal Rights in South Africa*: "The mechanisms that are supposed to oversee animal experimentation and safeguard the animals are deeply flawed. Animal ethics committees are inherently deficient because they are a self-appointed, self-policing, self-perpetuating peer review system where accountability is only to one's close colleagues. The Animal Protection Act offers no protection to animals in laboratories nor does it prohibit experimental procedures on them. This, coupled with the lack of official information about who conducts the experiments and what type they are, makes effective monitoring difficult."[219]

Ending the Madness

Animal testing is so abhorrent that ending the practice would seem like an ethical slam dunk. Indeed, that has been among the goals of countless animal protection organizations around the world since the 19th century. And though we've certainly seen progress—some countries, particularly Great Britain and India, have made enormous strides in replacing live animals with high-tech alternatives, for example—the bloodletting continues.

Animal advocates take a two-pronged approach in their opposition to vivisection, arguing that it is both inhumane (bad for the animals) and ineffective (bad for humans). The first approach has been met with middling success: activists armed with gruesome photos and eyewitness accounts of animal suffering have succeeded in halting the use of dogs in military wound labs, for instance, but not the use of rabbits in LD50 tests. The reality is that protesting the abusive nature of vivisection only goes so far because most people seem to view medical research on animals as acceptable, believing it somehow benefits society. Yes, it may be horribly cruel, but (the general public believes) vivisection leads to cures for diseases, and humans want to live—forever, if at all possible. Fear of death can be a powerful incentive.

But, as we have seen, animal-based bioresearch is inherently flawed, and that—not a focus on animal pain and distress—could lead to its downfall. "For 160 years now, anti-vivisectionists have tried the ethical approach," says Dr. Ray Greek. "They've tried to explain to society that it's really cruel to do this to animals. Well, guess what? That hasn't worked. Human nature is exactly what it was 160 years ago. I have very little respect for people who try to change the system doing the same thing over and over again and expecting different results. Einstein said that was the definition of insanity. Society views vivisection as a necessary evil: you don't have to sell society on the heinous nature of vivisection. What you *do* have to explain to society is that when the vivisector says, 'It's your child or this dog,' they are presenting a false dichotomy. It's not the child or the dog. In point of fact, vivisection has probably killed more humans than it has ultimately helped. That's what you have to convince society of."[220]

What You Can Do

Biomedical Research

Voice your objection to your tax dollars being used to fund experiments. If you live in the United States, tell Congress you don't want your taxes used to underwrite animal experiments. Every dollar the US government spends must be approved by Congress, and since virtually all federally funded research is paid for with tax revenue, it's important to let your elected officials know how you feel. You can find the members of Congress representing you, as well as phone numbers and links to contact them online, at www.contactingthe-congress.org.

You can also write to research-funding agencies, such as the National Institutes of Health:

Francis S. Collins, MD, PhD, Director
National Institutes of Health
Shannon Bldg., Room 126
1 Center Dr.
Bethesda, MD 20892
301-496-2433
francis.collins@nih.gov

In the United Kingdom, you can write to the Home Secretary and ask for the most progressive and compassionate laws governing animal research. You'll find contact details at www.homeoffice.gov.uk. You can also use the website of the British Union for the Abolition of Vivisection to lobby your MP. Visit www.buav.org/lobby-your-mp

In Canada, let your Member of Parliament (MP) and Member of the Legislative Assembly (MLA) know how you feel. Find your MP online at: www.parl.gc.ca/Parlinfo/Compilations/HouseOfCommons/MemberByPostalCode.aspx?Menu=HOC. You can find your MLA at www.leg.bc.ca/mla/3-1-1.htm

In Australia, you can find your federal electorate here: http://apps. aec.gov.au/esearch/

MPs in New Zealand can be found here: www.parliament.nz/en-NZ /AboutParl/GetInvolved/Contact/2/9/d/00PlibHvYrSayContact1-Contact-an-MP.htm

South African Members of Parliament can be located online at www.parliament.gov.za/live/content.php?Item_ID=36

When writing letters, be sure to make the following two points:

- Animal experimentation is an inherently violent and unethical practice, and you do not want your tax dollars used to support it.
- Testing on nonhuman animals is also bad science; therefore, funding for research into health and ecological effects should be redirected into using clinical, epidemiological, *in vitro*, and computer-modeling studies instead of laboratory experiments on animals.

Product Testing

- Only buy products from companies that don't test on animals! A comprehensive list is available at www.leapingbunny.org. Encourage your friends and family members to support humane companies as well.
- Let companies currently testing cosmetics on animals know that you will not buy their products until they stop. Most companies have toll-free numbers or websites you can use to contact them.
- Avoid pet foods that test on animals, including Iams, Eukanuba, and Natura Pet Products (owned by Procter & Gamble); Hill's Science Diet (owned by Colgate-Palmolive); Nestlé Purina/Friskies (Alpo, Bonio, Felix, Go Cat, Gourmet,

Omega Complete, Proplan, Spillers, Vital Balance, and Winalot); and these brands from Pedigree/Masterfoods (owned by Mars Inc): Bounce, Cesar, Chappie, Frolic, James Wellbeloved, Katkins, Kitekat, Pal, Pedigree Chum, Royal Canin, Sheba, Techni-cal, and Whiskas. The majority of pet food brands available in the UK are produced by Nestlé Purina/Friskies and Pedigree/Masterfoods. Pedigree also manufactures Thomas rabbit food and Trill bird food.

For information on pet food companies that *do not* test on animals, please visit: www.iamscruelty.com/nottested.asp

www.peta.org.uk/features/non-animal-tested-companion-animal-food/

Education

A student who rejects dissection takes a brave stand in defense of animals. You have every right to refuse to do something you believe is morally wrong, and your decision deserves respect from your classmates, teachers, parents, and school administrators. Here are some tips:

- When starting the new school term, determine when the dissection will take place and start the objection process as soon as possible. You may find that it takes several weeks before everything is resolved.
- When talking with your instructor, state your reasons for refusing to dissect. Emphasize that you cannot comfortably participate in dissection because of the values and beliefs you hold. Ask your instructor to respond as soon as possible to your request for a lab or other exercise without dissection. If he or she refuses your request, take your concern to the appropriate department head or dean.
- Suggest alternatives that will allow you to gain the same

knowledge as your classmates who participate in the dissection. Most students do not accept watching other students dissect as an alternative, as this puts them in the position of participating in the use of animals as educational tools. You should expect to be tested on the same material as the other students, provided it does not include a dissected animal, and you should not be penalized for doing an alternative project.

- Involve other students who oppose dissection and approach your instructor or department head as a group.
- It may help to put your statements in writing, either to help you speak with your instructor or to give directly to him or her to read before you discuss the matter. Keep a copy of any written statement you give to your instructor.
- Use the school media, especially the campus newspaper and radio station, as a forum for discussion. Introduce the ethical issues surrounding dissection at student government meetings.
- In the US, the National Anti-Vivisection Society offers a toll-free hotline for students who want to use alternatives to animals in life science courses without compromising their scientific ambitions: 1-800-922-FROG.
- For advice in Australia, contact Humane Research Australia at info@humaneresearch.org.au

You will also find these anti-dissection websites helpful:

www.dissectionalternatives.org/
www.teachkind.org/dissectalt.asp
www.frogsarecool.com/
www.humaneresearch.org.au/
www.h-ed.com.au/
www.humanelearning.info
www.animalexperiments.info

For a list of veterinary medical schools that offer alternatives, go to: www.animalearn.org/studentcenter_vetmed05.php

Donate your body to science, thereby saving animals from vivisection. Contact these organizations for more information:

Australia

Each State in Australia has its own Transplantation and Anatomy Act, and each Act enables people to bequeath their bodies for anatomical examination. Contact your nearest medical university for details.

Canada

Trillium Gift of Life Network – www.giftoflife.on.ca

New Zealand

Department of Anatomy
Auckland School of Medicine
Private Bag 92019
Auckland
Phone: 09 373 7599 ext 86703

Department of Anatomy and Structural Biology
Otago Medical School
PO Box 913
Dunedin
Phone: 0800 580500

United Kingdom

The Human Tissue Authority – www.hta.gov.uk

United States

Anatomy Gifts Registry – www.anatomygifts.org

Military Research

Around the globe, militaries' use of animals is as secretive as it is entrenched. But whether it's testing weapons or practicing battle-field surgery, their activities are funded by *your* tax dollars, so let your elected officials know how you feel. Use the websites listed above under "biomedical research."

Finally, I encourage you to adopt a rabbit from a shelter or rescue group. The more that people can see these wonderful animals as companions and not test subjects (or food or fur trim), the better educated the public will be. But first find out if a bunny is right for your home. A partial list of organizations you can contact for more information includes:

House Rabbit Society (US)
www.rabbit.org

Rabbit Rehome (UK)
www.rabbitrehome.org.uk

Rabbit Rescue Inc. (Canada)
http://rabbitrescue.ca

The Rabbit Sanctuary (Australia)
http://rabbitrescuesanctuary.blogspot.com

Rabbitron (US)
www.rabbitron.com

RabbitWise (US)
www.rabbitwise.org

SaveABunny (my local group, which rescued Nibbles and Sophie, to whom this book is dedicated)
www.saveabunny.org

Warren Peace Bunny Sanctuary (Canada)
http://wpbs.blogspot.com

Chapter 4

Poachers, Pills, and Politics:
The Persecution of Wild Animals

Mr. Speaker, I would like to see the six million seals, or whatever number is out there, killed and sold, or destroyed or burned. I do not care what happens to them. What [the fishermen] wanted was to have the right to go out and kill the seals. They have that right, and the more they kill the better I will love it.

—John Efford, former Minister of Canada's Department of Fisheries and Oceans

Blinking hard in the dim light, Jill Robinson steps into the quiet basement of a bear farm in China's Guangdong Province. It is 1993, and Jill has slipped away from a group of Japanese tourists who are being guided through the main grounds upstairs. For years she has heard about "bear farming," but as an animal advocate living in Asia, she wants to witness for herself the practice of draining bile from the gallbladders of live bears for use in traditional Chinese medicine.[1] As she moves deeper into the dark room, Jill is startled by a noise. *Pop-pop-pop-pop.* The din becomes louder and more frantic the nearer she gets to its source. Her vision now adjusted to the gloomy cellar, she sees them: dozens of endangered Asiatic black bears, each confined to a metal cage barely larger than the animal's body. The bears lie helpless in their barred coffins, fluids oozing from bloody wounds in their bellies, passing their lives in darkness. Jill has discovered the bear farm's "milking" facility.

"I was horrified by what I found," she says two decades later. "It was a torture chamber—a hellhole for animals, with the caged victims groaning in agony from the impacts of crude surgery and bile extraction. I took pictures of bears who had been declawed, had their teeth smashed out, were scarred from where their wounded bodies had grown into the cage bars, and had catheters and gaping holes in their abdomens from where the bile dripped out."

When Jill stepped within arm's length of some cages, the popping grew more frenzied, and she realized the sounds were guttural vocalizations of the bears, who were crying out in distress. To them, this Englishwoman was there to hurt them—not a surprising notion, considering that pain was all these bears had ever experienced at the hands of humans. As she looked around the basement and the cages supported off the floor, someone touched her shoulder. Jill turned and was face to face with a female bear reaching out with her paw. "Instinctively, but stupidly, I took it," she says. "She didn't hurt me as she had every right to do, but gently squeezed my fingers and looked into my eyes. I've never forgotten that moment, and to this day in presentations to children, I tell them the importance of receiving 'messages' and that ignoring or listening to them can change or shape our lives."[2]

That moment certainly changed Jill, who was determined to put a stop to the bear-bile industry. She founded Animals Asia soon afterward and saving Asiatic black bears, also called moon bears because of the large white crescent on their chests, has been one of her organization's chief projects. Since Jill began her campaign in the 1990s, the Chinese government has closed more than 40 bear farms, and nearly 300 bears have been released into the care of Animals Asia's Moon Bear Rescue Centre in Chengdu; more than 100 bears, meanwhile, are recovering in the group's sanctuary in Tam Dao National Park, near Hanoi, Vietnam.

Saving Bears

Asiatic black bears are natural forest dwellers who use their strong limbs and sharp claws to climb trees, where they can avoid contact with predators. Nature's most relentless predator, however, can simply shoot the treed animal and then use her remains to suit his purpose. Thirty years ago, killing bears outright was the preferred method for acquiring their bile, which is prized throughout Asia for its purported ability to treat just about every human ailment from the sniffles to epilepsy.[3] Before the 1980s, practitioners of traditional Chinese medicine (TCM) extracted bile from the gallbladders of dead bears, who were poached nearly to extinction. The Chinese government then endorsed the practice of bear farming, which they believed would be better for the bears in the long run. "That well-intentioned initiative was deeply flawed after bear farming boomed and we saw farmers continuing to take bears from the wild to replenish their stock," says Jill. "We also saw consumers preferring the 'real thing' and persisting in their demand for the wild-caught bile of poached bears."[4]

China's healers have a 3,000-year history of using bear bile, and it is available as powders, ointments, and pills. While its curative powers are likely overstated, bear bile does contain high concentrations of ursodeoxycholic acid, the active ingredient Western medicine uses to treat patients with the liver-wasting disease primary biliary cirrhosis.[5] Fortunately, Asian communities are beginning to accept plant-based alternatives, thanks to public-outreach campaigns explaining that bear bile conflicts with the TCM principle of being in harmony with nature. Unfortunately, as the market for bear bile in TCM declines, many farmers have introduced additional bear bile products, such as shampoo, wine, and tea. The trade in gallbladders is also extremely lucrative. In 1970, 1 kilo of bear gallbladder would sell for about US$200. Twenty years later, the price had jumped to between US$3,000 and US$5,000. Walk into a legal TCM market in Hong Kong today, and a kilo of gallbladder will go for as much as US$50,000.[6] That's an awful lot of incentive, and it's one of the biggest obstacles to combating the trade.

The demand for bile has led to such severe cruelty that bears killed quickly are actually the fortunate ones. In Chinese bear farms, the animals may be confined to constricting cages for as long as 30 years, often growing right into the bars. The bears frequently have their teeth cut back to gum level (exposing pulp and nerves) and the tips of their paws hacked off to stop the claws from growing, all to

215

make it safer for farmers to milk their bile. The psychological toll on farmed bears is obvious, with scars and open wounds from continually banging their heads against the bars. This stereotypic behavior is one of the key indicators of stress in animals held in captivity and a sign of ruthlessly poor welfare conditions.[7]

In Vietnam, where fewer than 100 Asiatic black bears remain in the wild and some 4,000 are confined in farms, the animals may suffer two methods of bile extraction. According to Animals Asia, bears either undergo a crude surgery every three months to remove the bile from their bladders—usually dying from infection after the fourth operation—or they are restrained and repeatedly jabbed with long hypodermic needles until the gallbladder is located. A pump is then attached to the needle and bile is drawn into a large glass bottle. Though the surgical method is no longer widely practiced, the latter procedure is as terribly unhygienic, and bears often suffer a lingering, agonizing death from peritonitis (abdominal inflammation).[8]

Despite outreach efforts and working with the government, there are at least 7,000 bears on 68 farms throughout China.[9] Many smaller farms have consolidated, and Animals Asia fears the number of bears could be as high as 10,000. Rehabilitating rescued bears takes months, and though they can never be returned to their native habitat, they have a permanent home with Animals Asia.

Wildlife Trade

Asiatic black bears are considered endangered under Appendix I of the 1973 United Nations Convention on International Trade in Endangered Species of Wild Fauna and Flora (CITES), which covers about 900 species and prohibits their international trade for commercial purposes.[10] Practitioners of TCM in countries such as Australia, Canada, the UK, and the US manage to keep supplies of bear bile stocked with the aid of smugglers, who transport the contraband in their personal luggage. This is but one type of crime in the global trade in illegal wildlife. Animals are either captured in the wild and sold live (as exotic pets, biomedical research subjects, or to zoos, safari parks, or hunting ranches), or they are killed and sold for their body parts (used as medical ingredients, food, fashion, ornamental objects, etc.).

The biggest markets for wildlife trafficking, according to the International Fund for Animal Welfare (IFAW), are the United States, China, the European Union, and Japan,[11] and it is generally considered by law-enforcement agencies to be the third most valuable illegal commerce in the world, rivaled only by illegal drugs and weapons. But that's just the economics of the trade, and it doesn't consider the animals. "Nobody asks how much murder costs the economy," says author Bryan Christy, who investigates the underground world of reptile smuggling in his book *The Lizard King*. Christy observes that the gravity of a crime, whether it's homicide or pilfering wildlife, is not a function of its economic impact. "What we really need to focus on is how many animals and plants are poached in a year, how many species are critically endangered, and how many lives are lost to poor transport, housing, etc., among wildlife, whether traded legally or illegally. Focus on the dollar value frames the issue as if wildlife is only worth caring about if it costs a lot. It's absolutely the wrong value system."[12]

The exotic-animal trade typically works like so: A local hunter snares an animal in a biologically rich nation and sells her to a broker, who takes his cut when he passes her on to a smuggler, who sneaks the animal into another country, where he sells her (if she survives) to a dealer in the private pet market, who finally sells her to a collector. By the time an animal goes from the forest into the hands of an affluent customer on the other side of the world, the price paid for her increases dramatically. A Hyacinth macaw captured in South America, for example, might earn the hunter a few dollars, but a buyer in Europe could pay up to US$20,000 for this beautiful, endangered bird. Indeed, the economic model of supply and demand also applies to wildlife trafficking—the rarer the animal, the more a customer is willing to pay—and it is disrupting biodiversity and hastening the demise of endangered species everywhere.

It is estimated that two-thirds of the animals smuggled alive from their habitat die in transit,[13] often from suffocation, thanks in large part to the inhumane methods used to secretly transport them on planes. Animals are bound and stuffed into toilet paper tubes, Thermos® bottles, cigarette packs, and stockings; they're hidden inside hollowed-out books, prosthetic limbs, and teddy bears; they're strapped to smugglers' legs and stashed under wigs. One courier bound for Dubai was nabbed at the airport in Bangkok with two leopards, two panthers, an Asiatic black bear, and two macaque monkeys—all crammed into a suitcase with his clothes. Fortunately for these animals, they were rescued before the suitcase had been loaded onto the plane.[14] Another smuggler made it out of Lima, Peru, on an airliner with 18 endangered titi monkeys stuffed into a girdle around his waist; two of the monkeys were dead when the plane landed in Mexico City.[15] Then there's the Swedish tourist traveling from Thailand to Australia who was arrested at Sydney Airport with eight snakes in his pants: four venomous king cobras and four emerald tree boas. The boas survived the nine-hour flight; the cobras did not.[16] Not that smugglers don't make an attempt to keep their contraband alive and well. In 2009, a writer for *Smithsonian* was offered a parakeet at a market in Ecuador. The writer asked hypothetically how he would get the bird onto an airplane. "Give it vodka and put it in your pocket," the seller said. "It will be quiet."[17]

Even upon reaching their ultimate destination, animals continue to suffer. An exotic animal might end up being the victim of a canned hunt or as a breeder in a captive-mammal hunting operation. He might be reduced to a tourist attraction as the denizen of a roadside menagerie, an unaccredited zoo, or a theme park. Locked into an enclosure completely inadequate for his needs, he might not even have enough space to turn around and could endure years of neglect. He may well be sold to a research facility or to a backyard hobbyist with little knowledge of wildlife—both scenarios could result in him living out his remaining years within a tiny, barren cage. According to a 2003 exposé in *Audubon* magazine, "Some wild pets, especially monkeys and apes, are adopted as surrogate children. They're christened, bottle-fed, diapered, dressed, and wheeled in baby carriages. But as the animals mature, the clothes restrict motion, atrophying muscles. Toilet training fails, and they begin to throw their feces. They masturbate in public, so they are spayed or castrated or confined in cellars and attics. They bite, so their teeth are extracted. They catch human diseases—measles, mumps, TB, shigellosis, and hepatitis A—so many die. Survivors are often taken back to the pet dealer, who allows that while he can't give a refund, he'll be glad to find the pet 'a happy home,' then sells it again."[18]

Cute exotic babies such as chimpanzees, kangaroos, and tigers grow into potentially dangerous adults, so no one should be surprised when they act on their natures and attack humans; these are not, after all, domesticated dogs and cats. Yet when tragedy inevitably occurs, the "pets" are frequently killed for simply being what they are: wild animals.[19] "Ironically, people's fascination with and deep need for animals fuels this lamentable trade," says Jim Mason of the Best Friends Animal Society. "Our long alienation from animals and our sense that wild nature is nearly gone stirs many people to want a last piece of it—a souvenir of sorts—embodied in a wild animal."[20]

Catching Animals

Birds are the most common victims of the illegal wildlife trade, and the methods used to catch them vary from country to country. Poachers in Africa and Latin America use nets, which is one of the few tools that can effectively target a species. Other techniques are less discriminate and usually result in the capture, injury, or death of other birds. Nylon loops strung around perches entangle any bird who comes into contact with them, leading to serious harm when the animal struggles to escape. Glue spread onto branches ensures that no bird leaves unharmed, including predatory birds who also get stuck when attracted to the trapped prey; both may languish there for a day or more before the poacher arrives, if ever. An even more haphazard practice is wing shooting; the goal is to wound the wing of a bird with pellets fired from a shotgun. Hunters blast into whole flocks, hoping to knock down a valuable bird or two and disable them for easy capture. Such an arbitrary and callous approach means more birds end up being killed than caught. Finally, one of the most environmentally destructive methods, especially popular with parrot poachers, is to cut down a nesting tree and steal baby birds. Wildlife dealers favor young parrots, since the birds more quickly bond with humans and can be taught to "talk" more easily.[21]

In targeting reptiles, insects, amphibians, and mammals for the black market, poachers possess an equally cavalier attitude. They'll employ nets, snares, or any other type of trap to get the job done. Leopard poachers in India deploy heavy wire traps along game trails; the devices, built from motorcycle clutch cables, tighten and cut through the animal's flesh and cause most of the leopard deaths in the state of Punjab.[22] To kill a larger animal such as a hippopotamus, poachers create snares with winch cables, guide wires from utility poles, or even the cable fencing that surrounds wildlife preserves where the hippos live.[23] And if the target is a baby elephant or primate, hunters will simply shoot the mother and take her orphaned offspring.

Making a Killing

When it's a body part such as tusks, skin, or horns the poachers are after, animals are usually gunned down. But gunfire can attract the attention of wildlife rangers and game wardens, so other lethal methods are being employed to suit the convenience of poachers. A favorite weapon is the poisoned arrow, which is growing in popularity in Kenya.[24] The toxin, made from acocanthera shrubs, can be applied to arrows and spears and has no antidote, as some ivory poachers in Tsavo East National Park discovered. After using the poison to kill an elephant for his tusks, they cooked and ate some of their victim's flesh; one poacher died and the others became severely ill.[25]

In addition to lacing spears and arrows with deadly toxins, some poachers construct wooden frames studded with long, poison-tipped nails and set the traps along forest paths, waiting for an animal to step on them. Poison is also placed in food, such as pineapple or cabbage, which poachers then leave for animals. Knowing an elephant's love of salt, they'll wrap an acid-filled plastic bottle with banana leaves soaked in saline and hang the bundle from a tree. Elephants find even the smell of salt irresistible, and they'll eat the bundle whole, releasing the acid inside them. In the case of a big cat or other carnivore, poachers will slaughter a chicken or goat, fill her stomach with poison, and leave the animal to be eaten. However the poison is administered, it almost always results in a lingering, agonizing death, and poachers generally don't wait until the animal is dead before they begin the gruesome work of harvesting body parts.

Pit poaching is a much older and more time-consuming procedure that entails digging a large hole, covering it with foliage, and waiting for a heavy animal to step on the camouflage and fall into the abyss. Hunters then murder the trapped animal, remove his horns or other parts, and bury him in the same pit. This is a labor-intensive scheme, however, putting the poachers at higher risk of getting caught.

In spotlighting (also called deer jacking, pit lamping, or jack lighting), night hunters in remote rural areas use high-intensity lights to stun and immobilize a deer long enough to shoot him, usually from a vehicle. The practice, illegal in the US, is popular among poachers who simply get a thrill from killing and will just leave the buck or doe behind.[26] Even licensed hunters abhor these poachers. In an otherwise profanity-laden hunter's forum responding to spotlighting, one poster wrote: "Loaded rifles across the seat, a high intensity light plugged into the cigarette lighter and a case of beer are the tools of the trade. ... It is not a sport it is a slaughter. There is no convincing such individuals to stop because they were not raised to know right from wrong. I hope the animals they have killed will be standing at the gates to heaven with antlers at the ready barring their entry and stomping their feet to announce to some hellish place that one more lowlife is coming down."[27] (Text left uncorrected.)

Mechanical traps and wire snares—perfectly legal in many US states—are among the most inhumane tactics poachers use, resulting in the victim dying from asphyxiation, dehydration, or starvation. The most common leg trap is manufactured commercially and seizes an animal with steel jaws that are activated by powerful springs when the release mechanism is stepped on. Tethered to the ground or a tree, these traps thwart the animal's attempts to get away; in some cases, she may attempt to gnaw her foot off to escape. Another spring-loaded trap, called the Conibear, is designed to catch the head of a small animal and quickly choke him to death or break his neck. Set and baited to kill indiscriminately, however, these traps often result in extremely slow and painful deaths, as many dog guardians have witnessed. When Grizzly, a 4-year-old Rottweiler, came running back to his Anchorage, Alaska, home with his head trapped in a Conibear, he was shrieking and thrashing wildly, covered in blood. He died on his way to the pet hospital, where it took four people to pry the trap from his head.[28] Snares made from wire cable are even more widespread. These are fashioned in the shape of a noose and tied to a tree. The snare catches animals around the neck, causing strangulation as they try to flee.

The newest poaching tactic involves tapping into a high-voltage power line and placing a live wire across a path where an animal will come into contact with it. This approach has been used to electrocute elephants, rhinos, leopards, tigers, deer, bears, peacocks, boars, and even (albeit accidentally) a few poachers.[29]

Whaling

Perhaps the most infamous example of profiting from wildlife is the remorseless whale slaughter that takes place each year in the Southern Ocean Whale Sanctuary surrounding Antarctica. Although many people are aware that Japan conducts this hunt, there remains a large segment of the public under the mistaken impression that efforts by Greenpeace and the Save the Whales! campaign of the 1970s put an end to the massacre of the Earth's largest mammals. And those who are ordinarily some of the most environmentally aware—young adults—are among the most confused. A study released in 2010 revealed that US college students are surprisingly uninformed about the status of whale conservation and US policy on commercial whaling; indeed, fewer than one-quarter of respondents said that they had ever heard of the International Whaling Commission (IWC), the institution responsible for the management of whale species worldwide.[30] Contrary to what some believe, commercial whaling is alive and well.

One of Japan's favorite hunting areas, the Southern Ocean Whale Sanctuary encompasses 19 million square miles (50 million square kilometers). It was established by the IWC as a haven for whales to recover from exploitation suffered in the 19th and 20th centuries, when many cetaceans were hunted to near extinction in pursuit of whale oil and whale bone. Since 1920, blue whales have declined in number by 96 percent, for example, and fin whales by 92 percent.[31] The IWC had already declared a moratorium on open-sea commercial whaling in 1986, but Iceland, Japan, and Norway—countries with entrenched whaling traditions—have defied the ban.[32] The commission set up the Southern Ocean as a protected area in 1994, with 23 of the 24 IWC-member nations voting in favor of the sanctuary. Japan opposed it, and has continued to hunt in the Southern Ocean by invoking a controversial exemption clause that allows killing the animals for "scientific research."[33] (Japan launched its scientific whaling program a year after the 1986 moratorium and has yet to produce a single peer-reviewed scientific paper.) Japanese biologists estimate that whales consume three to five times the amount of fish caught by the world's fishing fleets, and should thus be studied on economic and scientific grounds.[34] So far, about the biggest finding in their research of whales is that they eat krill.[35]

Japan's annual slaughter of whales has become an international point of contention, with conservationists and animal advocates loudly calling on the Japanese to halt its lethal research program. No anti-whaling organization has been more vociferous, or confrontational, than the Sea Shepherd Conservation Society. Every January and February finds the group and its all-volunteer crew plying the frigid Southern Ocean actively interfering with vessels from the Institute for Cetacean Research (ICR) as they search for whales to kill and "study." A registered nonprofit, ICR claims it has no commercial stake in the hunts, yet whale meat from their government-subsidized "research" continues to be sold in Japanese seafood markets. In 2013, Japan's fisheries minister publicly admitted his country is killing protected whales for food, vowing they'll never stop.[36] And though the spoils of the hunt are supposedly only available in the Land of the Rising Sun, whale meat sold illegally at a California sushi restaurant in 2010 was identified as having come from Japan's lethal research, suggesting that the meat from ICR hunts is even flowing into the global black market.[37] It's also apparently lining the pantries and pockets of the researchers on board. In 2010, two unnamed whalers came forward saying they witnessed crew members carrying large cuts of meat off the ship and even confronted them. "It happened on the container on the bridge," says one of the whalers. "I had to check the temperature every day and when I went in there, there was a staff member from the Institute of Cetacean Research packing something. When I yelled, 'What are you doing?' he then tried to hide the package by spreading his arms out. It was red meat from the tail. That is the highest quality whale meat."[38] The second whistleblower says at least one crew member built a house from the profits of the meat he took, while another used the money he earned to buy a car.[39]

To many animal advocates, killing an animal for food, clothing, entertainment, or even scientific gain is cruel. Others believe killing an animal is acceptable, provided the animal does not suffer in the process. But what constitutes "suffering"? Evidence is mounting that whales possess self-awareness, and this leads to a capacity to experience not just physical pain, but emotional distress. Neurobiologists such as Georges Chapouthier, director of the Emotion Centre at Pierre and Marie Curie University in Paris, say that whales rank right up there with some higher mammals in their ability to suffer. "Suffering supposes a certain level of cognitive functioning," he says, and data now suggests whales have that.[40]

The question of whether a whale suffers specifically during a hunt was answered when scientists from IFAW analyzed extensive video of whaling by the Japanese whaling fleet in the Southern Ocean and published their findings in 2007. The video depicts 16 minke whales being hunted and shot with high-powered harpoons guns; only two were hit in the brain and died instantly. The other whales, upon being harpooned, endured lengthy deaths lasting up to half an hour; the average time to death for those not killed outright was 10 minutes.[41] Discussing the death of one whale the team observed, IFAW scientist and whale expert Vassili Papastavrou says, "For some time the whale is seen breathing quickly at the surface. It is then winched up to the ship by the tail and is clearly still alive and thrashing around. It likely died from asphyxiation because its head was kept under water. This is how a whale was killed with observation boats in plain view. So what happens when no one is watching?"[42]

Sea Shepherd's goal is simple: disrupt the Japanese whaling fleet and turn their hunts into yen-swallowing sinkholes. The group's direct-action tactics include tossing stink bombs made of butyric acid onto whaling ships, sabotaging the enemy's propellers with cables, and using a Sea Shepherd vessel to block the transport of a whale from a harpoon boat to Japan's factory ship, where whale remains are processed. All these efforts eat into whaling profits by forcing the Japanese to buy and maintain security and defense systems, pay for surveillance flights to track the activists, expend additional fuel running from Sea Shepherd vessels, and, best of all, by cutting their kill quotas. Year after year, the whaling fleet returns to port with hundreds fewer whales than they set out to slaughter, and they place blame directly on Sea Shepherd.[43]

"All commercial whaling was ruled illegal in 1986 by the International Whaling Commission," says Paul Watson, who founded Sea Shepherd in 1981. "So commercial whaling is illegal. What Japan is doing, though, is they're targeting endangered whales in an established international whale sanctuary in violation of that commercial moratorium. And they're in violation of the Antarctic Treaty, the Convention for International Trade in Endangered Species, and they're also in contempt of the Australian Federal Court, which ruled they couldn't take whales in the Australian Antarctic Territory." All Sea Shepherd is doing, he says, is intervening to uphold the international law because governments don't have the economic or political will to do that.[44]

Did You Know?

There are whales alive today who were born before *Moby-Dick* was published in 1851.[45]

Fighting the Trade

Even those with the wherewithal to pursue wildlife crimes may find it frustrating. Not only is it difficult to apprehend those who raid the planet's forests, oceans, reserves, and rivers, but the higher up the supply chain a criminal reigns, the more likely he is to remain untouched. And when a smuggler *is* brought to justice, the penalty is often relatively light. Hisayoshi Kojima, who described himself as "the world's most wanted butterfly smuggler," received 21 months in prison when he was finally caught in 2006. His black-market butter-flies (many of whom he raised and killed himself) commanded huge sums, and Kojima got rich enough to maintain homes in Kyoto and Los Angeles. "He was able to produce butterflies for sale that are almost never seen in commercial trade, or even made available to university collections," says Special Agent Ed Newcomer of the United States Fish and Wildlife Service. "During the last months of our investigation, Kojima offered to sell me a variety of species of endangered or protected butterfly that had a collective value of more than US$294,000."[46]

To catch Kojima, Newcomer engaged in a three-year undercover operation, assuming a covert identity, gaining the smuggler's trust, and becoming his apprentice. He always wore a wire when talking with Kojima, and he was meticulous about collecting photos and other evidence to bring down the man who bragged that no cop or customs agent could stop him. In the end—he was nabbed at LAX with a box full of butterflies—the case against Kojima was so solid that he didn't even argue the charges.

When not posing as a potential buyer or some other confederate in crime, Newcomer looks like a federal agent right out of Central Casting; indeed, the trim former state prosecutor bears more than a passing resemblance to Kevin Costner as Elliott Ness in *The Untouchables*, down to the sharp suit and government-issue haircut. Not that you'll find his image in print or online. "I'd be busted down to management if my picture ever found its way onto Google," says the man who relies on his anonymity to catch bad guys, but he allows me to photograph several confiscated animal skins and ivory tusks spread across a large table. The skins, shrouds of a being's final moment on Earth, make me feel particularly sad. There's the skin of a dog imported from China. Two almond-shaped holes where the eyes were give the skin an eerie, Halloween-mask feel. The skin has been expertly dyed to resemble that of a leopard, and it lies next to a genuine leopard skin. Neatly folded beside the dog skin is a large swath of elephant hide. It feels surprisingly soft, and

Newcomer explains the skin is often used for pillow cases.[47]

Newcomer says the trade in wild animals and their body parts has become even more profitable thanks to the Internet, which has a devastating impact on wildlife because it has created a demand in the market for illegal specimens. He uses the online auction of an endangered Asian elephant head to illustrate his point. "Five people bid on something and one person wins. What do the other four people do? All of a sudden, they need to find themselves an Asian elephant head or some other body part." Poachers and smugglers are using Skype and online newspaper posts to aid their crimes, but Newcomer says Craigslist is the worst. "It's the Wild West of animal trafficking," since anyone can post a free ad and easily hide their identity.

One particular species imperiled by the Internet is a little brown forest dweller from Southeast Asia known as the slow loris. With a docile nature, plump body, and the large eyes of a Disney character, slow lorises have become a sensation on YouTube, where videos depict the animals in pet stores clutching cocktail umbrellas and being tickled. Such videos have kids throughout Japan, the Middle East, the UK, and the US coveting slow lorises, who are not only endangered and illegal to own but the world's only poisonous primates; as a result, traffickers commonly rip out the animals' teeth with pliers before selling them.[48] True to their name, slow lorises are sluggish, making it easy for poachers to steal the infants from their parents and then sell them at open-air markets in Indonesia for as little as US$20. It's now estimated that some 90 percent of these animals have been wiped out.[49]

Gorilla War

The most visible defenders of wildlife are several thousand forest rangers, who combat poaching in ecologically vulnerable landscapes throughout the world. "The work of rangers is often lonely, far from towns and villages, and often considered on the periphery of law enforcement," says John M. Sellar, senior enforcement officer for

CITES. "Many times, rangers are unable to call upon even the most basic logistics or support systems provided to operational law enforcement units."[50] Sellar adds that wildlife trafficking has become so lucrative that it's not unusual for rangers in Africa to engage in firefights against poachers who are armed with automatic weapons and rocket-propelled grenade launchers.

Not surprisingly, such gangs are well funded and often backed by the same transnational syndicates that support the drug trade and other smuggling operations. In fact, wildlife trafficking isn't merely connected to organized crime, it is itself an organized crime, complete with the internal structure, detailed planning, sophisticated document forgery, use of violence, and enormous profits that are the hallmarks of crime networks. Effectively targeting this kind of criminal enterprise is understandably challenging. Poaching is difficult to detect, criminals are highly motivated, and the hunters may even turn out to be members of a neighboring country's militia who regard endangered animals as just another cash crop to finance their agenda.[51] It is also extremely dangerous: the IFAW estimates that some 100 rangers are killed by poachers in Africa every year.[52]

The fighting has been especially violent in the Democratic Republic of the Congo (DRC), a war zone where more than 150 rangers have given their lives in recent years protecting eastern lowland gorillas and the country's iconic mountain gorillas from poachers. Some gorillas are sold to the pet trade, while others are killed for human consumption. This has led to a precipitous decline in great ape populations, especially among eastern lowland gorillas, whose numbers have dropped from an estimated 17,000 in the mid-1990s to about 5,000 today.[53] A recent report co-authored by the UN Environment Programme and INTERPOL warns that gorillas could disappear from Africa's Greater Congo Basin by the mid-2020s unless sufficient action is taken to halt poaching and protect their habitat.[54] The situation is graver than the UN predicted in 2002, when they estimated that only 10 percent of the gorillas' habitat (rainforests) would remain by 2032. That was before China's unforeseen demand for timber and minerals, much of which they now extract from Africa.

One promising consequence of stepped-up ranger patrols and other conservation work is the comeback of mountain gorillas, who survive in only two small patches of habitat: Uganda's Bwindi Impenetrable National Park and the fog-shrouded rainforests of the Virunga Mountains, a volcanic range straddling Rwanda, Uganda, and the eastern DRC. Between 1960, when biologist George Schaller estimated the mountain gorillas' population to be 450 in the Virungas, to 1973, when Dian Fossey and her colleagues put the number at 275, nearly half of these critically endangered animals were lost to poachers and disease. By 1981, the population had dropped to 254. But that decade heralded a turnaround, thanks in large part to Fossey's protection efforts, and a 1986 census revealed 293 mountain gorillas.[55] Meanwhile, Schaller believed there to be 120 to 180 mountain gorillas in the Impenetrable National Park as of 1960—a population estimated at 95 to 135 individuals 19 years later,[56] but that had jumped to 340 by 2003.[57] The most recent census, taken in 2010, counted 786 mountain gorillas left in the world.[58] While this number is still perilously low and the population remains fragile, it is an encouraging trend that we would not have seen without the heroic efforts of forest rangers and gorilla conservationists.

No Going Home

Unfortunately, there are not many happy endings for animals smuggled from their native habitats, even for those animals eventually recovered by authorities. Because the animals may have been exposed to a variety of diseases and parasites that might be passed on to other animals, repatriating them to their homes can be a dilemma. "Ideally, confiscated animals would be safely returned to the wild, but this frequently proves impossible," says Michael Hutchins, executive director and CEO of The Wildlife Society.[59] Consequently, animals may end up remaining in the country where they were recovered, provided an appropriate zoo, safari park, or rescue center can be found. According to Hutchins, "if an animal cannot be placed in a facility that meets the minimum requirements for its care, then the most responsible and humane alternative is euthanasia."[60]

Although both CITES and the International Union for the Conservation of Nature strongly recommend that confiscated wildlife be repatriated or at least rehabilitated and maintained,[61] smuggled animals are rarely returned and are all too frequently killed. "Almost every animal seized by the US Fish and Wildlife Service that I discuss in *The Lizard King* died," says Bryan Christy. "No one has done a study of the survival rate among wildlife confiscated by law enforcement in the US, but the mortality rate is in my experience very high. Except for especially rare animals which can be handed off to zoos, high-volume animals almost certainly die. Same is true around the world, though in some places those animals are sold to wildlife traders."[62]

Regrettably, the CITES treaty does not offer specific guidelines for authorities to use in finding appropriate homes for animals, and in addition to euthanasia as an option, CITES condones the sale or transfer of confiscated animals to commercial captive breeders or universities and research facilities. "CITES has failed wild animals because it does not provide for issues of ethics and compassion," writes Michelè Pickover of Animal Rights Africa. "It remains silent on the basic ethical question of whether it is even appropriate to engage in international trade. It appears to be concerned not so much with protecting species as with allowing trade in endangered ones, which makes it almost Orwellian in character. ... It operates on the premise that wild animals, even endangered ones, have an economic value and can be commercially traded, and because it accepts the concept of sustainable use as a way of managing wild populations, it regulates rather than prohibits trade."[63] Michelè adds that CITES is so weak and riddled with loopholes that many animal protection groups refer to it as "the animal dealer's charter."

Managing the Unmanageable

As animal populations go, coyotes are among the most adaptable and resilient—qualities that for more than 200 years have only exacerbated the contentious relationship North Americans have with these animals. Revered by some and reviled by others, coyotes range through much of Alaska and Canada, from the western United States to the Atlantic seaboard, and south through Mexico to Panama. Coyotes, once the alpha dogs of the Great Plains, are now being spotted in Florida's urban landscapes.[64] With a keen sense of smell, superb eyesight, and excellent hearing, coyotes are efficient predators who can detect prey up to a mile away and will eat just about anything, even transforming a city landfill into a buffet. They primarily hunt small animals such as mice, gophers, and rabbits, although as early European settlers pushed west and introduced cows to the land, the heavy-hoofed bovines grazed and trampled the vegetation that prey animals need to survive. In response, hungry coyotes turned their attention to the sheep, goats, and calves being conveniently fattened on remote pastures. They've also been known to consume domestic and feral cats, as well as little dogs.

Humanity's competition with coyotes for food and territory has only become more acute as civilization has expanded. Ranchers, farmers, and even governments have since declared war on coyotes, according to Camilla Fox, founding director of Project Coyote and wildlife consultant for the Animal Welfare Institute. "The coyote is the most persecuted predator in North America today," she says. "It's estimated that on average at least half a million coyotes are killed every year in the US alone—one per minute—by federal, state, and local governments and by private individuals." Because the animals are unprotected in most states, landowners are generally allowed to kill "nuisance" coyotes without a permit. Moreover, says Camilla, "Most states set no limit on the number of coyotes who may be killed, nor do they regulate the killing method."[65]

The US Department of Agriculture (USDA) is the main federal agency dedicated to coyote elimination through their ironically-named Wildlife Services program, which has nothing to do with servicing wildlife and everything to do with ensuring that vocal livestock owners and corporations earn a profit. In addition to coyotes, who make up about 90 percent of Wildlife Services' victims, the program targets badgers, bears, foxes, mountain lions, and other native carnivores, killing about 100,000 animals a year.[66] They've even been known to kill pets and endangered species. Gary Strader, a former hunter for Wildlife Services, used to catch coyotes with neck snares, and he recalls the time he'd accidentally strangled to death a federally protected bird. "I called my supervisor and said, 'I just caught a golden eagle and it's dead,'" says Strader. "He said, 'Did anybody see it?' I said, 'Geez, I don't think so.' He said, 'If you think nobody saw it, go get a shovel and bury it and don't say nothing to anybody.'"[67]

The lethal practices Wildlife Services uses to obliterate four-legged rivals from the land can be gruesomely cruel. Denning, for example, involves throwing carbon dioxide cartridges into a coyote den and, when the pups emerge, beheading them or smashing their skulls with shovels. Ignited canisters of sodium nitrate and charcoal—a deadly mixture—are another method; like exhaust fumes from a tailpipe, the resulting carbon monoxide is intended to asphyxiate the coyotes in their dens. The EPA warns that the highly combustible cartridges will burn with vigor until empty and could start a fire.[68] Indeed, Wildlife Services used to employ burning as a method to kill coyote pups, and since the species is unprotected in many states, it's not unlikely that a landowner today would put a lit match to gasoline or some other accelerant that has been sprayed into a den.

Among the most controversial coyote-execution methods is aerial gunning, in which sharpshooters and pilots hired by the USDA use helicopters and fixed-wing aircraft to chase down and fire upon predators. The targeted coyotes might be suspected of killing a rancher's livestock, or Wildlife Services might be trying to purge coyotes before farmed animals are brought into a grazing area. Either way, US taxpayers fund this program to protect the livelihoods of private sheep and cattle ranchers—and most have never even heard of it.

Animal advocates have long criticized aerial gunning as inhumane. "When they take that plane up, they kill every single coyote they can," says Strader, who worked with aerial gunning crews in Nevada. "If they come back and say, 'We only killed three coyotes,' they are not very happy. If they come back and say, 'Oh, we killed a hundred coyotes,' they're very happy. Some of the gunners are real good and kill coyotes every time. And other ones wound more than they kill. Who wants to see an animal get crippled and run around with its leg blown off? I saw that a lot."[69] Not only can strafing coyotes result in wounded animals who face a lingering death, but there is a psychological toll: loud gunfire and low-flying aircraft create fear, stress, and anxiety among all animals within earshot. Such noise can even damage the hearing of birds, deer, bighorn sheep, pronghorn, and other species, while the sudden presence of aircraft can cause survival responses that affect reproduction.[70] And when a lactating female coyote is shot, her dependent pups back at the den slowly die of starvation.

The tradition of killing coyotes, incidentally, is likely much less familiar to readers than the shooting of their canine cousin the wolf, thanks in large part to the efforts of former Alaska governor Sarah Palin—herself an avid hunter—who became notorious for encouraging airborne attacks on wolves in her state.[71] (Wolves are protected in many other parts of the US but were taken off the endangered species list in 2011.) Nevertheless, coyotes represent 83 percent of all the animals killed by aerial gunning.[72] How much of the public's money is underwriting this policy is anyone's guess. For more than a decade, the conservation group WildEarth Guardians has been petitioning the USDA to divulge its aerial gunning budget, even through the Freedom of Information Act and the intervention of Congressman Mark Udall, all to no avail. "Public accountability is not Wildlife Services' strong suit," says Wendy Keefover-Ring,

WildEarth Guardians' carnivore protection director.[73] What is known is that the overall amount allocated to the Wildlife Services program is just north of US$100 million a year.[74]

Other lethal measures include poisoning and trapping, both of which kill indiscriminately and with extreme suffering. Two common poisons used are sodium cyanide and sodium monofluroacetate, better known by its trade name, Compound 1080. In 1972, President Richard Nixon banned these substances for the control of predators in federal programs or on federal lands; however, following pressure from ranchers and the US Fish and Wildlife Service, the poisons were gradually reinstated by 1985. Today sodium cyanide is delivered using an M-44 device—an aluminum tube about the size and shape of a tent stake. Federal exterminators push the spring-operated device into the ground and bait the knob at the top with scent to lure predators. Once an animal tugs on it, the M-44 spews a cloud of sodium cyanide poison into his mouth and nose, and the cyanide powder reacts with the moisture in the animal's mouth, releasing hydrogen cyanide gas. Although its principal application is to kill coyotes and other predators, the M-44 may be triggered by anyone who disturbs it; consequently, these booby traps have also taken the lives of protected wildlife, including bald eagles, wolves, grizzly bears, and California condors, as well as dogs. The initial effects of sodium cyanide are dizziness, vomiting, and labored breathing, after which animals experience violent convulsions. It can take a coyote five minutes to finally succumb to the poison.

Still more appalling is the fate awaiting victims of Compound 1080. Developed as a toxic agent by German chemists in the 1930s, Compound 1080 was soon put to use killing rodents and coyotes in the United States.[75] It is now commonly delivered using the "livestock protection collar"—another ironic term, as it does nothing to protect the sheep or goat who wears the poison-filled rubber bladder around her neck; 1080 is released when a coyote or other predator bites into the collar while characteristically attacking

the animal's throat.[76] Death by Compound 1080 comes later—
sometimes 12 hours later—and it is agonizing. Montana rancher and
former State Senator Arnold Rieder describes a coyote's protracted
demise from 1080 as "a frenzy of howls and shrieks of pain, vomiting
and retching as froth collects on his tightly drawn lips... A scant six
to eight hours after eating his meal, Mr. Coyote is breathing his last,
racked by painful convulsions, [dying from] the most inhumane
poison ever conceived by man..."[77] Barbed wire and thorns also
puncture the collars, oozing deadly poison into the environment. In
addition to its horrific use on four-legged predators, Compound
1080 has been cited as a potential terrorist weapon, since it is
odorless, tasteless, relatively inexpensive, highly lethal, and has no
antidote; it could easily be added to food or water supplies.

Pre-dating poisons for targeting coyotes is the steel-jaw leghold
(or foothold) trap, which has operated on the same principle since its
invention in 1823: an animal steps onto a pan-tension device, the
spring-loaded jaws snap shut, and he is trapped in a vice-like grip,
sometimes for days. The pain of the steel jaws is excruciating. With
his talent for vivid description, author and Fund for Animals
founder Cleveland Amory put it this way: "Imagine having your
fingers crushed in a car door for 24 to 48 hours."[78] Naturally, most
animals desperately struggle to escape the anchored traps, thus
suffering fractures, torn tendons, blood loss, broken teeth, and self-
mutilation. Some die of starvation, exertion, exposure, or predation
before the trapper returns to kill them.[79] And, yes, animals have been
known to chew off part of a leg to free themselves.[80] Like poisons,
leghold traps do not distinguish between coyotes and other victims,
so they frequently snare or kill birds, reptiles, endangered species,
and companion animals. Both the American Veterinary Medical
Association and the American Animal Hospital Association have
condemned leghold traps as inhumane and advocate that the US get
on the ban wagon along with the 90 countries that have outlawed
them. The traps are illegal in Arizona, California, Colorado, and
Massachusetts, but so far legislative efforts to prohibit their use on

federal lands have been unsuccessful. (Among the other nations where leghold traps are still legal: Australia, Canada, China, France, Russia, South Africa, and Spain.)

Fruitful or Folly?

With all the effort, expense, and malice behind slaughtering 90,000 members of a single species every year, it's important to scrutinize the tangible results. Just how successful is Wildlife Services' "pest control" program? The results depend on whom you ask. The USDA, of course, defends its policy of targeting coyotes to support livestock producers. "This assistance can prevent predation and preserve the livelihood of farmers and ranchers across the nation," it says.[81] Those farmers and ranchers enjoy not having to compensate the government when Wildlife Services dispatches agents to shoot their arch nemesis, with each coyote costing up to US$1,000 to kill. "They're critical for the survival of the sheep industry—they perform an enormous role by protecting us from predators," is typical praise from a rancher.[82]

Conservationists tell a different story. Even after a century of non-stop slaughter, coyotes continue to flourish, and lethal methods of control can actually *increase* predation: studies strongly suggest that coyotes counter persecution by producing more coyotes. When not exploited, these animals live in packs, with only the alpha pair breeding once a year. Most of the other adult females in the group, though physiologically able to reproduce, are behaviorally sterile.[83] Environmental activist Chip Ward explains that killing the alpha pair, who do most of the hunting, throws the group structure into chaos. "Killing breaks down the pack's hierarchy so it resembles a gang of leaderless adolescents," he says. "When coyote couples are broken up by killing and pups die, the dynamic mating cycles are radically altered, resulting in fierce competition for females. Hormonal storms rage through the pack. As packs are broken up and disbursed or simply pushed away from their territories, coyotes end up competing for food in unfamiliar areas and cannot efficiently exploit their natural food webs." In the end, observes Ward, the USDA is simply turning coyotes into what the government claims to be fighting: livestock-killing predators.[84]

And they'll continue doing whatever it takes to survive. "Coyotes are incredibly adaptable carnivores who are able to live alone, in pairs, or in packs that are usually extended families," says Marc Bekoff, Professor Emeritus of Ecology and Evolutionary Biology at the University of Colorado–Boulder, who has studied the animals for more than 30 years. "Because of their flexibility in behavior and social organization, there is no such being as *the* coyote, and killing them in the name of population control or management has never worked and will never work because of their ability to live in a wide variety of habitats."[85] Indeed, Wildlife Services admits that, despite being hunted and trapped for 200 years, more coyotes exist today than when the US Constitution was signed.[86]

Others have examined the issue from an economic standpoint. In her in-depth analysis of how predator control in the US affects sheep production, wildlife biologist and economist Kim Berger casts doubt on the prevailing logic that wiping coyotes off the landscape will in any way benefit livestock producers. Berger found that, based solely on the number of carnivores shot, poisoned, gassed, beheaded, trapped, or otherwise killed, predator-control programs have been enormously successful. Yet ranchers, who have long singled out coyotes as the bane of the sheep industry, continue to go bust: 85 percent of sheep producers have gone bankrupt since the 1940s, despite the government killing more than 5 million predators.[87] "If predation losses are the primary cause of the sheep industry's decline," she writes, "then control, as practiced, has not been successful at reducing predation losses to the level necessary to make sheep ranching economically viable."[88] After crunching the numbers, Berger discovered that unfavorable market conditions—not coyotes—are by far the biggest factor in the decline in sheep production, especially the high cost of hay. As the price of hay rose 44 percent between 1966 and 1976, for example, sheep numbers dropped 44 percent during the same period.[89]

Killing Tournaments

That Wildlife Services kills coyotes as part of the US government's archaic wildlife damage management program (with taxpayers footing the bill) is certainly unconscionable, but there are those who kill these animals, and others, out of sheer delight. I'm not referring to the general "sport" of hunting—some of the more untenable examples of which I will address in Chapter 5—but festivals and tournaments focused on the death of a particular species. Emboldened by the moral fiction that coyotes are scavengers whose numbers must be reduced for the good of mankind, shooters are being drawn to "coyote calling" contests that offer thousands of dollars in prize money to participants who can "call in" and blow away the most or largest coyotes within a specified time period. Contestants use handheld devices or their vocal cords to mimic the cry of a rabbit, deer, or turkey in distress. They sometimes augment the deception with a decoy, all in an effort to draw the coyote into rifle range. Other participants use imitations of coyote vocaliza-tions—such as interrogation calls and challenge howls—to attract the animals. The voices are simulated using electronic gizmos or a wooden apparatus fitted with a reed that vibrates when blown through, much like a clarinet, to create a shrill, raspy call that sounds very much like a coyote.

Whatever the lure, a growing number of US states and Canadian provinces are permitting these killing competitions, which are organized by ranchers and promoted by sporting-goods stores, hunting-gear catalogs, gun clubs, local papers, and in specialty magazines like *Varmint Masters* and *Varmint Hunter*. Some calling contests have fanciful names like the Coyote Derby in Montana, the Predator Hunt Spectacular in Arizona, the North Dakota Coyote Classic, and the Kansas Predator Challenge. But no matter how these body-count events are dressed up, the cruelty is apparent as participants in this low-profile subculture leave countless wounded animals behind and chase coyotes with snowmobiles, occasionally running them over for fun and then bragging about it.[90] Protests from animal advocates have led to contest rules, though they are frequently ignored.

Prairie Dogs

When it comes to killing for gratuitous pleasure, few activities come close to the cruelty on display at contests where prairie dogs are the target. Contestants with high-powered rifles spend an entire day sitting at shooting benches and training their telescopic sights on a prairie dog colony, waiting for the animals to emerge from their burrows. Points are awarded not only for how many prairie dogs are killed, but for the violence a shooter inflicts. Killing two or more with one bullet earns extra points, as do specialty shots. A "chamois shot" refers to the bullet exploding the animal, propelling a large piece of their hide into the air; the "acrobat" (or "flipper") sends him cart-wheeling into oblivion; a head shot is known as "Hoover time"; and the "red mist," the most prized shot, turns the victim into a cloud of blood and vaporized viscera—providing what shooters call "instant visual gratification."[91] To enhance this gratification, shooters typically fire non-jacketed, hollow-point bullets that explode on impact.

Legal in every US state except Colorado (where killing numbers are restricted), these contests are nothing more than target practice for gun enthusiasts, who don't even bother retrieving the prairie dog carcasses—they're left to be scavenged, or to rot. "We have competitions to see who can flip one up onto the barbed-wire fence and hang it there," says one shooter, while another is delighted with the results of his marksmanship. "The head goes one way, the tail goes the other way, and everything in between just disappears," he says.[92]

Like coyotes, prairie dogs are Great Plains natives whom ranchers and the general public often regard as pests. Ranchers say the herbivorous, digging rodents compete with their animals for forage and create deep holes that horses and grazing cows supposedly trip in. (Lindsey Sterling-Krank, director of the Prairie Dog Coalition, says "The myth that cattle break legs in prairie dog holes is just that: myth. After years of asking ranchers this question, we have found not one example."[93]) Homeowners complain about the effects of burrows on their property. But prairie dogs are not the resilient survivors that coyotes are, and after decades of persecution, loss of habitat, disease, and use by the pet trade, their population has plunged by 95 percent.[94] Today, the five species of prairie dogs occupy as little as 2 percent of their historic ranges, which once spread over 12 states and portions of Mexico and Canada. Many scientists believe they may soon be extinct.[95] Their demise could signal the end of other species sharing their habitat, including owls, badgers, hawks, foxes, weasels, and especially the endangered black-footed ferret, for whom the prairie dog is nearly the only source of food. These rodents may be convenient targets for the "varmint militia," as they call themselves, but they are considered critical to balancing the natural order of North America's grassland ecosystems.

Pigs

Every March, hundreds of hunters and their dogs gather in Texas for the Hunt for the Hungry Hog Tournament. Contestants compete for more than US$3,000 in cash and prizes, awarded to the teams that kill the largest boar and sow, as well as to the team that brings in the longest tusk. The event's organizer, the Texas Dog Hunters Association, promotes this as the largest charity hunt in the United States. Donating the pig meat to feed some of the state's underprivileged residents may satisfy the group's conscience, but the cruelty of the competition is evident as dogs chase the hogs until they are exhausted and wait for the hunter to stab the pig to death with a knife. It's one more excuse to indulge in some barbarity while removing yet another "nuisance" animal from farmers' and ranchers' land.

Participants in this tournament are part of a subculture known as hog dogging (sometimes called hawg dawgin' or hog baiting), which turns trained dogs loose on wild boars inside pens. Judges rate dogs by how long it takes them to bring down the hog. During hunts like the Texas hog tournament, virtually anything can happen. Although they are only supposed to corner a hunted pig, "hog dogs" are trained to be aggressive and have been known to become violent when confronting their prey. One hog-hunting enthusiast tells of a time his dogs caught a sow several miles away. By the time he reached them, the dogs had attacked and eaten so much of the animal that they were passed out beside her. The hog was still breathing, even though her face had been chewed off from behind her ears to the end of her snout.[96]

Contest aficionados know well that it can take only an instant for fate to turn even the most skilled hunting dog into another victim. To protect their dogs from hogs' tusks—which are, ironically, canine teeth and the feral pigs' chief defense against attack—hunters wrap the hounds' necks with a "cut collar," which can be a single piece of wide, ballistic nylon or several leather collars strapped on side by side. Some dogs are also fitted with puncture-proof vests and chin guards. Despite these precautions, countless dogs have been gored and gutted by hogs, whose long, razor-sharp tusks can quickly slice open a belly.

In Australia, a similar "sport," called pig dogging, sets packs of hunting dogs loose on feral pigs. Practiced in the country's vast bushland, pig dogging has gotten tremendous support from the powerful hunting lobby, even while few of Australia's urbanites have heard of it. Fringe magazines like *Bacon Busters* and *Boar It Up Ya* glorify the savage nature of pig dogging: the cover of a recent issue boasted "Over 150 ripper piggin' pix." It's not uncommon to see children of hunters posing with mutilated animals. The violent subculture is extended online with discussion forums. "When your dog is swinging off a boar, there's no better feeling that you get," gushed one bloodthirsty hunter in a 2012 TV news exposé. "You can put me on any show ride and any Disneyland parks or whatever you got, but it won't give me the adrenalin that can. Nothing can."[97]

Rabbits

Like many other countries, New Zealand celebrates the Easter season with church services, chocolate eggs, and hot cross buns. But on the South Island, residents of the Otago region have another tradition: the Great Easter Bunny Hunt. Initiated in 1991, the annual contest involves teams of 12 shooters each, who come from all over New Zealand to kill as many rabbits as they can in 24 hours on the Good Friday prior to Easter Sunday. Although the teams compete for total prize money of NZ$3500, the most sought-after award is the trophy for the team that slaughters the most rabbits, who local farmers consider "pests."

Such wasn't always the case, however. New Zealand was rabbit-free until the 19th century, when some British settlers to the land thought it would be amusing to import rabbits from England, allow them to reproduce, and then hunt them down. (With the exception of bats, there were no land mammals in pre-European New Zealand, or Aotearoa, as the indigenous Māori call it.[98]) After a few attempts turning loose small rabbit populations that did not thrive, they were successfully introduced in 1862 and within 10 years the animals had bred so prolifically that they were nibbling their way through New Zealand's farms and vegetable gardens unchecked. Settlers tried to combat the population explosion by heading back to Europe for some weasels and ferrets—more non-natives—believing they would eat the rabbits. Instead of preying on rabbits, who were innately experienced with such wily predators, however, the weasels and ferrets discovered it was much easier to kill those native animals who were not used to being hunted by nonhuman mammals, all while alarmed scientists and conservationists shook their heads in dismay.[99] In 1876, the government passed the first legislation aimed at destroying rabbits throughout the country.[100] The animals have been in New Zealand's crosshairs ever since.

Every Great Easter Bunny Hunt results in more than 20,000 of the animals killed.[101] Hans Kriek, executive director of Save Animals From Exploitation (SAFE), a New Zealand-based advocacy group, says the hunt routinely involves first-time shooters injuring thousands of rabbits, who are then left to endure slow and painful deaths. "This hunt also sends the wrong message to young people, as the killing and wounding of animals is celebrated as a fun event and no concern is given to the suffering of the animals," he says. "The lack of respect shown to the killed animals further teaches kids that animals—and especially those considered 'pests'—are not worthy of consideration and can be abused at will."[102] Illustrating Hans' argument, one local newspaper reported that "with teams each sporting names such as Calici Crusaders, Hair Raising Mutineers, Cuniculus Terminators, Anti Pesto, and Oma Rabiti, a jovial atmosphere ensured the hunt was as much fun as it was competitive."[103]

There's no question that the overpopulation of rabbits is an issue that demands attention in New Zealand as it does in Australia, where rabbits were imported from England in 1859 and firmly established their population with the same unfortunate results.[104] But a killing contest like the Great Easter Bunny Hunt is clearly meant to serve as some sort of revenge—gunning down Peter Cottontail in a bit of twisted amusement—not a long-term solution. That the rabbits are killed in front of children on a religious holiday makes this event even more ethically troublesome.

After nearly 150 years of using bullets, leghold traps, electric fences, toxic gases, habitat destruction, poisons (including Compound 1080), and biological warfare against rabbits, New Zealanders should accept that these animals have become part of the landscape, if not the heart, of the country. The good news is that a non-lethal control method is now being developed in Australia, where researchers are using a virus called myxoma to induce infertility in female rabbits. If the myxoma virus sounds familiar, it's because Australians used it in the 1950s to destroy as much as 95 percent of the country's free-living rabbits,[105] and it's so virulent that it continues to kill nearly half the rabbits it infects today.[106] (The virus is transmitted by mosquitoes and fleas and was tried in New Zealand, but it didn't result in the same devastation due to inclement weather and a lack of suitable insects there.[107]) Today, thanks to pressure from animal advocacy groups, another large-scale release of lethal myxoma has been ruled out, and scientists at the Invasive Animal Cooperative Research Centre in Canberra are working to genetically modify the virus as a vaccine that will cause immunocontraception, a birth control method that uses the body's immune response to prevent pregnancy. The bad news is this research is being done at the cost of countless rabbits' lives.

Sharks

Up and down the eastern seaboard of the United States, from Maine to Florida, annual shark-killing tournaments attract angling teams eager to win their share of a pot that grows with every entrance fee and makes other hunting tournaments look small-time. One shark competition in New York is known for awarding the first-place crew more than US$100,000 in prize money.[108] Meanwhile, spectators young and old gather on the docks and wharves, cheering as each bloodied shark is offloaded from a boat to be judged. Not surprisingly, these are well-organized events that even attract corporate sponsors and are sometimes featured on TV sports channels. Considered a financial boon to local economies, the contests are also actively supported by governments and chambers of commerce.

One of the most popular competitions is the Monster Shark Tournament held in Martha's Vineyard, Massachusetts. If you're a movie buff, you may recall that much of the motion picture *Jaws* was filmed in Martha's Vineyard, which became the fictional resort town of Amity Island in the 1975 blockbuster. Unfortunately, the movie's success did much to fuel the misconception of the shark as a voracious maritime menace, and the annual Monster Shark Tournament capitalizes on that fallacy.[109] Three species of sharks are hunted, with prizes awarded for the biggest mako, porbeagle, and thresher sharks hooked and hauled back to the judging dock. There, amid high fives and back-slapping, sharks are weighed, hoisted by the tail, and dangled upside down for display on wooden gallows—sometimes while still alive. Between weigh-ins, an announcer calls out *Jaws* trivia questions.[110] The sharks are then torn apart with knives, their blood and entrails spilling out onto the wharf in full view of enthralled families.

Rivaling the carnage in Martha's Vineyard is the Star Island Yacht Club Shark Tournament held in Montauk, New York, at the tip of Long Island. Every year about 200 boats enter, each crew hoping they will be going home with a major chunk of the Calcutta pool that routinely exceeds half a million dollars. Teams angle for the largest blue, hammerhead, mako, thresher, and tiger sharks they can land during the two-day event. Since each boat is limited to one catch per day, sharks not meeting minimum weight requirements are de-hooked and thrown back into the ocean. But the standard fishing hook used, called a J hook, is a nasty piece of hardware with a barbed point that the shark often swallows whole ("gut hooking," to use the fishing parlance); when this occurs, the hook is left inside, where it can rip open the animal's stomach, puncture surrounding organs, and lead to peritonitis, gastritis, hepatitis, and pericarditis (inflammation around the heart).[111] Even without a hook in their stomachs, many sharks caught and released end up dead from the psychological stress and physical trauma of struggling for an hour or more at the end of a fishing line, being repeatedly gaffed with hooked poles, and gasping for oxygen.

Wherever the contest, one species contestants are not allowed to hunt is the great white—which is classified as endangered—but that doesn't mean these protected sharks aren't killed. During the 2010 tournament in Montauk, an angler brought in a great white shark, apparently excited to have captured a "man eater."[112] Despite explicit warnings by tournament organizers, this type of incident is not uncommon.

These celebrations of cruelty not only teach observers—especially children—that a shark's only value lies in the spectacle of his death, but with shark populations currently down 90 percent, they are ecologically irresponsible.

> "I am a man who loves the wild and all its citizens, and it is this love that sustains me. In the innocent eye of a baby seal, in the mournful eye of a dying whale, in the whispering of redwoods and pines, in the ingenuity of spiders and the free flight of birds I see the salvation of the Earth and even of our own species."[113]
> —Paul Watson

Kangaroos

There are many reasons behind the senseless slaughter of animals. Sometimes financial gain is the motivation—for the meat and dairy industries, for instance. In other cases, animals are targeted as a nuisance, as with coyotes and prairie dogs in the United States. Australia's kangaroo is thus doubly cursed. Shot, beaten, and clubbed for their flesh and skin, kangaroos are also victims of the debatable premise, perpetuated by farmers and ranchers, that the country's estimated 25 to 60 million 'roos are agricultural "pests" who compete with sheep for forage and destroy crops. With many Aussies convinced the destruction of these herbivorous marsupials is justified, the Kangaroo Industry Association of Australia (KIAA) makes a great effort to promote the animals as food and fiber resources. Overcoming the cultural reluctance to dine on Skippy has traditionally been a challenge, though kangaroo meat is becoming more accepted and it has long been a staple ingredient of dog and cat food.[114] In contrast, the skin trade is flourishing. "There is no practical or ethical justification for killing kangaroos, and the inevitable cruelty that accompanies both the commercial and recreational shooting of these magnificent animals makes it totally abhorrent," says Glenys Oogjes of Animals Australia. "Sadly, it seems very few Australians and even fewer tourists to this country realize our appalling double standards—an often-revered national icon that is shot mercilessly in the outback each night for financial reward."[115]

The primary objection made by most animal welfare groups is not that the kangaroos are being slaughtered, which is bad enough, but that the methods used for killing them are inhumane. Hunters are supposed to adhere to Australia's National Code of Practice, a set of guidelines intended to minimize the pain and suffering of targeted kangaroos. According to the Code, shooters must hit the country's most symbolic animal in the brain. Since hunting occurs at night at distances of 50 to 100 meters (164 to 328 feet), accurate shots to the head are difficult at best. (A separate Code of Practice allows non-commercial hunters to kill kangaroos and wallabies using shotguns.[116]) A 2009 report on the kangaroo killings commissioned by Animal Liberation NSW concluded that as many as 40 percent of kangaroos hunted are shot in the neck or body, rather than the brain, resulting in prolonged, painful deaths.[117] A kangaroo hit in the neck would not be considered acceptable—and therefore sellable—by industry standards, but hunters have a way around that. "Many just cut the neck really low down when dressing the kangaroo so you can't see the neck shot," says Nikki Sutterby of the Australian Society for Kangaroos.[118] (This is clearly done to disguise neck wounds, since severing the head low on the kangaroo's neck is not only very difficult, but it decreases the weight of the carcass and therefore how much the shooter will be paid for it.[119])

The Code also states that hunters must not kill protected species, and they should avoid shooting female kangaroos who have dependent young—two more directives that are impossible to fully comply with, particularly under nighttime shooting conditions. Only six of the 55 kangaroo species are allowed to be killed for commercial use—the Eastern Grey, the Red, the Western Grey, the common wallaroo (also called the Euro), the Bennett's wallaby, and the pademelon (a type of wallaby)[120]—but in the dark, who's to say which species of kangaroo is being destroyed? Furthermore, baby kangaroos are considered a worthless byproduct of the industry, so when a mother 'roo is targeted, her babies are also killed, multiplying the tragedy. Should a weaned baby (called a young-at-foot joey) escape being shot when his mother is killed, he hops off into the night to die by starvation, dehydration, or predation from foxes, hawks, or dingoes. There are also pouch joeys who are dragged from their dead or dying mother's pouch; after experiencing the trauma of mama's murder, these orphans get their heads cut off, bludgeoned, or bashed against the tow bar of a vehicle. Such are the killing methods recommended in the Code.

Because kangaroos are gunned down in remote locations of the Australian bush, and the hunts are not monitored, few observers ever witness the level of suffering animals endure. But at least one participant has spoken out. Former full-time kangaroo shooter David Nicholls writes:

> When the mother is killed, the young-at-foot joey is left to fend for itself, and any zoologist with knowledge of kangaroo habits would have to admit that its chances of survival are at best minimal. Panic, fear, starvation, or being preyed upon by the hundreds of foxes that keep tabs on kangaroo shooting, will end its life in a state of terror. This is not acceptable to reasonable, thinking people. Kangaroo shooting is inherently and overtly cruel by all standards that can be applied and would not be acceptable to reasonable thinking people, if they knew.
>
> The mouth of a kangaroo can be blown off and the kangaroo can escape to die of shock and starvation. Forearms can be blown off, as can ears, eyes, and noses. Stomachs can be hit expelling the contents with the kangaroo still alive. Backbones can be pulverized to an unrecognizable state, etc. Hind legs can be shattered with the kangaroo desperately trying to get away on the other or without the use of either. To deny that this goes on is just an exercise in attempting to fool the public.[121]

Nicholls (now a vegan and staunch animal advocate) explains how easy it is for a commercial kangaroo hunter to become desensitized and rationalize even the most egregious cruelties. "Shooting can be very arduous with extreme weather conditions, poor nutrition, and equipment failure," he says. "A few flat tires on a stinking hot or freezing cold night can soon turn the kangaroo into the 'enemy.' Mental and physical frustration adds to poor shooting and poor attitude, with existing terrible wounding rates accelerated. If you are shooting the 'enemy,' with the added justification of ridding a menace to landholders, a mind-set is in place to accommodate all kinds of atrocities being accepted."[122]

Until recently, one of the biggest commercial drivers of this AU$270 million (US$230 million) trade[123] was sportswear company Adidas, which insisted on manufacturing several lines of football (soccer) cleats from the skins of kangaroos. The company came under fire from the UK-based animal-advocacy group Viva!, which led a worldwide boycott of Adidas. In 2003, the US office of Viva!, established and directed by Lauren Ornelas, filed a lawsuit against the company for illegally selling kangaroo-skin shoes in California, one of its most lucrative markets. Adidas had been flouting a 1971 ban on the sale of certain animal parts, including those from kangaroo, in the state. "Californians weren't telling Australians how they should be managing their wildlife, but rather that California does not support the mass, inhumane killing of animals for their skin," Lauren says. "This is precisely why California banned the sale of seal fur and skins from Canada."[124] Faced with the court case, a very public black eye, and a subsequent drop in its share price, Adidas funded a US$436,000 lobbying effort to finally get the law amended to allow kangaroo parts.[125]

Then, in September of 2012, Adidas agreed to stop using kangaroo skin in its shoes, a decision hailed by animal advocates around the world. In their defense, Adidas said the skin they had been using was "waste" material from Australia's policy of culling kangaroos to preserve the flora and fauna of Australia, "which means that animals are not killed because of their skin—or because of our shoes," a company spokesperson told me in 2010.[126] But even if that were true, it would still not be a morally justifiable excuse, any more than Japan claiming that they're hunting whales for science, only to turn around and sell flesh from the animals they harpoon and butcher. In reality, Australia's kangaroo-skin and -meat trade isn't just thriving, it's growing by 7 percent a year, a rate that KIAA acknowledges is better than most other industries in the country, let alone a commercial venture in the rural sector.

Despite Adidas' decision, kangaroos are considered very much an economic resource, and environmental and animal protection groups including the Australian Conservation Foundation and Humane Society International have objected to the skin and meat revenue streams driving the 'roo massacre.[127] It's great when social-justice advocates make a stand, but it's even better when animal exploiters are forced to contradict their own rhetoric. In what certainly must have been discomfiting for the industry, Nicole Payne, manager of the Kangaroo Management Program, New South Wales Department of Environment and Conservation, admitted to the Administrative Appeals Tribunal in 2007 that the commercial slaughter of kangaroos is "Not designed to achieve population control or damage mitigation, but for commercial harvesting."[128]

Predator & Prey Urine

In nature, predatory animals mark their territory with urine. It's a powerful signal that prey animals and other predators understand, so it's little wonder that humans have found a way to exploit it. Sold in pump containers, animal urine is used primarily as a repellent; the odor of predators such as coyote, fox, bobcat, and wolf will supposedly keep deer, rabbits, and other hungry prey animals away from gardens and homes. Hunters and trappers use it to disguise their own scents so that animals don't smell the presence of humans. Trappers also douse traps with the urine of rabbits, for example, to lure predators, and hunters use prey urine to train their dogs to locate decoys.

Of course, animals in the wild won't simply fill a jar on command, and though you may never have heard of it, the market for their urine is substantial, so pee purveyors have created a way to meet demand. "The urine is collected from animals that are kept on farms and zoos," says Bill Graham, owner of Leg Up Enterprises, which claims to control 90 percent of the US market. "The urine is collected passively. The animals are not aware that it is being collected. They are conditioned to use an area of their habitat for urination, and the urine drains into vats and is filtered and strained."[129] Graham is wary about revealing who his suppliers are, though he says he has 10 of them. "They run the gamut from zoos to rehabilitation farms and people who keep foxes as pets."[130] A sales consultant for the Maine-based company adds that some of their profits "go back into supplying the animals with healthy living areas and quality feed so they can produce good urine."[131]

While this may sound innocuous enough, the animals are still being deprived of their freedom. Conditions are worse for animals whose urine is collected in fur farms. Beneath filthy cages, plastic buckets catch urine from foxes who are doomed to drape the shoulders of well-heeled heels. Activist Matt Rossell worked undercover for four months at an Illinois fur farm, gathering video and photographic evidence, so he could expose the suffering that is hidden from public view. Though its primary business was selling the fur of anally-electrocuted foxes, the operation where he worked also saved the animals' urine, which the owner then packaged in spray bottles for Kmart and other retailers to sell as a cover scent for hunters. "It was being continually collected," explains Matt. "The platforms the cages sat on were sloped such that all the urine drained down into five-gallon buckets." But first, the urine had to make its way through the feces that piled up under the cages, he says. "The urine drained through it and it was beyond disgusting. When I arrived it was utter filth, and the only time in four months that the place ever had the feces cleaned was after the owner got busted by the State Ag Department."[132] Photos of the mold-encrusted buckets, as well as caged foxes who had gnawed their limbs down to the bone, are among the powerful images that Matt captured and were later used to charge the farm's owner with animal cruelty—to which he pleaded guilty.

Seahorses

For a creature so remarkable, it's hard to believe the seahorse gets relatively little attention among animal protectionists. Part of the reason is likely because fish in general are too often ignored, even by animal advocates. But it's also probably due in part to the seahorse's size: even the species known as the giant seahorse only grows to be about 12 inches (8 centimeters) long, making him the Goliath of the seahorse universe. While seahorses may be small, the demand for them as pets and for use in traditional medicines in Asia, South America, and other regions is enormous; seahorse catches are declining, and studies suggest that some species populations have now dropped by 50 percent.[133] Even so, exploiters take about 24 million seahorses a year from oceans, supplying not only aquariums and apothecaries, but turning seahorses into decorations for use on key chains, earrings, bookends, Christmas-tree ornaments, and paperweights.[134]

As popular as seahorses are, though, they are still barely a blip on the world's radar screen. Walk into any bookstore and the titles you'll find devoted to seahorses, if any, are generally all juvenile fiction or nonfiction.[135] There might by a book or two on marine animals with a section on seahorses, but these intriguing fish don't get nearly as much shelf space as whales, great apes, big cats, sharks, and bears. Such an oversight only adds to the mystique seahorses have enjoyed for thousands of years. With their equine profiles, crowned heads, and prehensile tails like a monkey's, seahorses resemble creatures out of mythology more than denizens of the deep; in fact, ancient Romans believed seahorses pulled Neptune's chariot.[136] Like a chameleon, they use camouflage as a defense, blending into their surroundings, and the males even sport a marsupial-like abdominal pouch, from which they give birth to live offspring, thus helping to ensure the newborns' survival.

Unfortunately, their distinctive appearance and storied biology have made seahorses a favorite among fish-tank hobbyists, particularly in the US; but it's their use as a curative in Brazil, China, Indonesia, Japan, South Korea, and Vietnam that is the most serious threat to the animal's survival. The biggest demand is from practitioners of traditional Chinese medicine, who dry and grind seahorses into a powder that is used to treat ailments ranging from incontinence to difficult childbirths.[137] The most common complaint seahorse is prescribed for is impotence. "They have some other minor uses, but virtually all the supply used in Chinese medicine has gone to this one application," says Subhuti Dharmananda, director of the Institute for Traditional Medicine in Portland, Oregon.[138]

It is because of traditional medicine that CITES now regulates the trade in all known species of seahorses, now exceeding 35.[139] The 175 nations that have signed the agreement are responsible for limiting exports to protect the seahorse's survival. Convincing CITES to list the seahorse was an important step, and it was largely made possible by the efforts of a Vancouver-based team of marine conservation scientists who formed Project Seahorse in 1996 to ensure the long-term survival of these quirky fish. Sarah Foster, a biologist with the group, notes that as much as 95 percent of captured seahorses end up in the traditional medicine market. "That said, the eventual use of seahorses does differ across species, and for some it is exploitation for the aquarium trade that puts the greatest pressure on populations," she says. Seahorses come from two sources, says Foster. "The majority are caught as bycatch in tropical shrimp trawl fisheries, which have very high rates of bycatch."[140] These vessels trawl some of the most fragile marine habitats: coral reefs, estuaries, mangrove stands, lagoons, and seagrass beds, home to both shrimp and seahorses.[141] When crew members bring the shrimp nets onboard, they remove the seahorses, who are generally dead by this time, and set them aside to dry. Other defenseless seahorses are pillaged by hand, primarily by small-scale fishers. Those destined for the live trade are placed in water, while the rest are left to die of suffocation and dehydrate in the sun.[142]

Either way, seahorses are rapidly disappearing, says Healy Hamilton, director of the Center of Applied Biodiversity Informatics at the California Academy of Sciences in San Francisco. "Seahorses live in some of the world's most threatened habitats—the coastal oceans—where human impacts are really profound and severe. We don't know how many species of seahorses there are. Of the species that we know, we don't know very much about their geographic ranges. We don't know how seahorses are related to one another. We don't even know how long seahorses live. Really, what we only have been able to measure is very high declines in population numbers almost everywhere that they're harvested."[143]

Dwarf Seahorses

The dwarf seahorse, found in seagrass beds in the Gulf of Mexico, Florida, and the Caribbean, is threatened with extinction due to the decline of seagrass, commercial collection, boat propellers, and lingering pollution from the BP oil spill of 2010. In response, there's a move to give this one-inch-long creature protection under the Endangered Species Act. More than half of Florida's seagrasses have been destroyed since 1950, and in some areas losses are as steep as 90 percent.[144] As seagrass beds disappear, the seahorses vanish with them. Dwarf seahorses are not the only species that depends on seagrass ecosystems, but they've got my vote as the most adorable. Although male seahorses wrestle with one another for access to mates, once a pair has bonded, seahorse couples ignore other seahorses. These monogamous mates even greet each other every morning with a special dance.

Eaten to Extinction

As omnivorous consumers seek more exotic fare, they've threatened the long-term survival of many species. This is certainly not unprecedented: the dodo, great auk, and passenger pigeon—once considered to be the most abundant bird on Earth—are just three animals people have preyed upon and finally eaten to extinction in the last couple hundred years. Following are a few more animals who, without some drastic culinary intervention, could soon become memories of humanity's ignoble past.

Great Apes

Consuming so-called bushmeat, which may refer to any terrestrial wildlife, is particularly threatening to nonhuman primates in Africa. These animals are especially vulnerable because, rather than being widely distributed, they live mostly in the forested areas of central and west Africa; these regions are undergoing rapid economic growth, encroaching even further into primate habitats.[145] Though there is a long tradition of hunting great apes (chimpanzees, gorillas, orangutans, and bonobos) for animal protein, an influx of new logging roads has made it easier to reach and kill animals, and what was once subsistence hunting by forest-dwelling people has expanded and become drastically more commercialized.

Backed by foreign investors such as China, timber-company hunters armed with high-powered firearms venture deep into primate habitats, shoot all but the smallest animals, and carry the remains back to the logging camp, where some of the flesh is eaten.[146] The rest ends up in the hands of bushmeat dealers, who wrap the flesh in old newspapers or plastic bags and arrange for its transport to distributors in local towns or directly to illegal butcher shops.[147] But the illicit trade extends far beyond African borders, with Brussels, Chicago, London, Montreal, New York, Paris, and Toronto representing the largest markets.[148] In 2010, a European investigation concluded that 5 metric tonnes (5.5 US tons) of bushmeat is smuggled in personal baggage through Paris' Charles de

Gaulle Airport *every week*.[149] This is only a fraction of the 1 million US tons (907,184 metric tonnes) consumed around the world every year.[150] The Bushmeat Project, an organization devoted to education and reducing the demand for bushmeat, estimates that if the slaughter continues at its current pace, the remaining wild apes in Africa will be gone within 50 years.

Elephants

Images of elephants butchered for their tusks are so symbolic of animal cruelty that it may be surprising to learn that these beautiful animals are also hunted for their flesh. In many cases, their meat is actually much more valuable: while a poacher in Africa's Congo Basin might receive US$180 for the tusks of one forest elephant, the animal's flesh could sell for as much as US$6,000, thanks to a growing interest in exotic bushmeat. "When someone kills an elephant whose tusks don't weigh more than 500 grams [1 pound], it's not for the tusks—it's especially for the meat," says Omer Kokamenko, a ranger at Dzangha-Sangha National Park.[151] Forest elephants are more difficult to protect, as these animals dwell within dense vegetation, unlike their larger cousins, who roam the open savannas and are easier to observe. When wildlife biologists conducted their last comprehensive study of forest elephants in 1989, they estimated their population within the Congo Basin to be 172,400, nearly one-third of Africa's elephants at the time.[152]

Although elephants are also consumed in Asia—where the meat, especially from the pachyderm's trunk, is a popular aphrodisiac— few are hunted for food.[153] Instead, meat is taken from animals who have died from natural causes or who are accidentally killed by land mines, trains, or trucks.[154] Asia's population of wild elephants is thought to be about 25,000, while their numbers in Africa have dwindled from about 3 to 5 million in the 1940s to as few as 470,000 today.[155]

Frogs

Once regarded as a seasonal delicacy among French epicureans, frogs' legs can now be found throughout the year at school cafeterias, family dinner tables, market stalls, and restaurants worldwide. But as our hunger for frog meat increases, it contributes (along with global warming) to the collapse of frog populations. Humans eat as many as 1 billion frogs every year, and most of these animals are captured in the wild.[156]

Indonesia recently emerged as the world's leading exporter of frogs' legs. Villagers collect frogs from swamps and take them to a local cutting center for slaughter. "At the center, they're held down in groups and sliced in half through the belly while they're still conscious," says Rose Glover of PETA.[157] The upper body is then cast aside to join a twitching pile of frog torsos. It may take up to an hour for a frog to die.

"Amphibians are already the most threatened animal group yet assessed because of disease, habitat loss, and climate change," says Corey Bradshaw, associate professor at the School of Earth and Environmental Sciences, University of Adelaide. "Man's massive appetite for their legs is not helping."[158] Bradshaw co-authored a scientific paper on this topic, and he and his colleagues note that because of the frogs' roles as both prey and predator, their suscepti-bility to waterborne toxins, and an evolutionary history that straddles aquatic and terrestrial ecosystems, they are good indicators for environmental degradation.[159]

In addition to the cruelty involved in the frog-meat trade, killing frogs threatens world health. Because frogs eat mosquitoes and other insects, they help control the spread of malaria, encephalitis, West Nile Virus, and other vector-borne diseases. Declining frog popula-tions have a direct connection to an increased use of insecticides in farmland.

Pangolins

You may never have heard of them, but pangolins are the most frequently confiscated wildlife in Southeast Asia.[160] Although trade in these scaly anteaters has been banned by CITES since 2000, their flesh is considered such a delicacy that it's not uncommon for authorities to seize thousands of the animals aboard a single ship. Stricter monitoring of the trade by authorities has led some poachers to slaughter the animals first and then smuggle their flesh across borders as "goat meat."[161]

The pangolin has but one defense mechanism: a shield of hard, plate-like scales that allows the mammal to curl up into an armored ball. Unfortunately, these scales—prized for their use in traditional medicines—have made the docile, toothless, slow-moving pangolin even more popular among smugglers. Native to tropical regions in Asia and Africa, pangolins have been nearly wiped out in Cambodia, China, Laos, and Vietnam. Poachers are now encroaching on pangolin habitats further south in Asia, threatening to destroy their remaining populations in Java, the Malaysian peninsula, and Sumatra.[162] Records confiscated by Malaysian wildlife officials in 2009 revealed that just one local trafficking syndicate killed 22,200 pangolins between May 2007 and January 2009, but the actual figure could be much higher, since eight months' worth of logbooks were unaccounted for.[163] Traders have begun smuggling pangolins from Africa in an effort to satisfy diners in Asia.[164]

A chef in Guangdong, China, describes the fate that awaits pangolins in his restaurant: "We keep them alive in cages until the customer makes an order. Then we hammer them unconscious, cut their throats, and drain the blood. It is a slow death. We then boil them to remove the scales. We cut the meat into small pieces and use it to make a number of dishes, including braised meat and soup. Usually the customers take the blood home with them afterwards."[165]

Turtles

Turtles and their eggs have been popular delicacies for thousands of years. But with an insatiable demand for turtle meat in China, a growing population of foodies elsewhere in search of new gustatory experiences, and plenty of profiteers eager to make a buck, turtle populations around the world are shrinking. Most marine turtles are now considered protected and many are nearly extinct. With China's own turtle population decimated due to hunting and habitat destruction,[166] the country's food markets began importing the reptiles from Borneo, Indonesia, Myanmar, and Vietnam. Predictably, demand outstripped supply, and turtles have now all but disappeared from these countries, too. Chinese buyers have since turned to the United States, filling their pots with map turtles, mud turtles, red-eared sliders, snapping turtles, basking turtles, and others who inhabit the country's watersheds.[167] Lawmakers in turtle-rich Florida, worried that China could potentially eat the state's entire turtle population in a year, passed a law in 2009 that effectively ended commercial harvesting of the animals.[168] Alabama, Maryland, Mississippi, North Carolina, Tennessee, and Texas are among the states with similar bans.[169]

Turtle butchers at Chinese markets disassemble fully conscious beings. They begin with a hammer and chisel to remove the shell from the turtle's back and the plastron (the underside of the shell structure) from her abdomen. Even when the butcher slices off fat, cuts out several pounds of unwanted organs, and finally stacks his gruesome work on a display counter, the turtle is still alive and struggling.[170]

Because the life span of a wild turtle can be 60 years or more, females don't reach reproductive maturity until they are well into adulthood and large enough for her body to accommodate eggs.[171] On average, a female Hawaiian green sea turtle, for instance, won't lay her first clutch of 100 or so eggs until she is 25 years old. This makes turtle species especially fragile, since hunters take turtles who have likely never reproduced. Moreover, eggs are easily spotted on the beach, making them easy targets for poachers.

Turtles not targeted for eating can still become victims of the meat trade. A 2010 global assessment of turtle "bycatch" by the three major types of fishing—longline, gillnet, and trawling—found that nearly 9 million endangered sea turtles have been accidentally captured or killed over the past two decades. Bycatch occurs when giant nets or longlines with thousands of baited hooks snag animals other than what they are intended to catch. Turtles often perish by drowning or by swallowing sharp hooks that can become lodged in their throats and stomachs. Shrimp trawling is one of the worst bycatch offenders, with as much as 20 pounds of non-targeted animals yanked from the ocean for every pound of shrimp caught.[172]

Finally, turtles recently became victims in the trinket trade. Vendors outside subway and train stations in China offer live turtles inside plastic bags just 7 centimeters (2.8 inches) wide. Sold as key chains or good luck charms, the tiny bags are filled with brightly colored water and sealed shut to prevent leakage. How is the turtle fed? He isn't. According to one vendor, the water contains "nutrients" that will sustain the animal for months, though animal advocates in China argue that turtles trapped inside the bags quickly run out of oxygen.[173] Rumor has it that some customers have been eating the dead turtles.

Sea Urchins

It wasn't so long ago that sea urchins—those round, prickly creatures who live on the ocean floor—were considered the scourge of the deep. Not only can their painful sting be venomous, but they are voracious consumers of kelp, which the Japanese use for a traditional soup and which the US uses to manufacture agar for Petri dishes and a variety of other products. In the 1960s and '70s, local authorities in Southern California worked with dive clubs to organize urchin-killing parties: scuba divers armed with hammers would smash these spiky echinoderms to save kelp forests for the agar factories. Such killing sprees began winding down in the mid-'70s, as word spread that Japan's restaurant industry was paying 7 cents a pound for intact sea urchins.[174]

Today, thanks to millions of ravenous sushi fans, sea urchins have joined sharks and bluefin tuna to become one of the most prized marine delicacies—and one of the most threatened species. Especially popular among sushi connoisseurs are the sea urchins' reproductive organs. Their ovaries and testes are loaded with fat and used to make a sweet, creamy dish called *uni* (pronounced "ooh knee"). The appetite for North Atlantic sea urchin grew so rapidly that Maine's virtually unfished shallow coastal waters became the site of an aquatic gold rush for divers and draggers, who pulled 38 million pounds of urchins out of the ocean in 1994 and turned this former "marine weed" into the state's second most valuable sea creature, after lobsters.[175] By 2010, however, the industry was collapsing, with 2.6 million pounds of urchins removed[176]—a dramatic decline, to say the least, and a harbinger of unhappy tidings for the little sea urchin.

What You Can Do

In addition to talking to others about the abuses being perpetrated against animals, here are some actions you can take.

Bear Bile

Bear bile has been used in pharmacopoeia for thousands of years, yet it can be replaced easily and cheaply by herbs and synthetics. Support the work of Animals Asia, which is campaigning to end the untenable bear-bile trade. Learn more at www.animalsasia.org. Also check out Free the Bears (www.freethebears.org) and Bear Necessity Korea (http://bearnecessitykorea.com).

Illegal Wildlife Trade

Never buy souvenirs made from animals. Such items include elephant ivory, big cat and reptile skins, tortoise shells, feathers, furs, sharks' teeth, corals, seahorses, and seashells. Learn more from these organizations:

The Dian Fossey Gorilla Fund International
www.gorillafund.org

Humane Society International
www.hsi.org

International Fund for Animal Welfare
www.ifaw.org

Sea Shepherd Conservation Society
www.seashepherd.org

TRAFFIC
www.traffic.org

Coyotes

As tempting as it may be, never feed animals in the wild; this can lead to animals becoming habituated to humans. Moreover, once the humans-and-food connection has been established, coyotes increase in population because their hunting territories decrease, allowing more coyotes to establish packs. Project Coyote offers a variety of ways you can help ban the use of lethal chemicals and cruel traps, as well as other actions you can take on behalf of these persecuted animals. Visit www.projectcoyote.org for more information.

Killing Tournaments

Please speak out against any killing contests organized in your area. You can begin by contacting tournament organizers, local businesses, and editors of newspapers and magazines. Ask family and friends to do the same.

Kangaroos

You can support organizations that aid kangaroos, including:

Animals Australia
www.animalsaustralia.org

The Kangaroo Sanctuary
www.kangaroosanctuary.com

The National Kangaroo Protection Coalition
www.kangaroo-protection-coalition.com

Southern Cross Wildlife Care, an all-volunteer veterinary clinic
that treats Australia's sick and injured native species:
http://southerncrosswildlifecare.org.au

Seahorses

Consumers can greatly influence the seahorse trade by never buying
trinkets, jewelry, or other items made from these threatened animals.
If you take medicines that traditionally include seahorses as an
ingredient, please ask your practitioner for a treatment that uses a
plant-based alternative. For more information, visit Project Seahorse
at http://seahorse.fisheries.ubc.ca.

Eaten to Extinction

With so much delicious, nutritious plant-based food available,
there's no need to dine on animals—exotic or otherwise. Please visit
chooseveg.com, foodispower.org, goveg.com, vegansociety.com, or
viva.org.uk to find recipes and tips for a more compassionate diet. I
also encourage you to learn more about the bushmeat trade; a good
place to start is http://bushmeat.net.

Chapter 5

Ruthless Roundup: Animals Used in Sports

Who hears the fishes when they cry?
—Henry David Thoreau

It is well after sunset, and the summer sky above Omak, Washington, is a deep canvas of black. A dozen or so horses and their riders—all young men—are assembling near the top of a steep hill. A few of the men look back over the high desert valley toward the Cascade Mountains, barely discernible against a smattering of stars, but most look beyond the hill to the east and the wide swath of the Colville Indian Reservation that abuts the town. Omak has retained much of the frontier feel that marked its founding a century ago, with sawmills and apple orchards still dotting the landscape. It is this pioneer heritage, some say, that beckons rodeo enthusiasts here for the annual Omak Stampede: four days of chasing and roping frightened calves and riding bulls who've been prompted to buck. But it's the rodeo's event billed as "the World-Famous Suicide Race" that has brought spectators out on this August night.

At the crack of a starter's pistol, the riders whip their horses, who bolt ahead with startling power and reach a full gallop before blindly plummeting shoulder-to-shoulder over the brow of the sandy hill. Hooves sink into freshly groomed earth as riders lean back in their saddles trying to remain upright on the 62-degree slope—so steep, say equine experts, that horses cannot see where their legs are taking them.[1] The downhill sprint is supposed to last 225 feet (68 meters) before everyone hits the Okanogan River, but within moments a horse stumbles, pitching his rider and falling against another horse, who also loses his footing. The two animals tumble toward the water, tossed end over end, helpless to right themselves before finally sliding to a stop. Other horses, meanwhile, come cascading down the hill to the riverbank, where the path narrows like a funnel and they're all suddenly bunched together in a bottleneck of flesh and bone.

Nine horses—some riderless, others being struck with riding crops—jump into the cold, fast-moving Okanogan and swim for the other side 150 feet (45 meters) away. Races past have seen worn-out horses struggle and drown at this point, but not tonight. Each horse fords the deep current and comes trotting out of the water one by one, gaining speed as they climb the bank and gallop 400 feet (121 meters) into an arena filled with spectators. It's here that injuries sustained in the race become obvious, as the horses' adrenaline rush subsides and some animals limp to the finish line, panting and exhausted. Horses have been known to later collapse and die.

A tradition since 1935, the Omak Suicide Race is big business for a small town. Race organizers estimate the event brings in US$6 million, but the city, considering all the indirect revenue, says the economic benefit is probably twice that.[2] In the meantime, two dozen horses have been killed since 1983—the year animal rights groups began keeping count. Not included in that toll are the horses who succumb to their injuries after finishing the race or those who are killed during pre-trials. Supporters say it's all in keeping with the tradition of rodeos.

Rodeos

Rodeo events are supposed to fuse the sort of "frontier spirit" found at Omak with competition, turning such displays as bull riding, steer wrestling, and horse bucking into a sport. Rodeos are firmly associated with the Western United States, but they've also been held in Australia, Canada, Mexico, New Zealand, South Africa, South America, Spain, and even the United Kingdom (where rodeos were banned in 1934 under the Protection of Animals Act).

The exact origin of the rodeo is a topic of speculation. What we do know is that they gained popularity with the advent of the traveling Wild West shows that toured the US and Europe in the late 19th and early 20th centuries. Decades before this, rodeos were informal events in which ranch hands competed against one another for a cash prize put up by local ranchers. Some scholars argue the rodeo goes back to 1844, when Major Jack Hays of the Texas Rangers organized an event near San Antonio in which his Rangers matched their riding and shooting skills against those of Mexican vaqueros and Comanche warriors.[3] Centuries earlier, though, vaqueros were holding equestrian contests called *charreadas* on the haciendas of Mexico, and it's easy to argue that these competitions—a custom brought from Spain—gave birth to the modern rodeo.[4]

However they began, rodeos continue a long tradition of regarding animals as little more than objects. In her book *American Rodeo: From Buffalo Bill to Big Business*, historian Kristine Fredriksson observes that in 1860, cows and bulls were so abundant in Texas that they didn't even sell for a dollar each. "It is quite understandable that anything so plentiful and low in monetary value would be regarded as a downright nuisance," she writes.[5] Thanks to tireless breeding practices, the bovines used in rodeos today are still plentiful—and they're still handled with little thought for their welfare, let alone their intrinsic value as individuals. Typical of the sport's contempt for animals is the list of "humane rules" set forth by the Colorado-based Professional Rodeo Cowboys Association (PRCA), the rodeo industry's largest sanctioning body. An investigation by the nonprofit group SHARK (Showing Animals Respect and Kindness) revealed that these rules are virtually meaningless, but PRCA uses them as a tool for deflecting accusations of cruelty—as in, "We don't mistreat animals. We've got a collection of impressive-sounding welfare guidelines. We won't show 'em to ya, but we've got 'em." Actually, after 12 years of being prodded, PRCA finally provided SHARK with its list of 60 rules, which turns out to be—thanks to redundancies, duplications, and loopholes—20 rules, zero of which have evidently ever been enforced.[6]

Rodeos are comprised of timed competitions (such as roping and barrel racing) and rough stock events (riding a bucking horse or bull), and each has its own brand of abuse, practically none of which the public ever sees or hears about. Routine elements of the rodeo are fear and pain—indeed, these are what drive normally placid animals to behave as if they're "untamed" and make cowboys and cowgirls look like "heroes" in the arena. Calves and bulls charge through a chute at full speed not because they are ferocious, but because they are shocked with cattle prods or have their highly sensitive tails twisted. Likewise, bulls and horses are forced to buck with a leather or cotton flank strap fastened around their abdomen, just below the ribcage. Were it not for these cruel tricks, rodeos would not exist. Indeed, since Pittsburgh, Pennsylvania, banned the use of electric shocking devices, flank straps, and heel spurs, rodeos left the city and rode off into the sunset. While individual states or municipalities may regulate the treatment of animals used in rodeos, the US government generally excludes equines and bovines from the definition of "animal" under the Animal Welfare Act, so horses, cows, and bulls are afforded no federal protection in rodeos.

Cruelty for a Buck

As one of the fastest-growing forms of recreational animal abuse in the US, bull riding represents perhaps the most peculiar way to romanticize a cowboy "tradition," since these animals were never ridden in ranch work. But rodeos aren't known for celebrating common sense, and bull riding is a popular display of stupidity. What spectators come to see is a rider trying to stay mounted atop a frantically bucking bull for at least eight seconds. What they don't see is the device called a Hot Shot—not much bigger than a cell phone—that is sometimes used to deliver a 5,000-volt electric shock to the bull as he exits the bucking chute. Nor do audiences see the painful tail-twisting administered to the animals. Both of these practices are considered violations under PRCA rules, yet they continue to occur.[7] Flank straps are allowed, however, even though they cause bloody and painful wounds and friction burns on the animal's skin.[8]

Artificially inducing docile bulls to buck and thrash violently is all part of the act, which is played up by event hucksters, who characterize the bulls as "ornery, mean-spirited, crazed killers" and cowboys as brave champions man enough to tame them. Yet, watch any bull-riding event, and you'll see the bull continues to buck even after he throws the rider—thanks to the strap cinched around his groin. The myth of the fearsome bull is the biggest piece of propaganda rodeo announcers deliver to spectators.

Another iconic symbol of rodeos is horse bucking, in which riders compete to see who can stay on a tormented horse for a set amount of time. Once again, flank straps painfully tightened below the animal's ribcage ensure he bucks, and many riders also wear metal spurs, which dig into the horse's flesh to cause further aggravation. Like bulls, horses are shocked with Hot Shots just as they leave the bucking chute. PRCA allows this cruelty, but some rodeos have tried in vain to prevent it. Organizers of the Reno Rodeo told participants that shocking horses would not be tolerated during its 10-day event in 2012 and even installed cameras to monitor the bucking chutes. But when confronted later with undercover footage from SHARK showing one man secretly using Hot Shots on horses, a rodeo spokesperson admitted that cowboys had been found to be "messing with" the overhead cameras and the person who applied the shocks worked "really hard to stay out of camera view."[9]

Rodeo apologists say bucking events are safe for the horses. Yet try telling that to Strawberry Fudge, who died from head and neck injuries after she bolted from the chute at the Cheyenne Frontier Days Rodeo in 2009. Or Check Mate, who suffered a back injury at the same rodeo in 2011 and had to be euthanized. Or Sweet and Sour, who galloped headfirst into a metal arena gate at the Sedro-Woolley Fourth of July Rodeo and died instantly in 2011. Or Elvira, victim of the same fate at 2012's Orange Blossom Festival Pro Rodeo in Florida. And these are just the deaths found in a five-minute Google search. Horse-bucking events may be thrilling for the casual observer, but they can be murder on the horses.

Bum Steer

Rodeo promoters call it steer roping, but most fans refer to it as steer busting, and it's easy to see why. In this event, a steer bursts out of a chute and sprints across the arena as a contestant on horseback gives chase and tosses a lasso over his horns. The horse and rider then veer to the left so the rope is lowered along the steer's side and catches him just below the hip, pulling his hind legs abruptly out from underneath him. "Within a split second, the steer's head and neck are jerked 180 degrees and more, causing the animal to be violently tripped, rolled, and dragged for approximately 30 feet," says former rodeo veterinarian Peggy Lawson. "That's a 700-pound body being dragged by the neck, with the horns digging into the dirt. Sometimes the horns fracture. The stress to the neck is enormous." Dr. Lawson notes that the point of this mistreatment is to stun the steer sufficiently so the contestant can tie his legs for a score. When the animals are crippled from repeated abuse, she says, they are sent to slaughter.[10]

Steer busting (also called steer tripping or steer jerking) is one of those rare events that is even condemned by some within the rodeo industry for being so hard on animals. "Steer tripping is inhumane," says one longtime rodeo participant. "It is allowed in only a few states and should be outlawed by Congressmen. It breaks horns and necks, and many steers die a few days later of ruptured intestines."[11] That's especially harsh criticism when you remember it comes from a guy who spends his days jumping onto the backs of animals.

After observing a number of rodeos, anthropologist Elizabeth Atwood Lawrence writes that steer-busting spectators appear to be delighted by the animals' misery. "The commonest audience reaction to the steers' plight was laughter. ... A few people remarked genially about a steer who hit the ground especially hard, making such comments as 'he'll have a headache tomorrow,' or 'he won't feel much like eating for a while,' but they neither showed nor voiced regret or sympathy."[12]

Horse-Killing Spectacle

Every year at the Calgary Stampede—Canada's biggest rodeo—two traditions are practically guaranteed: the first is that enormous crowds will gather to cheer the chuckwagon race events; the other is that at least one horse, and probably more, will die on the track. Indeed, it would seem the whole point of chuckwagon races is for teams of four thoroughbred horses to pull carriages through a figure-8 course until at least one of the animals is killed. Since 1986, Calgary Stampede's chuckwagon events have claimed the lives of more than 50 horses.[13] In 2010, two horses dropped dead from heart attacks. It's little wonder the race is called "the half mile of hell."[14]

In addition to heart attacks, horses die from injuries sustained in horrific crashes or must be euthanized as a result of them. Three horses were killed in 2012 when a horse pulling a covered wagon driven by Chad Harden suffered a ruptured aortic aneurysm—a weak blood vessel in the heart that burst—and died. Not only did the entire team of horses go down, but a horse running behind them slammed into the back of the wagon. After euthanizing two horses with broken legs on the track, veterinarians began emergency surgery on a fourth. Harden gave a tearful press conference immediately following the disaster, saying the horses were like family.

From their 1923 birth as a spectator sport in Calgary, chuckwagon races are now a popular attraction at other rodeos in North America. (The US has a National Championship Chuckwagon Races event, held each year in Clinton, Arkansas.) Chuckers, as the sport's human participants are called, defend their pursuit, saying that pulling rigs competitively is a better life for the horses, most of whom come from the racing industry and would otherwise end up in a slaughterhouse.[15] Yet whatever concern they may feel for the animals is often belied by their need to appear masculine. Even Harden, who seemed genuinely grief-stricken when his three horses died on the race course, evidently reconsidered his emotional press conference: "I suppose I looked like a bit of a wussy," he told a reporter a few months later.[16]

Hunting and Fishing

That desire to be masculine is a driving force behind so many cruelties, from consuming meat to activities in which animals figure as unwilling opponents in antagonistic confrontations. And the more violent, the better. It is in risking their own life and taking another that many men would seem to find their place in the world.[17] Nowhere is this yearning to achieve masculinity through transcendence over nature more evident than in the "sport" of hunting. As the United States became more settled in the 19th century, this tenet was the central preoccupation of countless middle-class males, who viewed hunting as the principal means to restore a sense of manliness lost through urbanization. "The early conservationist hunters saw hunting as useful in building character, that is, male character," observed the late ecofeminist and activist Marti Kheel. "They argued that hunting was a necessary corrective for men who had become overly feminized by the encroaches of civilization," where physical work was becoming less relevant and boys were being raised and taught by women.[18]

Attitudes have changed little in the 21st century, though recreational hunters have brought their excuses for killing animals to a wider audience. In his online meditation on hunting, food writer Hank Shaw attempts to define the moral boundary between the gravity of taking a life and the hunter's unabashed merriment and back-slapping that follows it.[19] In doing so, Shaw stumbles over a bramble of ethical contradictions that are inherent in justifying the hunting of animals. He acknowledges, for example, a universal reality: "Everything wants to live," he writes, "and will try anything it can to escape you." Yet, when he's packing a firearm, Shaw just can't help himself, even as he professes sympathy for his prey. "It is a soul-searing moment where part of you marvels at the animal's drive to live—to escape!—at the same time the rest of you is consumed with capturing it as fast as possible so you can end this miserable business. This internal conflict is, to me, what being human is all about."

There may be some regrettable truth in that, but it is also true that humans are capable of demonstrating compassion, and every day, people reject the slaughter of animals for meat in favor of plant-based foods. Shaw hints at his own capacity for mercy in his essay. "I am not ashamed to tell you that I have shed a tear more than once when I've had to deliver the coup de grace to a duck," he writes. "I'm not sure what it is about ducks, but they affect me more than other animals. I always apologize to it, knowing full well that this is a weak gesture designed mostly to help me feel better. But it does help me feel better. At least a little. So I keep doing it."

Of course he does. He *wants* to, and like so many other unseemly habits and traditions—whether they be eating meat, attending a bullfight, or wearing a fur coat—apologists justify hunting under a broad banner of defenses, all designed to absolve the hunter of moral obligations. Killing "game" animals, argue hook-and-bullet types, keeps their populations in check. Some contend that wild animals, such as bears, elephants, and lions, might otherwise threaten public safety, while other animals can damage crops. Industry groups claim hunting is a wise and prudent use of renewable natural resources, that hunters are conservationists and stewards of the land, and that it's all about "getting back to nature." But the most offensive excuse has to be the one offered by those who say that the hunter enjoys a deep connection with his victim or honors the animal's spirit by killing her. Shaw falls into this ethical quagmire when he writes: "I am at peace with killing my own meat because for me, every duck breast, every boar tongue, every deer heart is a story, not of conquest, but of communion." Although the hunter is clearly trying to legitimize his acts, genuine communion involves a *shared experience*, not something unilaterally imposed by force.

I don't mean to pick on Shaw. Indeed, he's merely an example of the sort of archaic mindset that believes there's anything sporting— or masculine—about the act of killing a defenseless animal. "The game of stalking, shooting, and skinning other beings is compelled not by a need for food or fresh air, but by a selfish and sinister intent," writes animal advocate Jim Robertson. "Though they bill themselves as sportsmen, participants are never really happy unless they win. The sport hunter's ulterior motive is comparable to that of a rebuked child who torments a puppy to lift his sagging self-esteem or gain a feeling of power and control."[20]

> "Animals give me more pleasure through the viewfinder of a camera than they ever did in the crosshairs of a gunsight. And after I've finished 'shooting,' my unharmed victims are still around for others to enjoy."[21]
> —Jimmy Stewart

Secret Shame

The euphemistic language of hunting conceals the torment involved in taking another's life: animals are not "killed," but rather "taken," "bagged," "dispatched," "culled," 'harvested," or "managed." Fox hunters in England also use colorful terms like "accounted for" or "bowled over." Masked in these verbal dodges, however, is the shameful secret of how often victims are not swiftly "dispatched," but wounded and left to stagger in the woods for days, at last dying in agony. In one study of 493 hunted deer, 240 ran after being shot—even in the heart—and the aid of trained dogs was required to locate them, 19 of whom were found still alive and suffering.[22]

The estimates are slightly worse for bow hunters, who typically target deer. "Even the most skilled archer can't do much better than a 50 percent crippling rate," writes Robertson.[23] That figure tallies with investigations done by state wildlife agencies in Illinois and Texas, which found that bow hunters leave one deer wounded for every one they kill and retrieve.[24] Other studies are more forgiving—one concludes that archers fail to recover 18 percent of the deer they hit[25]—but any suffering of an animal is indefensible. Writing on a popular pro-hunting site, one archer describes hitting a deer with a poorly placed shot, but rather than going after her, he leaves the animal in the forest overnight. It was only when he returned the next morning that he found she had staggered 300 yards and finally died with a punctured lung.[26]

Eighteen percent is also the wounding rate of birds reported by US Fish and Wildlife, but other studies of duck hunters in Canada and the United States put the number at more than 30 percent, with similar results for geese. This means that, in these two countries combined, about 3.5 million ducks and geese suffer being hit with birdshot every year and are lost or fly away wounded.[27]

For some hunters, wounding an animal is actually part of the sport, as discussed in the comments section of an online article about hunting: "The conduct that worries me is the apparent acceptance of questionable shots to 'anchor' or slow down a running animal. Thankfully I haven't seen this first hand, but rather read (with disbelief) folks bragging about successfully tracking down some trophy buck after initially shooting it through the shoulder."[28]

Humans are frequently wounded as well, with hunters gunning down two-legged victims they've mistaken for a deer or some other forest creature, or sometimes shooting each other in supreme acts of stupidity, such as the moment in 2006 when then-Vice President Dick Cheney famously filled a hunting companion's face with birdshot. His friend recovered, and Cheney instantly became a punchline for late-night comics, but his blunder was emphasized by some sobering statistics. According to the International Hunter Education Association, approximately 1,000 people are accidentally shot by hunters in the United States and Canada every year, and about 100 of those injuries are fatal.[29] Hunters also take aim at companion animals like dogs and cats, mistaking them for coyotes, squirrels, or other targeted beings. In 2011, four dogs were mistakenly shot and killed in Maine alone.[30]

Sadly, there are hunters who go out of their way to attack humans, at least in England, where violence against activists who monitor hunts (called hunt saboteurs) now gets scant attention. When seven hunt supporters broke into an activist's car and beat him with sticks in December 2012, it wasn't the press that broke the story, it was the hunt saboteur community.[31] "These attacks still go on, and they're still underreported, under-policed, and under-prosecuted," says Kim Stallwood, an independent scholar and author on animal rights.[32] Authorities might see the activists as lacking credibility, partly because their presence at a hunt is interpreted as provoking an assault, or perhaps they're simply tired of them.

Tame Targets

Hidden within the world of hunting is a practice so plainly unethical that many recreational hunters consider it a disgrace to their sport—and that's saying something. Canned hunts, as the practice is known, take place on private land and cater to cowards for whom killing is strictly a business transaction. Advertised as "game ranches" or "hunting preserves," canned hunts offer those with little or no skill the opportunity to shoot animals trapped behind fences.[33] Worse still is that these aren't even wild animals: they have been "retired" from circuses, zoos, or wild animal parks or come from breeders. Often the animals are tame from being raised in captivity and treated like pets; they lack the instinct to flee from gun-toting humans.

That's just fine with canned-hunt patrons, who simply want a trophy to mount on their wall and can't be bothered with the time and effort required in traditional sport hunting. They pick their animal from a menu or photo, make their payment, and blast away. In some facilities, shooters even wait for and gun down animals when they arrive at the trough for their regular feeding. At one canned hunt in Michigan, for instance, the ranch owner's son led several Russian boars to their breakfast bin, where they were ambushed by customers armed with crossbows. Leaping out from behind a tree, one patron launched an arrow deep into a boar, who cried out in pain but could not escape the two arrows that followed, both from 10 feet (3 meters) away, and lay twitching for four minutes as the life oozed from him. "I was pumpin', man," the customer boasted into his buddy's video camera. "The first arrow was high. The second hit liver. The third took lung. I like it." He then grasped the animal by the ears and lifted his head off the ground for the camera. "I'll grab it like I grab my women," he said.[34] And while Safari Club International espouses the doctrine of fair chase, they argue this includes animals in captivity; at least one of their members paid for the privilege of shooting a tiger trapped in a horse trailer.[35]

The pay-to-slay industry is growing, and The Humane Society of the United States (HSUS) estimates there are more than 1,000 of these shooting galleries operating in at least two dozen states.[36] At canned-hunting ranches in the US, you can purchase and shoot elk, deer, bighorn sheep, eland, antelope, zebras, ostriches, leopards, turkeys, kangaroos, and more. Many of these animals have names. Bathsheba, John, Matthew, Paul, and Rachel, for instance, were pet African lions who were so comfortable around people that they'd lick their keepers' hands before they were killed at a hunting ranch in Texas.[37] Country singer Troy Gentry, meanwhile, shot a docile bear named Cubby inside an enclosure in Minnesota—and then bragged that he'd killed him in the wild.[38] Then there was Honker, a five-year-old reindeer who had been hand-fed and raised by an elderly couple in northern Iowa. When her husband died, the widow couldn't care for their animals, so she sold Honker to an auction house in Missouri. The auction house, in turn, sold Honker to a game farm in Wisconsin, where he was shot and killed.[39]

The cost for a canned hunt can range from hundreds to tens of thousands of dollars, with customers generally paying the highest prices for "trophy" animals with large antlers or exotic species like lions. At a typical canned hunt in Ohio, shooters pay up to US$9,800 to kill a whitetail deer and up to US$9,500 to shoot an elk, two of the most commonly killed animals in canned hunts.[40] Patrons of these contract executions have their choice of weapons, too: crossbow, shotgun, pistol, rifle, or muzzleloader—an archaic, single-shot firearm with such a slow reloading process that any animal not killed with the first try is certain to linger in agony. Whatever the weapon, whatever the targeted animal, many canned-hunt operators offer a "no kill, no bill" guarantee, assuring customers they won't leave empty-handed. Consequently, operators sometimes sedate animals with drugs to slow them down and make them even easier prey, as revealed in a 2011 undercover investigation by HSUS.[41]

As bad as the confined carnage is in the United States, the canned-hunt business is just as appalling elsewhere. Australia, Canada, New Zealand, and nations in Africa offer animals on ranches for the killing pleasure of paying customers. Indeed, affluent tourists from all over the world swagger into South Africa to take aim at captive-bred lions, who are reared in conditions resembling factory farms, with caged females used as breeding machines and their babies taken away shortly after giving birth. Like animals raised for food, lions here are selectively bred to make them bigger and thus more popular as "trophies."[42] (Wildlife expert Gareth Patterson writes of a canned-hunt customer who pumped a dozen bullets into one lion before the animal died—all because he didn't want to blemish the majestic head he planned to display.[43]) But before the lions are sent off to a canned hunt, breeders rent the cubs to facilities in which animal lovers pay to interact with them. While visitors to South Africa may delight in petting a live lion, they're actually subsidizing the country's lion-breeding industry and habituating the animals to humans before they become targets on a hunting ranch.[44]

Canned hunting has become so popular in South Africa that nearly twice as many lion trophies are exported from the country as from all other African nations combined.[45] With customers spending an average of US$40,000 per lion,[46] and about 1,000 lions killed in a single year,[47] breeding and killing lions is a multimillion-dollar business. Moreover, because it's only the head or skin of an animal that hunters want to take home, South Africa's canned-hunting industry is now enjoying a lucrative trade in lion parts to China and

Vietnam, where bones are turned into "lion wine," a popular aphrodisiac.[48] South Africa briefly abolished canned hunting in 2009, but lion breeders—not about to switch to a principled enterprise—got the law overturned.

"Cruel and Moronic"

Considering that pigeon shooting involves thousands of birds being released from spring-loaded boxes one by one so shooters can take turns blasting away at them with 12-gauge shotguns, this "sport" is the cruelest form of target practice. Shooters earn points when a bird's body lands in designated scoring areas. Meanwhile, girls and boys, generally 12 to 16 years old, collect surviving pigeons and are supposed to kill the birds by wringing their necks or decapitating them with shears. "I saw no one breaking any bird's neck that day," writes *The Philadelphia Inquirer* journalist Amy Worden, who witnessed a contest in 2012. "The shooters slammed them to the ground, whacked them against their boot heels, stomped on them. A teenager appeared to delight in the killing, laughing as he twisted his leg to smash birds into the ground." Some shooters, Worden says, grabbed injured birds off the ground "and punted them like footballs. Others threw birds unable to fly into the air and shot them at a few feet, as they exploded in a mass of feathers."[49] Many pigeons escape, however; for such birds, death comes slowly, though some live with their painful wounds.

In the US, these competitions are only held openly in Pennsylvania, with shoots in Berks County attracting the most notoriety, though illegal shoots have been popping up in South Carolina, Indiana, and Minnesota, says Janet Enoch of SHARK. "They are a lot like a dogfight in their secrecy and collusion with corrupt government officials."[50] Indeed, pigeon shoots are a violation of Pennsylvania's anti-cruelty law, yet district attorneys refuse to enforce it—a stance that continues to frustrate local humane societies. In 2009, Berks County Humane Society Police Officer Johnna Seeton filed three criminal citations charging the Pike

Township Sportsmen's Association with the "wanton and cruel treatment of pigeons" at its October 18, 2009, live pigeon shoot. (She even returned to the site *two days later* and found pigeons still struggling in pain after being struck in vital organs. These birds were humanely euthanized.) But the county's district attorney, John Adams, got the citations dismissed, arguing that shooting pigeons is not against the law in Pennsylvania. That he has taken campaign contributions from those who practice pigeon shooting may have something to do with his intractable position.[51]

The Humane Society of Berks County (HSBC) strongly disagrees with Adams, and in a rare public statement, they called on citizens to take a stand in this matter. After carefully examining the law, HSBC determined that pigeon shoots are in fact illegal. "We know lots of people run around saying the shoots are legal and have for years," reads the statement. "The fact that police and district attorneys in various counties, some with close connections to shooting groups, don't prosecute or even block prosecutions by Humane Society police officers doesn't mean they aren't a crime."[52] In light of a 2012 video taken by SHARK that shows participants at a Berks County pigeon shoot swinging, stomping, and kicking wounded birds, HSBC's executive director Karel Minor drafted an open letter to Adams offering the full resources of his office should the district attorney decide to prosecute. Adams never replied.[53]

Unlike traditional hunting, in which animals are eaten or at least valued as a trophy, shot pigeons are garbage in the eyes of hunters. This may explain why pigeon shooters defend their fun in part by claiming they are ridding the state of "rats with wings." Actually, most of the birds are captive bred or trapped and collected from places like New York City and deprived of food and water as they are transported by van. Pigeon brokers in Pennsylvania purchase the birds for US$2 each, then sell them to shooting ranges for up to US$4.[54]

There is some hope amid this gratuitous mass slaughter of birds. The most notorious of these contests in the United States—the long-running pigeon shoot held every Labor Day in Hegins, Pennsylvania—was finally shut down in 1999 after the Pennsylvania Supreme Court called the event "cruel and moronic" and ruled that humane officers could bring charges against pigeon-shoot participants.[55] Even the Olympic Committee, that arbiter of all things athletic, has declared that live pigeon shoots are not a sport.[56]

Hounded to Death

In 2004, sport hunters in Great Britain were indignant about a new piece of legislation being debated in Parliament that threatened to, according to the rhetoric, tear the very fabric of British tradition. The Hunting Act 2004 aimed to end hunting wild mammals with dogs throughout England and Wales as of February 18, 2005. (Scotland's Parliament had introduced a similar ban in 2002.) The law passed, and it's proved to be as contentious as it is monumental, with two types of hunting particularly affected: fox hunting, in which hunters mounted on horseback and on foot use dogs to pursue and kill foxes, and hare coursing, which involves teams of dogs chasing down wild hares, often tearing them to pieces. Shooting these animals is still legal; you just can't hunt them with hounds.

But that takes away all the fun, say hunt supporters—which is why the ban is unabashedly and abundantly ignored. Fox hunters ostensibly operating within the law don't chase a live fox, but rather follow a scent pulled across the countryside by a fellow hunter. They routinely flout the law, however, letting their dogs track and kill foxes. Since a dog "accidentally" attacking a fox he might locate does not fall outside the law, defiance of the ban has rendered it virtually meaningless. In the words of UK blogger Kate Holmes, "It's an official secret throughout the land—away from Westminster and all the townies—that fox hunting is going strong."[57] Though hunt saboteurs constantly witness red-coated hunters pursuing and killing foxes, prosecutions are relatively rare, in part because courts seem sympathetic to the hunters, whom Rod Liddle of *The Spectator* charitably describes as "braying high-born halfwits."[58] Said one judge who quit hunting when the ban was passed, "I felt I could not enforce the law Monday to Friday and break it on Saturday."[59]

It may not have the social distinction of fox hunting, but hare coursing has an equally long tradition in Britain—and it's also practiced despite the ban on hunting with hounds. In hare coursing, dogs pursue hares in flat, rural fields, usually after harvest season (August or September). A typical hunt begins with a line of participants and their dogs spreading out and disturbing a hare from her nest. The dogs are released, and bets are placed on which canine will be the first to overtake and catch his prey. Once the hare is killed, the body is discarded and everyone moves to a new piece of land for another round of torment.

All this illegal activity doesn't sit well with farmers, who continue to complain to authorities about violent confrontations with hare coursers. At least one farmer has had his barn set on fire. "Some farming families are genuinely scared of these people," says a landowner in Lincolnshire County. "They bully their way on to their farms and they say, 'Fuck off if you want to live.' And this can be 20 yards from your back door. There will be a fatality."[60]

Of course, there are plenty of fatalities among the hares, who die in the jaws of dogs, succumb later to injuries, or fall victim to capture myopathy, a stress-induced condition that may take hours or days to kill an animal after an intensely traumatic experience. Hares, like their lagomorphic cousin the rabbit, are fragile and even a mild level of fear can cause heart failure.[61] In countries where hare coursing is still a legal blood sport, such as Ireland and the US, dogs are sometimes muzzled, but this does little to reduce internal injuries or heart attack. Reports compiled in 2012 by Ireland's National Parks and Wildlife Service show that hares die from being mauled and pinned down by the much heavier greyhounds and that the animals are terrorized throughout the ordeal.[62] "Muzzling would not make coursing a humane sport," writes John Fitzgerald in his book *Bad Hare Days*. "Instead, it would just make the cruelty less visible."[63]

Hare or Rabbit?

They're both used for coursing—being pursued and killed by dogs for sport—but hares and rabbits have significant differences. For one thing, unlike hares, rabbits have been domesticated. Hares have longer ears and hind legs and can be distinguished from rabbits by the black markings on their fur. All rabbits (except the cottontail) burrow underground, where they bear their young and live in colonies, while hares give birth in nests at the surface and only come together to mate. The jack rabbit is actually a hare; the Belgian hare is in fact a rabbit.

Hooked on Cruelty

Hidden beneath the water's surface, fish live in a world that seems so different from our own. Perhaps that's one reason we rarely consider their well-being. These underwater aliens, with their scaly exteriors and limbless bodies, generate relatively little sympathy in their unseen universe. Are they intelligent? Do they feel pain? Is there anybody behind those blank eyes? No, no, no, cynics have long answered. All the easier, they say, to drag millions of these animals out of their watery world every year on barbed hooks. After all, these aren't like dogs or cats, who cry out when they're hurt or communicate with a facial expression we can recognize. Indeed, many "vegetarians" who wouldn't think of consuming the flesh of a pig, cow, chicken, or sheep have no qualms about eating a fish, somehow convinced they're not even animals.

The "sport" of fishing has two types of enthusiasts: those who hook a fish for display on a wall or possibly to consume, and those who release the fish after catching him. Both bear the burden of cruelty, but I'll wager that catch-and-release fishing is ultimately just as bad—and maybe worse. Hailed for its conservation of fish populations, catch-and-release is considered the ethical high ground among many anglers, yet studies show the harm caused to a fish who has been snagged and taken from the water is often invisible. Estimates on how many fish die within six days of being caught and released range from 16 to 43 percent.[64] This is a wide variance, but any way you look at it, with some 31 million recreational anglers making a total of 455 million fishing trips every year in the US alone, there are an awful lot of fish who end up killed by people who think they are doing these animals no harm.[65]

Fish experience high levels of stress from being caught, handled, and exposed to the air; even if they are set free, their feeding and reproductive behaviors may be forever inhibited by the ordeal, leading to a disruption in the ecosystem. Meanwhile, fishhooks can puncture vital organs such as the heart and lungs, leading to internal bleeding.[66] "No one would tolerate that sort of thing with birds. But we will for fish because they're underwater, out of sight," observes one angler who gave up recreational fishing because of the cruelty.[67]

Another hidden torment may include depressurization, common among fish caught in deep water, which can result in over-inflation of the gas bladder, gas embolisms, inability to submerge when released, internal and/or external hemorrhaging, and death.[68] The science tells us such harm is undeniable. Not so clear, at least among biologists and many who take pleasure in catching fish, is how the animal feels getting a sharp hook stuck in her mouth or—worse yet—swallowing one whole. A 2010 book by marine biologist Victoria Braithwaite, *Do Fish Feel Pain?*, seemed to sum up the debate very nicely: fish have nociceptors—sensory organs that respond to pain by sending messages to the brain—so, yes, they suffer when hooked or speared. And, as Dr. Braithwaite discovered, fish are also pretty smart. "It turns out that the stereotype of fish as slow, dim-witted creatures is wrong; many fish are remarkably clever," she writes. "For example, they can learn geometrical relationships and landmarks—and then use these to generate a mental map to plan escape routes if a predator shows up."[69]

Then, in 2013, the fishing world was abuzz about a new study suggesting that the presence of nociceptors isn't enough, and that the fish's brain is not sufficiently developed to detect painful stimuli; any reaction to being hooked is an unconscious one, or so say the paper's authors.[70] (It's significant that the lead scientist on the study is a fisherman.) Anglers were only too happy to tout this as proof they could go on hooking and killing guilt-free, but is this study conclusive? Many researchers say it's more speculation than science,[71] and animal protection groups like the RSCPA point to the large body of research indicating that marine life is quite capable of suffering. "There are a number of studies which we believe provide enough evidence to show that fish do feel pain and this remains our view," says a spokesperson with the charity.[72]

While the catch-and-release angler believes he's practicing an ethic, the "big game" fisher suffers no such pangs of conscience. These men and women hunt the oceans for large marine species such as tuna, sailfish, marlin, and swordfish, and reel them onto the decks of their boats, where the animals desperately writhe, gasp, and flap their gills in a fruitless attempt to get oxygen before they finally suffocate. Then they're hoisted high for a photo. Trophy anglers consider this all great fun. It's also a big sport, with fishing tournaments offering enormous cash prizes. Winning boats in one of the world's largest marlin-fishing contests, for instance, take home more than US$2 million.[73] But most deep-sea anglers will tell you they do it for love of the sport, and one of the elements they particularly enjoy is the fight that invariably ensues once a fish has been hooked. In fact, many fishermen will prolong the time it takes to land a fish just to see the animal struggle, an ordeal that causes fish additional fear, distress, and exhaustion.[74]

Animal Racing

A 21st-century time-traveler catapulted back 2,000 years or so to Greek or Roman antiquity would easily recognize the roots of modern animal racing. Inside the ancient hippodromes and stadiums, such as Rome's lavish Circus Maximus, teams of two or four horses pulled two-wheeled chariots and a driver in dramatic competitions. A dozen teams might be running in a race, which consisted of seven laps around the track. Crashes were frequent and violent and could be fatal to the horses and the charioteer (who was usually a slave); indeed, with their tight, 180-degree turns, racing stadiums were evidently designed to produce maximum carnage.[75] Equestrian events also included racing on horseback, but these were not as popular as chariot races, which had the allure of bloodshed to attract large crowds.

The tradition of racing animals continues, but with a twist: many of the abuses that were relished by sports lovers of the Classical world are now regarded as profound ethical concerns—at least in the eyes of animal advocates, if not explicitly those of spectators.[76]

Dog Sled Racing

Chariot races clearly find their modern counterpart in the chuck-wagon contests of rodeos. But they also bear more than a passing resemblance to today's grueling dog sled events. With teams of animals harnessed to a vehicle carrying a lone driver (a "musher"), canine-powered competitions like the annual Iditarod and Yukon Quest dog sled races—each featuring 1,000 miles of Alaska's unforgiving frozen wilderness—recall both the danger and callousness of ancient games. Dogs used are typically Alaskan huskies, a powerful breed with a dense coat that would seem ideally suited for snow-packed conditions. But like any animal, dogs suffer when driven to extremes—and they are driven hard during the nine to 18 days it takes a team of a dozen or more huskies to complete a race. Not every dog crosses the finish line, however. Dogs die from heart failure, pneumonia, internal bleeding, and choking on their vomit, which turns out to be a common occurrence. Others have drowned, been strangled in towlines, and run over by snowmobiles. In 1985, an Iditarod musher kicked his dog to death.[77] No one was keeping track of animal fatalities when the Iditarod was launched in 1973, but the Sled Dog Action Coalition says more than 140 dogs have perished—

an average of more than three per year in that race alone.[78]

That doesn't include the unknown number of animals who are simply disposed of. Mushers breed 50 or more dogs a year to find 15 to 20 outstanding runners, and those who are considered poor performers are often killed. Since getting to a veterinarian in Alaska and Canada for humane euthanasia can be a challenge, not to mention expensive, the heartless solution among mushers is to bludgeon or shoot the dogs in the head.[79] This practice, known in the industry as "herd control," didn't receive much attention until 2010, when a former musher who managed a recreational dog sledding business in British Columbia came forward to complain that his employer had forced him to kill one-third of the company's huskies—about 70 animals—over two April days in full view of all the dogs. So gruesome were the deaths he was asked to execute, said Robert Fawcett, that he filed a claim with British Columbia's Workers' Compensation Board saying he suffered PTSD. In his claim, Fawcett described how the huskies panicked as they witnessed their friends being stabbed and shot and tried desperately to defend themselves against the man they once trusted. The horrific details of the executions can be found in Fawcett's original workers' comp claim.[80]

Even dogs who survive long enough to "retire" may be destined for misery, since they pass the remainder of their lives isolated in kennels, tethered by a short chain. Some mushers have hundreds of canines they've bred. Joe Redington, co-founder of the Iditarod, admitted that he once had as many as 527 dogs.[81] "The aspect of the sport that has always most disturbed me is how the dogs are kept on a daily basis," says Ashley Keith, a former musher and Iditarod kennel employee who now rescues and rehabilitates abused sled dogs. "It is a common, accepted, and even preferred practice in the sled dog community to keep sled dogs on four- to six-foot [1.2- to 1.8-meter] chains attached to a plastic barrel or wooden house. For example, the kennel I worked for in Alaska didn't even use any type of bedding in the plastic houses except during the coldest months of the year. I was hired at the kennel in November, and the dogs still had just bare plastic houses without any straw bedding in them. I asked other mushers in the lower 48 states about this practice, and they said it was not uncommon. Many mushers view sled dogs as mere machines, and not as sentient individuals. Every dog deserves to be a part of the family. Unfortunately, most sled dogs never get the chance."[82]

Horse Racing

To fully appreciate the inherent danger of racing thoroughbred horses, we have to consider for a moment a slender bit of anatomy connecting the animals' legs to their feet. Sublimely powerful and graceful, thoroughbred horses weigh in excess of 1,000 pounds (453 kilograms)—all of it perched on ankles the same size as yours and mine. These ankle joints, technically called fetlocks, have literally been the breaking point for thoroughbreds, who are bred for extreme speed while their bones have gotten lighter and more frail.[83] One tragic and high-profile example is the filly Eight Belles, who ran her heart out in the 2008 Kentucky Derby and collapsed shortly after the finish line with compound fractures in both her front fetlock joints. Track veterinarians euthanized her moments later. She was three years old.

The global horse racing industry will tell you these animals live to run. The truth is, they are made to run—and they often die doing it. Shockingly often, it turns out. According to a 2012 investigation by *The New York Times*, an average of 24 horses pass away on US racetracks *every week*.[84] While the United States is arguably where most horses run and die, horse racing is a fixture in England and elsewhere, including just about every former British colony. Research by the charity Animal Aid reveals that some 370 equines are run to death in the UK each year.[85]

A number of factors have led to the rising toll in horses killed, and one cause that has been suggested goes back generations. Most of the horses bred for racing today trace their roots to one of just 28 horses—three stallions and 25 mares—who mated in England during the 17th and 18th centuries.[86] With such a shallow gene pool, the horse population can't help but encounter physical problems such as frail skeletal systems. In Britain, three times as many horses are being produced than 40 years ago, yet a decreasing proportion—currently only about 35 percent—are healthy enough to begin racing.[87]

Critics also point to the changing economics of the sport, where racetrack owners have had to devise new ways of attracting customers. One solution has been to add casino gambling to operations in Canada and the US. Slot-machine revenue has allowed for more lucrative race purses, which in turn has created incentive for trainers to push horses harder. This happens more frequently at so-called claiming races, where less-valuable horses run and where regulators often give the animals less protection from painkillers used to mask injury. You won't find an Eight Belles at one of these tracks, which represent the mainstay of US horse racing, but you will find death. In its month-long investigation, *The New York Times* found that horses in claiming races have a 22 percent greater chance of breaking down than horses in higher-grade races.[88]

In addition to liberal doses of painkillers, shady trainers are increasingly doling out an odd variety of performance-enhancing chemicals, including Viagra and drugs used to artificially bulk up pigs and cows before slaughter. Until recently, the most exotic substance was cobra venom, used to shut off the nerves that transmit pain.[89] Then, in 2012, US racing regulators confirmed what beforehand had only been rumor: trainers in several states were doping horses with dermorphin, a potent drug obtained from the skin of the *Phyllomedusa sauvagei*, commonly known as the waxy monkey tree frog.[90] Dubbed "frog juice," this chemical is more powerful than morphine as it numbs pain and produces a boost of hyperactivity—resulting in a much greater risk that horses will critically injure themselves.

Arguably the biggest tragedy of horse racing, however, is also the least publicized. The thoroughbred industry is now breeding more than 100,000 horses a year,[91] and doing so results in the deliberate killing of countless equines. That's because, like animals in factory farms, horses bred for racing are a commodity, and there's no room in the bottom line for compassion. In thoroughbred production, the largest segment of horse breeding, owners of mares may pay huge fees to have champion stallions brought in to "cover" (impregnate) their horse. Owners of studs can command in excess of US$100,000 for this service—due when the newborn foal has lived 48 hours—provided their stallion has the lineage and track record of a winner.[92] A stallion covering 100 mares or more a year means a multi-million-dollar return for his owners. But the industry is unpredictable, with racing experiencing peaks and valleys of popularity, and mare owners may decide that a foal is being born into unfavorable economic conditions. The fate of babies at the hands of some unscrupulous owners has been death—often shortly after birth, but sometimes through abortion.[93]

More and more, "surplus" horses are ending up in slaughterhouses in Britain, Japan, Mexico, and Canada. Figures released by the UK government in 2011 show that the number of horses and ponies being butchered for meat in England, Scotland, and Wales had risen by 50 percent from previous years.[94] Not even prize-winning performers are safe from the chopping block. After he failed to meet financial expectations as a stud, Ferdinand—the 1986 Kentucky Derby winner who retired three years later as history's fifth leading money winner at the time—was slaughtered for pet food in Japan in 2002. Ferdinand was, said one stable employee, "the gentlest horse you could imagine. ... He'd come over to me and press his head up against me. He was so sweet."[95]

Dog Racing

Sleek and swift, greyhounds seem born to run—a trait that unscrupulous owners, breeders, and trainers have been exploiting for maximum profit since the modern dog-racing industry was created as a gambling enterprise in 1919. It was then, at a racetrack near San Francisco, that an entrepreneur installed a mechanical rabbit on a rail that greyhounds would chase, giving birth to a new brand of industrialized abuse. It's since been exported to the UK, Canada, Australia, South Africa, New Zealand, Ireland, and countries throughout Asia.

Like animals in factory farms, confinement and death are what characterize the life of greyhounds in the racing industry. Dogs are kept in warehouse-style kennels in rows of stacked cages in which they are barely able to stand or turn around. Cages are built for convenience, not the comfort of the canine, and generally measure 34 inches high, 30 inches wide, and 43 inches deep—hardly enough space for an animal who is between 23 and 30 inches tall at the shoulder.[96] Yet this is how the dogs remain, with carpet scraps or shredded paper as bedding, for 20 or more hours every day. Their only respite comes when they are delivered to the track to compete or when they are taken out in large groups and allowed to relieve themselves. And while you'd think a champion dog would be fed the finest diet, the industry routinely gives its greyhounds "4-D meat"—flesh from diseased, disabled, dying, or dead animals (who died before reaching the slaughterhouse). This meat has long been a legal ingredient in pet food (see Chapter 1), for which it is first heated to destroy bacteria, but greyhound trainers feed it to the dogs raw, worried that cooked meat could hinder racing performance.[97]

Though commercial dog racing got its start in the US, it's actually now a bigger sport in Great Britain, where the £2.5-billion-a-year industry began in 1926 and continues to be taken to task for its relentless mistreatment of animals.[98] Every year, according to the UK-based League Against Cruel Sports, more than 13,500 "surplus" dogs are bred, with 4,000 of these going missing. Some are killed by vets, while others may be shot or simply discarded into a flooded quarry with a brick around the neck.[99] Because registered greyhounds have identifying tattoos on their ears, the bodies of many dogs have been found with the ears cut off.

If a dog does not suffer an early death—from heat stroke, say, or heart attack, or being euthanized after an injury—he will usually "retire" at age five. While greyhound-rescue groups do provide a glimmer of hope for these loving animals, rehabilitating and re-homing them has the unfortunate consequence of contributing to the constant cycle of exploitation, with the dog-racing industry pointing to adoptions as evidence that greyhounds retire to good lives. Moreover, breeders, trainers, racers, and owners may even take some credit for the hard work of rescue groups. "They will be able to boast of the adoptions as if they themselves were to thank for this one small bit of mercy," observe Erin Williams and Margo DeMello in their book *Why Animals Matter*. "On the other hand, some 'rescue groups' have been caught over the years selling their rescued greyhounds into biomedical research via class B dealers. This is perhaps the saddest end that these animals can experience in an industry that profits from suffering."[100]

What You Can Do

The first step toward helping nonhuman animals used in sports is to not participate in these activities and not patronize venues where animals are exploited. In addition, many events, such as rodeos and dog sled races, rely heavily on corporate sponsors; please let these companies know how you feel about the suffering they are subsidizing. You can also discuss your concerns with family and friends, and ask them to get involved. Please visit these organizations for more information about their campaigns:

Animal Aid (UK)
www.animalaid.org.uk

Animal Equity (UK)
www.animalequality.net

Animals Australia
www.animalsaustralia.org

Grey2K USA
www.grey2kusa.org

Greyhound Protection League (US)
www.greyhounds.org

Irish Council Against Blood Sports
www.banbloodsports.com

League Against Cruel Sports (UK)
www.league.org.uk

Liberation BC (Canada)
http://liberationbc.org

SAFE (New Zealand)
www.safe.org.nz

SHARK (US)
www.sharkonline.org

Vancouver Humane Society (Canada)
www.vancouverhumanesociety.bc.ca

Rodeos

- Learn about the corporations that want to profit from animal cruelty by visiting www.corporatethugs.com

Hunting

- Encourage your legislators to enact or enforce wildlife protection laws, and insist that non-hunters be equally represented on wildlife agency staffs.
- Before you support a wildlife or conservation group, ask if it supports hunting. Organizations such as the National

Wildlife Federation, the National Audubon Society, the Sierra Club, the Izaak Walton League, the Wilderness Society, and even World Wildlife Fund are pro-hunting.

Dog Sled Racing

Tell sponsors of dog sled races that you'll be boycotting their products and services as long as they continue to subsidize cruelty. This is not a complete list of races that exploit dogs, unfortunately:

Copper Basin 300
www.cb300.com

Eagle Cap Extreme
www.eaglecapextreme.com

Iditarod
http://iditarod.com/race/sponsors

Inland Empire Pacific Coast Championship
www.iesda.org

International Pedigree Stage Stop
www.wyomingstagestop.org/sponsors.php

John Beargrease Sled Dog Marathon
www.beargrease.com/sponsors/sponsor-page

Knik 200
http://knik200sleddograce.com/sponsors

North Pole Championships
www.northpolechampionships.com

Plum Creek Wilderness
www.100milewildernessrace.org

Sheep Mountain Lodge 150
www.sheepmountain.com/SheepMtn150.php

Tustumena 200
www.tustumena200.com/sponsors.html

Yukon Quest
www.yukonquest.com/site/current-yukon-quest-sponsors

Hare Coursing

Efforts to make hare coursing illegal in the US have failed, though it persists even in countries where it has been banned, such as England and Wales. About the most you can do in such cases is to ask courts to enforce the law. In Ireland, where participants engage in organized events, the major sponsor is Greyhound and Pet World, which provides financial backing to the annual hare coursing "festival" in which captive hares are terrorized and killed on a converted racecourse during three successive days. Please contact:

Greyhound and Pet World
Abbeyfeale, Co. Limerick, Ireland
Phone (from outside Ireland): 00 353 6831389; (from within Ireland): 068-31389
Email: greyhounds@eircom.net

Horse Racing

Some horses "retired" from the racing industry are lucky enough to be rehabilitated and re-homed, not abandoned or sent to a slaughterhouse. Even if you can't afford to adopt, these nonprofits would welcome your support. (Note: Not all of these groups are necessarily anti-racing.)

CANTER (The Communication Alliance to Network

Thoroughbred Ex-Racehorses)
www.canterusa.org

Gray Dapple Thoroughbred Assistance Program (US)
www.graydapple.org

Horse Rescue Australia
www.horserescue.com.au

Manes and Tails Organization (US)
www.manesandtailsorganization.org

No Day Off Equine Rescue (US)
http://nodayoffequinerescue.webs.com/

Racehorse Rescue Centre (UK)
www.racehorserescue.org.uk

ReRun, Inc. (US)
www.rerun.org

New Stride Thoroughbred Adoption Society (Canada)
http://newstride.com/

Thoroughbred Adoption Network (US)
www.thoroughbredadoption.com

Dog Racing
If you are interested in adopting a greyhound, please contact one of
these organizations:

Dog Rescue Ireland
www.dogrescueireland.com

Greyhound Adoption Program (Australia)
www.gapnsw.org.au

Greyhound Adoption Project (US)
www.adopt-a-greyhound.org/

Greyhound Companions of New Mexico (US)
www.gcnm.org

Greyhound Protection League (US)
www.greyhounds.org

Greyhound Rescue West of England
www.grwe.com

The Greyhound Sanctuary (UK)
www.thegreyhoundsanctuary.org

Greyt Exploitations (UK)
www.greytexploitations.com

National Greyhound Adoption Program (US)
www.ngap.org

Chapter 6

The Age of Aquariums: Animals in Entertainment

When I became disturbed about the treatment of the elephants, the continual beatings, including the baby Benjamin, I was told "that's discipline."
—Tom Rider, former circus employee

The *Dine with Shamu* show had gone well, and about two dozen tourists inside the stadium at SeaWorld Orlando began to file out after having a buffet lunch and watching trainers interact with killer whales, also known as orcas. Earlier that day, Tilikum, a 12,500-pound (5,600-kilogram) killer whale, had ignored some commands during a show in which he was supposed to perform such stunts as leaping from the water, swimming upside down, and splashing the crowd with his tail, but now he seemed better, even playful. One of the trainers, Dawn Brancheau, wearing a black-and-white wet suit that echoed the orca's coloring, lay in shallow water on a concrete ledge built into the side of the pool. Tilikum (or "Tili," as staff called him) mimicked her behavior, turning belly up while she held his flipper and talked to him. Moments earlier she had been feeding Tili, but she ran out of fish and was now spending a little time bonding with him. Perhaps the orca—who was two years old when he was seized in the open waters off Iceland in 1983 and has lived in captivity ever since—enjoyed a special connection with Dawn. She began working with otters and sea lions at SeaWorld in 1994 and was among the park's most experienced and careful orca trainers. "You can't put yourself in the water unless you trust them and they trust you," she once told a reporter about the whales she worked with.[1]

It was nearly time for Dawn to command Tili to swim deep into the tank and give spectators behind a special viewing glass a thrill.

But the whale had other ideas. Instead of waiting for the signal, Tili bit down on Dawn's arm. Whether startled or just professional, she remained smiling as she resisted, and the 6-ton marine mammal slowly pulled her into the pool.[2] Immediately another trainer, who was acting as Dawn's safety spotter, hit the alarm and 20 SeaWorld employees—everyone from food servers to paramedics—rushed to the scene. Confused spectators were hustled out of the stadium as several employees furiously reeled out a large net with which they hoped to corral Tili, who held Dawn in his mouth like a toy, diving deeper into the water and shaking her back and forth. A strong swimmer, Dawn managed to break free for a moment, reaching the surface and getting a gasp of air before the orca hit her with his nose. Once more she attempted to swim away, but Tili struck her body again. He took her in his mouth and began swimming frantically, only breaking the surface long enough to breathe. SeaWorld staff considered Tili a "possessive" animal, one who would not willingly relinquish an object, and he was intensely focused on Dawn. As trainers slapped the water, signaling the whale to let go, Tili only became more agitated. "The whale would not let us have her," trainer Jodie Ann Tintle later told investigators.[3]

We can't say for certain when Dawn died. What we do know is that the 40-year-old trainer suffered multiple injuries before dying of drowning and blunt-force trauma. Her neck was broken, her scalp had been torn from her head, and several ribs and her jaw were fractured. At some point during the ordeal, Tilikum had bitten off Dawn's left arm.[4] It was a gruesome way to die.

We also can't say with certainty what Tili was thinking during the 40 or so minutes before he was coaxed into a smaller pool and finally released Dawn's body from his jaws. But some animal advocates have suggested that intense frustration built upon three decades of imprisonment created a homicidal orca. In September 2011, the *Huffington Post* published a piece by PETA president Ingrid Newkirk, who wrote that: "Tilikum knew exactly what he was doing."[5] I asked Ingrid if she believed Tili wasn't just playing with

Dawn, but intended to kill her. "Yes, he didn't toy with her gently the way an animal does when playing," she responded. "Playing is a sophisticated concept, well understood in the animal kingdom, from the dog's play bow to the cat who retracts her claws, and so on. He was vicious with her, and who can blame him when he associated her with captivity? She was the human connector to his captivity every working day. Animals think, feel, are aware, have ideas, interests, frustrations, experience grief and anger and love, etc., as you know, and the reaction to being oppressed, repressed, suppressed over and over again is—as has been studied countless times in all manner of species, including our own—to lash out, to kill the oppressor."[6]

Turns out this opinion is shared by a number of whale experts. "I think he did know he was ending her life," says Howard Garrett, executive director of the nonprofit Orca Network in Washington State. "In general, orcas don't seem to act impulsively and are very aware of their surroundings and every move they make. The record of aggressive incidents in captivity run the full range from jaw-popping gestures and lunges to bites and near-drownings to killing. They seem to know how to almost kill someone, but not quite, and how to actually do it. The video of the interaction between Dawn and Tili seems to show he maneuvered himself, and possibly her as well, to the position where he could grasp her by the arm; then he very slowly pulled her in. His actions after that were much like the methods mammal-eating orcas use to kill their prey, ramming, shaking, and drowning. Tilikum was probably not a mammal-eating orca prior to capture, but he seems to have at least rudimentary proficiency in those methods."[7]

Emory University neuroscientist Lori Marino, who specializes in cetacean cognition and intelligence, says that dolphins and whales have highly developed brains and make very fine discriminations between different forms of prey in the natural environment. "In addition, there has not been a single case of a human death from an orca in the wild," she says. "So, I have no doubt that Tilikum's actions were deliberate in that he meant to harm Dawn Brancheau and probably kill her. He was not playing. I've discussed this with several colleagues who are either marine mammal scientists or are ex-orca trainers and none of them believe that Tilikum mistook Dawn for a toy or just played too rough with her. That explanation is, frankly, preposterous to those of us who know orcas. Now, I don't know what Tilikum's concept of death is like so we'll never really know what he was thinking when he attacked Dawn. But this was deliberate aggression."[8]

The death of Dawn Brancheau is actually the story of two tragedies. Since 1964, when marine parks began putting orcas on public display, we have learned enough to know that these killer whales should not be confined for exhibition. There's no question that living in the impoverished confines of captivity is a dreadful experience for marine mammals. Highly social animals, orcas are especially vulnerable when restricted to woefully small spaces like aquarium tanks and pools. These are some of the largest predators on Earth, reaching up to 32 feet (9.7 meters) in length. They travel as far as 100 miles (160 kilometers) in a single day and have been known to suffer depression when deprived of their family and the stimulation of life at sea. In captivity, they only survive, on average, another 13 years after being taken, yet wild male orcas can live 60 years and female orcas may reach 90.[9] A clue to the toll confinement takes on killer whales can be easily seen in their dorsal fins. In nature, these sleek, black fins stand straight and high, while in captivity, the dorsal fin of all adult males and many adult females collapses, or droops over to one side—a byproduct of the orca spending a lifetime near the water's surface, though scientists are unsure why this phenomenon occurs.

Hoping to distance themselves from any responsibility, SeaWorld officials were quick to label Dawn's death an accident, saying she had slipped or fallen into the water and drowned. But eyewitness accounts and the medical examiner's report quickly disabused that notion. Marine biologists and former SeaWorld trainers later added to the narrative, combining to paint a picture of an animal who had become unhinged by the loneliness, boredom, and physically detrimental life inside a watery prison. "I believe that although Tilikum is likely the most dangerous orca in captivity today, his homicidal tendencies have been produced by the conditions of his captivity, and are not the result of any physiological, genetic, or permanent mental derangement," says Garrett. "If he were relocated to a natural setting with room to move and without the daily demands of management and total sensory deprivation, there is no reason to believe he, or any other captive orca, would act aggressively toward humans."[10]

Tili had previously participated in the deaths of two people at marine parks—first at Sealand of the Pacific in Victoria, British Columbia, in 1991 and another at SeaWorld Orlando in 1999[11]—and it is clear that stress played a central part in his attack on Dawn. Lori, who has observed countless killer whales, believes that many captive orcas are at the mental and physical breaking point. "They suffer from stress-related diseases, shortened life spans, and show symptoms of psychological trauma seen in humans such as repetitive behaviors, hyper-aggression, and self-mutilating behaviors," she says. "Tilikum clearly had struck out before, and for some reason during this particular session with Dawn he snapped. Other killer whales have killed and attacked trainers as well as each other in captivity. But again, never in the wild. This shows that the level of stress and the confinement of captivity are too great for these animals. They cannot be psychologically healthy in captivity."[12]

So what happened with Tili? Jeff Ventre, a former SeaWorld trainer turned captive-animal advocate, offers a possible scenario. "I *think* that because she was out of food, Dawn Brancheau elected to do tongue tactile with Tilikum: she reached into his mouth and tickled his massive tongue. He may have enjoyed that, who knows. Then, he very quietly closed his mouth on her left forearm before she could withdraw her hand. Tongue tactile is a frequently used secondary reinforcer with marine mammals at SeaWorld and probably everywhere. For various reasons, Dawn elected to ride it out. The reasons might be as follows: 1. Give him a neutral response so as not to encourage similar behavior in the future (operant conditioning strategy); 2. She would have preferred to *not* bring attention to it because she would be in trouble because tongue tactile, while widely used, is technically against the rules; 3. It was her best 'way out' of the situation. Don't react, because if it's 'no big deal' to Tilikum, he is more likely to blow her off and let go; 4. When trainers activate emergency services and/or medical help—by screaming, for example—the situation becomes a legal one and adds to the incident log; 5. From a performance standpoint, SeaWorld trainers are trained to smile like everything is perfect at all times.

"So, Tilikum decides he's not done. He grabs Dawn and drags her a pretty far distance from right to left. After she hit the water, things got ugly. And I don't imagine that 'killer' whales feel guilt, perhaps like we would, after killing. From Tilikum's perspective, it likely just improved the quality of his day—and I don't say that jokingly. His days suck."[13]

In August 2010, the US Department of Labor's Occupational Safety and Health Administration (OSHA) cited SeaWorld for three safety violations related to Dawn's death and fined the company US$75,000—including the maximum US$70,000 penalty for the "willful" act of knowingly placing its employees at risk.[14] Rather than accepting responsibility, SeaWorld appealed, and in doing so, they exposed themselves to even harsher public scrutiny. Played out in a central Florida courtroom over two months, *SeaWorld vs. OSHA* brought to light the company's stubborn disregard for both its employees and the animals they work with. The court heard an orca "trainer" testify how he had nearly been killed by one of the park's killer whales—even viewing a videotape of the terrifying incident—and SeaWorld's vice president of veterinary services admitted on the stand that 14 of 20 orcas owned by the company have had their broken and worn-down teeth drilled out to prevent infection. This painful procedure is necessary because, in the stress and boredom of captivity, whales commonly chew on metal bars and the concrete corners of pools, breaking their teeth. The drilling of exposed dental pulp is done without any form of pain relief, and orcas cannot be given anesthesia.

But the hearing's biggest bombshell—and the one SeaWorld has tried to keep hidden for years—was the revelation that they had allowed a 12-year-old male orca named Taku to mate with his 29-year-old mother, Katina, who in 2006 bore the world's first fully inbred whale calf, whom the park named Nalani. "This type of incest is unknown in the wild. It is as unnatural and repellent in orcas as it would be in humans," says Naomi Rose, marine mammal scientist with Humane Society International and a staunch opponent of keeping whales in captivity. "SeaWorld no doubt did not mean for this incest to happen, but they allowed a 12-year-old male to remain in the same tank as his mother, simply assuming that he wouldn't mate with her. But why wouldn't he? He is a young, hormonal male, and he has been raised completely artificially and aberrantly. So has Katina, who was captured very young from the wild and was raised in a completely unnatural and artificial social structure, with no mentoring by competent older females on how to be an adult female orca." Had Katina been a normal wild female, says Dr. Rose, she never would have tolerated a sexual advance from her own son. "But in captivity, where everything is artificial and aberrant, Katina did not stop Taku from mating with her and they produced Nalani. SeaWorld will probably never breed her, given her genetic make-up and the possibility of genetic problems in any offspring."[15]

It took the judge months to review the *SeaWorld vs. OSHA* hearing record, which runs thousands of pages, but he ruled that SeaWorld was at fault for allowing its employees to interact directly with orcas, though he reduced the fines to US$12,000. The ruling affirmed that the marine park understood the potentially fatal risks involved in permitting trainers like Dawn to be in the water with Tilikum and other killer whales.

Keiko

The cetacean star of the 1993 film *Free Willy*, Keiko was for a time the most famous orca in the world. He had been taken from his family in the waters off Iceland in 1979 and sold to the marine park industry, where he spent most of his life performing tricks. The consequences of confinement were writ large on Keiko's body: his dorsal fin collapsed, he lost weight, and he developed a skin infection. In 1985, Keiko ended up at Reino Aventura, an amusement park in Mexico City, where he was kept in an enclosure designed for dolphins. It was in Mexico that Warner Bros. filmed *Free Willy*, which focuses on a young boy trying to save an orca, played by Keiko, from captivity. (Keiko did not appear in the two sequels.) In the wake of the movie's surprise success, life imitated art and advocates managed to free Keiko, whose health was failing, from his tiny tank and transfer him to the Oregon Coast Aquarium, where he was prepared for his return to the wild. Further rehabilitation in his native Iceland taught Keiko to catch his own food and reintegrate with orcas. He put on weight, his dorsal fin became upright, and his skin infection disappeared. In July 2002, Keiko was released but swam straight for Norway, apparently in search of human companionship. He died there of pneumonia on December 12, 2003, at age 27. The debate continues on whether or not Keiko's release was successful.

How Parks Get Their Orcas

Once aquariums and other marine parks got a taste of how lucrative it was to display large cetaceans like orcas, there was no going back—and there was no place in their ledgers for sentimental notions like compassion. The orca slave trade took off in 1965 when Ted Griffin, then owner of the Seattle Public Aquarium, captured a young whale, harpooning and killing her mother in the process.[16] The calf, the first in a long line of orcas to be given the name Shamu, was sold to San Diego's newly built SeaWorld for what would be half a million US dollars today.[17] Suddenly, marine parks everywhere were eager to shell out big money for these animals, and there were people willing to do anything for a piece of it.

Two of those people were Griffin and Don Goldsberry, partners in a whale-capture operation called Namu, Inc. Griffin and Goldsberry will go down in history as the developers of a technique for capturing killer whales that involves locating orca pods with airplanes, herding them into coves with boats and seal bombs (underwater explosives fishermen use to scare away seals), and blocking them in with huge nets. The nets are then closed around the whales, each whale is tied by his or her tail stock to a boat, and the boat drags them to shore, where the animals are dumped into containers and loaded onto trucks. It was a strategy they used many times, but never was it carried out with more venal determination than in the summer of 1970. On August 8, the crew of Namu, Inc., spotted some 80 orcas off the coast of Washington State.[18] Using speedboats and bombs, workers corralled the whales into a narrow inlet of Whidbey Island known as Penn Cove. Seven juvenile orcas from the group were chosen to be sold to various marine parks and the others were released, but not before four of the baby orcas became entangled in the nets and drowned, as did an adult whale trying to reach her dying calf.

"They had us cut the animals who were already dead open and put rocks inside their cavity, put anchors around their tails, and sink them," recalled Namu, Inc., employee-turned-activist John Crowe in the 1999 documentary *The Killer Whale People*.[19] This is precisely how Griffin had disposed of Shamu's mother in 1965, and he remained unapologetic, even as his greed killed more and more orcas. Rendering plants were usually happy to turn animal corpses into pet food or other products, but Griffin was worried they'd alert the media if he brought them four orcas at once, and sending the bodies to the state for research was not an option, since a government official had told him, "We are not the dumping ground for your dead whales."[20] So the baby orcas were hidden from view like victims of a mob hit.

Three months later, a fishing trawler caught some of the bodies in its net, and the captain unloaded them on a beach in front of a Seattle newspaper reporter. It was a public relations disaster for Griffin and Goldsberry, who were forced to admit their callous duplicity, though they clearly weren't losing any sleep over it. "If I have dead whales, I'm going to conceal it from the public, which is what I did," said Griffin.[21] Goldsberry was equally defiant. "At that particular time we had other animals in the net; we were busy," he told a TV news reporter in 1976. "I was sorry that we did kill animals, but there was nothing I could do, they were already dead, and I had to be concerned about the live animals. So we slit open their stomachs, put anchors on 'em, and sunk 'em, because no one else would take 'em."[22] People were outraged, and the incident helped push the passing of the Marine Mammal Protection Act in 1972, banning the capture and harassment of marine mammals in US waters. The theme park industry has a powerful lobby, however, and they convinced Congress to carve an exemption for marine mammals used in aquariums, marine parks, and zoos, claiming that these facilities are "educational" tools. In other words, the very industry whose reckless and lethal practices prompted the government to protect marine mammals was given a whale-sized loophole.

SeaWorld took full advantage of the exemption until March 1976, when Goldsberry, who had gone on to become their director of "collecting," finally pushed his luck too far. He'd spotted a family of orcas off the coast of Olympia, Washington's capital, and began his usual strategy of using aircraft, bombs, and speedboats to herd them into a waiting net. Perhaps he didn't notice that Puget Sound was filled with people enjoying the water that spring afternoon, or perhaps he didn't care, but Goldsberry now had witnesses, and they were shocked by the unfolding scene as terrorized whales cried out. One of those witnesses was Ralph Munro, who was sailing with his wife. "It was gruesome as they closed the net," Munro recalls, then an aide to the governor. "You could hear the whales screaming. Goldsberry kept dropping explosives to drive the whales back into the net."[23] Ironically, the entire operation was visible from the state's capitol dome, where the legislature was in session discussing the creation of a killer whale sanctuary in Puget Sound, and Evergreen State College, which happened to be hosting a conference on orca conservation.

Trapped inside Budd Inlet, the panicked orcas remained in the net for days as animal advocates tried to secure their release. A few activists even set out under the cover of darkness to cut the net, but they were turned away by an armed member of the capture crew. Although Goldsberry had a federal permit to collect four killer whales, the State of Washington filed a lawsuit, arguing that he and SeaWorld had violated permits that required capture methods to be humane. Facing an onslaught of negative publicity, SeaWorld agreed to release the Budd Inlet orcas and to cease taking killer whales from Washington waters and the state dropped their suit.

Without missing a beat, Goldsberry picked up and moved his capture operations to Iceland, where he found plenty of orcas. It was here, in November 1983, that Goldsberry helped take one female and two male killer whales from the frigid waters. The smaller whale was sent to Iceland's Sædyrasafnid Aquarium and confined in a small concrete tank for a year.[24] We can only imagine the distress the young orca must have felt, cut off from all that was familiar to him, the sights and sounds of the open ocean replaced by the monotony of swimming in tiny circles. In late 1984, he was shipped to Sealand of the Pacific, a marine park on Vancouver Island. The park was thrilled with their purchase and named him Tilikum, the Chinook word for "friend."

Lolita

Among the killer whales captured in Penn Cove in 1970 is Lolita, who is now the only orca housed at the Miami Seaquarium, living in the smallest whale tank in the world. Lolita's former tankmate Hugo died in 1980; after 12 years of service, his body was simply dumped at the Miami-Dade County landfill. Lolita still calls out using certain vocalizations that only her L pod family uses, which indicates she still remembers her time as a member of the Southern Resident community.

Artificial Insemination

Given the financial rewards of exploiting marine mammals, it's no surprise that facilities like SeaWorld would see breeding orca performers as a huge boon to their bottom line. But killer whales are rarely inclined to mate amid the unnatural conditions of a concrete tank (the case of Taku impregnating his mother being both an exception and an aberration). In response, marine parks came up with the same solution used in factory farming: manipulating the animals' reproductive systems. In 2001, SeaWorld San Diego announced the birth of Nakai, the first orca bred through artificial insemination.[25] The sperm "donor" was Tilikum.

Sperm collection has become as carefully rehearsed as any other act at SeaWorld. The male orcas are trained to turn onto their backs and present their phallus to be manually stimulated by trainers until ejaculation. The semen is collected in a plastic bag or bottle, it's frozen, and then stored for future use. Even after being involved in the deaths of three people, Tilikum is still used for his sperm. Indeed, he's gained famed at SeaWorld for fathering 18 calves so far.[26]

To inseminate the females—who are also trained to turn onto their backs—handlers insert an endoscope, a catheter, and the sperm directly into the uterus. SeaWorld, doubtless the company most eager to perfect the practice, is now able to induce ovulation in female animals, control their estrous cycles, and, according to the SeaWorld and Busch Gardens Reproductive Research Center, synchronize the cycles through "oral synthetic progestagen treatment."[27] Females who do not willingly submit to being inseminated are removed from the water and placed on foam pads for the 30-minute procedure. Impatient for more cetacean moneymakers, SeaWorld ignores the natural sexual maturity of whales, impregnating orcas as young as six years old. "This is absolutely too young," says Naomi Rose. "The age at first birth for wild females is about 14 to 15, which means they are impregnated at 12 or 13 at the earliest in the wild." She speculates that females in marine parks may be able to conceive much earlier than free-living females because life in captivity means they are often heavier: they are fed regularly and get less exercise. "It's similar to the trend in humans, where female puberty is reached in hunter-gatherer societies at 14 to 16, whereas in first world societies, where food is plentiful and young girls typically have more fat in their diet, they can reach puberty at 10 or 11." The result, says Dr. Rose, is an orca who is not socially ready to care for a calf, even for the brief time SeaWorld and other parks allow it. "Just because they are physically capable of pregnancy doesn't mean they are mature enough to be mothers."[28]

"These parks are taking a problem—like the animals' lack of normal social relations or normal reproductive life—and instead of doing something about that, they say, 'We'll just take what we need and create what we need,'" says Lori Marino. "So you have female whales who find themselves pregnant when they never had sex. You can just imagine how confusing that is to them."[29]

The latest "advance" in SeaWorld's bag of reproductive tricks is extracting sperm from dead animals to later insert into females. While the procedure, known as gamete rescue, is not all that remarkable—it's been around for years—what *is* notable is SeaWorld's hypocritical involvement. The company professes great concern for its orcas, beluga whales, bottlenose dolphins, and Pacific white-sided dolphins, yet it treats them like sperm banks, even when they're deceased.[30]

Dolphin Captivity

Orcas are the largest animals held by the "entertainment" industry, but in terms of numbers in captivity, they are far outweighed by their cetacean cousins, the dolphin.[31] The population of orcas being confined in facilities in North and South America, Europe, and Japan fluctuates a bit, but lately it's hovered at around 46.[32] We know this because organizations like the Orca Project and the Whale and Dolphin Conservation Society monitor their whereabouts. Meanwhile, there are so many dolphins held in aquariums, zoos, marine laboratories, oceanariums, hotels, theme parks, and so-called dolphinaria that no one can reliably keep track of their population, though estimates range from 1,000 to 2,000.[33] Somewhere on every continent except Antarctica you'll find a hostage dolphin. They're kept in conditions that can only be considered prisons. Among the most deplorable examples is the case of Misha and Tom, a pair of bottlenose dolphins abducted from the Aegean Sea and eventually dumped into a swimming pool in the center of a Turkish resort town. The facility's owner planned to create a swim-with-the-dolphins attraction, but the sight of Misha and Tom bobbing in the filthy, shallow, 40-by-56-foot (12-by-17-meter) pool was so pitiful that tourists complained, the owner fled, and rescue organizations stepped in. After two years of rehabilitation, the dolphins were returned to the ocean in 2012 and never looked back.[34]

Most dolphins held captive are not so lucky. Because the commercial enterprises that keep dolphins are in it for profit (and make no mistake, that's exactly what they're after), animals are placed in cramped, artificial conditions in which they're deprived of the ability to engage in nearly all their natural behaviors. Dolphins are highly intelligent, fast-moving animals, and in captivity they are forced to mark time by swimming aimlessly in circles. They also suffer impoverished social conditions, including the premature separation of mother and baby. Moreover, dolphins are acoustic animals who use echolocation (sonar) to communicate with one another and navigate the complex environment of the sea; in captivity, their sound waves bounce off the concrete walls. All these stressors can lead not only to a compromised immune system— making dolphins more susceptible to disease[35]—but often to aggressive acts on other animals, including chasing, biting, and head-butting.[36] Dolphins may even respond with self-destructive behavior. Renowned oceanographer Jacques Cousteau and his son Jean-Michel observed this firsthand when a dolphin they were keeping in a tank smashed his skull against the hard edge of the pool and died. "This was suicide, plain and simple," recalls Jean-Michel. "Nobody called it that, of course, but I was sure of it. We had killed that helpless dolphin by our mistreatment, our disregard."[37] The experience prompted the elder Cousteau to remark, "No aquarium, no tank in a marineland, however spacious it may be, can begin to duplicate the conditions of the sea. And no dolphin who inhabits one of those aquariums can be considered normal."[38] Ric O'Barry had a similar awakening. Ric has been passionate about dolphins for half a century, first as the guy who captured and trained the five dolphins used for the TV series *Flipper* (1964–1967), and then as an outspoken champion to liberate cetaceans from captivity. *Flipper* wasn't the earliest use of dolphins for entertainment—the New York Aquarium attracted crowds with an ill-fated dolphin exhibit in 1913, and in the 1930s, Florida's Marineland figured out how to force the animals to perform tricks for the first time—but the popular television show brought dolphins into people's living rooms every week and fueled the public's desire to see such a remarkable creature in person.

As a successful animal trainer and occasional actor on the show, Ric thought he had it all: money, sports cars, girlfriends. But with the growing popularity of *Flipper*, he began questioning the ethics of capturing and teaching dolphins to perform on cue. The turning point came in 1970 when Ric went to see Kathy, one of the dolphins who had played Flipper, at the Miami Seaquarium. Unlike humans and other mammals, for whom breathing is automatic, dolphins and whales are conscious breathers: every time they inhale, it's a deliberate act. "Dolphins can end their life whenever they want by simply not taking the next breath," Ric says. And that's just what Kathy did. With Ric watching, she stopped her breathing and died. "I don't know what Kathy was thinking for all the same reasons I don't know what you're thinking. But from my experience and from knowing her, I think it was suicide. I use the word 'suicide' with some trepidation, but I don't know another word to use. I've seen it many times since then."[39] The same year as Kathy's death, Ric founded the Dolphin Project, a group that aims to educate the public about captivity and, where feasible, free captive dolphins. It's Ric's way, he says, of trying to undo at least part of the mess he had a hand in creating.

In 2009, Ric worked with moviemaker Louie Psihoyos on the Oscar-winning documentary *The Cove*, which focuses on one of the world's most gruesome dolphin hunts. As with orcas, the capture of dolphins involves chasing the animals with boats until they are exhausted. Hunters then surround the pod with a net, yank the dolphins onboard, and drop them onto the deck. The crew picks the most desirable animals, generally the young ones, and throws the rest back into the water, forever disrupting the pod's social unity. Countless dolphins die from the shock of this practice. *The Cove*, however, documents a much more horrific practice, which takes place every year from September until about March off Taiji, a small fishing village on the rocky slopes of Japan's southeastern coast. Fishermen depart Taiji's harbor at first light in a flotilla of boats armed with long metal poles. They patrol the known dolphin migratory routes until they spot a pod, at which point the boats congregate and herd the animals toward town, banging on the long poles with hammers to create an acoustic wall below the water's surface. Taiji is positioned on a bay, and as the armada of hunters chases their prey toward land, they drive the dolphins into a narrow, shallow cove in the bay and block them in with nets. Representatives from nearby Dolphin Base (which has a swim-with-dolphin attraction) and the Taiji Whale Museum (which offers a live dolphin show) arrive and select individuals for the dolphin slave trade. The next morning is punctuated by cries and the frantic splashing of tail flukes as fishermen stab the remaining terrified dolphins to death with knives and spears, turning the water crimson. In the course of a six-month season, fishermen kill roughly 1,000 dolphins and sell the meat to local supermarkets for about US$500 per dolphin.[40] Live dolphins command considerably more: Ric estimates they can be sold for as much as US$150,000 apiece.

"Most of the dolphins captured at the cove are taken to facilities in Japan," says Ric. "Japan is the size of California, and it has 51 dolphin abusement parks. Fifty-one. It's amazing. That's more than all of Europe. They are substandard facilities. They are disposable dolphins for a disposable society. The fishermen capture them and drag them there kicking and screaming, they keep them for as long as they can, the dolphins die, they dump them, and they get more from Taiji. That's why the captures continue."

The conditions dolphins must endure make their lives incredibly stressful, says Ric, as they are constantly on display. "If you go to the zoo, take a look at the reptile exhibit and find a snake. You'll see that the snake is given more consideration than the dolphins at Marineland. You'll see that the snake has got tree limbs to climb on, he's got rocks to hide from the public if he wants to, grass—there's always something natural about the snake's habitat. But if you look at the habitat of a captive dolphin, you'll notice there's nothing there. It's just a blank, concrete box."

Lori Marino knows exactly why this happens. "The captivity industry feels that these animals are so appealing and so charismatic that you don't need anything else with them—and they don't want anything to get in the way of people being able to see them," she says. "They do that with elephants as well. Many of the displays are constructed so there's no place for the elephants to hide from the public—there's no way to get away from being seen. Zoos don't want the public paying a lot of money only to see an elephant hiding behind a tree." Incidentally, Lori once worked closely with dolphins. Indeed, in 2001, she and her colleague Diana Reiss conducted the groundbreaking study showing that these cetaceans recognize themselves in a mirror—evidence of self-awareness that until that time had only been seen in primates.[41] "That was done at the New York Aquarium," she says. "I began to realize there were ethical implications of working with individuals who are self-aware. They know they are in captivity, and they have a keen awareness of their circumstances." Then the two dolphins used in their study died after being transferred to another facility. It was a huge emotional blow. "At the same time, I learned about the Taiji dolphin drives and the role of the captivity industry in all this slaughter. I made the decision not to do any more work with captive animals. More importantly, I felt that knowing what I knew, it was more important to protect these animals than do research with them."[42]

Swimming with Dolphins

With the success of *Flipper*, people across the US wanted to swim with a dolphin, and it didn't take long for entrepreneurs and marine parks around the world to smell the money. Soon commercial enterprises began offering swim-with-the-dolphin programs. The United States has more than a dozen of these attractions from Hawaii to Maryland. Some of them are in facilities devoted to swimming with cetaceans, while others are in aquariums, marine parks, or dolphinaria (aquariums designed to showcase dolphins). The experience varies, for both the customer and the dolphins, between wading in a concrete tank to swimming in a sea pen in tropical waters. Whatever the case, these animals are held in captivity—prisoners in an industry that touts this as ecotourism. The programs market themselves to people with an affinity for dolphins and who are concerned about conservation. Little do consumers know that patronizing these facilities only perpetuates the suffering of the animals they love.

In the wild, dolphins spend 80 percent of their time well below the ocean's surface, exploring, playing, and hunting. Captivity turns the dolphins' natural world upside down, forcing them to spend 80 percent of their time at the surface, performing tricks and seeking the bits of fish tossed at them. Part of the enduring myth *Flipper* helped create is that dolphins are friendly and eager to bond with and assist humans. In reality, dolphins are free-spirited animals who prefer the company of their own species, thank you very much. They would rather enjoy the depths of the ocean than spend their time hanging out near the surface, as they are forced to do in dolphinaria. Phenomenal swimmers, these swift marine animals can travel for miles in a straight line and dive up to 1,000 feet (304 meters). In contrast, a dolphin in the US can be legally confined to a space that measures no more than 24 by 24 feet (7.3 by 7.3 meters) and just six feet (1.8 meters) deep.[43] For a human being, that's like spending your entire life trapped in an elevator—minus the stimulating music.

The booming business of swimming with dolphins is growing most rapidly in the Caribbean, where the competition for tourist dollars among cruise lines is fierce. Ships offer shore excursions with swim-with-the-dolphins attractions that are enormously lucrative, charging passengers about US$100 each, plus another US$100 for photographs of the experience.[44] Oh, and this type of money-making scheme isn't limited to exploiting dolphins. According to *The New York Times*, at least four of the largest marine parks in the United States invite visitors to don wetsuits and pet or be nuzzled by beluga whales for US$140 to US$250. "The Shedd Aquarium in Chicago offers couples, for US$450, a romantic wading experience that can culminate in a marriage proposal with Champagne, strawberries, and the beluga as a de facto chaperon."[45]

Dolphin-Assisted Therapy
Exploiting the belief that dolphins are enthusiastic about helping humans, a cottage industry now offers dolphin-assisted therapy

(DAT) as a form of treatment for people suffering a variety of mental or physical disorders. The origin of DAT is widely credited to Florida anthropologist Betsy Smith, who was inspired by observing two normally aggressive dolphins gently playing with her mentally disabled brother in 1971. It wasn't until the following decade, however, that DAT became a craze under the guidance of psychologist and entrepreneur David Nathanson, who claimed that supervised dolphin encounters offered short- and long-term improvements in the speech, language, and memories of neurologically impaired children.[46] How does DAT allegedly help? No one has offered a definitive answer, though it's been suggested that dolphin vocalizations, their echolocation sound waves, or the animals' supposed ability to alter human brain activity can bestow healing upon the afflicted.

Today, just about anywhere dolphins are imprisoned, you'll find a DAT program: Australia, the Bahamas, the Caribbean, China, Florida, Germany, Hawaii, Israel, Japan, Mexico, Mozambique, Russia, Turkey, and beyond.[47] Therapy commonly entails the patient swimming and interacting with dolphins in captivity while working on tasks such as hand-eye coordination. As an incentive, some children are only allowed in the water once they have produced the correct motor, vocal, or cognitive response.[48] The cost for treatment ranges from hundreds of dollars for a few hours of swim time to thousands of dollars for days-long programs.

Lori Marino has spent nearly 20 years evaluating the DAT field, and she argues that there's no science to support it. "There is absolutely no evidence that this is therapy," she says. Lori has co-authored two critical papers on dolphin therapy, one in 1998 and another in 2007. "We looked at the best evidence DAT can put out there. We looked at Nathanson's work and all the other studies, and we came to the same conclusion both times. I think this is a scam." She believes DAT exploits the most vulnerable, including desperate parents who are willing to try anything to help a child with a disability. "Parents are led to believe there is something special about dolphins that might help their child, but this is snake oil. It is exorbitantly expensive, it's dangerous, and many of the dolphins used in these facilities have been captured and are being held against their will. So, it's not a good thing for anyone except, I suppose, the people who are running the facilities and making a lot of money from it."[49]

Dolphin therapy is not regulated by any government authority overseeing health and safety standards for either humans or dolphins—in the US or anywhere else.[50] Animal welfare issues aside, this is a concern because dolphins can be unpredictable and even aggressive. Participants in DAT and swim-with-the-dolphin programs have been bitten, slapped, and rammed, resulting in lacerations, broken ribs, and punctured lungs.[51] It's fairly easy to imagine how astonished the eight tourists at Mexico's Dolphin Discovery marine park must have been when one of the "gentle" dolphins in the pool—stressed from 20 years of captivity—began targeting their limbs with his sharp, pointed teeth. One of the participants said the ensuing panic was like a scene from the movie *Jaws*, with thrashing, bleeding, screaming, and fleeing swimmers. An exaggeration, perhaps, but terrifying nonetheless: a wound on one woman's leg went down to the bone.[52] And you don't need to be in the pool to suffer injuries from dolphins. In 2012, a dolphin at SeaWorld Orlando leaped out of the water and attacked an eight-year-old girl who was feeding the animal, chomping down on her arm. "Everyone just imagines dolphins as smiling, non-biting animals with knobby teeth," said the child's mother. "You forget these are wild animals."[53] SeaWorld simply gave the girl's family a bandage and some ice and sent them on their way.

Circuses

The allure of the circus is centuries old, dating back to a time when itinerant acrobatic acts (juggling, tumbling, tightrope walking, and the like) merged with equestrian exhibitions to become England's new performance art. Even then, they were borrowing from the

---

Legacy of Cruelty

The spectacles of ancient Rome were staged in ornate arenas filled with circus acts and fights to the death. While we may cringe at stories of Romans killing animals and humans in the Coliseum—Emperor Trajan is said to have celebrated a triumphant battle with games that slaughtered 11,000 animals and 5,000 criminals, slaves, and prisoners of war[54]—it's only the humans who can claim any rights today. The arenas may have changed, but the animal exploitation continues unabated.

---

tradition of operatic exploitation established long before: the chariot races, staged battles, and trained animals seen in the amphitheaters of ancient Rome. By the 18th century, permanent arenas were constructed throughout Europe. When circuses went mobile, moving from town to town, a large tent was inevitable, and the Big Top was born. By now circuses had become akin to traveling zoos, with a menagerie of animals you wouldn't likely see otherwise coming right to your town by train. Not only were the animals exotic—even dangerous—but they were forced to do tricks: a tiger jumping through flaming hoops, an elephant balancing on a revolving ball, a bear dancing on his hind legs, a lion being "tamed" using a whip and a chair. Rival circuses became fiercely competitive, and entrepreneurs trying to surpass one another promoted their acts with bombastic lithographs filled with superlatives like "biggest," "grandest," and "best," usually accompanied by depictions of large animals. The Barnum & Bailey Circus even called itself "The Greatest Show on Earth."

Circuses have changed little in more than 100 years. They still often arrive by train, and promoters continue to use elephants, lions, and tigers in their advertising. Another element that remains is the hidden cruelty inherent in every circus performance that uses animals. Circus training methods involve physical punishment, deprivation, fear, and submission. Animals are frequently beaten, kicked, stabbed, and whipped to make them obey. An in-depth investigation by the nonprofit Animal Defenders International (ADI) found that animal abuse is part of the working culture in circuses throughout the US, UK, Europe, and South America.[55]

Nothing says more about the suffering animals endure in captivity than when they are finally driven to the breaking point and fight back. We saw this with Tilikum, and we continue to see it with animals in circuses. One of the most heartbreaking confrontations occurred in 1992, when Janet, a 27-year-old elephant who had been abused in circuses since being taken from the jungles of Southeast Asia in 1970, decided she'd had enough. It was a Saturday afternoon in Palm Bay, Florida, and the Great American Circus had set up a tent at the local college. During a show intermission, patrons were invited inside the ring for an "elephant ride" on Janet's back. Kathy Lawler, her two children, and three other kids are sitting atop Janet when the elephant suddenly resists her handlers, including head trainer Tim Frisco. She starts to slam her 8,000-pound (3,628-kilogram) body against the metal barrier of the ring, casting aside loosened sections with her trunk. Frisco shouts commands, but Janet ignores them, knocking the trainer over. In fact, she seems to target certain people. After breaking through the fence and running outside, Janet chases down a circus employee, flattening him. She even attacks Frisco's car, ramming it with her head.

A police officer there to provide traffic control, Blayne Doyle, tells Lawler to lower the kids to him, but Janet knocks him down. She lifts Doyle with her trunk and tosses him. Meanwhile, Lawler is able to hand the kids over to a circus worker on another elephant, and she leaps over to join them. Janet turns her rage toward a tractor trailer that had transported her to countless cities across the country, ripping off the vertical exhaust system and hurling it. Blood is now pouring from a large gash in her trunk. Taking a bullhook from a fallen elephant handler, Janet begins smashing this repellent "training" tool against the trailer. She heads back toward the circus tent, and a dazed Doyle, concerned for the lives of spectators, reluctantly fires all 14 rounds from his handgun into the elephant's ear. Janet screams in pain, but it doesn't even slow her down. Back inside the tent, people scramble for safety as Janet crushes bleachers. Doyle radios for armor-piercing ammunition and is joined by two other officers, who empty their guns into the panicked animal. She flees outside again and collapses in the parking lot, where an officer with a high-powered rifle kills her with two shots. Janet's body is hauled to a local dump.

Following the tragic incident, Frisco was charged by state officials with maintaining wildlife in an unsafe manner. In his defense, he claimed that Janet had always been an ideal performer and that the circus had never had a problem with her before. That's

Getting on the Ban Wagon

Like marine parks and zoos, circuses view animals as a commodity. The good news is that governments are beginning to ban this form of animal exploitation altogether. Austria, Bolivia, China, Costa Rica, Finland, Greece, the Netherlands, and Peru, among other nations, now prohibit the use of wild animals in circuses, as does England, as of 2015. After a major campaign by the nonprofit Save Animals From Exploitation (SAFE), circuses no longer use wild animals in New Zealand, though there has yet to be an outright ban. "The last circus using exotic animals closed in 2009," explains Hans Kriek, SAFE's executive director. "This circus had an African elephant who was relocated to a local zoo. Efforts are underway to get this animal to an elephant sanctuary in the US. We are now lobbying the government to introduce a permanent ban on the use of circus animals and we believe we will succeed in getting this ban introduced."[56]

not what Frisco had told Doyle during the chaos, however. "We can't control this son of a bitch," he'd told the officer.[57] "You'd better shoot this elephant before she gets out in that crowd and kills someone. She's a bad elephant and always has been a bad elephant."[58] I suppose being kidnapped from your family and undergoing years of torment can do that to someone.

Frisco was eventually acquitted, while Doyle has become a passionate anti-captivity campaigner. "I think these elephants are trying to tell us that zoos and circuses are not what God created them for," he said in 1994. "But we have not been listening."[59]

The Bullhook

It's little wonder that Janet would have regarded the bullhook with hostility. The use of bullhooks on elephants is considered common practice in the industry, and they are designed specifically to inflict pain. Also called an ankus, the bullhook is a rod with a combination steel hook and sharp tip at one end, much like a fireplace poker. Circus employees use various parts of the bullhook to dispense punishment, from applying pressure on a vulnerable area to delivering outright physical damage. Though it seems thick, an elephant's skin is actually quite thin in certain places, including the areas behind the eyes and ears, near the mouth, under the limbs, near the feet, and around the rectum. By pulling with the hook or stabbing the pointed tip in these highly sensitive spots, "trainers" torment elephants into becoming compliant. The bullhook is also wielded as a club, with circus workers inducing substantial pain by beating the animals on the head, face, legs, trunk, and back. To the extent that such assaults succeed in making a wild animal submissive, a part of that animal's spirit is destroyed. Such is the goal of "training" elephants, big cats, and other animals used in circuses.

In their study of the bullhook as a "training" tool, elephant welfare experts Gail Laule and Margaret Whittaker write that: "[N]o matter how gently the ankus may be used with an animal, at some point it had to be established as a negative reinforcer in order to be effective: that means causing enough pain and discomfort that the animal remembers, and seeks to avoid that experience by complying."[60]

The fear of such pain and discomfort is exemplified by the case of Benjamin, a four-year-old elephant with Ringling Bros. and Barnum & Bailey Circus, who was able to ride a bicycle, play musical instruments, and paint pictures with a brush held in his trunk, among other stunts. When Benjamin appeared on *The Today Show* and *CBS This Morning* to demonstrate such tricks, his handler, Pat Harned, claimed he'd taught the young elephant using food as a reward. Never did he mention the beatings he administered using a bullhook. In fact, two former Ringling Brothers employees had testified that they saw Harned routinely beat Benjamin in cities across the country.[61] So frightened was Benjamin of the bullhook that when Harned was transporting him from Houston to Dallas and they stopped overnight, the elephant spent most of the next morning hiding in a local pond. Harned called for Benjamin to come out. The little elephant refused. According to eyewitnesses, an infuriated Harned walked to the end of the pier and began striking Benjamin with a bullhook, prompting him to wade into the deeper side. But the circus "trainer" wasn't about to be bested by an animal, so he got into the water, the menacing bullhook raised in his hand. We can only speculate about the terror Benjamin experienced at the sight of Harned coming after him; what we know is that the physically healthy elephant suffered a heart attack and died in the pond. A USDA investigation report would conclude that Harned's use of the bullhook "created behavioral stress and trauma which precipitated in the physical harm and ultimate death" of the baby elephant,[62] though a later review of the case removed all references to eyewitness accounts and concluded that Benjamin simply had a heart attack and drowned. The USDA took no enforcement action.[63]

After years of denying the industry abuses elephants with bullhooks, Feld Entertainment, which owns Ringling Brothers, was sued by several animal protection groups for animal cruelty in 2009.

Brought to trial, company CEO Kenneth Feld was at last forced to publicly admit that he had seen circus employees hitting elephants with this nasty piece of hardware.[64] The bullhook is sharp enough to pierce an elephant's skin, so to prevent the public from seeing bloody wounds, the circus has a little secret called Wonder Dust. Developed to treat lesions on horses, Wonder Dust is a dressing power that acts as a caustic and drying agent for slow-healing sores. It comes in a bottle with a little spout through which the powder is applied with a gentle squeeze. Because it's charcoal-based, Wonder Dust is gray and thus closely matches an elephant's skin tone, effectively disguising the cuts and punctures bullhooks inflict.

The circus industry defends the use of the bullhook, saying it's simply used as a guide, like a leash on a dog or reins on a horse. Indeed, they are careful to always refer to it as a "guide" in public, never a "bullhook." Fighting a proposed ban on bullhooks in Atlanta in 2012, Steven Payne, a spokesperson for Ringling Brothers, told a local radio station: "The guide acts as an extension of the handler's arm and is an invaluable tool in the humane and safe handling of elephants."[65] Yet police considered the bullhook a dangerous weapon when they arrested activist Pamelyn Ferdin for possessing one at a circus protest in 1999.[66] During her arrest, Pamelyn pointed out that a nearby elephant "trainer" was carrying an identical bullhook to use on two circus elephants. Police ignored her.

In the same year as Pamelyn Ferdin's arrest, PETA released a shocking undercover video that showed the public once and for all how devastating circus "training" can be. The video shows Tim Frisco—the trainer from the infamous 1992 incident—viciously beating elephants as a demonstration to animal handlers. As the animal care director for Carson & Barnes Circus, Frisco instructs his trainees to use both hands when striking elephants with a bullhook and to dig the bullhook's sharp spike into their flesh and twist it back and forth until the elephants cry out in pain. "Sink that hook into 'em... when you hear that screaming then you know you got their attention... Right here in the barn," Frisco yells. "You can't do it on

---

The King's Ankus

"Wake again, Bagheera. For what use was this thorn-pointed thing made?"

Bagheera half opened his eyes—he was very sleepy—with a malicious twinkle.

"It was made by men to thrust into the head of the sons of Hathi [elephants], so that the blood should pour out. I have seen the like in the street of Oodeypore, before our cages. That thing has tasted the blood of many such as Hathi."

"But why do they thrust into the heads of elephants?"

"To teach them Man's Law. Having neither claws nor teeth, men make these things—and worse."

—Rudyard Kipling, *The Second Jungle Book*, 1895

---

the road... I'm not gonna touch her in front of a thousand people... She's gonna fucking do what I want and that's just fucking the way it is." He tells the animals, "I am the boss. I will kick your fucking ass." An elephant named Becky is a particular object of Frisco's wrath. "Becky! *Becky!* You mother*fucker!*" he yells as he beats her legs. She backs away and trumpets in protest. Frisco is visibly winded from the punishment he's delivering, and he wipes sweat from his brow. The man needs a serious anger-management intervention. (Is it any wonder Janet rebelled?) This violent display is in stark contrast to what Carson & Barnes claims on its website: "Our elephants are only trained through positive reinforcement."[67] Frisco's current employer, Cole Brothers Circus, evidently has no problem with his methods, since he works as an elephant "trainer," and we can only assume his tactics haven't changed.

Frisco may be the most notorious elephant abuser caught on video, but he's hardly the last. In 2011, Animal Defenders International videotaped an endangered Asian elephant named Anne being struck in the face and body with a metal pitchfork while being shackled with heavy chains in the winter quarters of the Bobby Roberts Super Circus in England. Her abusers are later seen repeatedly beating Anne in her arthritic leg—an abuse that the 57-year-old elephant visibly tries to cower from—all while she remains chained to the floor. The investigation led to the circus owners, Bobby and Moira Roberts, being charged with animal cruelty, though only Mr. Roberts was found guilty. He received a suspended sentence.[68]

Traveling

Moving animals from one venue to another presents its own set of welfare concerns. All the stresses characteristic of confinement are compounded as animals are cramped inside "beast wagons"— transport carriers that fit into trucks or trains—for long periods of time. During travel, the temperature is likely not regulated and food and water are limited or nonexistent. Two examples illustrate how dangerous these journeys can be. In the summer of 2004, a young lion named Clyde died in the sweltering boxcar of a Ringling Brothers train in the Mojave Desert. The company then tried to cover up the death.[69] Five years later, eight tigers and one lion were found dead after they had been driven in an unventilated circus truck for 20 hours across Siberia.[70]

For elephants, movement in trains and trucks is further constrained because they are immobilized in chains.[71] A lawsuit filed by a coalition of animal protection groups forced Ringling Brothers to reveal in 2008 that their elephants are chained in boxcars for an average of 26 continuous hours, often 60 to 70 hours at a time, when the circus travels. In some cases, the elephants have been chained on trains for 100 hours—that's four days without a break.[72]

Animals continue to be caged or shackled as circus tents and other facilities are erected. They spend a short time unconfined while they perform, though their freedom is severely restricted, and the cycle begins again. Animals are typically loaded in the late afternoon on a Sunday, remain inside "beast wagons" as all the tents and equipment are dismantled, packed, and loaded, and are kept huddled in their carriers as the circus travels to its next location.[73]

Research on the welfare of animals traveling in circuses has uncovered some stunning statistics. They spend 91 to 99 percent of their time confined in cages, carriers, or other enclosures that are typically one-quarter the size recommended for the same animals in zoos.[74] To conclude that the space provided for animals in circuses is four times smaller than what they're given in zoos—and that they spend most of their lives like this—reveals more about humanity's antipathy toward our fellow creatures than just about any other cruelty we subject them to. It's little wonder that elephants, bears, big cats, and other animals are literally going bonkers under the Big Top, engaging in repetitive, abnormal behaviors (such as self-mutilation) that we'll explore later in the chapter.

Hoping to ease some of the discomfort, at least in the United States, are backers of the Traveling Exotic Animal Protection Act (HR 3359), a bill that aims to amend the Animal Welfare Act by prohibiting the exhibition of any animal who has been transported within 15 days.[75]

Did You Know?

Most of the iconic trained seals found in circuses and marine parks are actually California sea lions. Unlike seals, sea lions have long front flippers and hind flippers that rotate under their body. This allows them to "walk" when they are out of the water, giving them extra mobility, and the ability to climb very well. Another physical feature that distinguishes sea lions from their seal cousins is their prominent ear flaps; seals lack external ears altogether.

Zoos

The cruelty of zoos is subtle. While many people believe that zoos are essentially sanctuaries in which animals have all their needs met, the truth of these facilities is buried in the bottom line: zoos are profit-driven institutions in which animals are exhibited for frivolous human amusement, and everything is prompted by the need to bring in customers, since entry fees remain the primary source of funding. In other words, zoo operations are dictated by the turnstiles, not the animals' lifestyles.

Zoos began as private menageries for entertainment and displays of wealth in historical lands such as Egypt, Greece, and Mesopotamia. It is said that the Hanging Gardens of Babylon—one of the seven wonders of the ancient world—were created in part to house King Nebuchadnezzar II's collection of exotic animals.[76] In 13th-century China, Kublai Khan's royal grounds held deer, goats, leopards, lions, hawks, falcons, camels, and, if we are to believe the writings of Marco Polo, 5,000 elephants, "all covered with beautiful clothes."[77] Over time, these ostentatious displays evolved into public zoological gardens, with animals confined in cages, tanks, or tiny habitats.

Today's zoos took centuries of trial and error, all at the expense of animals. What confounded European zookeepers most in the early years of the 20th century was that gorillas shipped from Africa never survived beyond a few days in captivity. German zoologist Alexander Sokolowsky observed in 1908 that gorillas "showed a total lack of engagement with their surroundings" and that "one notices immediately that the animals cannot get over the loss of their freedom."[78] Eventually, Sokolowsky reports, the gorillas would be found lying face down in their cage. It was clear to him that what killed these animals was captivity itself, which led them to experience a profound depression and simply give up living. (Despite his apparently compassionate speculation, Sokolowsky remained steadfastly in favor of captivity.) Zoo officials had similar trouble keeping chimpanzees alive for more than a few months. It wasn't until the 1930s that scientists discovered that gorillas and chimpanzees are extremely vulnerable to human diseases, especially respiratory infections, and that special precautions must be taken to protect them.[79] (As recently as 2012, studies revealed new evidence that even gorillas and chimps in sanctuary settings are susceptible to pathogens from humans.[80])

Actually, the history of zoos is a cheerless narrative of animals dying too young. Taking an animal whose instinct is to be free and forcing her into captivity is a death sentence. Cheetahs, for instance, face such chronic stress in zoos that they are plagued by a host of fatal diseases.[81] Clouded leopards, meanwhile, pair up with their mates early in life and suffer so much stress if introduced for mating as adults that males will sometimes kill females—something zoos took a long time to understand.[82]

Elephants provide another example. Despite veterinary care and the absence of predators, elephants live only about half as long in zoos as they do in the wild. According to a 2008 study from Oxford University, while the median lifespan of an Asian elephant in the wild is 41.7 years, the median lifespan for their zoo-born counterparts is 18.9 years (meaning that half die by that age and half later). The difference is even more dramatic for African elephants, whose median lifespan is 56 years in the wild, but only 16.9 years for those born in zoos. Even elephants in logging camps live longer, says the study, with a median age of 42 years.[83] What's behind these premature deaths? "Our two principal hypotheses are stress and being overweight," says Georgia Mason, a behavioral biologist and the lead researcher of the study.[84] When Dr. Mason and her team examined the causes in a follow-up study, they found that the poor treatment elephants commonly experience in zoos—including early separation of mothers and infants and frequent transfers from one facility to another—causes chronic and acute stress, impairing their health.[85] This is coupled with ailments such as cardiovascular disease and low fertility, which are closely tied to the obesity elephants endure in a confined environment like zoos, where they get little or no exercise.[86]

This lack of physical activity can be a problem for many species, yet zoos around the world have a habit of exacerbating the problem by moving some animals into small, off-exhibit areas during non-visitor hours. Elephants are commonly chained at night, supposedly to prevent them from fighting with each other, for instance.[87] "Whether animals are kept for only a part of each day in off-exhibit spaces or permanently, I think the practice really shows the hypocrisy of zoos," says biologist Rob Laidlaw, founder of Toronto-based Zoocheck. "If an animal needs space, stimulation, natural substrates or pasture, natural environmental conditions, social contact, and such during visitor hours, and on-exhibit spaces are designed—at least partially—with some of those needs in mind, those needs don't stop when visitors go home and staff leave. The so-called better zoos like to say their housing and husbandry practices

The Sad Life of Happy the Elephant

There was a time when she was the most famous elephant in the world. Happy was born in Thailand in 1971 and captured as an infant. She was shipped from one facility to another before ending up at the Bronx Zoo. It was here, in a 2006 experiment, that Happy recognized her reflection in a mirror, proving for the first time that elephants are self-aware.[88] She was an instant celebrity. The same year that Happy made headlines, the Bronx Zoo announced it would phase out its elephant exhibit and not take on new pachyderms. But the zoo reneged on its promise, acquiring additional elephants as friends for Happy, whose longtime companion had been killed by the zoo's two alpha females in 2002. One died from liver disease and another was adopted by the dominant elephants, leaving her alone. Today, Happy spends most of her time inside a large holding facility lined with elephant cages, which are about twice the length of the animals' bodies—a sight kept hidden from public view.[89]

are informed by science, but I think many of their management practices show that to be nonsense. Much of what they do is based on nothing more than human convenience."[90]

Surplus Animals

Some say the craze in exhibiting "glamour beasts" began in 1962. That's the year that Belle, an Asian elephant at Oregon's Portland Zoo, gave birth to a male named Packy. It marked the first time an elephant had been born in a North American zoo, and the impact was both swift and startling. *Life* magazine published an 11-page photo spread on the 225-pound (102-kilogram) arrival. Visitors came from all over the world, standing in lines half a mile long to catch a glimpse of the little pachyderm. The park's cash registers were ringing like never before, and the zoo capitalized on the Packy mania with toys, books, and clothing bearing his face. Suddenly, zoos recognized that baby animals are a driving economic force, and breeding large animals became a hallmark of the industry's ongoing effort to attract customers. (US zoos are also constrained by the Endangered Species Act of 1973, which restricts imports of threatened animals, so they operate breeding programs.)

Of course, zoos don't admit that's what they're doing. Instead, they breed animals under the guise of "conservation," ostensibly protecting species like polar bears, tigers, or elephants from extinction. But if conservation were really the goal, animals born in zoos would be released into the wild. Although some zoos do have captive breeding programs that reintroduce species into native habitats, these instances are the exception and they are rife with ethical considerations: how well can a zoo-raised animal survive in the wild, for instance, and how well can a degraded habitat—one that may have played a major role in the near-extinction of a given species—support that animal? Many conservationists would prefer zoos get out of the breeding business and support efforts to preserve wild habitats, where species can roam and proliferate naturally. As zoo historian and former zoo director David Hancocks observes, success rates for reintroducing animals into the wild are minuscule. When they do happen, "we all have reason to rejoice, but expectations that zoo-bred animals will repopulate the earth have sadly come to roost on a rather barren tree."[91]

But it's not just the zoo industry's poor record of getting animals back into their natural environment that's at fault here; it's the facilities themselves, and elephants are a tragic example of their failure. With substandard conditions and their blatant disregard for the overwhelming evidence that these animals suffer in captivity, zoos continue to abuse elephants. The situation has become so dire that the infant-mortality rate for African and Asian elephants is a staggering 40 percent—nearly triple the rate in the wild. A 2012 analysis by *The Seattle Times* of 390 elephant deaths in US zoos since 1962 found that most of them were caused by injuries or diseases directly related to their captivity. For every elephant born in a zoo, the paper found, two die.[92]

Then there's the issue of a restricted gene pool. Longtime zoo critic Dale Jamieson notes that the lack of genetic diversity among captive animals is a serious problem for zoo breeding programs, with the infant-mortality rate among inbred animals of some species being six or seven times that among non-inbred animals. In the 1960s and '70s, the industry was so determined to fill zoos with baby elephants that they recklessly bred father with daughter and brother with sister.[93] "What is most disturbing is that zoo curators have been largely unaware of the problems caused by inbreeding because adequate breeding and health records have not been kept," writes Jamieson. "It is hard to believe that zoos are serious about their role in preserving endangered species when all too often they do not take even this minimal step."[94]

Because zoos are limited by their size and financial resources, breeding programs create more animals than the facility is able to house and feed. Once babies outgrow their ability to bring in revenue, these "surplus animals" may face a number of grim fates. They may be sold to circuses, research labs, or roadside zoos. Many animals are simply euthanized, a solution that has become ever more common in Europe. The Copenhagen Zoo, for example, kills 20 to 30 healthy animals every year—including gazelles, hippos, and even chimpanzees.[95] The age of social media is making this course of action increasingly difficult, as officials from Canada's Aquarium des Îles-de-la-Madeleine learned in 2012. In an effort to attract tourists, the small marine park began displaying two baby harp seals who'd been captured on the spring ice by the Department of Fisheries and Oceans (DFO). By the waning days of summer, the pups had outlived their usefulness, but rather than returning them to the wild, the DFO ordered the animals killed. "The solution is like when you have a pet you no longer want to keep; in order to limit the suffering, you have it euthanized," explained the aquarium's president in a Radio-Canada interview.[96] Activists quickly created and shared online petitions via Facebook and Twitter, which generated signatures from thousands of outraged animal lovers, and the DFO was forced to rescind the death sentence and release the seals.

Not so lucky are the surplus animals whose abbreviated lives are spent as targets on ranches where customers pay enormous sums to fire bullets and arrows at exotic species. These "canned" hunts—so called because they take place in fenced enclosures where the animals are generally tame and kills are guaranteed—declare open season on lions, tigers, deer, and virtually any other animal a client wishes to destroy.[97] There are more than 1,000 properties across the US where animals may find themselves in the crosshairs of a canned hunt.

Back in the day, the link between these shooting galleries and zoos was more overt than now: in the 1930s, Texas hunting ranches were only too happy to take exotic surplus animals off the hands of the San Antonio Zoo.[98] In 1951, the San Diego Zoo began selling its surplus animals to Catskill Game Farm, a New York enterprise that dealt directly with hunting ranches. That arrangement ended in 1991, after the group Friends of Animals brought to light the zoo's relationship with the game farm.[99] But these zoos are not exceptional examples. Indeed, exploring the industry in a two-year investigation, the *San Jose Mercury News* discovered that "of the 19,361 mammals that left the nation's accredited zoos from 1992 through mid-1998, 7,420—or 38 percent—went to dealers, auctions, hunting ranches, unidentified individuals or unaccredited zoos or game farms."[100] Many reputable zoos have since distanced themselves from the paper trail, which has become obscured by the involvement of middlemen who buy animals at auctions and then sell them to owners of hunting ranches.

Although US zoos have a long history with hunting concessions, the profitable practice of turning last year's zoo babies into hunting trophies isn't limited to the United States. Serengeti Park, a zoo in northern Germany, recently sold three lions to a hunting preserve in South Africa.[101] The controversial enterprise also made headlines in Australia in 2009, when news broke that the Taronga Western Plains Zoo had sold 24 blackbuck antelope—a species with the sort of beautiful, spiraling horns that hunters would rather see hanging in a wood-paneled den—to a profiteer planning to open his own private game reserve, where he'll charge customers for the privilege of shooting these critically endangered animals.[102]

The Psychological Toll of Confinement

Even if an elephant, tiger, bear, chimpanzee, lion, or member of another non-domesticated species is not overtly abused, life in captivity is a grueling existence for these animals, who are not able to satisfy their natural needs while they are enslaved for human amusement. According to a study on circuses by ADI, many elephants spend 98 percent of their time chained by at least one leg; indeed, the circus industry norm is to shackle elephants overnight, either in tents or trailers, by both a front and hind leg. Meanwhile, horses and ponies spend up to 96 percent of their time tied with short ropes in stalls, or tethered to trailers, and tigers and lions pass as much as 99 percent of their days and nights in severely cramped cages on the backs of trailers.[103]

This incarceration can have such a damaging impact on animals that they gnaw on bars, pace, sway, swim in small circles, or even create self-inflicted injuries, such as chewing off fingers and toes or repeatedly hitting themselves in the face.[104] Biologists call these behaviors stereotypies, which refer to actions that are abnormal, repetitive, unvarying, and apparently functionless. At the Central Park Zoo in New York, a polar bear named Gus became famous in the 1990s for his habit of compulsively swimming around the pool in his enclosure. When not in the pool, he would pace, play with his excrement, or repeatedly bob his head. Some in the press called him the "bipolar bear." Gus' captivity had made him so unmistakably and abundantly neurotic that baffled zoo officials resorted to giving him the antidepressant Prozac. Such behavior-modification pharmaceuticals are now being routinely dispensed to an untold number of animals in zoos, where loneliness, frustration, and boredom literally drive them mad. Some patients are weaned off the drugs in a few months, while others spend the rest of their lives under the influence of mood-altering medication.[105]

It may be tempting to scoff at the notion that a phenomenon that seems so uniquely human as psychosis could be applied to animals, but emerging evidence may scientifically confirm that stereotypies are just what they look like: symptoms of mental illness. After observing 40 chimpanzees in six accredited zoological institutions in the United Kingdom and the United States, researchers from the University of Kent concluded that these animals are likely under severe psychological distress. Every single chimp they watched engaged in some form of maladaptive behavior, from repetitive rocking and pulling hair to eating feces and drinking urine, and this conduct could not be explained by sex, age, rearing history, or prior housing conditions. The study concludes that, despite environmental enrichment efforts by zoos, abnormal behavior is endemic among captive chimpanzee populations. "So how abnormal is the behavior of captive chimpanzees?" the researchers ask. "In 1,023 hours of focal animal sampling of wild chimpanzees in Uganda, none of the abnormal behaviors listed in this study were observed."[106]

Indeed, researchers very rarely see stereotypies among animals in the natural world, yet they are evident in nearly all captive species, especially in those who would otherwise enjoy large territories in their native environment. Elephants, for example, are nomadic animals who will roam up to 400 miles (644 kilometers) during a single migratory season,[107] and the home range of a male tiger can be up to 77 square miles (200 square kilometers).[108] Clearly, these are not animals who take well to being locked up. Little wonder the biggest stressor for animals in captivity is likely the inability to escape, even for a moment of peace away from *Homo sapiens*.[109] And it matters not a whit that most free-living species can be bred in captivity. Even after tens of generations of being bred for circuses and zoos, non-domesticated animals confined in cages and tanks are still highly motivated to perform certain activities seen in their wild counterparts—such as hunting and foraging—and these frustrated evolutionary instincts foster stereotypies.[110]

The stress of not being able to escape is especially significant for elephants and chimpanzees—psychologically complex species researchers now believe are capable of suffering post-traumatic stress disorder (PTSD). A condition characterized by extreme anxiety, PTSD can be the result of physical abuse, isolation, torture, deprivation, the threat of death, forced incarceration (captivity), and the loss or death (even the threat of death) of a loved one, events that are no doubt familiar to most animals in zoos and circuses. The science of diagnosing psychiatric disorders in nonhuman primates and elephants is fairly new, but researchers have made some discoveries that are both fascinating and disturbing. One study observed chimps living in sanctuaries who had been traumatized by some form of captivity and compared them with chimps living in the wild. Researchers found that 44 percent of chimps in sanctuary settings displayed the diagnostic criteria for PTSD, while a mere 0.5 percent of free-living chimps suffered the disorder (wild chimps may suffer trauma after experiencing an upsetting natural event, such as a lightning storm).[111]

Most elephants in captivity have endured successive traumas, and they are living without the cohesive communities that would normally help them cope. As a result, they exist in a state of chronic stress—something that even courts of law are beginning to recognize is appalling. In his rebuke of the display in which elephants Billy, Tina, and Jewel live at the Los Angeles Zoo, LA Superior Court Judge John L. Segal said, "Captivity is a terrible existence for any intelligent, self-aware species, which the undisputed evidence shows elephants are. To believe otherwise, as some high-ranking zoo employees appear to believe, is delusional." Judge Segal's withering criticism came as he ruled in favor of a lawsuit arguing that the Los Angeles Zoo mistreated the elephants. His censure of the facility was stunning, even to some animal advocates, but it didn't end there. The zoo, said the judge, "is not a happy place for elephants, nor is it for members of the public who go to the zoo and recognize that the elephants are neither thriving, happy, nor content." He was especially disturbed by the testimony of the zoo's senior elephant keeper, who claimed Billy's stereotypic head-bobbing was not abnormal behavior but a sign that the 27-year-old pachyderm was in good spirits, like a dog wagging his tail.

LA's zoo is a great example of a facility creating a habitat with the public in mind, rather than for the animals' benefit. The zoo had surrounded the enclosure with some natural-looking foliage to imitate what elephants experience in the wild—a life-sized diorama populated with living beings. "Oh, how lovely," visitors might say. "It looks just like a jungle. The elephants must love living here." Unfortunately, the vegetation is blocked with an electric fence: if the animals try to approach the bushes or trees they are naturally attracted to, they are shocked. In his ruling against the zoo, Judge Segal noted that: "It is one thing to place electric fencing between elephants and something they are not interested in. It is another thing to place such electric hot-wiring between the elephants and something they like, need, and use as part of their natural behavior."[112] Thus, the zoo frustrates the elephants by keeping trees in visual and sensory range but beyond access behind electrically-charged wires.

The Education Myth

Aquariums, zoos, wildlife parks, and other enterprises that exhibit animals justify their existence by claiming they promote conservation through education. As Rex Ettlin, former education program coordinator for the Oregon Zoo in Portland, put it: "A zoo exists to educate. Research happens, recreation happens, but above all is the intent to educate."[113]

Elephant behavior expert Gay Bradshaw offers a decidedly different viewpoint. "Zoos can no more be educational than prisons can be educational," she says. "There is nothing educational about seeing someone tortured. I think a zoo could be educational when there are no animals in it and people can tour it, like at Auschwitz. If you walk through a concentration camp or a prison, you don't need to see anyone there—you can feel the ghosts. You can feel the pain and suffering and the terrible things that have gone on. From that perspective, I think zoos should be made into museums."[114]

"Indeed," agrees Dale Jamieson, "couldn't most of the important educational objectives better be achieved by exhibiting empty cages with explanations of why they are empty?"[115] Trouble is, few people seem to bother reading zoo signage at all. In what are arguably the most enlightening insights into the educational value of viewing animals consigned to a life of captivity, studies examining the behavior of zoo visitors show that most of them ignore the descriptions and explanations posted in front of animal enclosures. Worse yet, visitors are generally indifferent to the animals themselves, typically only pausing to watch baby animals or those who are begging, feeding, or vocalizing. Researcher Edward Ludwig found that the most common expressions used to describe animals are "cute," "funny-looking," "lazy," "dirty," "weird," and "strange."[116] These results are echoed in a study conducted by Dale Marcellini, a curator at the National Zoo in Washington, DC. Marcellini discovered that people spent more time arguing with their kids, eating, and changing diapers than they did observing the animals. On average, they lingered for fewer than eight seconds per snake and spent about one minute with the lions, for example.[117] How tragic that visitors may take just a few fleeting moments to gaze at an animal, while the animals are forced to pass their entire lives looking back.

The message extrapolated from these studies is clear: people believe the animals locked away in undersized, impoverished enclosures are there for human amusement, not education. It certainly doesn't help that marine parks and zoos—even respected ones—offer acts featuring trained animals. Shows at the San Diego Zoo, for instance, include performances with kangaroos, sea lions, and cheetahs, to name a few. Which is one reason Jamieson concludes that: "Despite the pious platitudes that are often uttered about the educational efforts of zoos, there is little evidence that zoos are very successful in educating people about animals."[118]

Aquariums fare no better. How can visitors possibly understand the complex nature of dolphins, whales, or other marine life by watching them swim in a tiny tank or perform tricks? Facilities in the US are only somewhat hampered by the Marine Mammal Protection Act, which, as mentioned earlier, contains a loophole for parks that keep captive marine mammals: they can exhibit these animals—even force them to perform tricks—provided such displays have educational value. Consequently, marine parks assert their exhibits are educational, but in reality, they fall remarkably short of this obligation. Appearing before a Congressional subcommittee in 2010, Lori Marino testified that the information the marine mammal captivity industry provides about the animals on display is woefully inaccurate, and there is nothing to support the claim that visitors to marine mammal parks experience any change in attitude or learn anything measurable.[119] "In a nutshell," she writes, "there is absolutely no evidence that public displays of dolphins and whales (or other animals) are educational in any sense of the word."[120]

Other conservationists agree. Asked whether keeping captive marine mammals didn't help a species by promoting education, Jean-Michel Cousteau said, "The elation we feel in the presence of such a magnificent animal should not be used to justify the destructive assumption that we have the right to imprison these animals for our pleasure. That is a dangerous assumption and leads to the belief that all of nature is for our pleasure and we have the right to manipulate it. That is anti-educational. We need to educate people to cherish and respect animals and places they may never see or touch because they are a vital part of our own survival."[121]

So what lessons do zoos, aquariums, and other animal parks impart to visitors? I love what Stephen Kellert, social ecologist at Yale University, has to say about this. In his book *Kinship to Mastery*, Kellert characterizes visits to these facilities as contrived encounters with nature. He invites readers to consider whether viewing incarcerated wildlife produces a distorted picture of animals and their environment, compromising the potential for these beings to instruct and inspire humans with any deep meaning. In the end, he writes, "Many visitors leave the zoo more convinced than ever of human superiority over the natural world."[122]

Animals on Screen

Reports that 27 animals had died during the making of *The Hobbit* movie trilogy (2012–2013) were not only tweeted around the world, they highlighted one of the most under-reported and longest-running tragedies of the entertainment industry. Year after year, animals are featured in films, and year after year, animals are seriously injured or die as a result.

The American Humane Association (AHA), which monitors animal and insect welfare in movies and television and is perhaps best known for the "No animals were harmed..." disclaimer seen on end credits, gave *The Hobbit* its stamp of approval, meaning animals were deemed to be well-treated and safe on the sets and filming locations. Unfortunately, the same can't be said for the conditions in which the animals were housed and trained throughout the months-long shoot near Wellington, New Zealand. Animal wranglers working for the production of *The Hobbit* franchise said that the farm where horses, sheep, goats, and chickens were kept was a deathtrap filled with collapsed fencing, bluffs, and sinkholes created by underground water. A pony named Rainbow broke his back after running off an incline and had to be euthanized. Another horse, Claire, drowned in a stream after falling off a cliff. A dozen chickens left outside an enclosure were mauled to death by dogs. Six goats and six sheep died after falling into sinkholes. Other animals succumbed after exposure to cold weather. Rather than offer assurances that animals would be better treated on future films, director Peter Jackson distanced himself from the reports, which he claimed were from disgruntled members of the film crew.[123]

With its limited resources, the AHA can only monitor a handful of films outside the United States, and even scrutinizing productions in the US is a challenge, considering the enormous scale of the industry. Perhaps the most charitable thing we can say about the AHA is that the group has helped bring attention to the treatment of animals used in motion pictures, which have become considerably safer than they were in the 1930s and '40s, when Westerns ruled the cinema and horses were as expendable as fake bullets. In those days, galloping horses who tumbled on cue for the camera were brought down with hidden cables from a contraption called a "Running W"; animals often died from broken necks or were so badly injured that they were callously shot. One of the most notorious examples is the production of the 1936 Errol Flynn film *The Charge of the Light Brigade*, which killed dozens of horses using this cruel technique for the climactic battle sequence. (To his credit, Flynn was so appalled by the on-set carnage that he complained to the ASPCA.[124]) This movie, along with 1939's *Jesse James*, in which a blindfolded horse died after being forced off a high cliff, led to the AHA being granted oversight of animal treatment on film sets. Since then, any US production—films, television shows, commercials, even music videos—under contract with the Screen Actors Guild (SAG) or the American Federation of Television and Radio Artists (AFTRA) union must notify the AHA if animals are to be used. The organization then determines whether or not to send a safety representative to monitor the action.

The AHA's presence is no guarantee of safety, however. Two horses were killed on the set of the 2006 movie *Flicka* (one while filming an especially dangerous rodeo scene), and three thoroughbred horses died during the production of *Luck*, an HBO series about horse racing; the deaths resulted in the show's cancellation in 2012. Arguably no AHA-monitored movie, however, received the negative publicity leveled at *Project X* after its 1987 release. Inspired by actual events, the film stars Matthew Broderick and Helen Hunt and focuses on the ethics of the military exposing chimps to lethal doses of radiation—a subject that should have made *Project X* a feature-length advertisement for animal rights. Instead, the chimpanzees used for the film were routinely abused. According to one on-set witness, "Every day... I saw trainers beat the chimpanzees with clubs, blackjacks, and their fists."[125] Other people on the set offered similar accounts of cruelty, but retracted their comments citing concern for their future in the film industry.[126]

When television personality and animal activist Bob Barker got wind of the abuse on *Project X*, he prompted the Los Angeles Department of Animal Regulation to investigate. They found sufficient evidence to warrant filing felony and misdemeanor counts of cruelty to animals against six animal trainers from the film. But the Los Angeles District Attorney's office declined to prosecute, saying the statute of limitations for filing misdemeanor charges had expired, and the felony statute only applies to people who abuse an animal owned by someone else; since the film studio "owned" the chimps, its employees could not be guilty of cruelty. Undeterred, Bob placed ads in the trade publication *Variety* accusing the American Humane Association of negligence and incompetence. The AHA countered by slapping Bob with a lawsuit for libel, which his insurance company settled in 1994, over his objections.

While it's difficult enough to monitor the treatment of animals on a set, it's all but impossible to ensure that nonhuman "actors" aren't mistreated offsite. For the 1980 comedy *Any Which Way You Can,* for instance, an orangutan named Buddha was "trained" with a can of mace and a pipe wrapped in newspaper. Shortly before the production ended, Buddha took a doughnut on the set; his handlers brought him back to the training facility—the ironically named Gentle Jungle—and beat him with an ax handle for 20 minutes. A few months later Buddha was found dead in his cage from a cerebral hemorrhage. Another orangutan was used to promote the film.[127] More recently, the biggest star of the 2011 Depression-era drama *Water for Elephants,* about a veterinary school dropout who joins a traveling circus, is Tai, a four-ton pachyderm. AHA was there every day during filming. Scenes required Tai to perform headstands and stand on her back legs—tricks you'll typically find in a circus, but nothing you'll see an elephant do in her natural environment. To make Tai learn these stunts, "trainers" from the company Have Trunk Will Travel had beaten her with bullhooks and shocked her with stun guns years before, as revealed in an undercover video taken by Animal Defenders International in 2005.[128]

Since the AHA's oversight is largely funded by US$2 million in annual grants from SAG and AFTRA, with membership that includes producers and directors, some animal advocates and journalists have argued that the group is too cozy with the industry to be truly effective.[129] An investigation by the *Los Angeles Times* found that the AHA "lacks any meaningful enforcement power under the SAG contract, depends on major studios to pay for its operations, and is rife with conflicts of interest."[130] In response, the AHA says that there is no conflict of interest when it comes to funding, since an independent board oversees the money it is paid by the film industry. Yet, as the *Times* found, they have been slow to criticize incidents of animal mistreatment and quick to endorse the big studios. Four horses died during the filming of Columbia Pictures' *Running Free*, for example, and the handlers used whips, BB guns, and shock collars to train animals,[131] yet the AHA endorses the movie and offers no hint about these inhumane tactics in its online review.[132] Whistleblowers from within the AHA have also told the newspaper that senior management frequently ignores reports of animal mistreatment.[133]

Fortunately, filmmakers can now call upon an abundance of high-tech tools, and, as movies like *Rise of the Planet of the Apes* (2011) demonstrate, there is no longer any need to use live animals to convincingly tell a story. And, of course, no AHA representative is required.

Drawing the Line

Filmmaker Quentin Tarantino, never one to shy away from depicting violence in such movies as *Pulp Fiction* and *Django Unchained*, nevertheless sees no excuse for harming an animal. "That's absolutely, positively where I draw the line," he says. "I don't like seeing horses being yanked on cables from Running W's. I don't like seeing animals murdered on screen. Movies are about make-believe; it's about imagination. Part of the thing is we're trying to create a realistic experience, but we are *faking it*, and the faking it is the art. ... I don't even want to see an animal terrified."[134]

Animal Fighting

Animal fighting is one of the oldest forms of "entertainment." Many Romans were highly amused by blood sports, and as these spectacles became more elaborate and audiences grew weary of seeing only native species like bears and bulls killed in arenas, emperors began looking beyond the Mediterranean for exotic animals. Spectators were soon gawking at elephants, lions, leopards, hippos, crocodiles, and ostriches, all obtained by hunters and dealers in distant parts of Rome's extensive empire. Probably the best-known animal-vs.-animal contests today are fights that pit one dog against another and those in which roosters, often outfitted with razorblades on their legs, battle to the death. Though these particularly loathsome activities are now illegal throughout Australia, Canada, New Zealand, the United Kingdom, the United States, and many other countries, fighting rings manage to continue underground, where even attending one of these violent competitions is often a crime. Unfortunately, other forms of animal fighting operate with absolute impunity.

Bear Baiting

Here is a contest so sadistic—and so stacked in favor of one side—that it is only practiced in two places on Earth: South Carolina, where it is legal, and Pakistan, where it is not (at least not technically). Though the details may vary, the events are essentially the same: a declawed, defanged bear is staked to the ground and dogs trained to fight are released to attack him.

In Pakistan, bear baiting is practiced primarily by the Qalandar, an ethnic group known for performing with animals. After centuries of abusing "dancing" bears—a street act that is thankfully disappearing in Asia—Qalandar tribespeople have turned their affinity for ursine exploitation toward poaching and "training" these animals for dog-vs.-bear combat. Qalandar trap young brown bears and Asiatic black bears (generally killing the mothers) and keep them in cages. At five to 10 months old, the animals endure the pain of having their canine teeth pulled out and their sensitive muzzles pierced and a nose ring inserted—all without any anesthesia; Qalandar are well aware of the cruelty involved in this, since no one who inflicts these mutilations keeps his own adult bear, for fear of retaliation. Other bear cubs come from India, where trappers sell them to Qalandar through the same smuggling network that also sells bear gallbladders to China, Taiwan, Japan, and Korea.[135]

In a typical bear-baiting event, a bear is brought into an arena and tethered to a central pivot by a short rope. If the bear has experienced one of these contests before, he will likely have visible scars and may repeatedly "pop" his jaw—a sign of acute stress. Handlers let loose a pair of fighting dogs, usually terriers, who use their powerful jaws to grab and tear at the bear's most vulnerable areas: the muzzle, tongue, chin, and ears. Occasionally a spectator's dog will break away from the crowd and join the attack. The stand-off is over when the dogs bring the bear down or the dogs or their owner calls it quits.[136] Essentially defenseless, bears often sustain severe injuries, including ripped mouths and noses, torn ears, and lacerated flesh.[137]

Local landlords are the driving force behind these fights, says Fakhar-I-Abbas, director of the Islamabad-based Bioresource Research Centre (BRC), which has been working to eradicate bear baiting. "The events are intended to draw large crowds—and therefore more money—to village fairs in the landlord's territory. But mainly, the landlords want to prove they are above the law: defying the government ban against bear baiting is a way of flexing their political muscles." Dr. Abbas and his team appeal to landlords directly, explaining the miserable conditions the bears live in and how the fights leave the animals maimed and traumatized. "Over the past 10 years, over 80 percent of the landlords we spoke to agreed not to organize such events anymore," he says. "Our second approach consists in visiting mosques in regions where the practice exists and speaking to imams. We refer to Islamist teachings that condemn cruelty to animals, and ask them to denounce bear baiting in their Friday sermons, to help make the general public aware that the practice goes against their religion." In addition, BRC alerts authorities when they learn of a tournament taking place. "This has led to several successful raids during major bear-baiting events in recent years. But in some areas, the warlords are so powerful that they control the entire law enforcement apparatus. In these cases, police intervention is all but impossible."[138]

In South Carolina, bear baiting is called "bear baying" and is billed as an exercise for hunting dogs. (Some hunters use dogs to chase and force a bear to rise on his or her hind legs, making for an easier target in the wild.) As in Pakistan, the bears staked to the ground are captive animals whose teeth and claws have been removed. And like its Asian counterpart, the contests in South Carolina are raucous affairs that attract large, bloodthirsty crowds. "Although it's sold to the public as a training event, these are *clearly* exhibitions. There are grandstands with hundreds of people watching," says Andrew Page of The Humane Society of the United States (HSUS).[139]

Officially, dogs are only supposed to get the bear to stand without making physical contact, but in practice, frenzied dogs routinely use their teeth. A 2010 undercover investigation by HSUS documented one captive black bear being attacked for four hours as nearly 300 dogs took turns biting her.[140] "She was tortured all day long," says Andrew, adding that although major bear-baying events are held twice a year in South Carolina, bear owners rent the animals to private individuals who host contests in their backyards year round.

Orangutan Kickboxing

It may be the national sport of Thailand, but kickboxing takes on a decidedly twisted turn at the Safari World zoo just outside Bangkok. Here, orangutans dressed in brightly colored shorts and boxing gloves are forced to pummel each other for the tourist trade. Each performance features two male orangutans, who trade punches and kicks for 30 minutes—or until one of them is knocked down. A female orangutan in a bikini parades around the ring holding the round number.

Recognized by their reddish-brown hair and uniquely expressive faces, Asia's only great ape once ranged from China in the north to as far south as the island of Java. Decimated by palm oil production, deforestation, the zoo industry, and the pet trade, orangutan numbers have dwindled so drastically that they are now found only on Borneo and nearby Sumatra living in scattered bits of degraded forests—isolated bastions that are quickly vanishing. The situation is so dire that orangutans are listed as endangered under Appendix I of the Convention on International Trade in Endangered Species, meaning their presence in Thailand is most likely illegal. In 2004, Thai forestry police seized 69 orangutans from Safari World (36 of them were found in seven small cages behind the kickboxing arena), and the animals were eventually returned to Borneo, from where they had been smuggled.[141]

But the orangutan shows have made a comeback at the zoo, and animal advocates are campaigning for authorities to intercede again. Not only are the kickboxing matches dangerous, but orangutans forced to perform endure training methods that include beatings, food deprivation, electric prods, and drugs to make them compliant.[142] Laws protecting animals, particularly animals used for entertainment, are basically nonexistent in Thailand.

Horse Fighting

Like so many cruelties draped beneath the protective cloak of "cultural tradition," horse fighting is really about money. These gruesome competitions—held in China, Indonesia, the Philippines, and South Korea—feature two stallions who kick and bite each other until one of them is either too wounded or exhausted to go on or succumbs to his injuries. Wildly cheering spectators bet on the outcome, and the owner of the winning horse stands to earn a large cash prize. Local businesses even sponsor horses and tournaments, which are sometimes televised.

Contests are staged in stadiums, abandoned playing fields, racetracks—just about anywhere horses and blood-sport fans can gather. The stallions are provoked into fighting by the presence of an in-season mare, who is tethered in the middle of the arena and often sustains serious blows as the sexual rivals rear up and pummel each other with their hooves, explains veterinarian Dino Yebron with the nonprofit Network for Animals. "That mare," he says, indicating a terrified horse staked to the ground at one event, "has been out there in the sun all day. There may have been 10 or 12 fights. She'll have been mounted as many times. That's the winner's perk. You might say she's gang-raped. And she'll also be bitten, scratched, and kicked as the stallions fight it out. There's nothing noble or natural about the horse fight. This is a purely induced anger."[143]

Journalist and environmentalist Stanley Johnson, who investigated horse fighting in the southern Philippines for the UK's *Sunday Times Magazine*, provides an insider's look at a "tradition" claimed to be centuries old. "Inside the ring, two stallions, lathered in sweat and blood, fight each other to a standstill," he wrote. "They rear, gouge, kick and slash, competing for a tethered mare. At times they come to a trembling halt and almost nuzzle each other, before launching once more into a horrific attack. At other times, they race around the arena at full speed, causing the officials to slip quickly under the railings out of harm's way."[144]

In China, where these equine gladiator bouts are part of rural festivals, organizers sometimes add another cruel twist: losing horses are barbecued and eaten by spectators.[145]

Camel Wrestling

Onlookers may see more saliva than blood in a camel fight and therefore be tempted to regard this ancient pastime as little more than a comical clash.[146] But camel fighting—also called camel wrestling—shares an important characteristic with other staged animal contests: the mistreatment of other living beings for human amusement. Like horse fighting, organizers of camel matches goad the male animals into battle with the presence of a female in heat. To make them extra irritable, they may even be starved for months before a fight.[147]

Camel wrestling is most popular in Turkey, where tournaments attract 20,000 spectators and vendors sell *deve sucuk*—sausage made from camel flesh.[148] Fights take place in amateur football stadiums or anywhere flat soil is surrounded by sloping earth to create a makeshift amphitheater and accommodate the crowds. Using a series of head-butts and neck-slams, a dueling camel wins by making the other camel retreat, scream, or fall.[149] Matches usually last a few minutes, though some may go on for more than half an hour as the sexually-charged animals grapple in the dirt.

Organizers argue that camel wrestling dates back to the days of their nomadic ancestors, who held bouts in the desert that pitted the camels from one caravan against those of another. After the Turkish Republic was established in 1923, the government disapproved of camel wrestling, calling it a barbaric relic from a backward era. That changed in 1980, following a military coup, when the new regime declared camel fighting to be an authentic part of the country's culture and urged Turkish people to embrace it.

In addition to suffering injuries while fighting, camels are subjected to long periods of travel in open trucks as they are transported from one tournament to another. Camel-fighting expert Vedat Çalişkan notes that a camel named Alex was trucked 1,501 miles (2,417 kilometers) to participate in a dozen events during the 2007–2008 wrestling season, while another camel, Ufuk, travelled 2,230 miles (3,590 kilometers) for 10 competitions.[150] Most transport vehicles offer animals little or no protection from the elements.

Man vs. Animal

Two gloved fighters enter a boxing ring as a crowd sizes them up. After a little footwork, the first boxer, dressed in orange and blue, throws a preemptory jab, catching his opponent in the chin. The challenger, donning red-and-blue-striped shorts, shakes off the punch and responds with a fusillade of blows that forces his rival onto the ropes. Though clearly winning the round, the second fighter suddenly retreats, shuffling backward. It wasn't a referee who called him off; in fact, there *is* no ref in this fight. The pugilist has been yanked away by the first fighter's wife, who holds the end of a long tether attached to a harness wrapped around the other boxer's chest. What spectators are witnessing is a three-round bout between a kangaroo named Rocky and his "trainer," Javier Martínez, a former circus acrobat who doubles as Rocky's opponent in the boxing ring. When Rocky becomes too aggressive, Mrs. Martínez gives the tether a powerful tug, hauling Rocky off her husband.[151] So much for fair play.

Once a staple of circuses and carnival sideshows,[152] the man-vs.-marsupial boxing match now represents only a snapshot of how humans exploit animals for entertainment. But when framed as an unabashed disregard for our fellow creatures, it is a vivid picture of animal cruelty. Martínez has claimed he is not hurting Rocky, though videos of the two mixing it up in the ring show he is clearly striking the kangaroo in the face—with punches that seem to lift Rocky off his feet. According to PETA, at least two of Martínez's boxing kangaroos have died. One suffered from a condition called "lumpy jaw," which is caused by stress, poor hygiene and poor diet, among other factors.[153]

As abusive as it is, however, a human punching a kangaroo is hardly the most violent display of animal cruelty in the name of amusement society has managed to come up with.

Bullfighting

Bullfighting may enjoy a measure of social acceptance in some countries (France has even granted it cultural heritage status), but it is morally indistinguishable from dogfighting or cockfighting. Perhaps the only difference is that in bullfights, humans play a more hands-on role in the torment of vulnerable animals. By one reckoning, some 250,000 bulls are slaughtered each year in bullrings around the world.[154]

In Spain, the country most associated with this carnage, the traditional bullfight (*corrida*) is divided into three acts. In Act I, the bull enters followed by the *matador de toros* (literally, "bull killer") and his assistants, who chase the bull and begin to wear him down.

Men called *picadors* then ride in on blindfolded horses. The horses' eyes are covered so they can't see the charging bull, and they may even be doped up.[155] Because they are frequently gored to death, horses chosen for bullfights are generally old. The picadors stab the bull with lance-like spears in the neck, which prevent him from lifting his head. Act II signals the entrance of the *banderilleros*, who thrust brightly festooned harpoons called *banderillas* into the bull to induce further blood loss and slow the animal's reflexes. Finally, the matador takes over the torment in Act III. The matador's goal is to plunge a sword between the weakened bull's shoulder blades. The animals almost never die instantly, and even with the tremendous blood loss, they remain conscious as the matador cuts his ear off as a trophy. Fully cognizant and in indescribable pain, the bull is hauled from the bullring by ropes tied around his back legs. Jose Valle, an investigator with the nonprofit Igualdad Animal (Animal Equity), describes what happens next: "He's dragged into a small slaughter-house, where they hang him, skin him, and dismember him. I've been undercover in these places and I've seen the bull alive, although unable to move, still breathing after all the suffering he's endured in the bullfight, lying on the ground waiting to be hung and dismembered. Most people know the public side of the show—since it's sometimes aired on TV—but not this last horror."[156]

Thankfully, there is a ray of sanity amid all this gloom, and opposition to bullfighting has been gaining strength. It has already been outlawed in Argentina, Canada, Cuba, Denmark, Germany, Italy, the Netherlands, New Zealand, and the United Kingdom, and surveys show a growing revulsion for watching bulls being tormented and killed. In a 2006 Gallup poll, 72 percent of Spaniards indicated they had no interest in bullfighting, which was just 8 points lower than the citizens of Catalonia, the Spanish community that banned the barbaric pastime in 2011.[157] Meanwhile, 73 percent of Mexicans say they do not like bullfighting,[158] and 78 percent of Colombians cite animal cruelty as the reason they dislike it.[159] Best of all, younger generations show very little tolerance for this form of torture.

Faced with opposition to bullfighting in certain regions, promoters came up with a compromise: all the "thrills" and pageantry of the blood sport without the gore (or at least less gore). The best-known of these so-called "bloodless" bullfights are the Portuguese style, held as part of a religious celebration. Here, the bull is outfitted with a Velcro® pad on this back and the matador thrusts Velcro-tipped banderillas at him. These fights have become especially popular in California, where to-the-death bullfighting was banned in 1957. It's also in California that investigators have found animals in bloodless bullfights being hit with nail-spiked banderillas, which cause deep wounds.[160] At the conclusion of these matches, the bull is sent to a slaughterhouse.

Ironically, the "bloodless" bullfights in Portugal are violent versions of the style commonly named after them. Killing the bull in the arena is not permitted, explains Jose, but that doesn't prevent banderilleros and picadors from attacking him with harpoons and spears. "After that, and once he's exhausted, the bull is forced to kneel down on the sand. This supposedly proves how powerful men are. Then they pull out the harpoons stuck deeply into his flesh." Drawing these jagged weapons out of the animal's back removes large chunks of flesh, and the bulls are bleeding profusely as they are loaded up and sent hundreds of miles to a slaughterhouse in Santarém, the only facility in the country approved to kill bulls who have participated in bullfights. "So, in addition to the suffering inflicted during the bullfight, they have to suffer for many hours in the trucks with open and bleeding wounds until they are killed far away from the public. Every year, more than 4,000 bulls end up this way. The public has the illusion that this kind of bullfight is somehow acceptable in comparison with the Spanish way."[161]

Alligator and Crocodile Wrestling
At first glance, wrestling an alligator or a crocodile may not look like animal abuse. After all, if there's any blood spilled, chances are it is

human. But there's no question these animals are antagonized, unwilling participants, poked and prodded to get a reaction for audiences. "Alligator wrestling does stress the animal," admits one grappler. "I would much rather stand by the pit and educate people than put my body in harm's way. But people want to see it. They want to see the risk factor, the chance of a bite."[162]

Shows begin when an alligator is dragged by the tail into a ring, usually a sand pit. A performer jumps onto the alligator's back and uses both hands to apply pressure to the animal's neck, forcing his or her head down. He might torment the alligator with a stick or hit her on the nose until she opens her mouth, or he might force the animal onto her back—a move that can cut off oxygen to the brain and lead to the alligator losing consciousness. Hardly a way to treat anyone, let alone a species that's been around for 230 million years, surviving the dinosaurs.

Once a staple of the Florida tourist trade, alligator wrestling was originally performed by members of the Seminole and Miccosukee nations—Indian tribes that caught these animals for their flesh and skin. As paved highways pushed deeper into the state's landscape, indigenous people turned the pastime into a roadside attraction. Today, tourists will find organized wrestling at parks like the Everglades Alligator Farm, south of Miami, and Orlando's Gatorland, where handlers rope and yank alligators into service before each show. A relic of a bygone era, "man-vs.-gator" fights have been struggling for survival. "We stopped wrestling here because of the image," says an employee of the St. Augustine Alligator Farm. "Jumping on the back of an alligator—that's not a conservation message."[163]

Conservation is not the objective behind crocodile wrestling, either. Practiced primarily in Thailand, where these reptilian cousins of the alligator range widely in nature, crocodile wrestling is a popular tourist attraction at zoos and farms. These facilities, such as the Million Years Stone Park & Pattaya Crocodile Farm, are often grimy with too many animals crowded into each enclosure. A typical stunt show features a handler dragging a crocodile out of the water, prying the animal's mouth open with a stick, and then forcing his head inside—all to the applause of people who should know better. Occasionally the crocodiles strike back, as when one tormented animal snapped down on a performer's arm and began rolling.[164] The young man was eventually rescued, though it's unlikely he'll be using his arm to slap around large reptiles again.

Pig Wrestling

A popular activity at state fairs and other agricultural events, pig wrestling brings contestants together for what is promoted to be "harmless fun" as they try to catch a greased or muddy pig. Actually, these are not wrestling matches at all—that would imply that the pigs are willing participants able to fight back. No, these contests have the air of schoolyard bullies tormenting a child. If that sounds extreme, consider that it's typically several people—even teams of people—treating an animal like a football. In some cases, the object is to shove the pig into a barrel. There are even events geared toward children, who chase terrified piglets.

"We wanted to try something fun and exciting that everyone can have a really good laugh at," said one fair organizer planning a pig-wrestling competition in Utah. "It is going to be hilarious. Anyone who has ever seen it knows it is the funniest thing."[165] Well, certainly not for the pigs, who are tackled, kicked, yanked, pummeled, body slammed, and stomped on. Such rough handling can cause torsional stress on their joints, and they may suffer broken limbs or backs as well as serious internal injuries. Their fate gets worse, however, since the pigs are sent to slaughter after the fair.

What You Can Do

The first and most important step you can take to help animals exploited for entertainment is to not support the enterprises and institutions that profit from animal abuse. Marine mammal parks no longer exist in Great Britain, for example, not because they are illegal, but because the public has come to recognize the inherent cruelty of these facilities and stopped patronizing them. Aquariums, zoos, circuses, safari parks, etc., exist because of demand. So, as Ric O'Barry says, don't buy a ticket! This includes businesses that offer swimming-with-the-dolphins programs and hotels that keep dolphins. Moreover, share your concerns with family and friends. Here are some additional suggestions:

Circuses and Zoos

- Contact your local newspapers and television stations when a circus comes to town, letting them know about the cruelty often inflicted on animals who are forced to entertain.
- When a circus comes to your area, make sure the correct permits have been obtained. Also, contact your local law enforcement agency or humane society and ask them to make sure the circus follows local and state laws regarding the humane treatment of animals.
- Patronize circuses that do not use animals, such as Cirque du Soleil.
- Ask local school boards to ban circus promotions.
- If you live in the United States, support HR 3359—the Traveling Exotic Animal Protection Act. Call the US House of Representatives switchboard at 202-224-3121 and ask to be connected to your member of Congress.

Visit these sites for more information:
Animal Aid (UK)
www.animalaid.org.uk

Animal Anti-Cruelty League (South Africa)
www.aacl.co.za

Animals Australia
www.animalsaustralia.org

Captive Animals' Protection Society (UK)
www.captiveanimals.org

The Dolphin Project (US)
http://dolphinproject.org

Humane Society of the United States
www.humanesociety.org

Kimmela Center for Animal Advocacy (US)
www.kimmela.org

People for the Ethical Treatment of Animals (US)
www.peta.org

Performing Animal Welfare Society (US)
www.pawsweb.org

SAFE (New Zealand)
www.safe.org.nz

ZooCheck Canada
www.zoocheck.com

ZooCheck New Zealand
www.wildlife.org.nz/zoocheck

Animal Fighting

In addition to boycotting events and venues that feature fighting animals—whether they be bulls, camels, orangutans, pigs, bears, dogs, or any other species—please tell others about the cruelty of these contests. If your community does not offer tough laws against animal fighting, contact your legislators and demand increased penalties. The Animal Legal Defense Fund (http://aldf.org/) ranks the animal protection laws of individual states in the US and Canada. Here are some other ways to voice your opposition:

- Call or write to companies that sponsor and support bullfighting, expressing your disapproval.
- Refuse to stay at a resort that is currently building or already has a bullfighting arena as part of its recreation facilities. Let the resort know why you are opting for alternate lodging. Instead, visit the resort town of Tossa de Mar, which was the first town in Spain to ban bullfights and related advertising, or Barcelona, which banned bullfighting in 2011 and is quite vegan-friendly. (As I write this, there's a movement in Spain to give bullfighting cultural-heritage status, which could overturn local bans.) Refrain from eating at restaurants, patronizing tourist shops, or hiring local travel agencies that promote and advertise bullfighting—bloody or bloodless. Let them know why. If you see a travel book that includes details on attending a bullfight, write to the publisher and ask them to remove this information in future editions.
- If your taxes are funding bullfighting, contact your elected officials to let them know this is not acceptable. Encourage your friends and family to do the same. If you see a government-funded brochure, website, advertisement, or televised program that promotes bullfighting, contact the sponsoring government agency to register your strong objection.
- Anytime the topic of bullfighting comes up in print, send a letter to the editor explaining why bullfighting is cruel.
- Lend your support to organizations working to end bullfighting, such as Campaigns Against the Cruelty to Animals (www.catcahelpanimals.org), CAS International (http://cas-international.org), Humane Society International (www.hsi.org), and Igualdad Animal (www.igualdad animal.org).

Chapter 7

Animal Rites: Animals as Sacrificial Victims

"The multitude of your sacrifices—what are they to me?" says the Lord. "I have more than enough of burnt offerings, of rams and the fat of fattened animals; I have no pleasure in the blood of bulls and lambs and goats."
—Isaiah 1:11

With its 19th-century hearse house and leafy, single-lane roads, Bellevue Cemetery in Lawrence, Massachusetts, is the quintessential graveyard, an ethereal landscape of green hills punctuated by granite tombstones dating back to 1848. Lawrence itself is nicknamed "Immigrant City" and has long been witness to the varied customs that accompany an ethnically diverse population. So perhaps a woman walking through the cemetery carrying a live rooster wouldn't raise an eyebrow in Lawrence. As family members visited departed loved ones and Bellevue employees prepared the grounds for Memorial Day ceremonies two days away, the woman stopped at an old grave marker and placed candles around the burial site. Onlookers suddenly took notice of the woman as she drew a blade across the rooster's throat and sprayed his blood over the grave. She then set fire to the bird and the gravesite. Authorities charged her with a number of misdemeanors, including animal cruelty.[1]

For most people, even those who think nothing of eating meat, the notion of animal sacrifice is rather ghoulish. It is not uncommon for readers of Christian or Hebrew scriptures, for instance, to question the many references to sacrificing animals. Scholars explain that in most ritual sacrifices the animal serves as a substitute for the one doing the killing (whose sin or sins require a blood sacrifice), or that the animal is an offering to appease an angry god or to help seek the god's favor.[2] Yet killing an animal to propitiate a jealous deity seems to us now to be archaic—a gruesome remnant of an ancient order, or perhaps the final act in a ceremony secretly carried out amid the rhythm of drums on a Caribbean island. Students of religion know well that the Vedic priests of early Hinduism routinely engaged in animal sacrifices and that Buddhism and Jainism repudiated such violence, teaching that harming sentient beings hinders, rather than promotes, spiritual growth.[3] Though animal sacrifice in India gradually abated, it is not uncommon today, especially in rural settings. And as we'll soon see, even Judaism, which thousands of years ago killed animals as gifts to God, still practices a form of ritual sacrifice.[4]

Animal sacrifice is a contentious issue around the world. In the United States, followers of churches that engage in the ritual killing of animals have claimed protection under the First Amendment of the Constitution. Indeed, in 1993 the US Supreme Court overturned a lower court's decision that congregates of a Santería church in Florida could not slaughter animals as part of their religious practice.[5] In delivering the Supreme Court's ruling, Justice Anthony Kennedy cited an earlier court decision, writing, "Although the practice of animal sacrifice may seem abhorrent to some, 'religious beliefs need not be acceptable, logical, consistent, or comprehensible to others in order to merit First Amendment protection.'"[6] This form of animal cruelty may no longer be as common as it once was, but it remains an accepted form of worship around the world, and the theistic rationale for sacrificing animals is as deeply entrenched as the arguments touting the primacy of an animal-based diet. (Incidentally, because this chapter is concerned primarily with traditions or cults that still engage in animal sacrifice, I will not be exploring such ancient practices as those of the Roman or Hellenistic cultures.[7])

Judaic Sacrifice
Early Judaism observed two principal types of ritual sacrifice: burnt

offerings, in which an animal was slain and incinerated, and the sacrifice of salvation or peace, in which an animal was killed but only partially burned, the blood poured onto the altar, and the animal's flesh shared in a communal meal.[8] In both rituals, the slaughtered animals were meant to serve as a divine offering, act as a substitute for a person, and draw believers closer to God. Animal sacrifice was an intrinsic element of early Judaism, but one finds contrary views toward ritual killing in the Hebrew Scriptures. While the first nine chapters of Leviticus set forth a detailed structure for animal sacrifice, for example, Amos, Micah, and Isaiah were among the prophets who rejected such killing as an affront to God.

The Hebrew Bible recounts many instances of individual animal sacrifices (such as those made by Abel, Noah, and Abraham), but the majority of these animals died at the hands of priests at the Temple in Jerusalem. First built by King Solomon around 950 BCE, the Temple stood for more than 350 years, until it fell during the Babylonian invasion. The Jewish people were then held in Babylon as slaves for 47 years, and upon their return to the city, they rebuilt the Temple, and it flourished, with animal sacrifice as its central preoccupation, until the Roman army destroyed it in 70 CE following a revolt against Rome.[9]

Solomon used the best materials for the first Temple, which would be the heart of Jewish religious activity and house the Tablets of the Covenant—the Ten Commandments God had given to Moses. From using the finest stone to overlaying the walls with gold, the king spared no expense, and the Temple took seven years to complete. In keeping with Solomon's grand vision for the Temple, the altar for animal sacrifices was massive. Standing outside the Temple entrance, the altar was 15 feet (about 4.5 meters) high and 30 feet (about 9 meters) square.[10] The sacrifices themselves could be even more colossal: during the Temple's dedication ceremony, priests killed as many as 22,000 oxen and 120,000 sheep, whose flesh later fed the large crowd of worshippers. Historian Keith Akers has observed that "the temple resembled a butcher shop more than any modern place of worship."[11]

When the Jewish community constructed a new Temple following their Babylonian exile, they followed the same layout as the original, though they increased the Temple's height and made the sacrificial altar significantly larger, rising to 21 feet (about 6.5 meters). So that the priests could keep up with the never-ending demand for animals to kill, there were areas around the Temple where oxen, sheep, pigeons, and other animals involved in the sacrifices were held.

The rebuilt Temple with its many animals is the scene of one of the most vivid events of the New Testament: Jesus evicting the moneychangers. Often referred to as the "cleansing of the Temple," Jesus' only physically aggressive action on record has become a matter of some debate among biblical scholars and animal advocates, many of the latter arguing that Jesus was vehemently opposed to the Jewish custom of animal sacrifice. To them, the cleansing of the Temple was an act of animal liberation.

In ancient Israel, every Jewish citizen was required to come to the Temple once a year and offer a sacrifice—that is, pay to have a priest kill an animal on the altar to atone for one's sins. But only silver Tyrian coins could be used to purchase animals at the Temple, not the common Roman currency, which bore the graven image of the emperor, nor even the copper or bronze coins minted right there in Jerusalem.[12] In the open-air market in the outer courtyard sat moneychangers who earned a tidy profit exchanging coins into the proper currency with which devotees could buy animal victims. Burnt offerings required the purchase of an ox or sheep, though pilgrims of lesser means could buy turtledoves or pigeons. Temple priests reportedly shared in the blood money. Jesus denounced what had become of the House of the Lord, and the incident unfolds quickly as he enters the courtyard, overturns the tables, and drives away the moneychangers and the sellers of animals. Reverend Andrew Linzey, a leading animal rights theologian, suggests that: "The question to ask is: What did Jesus cleanse the Temple of? People making money, yes, but they were probably making money out of selling animals for sacrifice."[13]

Examining the Temple passage, which is described in all four gospels, most historians focus on the moneychangers, often citing the enormous authority Jesus must have exhibited to not be arrested by Temple police on the spot. To these scholars, Jesus was upset because the Temple had become a place of commerce. While three of the canonical gospel's authors—Mark, Matthew, and Luke—sum up the cleansing of the Temple in a couple of sentences, John offers another layer of detail. In John's narrative, an outraged Jesus fashions a whip out of short cords and drives out the cattle and sheep in addition to the moneychangers and animal merchants. It is this dramatic action that has inspired theological animal advocate Norm Phelps to declare: "The cleansing of the Temple is history's first recorded civil disobedience conducted at least in part on behalf of animals, and Jesus was the first animal liberator."[14]

This opinion is shared by a growing list of commentators who have scrutinized the Temple episode, searching for meaning in an act that threatened the very structure of Jewish tradition and thus precipitated Jesus' crucifixion. Why is it, these scholars ask, that although Jesus was devoted to the Jewish faith, there are no records of him ever participating in animal sacrifice? Echoing Norm's words, the theologian Stephen Webb writes: "The currency of expenditure in the economy of sacrifice is the lives of animals. Was the cleansing an indirect and symbolic statement about the intersection of religion and economics, or is it just as reasonable to think that Jesus saw the animals and was drawn to their liberation?"[15]

A gospel not included as part of the canon, and which now exists only in fragments, is more explicit than John on the matter of animal sacrifice. According to the Gospel of the Ebionites, Jesus says, "I have come to abolish the sacrifices; if you do not cease from sacrificing, the wrath of God will not cease from weighing upon you."[16] The Ebionites were early followers of Jesus who believed that his death was a sacrifice that rendered animal sacrifices meaningless—

a view that led them to embrace vegetarianism, since meat-eating at that time was linked to sacrifice.[17] (By killing animals to atone for sins, early priests had found a way to circumvent God's first commandment and make meat-eating pious.)

Not all animal advocates agree that Jesus was engaging in animal liberation at the Temple. Richard Bauckham has written extensively about theology and animals, and in his view, Jesus not only supported the sacrificial system but almost certainly participated in it.[18] Reverend Linzey, who has advocated for animals from both the pulpit and the press over the last four decades (he even edited the book in which Bauckham's argument appears), not only disagrees with his colleague's allegation, but observes that had Jesus engaged in animal sacrifices, Christians would have surely embraced it: "Why, we might ask, did the early Church effectively abolish a practice if it was personally endorsed by our Lord? I, for one, have long held that the cleansing of the Temple constituted a frontal attack on the Jewish sacrificial system. After all, what were they selling in the Temple? The answer is certainly not postcards and souvenirs."[19] Meanwhile, Matthew Scully, one of the most eloquent voices in the animal advocacy movement, demurs on the subject of the Temple cleansing, writing, "Though I have no biblical authority for this, I like to think some of the animals escaped in the confusion."[20]

Historians and animal advocates may quibble about Jesus' motivations at the Temple in Jerusalem, but its final destruction at the hands of the Romans meant there was no longer an altar upon which to sanctify the slaughtering of animals, and the sacrifices ended.[21] The 19th-century rabbi and scholar Abraham Geiger believed that animal sacrifice—at least as carried out by priests at the Temple—had run its course: "If the sacrificial idea had been a necessary element in Judaism, sacrificial service would certainly have outlived the destruction of the Temple, and attempts were made to continue it. But the very idea had become completely exhausted. Sacrifice had lost its hold upon the hearts and minds of the people..."[22] As a substitute for blood sacrifices, explains Rabbi

John Rayner, Jews proposed that prayers and good deeds would be just as acceptable to God, if not more so. "Nevertheless," he writes, "two thousand years later, Orthodox Jews still pray daily for the restoration of the Temple, so that sacrifices may again be offered; and though some of them don't mean what they say, which is bad enough, many of them do, which is worse."[23]

A Life for a Life

In his book *The Year of Living Biblically*, journalist Arnold Jacobs sets out to experience the Jewish rite of animal sacrifice as part of an effort to live according to all the moral codes expressed in the Bible. Yet, as we have seen, animal sacrifice in Judaism ceased at about the same moment that the Romans defiled the Temple in Jerusalem and razed the altar. Or did it? To satisfy the sacrificial obligations of his 21st-century experiment, Jacobs participates in the ritual of *kapparot* (in Hebrew; *kapores* or *shlogn kapores* in Yiddish), which is observed during the High Holy Days, the 10-day period between Rosh Hashanah (Jewish New Year) and Yom Kippur (the Day of Atonement). The ceremony, practiced by Orthodox Jews around the world, calls for a live rooster (for men) or hen (for women) to be swung in a circle three times above the penitent's head while he or she declares, "This is my exchange, this is my substitute, this is my atonement. This rooster/hen will go to its death while I will enter and proceed to a good, long life, and to peace."[24] The bird is promptly killed, and the animal's flesh is usually donated to the poor. Jacobs finds himself in New York City for the ritual where his guide, Rabbi Epstein, cautions him that kapparot is definitely not sacrifice. "You can only sacrifice at the Temple," the rabbi says, "and the Temple does not exist anymore."[25]

Though most Jewish literature is careful to avoid using the word "sacrifice" when describing kapparot—preferring to call it "a symbolic act of atonement," "a ceremony of expiation," or, even more accurately, "a ritual slaughter"—no semantic gymnastics can conceal that an animal is being killed in the name of religious tradition.[26] Temple or no Temple, we're talking about animal sacrifice here. Kapparot is repeated in public spaces and outside synagogues throughout the world, yet it dates not from the Torah, the Talmud, nor any other ancient Hebrew Scripture, but from the 9th century CE.[27]

Due in part to its medieval provenance, kapparot has been denounced by rabbis and other Jewish leaders for centuries and is now chiefly practiced by ultra-Orthodox Jews, who justify the killing by noting that the Hebrew word *gever* can mean both "man" and "rooster."[28] Rabbi Gilad Kariv, executive director of the Reform Movement in Israel, has called for Jewish followers to abolish kapparot, saying that: "Slaughtering chickens is an unfit custom that goes against Jewish feelings regarding animals." He stresses that atonement should be an inner spiritual endeavor, rather than an external ritualistic expression, especially when it results in cruelty to animals. "Anyone who walks through the markets can see that the manner in which the chickens are held before the kapparot is insufferable," says Rabbi Kariv. "There is no veterinary supervision and no concern for the feelings of these poor creatures."[29] Quoted in the Jewish daily *Forward*, Rabbi Tzvi Hersh Weinreb, executive vice president of the Orthodox Union, admitted there are issues with kapparot. "It's the very public nature and the pandemonium of slaughtering so many birds at one shot that necessarily involves problems," he said.[30]

Not all critics of the ritual are Reform Jews. Arguing against the use of chickens for kapparot in *New York Jewish Week*, Orthodox Jew Steve Lipman writes that even as he grasped the frightened bird by his legs and swung him aloft during his first encounter with the ceremony, he knew he never wanted to do it again. "I can't believe that the waving doesn't scare or hurt the bird, no matter how gently I hold it," he writes, adding that he has since followed the humane custom, long sanctioned by commentaries on Jewish law, of practicing kapparot by swinging money over his head and then donating it to charity. "Now the only pain is in my wallet."[31] Rabbi

Meir Hirsch, a member of an ultra-Orthodox sect in Jerusalem, decries the suffering the chickens experience in the name of religion. "You cannot perform a commandment by committing a sin," he says.[32]

Kapparot has also come under fire from animal advocates. Packed into small cages with other birds, chickens are routinely transported long distances and denied access to water and food. An investigation by PETA found that those birds who make it to the kapparot site alive are often mishandled, allowed to languish for hours in closed spaces, and may even end up bagged as garbage while still conscious after suffering ineffective kosher slaughter.[33] Other chickens have simply been abandoned, left to starve to death inside crates.[34] "Waving a slaughtered chicken around the head is a pagan custom that should be abolished," says Chedva Vanderbrook, a board member of the Jerusalem Society for the Prevention of Cruelty to Animals. "The slaughter poisons and hardens man's heart. It is absurd that people are asking for life by taking the life of another creature, especially when kapparot can be done with money."[35]

Karen Davis, a longtime advocate for chickens and other domestic fowl, is particularly sensitive to the abuse these animals suffer during the High Holy Days. "The birds used in kapparot are sometimes sitting for as long as week without food or water, usually exposed to the elements," she says. "Whole flatbed trailers bring the chickens in to places like Brooklyn and the Bronx, where they just sit stacked in crates or cages before the actual ritual takes place. They're being starved and dehydrated and left out in the rain. The birds are treated like rag dolls, like objects." From her home in Machipongo, Virginia, Karen and her nonprofit organization, United Poultry Concerns, have been campaigning for years to get Jewish communities to embrace humane practices and not use animals for kapparot. She believes the resistance to change is due in part to the fundraising role the ceremony plays in Jewish society: synagogues charge money for each bird, which covers the cost of the ritual and the kosher slaughter that is supposed to follow. "In order to have a chicken swung for you, you pay your particular synagogue twenty dollars or so," she says. "This is a money-making venture."[36] As if the killing of the hen or rooster isn't bad enough, Karen attributes further sinister consequences to kapparot: a misappropriation of the animal's very identity. "The ritual transference of one's own transgressions and diseases to a sacrificial animal constitutes an interspecies rape of that victim," she writes. "In both cases, the animal is treated as a receptacle for the victimizer's defilement."[37]

Though Jewish devotees claim using chickens in kapparot is part of religious tradition, there is also precedent for compassionate alternatives, such as the aforementioned currency or even beans. Rashi, the 11th-century rabbi and scholar, records the custom of weaving baskets from palm fronds and filling them with soil and beans two or three weeks before Rosh Hashanah. On the eve of the New Year, with the beans sprouting, adherents would circle the baskets overhead reciting "This in lieu of this; this is my exchange; this is my substitute" and throw the basket into a river.[38] It's a notion Aviva Weintraub, associate curator at the Jewish Museum in New York, advocates, especially as some within Judaism have not necessarily embraced kapparot. "Whereas many Jewish rituals such as the seder, tashlikh and bris have been adopted and reinvented by Jewish feminists and other Jewish subcultures, kapores has yet to engage these groups," she writes. "Perhaps a return to the earlier, vegetarian version (beans in a basket) would allow for renewed interest in the practice of shlogn kapores."[39]

Yom Kippur is the day when Jewish tradition says a person's fate is sealed for the year. How much more promising that year would be if it were to begin with kindness.

The Blood of the Lamb

It is generally accepted as an article of faith among Christians that Jesus was the "Lamb of God," whose crucifixion absolved humanity of the guilt that originated with the transgressions of Adam and Eve, and was perpetuated through their progeny. Jesus' death not only meant that God would forgive us, but it supposedly made the practice of animal sacrifice unnecessary. Yet, animal sacrifice has survived within Christian churches, particularly the Armenian Church.[40] At special ceremonies today, Armenians offer *madagh*, in which an animal is blessed and killed, with his or her flesh shared in a communal meal by neighbors, the poor, the sick, and the clergy.[41]

Archpriest Father Nerses Manoogian, pastor of the St. Gregory the Illuminator Armenian Apostolic Church in Philadelphia, explains that devotees offer madagh (literally, "sacrifice") either to thank God for granting a wish, such as regained health, or in memory of a loved one, asking God to have mercy on their soul. According to the Book of Ritual of the Armenian Church, before slaughtering the madagh animal, usually a lamb, a priest blesses a handful of salt, which is then fed to the sacrificial lamb to cleanse him before he is killed.[42] "The reason for lamb traces back to Jesus, who is the prototype lamb as described in the Gospel of John," says Father Manoogian. "So basically we use lamb because we know that the 'other lamb,' Jesus, was unblemished and delivered what was expected from him."[43]

In South Africa, Christian missionaries have managed to supplant many of the native faiths, but the notion of sacrificing animals is not altogether absent, even in the Catholic Church. After more than 150 years of acculturation in the country, the Church is beginning to accept ritual sacrifice, at least grudgingly, as a way to retain laity on a continent known for its polytheistic tribal religions. It's part of a post-apartheid inculturation led by a coalition of South African Catholic priests who want to celebrate mass with indigenous practices, including the veneration of ancestors. Because blood is symbolic of life, they say, Christian worshippers can come into communion with their ancestors through the blood of animals. Among the movement's leaders is Archbishop Buti Tlhagale of Johannesburg, who concedes that Jesus' death eliminated the need for sacrifices but argues that African members of the Church can still engage in animal sacrifice by offering the blood to departed relatives. "Animal sacrifice has a special place in the scheme of things and is celebrated in almost all African families," he says. "We have kept it out of the Church of God for too long. It is time we welcomed it openly into the Christian family of the living and the dead."[44] Archbishop Tlhagale's views have garnered support from parish priests like Father Victor Phalana, who sees nothing wrong with killing animals in the name of religion. "It's not appeasing God—the sacrifice of Jesus was enough—but it's bringing the ancestors into the communion of the living," he says.[45]

Critics, both within and outside the animal rights community, have expressed concern that a Christian church would support killing animals for any form of religious rite. "Animal sacrifice is literally a step backwards into a pre-Christian age," says Reverend Linzey. "At best, it reflects a well-meaning, but misconceived, attempt to adapt the Gospel to a prevailing culture. At worst it signals a fantastic failure to understand atonement theology: Christ is the one true Lamb who saves the lambs!"[46] Meanwhile, Christopher Howse, columnist for the *Daily Telegraph*, writes that: "To sacrifice a goat during Christian worship had never seemed remotely within the bounds of propriety to me."[47]

Propriety or not, the violent sanctification of animals is widely practiced among Christians, and not just clerics. Pious devotees throughout the world celebrate Easter by eating lamb, a tradition borrowed from Judaism, in which a male lamb is sacrificed at the Temple on the eve of Passover. Thus, people who today would never countenance animal sacrifice are participants in this very act, albeit obliquely, when they observe the death and resurrection of Christ by eating the "Lamb of God." Christians maintaining "tradition" by eating lamb or other animal flesh at Easter might want to consider the possibility that Jesus himself celebrated a meat-free Last Supper (Passover). "It could be argued that Jesus jettisoned the traditional Passover meal, which would have been the sacrifice of the lamb, and took bread and wine—vegan elements—as substitutes for the whole tradition of animal sacrifice," says Reverend Linzey.[48] Linzey's view has gained traction among many historians, who, through a careful reading of the New Testament, the Dead Sea Scrolls, and commentaries by early Christians, suggest Jesus did not eat meat. A 3rd-century manuscript written in Aramaic (the language Jesus probably spoke) and discovered in the Vatican archives a century ago, is just one of many documents to proclaim Christ was a vegetarian.[49]

To those who may regard a comparison between animal sacrifice and eating animals to be a stretch, remember that sacrifice was, at least for the ancient Hebrews, a justification for eating meat. Moreover, today's industrialized "processing" of animals from living beings into bits of protein products resembles nothing so much as a secular ritual carried out by men using a specially sanctioned set of instruments, procedures, garb, and locations. In comparing animal sacrifice to a variety of other animal abuses, religious historian Bruce Lincoln defines the act as "a logic, language, and practice of transformative negation, in which one entity—a plant or animal, a bodily part, some portion of a person's life, energy, property, or even the life itself—is given up for the benefit of some other species, group, god, or principle that is understood to be 'higher' or more deserving in some fashion or another."[50] It is by no means an exaggeration to view eating animals through this prism and see that it is a form of animal sacrifice.

The Age of Kali

Rising from a gently sloping riverbank, India's Kalighat Temple is a study in contrasts. While the temple's tranquil architecture of distinctive Bengali design—a unique, eight-roof hut pattern enlivened with colorful accents—creates a peaceful oasis in teeming Kolkata (Calcutta), the serenity is marred by bloodshed. Every day, votaries bring young goats to Kalighat as an offering to Kali, the temple's patron goddess. Each goat is ritually washed and purified before his neck is secured in a Y-shaped wooden brace and he is beheaded with a single stroke of a heavy blade. Of the many Hindu temples engaging in animal sacrifice, it is fitting that this one should be among the most infamous. Kali is, after all, the bloodthirsty goddess of destruction, and Kolkata is her city. Kalighat welcomes thousands of visitors a day, pilgrims and tourists alike, all drawn to the site where legend says a toe of the goddess Sati (an aspect of Kali) fell to Earth following a flash of rage.[51]

Kalighat Temple is a microcosm of India itself. With a population that is 80 percent Hindu, India is home to more vegetarians than any other country;[52] at the same time, it is steeped in the blood of animals, sacrificed to placate a variety of fierce deities or petition their protective powers. I should note that not all Hindus agree that animal sacrifice belongs in their religious observance, and many have spoken out against it. But those who do practice it—primarily in the eastern states of Andhra Pradesh, Assam, Orissa, and West Bengal—subject animals to a variety of grisly ritual deaths, including decapitation, impalement, suffocation, disembowelment, and drowning. An especially gruesome fate awaits young goats at a particular temple in Andhra Pradesh, where a priest kills the animals by tearing into their throats with his bare teeth.

It's reasonable to demand how such abuse could be legal. India has enacted legislation attempting to safeguard animals, but these laws, such as the Prevention of Cruelty to Animals Act, fall well short of banning the abusive treatment of animals in the name of religion. In response, the Indian states of Andhra Pradesh, Gujarat, Karnataka, Kerala, Pondicherry, Rajasthan, and Tamil Nadu have passed laws prohibiting animal sacrifice, yet enforcement is at the whim of local officials. The Andhra Pradesh Animals and Birds Sacrifices Prohibition Act, for example, defines sacrifice as the killing or maiming of any animal or bird for the purpose of any religious worship or adoration—yet the law would seem all but useless in a state where the Animal Welfare Board of India has found 124 temples routinely engaging in animal sacrifices.[53] In addition to priests who bite into the jugular veins of helpless goats, Andhra Pradesh is home to the little-known practice of Mailatheppa. Meant to appease the spirits of the recently departed, Mailatheppa entails strapping hens to bamboo poles and drowning them, often dunking the birds repeatedly, in the fabled Krishna River and discarding their bodies in the water like so much worthless flotsam.[54] In many cases, authorities simply look the other way because animal sacrifice in India, as in other cultures, is a business as well as a tradition.

Studying the various reasons Hindus engage in ritual slaughter, David Kinsley, professor of Religion at McMaster University, Canada, speculates that worshippers may sacrifice animals to certain deities in order to "feed" their mythological exploits. In the case of Durgä, an aspect of Kali identified with creation, vegetation, and crops, Kinsley writes:

My suggestion is that underlying blood sacrifices to Durgä is the perception, perhaps only unconscious, that this great goddess who nourishes the crops and is identified with the power under-lying all life needs to be reinvigorated from time to time. Despite her great powers, she is capable of being exhausted through continuous birth and the giving of nourishment. To replenish her powers, to reinvigorate her, she is given back life in the form of animal sacrifices. The blood in effect resupplies her so that she may continue to give life in return. Having harvested the crops, having literally reaped the life-giving benefits of Durgä's potency, it is appropriate (perhaps necessary) to return strength and power to her in the form of the blood of sacrificial victims.[55]

Both the appropriateness and necessity of animal sacrifice are easily challenged, however, and practitioners know it. In her visit to Kalighat, Sanjukta Gupta, a specialist in Hindu religion, says the Haldar family, hereditary owners of the temple, are worried about negative publicity and make efforts to preserve the bloodshed. "I encountered total hostility to my taking a photograph of the temple precinct," complains Gupta, "lest I try to capture with my camera the cruel custom of decapitating a poor goat."[56]

A Plea for Compassion

As the world's only Hindu kingdom, Nepal, India's northern neighbor, also shows its devotion to Kali by killing animals. Tucked into a valley between two mountains, Dakshinkali Temple near Kathmandu is infamous for the hundreds of animals ritually slaughtered every week. Temple executioners saturate Kali's shrine with the spurting blood as the panicking animals struggle to escape. Describing the chaos of hundreds of people competing for their opportunity to appease the goddess, journalist Richard Ehrlich noted how the crowd at Dakshinkali pushes and shoves their way to the sacrificial spot, "walking barefoot in huge puddles of blood."[57] Elsewhere in Nepal, animal sacrifices have been used to bless a new car or to keep an aircraft in working order. In the latter example, officials from Nepal's state-run airline beheaded two goats in an effort to appease Akash Bhairab, the Hindu god of sky protection, and keep their two Boeing 757s flying properly.[58]

This Himalayan nation is also known for what certainly must be the most karmically ironic sacrifice anywhere: the one-day slaughter at the Rajdevi Panchawati Temple in southeastern Nepal. In a bid to honor the goddess Rajdevi, an aspect of Durgä, Hindus kill animals on the only day during the year the temple allows blood sacrifice: May 20. Meanwhile, Buddhists celebrate the birth of the Buddha (Buddha Purnima) during the month of Vaisakh (April–May) when the moon is full. Buddha Purnima is also regarded as Nonviolence Day, yet when May 20 is endowed with a full moon, the Hindu and Buddhist observations overlap, and the blood runs all day at Rajdevi Panchawati Temple without regard for a spiritual leader who not only preached against the taking of sentient life, but who some scholars maintain was a vegetarian.[59] Whatever his views on eating meat, the Buddha, who was born in Nepal, would undoubtedly be appalled by the suffering when the anniversary of his birth coincides with a massive crowd of devotees descending upon Rajdevi Panchawati with their sacrificial victims. Inside the temple, thousands of goats, chickens, ducks, and pigeons are killed by those wishing to gain favor with a goddess recognized for granting wishes. Temple priest Dambar Bahadur Bhatta acknowledges the paradox that last occurred in 2008, but claims there's no changing tradition. "We've been compelled to offer such sacrifice on Buddha Purnima despite knowing the relevance of the day, as Goddess Rajdevi receives such offerings only on this particular day," he says.[60]

But of all the ritual killings carried out in Nepal, or anywhere else, none can compare to the mass carnage that takes place during the Gadhimai Jatra Mela. Held every five years at the Gadhimai temple near Nepal's southern border, the festival attracts about five million devotees, mostly from India, and is marked by the killing of hundreds of thousands of animals, all to appease Gadhimai, the Hindu goddess of power. At the 2009 festival, some 250,000 animals were massacred in two days. Though a wide variety of animals are killed, witnesses say the slaughter of the buffaloes is the worst spectacle. Men armed with swords enter an enclosed yard containing approximately 20,000 buffaloes. As they begin hacking away, the butchers are sometimes able to behead the animals with a single blow, but as the men tire, it can take as many as 25 strikes of the blade to kill a buffalo. First the men cut the hind legs, forcing the buffalo to the ground; then they begin chopping at the neck until the writhing animal is finally beheaded. Baby buffaloes bleat for their mothers; the babies are hacked to death, too. Animal advocates around the world continue to call on Nepal to end this massive display of agony, but authorities cite that age-old excuse: tradition. The real motivation may be economic, however—organizers of the 2009 festival estimated they earned €2 million (about US$3 million) from sales of carcasses and hides.

Pleading with his fellow Nepalis to shun violence, Tirtha Bahadur Shrestha, a respected naturalist, contends that animal sacrifice has no place in a modern world. "Our enemies today are not demons," he says. "It is superstition, fatalism, poverty, and social inequity that plague our society. We will defeat and overcome these ills by being more humane and caring ourselves, by showing civilized behavior. Decapitating a bleating buffalo or goat should not be the symbol of the Nepali civilization." Shrestha is calling for a "New Nepal" in which Hindus embrace compassion over cruelty. "It is morally wrong to torture fellow creatures, but to do so in the name of religion is a sin. The government should set an example by stopping official sacrifices."[61]

Creed or Commerce?

Shrestha is not alone in his crusade. Indeed, animal advocates throughout the Hindu world are campaigning to end the use of animals as sacrificial victims. Groups such as India's People for Animals, the Visakha Society for Protection and Care of Animals, and PETA India have targeted blood sacrifice as a barbaric and uncivilized practice that is not in keeping with the true spirit of Hinduism.

Part of the growing debate concerns the role money plays in blood rituals, where the commodification of animals is just as entrenched as in factory farming and other forms of exploitation. Sacrifice has created a profitable business for butchers, clerics, animal dealers, and lenders, all of whom have a vested interest in seeing the practice continue. Maneka Gandhi, founder of People for Animals, explains that many Hindu temples are leased to contractors, and all monetary offerings go into a treasury shared by the temple trust, trustees, and their families. "Colluding with butchers and moneylenders, priests and contractors promote animal sacrifice within nearby villages, often compelling impoverished residents to borrow money to afford sacrificial animals," she says. "Then the animals are butchered behind temples in unhygienic conditions, creating public health problems."[62] While proponents of animal sacrifices would like villagers to believe the killing will result in an economic bounty, in truth it only lines the pockets of those conspiring to bring misery to animals and Hindus alike.

Hinduism also bolsters the trafficking of animal remains. People for Animals has been investigating this illegal trade for years and has discovered countless body parts from protected animals slaughtered for religious objects. Tiger and panther claws, peacock feathers, cobra-bone necklaces, buck horns, monkey skulls, and ivory decorations are but some of the paraphernalia on display in temples and in shops that specialize in Hindu artifacts. According to Maneka, many swamis contribute to the poaching of animals by sitting on deer and tiger skins or donning them at festivals. "Many who congregate in Allahabad for the Kumbh [a massive Hindu pilgrimage] openly wear big cat skins which I am sure they sell and regularly replenish," she says. "No wonder these Hindu priests just won't give up animal sacrifice." Maneka reveals that priests in the Andhra Pradesh temple town of Tirupati routinely capture and whip civet cats, an endangered species, to extract a yellow secretion from the animal's anal glands. The priests then charge a fee to apply the substance to the forehead of devotees.[63]

Islamic Feasts

Kareem Khan was about to betray someone he loved. The devout Muslim was preparing for the festival of Bakri Eid, an Islamic holiday that traditionally includes animal sacrifice, and he soon would have to kill a goat. But unlike the victims of blood sacrifice in other religions, goats or other animals destined for ritual slaughter on Bakri Eid commonly live with the family that will eventually murder them.[64] The Khans lovingly reared their goat, even giving him a name. "I brought up Golu Mian as my own son, fed and cared for him regularly," said Khan, "and now I have to kill him."[65]

While many Muslim families struggle with this emotional dilemma, it's clearly the animals who bear the true burden during Bakri Eid, which commemorates the prophet Abraham's willingness to sacrifice his son for Allah.[66] According to Jonah Blank, whose book *Mullahs on the Mainframe* focuses on life among a community of Indian Muslims, animals are supposed to be killed by someone skilled with a knife, but many are subjected to horrific, lingering deaths. Blank describes in agonizing detail the suffering of a particular goat during Bakri Eid:

> One of the goats whose sacrifice I witnessed spent several lengthy minutes bleeding its life away: for the first thirty seconds it lay thrashing on the pavement, its head bent back at an angle nature never intended. Then the animal settled into a confused state: still alive—but stunned to be staring directly at the hide covering its own spine. A few moments after the butcher had moved on to the next animal, the goat seemed to recover from its initial shock. Its nose began to twitch, its breathing became more labored, its legs began kicking with all their waning strength. The death-throes lasted at least two more minutes. Each time I thought the animal had finally sunk away, the nearly decapitated goat would start kicking again with renewed vigor, trying one last, fruitless time to scramble back to life.[67]

This account of blatant cruelty epitomizes the need for religious reform, and indeed some Muslim critics now recognize that such inhumane treatment of animals violates Islamic teachings. "Sacrifice is not a pillar of Islam," argues Muslim activist Shahid 'Ali Muttaqi. "Animals are mentioned in the Qur'an in relation to sacrifice only because in that time, place, and circumstance, animals were the means of survival." 'Ali Muttaqi explains that when the Qur'an was written in the 7th century CE, the desert-dwelling people of Arabia were intricately connected to the cycle of life and death, and they killed animals for food. "But let us not assume for a minute that we are forever stuck in those circumstances, or that the act of eating meat or killing an animal is what makes one a Muslim." Islamic sacrifice is not about blood atonement or seeking God's favor through another's death, he says. "In Islam, all that is demanded as a sacrifice is one's personal willingness to submit one's ego and individual will to Allah."[68]

Animal sacrifice becomes an operatic bloodbath during the Hajj, when two million Muslims from around the world make a once-in-a-lifetime pilgrimage to Mecca, Saudi Arabia, the holiest site in Islam. At the culmination of the Hajj, every pilgrim is enjoined to kill at least one four-legged animal, with goats and sheep being the most common sacrificial victims.[69] Hajj-related animal sacrifice has become so popular that every year more than four million sheep are shipped to the Middle East from Australia to help meet the demand.[70] As we saw in Chapter 1, the animals endure many weeks at sea on huge, overcrowded transport vessels. Before they even reach port, a large percentage of these sheep die from exposure, starvation, disease, and being trampled or suffocated by other animals. It's all part of a profitable business in which ranchers, animal dealers, and butchers enjoy the blood money earned from exploiting sacrificial victims.

'Ali Muttaqi has called on Islam to end the vicious practice of animal sacrifice. "It's not enough to acknowledge that the situation is unfortunate," he says. "We as Muslims must not only change our own actions that help create this situation, but also speak out for the protection of Allah's innocent creatures. We're not living 1,400 years ago, and whether some of us like it or not, the world is changing."[71]

"Religious freedom cannot be unlimited. For us religious freedom stops where human or animal suffering begins."[72]
—Marianne Thieme, leader of the Dutch Animal Rights Party

The Way of the Saints

After examining an extensive amount of scholarship on animal sacrifice, I think it's safe to say that over the last 30 years no faith system has garnered more attention for the ritual killing of animals in the United States (or perhaps anywhere) than the Caribbean religion of Santería. The roots of Santería go back to the traditional beliefs of the Yorubas, a tribe from the West African nations of

Nigeria and Benin, who brought the religion to the West Indies as slaves in the 16th century. In Cuba, it merged with certain Roman Catholic beliefs and evolved into modern-day Santería, where its spirits, or orishas, are reached through animal sacrifices. Following Fidel Castro's revolution in Cuba in 1959, exiles brought the religion to the US. Santería means "way of the saints" and refers to the correlations between the Catholic saints and the orishas of Yoruba.[73] Most of the animals ritually killed in Santería are eaten, though animals used in cleansing rituals, such as chickens, are simply thrown away, since they are considered to be imbued with the negative energy of the person being cleansed.[74]

Owing in part to the Supreme Court's 1993 ruling, mentioned at the beginning of this chapter, Santería is never far from the controversy when animal sacrifice is debated in the United States. The case began in 1987, when the Church of the Lukumí Babalú Ayé announced plans to build a church, school, and cultural center for its 300 members on land they leased in Hialeah, Florida, a blue-collar city of 200,000 people near Miami. It would be the first formal place of worship in Florida, possibly even in the country, for Santería. Hialeah residents, citing concerns about animal cruelty, petitioned the city council to keep the new church out of their backyard.[75] Hialeah officials quickly passed several ordinances prohibiting animal sacrifice, leading the church to file a lawsuit against the city on the grounds that their First Amendment rights to freely exercise religion had been violated. After years of legal wrangling in state and appeals courts, the case was heard by the US Supreme Court, which unanimously invalidated the city ordinances that had outlawed animal sacrifices.

The high court's decision has led to a bookcase full of texts and philosophical discourse—not to mention an endless stream of opinions found in ubiquitous blogs and video postings—all centered on the religion's practice of ritual slaughter. Some have observed that the Supreme Court's decision flatly affirmed the right of religions to sacrifice animals, but animal law expert Bruce Wagman says the ruling is not that simple. "The court *did* uphold the sacrifice, but it basically upheld the sacrifice because it was a recognized religious practice and the law barring it was directed at the religion and the religious practice," says Bruce, who uses the Lukumí case in classes as an adjunct professor of animal law at several law schools in California. "So because the ordinances written by the City of Hialeah were clearly intended to target religious practice, the court upheld the sacrifice." While the decision does not mean that animal sacrifice is explicitly legal in the US, Bruce says the real question, at least from a legal standpoint, is whether authorities could prosecute someone engaged in animal sacrifice by applying a general anti-cruelty statute. "I think the answer, even from the Supreme Court's precedent, is yes," he says, noting that states can enforce their anti-drug laws by prosecuting and imposing sanctions on people who, for example, consume peyote as part of a religious sacrament.[76]

As Justice Kennedy said, residents in the US find animal sacrifice abhorrent, and authorities attempt to ban it by bringing Santería practitioners to court. But santeros (as the religion's priests are called) are fiercely protective of their sacrificial tradition, and judges continue to support their right to free exercise of religion. In 2009, a federal appeals court reversed the ruling of a US district court that had barred a Santería priest from sacrificing animals in his Texas home. The priest, Jose Merced, claimed that by practicing his faith in the privacy of his house, he didn't harm anyone. Merced, clearly oblivious to the insensitivity of his remark, didn't take into account the suffering of the turtle, the 20 chickens, and the nine larger animals, such as goats or sheep, he slaughtered every time he ordained a new priest.[77]

Santeros sacrifice animals in a wide variety of Santería rituals, including marriages, funerals, and to heal the sick. For the actual killing, the priest holds an animal on his or her side and raises the animal's head with one hand while inserting a four-inch blade into the neck with the other, pushing all the way through.[78] In his expert testimony during the Church of the Lukumí Babalú Ayé lawsuit, veterinarian Michael Fox of The Humane Society of the United States established that this method of severing both carotid arteries is not humane, nor is it reliable or painless. Furthermore, Dr. Fox testified that the animal being killed is likely to experience stress and fear, since animals are often kept in close confinement with animals other than their own species while awaiting sacrifice, causing significant stress. Finally, he said, an animal brought into a room where other animals had just been killed would perceive the bodily secretions of those deceased animals. Animals who experience fear often secrete chemical metabolites known as thermones, and the odor of these thermones can trigger an intense fear reaction in other animals who detect those odors.[79] As attorney Anna Charlton of the Rutgers Animal Rights Law Center puts it, "The Santería killing is done with a stab through the neck. You've got a stabbing and a sawing action, and it's not what we consider humane slaughter. We set up minimum standards for slaughter, and they don't match it."[80]

Closely aligned with Santería is an Afro-Brazilian religion known as Candomblé, which fuses Catholicism with African and indigenous Indian beliefs. Like Santería, Candomblé was developed as a result of the slave trade, and adherents rely on animal sacrifice to commune with orishas. Researchers in South America recently gained the trust of local practitioners and uncovered details about ceremonies involving spirit worship. According to their findings, priests in Candomblé kill domestic and wild animals—including the threatened yellow-footed tortoise (*Chelonoidis denticulata*)—through strangulation and decapitation as a way to "nourish" orishas and earn their favor.[81]

Double Standard

Among the arguments used by the Church of the Lukumí Babalú Ayé in its lawsuit against the City of Hialeah is an ethical dilemma that many critics of other animal cruelties, such as dogfighting or the fur industry, also struggle to reconcile: if one accepts the premise that it is morally wrong to torture and kill an animal, is it morally acceptable to eat them? After all, turning living beings into food products today means that billions of animals are raised and killed every year in conditions that are, to be fair, routinely more horrific than those involved in sacrifice. In his lengthy critique of the Lukumí case for *Animal Law Review*, attorney Henry Mark Holzer asks "… if animals can be murdered in Hialeah, and, for that matter, everywhere else in the United States, for virtually any reason (or no reason) at all, how can the Constitution, which protects the free exercise of religion, prohibit the killing of animals for religious purposes?" But Holzer is no sacrifice apologist; he's merely highlighting the intrinsic paradox of the city's argument—one not lost on the justices. "Although there are anti-cruelty laws purporting to protect animals in every state," Holzer writes, "they are no impediment to production and slaughter for food, to experimentation for 'science,' to hunting for 'conservation,' to fishing for 'sport,' to 'ranching' for fur, to performance for 'entertainment,' and on and on. I mention this because the [Supreme] Court knows it… well. There isn't an Animal Rights person, let alone an ethical vegetarian, among them."[82]

Attorney and ethical vegan Gary Francione, who represented the American Society for the Prevention of Cruelty to Animals in New York City when Santería practitioners sued them in 1983, goes a step further, challenging non-vegan critics of animal sacrifice to put their morals with their mouth is and stop eating meat, eggs, and dairy foods. He points out that the best justification non-vegans can offer for inflicting pain and death on animals is that they taste good. "We do not need to eat animals to be optimally healthy and animal agriculture is an environmental disaster," Francione observes. "The Santería practitioners believe that animal sacrifice is necessary for spiritual reasons. They actually have a *better* reason for animal exploitation than most non-vegans do."[83]

So what makes one animal worthy of our protection and another one a meal? The staunchest animal advocates (i.e., those who reject all animal exploitation) have confronted omnivores with this contradiction for years, as when activist Henry Spira and former *New York Times* advertising artist Mark Graham designed an ad featuring a kitten and a piglet looking at each other; the copy reads: "Which do you pet and which do you eat? Why?"[84] Matthew Scully explored this question in a feature for *The American Conservative*, and, after asserting that a dog and a pig are moral equals, suggested that "it's only human caprice and economic convenience that say otherwise. We have the problem that these essentially similar creatures are treated in dramatically different ways, unjustified even by the very different purposes we have assigned to them. Our pets are accorded certain protections from cruelty, while the nameless creatures in our factory farms are hardly treated like animals at all."[85]

Animal sacrifice practitioners have relied on the implied hypocrisy of favoring companion animals over other animals to help defend ritual slaughter. "Unfortunately, we live in a society that is largely blind to its own confused double standards of morality," writes Migene González-Wippler in *Santería: The Religion*. "Many of the people who condemn the ritual sacrifices of Santería have no pangs of conscience when they eat lobster, shrimps, crabs, or crayfish. But these animals are boiled alive so that they may be eaten. … Why is it that killing animals in a slaughterhouse is allowable but killing them in a place of worship is not?"[86]

The answer, at least to the steadfast advocate, is that killing an animal for exploitation, whether such exploitation is for a meal or to offer blood to a deity, is never acceptable; as sentient beings with their own interests, animals should be left alone. "Thus, for the animal rights movement, the message is clear: it must redouble its effort to eliminate all forms of cruelty to animals," writes Holzer. "Then, neither Santeríans nor anyone else will be able to justify their obscene, religious practices on the ground that everyone else is mistreating animals for reasons considerably less important than the free exercise of religion."[87]

Hmong Rituals

Following the Communist takeover of Laos in the 1970s, vast members of an ethnic community known as the Hmong, facing genocide, fled to other countries, including the United States. This wasn't their first migration; the Hmong (pronounced "mong") had been forced from their native land in eastern China into Laos and other parts of Southeast Asia centuries earlier.[88] Today, the Hmong population in the US is more than 180,000.[89] The Hmong are justly proud of their culture, which includes a rich tradition in music, dance, and art. Many Hmong also follow an ancient religion that combines animism with some elements of ancestor worship. At the center of this Hmong religion is the shaman.

In Hmong society, the shaman is a healer who is gifted with the ability to pass between the permeable barrier that separates the material world and the world of spirits in his pursuit of a cure for the sick. Causes of illness may include doing one's laundry in a lake where a dragon lives, pointing at a full moon, and urinating on a rock that resembles a tiger. But by far the best way to become physically or mentally ill, say the Hmong, is for the soul to become separated from the body after a moment of anger, a period of grief, or a variety of other reasons. According to the Hmong's shamanic cosmology, the human body is the host for a number of souls, and a soul separated from the body or stolen by an evil spirit often requires the intercession of a shaman.[90]

While these superstitions may elicit a snicker from some Westerners, there is nothing amusing about the fate that awaits animals used to treat mental and physical ailments in Hmong culture. Shamans routinely sacrifice animals to negotiate with spirits for the soul of the inflicted person.[91] In a typical healing ceremony, the shaman ties a string or cord around a small pig and wraps the string around the patient. Chanting loudly, the shaman then enters a trance while observers restrain the terrified pig, who is eventually carried to a table or bench and bled to death as his shrieks inevitably ebb away. The ritual is repeated with another young pig, who is also

killed, and their flesh is used to feed the shaman and others in atten-
dance.[92] Pigs are the preferred sacrificial victims for the Hmong
healing ceremonies, though if they cannot be obtained, chickens will
suffice.[93]

This is not to suggest that the Hmong only sacrifice animals for
healing. In very traditional households, such as those in China, the
Hmong shaman might be summoned to sacrifice chickens and pigs
simply to rid a young boy or girl of an inappropriate infatuation.[94]
Or if someone in a household has been experiencing a series of
misfortunes, a shaman can perform a ritual in which he, a child, and
the patient chase a dog around the house. The dog is finally led
outside, where he is killed and dismembered; his head is buried
beneath a village gate, while his paws are displayed to ward off evil
spirits.[95]

Hmong also kill animals to commemorate births, to sanctify
marriages, and to practice "soul calling," which may be used to
invite an ancestor to be reborn into the body of a new baby and
determine if the call for reincarnation has been successful. In her
bestselling book about Hmong culture, *The Spirit Catches You and You
Fall Down*, author Anne Fadiman recounts how an elder from a
Hmong clan brought two live chickens to a party celebrating the
birth of a baby girl. The man stood in the doorway and chanted for
the soul of a departed relative to occupy the baby's body. The
chickens were then killed, partially boiled, and examined to see if
their skulls were translucent and their tongues curled upward—both
believed to be signs the ancestor was pleased with her rebirth.[96]

Although these killings are cruel enough, they are no match for
the carnage involved in Hmong funerals, elaborate affairs that follow
a rigorous protocol. Some may last a few days, while the burial
ceremony for an elder, deeply respected member of the community
may go on for nearly two weeks. Throughout the event, tradition
holds that at least one pig must be sacrificed each day of the funeral,
and other animals are sacrificed for various purposes.[97] A rooster
might be killed because he can see a dead person's soul and will

accompany the deceased into the spirit world, while a cow might be sacrificed to serve as a dowry for a dead female in the afterlife.[98] Family members of the deceased must provide animals to sacrifice on the day of the burial, and with a large clan, the slaughter can be extensive; animals killed are usually oxen, who are bludgeoned with a mallet.[99] For a dead parent, every grown son and son-in-law is expected to provide an ox, while daughters can pool their financial resources and collectively offer just one. In rural Hmong households, such as those in Asia, the oxen are lined up in the front yard of the dead person's home, connected with a string to the deceased, and murdered with an ax one after the other.[100] Within a year of the burial, this chaotic, bloody scene is repeated with a mortuary rite called *tso plig* ("release the self"), which is intended to prevent the soul of the deceased from troubling its descendants. In the years after the tso plig sacrifices, however, should a member of the family be afflicted by a serious illness, a shaman might proclaim that the departed soul needs still more animals in the afterlife. To appease the troublesome soul, the funeral rite is again repeated, with the deceased's sons, sons-in-law, and father-in-law contributing pigs to be killed every day of the ritual. A cruel finale to the ceremony takes place as the dead person's family gathers and, in the words of anthropologist Nicholas Tapp, "as many bulls as possible should be sacrificed."[101]

Predictably, such practices have not found general acceptance outside the Hmong Diaspora. According to Nachee Lee, former executive director of the Hmong Cultural Center in St. Paul, Minnesota, site of one of the largest Hmong populations in North America, "Some non-Hmong individuals disagree with how the animals are slain for the sacrifice and may view it as animal cruelty, such as a chicken's throat being slashed or a cow's head being hammered to death."[102] A 1995 case in Central California, home to another large Hmong community, illustrates Lee's point. Hoping to appease an angry spirit causing his wife's diabetes, Chia Thai Moua, a Hmong shaman who had emigrated from Laos to Fresno in the

1970s, recited an ancient chant on the front porch of his house while a club-wielding relative beat a three-month-old German shepherd to death.[103] After a horrified neighbor reported him to police, Moua explained that the dog's keen night vision and sense of smell can track down elusive spirits and barter for a person's lost soul.[104] (The outrage expressed by the general public in this case, including letters to editors and to the district attorney calling for Hmong refugees to move back to Laos, reflects the cognitive dissonance discussed earlier: while most people in the US would agree it is morally wrong to crush a puppy's skull at home, relatively few people speak out against the killing of dogs in medical research labs or express outrage that "retired" greyhounds are killed after their racing days are behind them—perhaps because such animals are not on someone's private property and therefore not considered a "pet.") In the end, Moua received probation, community service, and a small fine.[105]

Exploring the many rituals of the Hmong, one is left with the impression that their lives are pervaded by cruel and ceaseless death. Perhaps so. Fadiman recalls that nearly every Hmong family she met in Merced, California, sacrificed animals. "In fact, a fourteen-year-old boy I knew, a member of the Moua clan, once complained that he hardly ever had enough free time on weekends because his parents made him attend so many of his relatives' *neeb* [sacrificial] ceremonies."[106]

In justifying his culture's practice of animal sacrifice, Lee explains that, according to a Hmong legend, animals brokered a deal with humans long ago: If the humans would provide them with food and shelter, the animals would allow the humans to kill them for food and sacrifice. Undoubtedly seeing no downside to this selfless offer, the Hmong agreed and began their tradition of domestication and blood sacrifice.[107] Such folklore is not uncommon in other traditions; Winnebago tribal mythology tells of a hare who convenes with animals to determine which of them will give humans their permission to be eaten and which will allow themselves to be exploited for transportation and heavy labor.[108] These fanciful ratio-nalizations for animal cruelty are more than just oral histories; they hint at humanity's need for both solidarity with and, more tellingly, the forgiveness of the animals they oppress. It's as if in their hearts human beings recognize the injustice and must seek outside influ-ences to legitimize their domination of nonhuman animals—or, indeed, even fellow human beings, as we find a similar dynamic in the subjugation of African slaves in the US 200 years ago. Slaveholders looked to the Bible and quoted Ephesians in Sunday sermons: "Slaves, obey your earthly masters with respect and fear, and with sincerity of heart, just as you would obey Christ. Obey them not only to win their favor when their eye is on you, but like slaves of Christ, doing the will of God from your heart."[109]

Needless to say, even scripture didn't keep an unjust practice from finally being banned.

Vodoun

Think of "Voodoo" and two images likely come to mind: zombies and animal sacrifice. But while reanimated human corpses are largely the stuff of B movies and horror fiction, the blood sacrifices in the African religion known by practitioners as Vodoun are as grim as anything Hollywood could create. Animals killed in the rituals of Vodoun (also known as Vodou, Vudu, and Vodun) are usually goats and roosters, though Vodounists believe each *lwa* or *loa* (a pantheon of supernatural beings) has its own preference, which may also be a snake, lion, leopard, bull, sheep, crab, alligator, or crocodile.[110]

Before the animal can be sacrificed, his or her compliance is necessary, so the animal is offered food. If they accept, it is considered agreement. If they reject the food, another animal is chosen.[111] Dowoti Désir, a Vodoun priestess, acknowledges that there's something inherently unjust about sacrificing an animal. "Essentially, I apologize for taking away its life," she says. "I didn't give it; it's not my right to take it away. But at the same time, I know I need it." Her "need" is based on the premise that an animal's life is a substitute for her own or someone else's. This is a common theme within the sacrificial cult, putting human desires above those of all other species. "When I need to use a rooster in a ceremony, I ask its permission," says Désir. "I ask its forgiveness, because I am fully aware that at any point in my life, it could be *my* head that is being taken away. Having your head taken away probably won't happen in a ceremony like this, but when you don't get the job you need, or something horrible happens to you on your way to work, or your child has a debilitating illness—essentially, it is the same."[112]

Uh, actually, it's not the same thing. Moreover, I find it difficult to imagine that any animal would give his or her consent to being murdered for any reason, least of all to help someone land a job. "Asking" animals to acquiesce to being blood victims is another instance of sacrificers expiating their guilt before the deed is done. Throughout the sacrificial tradition there is the concept that the animal is in some way a willing participant in the ritual. In Hinduism, for example, a priest asks a deity's permission to sacrifice an animal, since the animal is considered the property of the gods. Then the victim must be persuaded to allow him- or herself to be killed peacefully for the benefit of humans. Should the victim not remain calm, it is a sign that the animal has not granted permission, and there is a fear that he or she could return as an evil spirit to exact revenge.[113] There is even a persistent belief in India that the flesh of animals killed for food is poison because such animals died in fear, while the flesh of sacrificial victims is sweet, since these animals died "willingly."[114]

Beyond Religion

Blood sacrifices may transcend religion, but not ritual. Even the act of loved ones gathering to eat meat—communally consuming the flesh of an animal—is rich in ritualistic metaphor. Suggesting the very patriarchal cultures that loom so large in the early history of animal sacrifice, it is the "man of the house" who has traditionally carved the roast at dinnertime: presiding at the head of the table, sharp knife in hand, the man solemnly cuts deep into the animal corpse as liquid oozes from the cleaved flesh. The special apron sometimes worn while slicing and serving meat is also reminiscent of the sacrificial cult, while the celebratory mood of those at the holiday ("holy day") table imbues the moment with an air of significance. Moreover, the meal is frequently accompanied by a prayer or scripture reading, further perpetuating the sacrificial symbolism. Some families even use a special room for holiday meals, echoing the use of a temple or altar for performing the divine offering.

When it comes to sacrifices in the United States, sacred or secular, no animal is more oppressed than the turkey, with more than 45 million of these sensitive animals killed and eaten every Thanksgiving.[115] Ironically, this holiday is often a time for remembering those who have paid the ultimate sacrifice and given their lives defending freedom. In examining how the noble turkey could have been transformed into the national victim, I turned again to Karen Davis as well as to Brian Luke, who explores the role gender plays in the sacrifice of animals in his book *Brutal: Manhood and the Exploitation of Animals*. Brian sees a clear connection between sacrifice and how consumers in the United States view turkeys at Thanksgiving. "Historically, meat-eating was almost entirely sacrificial," he says. "People did not eat meat unless it was ritually sacrificed. Whereas in our time, it's just a product on the shelf with, for a lot of people, no lingering images of sentience or evidence that the creature had to be killed. That's all changed at Thanksgiving. The sentience of the turkey is really brought to the forefront of the imagery around Thanksgiving."

Brian posits that this imagery—cartoons, greeting cards that mock turkeys, articles describing the slaughter process, etc.—is meant to emphasize the turkey as a living being. "There's not really a sacrifice in the sense of a full display of power unless there's an understanding that there's a victim," he says. "So what's going on here is a ritualized display of power. To do that, you need to construct the victim, and that happens in a society where we've largely forgotten that animals are sentient before they're made into meat." Standing in sharp relief to this annual focus on the sentience of turkeys is the propaganda system that leads people to repress reminders that when they consume meat they're eating a dead animal. "At the same time," says Brian, "we don't really forget. We bring it out and accentuate it—almost exaggerate it—at certain key points, and those are the points where we *want* to remember that the animal is sentient, can feel pleasure and pain, has a drive to survive, and must be killed against their will. I think Thanksgiving is one of the key examples of that."[116]

Karen Davis, who offers an illuminating history of turkeys in *More Than a Meal: The Turkey in History, Myth, Ritual, and Reality*, suggests that the nascent practice of ridiculing this animal through imagery, jokes, and "games" such as turkey bowls (in which participants roll a frozen turkey at a set of bowling pins) serves to demonstrate our superiority over other animals and our power to consecrate such "inferior" beings through the Thanksgiving sacrifice. "The carnivalization of the turkey functions as a magic formula for conquering our fear of being a 'turkey,'" she writes. "We poke so as not to be poked at. By devouring another, we master our fear of being devoured. ... A pathetic bird, conceived in the mind of Man, is purified and redeemed by being absorbed back into the bowels of Man."[117] Also perpetuating animal sacrifice, in Karen's view, is something much more troubling. "I think one of the main characteristics of many humans is a desire to have somebody suffer and die for them," she says. "Some people like the idea that turkeys and other animals have to suffer and die for us to live."[118]

Karen agrees with Brian that Thanksgiving is as much about the turkey as a sacrificial victim as it is about who wants dark meat and who wants white—maybe even more so. It's critical, she believes, that the bird is not transformed into just another meal. "To do so would diminish the bird's dual role in creating the full Thanksgiving experience. In order to affect people properly, a sacrificial animal must not only be eaten by them; the animal's death must be 'witnessed by them, and not suffered out of sight as we now arrange matters,'" she writes, quoting that keen observer of social rituals, Margaret Visser.[119]

The animal's death must also be shared by the country in order for the turkey's sacrifice to bring an entire society together, says Brian. "I think one of the ways that shows up so strongly is how insistent we are that everybody eats turkey," he says. "It's hard for most people to imagine celebrating Thanksgiving without eating turkey; in fact, some people call it Turkey Day. I think the real drive behind that is that the point of the holiday is to unify the nation, and if you don't participate in the main way we come into unity with each other, it's not working." Advocates of turkey-eating ensure that everyone from prisoners to the homeless partakes in the sacrificial bird. "There's this effort to make sure that no matter what someone's status in society, no matter how poor they are, they get some Thanksgiving turkey, because it's supposed to bring us together as Americans."

Another important component of the sacrifice ritual carried out at the dinner table is the veiled threat against humans, serving as a way to exercise patriarchal control over society. "By virtue of the man carving the turkey, he's implicitly threatening his underlings, who could be the women and children in his household," says Brian. "Of course, we don't live in a patriarchal society, at least not in the traditional sense, yet we still have this once-a-year ritual where the man has to be the one who actually cuts into the bird. When we *did* live in a patriarchal society, this was a very good way of communicating threats to everybody in the household." The classic example of this, says Brian, is the Judeo-Christian story of Abraham ready and willing to sacrifice his son Isaac; at the last moment, God intervenes and Abraham sacrifices a ram in his son's stead.[120] Brian believes the annual "presidential pardon" of a turkey shares something in common with the story of Abraham, as the president's benevolent act implies his capacity to kill and his decision not to.[121] "The freeing of the one symbolic turkey is really a way of communicating in a very visceral way the power of the chief executive over life and death," he says. "What's implied is that the power we are actually exercising over turkeys could be applied to certain groups of people by certain other groups of people; namely, the men in charge of politics and the military and so on have the ability to kill whatever group is designated as outside the pale, whether it be a condemned criminal or somebody designated a terrorist."[122]

Laboratory Rituals

If animal sacrifice can be defined as ritualized killing, it is hardly a stretch to view animal testing with the same lens we use to scrutinize kapparot, Santería, Hmong ceremonies, or any other blood ritual. In fact, with today's biomedical researchers cloaked in white lab coats reminiscent of priests' robes and worshipping at the altar of science, there could hardly be a more apt comparison, a point driven home by Brian Luke in *Brutal*. "In its overt organization, vivisection differs little from ancient religious rituals of animal sacrifice," he writes. "Beyond this structural congruence there is also a direct line of historical continuity between the sacrificial altar and the necropsy table. Indeed, the established technical term for killing an experimental animal is 'sacrifice.'"[123] Brian is not the first person to make this observation, of course, and we are again reminded of the definition of animal sacrifice offered by Bruce Lincoln, who specifically notes that animals are regularly sacrificed in research labs.[124]

Nearly every scholarly examination of animal sacrifice in the last 40 years cites the work of Walter Burkert, whose influential study on the subject, *Homo Necans*, was first published in German in 1972 and translated into English a decade later. A religious historian of some prominence, Burkert asserts that early humans took their genetically-based hostility toward one another and channeled it into hunting animals. As humans domesticated animals and no longer had to rely on hunting for survival, says Burkert, animal sacrifice became their outlet for violence.[125] Is it not axiomatic that animal testing would follow suit, displacing the "primitive" act of religious sacrifice as the next link in the chain of human aggression?[126] It certainly rings true for animal advocates like Karen Davis, who is offended by the common practice of projecting human weaknesses into turkeys and other animals before we kill them. "That's the whole basis of animal experimentation to cure human diseases," she says. "You take a healthy animal and you inflict human ailments into their body, and they suffer and die for our health and recovery from our illnesses. There are very deep psychological—and, in my opinion, genetically-based—impulses that help explain the kinds of societies, rituals, and activities that prevail."[127]

These profound psychological entanglements in our relationship with animals have fueled the fallacy that the lives of some species are less important than others, and it contributes to the practice of sacrificing animals for human benefit.

What You Can Do

Animal sacrifice is deeply entrenched within the religions and cultures that practice it. Nevertheless, you should always notify authorities if you know of any instance of animal sacrifice or of animal mutilations (mutilated corpses are often discarded in public places). Here are some additional suggestions:

- Find out who in your area (city, state, etc.) investigates and enforces anti-cruelty laws. This may be your local humane society or SPCA. Contact them if you discover evidence of animal sacrifice.
- Contact organizations that campaign against animal sacrifice, such as PETA, PETA India, People for Animals, and United Poultry Concerns.
- Keep your animal companions indoors, on leashes, or closely supervised so they're not stolen. Be especially careful to keep cats indoors on Halloween.

Kapparot

Please contact the following Orthodox organizations and ask them to promote the use of money instead of chickens for kapparot ceremonies:

Israel

Seymour J. Abrams Orthodox Union Jerusalem World Center

22 Rechov Keren Hayesod

P.O. Box 37015

Jerusalem 91370

Israel

(02) 560-9100

Email: israelcenter@ou.org

UK

The London Beth Din

305 Ballards Lane

North Finchley

London N12 8GB

020 8343 6270

Email: info@bethdin.org.uk

US

National Committee for Furtherance of Jewish Education

824 Eastern Parkway

Brooklyn, NY 11213

718-735-0200

Orthodox Union

11 Broadway

New York, NY 10004

212-563-4000

Rabbinical Council of America
305 Seventh Avenue, 12ᵗʰ Floor
New York, NY 10001
212-807-7888
Email: office@rabbis.org

Finally...

If you celebrate Easter, Thanksgiving, or any other holiday by eating animals, please consider enjoying a plant-based meal instead. For information and recipes that will help make compassion the center-piece at your holiday feast, see *The Vegan Table: 200 Unforgettable Recipes for Entertaining Every Guest at Every Occasion* by Colleen Patrick-Goudreau, or visit one of these websites:

- CompassionateCook.com
- ExploreVeg.org
- FoodIsPower.org
- GoVeg.com
- VeganMexicanFood.com
- VegCooking.com
- VegNews.com
- Viva.org.uk

Chapter 8

Conceptual Cruelty: Animals Used in Art

The study of art that does not result in making the strong less willing to oppress the weak means little.
—Booker T. Washington, educator

Tucked in among exclusive boutiques bearing such names as Armani, Cartier, Ralph Lauren, and Louis Vuitton, Sotheby's auction house is right at home along London's fashionable New Bond Street. It's the sort of high-end shopping district where you don't inquire about the price of an item: if you have to ask, you probably can't afford it. Inside Sotheby's, amid the imposing walls with their grand scale, art enthusiasts washing down foie gras with vintage champagne seemed unconcerned by the astronomical bids being showered on hundreds of pieces in September 2008. Many of these works finally went for double, triple, or even quadruple what Sotheby's expected they'd fetch. In the end, it was a sales record for a single artist, with bidders paying US$198 million (£111 million) for 218 pieces by Damien Hirst—10 times the previous record, which was set for works by a guy named Pablo Picasso.

Unlike Picasso, however, Hirst uses animals and insects, killed so they may be embalmed, sliced open, pickled, ground up, covered in resin, or otherwise presented as "art." The highest price in the Sotheby's auction was paid for a calf who had been embalmed and positioned on a marble plinth, his hooves and horns covered in gold. A shark suspended in a tank of formaldehyde was another top seller. Sadly, that well-heeled collectors would pay millions for displays of cruelty that have been frozen in time says as much about certain people as it does about Hirst. (Reviewing Hirst's work the day before the Sotheby's auction, Peter Conrad, the acclaimed critic for the *Observer*, marveled at the exhibit's "witty inventiveness, the ingenuity of its manufacture and its sheer beauty."[1])

Born in Bristol, England, in 1965, Hirst has become the bad boy of the British art scene. In 1994, US Customs held up one of Hirst's non-preserved dead-animal displays en route to New York City, citing concerns about health: apparently the stench of rotting flesh caught their attention. Other Hirst creations include a crucified sheep, a bull's heart punctured with a variety of surgical instruments, and a kneeling sheep holding a prayer book—all part of his "Death of God" series.

Before his recent taxidermy-as-art period, Hirst made a name for himself creating colorful compositions that resemble the stained-glass windows of churches. Look closely and you'll see that the collages are made from thousands of dismembered butterfly wings. "One has to wonder if Hirst was the sort of demented child who would pull the wings off flies for fun," said Dawn Carr, PETA's European director, in 2003. "He certainly has become that sort of an adult. Butterfly wings are beautiful on a butterfly, but tearing small creatures to bits is not art, it's sadism."[2] Indeed, Hirst seems to relish inflicting death upon insects. Measured by the number of lives lost, his 2012 installation at London's Tate Modern, "In and Out of Love," is surely his most offensive, with some 9,000 butterflies killed during the 23 weeks of the exhibition. Trapped inside two windowless rooms at the gallery were butterflies of the Owl and Heliconius species, which live for up to nine months in the wild. Those used in Hirst's display died so quickly—surviving for between a few hours and several days—that they had to be continuously replenished 400 butterflies at a time. Some of them perished after being trodden underfoot, and others were killed when visitors swatted the gentle insects off their clothing.[3]

"We don't care what Hirst sculpts or paints, but when he 'procures' animals, and he pays for them to go through pain and suffering and death, he might as well be doing it to children," says PETA's Jenny Woods. "It is simply not acceptable to contribute to and encourage animal suffering for art. His pieces are cheap shots at the expense of animals and are more like crime scenes than art exhibits."[4]

Hirst has defended his work, noting that animals are continually killed in slaughterhouses. It's an argument other artists and gallery owners have offered as well; they claim it is hypocritical to criticize those who kill animals for the sake of artistic expression when most people gorge on animal flesh every day. Moreover, they claim artistic freedom not only supersedes the humane treatment of animals, but it is the artist's responsibility to challenge, shock or even offend the sensibilities of a public that has grown numb from reality TV and information overload. Indeed, in its treatise on free speech vs. censorship, the American Civil Liberties Union even declares that "a free society is based on the principle that each and every individual has the right to decide what art or entertainment he or she wants— or does not want—to receive or create."[5]

What, then, are we to make of Hirst and his ilk using violence against animals as a leitmotif? Are such people truly fulfilling a need in society? Should they and their creations stand outside respect for life; should they hover somewhere in that gray area between the confrontational and the cruel?

Conceptual Cruelty

Others have asked, is this art? Critics with debased taste agree it is, placing even the most perverse exhibitions under the category of "conceptual art"—that is, displays that reject the aesthetic values traditionally associated with art and instead strive for an idea or intellectual experience. The question, however, isn't whether or not a piece qualifies as art, but whether it is morally acceptable to subject an animal to pain and suffering for the *sake* of art (or any other pursuit intended to entertain us).

Ever since conceptual art emerged as a movement in the 1960s, its practitioners have pushed the boundaries of taste, offering creations that defy explanation and provoke public debate. In 1965, a chair positioned between a photograph of a chair and a dictionary definition of the word chair could be considered intellectually stimu-lating.[6] Today's artists have crossed a philosophical threshold as some resort to transforming life into death; in doing so, they not only ignore the interests of another sentient being, but they negate what should be obvious to an artist: that animals and insects are themselves works of art whose very existence inspires the kind of cognitive experience conceptual artists claim they want to compose.[7] Sadly, there are those who feel they must destroy in order to create.

Using animals for artistic expression goes back well before the conceptual art movement, of course. Evidence has shown, for instance, that the Dogon people of Mali, famous for their carved masks and other artistic designs, were using animal blood-based paint to decorate their sculptures back in the 13th century.[8] More recently, the Federal Subsistence Board, which is comprised of several agencies within the US government, gave subsistence hunters in Alaska permission to sell non-edible parts of wildlife—such as bones, claws, and fur—if they turn them into artwork first. This means that artists can sell handicrafts fashioned from the remains of animals killed under federal subsistence laws, such as caribou, moose, or whales.[9]

While these forms of animal exploitation are troubling to some people and "art" to others, it is the nascent trend of nausea-inducing works serving no higher purpose than to let people gawk at the suffering of innocents that has attracted the greatest outrage.

Artists such as Hirst who revel in death often claim they are reminding the public that we are all mortal. Some sadistic artists take this *memento mori* approach a step further, summoning the public to witness the loss of life—or even cause it. Chilean-born Danish artist Marco Evaristti created an art installation featuring 10 working kitchen blenders, each filled with water and a live goldfish, and invited the public to turn a blender on. The idea, said Evaristti, was to illustrate the fine line between being and nothingness—and tempt the vagaries of human nature. The installation has been displayed at a number of venues, but it was at the Trapholt Art

Museum in Kolding, Denmark, that one museum visitor accepted Evaristti's suggestion and killed two fish in 2007. Did the patron meditate on mortality, pondering the grand, existential questions Evaristti claims he wanted to highlight? It's doubtful. What's more likely is that the button-pusher was indifferent to another's suffering and simply wanted to see what it would be like to pulverize a live animal. That it could be done in the socially sanctioned milieu of a museum no doubt made the act all the more enticing.

Danish authorities fined Peter Meyer, director of the Trapholt Art Museum, for cruelty to animals. But Meyer appealed the fine, arguing that artistic freedom was at stake. "It's a question of principle," he told the court in Kolding. "An artist has the right to create works which defy our concept of what is right and what is wrong."[10]

After hearing from the blenders' maker, Moulinex, that the animals probably died within one second, the judge ruled the fish were killed humanely and that Meyer was not guilty of animal cruelty. Interestingly, the senselessness of the act—liquefying two goldfish in the name of "art"—was apparently not considered; rather, artistic expression trumped the lives of helpless animals, and no one was held accountable.

Shortly after the Kolding cruelty case, Evaristti's kill-a-goldfish-in-a-blender exhibit opened at the Kunstraum Dornbirn Gallery in Austria. Animal activists were waiting. They broke in after closing time and smashed the empty kitchen appliances.

Even when death is not an artist's intention, killing animals may still be the consequence of exploiting sentient life in the name of creativity. Brazilian artist Cildo Meireles probably had no desire to harm animals when he thoughtlessly filled three aquariums in his conceptual installation with 55 Glass Fish and Ghost Catfish. Nevertheless, by the time Meireles' 13-week-long exhibition at the Tate Modern museum in London had ended in January 2009, 12 of the fish were dead. Glass Fish can live up to three years in their natural environment, which is the fresh or brackish waters of India,

Burma, and Thailand. Ghost Catfish are freshwater fish from Indonesia who may live up to five years. Both species are translucent, allowing onlookers to view their skeletons and internal organs. Because Meireles was more concerned with visual impact than ethics, it is likely the animals' transparent quality that inspired him to include the Glass Fish and Ghost Catfish in his exhibit.

According to a statement from the Royal Society for the Prevention of Cruelty to Animals, "The RSPCA opposes any so-called 'art exhibition' that causes animals of any species distress or suffering. The RSPCA believes that fish are capable of feeling pain and suffering, they therefore should be treated with respect and in a manner that minimizes the risk of harm. ... If this art exhibition involved dogs, then there would be a national outcry; why should the use of fish be any different?"[11]

Hungry and Homeless

The RSPCA is right about a public outcry over dogs. In fact, the most infamous animal-related art display in the last decade is undoubtedly a gallery installation by Costa Rican artist Guillermo Vargas Jiménez, who tied a malnourished dog to a wall in the Códice Gallery in Managua, Nicaragua. Jiménez, who uses the name Habacuc, reportedly paid some local children to bring him a stray dog from the streets. Habacuc named the dog Natividad, and his apparent intention was to let the animal slowly die of starvation while gallery patrons placidly strolled by. Titled *Exposición No. 1*, the display is better known as *Eres Lo Que Lees* ("You Are What You Read"), the words meticulously spelled out on the gallery wall in bits of dry dog food.

In an interview with the Spanish-language Univision Network, Habacuc said the installation was meant to draw attention to people's apathy—the way they look away when they see something unpleasant on the street. "Look how many dogs can be seen on the streets and how many you have seen while you're traveling here in Central America," said Habacuc, who claimed to have three dogs and three cats, rescued from the streets. "Nobody does anything."

Eres Lo Que Lees was displayed for three days in August 2007 and quickly became an Internet phenomenon, with outraged people around the world blogging about Natividad, posting photographs of him on websites, and viewing videos of his suffering on YouTube. Perhaps that was Habacuc's real objective all along: What better way to garner some free publicity than through a blogosphere of furious animal lovers? Fueling people's anger was a report that Habacuc had been invited to display *Eres Lo Que Lees* at the *Bienal de Artes Visuales del Istmo Centroamericano* (Visual Arts Biennial of Central America) exhibition in Honduras in 2008–2009. Thus began a wave of online petitions hoping to prevent Habacuc from repeating the cruelty at this prestigious event. Although Habacuc did represent Costa Rica at the Biennial, held at the Museum of National Identity in Tegucigalpa, exhibition rules did not allow for any live animals to be used.[12]

That *Eres Lo Que Lees* is cruel there can be no question. No animal deserves to be tethered to a small area with a hard floor for long periods and denied access to water and food. But just how far Habacuc carried the abuse has been the subject of some debate. At first it was reported that Habacuc let Natividad die. Then Juanita Bermúdez, director of the Códice Gallery, told a reporter for the *Observer* that Natividad escaped after the first day. "It was untied all the time except for the three hours the exhibition lasted and it was fed regularly with dog food Habacuc himself brought in," she said.[13] Several animal groups, including The Humane Society of the United States and the World Society for the Protection of Animals, looked into the case, though none could conclusively determine what became of Natividad.

Animal advocates had another opportunity to stand up for dogs in Drogheda, a port town on Ireland's eastern coastline. There Dublin conceptual artist Seamus Nolan unveiled a winter 2009 showing of two dogs borrowed from a local animal shelter inside two pens at the Droichead Arts Centre. Like Habacuc's display,

Nolan's *If Art Could Save Your Life* exhibition was allegedly intended to encourage patrons to consider the plight of homeless dogs. Although it seems the gallery fed and watered the dogs, their description of the display leaves no doubt the Droichead Arts Centre considered the animals to be commodities.[14] "The product of a human value system, these objects without use are in a sense the waste product of man," reads the description in part. "They have become material which has had its value extracted or to use a popular metaphor consumed."[15]

When they heard about Nolan's planned exhibition, activists from Ireland's Animal Rights Action Network (ARAN) quickly mustered their resources, contacting both the artist and the Droichead Arts Centre. "Shortly after this we drafted an email action alert for our members and supporters to take action," says ARAN founder John Carmody. "We asked them to write to the Drogheda Arts Council and Louth County Council asking them to leave the two live dogs out of the 'art' project."[16] ARAN also reached out to the press, and sympathetic members of the media were only too willing to voice their disgust. "Well, if he's trying to make the point that he's nothing but a jerk who is happy to exploit two already traumatized dogs merely to impress his pseudo friends, then he has succeeded admirably," wrote *Irish Independent* columnist Ian O'Doherty, who added the phone number for the Droichead Arts Centre and encouraged his readers to "give them a bell and tell them how much you admire them for abusing defenseless dogs."[17]

Nolan's installation opened as scheduled. A local veterinarian even commented that the two dogs—a four-year-old Jack Russell terrier and a cross-terrier about one year old—would be just fine during the three-week run of the exhibition, saying that conditions in the gallery were "better than the dog pound."[18] Happily, the display garnered so much attention that the dogs were adopted and *If Art Could Save Your Life* closed two weeks early. "After the second full day of the exhibition, we were approached to have both of them adopted by separate people, so after contacting the county vet,

Gareth Shine, we decided to proceed with giving them homes," says Marcella Bannon, director of Droichead Arts Centre.[19] Moreover, Nolan promised to collaborate with ARAN on a future project that will use photographs to raise awareness about the plight of dogs in Ireland's animal shelters.

Regrets Only?

At least one abusive artist has apologized for his crimes against animals. In 1977, 25-year-old Tom Otterness video-taped himself shooting to death a puppy he had adopted from a local shelter and taken home to care for. The resulting piece of "art," titled *Shot Dog Film*, was even featured on a New York City cable channel one Christmas evening. Now known for his whimsical sculptures that adorn parks and other community spaces, Otterness characterizes the infamous killing as a youthful indiscretion. "It was an indefensible act that I am deeply sorry for," he said in 2008. "Many of us have experienced profound emotional turmoil and despair. Few have made the mistake I made. I hope people can find it in their hearts to forgive me."[20] Some skeptics believe the artist's contrition is merely an attempt to advance his career. More than 30 years on, Otterness' animal cruelty ignites fervent debate whenever he is selected for a public art commission.[21]

Snuff Film

One might suppose that animals would enjoy a higher degree of respect in a city named in honor of Saint Francis, the patron saint of animals. That is sadly not the case, as was demonstrated when the San Francisco Art Institute (SFAI) sponsored an exhibition called *Don't Trust Me* at a local gallery in March 2008. The work of Algerian-born artist Adel Abdessemed, *Don't Trust Me* featured six televisions displaying video images of six different animals—a goat, a horse, an ox, a pig, a sheep, and a baby deer—being bludgeoned to death with a sledgehammer. Each video shows an animal tied to a wall by one leg; suddenly, someone delivers a blow to the animal's head. The blunt-force trauma causes the animal to collapse, and then the video loops back to the beginning.[22]

The SFAI's press materials not only claim the animals died instantly, but they invite gallery patrons to believe that Abdessemed has some larger agenda in mind: "Each killing occurs so quickly that it's difficult to determine definitively what has happened. Do these incidents represent slaughter or sacrifice? What are their social, cultural, moral, and political implications? Or are such questions now verging on irrelevance, as if something else altogether were taking place (or about to), something wholly other, unforeseen, unexpected?"

The exhibition was scheduled to remain on display until May 31, 2008, but animal welfare groups, animal activists, and outraged members of the public had other plans. Calling Abdessemed's display "snuff films," activists demanded that SFAI close the exhibition. SFAI was unrepentant, saying that the images are "of events that took place—and regularly take place—in the real world, on a regular basis."[23] Never in its 137-year history had SFAI closed an exhibition due to public pressure, and it wasn't about to start now.

Jan McHugh-Smith, president of the San Francisco SPCA, was among those who condemned the exhibition, describing it as barbaric and depraved. "This type of work, masquerading as art, degrades the reputation of everyone associated with it," she said. "There is no artistic merit in cruelty to, and suffering of, living creatures. Nor is there any social or cultural message so imperative that it warrants such gratuitous brutality and callousness. This shameful exhibit calls into question the humanity of the 'artist.'"[24] Other groups, including PETA and Farm Sanctuary, also campaigned against the display, urging their members to contact SFAI and ask that they cancel it. But it was In Defense of Animals

(IDA), just over the Golden Gate Bridge in Marin County, that got things rolling, and it all started with a phone call.

"KTVU had gotten an anonymous tip from someone who had attended the opening party for the *Don't Trust Me* exhibit and was disturbed by what he saw," says activist Val Mizuhara, who was working for IDA. The following day, March 19, an assignment editor at KTVU, a San Francisco television station, emailed Val. "They contacted me because I was the IDA person they would usually go to," she says. "They wanted me to check out the exhibition and decide, as an animal rights person, if I thought it was offensive and gratuitous violence against animals. That's how the anonymous tipster had described it; he thought it was just snuff videos."

With a KTVU crew standing by in the city waiting for her call, Val immediately headed for the Walter and McBean Galleries on Chestnut Street, adjacent to the art institute. "It was dark inside, all cement," she says. "In the lobby, there was one television monitor with a looped video showing a horse getting hit over the head with a sledgehammer and collapsing. The person at the front desk was just sitting there like nothing was happening." But not everyone was so blasé. "One couple walked in and was so disturbed by the video that they left. Somebody else walked into the lobby, saw the horse get bludgeoned and turned right around." Val called KTVU, which raced over and covered the controversial exhibition on the evening news. IDA quickly initiated an email alert to their members, and the email went viral, resulting in people from all over the world contacting the school.[25]

Then things got nasty.

Before we explore how this dispute escalated, let's take a moment to consider the animal advocates' viewpoint regarding this display. I believe many activists would agree that allowing the public to witness the slaughtering of animals for food would, in the long run, prove beneficial to animals since it would certainly create more vegetarians; indeed, undercover videos often have just that effect on meat-eaters, allowing them to see the horror involved in killing and disassembling animals to turn them into "chops," "steaks," and "nuggets." The point of contention with *Don't Trust Me* (the very name eerily portends cruelty) is that animal abuse is being commercialized. What animal advocates objected to with this piece was how it framed the killings as if they were artistic expression, in essence trivializing the death of a defenseless animal by transforming it into entertainment. Activists are similarly exasperated when they hear a hunter claim he "honored the animal" before shooting him or her. The activist's retort is often something along the lines of, "Hey, Hemingway, how about honoring animals by letting them *live*?"

The fundamental issue with the San Francisco installation—and, indeed, all the "art" displays in this chapter—is that through the exhibition of animal suffering, art patrons become consumers of cruelty. Their support of the artistic expression claimed to inform these examples of animal abuse is tacit approval that such cruelty is not only acceptable, but a model of human creativity.

These weren't exactly the words activists were using when they finally threatened SFAI, however. In an editorial for the May 2008 issue of *The Art Newspaper*, SFAI president Chris Bratton wrote that faced with "threatening e-mails, phone calls, and letters, all echoing themes of surveillance, control, and violent punishment, addressed to numerous board, staff, faculty, and their families," SFAI made the unprecedented decision to close the display.

Kalista Barter, who was working for IDA during the SFAI campaign, says the school blamed her organization for the threats they'd received. "They said we were asking our members to send such emails," she says.[26]

In his editorial, Bratton complained that in wanting to halt Abdessemed's exhibition, animal activists were engaging in censorship. My guess is if the display had featured puppies and kittens being bludgeoned to death, Abdessemed would have found himself under criminal investigation—if the exhibition even made it to a public venue. "But," many will argue, "we're talking here about animals killed for food," as if that makes everything all right. And thus the cycle of debasing nonhuman animals continues.

As if to prove my point, Abdessemed was back the following spring with another arena of cruelty called *Usine*. This short video, exhibited at a New York gallery, featured predatory species like dogs, snakes, and scorpions thrown together with chickens, frogs, and mice into a concrete pen. The violence is quick and painful: a dog attacks a rooster; the dogs attack one another; a snake slowly crushes a frog. As with *Don't Trust Me*, Abdessemed shot the *Usine* footage in Mexico, where animal fighting is not illegal. Of the display, *The New York Times* art critic Ken Johnson wrote: "I think that Adel Abdessemed's video of animals fighting and killing each other (at the David Zwirner gallery) is the most appalling and evil work of art I have ever seen. Michael Vick went to prison for far less."[27]

"I don't believe in the concept of hell, but if I did I would think of it as filled with people who were cruel to animals."[28]
—Gary Larson

Photo Insensitive

At first, the photographs taken by Nathalia Edenmont look like she created them with a software program. A rabbit's head protrudes from an elaborate paper collar. A cat's head is mounted on a vase. The upper bodies of five white mice are appended like finger puppets to a human hand. Yet Edenmont uses cruelty, not digital trickery, to achieve her ends: she killed and decapitated the animals only moments before the photographs were taken, positioning their heads in colorful ruffs or some other fanciful tableau. The animals' eyes are open, even alert, their placid faces belying the violence of their fate. The ghoulish creations have earned Edenmont a variety of scathing insults from the general public—none of which I suspect bothers her in the least—and praise from many art aficionados.

One such supporter is Björn Wetterling, owner of a Stockholm gallery that has displayed Edenmont's work for years. Wetterling has insisted, evidently without a trace of sarcasm in his voice, that Edenmont is in her own way a crusader for animals. "Her work calls into question the hypocrisy in the debate surrounding animal rights," he has said. "Is it better to kill animals for makeup than for creating art?"[29] Wetterling has also observed that Edenmont's mother was murdered when the artist was 14, and the trauma of this event may have some connection with her killing and dismembering of mice, cats, rabbits, and birds. He's even encouraged her to move beyond small animals. "Her work is very important, [and] it is very important for her that the animals she uses are treated well," he said. "I have tried to get her to try to work with larger animals, like dogs."[30]

As we've seen, animal advocates have had some success shutting down art displays that involve animal cruelty. When he learned that Edenmont's photos would be on display at the Wetterling Gallery, PETA activist Andrew Butler decided to do something about it. It was February 2004. The weather was bitterly cold, but Andrew was determined to protest outside the gallery until the exhibition was withdrawn. "I went to the gallery where the photographs were being shown, took out a sign reading 'Cruelty Is Not Art' and said I would remain there 24 hours a day until the exhibition was removed," he says. "I was there when the gallery owner arrived in the morning, and I was there when he left in the evening. I spoke to everyone who came to the gallery, explaining why they shouldn't go to the exhibition. Many people turned away." After five snowy days and nights of Butler protesting, Wetterling cancelled the exhibition. "I think you win support and sympathy simply by acting on what you hold to be morally right and true," Andrew says.[31]

That moral high ground seems to be foreign soil for most art galleries, which often welcome controversial artists as a way of demonstrating their commitment to creative expression and free speech. (It doesn't hurt that controversy also attracts attention—and patrons.) But some galleries do draw the line at animal cruelty.

Appalled by Edenmont's morbid oeuvre, Irina Meleshkevich, director of Moscow's Manezh art gallery, wrote of the Russia-born artist: "Her aspiration of turning the act of killing live creatures with her own hands into an arrangement in the style of a fashion magazine betrays an attempt at gaining recognition at the cost of any scandal. Sadly, the author is trying to turn a perversion into an artistic event. As newspapers reported, 'the artist' maintains that the whole operation should be completed in no more than fifteen minutes, because otherwise 'the eyes of the animals tend to glass over, and the effect of living nature and freshness is lost.'"[32]

Taxidermy as Art

Trying to outdo Damien Hirst, some artists are turning to stuffed animals with a twist: fusing hooves, feathers, beaks, and other body parts to create shocking hybrids. The results—such as winged cats, conjoined squirrels, or antlers appended to the head of a rabbit—have become both praised and pricey, with some pieces selling for tens of thousands of dollars. The trend has also gained a moniker: rogue taxidermy.

While fabricated mutants are not exactly new—PT Barnum, for instance, had a special fondness for a fish tail stitched to the body of a monkey, which he pawned off on 19th-century ticket-buyers as the mythical Fiji Mermaid—the abstract creations of rogue taxidermy have become a hot commodity in posh circles. Among the best-known of these alternative taxidermists is Sarina Brewer, who calls her art "custom creatures" and has been lauded in museums and galleries around the world. Brewer says all the animals she uses are victims of some other industry, such as food production or the pet trade, but they are victims nonetheless. Their dignity as beings is utterly destroyed when they become mere displays, their bodies transformed into surreal mutations to please patrons of the macabre. Would we tolerate such disrespect if the animals used were human beings? Not very likely.

Other rogue taxidermists are quite happy to let animals die

specifically to be stuffed and spliced. Enrique Gomez De Molina has carved a name for himself with sculptures that combine multiple body parts: his "Pandora," made from a deer, an antelope, dik-dik horns, a coyote, and two swans, for example, suggests something right out of Narnia or Hogwarts. De Molina's other creations have included fragments of crabs, hippos, wild boars, and emus. In 2009, his work attracted the attention of US Fish and Wildlife Services, which intercepted two packages shipped from Indonesia to De Molina in Miami. One of the packages contained the skin of a Java kingfisher, the skin of a collared kingfisher, a mounted lesser bird of paradise, the skin of a juvenile hawk-eagle, and carcass remnants of a slow loris and lesser mouse deer. Further investigation revealed that De Molina would select endangered and threatened species from photographs supplied by wildlife smugglers, mostly in Asia.

Cruelty-Free Taxidermy

Berkeley sculptor Aimée Baldwin doesn't need feathers or body parts to put beautiful animals on display. Carefully arranging hand-cut crepe paper feathers over an individually-shaped foam and papier-mâché body, Aimée fuses art and conservation into strikingly realistic paper depictions of common and extinct birds—a pursuit she calls "vegan taxidermy." Her pieces take anywhere from 10 to 100 hours of painstaking work, all to fashion specimens worthy of a museum. Aimée launched her line of vegan taxidermy after many years working for a company that cranked out mass-produced products. "I wanted my personal work to be something that I could feel good doing, both through enjoying my own interaction with the medium, and by feeling good about the underlying complex relationships that my own art would build between myself and the world I live in," she says.[33]

Some of the pictured animals—including a wooly stork, a slow loris, and a hornbill—were alive at the time of the photos and later shipped to him dead.

Needless to say, De Molina's actions were not just cruel; they were illegal. He clearly understood this, since he instructed sellers to wrap his prohibited items in carbon paper to avoid detection. In 2012, a federal court sentenced him to 20 months in prison for trafficking in endangered and protected wildlife.[34] Like so many other conceptual artists who claim their exploitation of animals is intended to raise awareness about environmental or welfare concerns, De Molina says he wants his work to bring attention to the plight of animals worldwide. His arrest and conviction did just that.

Torture Is Skin Deep

Although the creations of Belgian artist Wim Delvoye have been called everything from "bizarre"[35] (x-rays of his friends engaging in sex) to "pungent"[36] (a machine that duplicates the *entire* human-digestion process), one word best describes his tattooing of live pigs: cruel. Delvoye hasn't just tattooed a few pigs; since he embarked on his pig-tattooing venture in the 1990s, he's created a complex enterprise devoted to this painful endeavor, churning out dozens of pigs who have been forced to endure the tattoo needle. He calls it his "Art Farm." Tucked into a tiny village near Beijing, Delvoye's Art Farm employs a host of caretakers and tattoo artists who have found a new way of commodifying animals. Indeed, it is clear that Delvoye is interested in these intelligent, sensitive animals only as products.

"I was interested in the idea of the pig as a bank—a piggy bank," he says. "I didn't have the concept formulated yet, but I decided to place some small drawings onto these living organisms and let them grow. From the beginning, there was the idea that the pig would literally grow in value, but I also knew that they were considered pretty worthless. It's hard to make something as prestigious as art from a pig. It's not kosher."[37]

To comprehend the cruelty behind Delvoye's work, it's important to first understand how tattoos are created. A tattoo is essentially ink introduced into the skin through thousands of tiny puncture wounds. When tattooing a human, the tattoo artist uses a handheld electric machine with one to 30 needles soldered to a needle bar to rapidly deliver pigment through the top layer of skin (the epidermis) into the second layer of skin (the dermis).[38] Today's needles can administer 30,000 punctures per minute. As someone who has been tattooed, I can attest that the procedure is indeed painful, though each person has his own threshold of pain, and the location of the tattoo and size of the design will also dictate how much the tattooing process hurts and how much a person bleeds. But for a human, the pain experienced in getting a tattoo is both a consequence of one's own volition and a rite of passage: you bear it, knowing that you will always carry this symbol with you. Whether it honors a loved one, celebrates an important event, or just looks cool, a tattoo literally marks a person for life—*but it's his or her choice.*

Perhaps in some alternative porcine universe a pig may pay to get an anchor inked to his limb, but here on planet Earth, most nonhuman animals are bred to serve the whims and appetites of people. So forcing a pig to suffer a painful and what must seem to them confusing experience is not much of a challenge, as evidenced by the online videos of Delvoye tattooing pigs in China. Delvoye, tattoo machine humming in his hand, can be seen tracing over his handiwork on the animal's shaved skin as one or more assistants restrain the bewildered pig. Even sedated, the pig is clearly not enjoying this, and he struggles to get away as a handler pins him onto a table.

Some people argue a pig's skin is so thick that he or she does not feel anything. But anyone who has spent time with these animals outside of factory farms—anyone who has scratched a pig's back or rubbed a pig's belly—knows the exquisite joy they feel when having their skin patted. I have watched pigs at sanctuaries literally fall over onto their sides, close their eyes, and grunt in delight as I scratched their stomachs.[39]

To date, Delvoye and his cohorts have covered pigs with tattoos ranging from skulls, hearts, and crosses to Louis Vuitton logos, Murakami cherries, and elaborate Disney characters.[40] While some of the tattooed pigs remain on the farm as "living art pieces," Delvoye is just as happy to have a pig slaughtered so his or her skin can be stripped off and displayed on a wall. Other pigs bearing the artist's sketches have been killed and stuffed, their heads tilted up slightly as if hoping to be petted. "The idea for Art Farm is not only to produce art but to harvest art," Delvoye says.[41] In fact, it seems his pigs only become "art" (and profitable) once they're dead. "No one wants to give a penny for an electronic tattoo on a live pig," he says. "But if the pig dies, it's art. Then it's a pigskin, it can be stuffed; it becomes a commodity. It's really strange that it has to be dead to become that. It is rarely art before it becomes a commodity."[42] He began tattooing pigs in Belgium, but he now reportedly rents the land for his farm in China because of the country's lack of animal welfare laws.[43] Ironically, Delvoye was scheduled to have eight of his pigs displayed as part of the Shanghai Contemporary Art Fair, but shortly before the event opened in September 2008, Chinese officials declared that the tattooed pigs were in bad taste and the Art Farm exhibit was removed from the exhibition. Another irony: Delvoye is a vegetarian.

A Brush with Death

Among the many tools of the fine artist, a paintbrush may not seem like much. A narrow handle, usually made of wood, at one end and a tuft in the other, the two parts bound together with a metal sleeve called a ferrule. The entire paintbrush may be the size of a pencil, easily lost amid a boxful of misshapen paint tubes, smeared rags, and toxic solvents. Yet even the smallest brushes represent great suffering when the tufts are made from animal hair.

Although no part of the world has a corner on the paintbrush market, animals in Asia, especially China and India, are most likely to get the short end of the paintbrush stick. And nearly any mammal is fair game. Indeed, a list of species whose hairs are used for paint-brushes reads like a Noah's Ark of animal abuse: badger, bear, cat, deer, hog, mink, mongoose, monkey, rabbit, sable, sheep, tiger, and weasel are but a few of the creatures whose suffering contributes to the paintbrush trade. Suppliers for brush manufacturers pull the hairs from every possible part of an animal's exterior, including an ox's ears, a horse's tail, a pony's belly, and a pig's back. Even goat eyelashes and squirrel and rat whiskers may end up as tufts. After hairs are removed from the animal, they are boiled to clean them and to satisfy health restrictions for export. This preparation also stabilizes the animal-hair bristles so that when they are set into a brush they won't warp.[44]

Visiting a local art-supply store, I had difficulty discerning many of the animal-hair brushes from their synthetic counterparts. "Manufacturers sometimes make synthetic brushes to look like animal hair," Kathleen Myers, owner of Petaluma Art & Earth, tells me. She's curious about my interest in brushes, and when I explain the cruelties that go into making a paintbrush from animal hair, she knits her brow and her shoulders droop. "There's so much we do to animals," she says with a sigh. She waves a hand, the creases etched black with dried paint, across a column of brushes standing at attention and explains the traditional preference among artists: animal-hair brushes for oil-based paints and man-made bristles for watercolor and acrylic. Not surprisingly, there's a significant cost difference, with brushes made from animals selling for as much as five times the cost of synthetic filament. Myers leans closer to me. "Sable brushes are supposed to be the best," she says in a lowered voice, her eyes skirting the store, "but some synthetics are actually better."[45]

A paintbrush made from sable, native to Russia, is prized for its ability to quickly return to its pointed shape while being used on a canvas or other surface.[46] Because hardy sable hairs command the highest price, thick-furred sable are trapped or shot in Russia's frigid Siberian forests. They are also raised in the country's fur farms, which became a major component of Russia's agricultural production after World War II.[47] The sable, looking not unlike a hybrid of a cat and a weasel, is a cousin of both the weasel and the mink, but sable fur surpasses all others in silky density and luminous hues of beige, brown, gold, silver, and black.[48]

Far to the south of Russia, through the heart of China on the subcontinent of Asia, animal advocates in India have been struggling for years to save the mongoose, whose fur and tail hairs are in such demand for fashion and high-quality paintbrushes that the animal is now endangered and protected under India's Wildlife Protection Act. The mongoose has for centuries held a special place in Indian literature and society. In *The Mahabharata*, one of Hinduism's great sacred texts, a mongoose plays a central role in explaining how a poor, hungry man offering all his food to a beggar could have more power than the animal sacrifices carried out by kings.[49] Another ancient tale, "The Mongoose and the Farmer's Wife," is the story of a pet mongoose who kills a cobra, saving the life of a couple's newborn son. Indeed, it is the mongoose's courage and fighting ability that has endeared him to Indians, who have relied on the animal to help control the population of rodents and poisonous snakes.

Not that this matters to poachers, of course. Motivated by easy income, hunters capture mongooses by chasing them into a net or injure the animals with a pellet gun, making them easier to catch and throw into a sack. Poachers then usually beat the mongoose to death, though some suffer a worse fate. "Such is the pressure of the demand for paintbrushes for children that sometimes the hair is plucked by hand when the animal is still alive and then the wounded, pellet-filled, bloody bodies are thrown in a heap to die slowly and in extreme pain," writes Maneka Gandhi, founder of People for Animals (PFA), India's largest animal welfare organization. "Each mongoose yields only 10g of hair as it is only the tail hair that is taken. Several mongooses have to be killed for a single paint-brush."[50]

Enforcing India's anti-poaching laws has been difficult, with forest staff lacking even the most basic equipment, such as flashlights, vehicles, and firearms. Anti-poaching camps are often primitive sites without sanitation or protection from the elements, and guards' salaries are paid late.[51] Yet poaching is only half the problem. Like other animal cruelties, the illegal wildlife trade is fueled by market demand, making those who purchase products fashioned from protected animals culpable as well. "The end consumer is as much a partner in wildlife crime as the trader or the poacher," says Samir Sinha of TRAFFIC India, a wildlife-trade monitoring network.[52] Samir and his team are thus working with the World Wildlife Fund (WWF) to educate some of India's youngest artists why they shouldn't paint with brushes made from mongoose hair. "We do a lot of work with WWF India with schools and school children to make them aware on issues of illegal wildlife trade," he says. "We also have developed a short film and a series of leaflets for raising consumer awareness on such issues."[53] (Part of the awareness campaign is teaching people the difference between animal-hair and synthetic brushes. Animal-hair brushes have uneven colored bands, while a synthetic brush is a single color.)

Another organization crusading against mongoose poaching is the New Delhi-based Wildlife Trust of India (WTI). Since 2002, when WTI became aware of the paintbrush trade's use of the mongoose, the nonprofit has made great strides to eliminate the illegal trade in mongoose hair. The vice chairman and trustee of WTI is Ashok Kumar, who also heads the organization's law and enforcement division. Until WTI began investigating the use of mongoose hair in paintbrushes, Ashok told me, the Indian government gave the animals little notice. "This meant that the penalty for trade in this species was a small amount of fine," he says. Using a hidden video camera, WTI conducted a series of undercover investigations at trade centers where brushes are made and turned their videotape over to authorities. The situation suddenly changed. "Seizures and arrests took place across manufacturing centers in Northern India and shops selling these brushes in many parts of India wherever there was information that manufacture and sale is taking place," says Ashok. "This was followed up by awareness campaigns among users, artists and school children."[54]

The trade in mongoose hair has been reduced but not eradicated, so WTI and PFA combine awareness campaigns with raids on manufacturers and stores where mongoose-hair paintbrushes are made or sold to the public. These efforts have pushed much of the trade in mongoose north to neighboring Nepal, where the animal is not protected by the government. A survey conducted by Wildlife Conservation Nepal found three paintbrush manufacturers using mongoose hair in Kathmandu, Nepal's capital, and nearby stationery stores selling mongoose-hair paintbrushes. With India cracking down on the illegal trade, it is likely Nepal will pick up the slack.[55]

Like animal fur used in fashion, the paintbrush industry has a perfectly good and humane substitute. Technology has led to the development of synthetic filament for brush bristles that is superior in many respects to brushes made from animals. Usually fashioned from nylon or polyester, synthetic-bristle paintbrushes are easier to clean, are not as likely to break, and aren't damaged by paint and solvents like animal hair is. They're also versatile: synthetic brushes work well with oil, watercolor, or acrylic paints.[56]

Art as Activism

In contrast to the shocking cruelty some artists display, compassionate painters and illustrators such as Dan Piraro, Gale Hart, and Sue Coe use their talents to draw attention to animal suffering. In his popular syndicated comic panel *Bizarro*, Dan regularly takes aim at agribusiness, vivisection, and other abuse; Gale agitates for animals through sculpture, graphics, and other media; while Sue, whose paintings raise awareness about factory farming and other social injustices, describes the purpose of her work as "a mission to be effective in convincing people to change from a diet of corpses to a plant-based diet."[57] Her haunting *Sheep of Fools* collection, for example, documents the experiences of sheep aboard the *Uniceb* in 1996; the cramped live-export vessel caught fire and sank as the animals were being transported from Australia to Jordan. Dozens of graphite, gouache, and watercolor illustrations vividly depict the disaster and the fate of 67,000 sheep, who burned to death or drowned in the Indian Ocean while the *Uniceb* crew abandoned ship.

Sue, a native of England now living in the US, says her compositions inspire dialogue about how humans treat nonhuman animals. "I find that if the work is done well, people will look closer, move into the drawing or painting, and not dismiss the images as propaganda. I am not telling people what to think, but to give a thought to those billions of others, rendered mute and invisible. Our complicity by our silence, our complicity by choosing convenience over change, our complicity in not even taking control of what is on the end of our fork, will be the eventual demise of our species. Despite ideas of individualism, very few of us speak out about anything. Politics has become consumer choice, but as social conditions continue to worsen, a new culture will be born out of the ruins."[58]

Attacking the very complacency Sue decries is Jonathan Horowitz, who has brought the fight to the abuser-artist's home turf: conceptual art. His installation titled *Go Vegan!* includes a gallery of 200 well-known vegetarians, a collection of farmed-animal portraits, scenes of commercial slaughter, and a block of tofu suspended in water. When the display was unveiled in New York City in 2010, it was staged in the perfect setting: a meatpacking plant turned art gallery. The result was all the more unsettling because the facility's former incarnation remained virtually untouched. Still present amid the soybean curd and images of chickens were the butchery's stainless-steel surfaces, large floor drains, meat hooks, and walk-in cooler that practically reeked of death.[59]

"The perceived non-threatening nature of vegetarianism as a subject for political art conceals its potency as a stand-in for other highly charged social issues of our day, ranging from war to AIDS," says Jonathan. "When one examines the troubling contradictions—astonishing cruelty, environmental and health risks, economic imbalances—involved with the business behind and mass consumption of meat, vegetarianism takes on the urgency of much larger debates in which the survival of the human race is at stake. Every year, as the connection between meat consumption and climate change becomes more apparent, the words of Albert Einstein become more and more prophetic: 'Nothing will increase the chances for survival of life on Earth as much as the evolution to a vegetarian diet.'"[60]

> "My least favorite human trait is the arrogant and small-minded belief that we are the only species that matters."[61]
> —Dan Piraro

"With paintbrush and sculpture tools, an artist creates, not destroys life with instruments of death," says Peter Hamilton, founder of the Vancouver-based Lifeforce Foundation. "The latter have no artistic talent and some probably cannot even draw."[62]

Peter, an artist and former art instructor, may be better known as the man who saved Sniffy the rat. In December 1989, conceptual artist Rick Gibson announced plans to crush Sniffy between two canvas-covered blocks of concrete the following week, thereby creating a diptych of death. The public probably wasn't terribly surprised by Gibson's press release—he had previously been in the news for eating a human testicle, and his gallery exhibition of human-fetus earrings got him fined for "outraging public decency"—but animal advocates quickly denounced his plan to kill an innocent rodent from a pet store. In fact, before Gibson could carry out his performance in front of the Vancouver library, Peter and some fellow Lifeforce activists removed the concrete blocks from Gibson's rented moving van as the bewildered artist looked on.[63]

(Though media at the time referred to Lifeforce as a "militant animal rights group," the organization actually advocates on behalf of humans and the environment, in addition to animals.[64])

With his execution paraphernalia confiscated, Gibson returned Sniffy to the pet store and then faced a hostile gathering of about 300 people outside the library. One man whacked the artist in the back of the head with his hand, shouting "They should drop a brick on *your* head!" Gibson pushed his way through the angry crowd, some of whom chased him down the street and into a hotel lobby.[65]

"Violence towards animals leads to violence towards people," Peter told the news media. And Sniffy? Peter promptly bought him from the pet store and placed him with a loving guardian in the suburbs.

I asked Peter for his thoughts on using "creative expression" as an excuse for the exploitation of animals. "Most serial killers tormented animals when young," he says. "It also instills into some young minds that this is acceptable, and more animals could be harmed. It doesn't take an artist to decapitate a living creature; it takes a very disturbed person. A true artist would paint or sculpture the images. Seeking publicity by the exploitation and killing of animals must not be condoned by any society that seeks to be compassionate. The people and their promoters are perpetuating violence."[66]

Truly, some artists suffer for their work; some artists make others suffer.

What You Can Do

- Never patronize art galleries or other exhibitions that feature animal abuse in any form, as doing so only encourages artists to continue such work and encourages galleries to display more of these cruelty-based installations.
- If you learn of an "artistic" display that uses animals, speak up. Voice your concern in letters to editors of local newspapers and to gallery directors. It's important they know

the public won't tolerate animal cruelty.

- Ask legislators to support laws that make it a crime to commission animal abuse for the purposes of creating media or an exhibit.
- Consider demonstrating outside the gallery, informing the public about how animals suffer in the name of "art."
- If you're a painter, use synthetic brushes rather than those made from animal hair. Most synthetic brushes will be a single color, while the tufts of animal-hair brushes have unevenly colored bands. If you're unsure about a brush, ask the manufacturer or the person who buys brushes at the art store.
- If you're a parent or guardian of a child, inform officials and teachers at his or her school about the plight of animals killed for paintbrushes and ask that they only buy synthetic brushes for students to use.

Chapter 9

The Horse Before the Cart:
Working Animals

We must use her now, while we can. Once she gives birth, she is useless for a long time.
—Broker in a Burmese teak forest on why he forces a pregnant elephant to pull 2-ton logs

The year is 1889 and Friedrich Nietzsche, the renowned German writer and philosopher, is living in Turin, a city in northern Italy he dearly loves. On the 3rd of January, Nietzsche leaves his lodgings at number 6 Via Carlo Alberto and makes his way toward Piazza Carlo Alberto, a picturesque square surrounded by tall houses, just a few steps away. In the piazza, Nietzsche observes the driver of a hansom cab violently whipping his exhausted horse. Sadly, a coachman beating a horse was not an uncommon sight in 19th-century Europe, where much of commerce and transportation used these animals to pull carts, carriages, and omnibuses. Distraught by the scene, a sobbing Nietzsche throws his arms around the equine's neck. Bystanders are not terribly surprised by Nietzsche's overwhelming display of compassion and remember that the mercurial existentialist has a reputation for being unstable. Yet Nietzsche seems positively unhinged by the cruelty he's witnessed. He collapses in the street and has to be carried back to his room.

Nietzsche reportedly never speaks again, and he dies 11 years later.[1]

Many scholars have pointed to this event as the catalyst that triggered Nietzsche's flagging mental state (in their obituary for him, *The New York Times* described Nietzsche as "hopelessly insane"[2]), and while his dementia was probably the result of other influences, it is not difficult to put yourself in the philosopher's place as he intercedes on behalf of an abused animal. Around the world, horses, dogs, camels, yaks, elephants, dolphins, donkeys, and oxen have all been pressed into doing work that is either too strenuous or considered too dangerous for humans. It's not been a pleasant experience for the nonhuman animals, who are forced to toil at the end of a whip or other physical violence, leading more than a few animal advocates to equate this treatment with slavery.[3] Whether they strain under the burden of enormous loads, transport tourists up steep inclines, or are yoked to plows, the individuals euphemistically referred to as "working animals" endure as much suffering as they did more than a century ago, and there are too few Friedrich Nietzsches speaking out for them.

Working animals can be placed into two general categories: those whom humans have domesticated, such as dogs and horses, and those who, for all their outward tameness, retain a wild spirit — think elephants and dolphins. In one group, an evolutionary lottery bestowed the domesticity gene upon species put to work on farms; in another, animals born in their natural habitat have been taken and forced to perform labor. To elaborate on this distinction, we turn to biologist Jared Diamond, who explains the difference between the elephants used by the military commander Hannibal to cross the Alps in 218 BCE and the large animals used on farms. "Elephants have been tamed, but never domesticated," he writes in his Pulitzer Prize-winning book *Guns, Germs, and Steel*. "Hannibal's elephants were, and Asian work elephants are, just wild elephants that were captured and trained; they were not bred in captivity. In contrast, a domesticated animal is defined as an animal selectively bred in captivity and thereby modified from its wild ancestors, for use by humans who control the animal's breeding and food supply."[4]

Horses

Although the hansom cabs of Nietzsche's day may seem quaint, they continue as vehicles for hire in many of the world's most congested cities, including New York, Rome, and Mumbai. Wherever they are, the horses who pull carriages, coaches, and buggies today have been conferred much of the same agony their equine ancestors suffered. So ubiquitous were urban workhorses in the 19th century that the cruelties inflicted upon them inspired the first successful animal rights campaign and the first generation of welfare reforms in the United Kingdom and the United States.[5] It was a time ripe for change: every year in the US, some 25,000 overworked horses died from pulling streetcars.[6] Not only were humane laws introduced, but attitudes about cruelty began to change.

Society still has a long, long way to go. New York City has the highest horse-drawn carriage accident rate in the country—and a fair share of compassionate celebrities—so it's no surprise this is home to the world's highest-profile campaign to end the industry.[7] (For his Manhattan-produced sitcom *30 Rock*, actor Alec Baldwin agreed to appear in a scene featuring a horse-drawn carriage only because he was allowed to call them "rolling torture wagons for nature's most dignified creature.") The city has more than 200 horses shuttling tourists around busy streets. It is grueling work for the animals, who are wedged between the carriage shafts for nine hours a day, seven days a week. Their reward at the end of a shift is to be returned to cramped, multistory "stables." Here the stalls, legislated at 64 square feet (6 square meters) minimum, are less than half the size suggested by the New York State Department of Agriculture and Markets Horse Health Assurance Program, which recommends stalls be 144 square feet (13 square meters) for mid-sized horses and 196 square feet (18 square meters) for larger draft horses.[8] Most of the stalls are on the upper levels, accessed by a steep ramp.

"These stables do not give the animals adequate ventilation, or bedding, or grooming, or time off," says horse advocate Sally Eckhoff, whose book *Beastly Life: A History of American Working Animals* explores how equines and bovines helped build the United States. Nor do the carriage companies give the animals any relief from severe weather, she says. "In the summertime, when the pavement gets to be 120 or 140 degrees, they're out there in front of the Plaza Hotel wearing metal shoes. The horses don't look good, because they're not healthy. Every single fricking year one collapses from heat exhaustion, and it takes a tremendous amount of abuse to get a horse to fall over. It doesn't just happen; they are amazingly tough animals. The carriage companies just consider it part of the price of doing business."[9]

In fact, the New York companies have made working in all weather a standard practice. On August 27, 2011, as Hurricane Irene forced residents to flee sections of the city and the entire transit system was shut down for the first time in history, dozens of horse-drawn carriage operators smelled opportunity and were trolling the stormy streets. Do they realize that the law prohibits them from operating during "ice, heavy rain, or other slippery conditions"?[10] Of course they do. Moreover, they routinely deny horses nearly all their natural behaviors.

"Every horse in New York's carriage industry should have—and rarely gets—a daily turn-out in which he or she is given a period to relax with a compatible stable buddy in a large enclosure where they can roll, mutually groom each other, lie stretched out, and generally obtain relief from their arduous shifts and the discomfort of tight-fitting harnesses," says Holly Cheever, an equine veterinarian. "In so doing, they satisfy both behavioral and physical needs. During the six years that I inspected the city's carriage horses on the street and in their stables, I found their housing and routine care to be unacceptable. I noted repeated violations of basic humane equine husbandry and care principles, including horses who were not given enough water during their work shifts, horses who were given insufficient hoof care and shoeing—adding to their likelihood of developing or exacerbating lameness—and stables that were distressingly substandard, with poor hygiene, temperature control, and ventilation." Dr. Cheever also found that a large percentage of drivers were not familiar with horses and had no prior experience as carriage drivers in a hazardous urban environment. "I'd like to see the industry phased out and replaced with something else for tourists, like electric-powered classic cars," she says.[11]

Horses on city streets face a variety of hazardous risks, such as close proximity to dangerous traffic, becoming tangled in equipment, heavy exhaust fumes, leg ailments, and a host of other perils, any one of which could result in the animal's death. It is not uncommon for city noises like car horns, police sirens, and construction clamor to spook a horse, sending her into the street to be struck by a vehicle. Such was the case with Spotty, a five-year-old horse who was euthanized after he was startled and bolted into a station wagon near Central Park, breaking his leg.[12] A similar fate befell Smoothie, a mare who became frightened by the sound of a drum, plowed into a tree, and moments later lay lifeless on the pavement.[13]

"The media never talks about the industry being inhumane and unsafe," says Elizabeth Forel, president of the Manhattan-based Coalition to Ban Horse-Drawn Carriages, an all-volunteer nonprofit founded after Spotty was killed in 2006. Elizabeth sees the campaign to end horse-drawn carriages in the city as a political fight, which she adds is another element the media never addresses. Filmmaker Donny Moss, who explores the carriage industry in his 2008 documentary *Blinders: The Truth Behind the Tradition*, says the controversy revolves around New York City Council Speaker Christine Quinn, criticized as a supporter of horse-drawn cruelty. "Since 2007, Quinn has used her power as Speaker to block the legislative efforts to ban horse-drawn carriages from New York City," he says. "In 2010, she fast-tracked a bill through the city council giving carriage operators a rate hike and disguised it as a law that would reform the industry. There is *nothing* in the law that improved the lives of carriage horses."[14] The law, which doubled carriage fares, gives horses five weeks of vacation a year, but as Elizabeth points out, "A carriage horse doesn't need a vacation—that's a human concept. What they need is a daily turn-out to pasture, something they are denied in New York City."[15] Elizabeth and Donny are among many activists who contend that no amount of regulation or enforcement can make the operation of horse-drawn carriages in New York City humane or safe. "Reform has never worked," Donny says. "The horses are in as bad a shape now as they've ever been."[16]

Clearly, not every city with horse-drawn carriages is as congested as Manhattan (though some are worse)—nor is the issue always as complicated.[17] But the danger is much the same, whether we're talking about streets in the United States, Canada, India, Italy, Austria, China, Australia, or anywhere horses share roadways with cars and trucks. One of the biggest risks is respiratory disease. "Horses working in traffic lanes alongside motorized vehicles are constantly nose-to-tailpipe, whether waiting for their next fare by the curb or moving in the traffic lane," says Dr. Cheever. "A study of New York City's horses from 1985, when they only worked in Central Park, shows that they suffered significant lung tissue damage and cellular changes due to their exposure to the noxious emission fumes of the vehicles—and this at a time when the horses were not out on the city streets, as they are now."[18]

William Wilberforce

As a Member of Parliament and social reformer, William Wilberforce (1759–1833) is perhaps best remembered for helping to abolish slavery in Great Britain. But he was also one of the founders of the Royal Society for the Prevention of Cruelty to Animals. One anecdote handed down by his great-grandson tells of Wilberforce walking near Bath when he saw a man violently whipping a horse who was struggling to pull a load of stone up a hill. Wilberforce pleaded with the man to stop abusing the helpless animal. Angered by the interference, the man turned and cursed the politician—then recognized him. "Are you Mr. Wilberforce?" he asked, suddenly filled with shame. "Then I shall never beat my horse again!"[19]

Citing just this sort of cruelty to animals, Israel outlawed carriages, carts, and wagons pulled by horses and donkeys on city streets in 2013. The animals had been severely neglected, with some dying of hunger or exhaustion.

Donkeys and Mules

You'll find them throughout the developing world: blistering-hot kilns that produce a never-ending supply of bricks for use in local houses, schools, shopping malls, office buildings, and hospitals. India alone makes 140 billion bricks a year, all in open-air factories that rely on manual labor. It takes a tremendous toll on workers, including the donkeys, horses, and mules who are forced to carry cumbersome loads of bricks from the kilns to building sites. Their abbreviated lives are characterized by extreme temperatures, difficult terrain, poor nutrition, and disease. In suburban Delhi, India's capital, more than 3,000 donkeys work in kilns seven days a week, at least eight hours a day. Some are owned by the factories, while others are owned by families trying to eke out a living in an ever-oppressive industry. At night, many donkeys are hobbled with short ropes and left to root through garbage for nourishment. The ropes leave deep abrasions, but because most of their owners are poor, donkeys rarely receive veterinary care. If they are injured or too sick to work, chances are they will be abandoned. Weakened donkeys are sometimes attacked and eaten by roaming packs of dogs.[20]

The situation is just as grim for donkeys who toil in brick bondage in Afghanistan, Egypt, Nepal, and Pakistan. A study by the charity Animal Nepal found donkeys and children as young as six working side by side under extremely dangerous and unhealthy conditions in Kathmandu Valley, where some 500 brick factories pollute the landscape.[21] Here children stack unfired bricks onto the backs of donkeys and guide them to a circular brick kiln—a giant outdoor furnace that becomes even more unbearably hot beneath the scorching sun. Later, they pack fired bricks onto the animals' backs for the return trek, which may include hauling their heavy cargo up steep hills to reach remote building sites. Donkeys are typically laden with 45 to 55 bricks, each weighing about 5.7 pounds (2.6 kilograms), meaning these animals are burdened with anywhere from 256 to 313 pounds (116 to 142 kilograms)—even more if her handler chooses. Meanwhile, equine experts recommend a large, healthy donkey never be loaded down with more than 176 pounds (80 kilograms).[22]

There are no healthy donkeys working in brick kilns, however, and one of the chief ailments is directly linked to the loads they transport: saddle sores, which are inflicted by the pressure, friction, and rubbing of the saddle or cinch against the skin. The majority of these injuries are caused by uneven weight placed on the muscles of the animal's back.[23] Wounds can be deep, and they're usually left untreated, which leads to infection. According to Animal Nepal, most donkeys have saddle sores and all suffer from dehydration and malnutrition. Not surprisingly, their lives are miserably brief. While the life expectancy of a donkey in Europe or the US is 40 years or more, a "brick donkey" may only survive 18 months. Whipped and beaten with sticks and rocks to move faster, these equines endure some of the harshest treatment of any working animal. The nonprofit Society for the Protection of Animal Rights in Egypt tells of one donkey owner who was so enraged because his exhausted animal had collapsed that he ignited some hay and brought the flames to the donkey's stomach, forcing him onto his feet and back to work.[24] A few compassionate brick kiln owners have refused to exploit donkeys. "I have seen how they are treated at other places," says the manager of one factory. "They are beaten, starved, traumatized, and made to work till they drop dead. They too are living beings; it's an offense to treat workers like that."[25]

Like their equine cousins, mules and horses are forced to work in brick kilns, though they fare somewhat better than donkeys. "Mules and horses are more expensive and therefore better treated," says Lucia de Vries, director of Animal Nepal. "Having said that, today we had to euthanize a mule with a broken leg. We found him during one of our vaccination camps. His leg was broken a month ago when transported in a truck from India. His owner did not bother to inform us because he wanted to get his cut from the factory owner, who pays per equine. We could have saved the mule's life if we had known about that. The mule, whom we called Himal, suffered tremendously as the leg was badly infected."

> "The worst thing we can do to the abusers and the best thing we can do for the animals is to bear witness to the abuses and document them for others to see. The power of the image cannot be diminished, and the truth cannot be denied."[26]
> —Colleen Patrick-Goudreau

Elephants

Elephants have been exploited for their strength and intelligence for thousands of years. An army fronted by a column of enormous pachyderms, for instance, was a fearsome foe—something ancient Greek and Indian warriors knew well. But they also toiled in agriculture, and while the elephant's value on the battlefield happily diminished with the advent of the cannon centuries ago, human enterprises continue to force them into forests and fields. The most prominent of these abusers is the timber industry, which uses elephants for physically demanding work such as dragging heavy logs to rivers for transport. Ironically, the industry seems to be wiping out the very species it enslaves. As companies in Southeast Asia lay waste to acres of highly prized teak trees, the animals who rely on this habitat for survival—notably elephants—disappear. Laos, for example, once boasted a colossal elephant population, but now only 600 remain in the wild, while another 420 are used to harvest timber.[27] Perhaps the forests and elephants will vanish at the same time.

No country, however, can match Burma's use of elephants. Laos' northwestern neighbor, Burma exploits an estimated 4,500 captive elephants—the largest number in the world—for the logging industry, including 2,500 owned by the state-run Myanmar Timber Enterprise (MTE).[28] Capturing elephants from the wild for non-scientific purposes is prohibited in Burma, but MTE continues taking them from the forests as hunters target areas with the highest concentrations of the animals. To capture an elephant, trainers ride domesticated elephants and slip a noose around the neck of a free-living one. More ropes are tied around the animal, and if he's particularly difficult to control, his head is tied to the ground so that he'll choke if he tries to escape.[29] Focusing their capture efforts on the largest population cluster results in breaking up the most viable and sustainable herds and further fragmenting the total number of wild elephants. All of MTE's elephants are branded with acid.[30]

According to an investigator who observed Burmese elephants dragging logs with chains, the work is painfully arduous for the animals, despite their immense size. "The logs needed to be pulled up quite a steep incline and along steadily rising ground to the dirt road," writes Charles Begley of the nonprofit EleAid, "a total distance of about two miles. The steep drag was difficult for all of the elephants and they were all straining and pulling hard. It caused particular problems for the smallest elephant (with the largest load). She cried out with each pull and was clearly in great distress, which was difficult to witness. In addition to the burden of the weight, the chains opened sores on both of her flanks."[31]

Because of its secrecy, one aspect of the industry that Charles was not privy to during his investigation is the elephant-training process. Known as "the crush," since its goal is to break an animal's spirit, the "training" involves tying up a young elephant between trees and beating him for days or weeks and withholding food and water, torturing him into submission. Photojournalist Brent Lewin, who has been documenting the plight of Asian elephants since 2007, managed to negotiate his way into a crushing session and was appalled by

Elke and Krungsee

Rehabilitating animals who have been tortured and abused is a long process requiring exceptional patience. Among those specializing in this is Elke Riesterer, a body therapist who works with all species. One of her patients was a 40-year-old elephant named Krungsee, who stepped on a landmine while logging and spent years at a rescue center in Thailand.

"Krungsee was in severe pain from her injury and the years of hard labor," remembers Elke. "Her routine at the hospital was a daily hobble down from her space on the terraced hill, where she was chained each evening, to the cement floor of the veterinarian station. She had become very disconnected from the rest of her body, most of the time staring into space with a glazed look. As a result of holding up her leg for three years to compensate her injury, her muscles had atrophied. Her profound hurt showed when I moved my hand toward her stomach because she awoke immediately and reacted by lifting her rear left leg and pulling it forward protectively out of my reach, until, after a while, I approached and began to brush her with a soft broom. Little by little, her body softened, she sighed big deep breaths, eyes closed half shut, and tears ran down. When we finished the session, she coiled her trunk toward the back to touch my face that was also wet with tears."[32]

After three weeks of acupressure and massage therapy, Krungsee was standing on her injured leg—and the center's once-skeptical veterinarian asked Elke to teach his tech assistant her healing techniques.

what he saw. "The baby elephant was terrified and started crying," he says. "The biggest difficulty I experienced was not being able to put a stop to it. There was a point when the elephant just resigned to what was happening and stood still, the life in her eyes disappeared. It was a look that was haunting."[33] MTE admits the crush method is cruel and that deaths of baby elephants are not uncommon.[34]

Elephants illegally captured in Burma are often smuggled across the porous jungle border into Thailand, where the pachyderm population has declined dramatically, from 300,000 at the beginning of the 20th century to possibly fewer than 1,000 today.[35] Logging has been banned here since 1989, but elephants are crushed into obedience for use primarily in the entertainment and tourist trades, though they are sometimes forced into service for illegal logging, says Sangduen "Lek" Chailert, who advocates for the rights of Thailand's national animal. Lek's lifelong devotion to these charismatic individuals began when her grandfather, a shaman, received an elephant named Tongkum ("Golden One") in return for saving a man's life. She has since become one of the most ardent and vocal activists campaigning for the species. "I have been researching elephant logging in Burma, Laos, Thailand, Cambodia, Indonesia, and India since 1992," Lek says. "The way they treat elephants in the logging industry is terrible. Many of them suffer. Many of them are dying but still work. I ask owners when an elephant can get rest— some answer, 'When they fall down.'"[36] In 1996, Lek and her husband, Adam, founded the Elephant Nature Park sanctuary in northern Thailand, where elephants rescued from logging, tourism, and street begging can heal and thrive.

Dolphins and Sea Lions

In 2012, when Iran threatened to close the Strait of Hormuz with explosives—blocking the millions of gallons of oil that move out of the Persian Gulf every day—the White House had a secret weapon on standby: dolphins. Through its Marine Mammal Program, the US Navy keeps about 80 bottlenose dolphins trained to detect mines with their natural sonar, and the animals could have been deployed from their base in San Diego. Cooler heads prevailed during that political crisis, but dolphins have been on call to locate underwater explosives since the 1960s. During the 2003 invasion of Iraq, the Navy used nine dolphins to help clear more than 100 mines and underwater booby traps planted by Saddam Hussein's forces. The operation prompted condemnation from Cetacean Society International president William Rossiter. "Even wars have rules," he said. "It is evil, unethical, and immoral to use innocents in war, because they cannot understand the purpose or the danger, their resistance is weak, and it is not their conflict."[37]

The Navy says dolphins only locate mines and drop acoustic transponders nearby, so that divers can destroy them. But any situation that is too dangerous for a human is too dangerous for a nonhuman animal. Though it's unlikely that a dolphin could accidentally detonate an explosive device (sea mines are set off by large metallic objects, like a ship's hull), their work makes them targets. Had the diplomatic standoff with Iran resulted in dolphins being dispatched to the Strait of Hormuz, Iran's military—doubtless aware of the US plan—would have been shooting at every creature in the Persian Gulf with a dorsal fin.

Ironically, Iran may have its own marine mammal arsenal, which it reportedly purchased from Russia in 2000. Trained by the Soviet Navy to attack ships and enemy frogmen, the dolphins, sea lions, walruses, and a beluga whale were part of a Russian project that ceased when the Soviet Union crumbled and funding dried up. Oil-rich Iran was apparently only too happy to take the 27 highly skilled animals off their hands, so they were all transported to the Persian Gulf, where their activities remain a mystery. Among the tasks the animals had been trained for in Russia are offensive tactics using harpoons strapped to their backs and suicide missions using mines that would explode on contact with an enemy ship—a scheme that reportedly killed 300 dolphins during test runs.[38] They are also allegedly able to drag an adversary to the surface to be taken into captivity.[39]

Cetacean expert Lori Marino is one of many marine mammal

advocates who object to dolphins being used as mine sweepers. "I am opposed to the use of dolphins in the military for any purpose for the same reasons that I am opposed to captivity in general," says Lori, who believes the animals might be placed in harm's way. "There is a clear risk. Additionally, dolphins in the Navy have been deployed in the Middle East and in places where the temperatures of the oceans are not healthy for them." Lori also notes that prior to 1999, when the Navy stopped capturing dolphins in the wild, they acquired some from Japan's notorious Taiji dolphin drives. (Former CBS television news director Hardy Jones exposed this dirty little secret in 1990 when he filmed a group of men in Taiji harbor taking Risso's dolphins, who were then shipped to Hawaii and ended up in the Navy's Marine Mammal Program.) "And, finally, the Navy conducts invasive research on dolphins, examining everything from brain structure to unihemispheric sleep and echolocation. So, to put it in plain terms, it is not a good thing to be a dolphin in the Navy."

Longtime dolphin advocate Ric O'Barry agrees. In the 1960s, when he was working as an animal trainer on *Flipper*, Ric was approached by the CIA and asked if he would take charge of trans-forming dolphins into weapons of war. "In those days, nobody knew for sure that it could be done," Ric recalls. "But it seemed like a natural idea to go from dolphins leaping through hoops to dolphins affixing magnetic mines to enemy ships. In fact, that very idea was used in one of the *Flipper* episodes." Though Ric isn't allowed to reveal exactly what the government officials said they hoped to accomplish, it's clear that their plans included the same kinds of suicide missions the Soviets later tested dolphins for. "It's easy to make fools of cooperative creatures, and an unscrupulous person would find it simple to fit a bomb on a dolphin's snout and lovingly induce him to ram a boat and blow himself up."[40] Appalled and disgusted by the government's request, Ric instantly rejected it. The Navy, of course, proceeded with its program, and however deeply the complete nature of their activities is shrouded in military secrecy, it's not difficult to imagine they'd have no qualms about turning dolphins into unwitting kamikazes for the sake of "national security."

Another way of arming dolphins involves outfitting them with a large hypodermic syringe that injects a high-pressure discharge of compressed carbon dioxide into an enemy diver when the dolphin bumps him; the pressurized gas then forces the man's internal organs out through his body's orifices, literally blowing him up. James Fitzgerald, former chief of the CIA's Office of Dolphin Research, says that this tactic, known as the Swimmer Nullification Program, was responsible for the deaths of a number of Vietcong divers during the Vietnam War.[41]

According to defense contractors and others who have spoken out and criticized the Navy's Marine Mammal Program, dolphins have been beaten and some 20 percent escape every year, many with a so-called anti-foraging device (AFD) still secured to their snouts.[42] These devices—really just a strip of Velcro that keeps the dolphin's mouth closed—are the Navy's way of controlling the animals in the open sea: dolphins who return from missions are rewarded with food. The Navy attempts to find missing dolphins using a "recall pinger" that the animals can hear from a great distance, but anyone with an AFD attached who doesn't come back is doomed to starvation.

In May 1996, after two years of rehabilitation work, Ric released two dolphins the Navy had "retired" and turned over to him. Ric maintains Buck and Luther were fully prepared for life on their own, and he set them free 12 miles off the coast of Florida. But he'd made one mistake, at least in the eyes of the government: he never got the Navy's permission to liberate the dolphins. His team had applied for the necessary permit and then received a 15-page fax asking them for proof that the animals would never come to any harm in the open ocean. "'Prove to us that dolphins are capable of breeding in the wild and the predators are not going to attack them.' All kind of ridiculous things that you can't possibly prove," Ric later told PBS' *Frontline*. "In other words, this says, 'No, you can't have a permit.'

Ironically, if I wanted to take the same two dolphins and exploit them in a swim program somewhere in Honduras or out of the country, legally you could do that. They'll help you do that. It's only when you want to do the right thing they stop you."[43] So when Ric went ahead and released Buck and Luther, the Navy used a recall pinger to bring them back. "Fact is," says Ric, "that release was sabotaged because it had the potential to open the door of freedom for all Navy dolphins. This was a major threat to the entire program and had the potential to end the flow of millions of dollars to the civilian corporation that runs this program. After they were recaptured, Buck was sent to the Dolphin Research Center, a captive operation. He spent a few years there painting pictures for tourists before he died of terminal captivity. Luther was flown back to the polluted waters of San Diego Bay and back into active duty in the Navy."[44]

Nearly as adept at swimming as Atlantic bottlenose dolphins are California sea lions, 40 of whom are now being used by the US Navy in a variety of military applications.[45] In addition to locating bombs like their fellow marine mammals, sea lions are trained to detect an enemy diver and place a clamp onto his leg. The spring-loaded clamps are tethered with a long cable, enabling security forces to haul the intruder onto their ship. ("Swimmer interdiction" is the fancy name for this.) The Navy says that sea lions, superior swimmers with extraordinary underwater vision, can cuff a saboteur before he even knows what's hit him. But here again we see the military using animals for maneuvers considered too dangerous for humans. Like mine-sweeping dolphins, sea lions can be targets, and they would be easy prey for an armed adversary. Also like conscripted dolphins, sea lions are kept in captivity and denied many of their normal behaviors, including foraging for food, choosing their mates, and exploring their natural environment. These animals are apolitical—they have no say in matters of terrorism, war, or disputes over oil—and deserve better than to be forced into service for human benefit.

What You Can Do

It's clearly easier to help some working animals than others. Not patronizing horse-drawn carriages, for example, is simple enough. And if your city allows carriages on city streets, urge your lawmakers to propose legislation that will ban it. Assisting the elephants, donkeys, mules, marine mammals, and others who toil in jungles, factories, and oceans—often under the threat of physical violence—is more challenging. Raising awareness is an important step: talk to family and friends about this issue and tell them why you believe it's cruel to turn animals into laborers. You can also lend your support to organizations that help working animals around the world. Below are some general and more specific charities that would appreciate your donation or other assistance.

Charities that assist working animals include

Animal Aid Abroad (US)
www.animalaidabroad.org

Animal Care Association Pakistan
www.facebook.com/a.c.a.pak

Animal Rahat (India)
http://animalrahat.com

Pakistan Animal Welfare Society
http://pawspakistan.org/

People for Animals (India)
www.peopleforanimalsindia.org

PETA India
www.petaindia.com

Society for Protection of Animal Rights in Egypt
www.sparelives.org

Horses

Coalition to Ban Horse-Drawn Carriages (US)
www.banhdc.org

Horses Without Carriages International
www.horseswithoutcarriages.org

Peace Advocacy Network (US)
www.peaceadvocacynetwork.org/HDC

Working Animal Advocates (US)
www.workinganimal.org

Donkeys and Mules

Animal Nepal
www.animalnepal.org

The Asswin Project (UK)
www.theasswinproject.org.uk

The Brooke (UK)
www.thebrooke.org

The Donkey Sanctuary (UK)
www.thedonkeysanctuary.org.uk

The Gambia Horse and Donkey Trust
www.gambiahorseanddonkey.org.uk

Elephants

Boon Lott's Elephant Sanctuary (Thailand)
http://blesele.org/

Bring the Elephant Home (Thailand)
www.bring-the-elephant-home.org

Elephant Conservation Network (Thailand)
www.ecn-thailand.org

Elephant Nature Park (Thailand)
www.elephantnaturepark.org

Dolphins

The Dolphin Project (US)
http://dolphinproject.org

International Dolphin Watch
www.idw.org

Kimmela Center for Animal Advocacy (US)
www.kimmela.org

Whale and Dolphin Conservation International
www.wdcs.org

Chapter 10

Secret Abuse: Sexual Assault on Animals

Eroticism is a representation, a ceremony of transfiguration: men and women make love like lions, eagles, doves, or praying mantises; neither lions nor praying mantises make love like human beings. We humans see ourselves in animals; animals do not see themselves in humans.

—Octavio Paz, poet

Had you opened the *Los Angeles Times* on the morning of June 11, 2008, the following headline and story would have doubtless grabbed your attention:

9th Circuit's Chief Judge Posted Sexually Explicit Matter on His Website

One of the highest-ranking federal judges in the United States, who is currently presiding over an obscenity trial in Los Angeles, has maintained a publicly accessible website featuring sexually explicit photos and videos.

Alex Kozinski, chief judge of the US 9th Circuit Court of Appeals, acknowledged in an interview with *The Times* that he had posted the materials, which included a photo of naked women on all fours painted to look like cows and a video of a half-dressed man cavorting with a sexually aroused farm animal. Some of the material was inappropriate, he conceded, although he defended other sexually explicit content as "funny."[1]

That the article concerned bestiality and humiliating images of women was bad enough; that it involved a prominent judge with a glib attitude served to show how pervasive this form of animal abuse is.

Of all the cruelties subjected upon animals, sexual contact with them is the least understood and arguably the most insidious. It is also among the biggest social taboos—a shameful practice veiled in a culture of silence. This may help explain why sex assaults on animals get so little attention in the media. It's not that news editors aren't eager to chronicle stories that inspire shock and bewilderment; they're happy to oblige when they learn of disturbing events. But fornicating with animals thrives in a well-hidden subculture that attempts to blur the line between exploitation and consent (if such a line indeed exists). Not so long ago, when a perpetrator was caught in the stable with his pants down, so to speak, the act was quickly labeled bestiality. And while that may still be technically accurate, apologists argue the practice should not only be destigmatized but, under certain circumstances, sanctioned.

Dictionaries define bestiality as sexual relations between a human being and an animal. Although such a description might bring to mind randy farm boys and compliant barnyard animals, the legal definition is much more to the point: bestiality is sexual molestation.[2] Like the depictions of women on Judge Kozinski's website, bestiality is both exploitive and degrading. Even the term *bestiality* is a form of debasement, since it both refers to animals as beasts and implies they are the instigators—rather than the victims—of sexual contact, suggesting they are as culpable as their abusers. "If we call it sex with animals, and recognize that it is forced sex, we reclaim the animal's perspective as a central concern," says Carol Adams, author of *The Pornography of Meat*. "I believe that it is more prevalent than we can measure and that it is not harmless; it is always animal abuse."[3] (I use the term *bestiality* in this chapter to categorize historical sex with animals and distinguish it from other types of human-nonhuman sex assaults.)

Bestiality

Once known as a "crime against nature," bestiality has long figured prominently in popular culture. In classical mythology, the Greek god Zeus transformed himself into a swan to have his way with

Leda, a white bull to kidnap Europa, and an eagle to carry off Ganymede. Renderings by renowned artists have brought these scenes to life, with Rembrandt's *The Rape of Ganymede* being perhaps the most well-known. The gods of antiquity, however, evidently didn't approve of humans engaging in such behavior with animals. According to an epic poem by Girolamo Fracastoro, Apollo, displeased that a shepherd named Syphilus was violating his sheep, punished him with a sexually transmitted disease. Meanwhile, Christian scholars have observed that it was the Holy Spirit in the form of a dove who impregnated the Virgin Mary. Fairytales such as *Beauty and the Beast, Little Red Riding Hood,* and *The Frog Prince,* as well as the ballet *Swan Lake,* also delve into bestiality themes. More recently, a 2011 episode of the television series *CSI: Crime Scene Investigation* featured a storyline in which a Japanese character performs in live sex shows with an octopus—a subculture known as *shokushu goukan,* or tentacle porn. Even King Kong, the quintessential simian of the cinema, was portrayed as being in love with a woman, and the eponymous film invites viewers to sympathize with his amorous desires: producers playfully used the "tall dark stranger" fantasy as a tagline for the movie.

The history of sex with animals is both extensive and pancultural. Some scholars believe the practice may be 40,000 years old.[4] A cave painting from about 8000 BCE, found in the Camonica Valley of northern Italy, depicts a man sexually assaulting a donkey. A rock engraving from eastern Siberia portrays a Neolithic man trying to penetrate an elk. Similar ancient artwork and other archeological evidence of bestiality has been unearthed in France, Sweden, Greece, India, the Middle East, Africa, China, and throughout the Americas. In the creation myth of the Inuit, Sedna, goddess of the sea, is said to only find sexual satisfaction with dogs.

By the Middle Ages, Europeans considered bestiality a grave sin linked to the concept of demonic intercourse, since it was believed that Satan would turn himself into an animal—most commonly a dog, goat, or snake—in order to copulate with humans. At the same time, animals were sexualized in literature through depictions of them in both illustrations and comparisons to female humans.[5] Moreover, sex with another species was prohibited because it served no reproductive purpose—a ban that seems to contradict the prevailing thought of the time that people could couple with predators such as bears and spawn offspring with superhuman traits.[6] Contrast these attitudes with the explicit interspecies sex on display in the sandstone carvings of the elaborate Lakshmana Temple in Khajuraho, India, produced more than a thousand years ago.

During the Renaissance, Western law books referred to bestiality as *"offensa cujus nominatio crimen est* (the offense the very naming of which is a crime)" and punishment was swift, generally by burning both parties alive.[7] Such executions were carried out per Judeo-Christian tradition, as outlined in the Book of Leviticus, in the belief that bestiality was an act in which a human and an animal collaborated in service of the devil. The only hope for the nonhuman animal was if a respected citizen testified that the cow, sheep, horse, goat, dog, cat, or pig was known to be virtuous and law-abiding. An English statute of 1533, known as the Buggery Act, made bestiality (and homosexuality) a crime punishable by death, though prosecutions were rare.

In the colonies of North America, Puritans equated bestiality with witchcraft and would kill the animal victim in front of her human abuser just before he too was put to death. When Thomas Granger of Plymouth was caught fornicating with a mare in 1642, he quickly confessed to having also sexually assaulted a cow, two goats, five sheep, two calves, and a turkey, all of whom, along with the horse, were slaughtered before he was fitted with a hangman's noose. The nonhuman animals' bodies were then "cast into a great and large pit that was digged of purpose for them, and no use made of any part of them."[8] In 1641, when a sow gave birth to a dead, deformed piglet, the clergy of New Haven Colony interpreted the event as a divine finger pointing to a bald, one-eyed servant named

George Spencer—the piglet was completely hairless and had "butt one eye in the middle of the face."[9] Spencer admitted to abusing the sow, recanted when he learned his confession would seal his fate on the gallows, then confessed his guilt again. Then he recanted once more. (He was apparently unsure which plea would spare his life.) Impatient magistrates finally ordered the unfortunate sow to be stabbed to death under the gaze of the unrepentant Spencer, who was then executed.

Attitudes changed around the time of the French Revolution (1787–1799), when Enlightenment thinkers advocated that morality should be considered a matter of conscience, not law, and people began speaking out against the death penalty. Gradually, sex with animals lost its status as a capital offense, not just in France, but throughout most of Europe.[10] Of course, animals were still considered non-sentient objects—soulless machines, in the words of the French philosopher René Descartes—and there is little evidence to suggest that the sexual abuse they suffered was looked upon as cruel.

But cruel it is. Injuries to animals resulting from sexual molestation include internal bleeding, torn rectums, ruptured organs, and bruised vaginas and cloacae (the posterior orifice through which a hen lays her eggs). Small animals such as cats, birds, and rabbits are especially vulnerable to harm. A particularly disturbing example occurred in 2006, when unknown assailants in Arizona used a blunt object to sexually assault a pair of six-week-old puppies, who later died from internal injuries and bacterial infection.[11] While physical damage may be apparent, not so clear is the psychological and emotional trauma animals endure. Imagine the confusion a companion animal must feel to be raped by his or her human guardian—the person they rely on for food, shelter, and protection.

Despite such cruelty, ethicist Peter Singer has challenged society's attitude on sex with animals, calling the taboo of interspecies sex unnatural. In his review of the bestiality apologia *Dearest Pet*, Singer argues that, while sex that results in an animal's death should be a crime, certain contact may be morally permissible. "Who has not been at a social occasion disrupted by the household dog gripping the legs of a visitor and vigorously rubbing its penis against them?" he writes. "The host usually discourages such activities, but in private not everyone objects to being used by her or his dog in this way, and occasionally mutually satisfying activities may develop."[12] Yet encouraging such behavior, regardless of what satisfaction a dog may derive from it, is just another objectification of the animal. Moreover, argues Singer, many other forms of human sexuality that were once considered deviant are now mainstream—so why not sex with animals? "I think perhaps the diagnosis here is that it's something to do with this gulf that we like to have between ourselves and animals," he says. "I don't see much of a basis for that."[13]

Two things make Singer's remarks particularly significant. First, deservedly or not, as the author of *Animal Liberation*, he has been hailed as the father of the modern animal rights movement, making him an influential voice in matters related to the welfare of nonhuman individuals. Animal advocates felt betrayed when Singer's comments in support of bestiality were published in 2001, and his views on humans engaging in sex with animals continue to disappoint many who recognize the abusive nature of this practice. (His defense of bestiality has also become low-hanging fruit for anyone looking to ridicule the animal rights cause.) Second, Singer is a prominent, if controversial, philosopher. He's a professor of bioethics at Princeton University and an ethics professor at the University of Melbourne. He has written or edited more than 25 books, co-founded the Great Ape Project, and received more honors and accolades than he probably has space in his office to display. In short, his opinions carry weight. Indeed, he's arguably the most well-known intellectual to publicly countenance a practice that most people recognize as animal exploitation.

Singer's comments on behalf of sex with animals are informed by the utilitarian moral principle, which holds that the most ethical action is the one that produces the greatest amount of pleasure to the most people. From his perspective, then, copulating with another species is just fine if it results in an increase in overall gratification. The problem here should be obvious: nonhuman animals can no more give their consent to a sexual relationship with a human than a child can.

By the Numbers

Just how many people engage in sex with animals is unclear. Those who sexually prey upon animals are, not surprisingly, apt to keep that information to themselves or within a small group of fellow abusers (such as those in the so-called "zoo" community). In surveys conducted in 1948 and 1953, social researcher Alfred Kinsey reported that an average of 8 percent of the male population in the US had sexual contact with an animal at least once, though data suggested that some 40 to 50 percent of boys living in rural areas did, a conclusion that has been challenged as exaggerated.[14] Kinsey found a much lower statistic among women—about 3 percent.[15] Two decades later, studies by Morton Hunt revealed lower statistical evidence of bestiality among both genders: 1.9 percent of women and 4.9 percent of men reported having at least one sexual encounter with an animal.[16]

Zoophilia

In the 21st century, bestiality enjoys a modicum of social tolerance, often regarded more as benign contact than something to merit persecution. A certain segment of those who practice bestiality has even entered the realm of fringe movement. Calling themselves "zoophiles," they consider their "zoosexual activity" to be consensual and that what they are engaged in is a product of mutual attraction. For zoophiles, there is an emotional involvement with the animal that transcends the sex act; they say the relationship is about love, not objectification. Florida resident Malcolm Brenner, for example, was married twice yet insists to this day that the love of his life was a dolphin he had sex with while photographing her at an aquarium in 1970.[17]

Psychotherapist Hani Miletski has people like Brenner in mind when she argues that zoophilia is a legitimate sexual orientation and is not the same as bestiality. "Those who are bestialists tend to use animals as masturbation machines for their own sexual gratification," she says. "That doesn't mean they are abusing the animals in the process, but they may, depending on the animal involved, and how they go about it. Zoophiles, or 'zoos,' are sexually and emotionally attracted to animals, as in a sexual orientation. They will usually have sexual relations with animals as an act of love, and if the animal is not interested, they—the humans—will not pursue it. For zoos, it's important that the animals want and enjoy what they are doing together. They see the animals as equal partners, and some treat them as spouses."[18] Clearly, Dr. Miletski falls well short of condemning sexual contact with animals; indeed, her book *Understanding Bestiality and Zoophilia* is one of the few scholarly works on the topic to sympathize with animal abuse. Her opinion offers a disturbing insight into what may be a growing acceptance of sexual assaults on animals.

Zoophiles (I'll use the term they prefer in the context of this chapter) say they have a preference for nonhuman animals as sexual partners, often even to the exclusion of humans, and maintain that they are in no way hurting them. "Laws prohibiting zoophilia are enforced even in the absence of any discernible harm to the animal resulting from such acts," argued outspoken zoophile Brian Cutteridge of Vancouver, British Columbia, in a 2010 academic paper.[19] Ironically, Cutteridge was arrested later that year and charged with bestiality when the veterinarian for his Rottweiler and Golden Retriever noticed the female dogs suffered more than their share of internal infections—a symptom of sexual abuse. Cutteridge, a former veterinary office worker, pleaded guilty and received a suspended sentence.[20]

But not all zoophiles actually engage in intercourse with animals. Josef Massen has identified nine forms of zoosexual activity:

1 Incidental experience and latent zoophilia.
2 Zoophilic voyeurism.
3 Frottage (rubbing against animals for sexual pleasure).
4 The animal as a tool for masturbation.
5 The animal as a surrogate for behavioral fetishism (such as zoosadism, which we'll explore in a moment).
6 The animal as fetish (fixation on one specific kind, breed, or individual).
7 Physical contact and affection.
8 The animal as a surrogate for a human sex partner.
9 The animal as a deliberately and voluntarily chosen sex partner.[21]

There are clearly shades of exploitation here, from getting off watching another species have sex to forcing oneself on an animal— all within the realm of zoophilia. Incidentally, veterinarians hate that term, since it focuses on the human perpetrator and ignores the harm it inflicts upon animals. Vets are, after all, the people who are often the first to discover and treat injuries caused by bestiality. (Given the anatomical differences between *Homo sapiens* and other species, sexual contact is frequently painful, even fatal.[22]) Yet even among those who practice veterinary medicine, bestiality is considered taboo and is rarely discussed. "This is odd, because in the main veterinarians tend to be fairly robust about 'difficult' subjects (such as sexual matters) yet on the sexual abuse of animals there has been a major silence," writes Helen Munro, BVMS, in *The Veterinary Journal*. "One wonders why? Is it that veterinarians have difficulty in facing up to the fact that an animal has been a victim of sexual abuse?"[23]

In fact, observe forensic veterinary experts Melinda Merck and Doris Miller, sexual abuse doesn't even seem to be included as a possible diagnosis for vaginal, anal, rectal, or genital lesions in veterinary textbooks.[24] Drs. Merck and Miller argue that in many cases, animals who allow rectal or vaginal penetration—even if they appear not to resist—are actually being coerced. "This type of assault would be extremely painful and the lack of resistance could indicate the animal was under the effects of a drug. It may also be an indicator that the animal has been trained and conditioned to accept the assault, an indicator of chronic abuse."[25]

Anyone with any doubt about whether or not zoophiles exploit animals can refer to a 1983 study on the motivations for zoophilia, in which participants cited how effortless it is to use animals for sexual gratification, because there is no negotiation required—there is no need to bargain or play "mind games." (This was especially true for men, who rated "emotional involvement" with an animal the least important aspect of their zoophilic behavior, while women gave it the highest rating.)[26] "Animals are much easier to understand than women," said Michael Kiok, the chairman of the German group Zoophile Engagement for Tolerance and Information when Germany moved to ban bestiality in 2012.[27]

Clearly, it's easy to get what you want when someone can't complain or report you.

Institutionalized Assault

Writing in *Transgressive Sex: Subversion and Control in Erotic Encounters*, anthropologist Rebecca Cassidy accuses modern authors—including psychologists, sexologists, and scholars—of reinforcing stereotypes about bestiality. While I don't share her belief that sex with nonhuman animals is an appropriate lifestyle choice, Cassidy ends her piece with one observation that rings true to me: "In thoroughbred reproduction, the animal sex act with which I am most familiar, the mare is restrained by human handlers using a selection of ropes and harness, including hobbles on its feet and a twitch on its nose. The stallion must cover the mare 'naturally' (according to the rules of horse racing), but human-assisted foreplay is tacitly permitted. Artificial insemination, banned for use in thoroughbred reproduction, permits a sexual manipulation of animals that differs only from zoosexual acts by virtue of its motivation (economic as opposed to sexual) and the context in which it takes place (down on the farm as opposed to in the bedroom)."[28]

Indeed, the exploitation of an animal's reproductive system is as much a sexual assault on her (or him) as forced intercourse. Artificial insemination (AI) is a routine abuse for cows, sheep, pigs, and turkeys in factory farms, and it's used to breed some primates in research facilities. AI is especially common in the dairy industry, where cows are constantly impregnated using an apparatus animal agribusiness calls a "rape rack." Once the cow is strapped in, she is often inseminated by a human who manually inserts bull semen, though sometimes a bull is brought in to mount her. Inherent in AI is the potential for causing the cow a good deal of pain and distress. "For this reason student inseminators need considerable practice," writes author Sue Cross. "At first they are very slow and their inexperience often causes severe damage, particularly to the rectum, anal sphincter, and reproductive tract. So great is the likelihood of injury that the industry advises that 'novice inseminators'—for welfare reasons—practice on cows that are to be slaughtered the same day."[29]

Pigs and sheep are similarly immobilized for AI using rape racks—a term that is as accurate as it is ugly.[30] In many ways, the rape rack is the crucible on which all who consume meat or dairy products must weigh their collective conscience, the place where we must surely agree that society's abuse of animals has exceeded any reasonable measure of sanity. How can we possibly reconcile a world where a device like this not only survives, but is legitimized as a standard business practice? In the words of feminist writer Carolyn Zaikowski, "As long as the rape rack exists, we will live in a world of

Secret Abuse: Sexual Assault on Animals

rapists."[31]

While female animals are sexually manipulated for food production and other industries, male animals are objectified as well, either masturbated for their semen or conditioned to ejaculate into an artificial vagina.[32] The most controversial method for obtaining semen, however, even among some agribusiness veterinarians, is to insert an electric probe into the animal's rectum and press it against his prostate gland. An electric shock is delivered until the animal involuntarily ejaculates. This procedure, known as electroejaculation, can cause extreme pain, with animals writhing in agony and fighting against their restraints.[33] (This is also the technique used to obtain semen from almost all wild animals held in captivity.) Farmers say the need for efficiency requires AI, though this institutionalized sexual assault on animals never considers the victim.

In the turkey business, it isn't just efficiency that necessitates AI, it's the size of modern turkeys. Because consumers want the white meat—and lots of it—that comes from the bird's breast, today's turkey is the product of decades of selective breeding, resulting in morbidly obese animals who grow rapidly.[34] So large are tom turkeys that they can barely keep themselves upright, let alone get close enough to a hen turkey for mating. With the tom's natural evolutionary fitness long bred out of him, the industry now resorts to artificial insemination. In their book *The Way We Eat: Why Our Food Choices Matter*, Peter Singer and Jim Mason recount their experience working on a Missouri turkey farm, where they chased down and grabbed toms for semen collection. "Our job was to catch a tom by the legs, hold him upside down, lift him by the legs and one wing, and set him up on the bench on his chest/neck, with the vent sticking up facing the worker who actually collected the semen," they write. "He squeezed the tom's vent until it opened up and the white semen oozed forth. Using a vacuum pump, he sucked it into a syringe." Then they moved over to the hen house, where they proceeded to "break" the hens, first by grasping a bird by her

455

legs and crossing her ankles to hold her with one hand. "The hens weigh 20 to 30 pounds and are terrified, beating their wings and struggling in panic. They go through this every week for more than a year, and they don't like it." The hen breakers push the turkey onto her chest and pull her tail upward to expose the vent. "At the same time, you pull the hand holding the feet downward, thus 'breaking' the hen so that her rear is straight up and her vent open." The inseminator then pokes the tormented bird with a semen-filled straw connected to compressed air, which blows the semen into her oviduct. "Each breaker 'breaks' five hens a minute, or one every 12 seconds."[35] One hundred percent of large-scale, commercially bred turkeys in the US are sexually violated and artificially inseminated in this manner. We then steal their babies.

Zoosadism

Singer and Mason didn't enjoy their stint as animal abusers—they called the work dirty and disgusting, and they lasted all but one day on the farm—but there are those for whom harming or even killing animals is an aphrodisiac. Indeed, these so-called zoosadists derive intense pleasure from inflicting pain. Zoosadism gets its name from the Marquis de Sade (1740–1814), the infamous French aristocrat known for sexually abusing women and children, among others. He apparently never met a cruelty he didn't relish, including a practice performed in Parisian brothels in which a customer rapes a turkey held by a prostitute. He writes: "The girl holds the bird's neck locked between her thighs, you have her ass straight ahead of you for prospect, and she cuts the bird's throat the same moment you discharge."[36] This perversion, known as avisodomy, is still common among male zoosadists, who will penetrate a chicken or goose, wring her neck, and get stimulated by the constriction and spasms of her cloaca sphincter as she dies. Rabbits are likewise used in this way, with the perpetrator strangling his victim or breaking her neck and then getting aroused by the animal's death throes.[37]

Zoosadistic activity can include much larger animals as well. For decades, police in Europe and the United States have been examining a string of puzzling cases in which horses are stabbed and mutilated. Today, so-called "horse ripping" is considered a new criminal phenomenon. Incidents are especially common in England, where hundreds of ponies and horses have been found with deep lacerations to their genitalia—sometimes it's been completely removed. While some investigations have dubiously linked these crimes to occult practices (at the scene of one attack, police found stones depicting five-pointed stars in the surrounding fields[38]), evidence suggests zoosadism as a motivating factor in many of these cases. In one of the first serious studies of horse ripping, a researcher examined 1,035 violent crimes committed against horses in Germany between 1993 and 2000 and found that one-quarter of them involved injuries to the animals' genitals and that most of the victims were female. So sexualized were these attacks that the researcher characterized them as rapes.[39]

Research suggests that many zoosadists were themselves once victims of sexual assault. A participant in Dr. Miletski's survey, identified as "Isaac," recounted that he had been raped by two men before he'd reached puberty and suffered a series of other molestations. Not that this excuses his abuse of animals—not by a long shot.

> "I look out into the world and I see a deep night of unthinkable cruelty and blindness. Undaunted, however, I look within the human heart and find something of love there, something that cares and shines out into the dark universe like a bright beacon. And in the shining of that light within, I feel the dreams and prayers of all beings. In the shining of that beacon I feel all of our hopes for a better future. In the shining of the human heartlight there is the strength to do what must be done."[40]
> —John Robbins

Isaac began experimenting sexually with animals at age 7, and went on to engage in years of bestiality, culminating in a sociopathic disregard for other species. "I have raped female and male pups," he boasted. "I have slit open the bellies and used the hole for a place to fuck!" His violent abuse included cats, dogs, horses, sheep, goats, chickens, and rabbits. "I like making love [sic] and fucking dogs and critters," he said.[41]

If one definition of sadistic sex is someone forcing himself onto someone else for sexual gratification, it could be argued that any sex with an animal could be considered zoosadism.

The Psychology of Abuse

What are we to make of people like Isaac—or, for that matter, anyone who sexually abuses an animal? Many of the participants in Dr. Miletski's survey reported being sexually, physically, or emotionally abused as children: 45 percent of the women and 46 percent of the men said they'd been emotionally abused; 27 percent of the women and 21 percent of the men reported being physically abused; and 36 percent of the women and 40 percent of the men replied that they'd been sexually abused. This is certainly not to imply that every abused kid grows up to become a bestialist, but the incidence of childhood victimization among those who sexually assault animals as adults does seem to suggest that the abuse, coupled with some other trauma or dysfunction, may predispose them to this pattern of behavior.

Since 1952, the standard manual used by psychologists, psychiatrists, and other mental health professionals to diagnose patients in the United States has been *The Diagnostic and Statistical Manual of Mental Disorders*, popularly known as DSM. The text has gone through several major revisions, and it wasn't until the third edition, DSM-III, that zoophilia made an appearance and was classified as a mental disorder. When the diagnostic committee made slight revisions to DSM-III, however, they removed zoophilia as a formal disorder and listed it under the diagnostic label "paraphilia not otherwise specified," noting that "zoophilia is virtually never a clinically significant problem by itself."[42] (Paraphilias are psychosexual disorders in which arousal and gratification depend on behavior that is atypical and extreme.) In other words, DSM rates bestiality/zoophilia as a deviant, though essentially victimless, sexual indulgence.

Yet not only are nonhumans victimized, but this sexual abuse is one of the early warning signs of the abuse of human beings. There is a growing body of empirical evidence that violent offenders don't begin their aberrant behavior by assaulting people—they evolve by torturing animals and insects. And every decade offers its own chilling example. Albert DeSalvo, the serial killer known in the 1960s as the Boston Strangler, trapped dogs and cats and then shot them with arrows. In the summer of 1976, New York City slept in fear of David Berkowitz (Son of Sam), who as a child killed small animals, including his mother's beloved parakeet.[43] The mid-'80s were marked by the sociopathic murders committed by Richard Ramirez (The Night Stalker), who as a teen had a fondness for stabbing and gutting animals. Jeffrey Dahmer, finally caught for a spree of killings and sex crimes in 1991, impaled the heads of cats and dogs on sticks. Even early criminologists saw a disturbing link between animal abuse and human abuse. The most notorious murderer of the 1920s, Peter Kürten (The Vampire of Düsseldorf), started engaging in bestiality at a young age and progressed to stabbing sheep while raping them.

Every criminal is unique, but one of the biggest predictors of domestic abuse, homicide, and other assaults against people is cruelty accompanied by a sexual interest in animals. In one study of 44 serial killers, 32 reportedly injured or killed animals, and 24 of them also tortured the animals, either through sexual assault, strangulation, or some other agony. Many of these killers created their homicidal "signatures" by practicing on animals. Arthur Shawcross (The Genesee River Killer), for example, engaged in bestiality as a youth and went on to rape at least two of his human victims.[44]

Using Animals for Domestic Battery

One of the most humiliating forms of abuse occurs when a perpetrator uses an animal to sexually assault his human victim. Seen primarily in situations of domestic violence, these cases generally involve women compelled by their partners to engage in sexual activity with dogs or other species. In one study, 41 percent of women in physically violent relationships and 5 percent of those in non-physically violent relationships had also experienced some form of forced sexual contact with an animal, or it was requested of them.[45]

"Forced sex with animals is an indication of how abusive men extensively sexualize and objectify their relationships, including their relationships with other animals," writes Carol Adams. "From the abuser's point of view, he is sexually using an animal as an object, just as others may use baseball bats or pop bottles. The animal's status as an object is what is important in this instance." Whereas the voice of the human victim is suppressed out of shame, the other victim, Carol observes, is regarded as voiceless since animals do not communicate in a language we recognize. "Both victims experience the unspeakable and are made unspeakable as well."[46]

Abusive partners may also harm or even kill the animal companions of their human victims—or threaten to—as a way to inflict terror and exert control. One disturbing example comes from a study by sociologist Clifton Flynn, who interviewed clients at a South Carolina shelter for battered women. Among these women was Mary, whose first and second husbands had both sexually assaulted her Boston terrier, Belinda. Mary also had a Doberman named Hans. One day, Belinda and Hans tried to intervene as Mary's second husband was assaulting her. In retaliation, he hung Belinda with a clothesline, though Mary was able to save her. He also deliberately ran Belinda over with his motorcycle, then buried her alive. Mary rescued the terrier once again, but her husband eventually murdered Belinda in what Mary characterized as a satanic ritual.[47]

While these incidents are upsetting, it's important to bear in mind that they are typical of the kind of cruelty abusive partners are capable of. Making matters worse is that most domestic violence shelters do not allow animals, so battered women who escape their abusers are often forced to leave their nonhuman companions behind to be further victimized.[48]

Flynn takes other sociologists to task for viewing animals merely as collateral damage in situations of domestic violence and ignoring their role as central participants. "This perspective is harmful to the women as well as the animals," he writes, "as it tends to devalue their nonhuman relationships, which may be the most meaningful and valuable ones in their lives."[49] Time and time again, Flynn reports, battered women turned to their companion animals for the comfort of unconditional love immediately after being abused by their partners.

The only way to make forced sex with animals more unthinkable is to turn it into child molestation. "The sexual abuse I endured was perpetrated by my kindergarten teacher and her partner," writes "Kate" on the rape survivor's support site Pandora's Project (pandys.org). "As the abuse progressed, it eventually included the dog the children at the centre played with. The first time I remember it happening, the man held me to the floor by sitting on my stomach, pulled my legs apart, and encouraged the dog to lick my 'private area,' while they both watched. Saying that even now brings a wave of disbelief that it could truly have happened, and humiliation, but at the time it was a million times worse and I wanted to sink into the ground and disappear, anything to get away from that room. I was also made to masturbate the dog, with the man giving me instructions on what to do, afterwards telling me how dirty I was, how my 'secret' was safe with him. It didn't go much further than this, but I remember it happening many times. I was only four years old, but even then I knew that what was happening was very, very wrong and something to never tell about."[50]

Crush Videos

While there are those who get sexual pleasure from torturing animals, there are those who equally enjoy seeing someone step on small animals and insects. Crush videos cater to these individuals, who derive sexual gratification from watching women use their feet to torture and slowly kill their victims. It's a deviant industry that has flourished in a world with easy access to video cameras and the Internet. There is some question about whether it is women's feet or the animals' torture and death that are the crush fetishist's primary stimulus, but such debate is meaningless to the victims, who always end up dead.

In a typical crush video (and I warn you, this paragraph is graphic), the camera focuses on a guinea pig fastened to the floor, his limbs akimbo and secured with tape. As the camera pulls back, we see the red high-heel shoes of a woman stepping around the animal. "You are my victim," she says softly. "Are you frightened, little man, hmm? You know that your destiny is under my heel. Squirm for me... No, you're mine, little man, to torment and torture." The guinea pig squeals in pain as the woman uses the pointed heel of her shoes to break each of his tiny legs, then crushes his back with her toe. The torture continues for half an hour, with the bones of his little body methodically broken and cigarette burns delivered to his fur, until the woman finally drives a spiked heel into his head, killing him.[51]

As Carol Adams observes in her book *The Pornography of Meat*, crush videos exploit two fundamental stereotypes: that women are supposed to be scared of small animals, and that women are supposed to care about animals. "Clearly women have been the majority in animal activism. Pornographers have fun with the idea that women destroy animals rather than protecting them."[52]

Yet women have also been found to enjoy this particular fetish. One mother of three, known to the media only as Anna B., was arrested in Milan after she'd posted dozens of videos online that showed her squashing the life out of animals while wearing stockings and stiletto heels. It was the first prosecution under Italy's 2010 law banning crush videos. "This case was brought to our attention following a tip off to us and we acted immediately to bring this woman to justice," said Paolo Iosca, a lawyer representing the Italian Anti-Vivisection League. "The videos she posted showed her semi-naked, wearing tights and high heels and crushing innocent animals such as rabbits, chicks, and mice to death. They were particularly crude and offensive."[53] The court fined her US$5,400 and let her go with a suspended sentence.

Crush Videos: Sadistic or Masochistic?

While it's tempting to label those who obtain sexual gratification from watching animals being crushed "sadists," there's more than a little masochism present as well. "Masochists often suffer from personality disorders in which they are only able to experience feelings in the context of situations where they are hurt or in pain," explains Kevin Volkan, professor of psychology at California State University Channel Islands. "These people need to surrender their needs and identity and experience extremely disturbing things to feel that they exist and to feel pleasure." In terms of crush videos, says Dr. Volkan, "It is possible that masochists identify with the animals being tortured and killed, actually seeing themselves as the animal being crushed, and these individuals obtain sexual gratification through this identification."[54] In other words, the desire to watch animals being crushed may be sadistic, but mentally putting oneself in the place of the animal is masochistic.

Legislation

Laws applicable to crush videos and the actual practice of torturing and crushing animals vary by region and country. For instance, they are perfectly legal in China, where animal cruelty laws are virtually nonexistent. They are illegal in the UK, Greece, the Philippines, and, as mentioned, Italy, where laws are stricter. Crush videos are also prohibited in the United States, though identifying and prosecuting offenders has been a challenge. It hasn't helped that, until recently, many lawmakers were shamefully ignorant on the issue. When Susan Creede, an investigator with the Ventura County District Attorney's Office in California, testified before the House Subcommittee on Crime in 1999 about her undercover work in the crush community, committee members were disgusted and stunned in equal measure—stunned perhaps more than anything that they had never heard of such a thing. "I will say this is shocking and that is not a word we use too often because the subcommittee sees a lot of pretty horrible things, being the Crime Subcommittee," said Florida Congress member Bill McCollum, who chaired the subcommittee.[55]

For nine months, Susan trolled foot-fetish chat rooms online and used web-based bulletin boards to communicate with crush enthusiasts all over the world. Everyone went by an alias. Susan called herself "Hot Heels" and "Minnie." She gradually gained people's confidence, and they opened up to her about the source of their sexual fixation on animal cruelty. "For many of them the fetish developed from something they saw at a very early age, usually before the age of five," she explained. "Most of these men saw a woman step on something. She was usually someone who was significant in their lives. They were excited by the experience and somehow attached their sexuality to it." As these men grew older, they eroticized the feet of dominant women, imagining scenarios in which the women had the power to crush the life out of them. "Many of these men like to be trampled by women," Susan told the subcommittee. "They prefer to be hurt and the more indifferent the woman is to their pain, the more exciting it is for them." The ultimate fantasy for these men is to be crushed to death—certainly more a masochistic aspiration than a sadistic one—but since that is out of the question (for most men, anyway[56]), they've transferred the focus of their desire onto seeing a woman stomp on a live animal or insect. "I was once instructed on how to torture a dog on video, step by step. I was told to purchase the dog at a place that would not check on the animal at a later date. I was told to make the video immediately after purchasing the animal to avoid the risk of becoming attached. I was told to make the crushing incident last ninety minutes before the animal actually died."[57]

In May 1999, Susan and her team hit pay dirt: a California producer of crush videos named Gary Thomason contacted her through a chat room and passed along a video clip he'd made of a woman stepping on a mouse and a rat. He asked Susan if she'd be interested in crushing animals on camera. Susan agreed and made arrangements to meet Thomason at his Long Beach apartment the following month to make the video. When she and another female undercover officer arrived, Thomason went to a local pet store and returned with five large rats. He closed the blinds, locked the front door, and taped a struggling rodent to the top of a glass table, which allowed a camera to record an animal's agonizing demise from below. At this point, Susan uttered a prearranged code word and police burst in, arresting Thomason. Officers found dozens of crush videos in Thomason's closet and eventually recovered the one he had sent to Susan. That video showed the deaths of 12 animals—six baby mice, four adult mice, and two rats. "They were all taunted, maimed, tortured, mutilated, disemboweled, and ultimately slowly killed under the heel of a shoe," according to court records.[58] Thomason and his girlfriend, Diane Chaffin, under whose feet the animals died, were charged with three felony counts of cruelty to animals. Chaffin pleaded no contest, but when Thomason was eventually convicted, he appealed, arguing that the animals he destroyed were "pests." The appeals court disagreed, saying the animals were clearly killed for sexual gratification and profit.

With the Thomason and Chaffin case making headlines, California Congress member Elton Gallegly introduced the Depictions of Animal Cruelty Act (HR 1887, also known as the

Crush Video Bill), which passed in the House by a landslide and in the Senate by unanimous consent. Although the cruelty depicted in crush videos was already illegal in most states, it could rarely be prosecuted because the nature of the videos made identifying perpetrators nearly impossible, timelines affecting statutes of limitations were difficult to establish, and criminals moved their videotapes through interstate commerce to avoid prosecution. HR 1887 was designed to close these loopholes, and President Bill Clinton signed the bill into federal law in December 1999.[59]

Opponents of the statute—as diverse as the hunting lobby and *The New York Times*—argued that it infringed on the First Amendment freedom of expression, and they anxiously awaited the moment when it was challenged. Their wish was granted a decade later, when *United States v. Stevens* was argued in the Supreme Court. In 2005, Virginia resident Robert Stevens had been convicted of violating the ban on animal-cruelty depictions, by now known officially as Section 48 of Title 18 of the US Code. Stevens had been selling videos that showed dogfights and so-called "hog-dog fighting," including graphic footage of a pit bull mutilating the lower jaw of a live pig. He also provided voiceover narration on each video. The trial court determined that the videos had none of the serious religious, political, scientific, educational, journalistic, historical or artistic value that would exempt the videos from Section 48's prohibitions.

Sentenced to 37 months in federal prison, Stevens challenged the lower court's ruling on First Amendment grounds. The Third Circuit Court of Appeals agreed with him, invalidating Section 48 as a violation of the First Amendment. The Third Circuit concluded that the government's interest in barring the depictions of animal cruelty didn't rise to the level of a compelling governmental interest necessary to create a new category of speech not protected by the First Amendment. The government appealed, and the Supreme Court heard oral arguments on October 6, 2009. Some observers believed that since the Court has ruled the government can constitutionally prohibit images of child sexual abuse, it should also be able to ban images of animal abuse. Many legal pundits recognized this argument wasn't going to sway the highest court in the land, and they were not surprised when the justices, in an eight-to-one decision, ruled Section 48 to be unconstitutional. Among those unsurprised was law professor Edward H. Levi of the University of Chicago, who pointed out that although the US forbids child sexual abuse in all circumstances, society loses little sleep over the inhumane treatment of nonhumans. "For example," he writes, "although some people find it troubling, we permit hunting, we experiment on animals for medical reasons, and we slaughter tens of millions of animals annually for food. The allowance of such conduct clearly reveals that our society does not consider animal abuse on a par with child sexual abuse."[60]

One day after the Supreme Court struck down Section 48, Congress member Gallegly introduced a new bill that applied only to crush videos. It was signed into law in 2010. "The new law, the Animal Crush Video Prohibition Act, essentially labels crush videos as 'obscene,'" explains attorney Matthew Liebman of the Animal Legal Defense Fund, which had filed an *amicus* brief in 2009 encouraging the Supreme Court to recognize the protection of animals as a compelling government interest and uphold Section 48. "The Supreme Court has long recognized 'obscenity' as unprotected speech, so the aim of the new law is to fit crush videos into an existing First Amendment exception instead of asking the Court to recognize depictions of cruelty as an entirely new class of unprotected speech, which it refused to do in *Stevens*."[61] Unfortunately, the first prosecution under the new statute—against a Houston, Texas, couple caught with some 27 videos of animals being tortured and killed—was tossed out of court in April 2013. A federal judge declared that the ban on depictions of animal cruelty is unconstitutional under the First Amendment.

What You Can Do

- Unfortunately, sexually assaulting an animal is not a crime in every county, state, or country. If it's not illegal where you live, work with legislators to enact or strengthen animal sexual abuse laws.
- Those who sexually prey on animals often understand that the taboo nature of their practices means their assaults may go unnoticed or even ignored. Please do not disregard the signs of animal cruelty, which—in the case of sexual abuse—may include physical injuries or blood around the animal's backside.
- If you witness or suspect animal abuse, contact your local humane society or police department.
- Be aware that a child's sexual abuse of an animal may be a warning sign that he or she is a victim or witness of physical, sexual, or emotional abuse.
- Visit www.nationallinkcoalition.org for additional information.

For Veterinarians

Veterinarians are often the first to recognize evidence of sexual assaults on animals, including infections, fur loss or fur matting, and tail injuries. Vets should also look for additional signs of abuse or neglect, such as illness, malnutrition, unclean or inadequate living environment, and the presence of penetrative objects (often in the form of adult sex toys) in the animal's living area (possibly bloody or stained). Other warning signs include a family history of animals disappearing or dying at a young age; explanations about injuries that don't seem accurate; injuries in different stages of healing; families using a series of different vets (to help conceal serial abuse); and families keeping one animal in a private location, such as a basement or garage, while other animals are in the house or backyard. These clues may not necessarily indicate a case of sexual assault, but veterinarians should contact the appropriate humane or law enforcement officials if they find bruises, tears, or abrasions around an animal's anus or genitalia.

While there is some debate among veterinary professionals about their role in addressing animal cruelty—some vets feel the duty of client confidentiality supersedes any obligation to report abuse—the American Veterinary Medical Association clearly states that it is the responsibility of veterinarians to report cases of animal cruelty, animal abuse, or animal neglect to authorities, adding, "Such disclosures may be necessary to protect the health and welfare of animals and people."[62] Likewise, the UK's Royal College of Veterinary Surgeons asserts in the confidentiality section of their Code of Conduct that veterinarians may divulge information to a third party "where in an exceptional case they are clearly of the opinion that animal welfare or the public interest is so endangered as to outweigh any obligation to the owner."[63]

For Human Victims

Finally, if you are the victim of domestic violence—whether it involves a nonhuman animal or not—please seek help from one of these agencies:

Australia: call 1800RESPECT at 1800 737 732 or visit www.1800respect.org.au

Canada: call the National Domestic Violence Hotline at 1-800-363-9010

New Zealand: call Women's Refuge at 0800 733 843 or visit www.womensrefuge.org.nz

South Africa: call the Stop Women Abuse help line at 0800-150-150 or visit www.stopwomenabusehelpline.org.za

UK: call Women's Aid at 0808 2000 247 or visit www.womensaid.org.uk

US: call the National Domestic Violence Hotline at 1-800-799-7233 or visit www.thehotline.org

Worldwide: visit the International Directory of Domestic

Violence Agencies for a global list of help lines, shelters, and crisis centers: www.hotpeachpages.net

Chapter 11

Achieving Moral Parity

The true struggle is between animals and humans.
—George Orwell, *Animal Farm*

In the years I spent researching and writing this book, examining the tortures animals endure at the pleasure of humans, I often wondered: What makes some people care passionately about animals, while other people can turn a blind eye to their suffering? What will it take for *everyone* to acknowledge the obligation we have to the creatures with whom we share this planet and recognize that they deserve full moral parity with human beings? Struggling with such questions, I turned to some of the prominent ethicists, writers, and philosophers whose work has inspired a generation of animal advocates. They are:

Carol J. Adams, a feminist-vegan writer who explores the links between species oppression and gender oppression. She is the author of *The Sexual Politics of Meat: A Feminist-Vegetarian Critical Theory* and *Living Among Meat Eaters: The Vegetarians' Survival Handbook*, among many other books.

Harold Herzog, who has been examining the complex psychology of our interactions with other species for more than two decades. He is particularly interested in how people negotiate real-world ethical dilemmas, and he has studied animal activists, cockfighters, veterinary students, animal researchers, and ex-vegetarians. A professor of psychology at Western Carolina University, Dr. Herzog is the author of *Some We Love, Some We Hate, Some We Eat: Why It's So Hard to Think Straight About Animals*.

James McWilliams, professor of history at Texas State University–San Marcos. Dr. McWilliams has emerged in recent years as a leading voice in the movement, and he blogs frequently about animal issues at james-mcwilliams.com. His books include *Just Food: Where Locavores Get It Wrong and How We Can Truly Eat Responsibly, The Modern Savage,* and *The Politics of the Pasture: How Two Oxen Sparked a National Discussion about Eating Animals.*

Marc Bekoff, professor emeritus of ecology and evolutionary biology at the University of Colorado–Boulder, who is a fellow of the Animal Behavior Society and is a faculty member of the Humane Society University. In 2000, he co-founded, with Jane Goodall, Ethologists for the Ethical Treatment of Animals. His latest book is *The Animal Manifesto: Six Reasons for Expanding Our Compassion Footprint.*

Mylan Engel, Jr., associate professor at Northern Illinois University, where he teaches animal rights, epistemology, philosophy of religion, and metaphysics. Dr. Engel is executive secretary of the Society for the Study of Ethics and Animals. He is the co-author (with Kathie Jenni) of *The Philosophy of Animal Rights.*

Richard Ryder, a psychologist and philosopher, regarded as one of the founders of the modern animal rights movement. While at Oxford in 1970, he coined the word "speciesism" to describe the widely held belief that the human species is inherently superior to other species with rights or privileges that are denied to other sentient animals. His books include *Animal Revolution* and *Victims of Science.*

I asked them all the same questions, though they didn't always want to respond to every one of them. Perhaps their insights can help make sense of a world in which animal exploitation is as common as it is accepted.

Why do some people care so deeply about the suffering of animals, while other people ignore this suffering or even cause it?
CJA: I believe everybody has the potential to care, and this is the argument that is made in *The Feminist Care Tradition in Animal Ethics* that Josephine Donovan and I edited. The approach I take is not that I have to teach people to care, but I have to help people discover that

they already have the ability to care and it's been socialized out of them. In other words, I think that we all care. One of the results of that is that people are frightened by the intensity with which they *can* care for animals. That intensity and awareness of it makes them wary; they think, "It's going to be too painful to care." Look at examples. When people find out about whales trapped under ice, when people are given specific examples of individual animals suffering, they often respond. Other people, when you try to talk to them about factory farming or dogfighting or cows and veal calves and why people shouldn't drink cow's milk, they say, "Please don't tell me." They don't want to know, because they're aware of their ability to care. I believe that people think that caring that deeply will kill or disable them, because we have not modeled how to care well—care well in the sense of caring about other animals and how to live with this kind of caring ability and not let it destroy you.

One of the things I believe is that animal activists have learned that caring makes us more *human* as it makes us more *humane*. We've learned that grief will be a constant companion. The grief doesn't kill us, but there are going to be days or hours in the day or minutes in the hour when we say, "This is terrible information." We rightly feel sad when we learn this information, and this shows how humane we are.

This is the feminist intervention into animal ethics. We don't have to convince anybody to care. What we have to do is show people that their ability to care enhances their life, rather than disabling them.

HH: Psychologists don't have a complete answer to this question, but several factors are known to be associated with involvement in animal protection. The biggest factor is gender. Women make up between 75 and 80 percent of individuals involved with animal protection at all levels—from sea turtle rescuers to full-blown animal activists. This gender ratio has not changed since the origins of the animal protection movement in the 1860s. Studies have also shown that animal activists tend to have high levels of two moral emotions: the positive emotion of empathy and the negative emotion of disgust. In addition, animal activists score higher than average on several personality dimensions. These include the traits of "openness to new experiences" and "worry/anxiety." Finally, animal protectionists tend to ascribe higher levels of mental abilities to other species than do non-activists.

JM: I couldn't advocate for animals if I didn't deeply believe that humans are not only generally good, but that we have a deep desire to live in a world where suffering is minimized. What's the point of life if this maxim were false? The primary difference between those who are indifferent to animal suffering and those who care deeply about it comes down to the extent to which we have realized and appreciated the powerful human potential for compassion and empathy.

While innate, these expressions of human goodness do not just happen. They have to be nurtured over time, coaxed out of us with love, and affirmed. This complex process faces innumerable cultural, social, and economic barriers, but its force is inexorable—it *needs* to happen. In many respects, it is this primal need that makes us human. The extent to which we open our heart to this process is the extent to which we become predisposed to treating nonhuman animals with dignity.

Everyone interacts with this process of moral enlightenment differently, in unique terms—it took me until my mid-30s to embrace it—but everyone is at least *somewhere* on the vast continuum of living a life that seeks to reduce suffering for humans and nonhumans alike. As an activist, I work to push people in the right direction on what at times seems like an endless continuum of compassion.

MB: I think there could be a number of different reasons. I imagine that the way in which people are reared plays some role, along with some as-yet-unknown genetic factors. I was raised in a compassionate and loving household, and my mom was extremely caring and empathic, although she was afraid of dogs because she'd been bitten when she was young. As a result, I lived with a goldfish and my grandparents lived with a cat and dog and I remember they loved them both. I think there's a general development environment that favors the development and expression of a caring ethic. My folks told me that I "minded animals" from the time I was very young and always was asking them what animals were thinking and feeling. I was always concerned about animal well-being. I once yelled at a man for spanking his dog and the guy came after my dad!

ME: I believe that most people care deeply about the suffering of animals. When I show my students documentary films that reveal the cruel, inhumane animal husbandry techniques commonplace in today's factory farms, virtually all of them are shocked and horrified at witnessing such inhumane treatment and the terrible suffering that it causes innocent, helpless animals. Many of these students are so upset by the animal suffering they are witnessing that they are actually brought to tears. If people didn't care deeply about animal suffering, they wouldn't be so upset by it. In their reaction papers, nearly all students find the inhumane treatment of animals in factory farms disgusting and morally reprehensible. Moreover, most insist that such treatment of factory-farmed animals ought to be illegal, even if they are personally unwilling to give up eating animal flesh.

That brings us to the question of why so many people still are (or at least seem to be) indifferent to the immense suffering that farmed animals are forced to endure. I think that much of this indifference is due to ignorance—most people simply don't know how badly the animals are treated in modern factory farms. They may still carry around images in their heads of "happy farms" where the animals frolic freely and where, after having had a wonderful life, they are killed quickly and humanely. They may realize that the animals suffer somewhat at the end of their lives when they are slaughtered, but they mistakenly think that the process is swift and relatively painless. They have heard about the Humane Slaughter Act and think that it is enforced. In short, many people ignore the plight of farmed animals because they have convinced themselves that there really is no plight.

What makes me think that people's indifference is based on ignorance as to what is really going on in factory farms? The fact that each semester I witness students' reactions to learning about the plight of factory-farmed animals, both their reactions to descriptions of factory farms and their reactions to films documenting firsthand the inhumane treatment to which farmed animals are subjected in factory farms; and as I said, they are consistently appalled by that treatment. Some are appalled to the point of becoming vegetarians. Others insist that they will make a conscious effort to eat less meat. And even those unwilling to alter their dietary practices think that laws should be enacted that make inhumane farming practices illegal.

If people are naturally empathetic and compassionate where animal suffering is concerned, as I have suggested, then why are some people able to work in factory farms and slaughterhouses and capable of treating animals so inhumanely? The answer, I think, lies in two well-documented psychological phenomena: 1. Desensitization. People tend to become desensitized to what would normally be psychologically distressing experiences through repeated exposure to those experiences. This desensitization process is a defense mechanism that allows us to cope psychologically with such traumatic experiences and events. 2. Deference to authority. People also have a natural tendency to defer to authority figures, even when those authority figures are instructing them to do something that they themselves would ordinarily think wrong, as was demonstrated by Stanley Milgram in his famous experiments on obedience. In one of these experiments, the test subjects were instructed to administer shocks of increasing strength to another human being whenever that other human being answered a multiple choice question incorrectly. Milgram found that 65 percent of the test subjects were willing to administer what they thought were lethal 450-volt shocks to these other human beings, as long as they were instructed to do so by the scientist conducting the experiment. Based on these experiments, Milgram concluded: "Ordinary people, simply doing their jobs, and without any particular hostility on their part, can become agents in a terrible destructive process. Moreover, even when the destructive effects of their work become patently clear, and they are asked to carry out actions incompatible with fundamental standards of morality, relatively few people have the resources needed to resist authority."

Desensitization and deference to authority help explain why otherwise decent, compassionate people can become capable of treating animals so badly. Many, if not most, people who work on farms grew up on farms. From the time they were small children, they were witness to the cruel treatment of animals, e.g., they witnessed castration, branding, dehorning, teeth-pulling, ear-tagging, etc., all being performed without anesthesia. In many cases, these children are deeply troubled by what they see, but over time they become desensitized to animal suffering. Once they get a little older, they are instructed to perform these inhumane procedures themselves by authority figures—usually their parents or relatives—that they look up to and respect. In addition, these same authority figures provide rationalizations to help them cope with what they are doing to the animals.

I have firsthand knowledge of some of these rationalizations. When I was ten years old, I witnessed my cousins castrating piglets on my uncle's hog farm. The procedure was horrific. One of my cousins held the piglet upside down by his hind legs, and the other took a razor blade and slit the scrotum twice. She then reached into the scrotum with her index and middle fingers and simply ripped the testicles out of the piglet's body—the vas deferens wasn't cut with the razor blade; the testicles were simply pulled out of the piglet's body until the vas deferens snapped. After removing the testicles in this way, she applied an antiseptic spray to the scrotum of the squealing piglet and then dropped the piglet in the dirt. These piglets were in such agony from the procedure that they couldn't move their hind legs. They dragged themselves by their front legs to the farthest corner of the pen where they were being housed and lay there, squealing and whimpering. Shocked by what I was witnessing, I asked my cousins whether they thought castrating the piglets in this way caused the piglets to suffer. Their matter-of-fact reply reeked of rationalization and indoctrination: "Yes, it causes them terrible suffering, but they won't remember it. So, it doesn't matter." Still deeply troubled by what I had seen, I approached my father, who himself had grown up on a hog farm, and asked him about the procedure. He told me that we had to eat to survive and that God put animals here for us to eat. He also told me that the castration was necessary so that the animals would grow better and be easier to raise. As a ten-year-old, I recall thinking that if that's what God intended, then it must be okay. At that time, I had no idea that we could easily meet all of our nutritional needs with a plant-based diet. I was still bothered by what I saw, but if it was God's will, who was I to object?

I mention this anecdote, *not* because I think that a loving God would approve of our horrific maltreatment of farmed animals *nor* because I think it okay to cause a being to suffer provided that being won't remember the suffering—I don't think either such thing. I mention it because I'm confident that most children raised on farms are told similar self-serving stories that allow them to cope with and rationalize the inhumane treatment of the animals in their care. After hearing these rationalizations over and over from authority figures they look up to and respect, what was once troubling to do to an animal becomes "acceptable" and more or less routine.

It is worth noting that even with all the desensitization that comes with routinely mistreating and slaughtering animals, slaughterhouses have some of the highest worker turnover rates of any industry in the country, and slaughterhouse workers have one of the highest rates of alcoholism of any occupation. So, at some level, even the people abusing these animals day in and day out must be bothered by what they are doing, for they turn to alcohol to numb themselves on a regular basis.

RR: Everyone has a streak of compassion within them. This can, however, be overruled by various forces, most commonly by custom or anger. A soldier or a slaughter man becomes used to killing—it becomes customary. If it is regarded as customary and meets with the approval of others, especially those in authority, then most normal people will do it. Stanley Milgram, the American psychologist, found that about 60 percent of normal subjects would give apparently lethal shocks if told to do so by someone in a white coat. On the other hand, anger plays a part with many so-called psychopaths: they are chronically angry because of the way they have been treated and sometimes take it out on animals. They can go on to take it out on innocent humans too.

With so many animals abused and exploited in the world, how do caring people not lose their faith in humanity?
CJA: Well, there are going to be days that we *do* lose our faith; I think that's part of our grief, and I think that's an honest response. We feel disillusioned when people know what's going on but still don't change. But that is the challenge of every social justice movement that's ever been known in the world: How do good people do bad things? We might never reconcile ourselves to the fact that people educated about animal cruelties continue to cause harm. One way we handle that is by reassuring ourselves that not all people do that, and that change is possible. We remind ourselves that *we* have been in a process of change, and we can become models for other people about how to change. We make sure that we never think that we've done it all and that we understand that other people might see *us* as culpable for something because we're not aware of corollary social justice movements. You know, for years and years and years there

was a farm workers' boycott of grapes. So if a vegan thinks they've done it all and they were eating grapes that the United Farm Workers union was asking us to boycott, that's an example that we haven't figured it all out. This goes back to the feminist approach to animals, that this is not something apart from or separated from other social justice movements. So, we don't think, "All I have to do is care about animals."

HH: This can be really tough. I once interviewed several dozen activists for a research project. Some were cheerful and optimistic and felt their involvement in animal rights gave their life meaning. Others, however, suffered from "compassion fatigue." They were discouraged and on the verge of burnout. The activists dealt with this in different ways. The most interesting was a man who told me that once a year, he would take a "moral vacation" by flying to the Bahamas for a couple of weeks, lying in the sun, not thinking about animal issues. This worked for him, but I suspect that it would not be possible for others.

Because I am not an activist, I hesitate to offer advice on this issue, but I think that a good place to start would be to link up with other like-minded people and form support groups. I think is it healthy to recognize that complete moral consistency is nearly impossible and can actually drive people out of the movement. I call this "the activists' paradox": the idea that the clearer your moral vision, the harder it can be to live up to your own standards.

JM: Caring people do not lose faith in humanity because they can't lose faith in humanity. It's not an option. Do that and you stop caring. You undermine not only your effectiveness as an advocate for animals, but your humanity as well. Stop caring and you snuff the embers that burn in our hearts to leave a better world than the one we entered.

Caring people have to be thinking people. I say this because it requires considerable reflection on the human condition to understand why good people perpetuate and condone systematic animal suffering. Advocates for animal rights inevitably live on the brink of burnout. I grapple with it every day of my life. Still, thinking deeply about the external factors that allow humans to accept suffering illuminates two critical points: a) we all have the potential for improvement; and b) much of the suffering humans perpetuate is done unthinkingly. Oh, and as you have sensed, points a and b are intimately connected.

Most of us, in other words, are trapped in cultural and social and economic frameworks that nurture unthinking behavior. While these frameworks can be daunting in their seeming permanence, there is power in identifying them. Indeed, identifying them is a necessary prerequisite for dismantling them. When we begin to dismantle the structures that blind us to compassion for animals, even tentatively, our unthinking decisions become not only thinking ones, but feeling ones. Compassionate ones. Watching this shift in perspective happen for even one person is enough to counteract all the doubt and fear and frustration that come with the territory of animal activism.

MB: I look for small incremental changes and know, especially in my heart, that there are people all over the world who are working for animals. I travel a lot and see this firsthand. I'm not a blind optimist or dreamer, and I know about the rampant abuse and exploitation, but there are good things happening, and I look to those for inspiration and hope. I also work with children, as they are the ambassadors for a better future world. We need to tap into the compassionate and empathic side of kids to ensure that they will become compassionate, proactive activists as they grow up. I suppose that while there are people out there who behave in reprehensible ways, there are also people who give their all for animals, and they are my models and heroes. I am always looking for people who can help us expand our compassion footprint. I believe that we are born to be good and that we can tap into our inherent goodness, kindness, compassion, and empathy to make the world a better place for all beings. This is one of the main messages of my latest book, *The Animal Manifesto: Six Reasons for Expanding Our Compassion Footprint.* I like to keep in mind what Henry Spira, founder of Animal Rights International, did in the 1970s working from his small apartment in New York City. Spira and his grassroots organization were responsible for having federal funding pulled on a project in which researchers at the American Museum of Natural History performed surgery on cat's genitals and pumped them with various hormones to see how the mutilated cats would behave sexually. Spira also formed the Coalition to Abolish the Draize Test, a horribly painful test that involves using rabbits to test eye makeup.

ME: The main reason I don't lose faith in humanity is because I believe in the power of education. Every semester I see people make the conscious, compassionate choice to stop eating animals after they learn about the inhumane way in which these animals are raised. Most people have been taught that they need to eat meat and dairy products in order to be healthy. They are constantly bombarded with television commercials telling them that "milk does a body good" and that beef is "real food for real people." Most people are not intentionally cruel or malicious. Most people are, however, misinformed. I actually find it encouraging just how many people do give up meat and dairy products after: 1. Learning that such products aren't necessary for good health; and 2. Becoming informed about the institutionalized cruelty inherent in modern animal agriculture, especially given the fact that so many of these people were subjected to years of indoctrination aimed at instilling in them the desire for a meat-based diet.

When I attended the 1996 World Congress for Animals, I had the opportunity to hear Rue McClanahan speak on behalf of animals. To this day, I vividly remember one thing she said: "Cruelty can't stand the spotlight!" I think that she is right. I'm confident that as more and more people become informed about how badly farmed animals are mistreated, they will insist that farmed animals be treated humanely. We already see this happening throughout the European Union and in selected states here in the United States. The European Union has banned the use of veal crates and passed legislation requiring the elimination of battery cages for hens and the elimination of gestation crates for sows. In the US, several states are phasing out the use of gestation crates for sows. California has also passed legislation eliminating veal crates and battery cages. The electoral margins by which these laws have passed reveal that even people unbothered by the thought of eating animals still think that those animals should be treated humanely while they are being raised.

RR: Maybe if people joined the thousands of others who work hard to reduce animal suffering they would see that all of us have a compassionate side as well as a selfish side. Humanity is a mixture. None of us are entirely without compassion.

How has the world changed over the last 20 years in its treatment of animals? Are we getting better—or worse?
CJA: Yes (laughs). Twenty years ago, *The Sexual Politics of Meat* came out. At that point, I dedicated it to "six billion land animals"—that was the number who were killed every year in the United States to become people's food. Now I think we're over *nine* billion land animals. One of the impacts of that is that people stopped eating flesh from four-legged animals and started eating more two-legged animals, like chickens. That's not an advance. Also, look what's happening to sea animals. My God, what a crime! I think that in terms of individual animals, some may be better off than they were 20 years ago, but the whole institution is still corrupt, and the change has to be with the consumer. Veganism is a boycott. Veganism is also an affirmation. That's where I see the change in 20 years—such a growth in vegan culture, vegan restaurants, vegan cookbooks, vegan blogs, even the word "vegan." I think all of that is

a change for the positive, so that when people want to think about being vegan, there are so many more resources. On the other hand, veganism comes to be seen as an individual lifestyle, rather than this social justice worldview. And while it is enacted as a lifestyle, it arises because we want to change the world.

HH: In many ways, things are better for animals. For example, the success of spay-and-neuter programs has reduced the number of dogs and cats euthanized in animal shelters by nearly 90 percent. And, more people are buying cruelty-free products and purchasing meat they believe has been raised humanely.

However, the problem is that as our society's desire to protect animals has increased, so has our desire to eat them. When Peter Singer wrote *Animal Liberation* in 1975, the average American ate about 170 pounds of meat a year; now we are up to an average of 240 pounds a year. And the number of animals killed because they taste good has more than tripled, from 3 billion in 1974 to over 10 billion in 2012. Further, as countries like China and India have gotten wealthier, their citizens' desire to eat meat has skyrocketed. I hate to say it, but the campaign to moralize meat has been a failure.

JM: We're getting better, no question. One optimistic trend that has developed over the last 20 years is a widespread awareness and condemnation of animal suffering in factory farms. I view this development as a major consciousness-raising shift down the continuum of compassion. Even if the vast majority of those who abhor factory farming on the grounds of animal welfare still eat animals, we cannot discount the significance of this massive upsurge in enlightenment.

Not only should we not discount it, we must capitalize on it— push it to its logical conclusion. The book I'm now writing, called *The Modern Savage*, does exactly this. It asks those who oppose factory farming on welfare grounds but still eat animals from non-industrial farms to explore the nature of their opposition to factory farming.

Once consumers recognize that they ultimately care about the treatment of animals in factory farms because those animals are deserving, as sentient beings, of moral consideration, it's a short, downhill journey to the conclusion that we should not be—at the least—eating them at all, no matter how they were raised.

If nothing else, the fact that this argument of mine even has an audience at this point in time is, in a weird way, indicative of substantial progress.

MB: My answer can vary from day to day, but there are some significant positive things happening, and I devote sections of *The Animal Manifesto* to the progress we are making. These include universities and schools that are abolishing dissection, even in India and Russia; the passage of Proposition 2, granting more protection to factory-farmed animals; granting rights to great apes in Spain; and seeing young kids give up birthday gifts and allowances to help animals and habitats.

ME: It's a mixed bag. On the plus side, as I noted earlier, the inhumane treatment of farmed animals is coming under critical scrutiny in developed nations. For example, the European Union banned the use of veal crates and passed legislation calling for the total elimination of battery cages and gestation crates. Following the EU's lead, a number of states in the US have passed legislation aimed at improving the conditions in which farmed animals are forced to live. In November 2008, by an overwhelming 63.3 percent margin, California residents voted in favor of Proposition 2—a ballot measure banning veal crates, gestation crates for sows, and battery cages for hens in the state by the year 2015. Reflecting this same moral consciousness, Colorado and Arizona have passed similar measures that require the phased-out elimination of both gestation crates for sows and veal crates. Florida and Oregon have also passed legislation aimed at abolishing the use of gestation crates. In addition to legal sanctions, a growing number of corporations, such as Whole Foods and Chipotle, are now imposing even stricter humane farming standards on the farmers who supply their products. While these changes do not go far enough, they certainly make farmed animals' lives better than they otherwise would have been.

Unfortunately, at the same time that the inhumane treatment of farmed animals is coming under critical scrutiny in Western nations, factory farm technology is being exported to Third World countries. As a result, the number of animals whose interests and well-being are systematically ignored in factory farms is dramatically increasing throughout the world. Not only is this horrible for the animals themselves, it is also tragic for the people living in these developing countries, as their largely plant-based, traditional ethnic diets are being replaced with less healthful meat- and dairy-based diets.

RR: A little bit better. The EU now has a score of laws giving some protection to animals, and China has just published its first ever draft bill on animal welfare. Now we must push for a UN charter for animals.

What will it take for humans to move beyond seeing animals as "tools" and regard them as sentient beings with their own interests?

CJA: Well, I think the presumption is that people will stop treating them as tools if they see them as sentient beings. But we use sentient beings as tools all the time. I don't think it's an either/or thing. I think all the new information coming out about animals' capabilities, animals' consciousness, the social communities animals have is helpful. It's kind of like the accumulation of a snowball into something bigger and bigger. The more there is, the more that has to be dealt with. But I think the process of objectification is, which is what I think you're getting at, how do we stop objectifying animals? Well, as long as objectified animals are fulfilling a need humans believe they have the right to be fulfilled, then they are going to stay objectified and humans will just build greater excuses for why they're doing it. We know they've already done that around slavery and the Holocaust and women being beaten by their husbands and girlfriends being raped. The justification of objectification goes back as far as Western civilization, it seems. A different way of asking the question "How does change happen?" is "How do we help people see that their selfishness and narcissism are unfulfilling, killing them and the planet, and that on the other side of change is something fulfilling?" You don't lose pleasure changing; you change what gives you pleasure.

Everybody says, "I don't want to give up my hamburger." Sometimes I'll just say, "Well, it's nice to know how selfish you are," which doesn't get me very far. There's this saying by the Buddha: "You don't have to carry the canoe once you've crossed the stream." So, there is the process of change, and during that process of change you probably have to learn some new recipes. The average person only really cooks eight basic recipes. You might have to learn a cheese sauce from nutritional yeast instead of from cow's milk cheese. The process of change interrupts habit. But on the other side of the process of change is a delightful way of living as well. It's not like we're saying, "Become a vegan and give up everything you enjoy." It's a transvaluation of values. We're saying there are lots of wonderful ways to live as a vegan. In *Living Among Meat Eaters* I say: "Change is hard, but not changing is just as hard." It's just that meat-eaters haven't realized it yet. They're spending so much time *not* changing—justifying why they have a right to their hamburger— they could be using all that energy changing. And they're not helped by people like Mark Bittman or Michael Pollan, who find ways to justify being carnivorous. Both of those people, and especially Pollan, have stopped viewing animals as objects. In one sense, it acknowledges some aspects of animals' sociability and animals' capacities, but they still have a human-centered view of the appetite.

What we're doing is changing two things simultaneously. We're changing the human-centered view of the appetite. We're saying,

"How you decide what you're going to eat is not something you decide just based on what you like." And we're changing what's in the basic repertoire of the average eater. We know that vegetarians eat far more diverse vegetables than the meat-eater—we're probably eating much more diverse grains and beans, we're probably aware of more herbs and spices to use. So, we're changing people on two levels, and it has to happen at the same time, and that's sometimes hard. I think people want to hold to the human-centered view of the world because it's safe and because it's secure and because it's what they were taught as children. Every one of us as a vegan is standing up to people and saying, "Your parents lied to you when you were little." We might not say that literally, but everything we're saying is saying that. People don't want to hear that.

JM: This question highlights the profundity of what animal rights advocates are ultimately seeking to do. We're not only working to get people to stop eating, wearing, and using animals. Yes, that's critical, but we're also seeking a fundamentally new way of conceptualizing power, hierarchy, and justice. We're seeking an enlightened shift in consciousness about how humans live, and relate with each other and nonhumans, in the natural world. We're seeking, in other words, a multifaceted revolution.

What this means is that our activism—in fact, every aspect of our engagement with the world around us—is necessarily marked by the incessant questioning of preexisting structures of authority as well as the concomitant quest to raise awareness of injustice in a way that is humble and respectful of the fact that everyone comes to Jesus in his own weird little way.

The hardest part of waking up every morning and banging into a world marked by conventions that you find loathsome is knowing that, in working to reshape something as basic to life as the human understanding of its place in the world, you'll never see the changes you espouse come to fruition. I don't mean to sound discouraging here, but it's true. The deeper nature of the change that animal rights activists seek will be realized, but not in our lifetime. History tends not to work that fast. Activists must take inspiration in small steps.

MB: When people see that we are all interconnected and that what happens to other people and to other animals affects them, we will be making great progress. While there are more than enough scientific data that show that animals are far more than we give them credit for—they are intelligent, adaptable, emotional beings who also display moral intelligence, or what I call "wild justice"—it's not a matter of research but a change in people's perceptions of who we are and who "they" are. We're looking at a social movement that will entail a paradigm shift in how people value the wonderful webs of nature that encompass all beings. Thomas Berry's reminder that we are all integral members of a community of subjects and that we're not merely a collection of objects is a good bumper sticker. Along these lines I'm working on a broader project with Dr. Sarah M. Bexell concerning the ways, and reasons why, people ignore nature— why we fail to act proactively when significant losses in biodiversity are staring us right in the face, why we allow critical habitat to be destroyed as we attempt to recreate or restore ecosystems that have been demolished because of a lack of concern on our part, why we over-produce (we're in the Anthropocene [epoch] and people are the main problem because there are far too many of us along with a concomitant loss of connection to other people and to nature), and how social science and conservation psychology must be brought into discussions of how we can best move ahead.

ME: Our psychological attitudes toward animals have always been of a schizophrenic nature. We care deeply about animals and don't want them to suffer, until we think that their suffering is necessary for some human benefit—even if that benefit is itself unnecessary. We then think that human interests trump the welfare of animals. For example, the overwhelming majority of Americans oppose killing animals for fur coats and oppose testing cosmetic products on animals, because they see these practices as causing animals to suffer *for no good reason*; no one in modern societies needs a fur coat to survive or stay warm, and we already have more cosmetic products than we could ever need. Causing animals to suffer for unnecessary products like furs and new cosmetics is *gratuitous*—it serves no significant human need.

I think that one of the most important and effective steps toward getting humans to stop viewing animals as "tools" and to start respecting them as conscious, sentient beings with interests is to convince people to stop eating them. When one is dining on animals three times a day, it is psychologically difficult, if not impossible, to allow oneself to think of animals as the type of being who deserves moral consideration, for if one thought that animals deserved moral consideration while continuing to eat them, then one would have to think oneself immoral for ignoring their interests and failing to show them the consideration they are due. But our attitudes toward animals change once we stop eating them. Franz Kafka aptly described this shift in attitude: "Now I can look at you in peace; I don't eat you anymore." Once one stops eating animals, one frees oneself psychologically to acknowledge that animals have interests that should be respected, because one is no longer guilty of violating those interests. This is one situation where animal liberation is human liberation.

But how does one persuade a person to stop eating animals before that person has acknowledged that animals are sentient beings who deserve moral consideration? Since most humans are only willing to recognize the interests of animals when they don't think those interests clash with their own, I think that one of the best ways to get people to stop eating animals is to provide them with cutting-edge nutritional research that documents the health problems caused by consuming meat and diary products. Once people come to realize that eating meat and other animal products has a huge downside—increased risk of coronary artery disease, stroke, obesity, diabetes mellitus, osteoporosis, and some forms of cancer—they no longer regard eating animals as being in their own interest. Once people realize that eating animals isn't in their self-interest, that realization frees them to admit that animals have interests and to act in ways consistent with this admission.

RR: Unfortunately, we are all selfish. We have to be, up to a point. Yet the whole point of morality is to improve our treatment of *others*. In the definition of "others," of course, I include nonhuman animals. Darwin pointed out that we don't differ qualitatively from the other animals, only in degree. It has taken a hundred years for Darwin's moral message to sink in. As the other animals are our evolutionary brethren we should treat them as such. Yet we go on being obsessed, small-mindedly, with our own species. Such speciesism is as absurd and unjustified as racism or sexism. I have seen education and media support substantially eradicate racism by, say, 50 percent in 40 years in Britain. Let's hope the same will happen with speciesism.

What lessons can animal advocates learn from other social justice movements, such as women's suffrage, the abolition of human slavery, and the struggle for civil rights?
CJA: Well, let's talk about women's suffrage for a moment. In 1848 Elizabeth Cady Stanton was one of the people who attended a meeting of largely middle-class white women in upstate New York. They issued a series of resolutions, which was modeled on the Declaration of Independence. She penned in at the last minute the right to suffrage—the right to vote. In 1848, this was a highly controversial thing, to ask for that. The husband got the woman's property when they married; he could divorce her, but she couldn't divorce him; she got the kids. There were a lot of problems with men abusing alcohol at this point. So many issues, but suffrage was the one that was seen as so radical and impossible. What happened after the Civil War was that they decided they would concentrate on suffrage as the first plank of many that were needed for women's change. By the time women got the right to vote—which was after

World War I, and some people viewed it as women got the right to vote as a reward for their World War I work—it had become so associated with women's rights that many people stopped working for other things. The Equal Rights Amendment was introduced in 1923, but we still don't have an Equal Rights Amendment in the United States. It did not pass at the state-ratification level in the 1980s. So, one thing for us to learn is that we should never assume that any of those movements have succeeded. Women are not yet accorded equality with men in the United States and in most countries. We should never say, "Oh, that's all taken care of." We should never assume that. For instance, are people reconciled to factory farming by believing that cows and pigs are better treated in states where we've eliminated the gestation crate or other welfare-related changes? Does it reconcile people to animals' oppression?

People can find a way to justify almost anything. So we have to be careful when we go to argue about some aspect of animal oppression to understand how manipulatively self-justificatory people can be. Human slavery was justified and is still being justified. That we've got human slavery throughout the world right now, predominantly women and children, is cautionary. It's always one step forward and two steps back. And I don't say that pessimistically. I think that if we understood that, that would be an optimistic thing, that it's only two steps back.

I think the other thing to learn is that oppressors really like having hierarchies. Hierarchies feed oppression because it allows for valuation: those at the top are more valued than those at the bottom. Oppressors like hierarchies that keep animals on the bottom because then you can do to humans what you do to animals if you say that the humans are like the animals. So it feeds oppression to have animal objectification. And it's not just animal oppression that gets fed by that hierarchy; it's whatever people are being lowered, lowers the status of animals. People of color, working-class women—it depends on the occasion and what the oppression requires.

HH: First, that moral progress is a long slog. Women and people of color still do not have economic and political parity in the United States. Second, when it comes to the biggest source of animal suffering, our desire for cheap meat, I suggest that animal advocates look to the anti-smoking movement rather than social justice movements. The logic of animal liberation is based primarily on fairness. For the most part, this has not motivated a huge number of people to stop eating meat. I suggest that activists work on framing meat as: (a) bad for your health; and (b) a disgusting habit. I expect more people gave up beef when they realized that beef cattle in feedlots spent their day wading knee deep in feces than were moved by the "meat is murder" argument.

JM: A lot. We need to study these movements in depth. Doing so would drive home a number of critical lessons, but I'll just mention two that I've learned (as a professional historian) by examining the history of social reform in the United States.

First, the single most debilitating factor for every movement you mention came from within. Internal factions that are deemed irreconcilable have systematically weakened the message and effectiveness of these reform movements. While differences are important, and dialogue is healthy, factionalism is counterproductive. Plus, internal strife is typically more about the narcissism of small differences than fundamental disagreements over basic issues. In any case, infighting should be avoided at all costs. (Of course, it never is avoided, but I still feel it should be said.)

Second, advocates should never fear articulating a vision that will be perceived by the conventional wisdom as too radical. You can't be too radical about seeking justice. Again, in every movement you mention above, there were voices that at first were dismissed as too impractical. A hundred years later, their impractical vision was commonly accepted. The lesson is important: if someone hadn't been bold enough to state that message, it would never have come to fruition. Those who seek a middle ground approach to change need to be careful about dismissing the more radical voices in their midst. And the radical voices need to be tolerant of those who go about matters more pragmatically.

MB: Many. First, we can all see that the hard work ultimately pays off and that keeping positive and focused is critical. We also can see that while reactive social movements can work, seeing problems brewing and jumping on them in a proactive way will make the work we need to do easier. It's always easier to prevent fires from starting than to put them out.

RR: In many ways, although unsung, the animal protection movement since 1970 has achieved far more than some other social justice movements. Although largely ignored by the media and political commentators, we have achieved improved attitudes and legislation globally. Considering the continued speciesism of many politicians and media people—and the total speciesism of most governments and all churches—that's not bad. Of course, there is still a mountain range to climb. The churches are, frankly, beneath contempt in their callousness towards God's creatures.

What role, if any, do you think incrementalism plays in the animal rights movement? Do you feel the "welfare" message weakens the "abolition" message?
CJA: I saw recently that Steve Best was challenging Gary Francione* to a debate. And I thought, this is so macho. Like it's one or the other, either/or. "I'm going to prevail; I'm going to beat you to a pulp philosophically." I don't know that I want to reduce anything that's part of trying to create the kind of human beings we want to be. I really respect websites that look at the myths of "humane" meat, because I don't think there could ever be humane meat. I would not participate

---

*Steve Best and Gary Francione are outspoken university professors who strongly support the idea of total liberation for animals.

or accept any movement that would posit that. On the other hand, I think suffering is a terrible thing, and who am I to say that a reduction in suffering is measurable or condemnable? I don't know. I think sometimes our powerlessness makes us flail against each other, which in the feminist movement is called horizontal hostility. I think debates are healthy within a movement. I think personalizing the debates and trying to destroy the people who share your beliefs is not healthy, and I don't think we ever need to reduce a debate to be so absolutely about an individual that we then disown that individual. We've *all* changed. Most of the people in this movement did not grow up vegan. We are our own testimony to the power of change, and I don't think we should ever forget that. I'm for multiplicity. If we were able to model that multiplicity, we could perhaps be more inviting.

HH: Incrementalism plays a huge role. The fact is that most people have trouble giving up meat. Indeed, nearly 70 percent of self-described "vegetarians" do occasionally eat flesh, and three out of four vegetarians will eventually revert to omnivory. People are put off by what they perceive as the self-righteousness of purists who say that unless you are a vegan, you have no right to criticize other forms of animal cruelty. I think that activists would do well to encourage people to take whatever steps they can to reduce suffering. These baby steps sometimes open the door for bigger changes in lifestyle.

JM: The politics of animal emancipation are complex. On the one hand, we could argue that the more internal disagreement that rages within the animal liberation movement the better. James Madison, the father of the US Constitution, promoted a "theory of faction" in which he envisioned a political milieu where "interests would counter interests" as the project of republicanism lurched ahead. He viewed the chaos of dispute as healthy. On the other hand, when faction reaches a point at which the center cannot hold—or, to put it differently, the ultimate goal gets lost in internecine (and often human-centric) disagreements over tactics—it undermines any potential that disagreement will be healthy.

When it comes to promoting animal rights, I'll confess to being on the fence over the question of approach—and that's likely where I'll remain, for reasons that I hope will be clear. Radical abolitionism obviously has the strongest appeal to me. However, I'm not prepared to dismiss "gradualist" or other peripheral tactics (health/ environment) out of hand.

While the abolitionist message is the most bold and direct approach, both tactics have a place in the larger quest to eliminate systematic and intentional animal exploitation. There are already so few voices supporting the interests of animals that it seems counter-productive to squelch any particular voice over tactical disagreements. I certainly think that efforts to enlarge cages in factory farms—or promote vegan conversion on strictly health grounds—are shortsighted and symbolic at best. That said, I'm willing to tolerate shortsighted and symbolic methods rather than waste time trying to convince these groups that my approach is morally superior. This is called pragmatism.

A useful analogy to consider when pondering the problem of tactics is the abolition of slavery in the United States. There were gradualists and there were abolitionists. They disagreed on tactics. Often viciously. However, in the end, both groups played critical roles in ending slavery as an institution. This point is important for animal advocates to recognize.

The gradualists were critical in ending northern slavery—yes, there was northern slavery before 1830 (25 percent of New York City was slave in 1776, for example). Most northern states ended slavery gradually as a state constitutional measure—New Jersey allowed slavery well into the 1820s. The decision to end slavery had nothing to do with the immorality of slavery, but rather basic economics— northern labor did not want to compete with slave labor for jobs.

The abolitionists, of course, ended slavery nationally. They did so on solid moral grounds and were led by men and women who we consider today to be heroes: William Lloyd Garrison, Frederick Douglass, Harriet Beecher Stowe, John Brown, etc. They infused the gradualist approach with moral fervor, changed the nature of the debate, and turned slavery into a barbaric relic of the past. While abolitionists disagreed with gradualist tactics, in the end the abolitionists and the gradualists each played critical roles in ending slavery.

This little history lesson might be useful to keep in mind as vegan activists go about tearing into each other over the best way to reach the finish line. Failure to do so is to place our own interests ahead of the animals we want to help. Let's have our debates, but let's also keep them from derailing the project of improving the lives of animals.

MB: I think incrementalism clearly is important and forces us to be patient, very patient, as we work to make the world a better place for animals. We just need to accept that social movements take time and we must look to the social sciences in order to understand how long-lasting social and attitude changes develop and how they're maintained. I'm not sure how the "welfare" message weakens the "abolition" message, but I have seen people make the slide "to the left," if you will, and begin by being concerned with welfare and seeing that "good welfare is not good enough." I'm careful not to push people too far too fast and have seen remarkable shifts in attitude and action with time and by not being in the face of people who disagree with me. It's best to confront the position a person takes, not the person themselves. Once you put someone on the defensive, the exchange is over.

ME: The question is important and a hotly-debated one among those working to help animals. Animal welfare activists want to improve the lot of farmed animals now by improving their living conditions now. Abolitionists insist that these incremental improvements in animal husbandry techniques only serve to further entrench the view that animals are property and a mere means to our ends. Abolitionists also tend to think that if people believe that the animals had a good life on the farm, they will feel less guilty about eating them.

The first thing to realize about the question of whether or not incrementalism helps or hurts the animal rights movement is that the question is an empirical one. It is not knowable *a priori*. We simply don't know *a priori* whether improving the conditions in which farmed animals are raised will further entrench the view that animals are mere means, or whether it will have the opposite effect of getting people to put two and two together and concluding: "If animals deserve so much moral consideration that we owe them humane living conditions, perhaps they deserve so much consideration that we shouldn't kill them at all." I'm not claiming that the latter reaction is any more likely than the former. I am claiming the question is an empirical one that cannot be resolved in our armchairs. We will simply have to see whether passing measures like Prop 2 makes people less concerned with animal well-being or more concerned to the point of stopping eating them entirely.

I wish both sides of this volatile and often divisive debate would remember that while animal welfare activists and animal rights activists don't share every goal, they do share one goal: both want to improve the lot of animals by reducing the amount of human-generated animal suffering and exploitation in the world. Instead of focusing on their common goals, animal rightists and animal welfarists often clash over the best way to help animals with the end result that the animals lose.

Just as other social justice movements did not gain widespread appeal overnight, it's unrealistic to think that we are going to abolish animal agriculture in one fell swoop. Sadly, animal agriculture is going to be around for the foreseeable future, which means that billions of animals will continue to be housed in factory farms. If we can't prevent that now, at least we can take steps to improve the quality of their lives while they are here. The fight for civil rights and women's rights took decades of continuously struggling for the just treatment of minorities and women. First, minorities and women fought for and won the right to vote alongside white males. Then, they fought for and won the right to attend the same colleges and universities as white males. Though we have not wiped out all forms of discrimination directed toward minorities and women, look how far we have come! Lots of small steps got us to this more just society. For the sake of animals, I hope that we refuse to let the best be the enemy of the good. We can take steps to improve animals' lives now, while working to end all forms of animal exploitation in the future. These goals are not mutually exclusive; they are cut from the same cloth.

RR: Not at all. One has to fight right across the board from a range of positions and using a range of non-violent tactics.

Notes

Introduction

1. Gerald Carson, *Men, Beasts, and Gods: A History of Cruelty and Kindness to Animals* (New York, NY: Charles Scribner's Sons, 1972), 4.
2. Jennifer Viegas, "Chickens worry about the future," *Discovery News*, July 15, 2005.
3. Charles Q. Choi, "Ravens Use 'Hand' Gestures to Communicate," *Scientific American*, November 29, 2011.
4. Fiona MacRae, "Elephants grieve for lost relatives," *Daily Mail*, August 8, 2006.
5. Rowan Hooper, "Death in dolphins: do they understand they are mortal?" *New Scientist*, Issue 2828, September 1, 2011.
6. David Brown, "A new model of empathy: the rat," *Washington Post*, December 8, 2011.
7. "Chickens are capable of feeling empathy, scientists believe," *Telegraph*, March 9, 2011.
8. Steve Connor, "Captive chimps choose to help their neighbours," *The Independent*, August 9, 2011.
9. Rob Waugh, "Chimps may have the ability to understand language too—humans just get more practice, say researchers," *Daily Mail*, November 1, 2011.
10. Justin Nobel, "Do Animals Commit Suicide? A Scientific Debate," *TIME*, March 19, 2010.
11. Jason Castro, "Do Bees Have Feelings?" *Scientific American*, August 2, 2011.

Chapter 1

Henry Pace is quoted from *Diet for a New America* by John Robbins (Stillpoint Publishing, 1987).

1. Chris Brooke, "Larry, the 'luckiest' lamb alive," *Daily Mail*, March 17, 2006.
2. Lucy Thornton, "Saved from the Chop," *Mirror*, March 17, 2006.
3. Chris Brooke, "Larry, the 'luckiest' lamb alive," *Daily Mail*, March 17,

2006.

4. "Livestock's Long Shadow: Environmental Issues and Options," released by the Food and Agriculture Organization of the United Nations (FAO), November 29, 2006. Although the report claimed that the meat industry surpasses transportation as the world's leading contributor of greenhouse gases (18 percent vs. 15 percent), one of the authors, Dr. Frank Mitloehner of the University of California–Davis, has since identified a flaw in how emissions were compared. To calculate the impact of animal agriculture, the FAO report's authors relied on a method called life-cycle assessment, which charts the emissions of every element of raising meat, beginning with the carbon costs of clearing land for planting the grain the animals eat, and following it until a package of beef is sitting in the supermarket. Dr. Mitloehner says the figure for transportation-related emissions they used only counted those produced when vehicles burn fossil fuels, not the full production cycle of petroleum. This in no way undermines the report's findings that nearly one-fifth of human-induced greenhouse gas emissions are attributable to animal agriculture.

5. Jonathan Safran Foer, *Eating Animals* (New York, NY: Little, Brown and Company, 2009), 92–93.

6. Gene Baur, *Farm Sanctuary: Changing Hearts and Minds About Animals and Food* (New York, NY: Simon & Schuster, Inc., 2008), 150. Reprinted with the permission of Touchstone, a division of Simon & Schuster, Inc.

7. http://farmusa.org/statistics11.html

8. Karen Davis, *Prisoned Chickens, Poisoned Eggs: An Inside Look at the Modern Poultry Industry*, revised edition (Summertown, TN: Book Publishing Co., 2009), v.

9. Forty-seven billion chickens divided by 365 days a year = 128,767,123 chickens per day; 128,767,123 divided by 24 hours = 5,365,296 per hour; 5,365,296 divided by 60 minutes = 89,421 per minute; and 89,421 divided by 60 seconds = 1,490 chickens killed every second. See http://farmusa.org/statistics11.html for global slaughter data.

10. www.humanesociety.org/news/resources/research/stats_slaughter

_totals.html

11. William Grimes, "If Chickens Are So Smart, Why Aren't They Eating Us?" *The New York Times*, January 12, 2003.

12. John Fraser Hart, *The Changing Scale of American Agriculture* (Charlottesville, VA: University of Virginia Press, 2003), 114.

13. Sally Kneidel and Sara Kate Kneidel, *Veggie Revolution: Smart Choices for a Healthy Body and a Healthy Planet* (Golden, CO: Fulcrum Publishing, 2005), 74–75.

14. Australian Chicken Meat Federation: www.chicken.org.au

15. Phil Brooke, "Defra Consultation on Proposed Legislation and Codes for Broiler Chickens," Compassion in World Farming, April 2009.

16. Correspondence with Ian Duncan, chair of animal welfare in the Department of Animal and Poultry Science at the University of Guelph (Canada), September 16, 2009. According to Dr. Duncan, males are now typically slaughtered after just 38 days, while females, who grow slightly slower, are killed at about 42 days of age.

17. Martin Blaser, "Antibiotic overuse: Stop the killing of beneficial bacteria," *Nature*, Volume 476, August 25, 2011.

18. Tom Philpott, "The Meat Industry Now Consumes Four-Fifths of All Antibiotics," *Mother Jones*, February 8, 2013. www.motherjones.com/tom-philpott/2013/02/meat-industry-still-gorging-antibiotics. Also noteworthy: Upon accepting the Nobel Prize in 1945, Alexander Fleming, who discovered penicillin, warned that exposing microbes to concentrations of the antibiotic insufficient to kill them would merely produce penicillin-resistant bacteria.

19. www.wired.com/wiredscience/2011/11/eu-farm-antibiotic-use/

20. Rob Stein, "Drug-Resistant Staph Germ's Toll Is Higher than Thought," *Washington Post*, October 17, 2007.

21. Andrew E. Waters, Tania Contente-Cuomo, Jordan Buchhagen, Cindy M. Liu, Lindsey Watson, Kimberly Pearce, Jeffrey T. Foster, Jolene Bowers, Elizabeth M. Driebe, David M. Engelthaler, Paul S. Keim, and Lance B. Price, "Multidrug-Resistant Staphylococcus Aureus in US Meat and Poultry," *Clinical Infectious Diseases*, April 15, 2011.

22. www.meatami.com/ht/a/GetDocumentAction/i/56994

23. Lance B. Price, Marc Stegger, Henrik Hasman, Maliha Aziz, Jesper Larsen, Paal Skytt Andersen, Talima Pearson, Andrew E. Waters, Jeffrey T. Foster, James Schupp, John Gillece, Elizabeth Driebe, Cindy M. Liu, Burkhard Springer, Irena Zdovc, Antonio Battisti, Alessia Franco, Jacek Żmudzki, Stefan Schwarz, Patrick Butaye, Eric Jouy, Constanca Pomba, Concepción Porrero, Raymond Ruimy, Tara C. Smith, D. Ashley Robinson, J. Scott Weese, Carmen Sofia Arriola, Fangyou Yu, Frederic Laurent, Paul Keim, Robert Skov, and Frank M. Aarestrup, "*Staphylococcus aureus* CC398: host adaptation and emergence of methicillin resistance in livestock," *mBio*, February 21, 2012, Volume 3, Number 1.

24. "The Problem of Antibiotic Resistance," National Institute of Allergy and Infectious Diseases, National Institutes of Health fact sheet, Office of Communications and Public Liaison, April 2004. www3.niaid.nih.gov/topics/AntimicrobialResistance/default.htm_

25. Michelle Roberts, "Europe 'losing' superbugs battle," *BBC News*, April 6, 2011.

26. www.gpo.gov/fdsys/pkg/FR-2011-12-22/html/2011-32775.htm

27. Dale Keiger, "Farmacology," *The Johns Hopkins Magazine*, June 2009.

28. Gardiner Harris, "Steps Set for Livestock Antibiotic Ban," *The New York Times*, March 23, 2012.

29. Gardiner Harris and Denise Grady, "Pfizer Suspends Sales of Chicken Drug with Arsenic," *The New York Times*, June 8, 2011.

30. Donald L. Sparks, *Advances in Agronomy*, volume 87 (San Diego, CA: Elsevier Academic Press, 2005), 7.

31. Amy R. Sapkota, Frank C. Curriero, Kristen E. Gibson, Kellogg J. Schwab, "Antibiotic-resistant enterococci and fecal indicators in surface water and groundwater impacted by a concentrated Swine feeding operation," *Environmental Health Perspectives*, July 2007.

32. Donald D. Bell, Mack O. North, and William Daniel Weaver, *Commercial Chicken Meat and Egg Production*, fifth edition (New York, NY: Springer, 2002), 243.

33. Sigrid Boersma, "Managing rapid growth rate in broilers," *World Poultry*, volume 17, No 8. 2001.

34. Conversation with Paul Shapiro, July 30, 2012.

35. From his blog post "The Amnesia-ville Horror," June 12, 2012: http://james-mcwilliams.com/?p=1621

36. Correspondence with Ian Duncan, September 3, 2009.

37. Correspondence with Dominic Elfick, director of research and development for Aviagen, August 16, 2009.

38. Correspondence from Suzanne Millman to Pattrice Jones of the Eastern Shore Chicken Sanctuary, May 22, 2002.

39. Neville G. Gregory and Temple Grandin, *Animal Welfare and Meat Production* (Wallingford, UK: CABI, 2007), 17.

40. Bernard E. Rollin, *Farm Animal Welfare: Social, Bioethical, and Research Issues* (Hoboken, NJ: Wiley, 2003), 119.

41. Correspondence with Ian Duncan, September 3, 2009.

42. *Unnatural Breeding Techniques and Results in Modern Turkey Production: A Farm Sanctuary Research Report*, January 2007.

43. Ibid.

44. Andrew F. Smith, *The Turkey: An American Story* (Champaign, IL: University of Illinois Press, 2006), 97.

45. Karen Davis, *More Than a Meal: The Turkey in History, Myth, Ritual, and Reality* (New York, NY: Lantern Books, 2001), 75.

46. Jim Mason, "In the Turkey Breeding Factory," *Poultry Press*, Fall–Winter 1994.

47. Ibid.

48. "Artificial Insemination," *The Merck Veterinary Manual*, 2008. www.merckvetmanual.com

49. Jim Mason, "In the Turkey Breeding Factory."

50. Barry H. Thorp, "Diseases of the musculoskeletal system," from *Poultry Diseases*, 6h edition, edited by Mark Pattison (Philadelphia, PA: Elsevier Limited, 2008), 484.

51. In July 2011, The Humane Society of the United States brokered a deal with the US egg industry that would have them jointly seeking federal legislation to improve the housing conditions of egg-laying hens. Once fully implemented at the national level, actual floor space for each bird would increase from the current standard of 67 square inches to 124

square inches for chickens who lay white eggs and 144 square inches for larger birds who lay brown eggs. The move to these "enriched colony" cages, with perches and nesting boxes, would have a 15- to 18-year phase-in period, however, and there is no guarantee the legislation will be enacted.

52. PLM Van Horne and TJ Achterbosch, "Animal welfare in poultry production systems: Impact of European Union standards on world trade," Agricultural Economics Research Institute, Wageningen University and Research Center, the Netherlands, 2007.

53. Review of the Welfare of Animals in Agriculture: Hearing Before the Subcommittee on Livestock, Dairy, and Poultry of the Committee on Agriculture, House of Representatives, One Hundred Tenth Congress, first session, May 8, 2007, 129.

54. Associated Press, "'Zombie Chickens' Hatch Debate Over Older Chickens' Fate," San Jose Mercury News, December 5, 2006.

55. Page 20 of the AVMA Guidelines on Euthanasia (June 2007) states that: "Maceration is believed to be equivalent to cervical dislocation [necking breaking] and cranial compression [bashing in the skull] as to time element, and is considered to be an acceptable means of euthanasia for newly hatched poultry by the Federation of Animal Science Societies, Agriculture Canada, World Organization for Animal Health (OIE), and European Union." Animal rights advocates have long criticized the AVMA's Animal Welfare Committee for its membership of pro-industry veterinarians who seem to have more interest in hunting, trapping, rodeos, and other forms of cruelty than in the humane treatment of animals.

56. Statement by Karen Davis at www.mercyforanimals.org/hatch ery/expert-statements.asp

57. Conversation with Nathan Runkle, December 11, 2009. MFA's investigation took place inside Hy-Line International in Spencer, Iowa. According to Nathan, the industry is trying to develop a method to identify male chicks while they're still inside the eggs so they can kill them before they hatch.

58. Jerry Hopkins, Extreme Cuisine: The Weird & Wonderful Foods That

People Eat (North Clarendon, VT: Tuttle Publishing, 2004), 164–165.

59. Margaret Magat, "Balut: Fertilized Duck Eggs and Their Role in Filipino Culture," *Western Folklore*, Volume 61, No. 1, 2002.

60. Ibid.

61. Conversation with Karen Steuer, director of government relations for the Pew Environmental Group, October 19, 2011.

62. Consumers Union, "Downright Scary! Cows Fed Chicken Feces, Recycled Remains," press release, October 29, 2009. From www.consumersunion.org/pub/core_food_safety/015272.html

63. W. Michael Scheld, William A. Craig, and James M. Hughes, *Emerging Infections*, Volume 2 (Herndon, VA: American Society for Microbiology, 1998), 2.

64. After the United States encountered its first case of BSE in 2003, the FDA halted the practice of feeding poultry litter to beef cattle; some scientists expressed concern that the infectious agents of BSE could be passed to cattle from spilled feed or manure. In response, the FDA mandated the removal of all cattle tissues that have been shown to carry infectious agents of BSE (the brain, trigeminal ganglia, tonsils, spinal cord, dorsal root ganglion, and distal ileum of the small intestine) from poultry diets, and poultry litter was again approved as a feedstuff for beef cattle in 2005.

65. Conversation with Dr. Michael Greger, November 2, 2009.

66. Jerry Hirsch, "FDA urged to ban feeding of chicken feces to cattle," *Los Angeles Times*, October 31, 2009.

67. Correspondence with Steve Roach, November 10, 2009.

68. According to the Physicians Committee for Responsible Medicine, chicken manure often contains *Campylobacter* and *Salmonella* bacteria, which can cause disease in humans, as well as veterinary drug residues, intestinal parasites, and toxic heavy metals such as arsenic, lead, cadmium, and mercury. These bacteria and toxins are passed on to the cattle via poultry litter and can be ingested by humans who consume meat that was contaminated by feces during slaughter.

69. Correspondence with Steve Roach, March 9, 2010.

70. Jerry Hirsch, "FDA urged to ban feeding of chicken feces to cattle," *Los

Angeles Times, October 31, 2009. The FDA banned the use of poultry litter as cattle feed in 1967. They revoked the ban in 1980, turning the responsibility for regulating the substance over to state agricultural agencies, though few monitor it.

71. Stephen Chapman, "Madness About Mad Cow Disease," *Chicago Tribune*, April 26, 2006.

72. Sam Hananel, "Government asks court to block wider testing for mad cow," *USA Today*, May 9, 2008.

73. US Recall News, March 10, 2011. www.usrecallnews.com/2011 /03/12485.html

74. Michael Moss, "The Burger That Shattered Her Life," *The New York Times*, October 3, 2009.

75. "Feeding Poultry Litter to Beef Cattle," Akey, Inc. www.akey. com/ruminant/beef_briefs_feedlot/fb%20feeding%20poultry%20litter %20to%20beef%20cattle.pdf (Akey is a nutritional services company that assists the feed, livestock, and poultry industries.)

76. Conversation with Dr. Michael Greger, November 2, 2009.

77. Conversation with Rick Dove, October 26, 2011.

78. Conversation with Dr. JoAnn Burkholder, October 27, 2011.

79. David Foster Wallace, "Consider the Lobster," *Gourmet*, August 2004. In the issue, Editor-in-Chief Ruth Reichl of the now-defunct magazine calls Wallace's feature "hilarious, thought-provoking, very uncomfortable," and admits: "I wasn't quite prepared for this." Wallace, a huge writing talent who tragically took his own life in 2008, no doubt secured an equally huge paycheck for writing the piece, and *Gourmet* would have had to pay him whether they ran the article or not. After the issue came out, Wallace told *The Boston Globe* that Reichl would not allow him to identify PETA's video *Meet Your Meat* by name. "My impression was that Ruth absolutely loathed PETA, and some of their advertisers do, too," he said. (Alex Beam, "Lobster tale lands writer in hot water," *The Boston Globe*, August 5, 2004.)

80. A study published in 2013 found that crustaceans experience the world, including pain, much like humans do. See Barry Magee and Robert W. Elwood, "Shock avoidance by discrimination learning in the

shore crab (*Carcinus maenas*) is consistent with a key criterion for pain," *Journal of Experimental Biology*, Volume 216, Issue 3, February 1, 2013.

81. According to a report by the Food and Agriculture Organization of the United Nations, global marine catches have leveled off, hovering at around 85 million tons per year. A study by fishcount.org.uk did attempt to calculate how many wild fish are caught each year; they estimate the number to be 1 trillion (see Alison Mood, "Worse things happen at sea: the welfare of wild-caught fish," fishcount.org.uk, August 2010).

82. Correspondence with Dawn Carr, February 11, 2010.

83. Robert R. Stickney, *Aquaculture: An Introductory Text*, second edition (Wallingford, UK: CABI, 2009), 1.

84. Brian Halweil, *Farming Fish for the Future* (Washington, DC: Worldwatch Institute, 2008), 13.

85. Elisabeth Rosenthal, "Another Side of Tilapia, the Perfect Factory Fish," *The New York Times*, May 2, 2011.

86. Food & Water Watch, "How Can Farmed Salmon Impact Your Health and the Environment," June 2009. http://www.foodandwater watch.org/factsheet/how-can-farmed-salmon-impact-your-health-and-the-environment/

87. Adam Anson, "Trailing the Answer to Farmed Fish Escapes," *TheFishSite.com*, April 2009. www.thefishsite.com/articles/631/trailing-the-answer-to-farmed-fish-escapes

88. Philip McGinnity, Eleanor Jennings, Elvira deEyto, Norman Allott, Patrick Samuelsson, Gerard Rogan, Ken Whelan, and Tom Cross, "Impact of naturally spawning captive-bred Atlantic salmon on wild populations: depressed recruitment and increased risk of climate-mediated extinction," *Proceedings of the Royal Society B: Biological Sciences*, July 2009.

89. Eva B. Thorstad, Ian A. Fleming, Philip McGinnity, Doris Soto, Vidar Wennevik, and Fred Whoriskey, "Incidence and impacts of escaped farmed Atlantic salmon *Salmo salar* in nature," World Wildlife Fund, 2008. ftp://ftp.fao.org/FI/DOCUMENT/aquaculture/aj272e00.pdf

90. Øystein Aas, Anders Klemetsen, Sigurd Einum, and Jostein Skurdal,

editors, *Atlantic Salmon Ecology* (Oxford, UK: Blackwell Publishing Ltd., 2011), 268.

91. Theresa M. Bert, editor, *Ecological and Genetic Implications of Aquaculture Activities* (Dordrecht, The Netherlands: Springer, 2007), 5–8.

92. Jeffrey Moussaieff Masson, *The Face on Your Plate: The Truth About Food* (New York, NY: WW Norton & Company, 2009), 123.

93. Marion Nestle, *What to Eat* (New York, NY: North Point Press, 2006), 209.

94. Robert R. Stickney, *Aquaculture: An Introductory Text* (Wallingford, UK: CABI, 2005), 167. Species commonly stripped of their eggs include carp, Atlantic and Pacific halibut, rainbow trout, striped bass, and Atlantic salmon.

95. "Spawning," Virginia Institute of Marine Science, College of William & Mary, http://web.vims.edu/vsc/spawning/

96. Nan Unklesbay, *World Food and You* (Florence, KY: Routledge, 1992), 199.

97. Malden C. Nesheim and Ann L. Yaktine, *Seafood Choices: Balancing Benefits and Risks* (Washington, DC: The National Academies Press, 2007), 42.

98. *The State of World Fisheries and Aquaculture 2012*, Food and Agriculture Organization of the United Nations FAO Fisheries and Aquaculture Department, Rome, 2012. www.fao.org/docrep/016/i2727e/i2727 e00.htm

99. Andrew Purvis, "Farmed Fish," *Observer*, May 11, 2003. According to animal activist Maneka Gandhi, founder of India's People for Animals, it can take up to 15 minutes for a fish to suffocate.

100. Maneka Gandhi, "Hazards of fish factories," *Bihar Times*, October 20, 2009.

101. The Humane Society of the United States, "An HSUS Report: The Welfare of Animals in the Aquaculture Industry," 2008.

102. A. Ardura, JL Horreo, E. Hernández, A. Jardon, IG Pola, JL Martínez, E. García-Vázquez, "Forensic DNA analysis reveals use of high trophic level marine fish in commercial aquaculture fish meals," *Fisheries*

Research, volume 115, March 2012.

103. Paul Roberts, *The End of Food* (New York, NY: Houghton Mifflin Harcourt Publishing Co., 2009), 270.

104. Mark Bittman, "A Seafood Snob Ponders the Future of Fish," *The New York Times,* November 15, 2008. To be precise, tunas are not farmed, but ranched—they are corralled from the wild and brought into tethered pens. Apparently, no one has been able to raise tuna from eggs.

105. Tom Philpott, "Taras Grescoe on factory salmon farming," *Grist,* July 15, 2009. www.grist.org/article/2009-07-15-taras-grescoe-on-factory-salmon-farming/

106. "Marine Aquaculture in the United States: Environmental Impacts and Policy Options" Pew Oceans Commission, June 2001.

107. Marian Burros, "Issues of Purity and Pollution Leave Farmed Salmon Looking Less Rosy," *The New York Times,* May 28, 2003. Salmon farmers even have the option of choosing the shade of pink they want their fish to be from a color chart called the SalmoFan, made by Swiss chemical giant Hoffmann-La Roche; colors range from #20 (pale salmon pink) to #34 (bright orange red).

108. www.marineharvest.com/en/Systempages/Global-leftmenu/FAQ/#predators

109. www.marineharvest.com/en/Systempages/Global-leftmenu/FAQ

110. Correspondence with John Robins, February 7, 2010.

111. Adam Yamaguchi and Zach Slobig, "Can bluefin tuna farms work?" *Los Angeles Times,* July 21, 2011.

112. www.bbc.co.uk/news/world-asia-20919306

113. Eli C. Minkoff and Pamela J. Baker, *Biology Today: An Issues Approach,* second edition (New York, NY: Garland Publishing, 2001), 606.

114. H. Bruce Franklin, "Net Losses: Declaring War on the Menhaden," *Mother Jones,* March/April 2006.

115. Paul Greenberg, "A Fish Oil Story," *The New York Times,* December 15, 2009.

116. H. Bruce Franklin, *The Most Important Fish in the Sea: Menhaden and America* (Washington, DC: Island Press, 2007), 5–6.

117. Patrick Lynch, "Whether Fish, Forests or Fires, the Issues Are All

Heated," *Daily Press* (Newport News, Virginia), March 18, 2007.

118. G. Tyler Miller and Scott Spoolman, *Living in the Environment: Principles, Connections, and Solutions* (Belmont, CA: Brooks/Cole, 2009), 96.

119. Ken Kieke, "Shark's Fin: No Longer on the Menu," www.culture.tw, September 15, 2008; and Frederick J. Simoons, *Food in China: A Cultural and Historical Inquiry* (Boca Raton, FL: CRC Press, Inc., 1991), 432.

120. Liang Qiwen, "Watch out for Shark Fin Soup," *China Daily*, May 21, 2005.

121. Correspondence with Erik Brush, May 16, 2010. A 2012 study estimated that 100 million sharks are killed every year (see Boris Worm, Brendal Davis, Lisa Kettemer, Christine A. Ward-Paige, Demian Chapman, Michael R. Heithaus, Steven T. Kessel, and Samuel H. Gruber, "Global catches, exploitation rates, and rebuilding options for sharks," *Marine Policy*, December 21, 2012).

122. Conversation with Randall Arauz, May 3, 2010.

123. World Wildlife Fund bycatch fact sheet, June 2009: http://wwf.panda.org/?166941/bycatch-factsheet

124. Conversation with Randall Arauz, May 3, 2010.

125. Source: www.hsus.org/web-files/PDF/hsi/shark-finning-regulations-2010.pdf. Shark fins can be imported into some countries that ban shark finning, such as the US, if the entire animal was caught and used.

126. Source: Animal Welfare Institute, "Sharks at Risk" brochure, www.awionline.org.

127. *Survey on shark consumption habits and attitudes in Hong Kong*, University of Hong Kong Social Sciences Research Centre and BLOOM, April 2011.

128. www.cites.org/eng/news/pr/2013/20130314_cop16.php

129. Peter Trutanich, "Eastern Tropical Pacific tuna fisheries," *INFOFISH International*, April 2005.

130. *Consumer Reports*, "What 'dolphin safe' means," June 2001.

131. The bottlenose dolphin, Hector's dolphin, Indo-Pacific-humpback dolphin, Indus River dolphin, Irrawaddy dolphin, spinner dolphin,

spotted dolphin, and Yangtze River dolphin are among the many cetacean species whose populations have declined or are threatened.

132. Jay Alabaster, "Hayden Panettiere in Japan to Aid Dolphins," *Associated Press*, March 26, 2010.

133. Boyd Harnell, "Eyewitness to slaughter in Taiji's killing coves," *The Japan Times*, February 14, 2007.

134. Boyd Harnell, "Eyewitness to slaughter in Taiji's killing coves."

135. Dolphins are killed in other remote Japanese bays, including those at Futo, Ito, Izu, and Nago—as well as in Peru, the Solomon Islands, and the Faroe Islands—but Taiji's "drive hunt" remains the most notorious.

136. Larry Rohter, "In a Killing Cove, Siding with Dolphins," *The New York Times*, July 16, 2009.

137. Patricia Thomson, "Exposing a Secret Slaughter: *The Cove*," *American Cinematographer*, August 2009.

138. Andrew O'Hehir, "Who Killed Flipper?" *Salon.com*, January 22, 2009.

139. Richard "Ric" O'Barry, CNN, September 18, 2008.

140. Richard O'Barry, with Keith Coulbourn, *Behind the Dolphin Smile* (New York, NY: St. Martin's Press, 1988), 13–14.

141. "EWA Calls For Export Ban on Horses, Cites Chemical Poisoning," http://horsebackmagazine.com/hb/archives/9209, June 2, 2011.

142. Larry Rohter, "In a Killing Cove, Siding with Dolphins," *The New York Times*, July 16, 2009.

143. Not all animals are required by law to be humanely slaughtered, however. In the US, for example, the federal Humane Methods of Slaughter Act specifically excludes "poultry," which means the overwhelming majority of animals killed for food—chickens and, to a lesser extent, turkeys, ducks, and geese—are exempt from the law and can be mistreated in the extreme, provided the abuse is considered "standard practice" within the industry.

144. This can be an exceedingly long and frustrating process, though. Here's just one example: After years of effort by the USDA to bring the New Square kosher poultry slaughterhouse in White Plains, NY, into compliance with the federal Poultry Products Inspection Act, a judge finally ordered the facility closed in December 2009. During a visit to

the plant in April of that year, federal investigators reported finding poultry residue on walls, light fixtures, and the manager's office. The employee bathrooms didn't even have soap!

145. This particular illegal butcher shop in Daxinzhuang village, at the remote Zhangjiawan township, sold tainted pork every day to restaurants and markets all over Beijing. When the property was raided, officers from the Commerce Committee and the Animal Quarantine Office found 20 dead pigs with purple skin. The owner told undercover reporters from the *Beijing News* in November 2009 that many of the pigs had died of diseases like fever and others died from the winter cold.

146. "Prison Sentences for Men Operating Illegal Slaughterhouse," Hillside Animal Sanctuary newsletter, winter 2005.

147. This doesn't prevent tens of thousands of horses from being exported to Canada and Mexico every year to be killed for human consumption. The federal Prevention of Equine Cruelty Act (HR503/S727) would prohibit both the domestic slaughter of horses for human consumption and their export for that purpose.

148. Conversation with Richard Couto, January 14, 2010.

149. Colleen Patrick-Goudreau, *Vegan's Daily Companion: 365 Days of Inspiration for Cooking, Eating, and Living Compassionately* (Beverly, MA: Quarry Books, 2011), 212.

150. According to Lester C. Friedlander, DVM, former chief inspector for the USDA, captive bolt guns, which are designed to stun cattle and render them insensible to pain before slaughter, are generally not effective on equines, whose skulls have a different physical structure than those of bovines. (My thanks to Ellen-Cathryn Nash for sharing this insight with me.)

151. Horse meat has been found on menus in the United States. Perhaps the most notable example is the case of The Hump, a trendy sushi restaurant in Santa Monica, California, which was the subject of a sting operation in 2010. Two members of the team that made the Academy Award-winning documentary *The Cove* visited the restaurant several times and were able to order horse and whale meat. The activists

captured the exchange with a hidden camera, and the US attorney's office filed charges against The Hump soon after.

152. Details on Bravo Packing come from conversations with Amanda Sorvino on February 11, 2010, and Ellen-Cathryn Nash, March 12, 2010. Amanda and her father founded Pennsylvania-based Horsefellas, an equine rescue organization whose name recalls the 1990 film *Goodfellas*, in which Paul Sorvino plays a mob boss. Ellen-Cathryn Nash's New Jersey-based nonprofit Manes and Tails also rescues and rehomes horses.

153. Peter J. Sankoff and Steven William White, editors, *Animal Law in Australasia: A New Dialogue* (Sydney, Australia: The Federation Press, 2009), 154.

154. Michael C. Appleby, V. Cussen, LA Lambert, J. Turner, L. Garcés, editors, *Long Distance Transport and Welfare of Farm Animals* (Wallingford, UK: CABI, 2008), 344.

155. As reported by Richard Carleton on Australia's *60 Minutes*, September 21, 2003. The ship worker he interviewed wished to remain anonymous.

156. John Keniry, Michael Bond, Ivan Caple, Lachlan Gosse, and Murray Rogers, *Livestock Export Review: Final Report. A report to the Minister for Agriculture, Fisheries and Forestry*, December 23, 2003.

157. Peter J. Sankoff and Steven William White, editors, *Animal Law in Australasia: A New Dialogue* (Sydney, Australia: The Federation Press, 2009), 159–161.

158. Correspondence with Glenys Oogjes, March 1, 2010.

159. Jennifer O'Connor, "4-H: Cruel to animals and kids," *Chicago Tribune*, November 2, 2009.

160. Mark Hawthorne, "The Ag Class Hypocrisy," *Satya*, May 2006.

161. Terry Smith, "Poultry project yields life lessons," *Idaho Mountain Express*, November 11, 2009.

162. Karen Davis, "Poultry Project Was Misguided" (letter to the editor), *Idaho Mountain Express*, November 18, 2009.

163. Terry Smith, "Poultry project ruffles feathers," *Idaho Mountain Express*, November 11, 2009.

164. Karen Davis, "Idaho School Arms Children with Knives to Kill Chickens," *Poultry Press*, Winter–Spring 2010.

165. In the end, the school announced Lou's remains would not be fed to students, since by law animals destined for human consumption cannot receive pain medication within 30 days of slaughter.

166. http://james-mcwilliams.com/?p=2401

167. Mark Hawthorne, "The Ag Class Hypocrisy."

168. Christine Rossouw, "Vandals trash school; Animals killed in attack," *The Reporter* (Queensland, Australia), February 7, 2011.

169. Mark Hawthorne, "The Ag Class Hypocrisy."

170. "School's chickens beaten to death," *BBC News*, June 24, 2009.

171. Mark Hawthorne, "The Ag Class Hypocrisy."

172. "Boys, 11, Killed Tame School Hen During Break-in," thestar.co.uk, May 10, 2010.

173. Conversation with Hans Kriek, July 24, 2011.

174. www.agritech.org.nz/dairy.shtml

175. Jill Galloway and Mark Hotton, "Vets Support Reducing Calf Induction Numbers," *Manawatu Standard*, August 10, 2010.

176. Frances Sizer and Ellie Whitney, *Nutrition: Concepts and Controversies*, eleventh edition (Florence, KY: Brooks/Cole, 2007), 121. The specific lactose intolerance percentages the authors provide on these ethnic groups are 85–100 percent of Asians and 70–95 percent of black Africans. I simply averaged the figures.

177. P. Sainath, "There's No Such Thing as a Free Cow," Counterpunch.com www.counterpunch.org/sainath12162006.html

178. Correspondence with Andrew Tyler, February 4, 2010.

179. Sam O'Neill, "Why You Should Always Look a Gift Goat in the Mouth," *The Times*, February 15, 2006.

180. Sam O'Neill, "Critics Urge Charities to Give Up the Goat," *The Times*, November 30, 2006.

181. Andrew Tyler, "Don't follow the herd and give a cow for Christmas," *The Independent*, November 27, 2006.

Chapter 2

The quote from journalist Brendan O'Neill comes from his article "I'd rather wear fur than go naked," *The Guardian*, March 19, 2007. The full paragraph this quote comes from reads: "And yes, even fur is humane. To turn an animal into a fur coat is to ennoble it. As a fashion item, an animal acquires significance far beyond its own natural existence. Indeed, the only true 'purpose' in the life of a mink or rabbit is that bestowed on it by the hunter, skinner and fur-maker—through their efforts, an animal is elevated from an instinct-driven bundle of reflex responses to an item worthy of being displayed in Paris, London and New York. Through human endeavour and labour an animal is given a use and meaning that nature could never have designed for it. What is a mink but a wild beast scrabbling for food along riversides, destined to die and rot in the shade of a tree? The mink worn by Kate Moss was spared this fate and made into something memorably beautiful."

1. Nancy Armour, "Animal Rights Group Unhappy with Weir Wearing Fur," *Associated Press*, January 26, 2010.

2. http://nymag.com/daily/fashion/2010/06/johnny_weir_on_his_fab ulous_cl.html

3. American Veterinary Medical Association, "AVMA Guidelines on Euthanasia," June 2007.

4. Matt Rossell, "How to Discuss the Fur Industry," Live Let Activism Series (www.letlivefoundation.org), November 15, 2009. Matt has worked undercover investigating fur farms in the US.

5. Diane L. Beers, *For the Prevention of Cruelty: The History and Legacy of Animal Rights Activism in the United States* (Athens, OH: Swallow Press, 2006), 189.

6. Malwina Gudowska, "Is the Fur Still Flying? (not here, it would seem)," Calgary Herald, December 17, 2010.

7. Elizabeth Day, "Would you rather go naked? Not any longer," *Observer*, November 22, 2009.

8. Eric Wilson, "Fashion Feels Fur's Warm Embrace," *The New York Times*, March 10, 2010.

9. "Fur industry untouchable," *Reuters*, March 6, 2008.

10. Correspondence with Dan Mathews, February 14, 2013.

11. www.hsi.org/issues/fur/facts/fur_trade_europe.html

12. Hsieh-Yi, Yi-Chiao, Yu Fu, Barbara Maas, and Mark Rissi, "Dying for Fur: A Report on the Fur Industry in China," East International/Swiss Animal Protection, January 25, 2007.

13. Tom Regan, *Empty Cages: Facing the Challenge of Animal Rights* (Lanham, MD: Rowman & Littlefield Publishers, Inc., 2004), 108.

14. Tom Regan, *Empty Cages: Facing the Challenge of Animal Rights*, 108–109.

15. Donald M. Broom and Andrew Ferguson Fraser, *Domestic Animal Behaviour and Welfare*, 4th edition (Wallingford, UK: CABI, 2009), 309.

16. Hsieh-Yi, Yi-Chiao, Yu Fu, Barbara Maas, and Mark Rissi, "Dying for Fur: A Report on the Fur Industry in China."

17. PETA Investigation Exposes Chinchilla Cruelty, www.peta.org/feat/chinchilla/account.html

18. Hsieh-Yi, Yi-Chiao, Yu Fu, Barbara Maas, and Mark Rissi, "Dying for Fur: A Report on the Fur Industry in China."

19. Vivi Lin, "China's northern fur farms grow despite furor," *Reuters*, January 19, 2009.

20. "What Impact Has Activism Had on the Fur Industry?" *Scientific American*, June 15, 2009. Data collected in 2008 by the USDA's National Agricultural Statistics Service puts the number of US mink farms at between 274 and 283; however, Peter Young, who conducted an extensive survey of US fur mills in 2009, suggests there could be more, since most states do not require fur farms to be licensed.

21. Correspondence with Peter Young, July 15, 2010. The results of his investigation can be found in "The Blueprint: Fur Farm Intelligence Project Report," from Voice of the Voiceless and *Bite Back Magazine*, 2009.

22. Marc Bekoff, *Encyclopedia of Animal Rights and Animal Welfare*, Second Edition, Volume 1 (Santa Barbara, CA: Greenwood Press, 2010), 560.

23. "Welfare Implications of Leghold Trap Use in Conservation and Research," American Veterinary Medical Association, Animal Welfare Division, April 30, 2008.

24. Tom Regan, *Empty Cages: Facing the Challenge of Animal Rights*, 111.

25. www.statesassembly.gov.je/documents/hansard/47813-4.htm

26. Peter S. Wenz, *Beyond Red and Blue: How Twelve Political Philosophies Shape American Debates* (Cambridge, Massachusetts: MIT Press, 2009), 308.

27. Tim Unruh, "Dog Caught by Trap, Dies," *Salina Journal*, March 13, 2009.

28. Bruce T. Batchelor, *Nine Dog Winter* (Victoria, BC: Agio Publishing House, 2008), 351.

29. Jim Spencer, *Guide to Trapping* (Mechanicsburg, Pennsylvania: Stackpole Books, 2007), 22.

30. Jordan Curnutt, *Animals and the Law: A Sourcebook* (Santa Barbara, CA: ABC-CLIO, Inc., 2001), 215.

31. The Humane Society of the United States report, "What Is That They're Wearing?" http://www.humanesociety.org/assets/pdfs/What-is-that-they-re-wearing_FurBooklet.pdf

32. PETA fact sheet, "Inside the Fur Industry: Factory Farms," http://www.peta.org/issues/animals-used-for-clothing/inside-the-fur-industry-factory-farms.aspx

33. David Graham, "How Canada gets dog and cat fur from China," *thestar.com*, June 30, 2012.

34. Maria Halkias, "Neiman Marcus settles Humane Society's fur lawsuit for $25,000," *The Dallas Morning News*, February 2, 2010.

35. www.fashionencyclopedia.com

36. There is nothing about this activity that can be called a hunt. The targeted seals are helpless on the ice; sealers simply walk up and crush the animal's skull.

37. Once her pup is weaned, the female harp seal is ready to mate again. She then returns with the herd to the Arctic and, if pregnant, will gestate her pup for about 225 days, after which she will return to the Gulf or the Front to give birth.

38. Mark Glover, interviewed by Anna Bruce-Lockhart, "Campaigners see red over seal hunt," *The Guardian Weekly*, March 31, 2008.

39. Farley Mowat, *Sea of Slaughter* (Mechanicsburg, Pennsylvania: Stackpole Books, 2004), 335.

40. Presentation by Nigel Barker at the Taking Action for Animals conference, Washington, DC, July 24, 2010.

41. William Chemko, "Most Canadians Don't Support the Seal Hunt," *Vancouver Sun*, March 17, 2010.

42. Alex Panetta, "Jean eats raw seal heart to show support for hunt," *The Star*, May 25, 2009.

43. Activist François Hugo notes that the Canadian harp seal population numbers 6 million, of which 1.2 million pups are born annually, and the government awards an annual quota of 300,000. That's about 5 percent of the population, and 90 percent of these seals are shot prior to clubbing. Meanwhile, the Namibian Cape fur seals number 800,000, of which 200,000 pups are born annually; of these, about 120,000 inhabit the three seal colonies targeted for culling. He estimates that 40 percent of the pups in targeted seal colonies die from natural causes, leaving about 70,000 surviving young seals to be clubbed (shooting of Cape fur seal pups is not permitted). Yet the Namibian government sets the annual quota at 85,000. "The cull therefore kills all the pups," says François.

44. According to CITES, "Appendix II includes species not necessarily threatened with extinction, but in which trade must be controlled in order to avoid utilization incompatible with their survival." Source: www.cites.org/eng/disc/how.shtml

45. Stephen P. Kirkman and David M. Lavigne, "Assessing the hunting practices of Namibia's commercial seal hunt," *South African Journal of Science*, Volume 106, Number 3/4, March/April 2010.

46. Michelle Theriault, "Namibian Seal Hunt to Go on, 90,000 to Be Clubbed," *US News & World Report*, July 6, 2009.

47. Reynard Loki, "Exclusive Interview with François Hugo, Founder, Seal Alert-SA," *13.7 Billion Years*, July 14, 2009: http://www.13point7billion.org/2009/07/137-billion-years-exclusive-interview.html

48. Eleanor Momberg, "Seal cull placed on hold pending deal," *The Sunday Independent*, June 28, 2009.

49. Correspondence with François Hugo, May 19, 2010.

50. Information provided by Francois Hugo, May 20, 2010. Conversions

based on exchange rates on February 21, 2013.

51. Reynard Loki, "Exclusive Interview with Francois Hugo, Founder, Seal Alert-SA."

52. Tom Rhodes, "In Namibia seal hunt, journalists said to become prey," Committee to Protect Journalists, www.cpj.org/blog, July 17, 2009.

53. Tony Halpin, "Slaughter of the seals in Russia is stopped by Vladimir Putin," *Times Online*, March 20, 2009.

54. Andrei Ajamov, "Karakul as the Golden Fleece of Uzbekistan," Ferghana Information Agency (Russia), July 27, 2007.

55. Eric Wilson, "The Lamb on the Runway," *The New York Times*, August 11, 2005.

56. The Humane Society of the United States, "Karakul Sheep and Lamb Slaughter for the Fur Trade," March 2001.

57. Ibid.

58. *Dateline NBC*, December 11, 2000.

59. www.furisgreen.com

60. www.furisgreen.com/renewable.aspx

61. "Fur: sustainable resource or fashion faux pas?" *CBC News*, March 20, 2008

62. Marijn Bijleveld, Marisa Korteland, and Maartje Sevenster, "The environmental impact of mink fur production," CE Delft, January 2011. www.ce.nl/publicatie/the_environmental_impact_of_mink_fur_produ ction/1131

    In many cases, fur has impacts that are a factor 2 to 28 higher than textiles, even when lower-bound values are taken for various links in the production chain.

63. Ken Beck, "Local fur trapper pursues a 'dying' way of life," *The Wilson Post*, February 23, 2010.

64. For a time, it seemed the beaver was also doomed to this fate, but fashion trends intervened. So popular were beaver coats and hats in the 19th century that the animals were trapped to near extinction in North America. That beavers exist today is thanks to the changing whims of style-conscious consumers: by the 1930s, the demand for their fur had declined.

65. David Whyte Macdonald and Claudio Sillero-Zubiri, *The Biology and Conservation of Wild Canids* (New York, NY: Oxford University Press, 2004), 197.

66. Michael Robotham, Chris Smith, and Hector Valenzuela, "Testing for Soil Nitrogen and Phosphorous for Environmental Pollution Monitoring," College of Tropical Agriculture and Human Resources, University of Hawaii, January 2004.

67. "Toxic Fur: The Impacts of Fur Production on the Environment and the Risks to Human Health," The Humane Society of the United States, January 29, 2009.

68. "Fur–the fake debate," *The Independent*, November 23, 2004.

69. www.asa.org.uk/ASA-action/Adjudications/2012/3/European-Fur-Breeders-Association/SHP_ADJ_164462.aspx

70. "The Reality of Commercial Rabbit Farming in Europe," Coalition to Abolish the Fur Trade, 2007. www.rabbitfur.org

71. Diane Wells, "Meat Rabbits and Overcoming the Easter Bunny Syndrome," *Farming: The Journal of Northeast Agriculture*, June 2010.

72. Susan E. Davis and Margo DeMello, *Stories Rabbits Tell: A Natural and Cultural History of a Misunderstood Creature* (New York, NY: Lantern Books, 2003), 275.

73. Food and Agriculture Organization of the United Nations, "Rabbit: Skin, Slaughtering and Production of Quality Pelts," 2006. www.fao .org/teca/content/rabbit-skin-slaughtering-and-production-quality-pelts

74. Food and Agriculture Organization of the United Nations, "Rabbit: Skin, Slaughtering and Production of Quality Pelts." www.fao.org/teca /content/rabbit-skin-slaughtering-and-production-quality-pelts

75. "The Reality of Commercial Rabbit Farming in Europe."

76. "The Rabbit: Husbandry, Health and Production." www.fao.org/ docrep/t1690e/t1690e0a.htm

77. National Council of Wool Selling Brokers of Australia.

78. ANZFAS (Australian and New Zealand Federation of Animal Societies), "Extensive Sheep Husbandry," Submission to the Senate Select Committee on Animal Welfare, 1989.

79. Elizabeth Wayland Barber, *Women's Work: The First 20,000 Years: Women, Cloth, and Society in Early Times* (New York, NY: WW Norton & Company, Inc., 1994), 97.

80. John L. Capinera, *Encyclopedia of Entomology*, Volume 3 (New York, NY: Springer, 2008), 335–337.

81. Flystrike can affect any breed of sheep. Because Merino sheep have wrinkled skin, and because they comprise 70 percent of the sheep in Australia, this is the breed to undergo the most mulesing procedures.

82. Leland S. Shapiro, *Pathology and Parasitology for Veterinary Technicians*, Volume 1 (Clifton Park, NY: Delmar Learning, 2005), 125.

83. RE Chapman, LR Fell, and DA Shutt, "A comparison of stress in surgically and non-surgically mulesed sheep," *Australian Veterinary Journal*, volume 71, August 1994.

84. JL Barnett, PH Hemsworth, EC Jongman, and JP Morris, "EEG changes in 4-week-old lambs in response to castration, tail docking, and mulesing," *Australian Veterinary Journal*, volume 78, May 2000.

85. Correspondence with Ingrid Newkirk, August 12, 2010.

86. Letter to Julia Gillard, Prime Minister of Australia, from Ingrid Newkirk, President, People for the Ethical Treatment of Animals, July 7, 2010.

87. Neville G. Gregory and Temple Grandin, *Animal Welfare and Meat Production*, second edition (Wallingford, UK: CABI, 2007), 48.

88. Correspondence with Glenys Oogjes, August 14, 2010.

89. John M. Sellar, "International Illicit Trafficking in Wildlife," *The Police Chief*, June 2007.

90. Tara Donn and Bonnie C. Yates, *Identification Guidelines for Shahtoosh & Pashmina*, US Fish & Wildlife Service, Ashland, Oregon, 2002.

91. David Schoenbrod, Richard B. Stewart, and Katrina M. Wyman, *Breaking the Logjam: Environmental Protection That Will Work* (New Haven, CT: Yale University Press, 2010), 145.

92. International Fund for Animal Welfare/Wildlife Trust of India, *Wrap Up the Trade*, 2001.

93. John M. Sellar, "International Illicit Trafficking in Wildlife," *The Police Chief*, June 2007.

94. George B. Schaller, "An Antelope of Fashion," *China's Tibet Magazine,* December 29, 2007. http://en.tibetmagazine.net/zztj/200803/t2008 0312_51637.htm

95. Richard B. Harris, *Wildlife Conservation in China: Preserving the Habitat of China's Wild West* (New York, NY: ME Sharpe, 2008), 142.

96. www.wildaid.org/endangeredspecies/index.asp?ID=10&MORE=Show

97. George B. Schaller, "An Antelope of Fashion," *China Tibet Magazine,* December 29, 2007. http://en.tibetmagazine.net/zztj/200803/t20080 312_51637.htm

98. Jeffrey Moussaieff Masson, *The Pig Who Sang to the Moon: The Emotional World of Farm Animals* (New York, NY: Ballantine Books, 2003), 182–183. Ironically, down is a terrible insulator for human-made products once it becomes wet, as anyone who's been caught in the rain wearing a down jacket will attest.

99. An early and notable win for animal advocates was the US campaign against feathers used in ladies' hats that began in the late 1800s. At the time, millions of wild birds were killed each year to satisfy the demand for trendy chapeaus bearing everything from a simple gull feather to a stuffed bird. Many states banned plumage sales, and in 1900 the US Congress passed the Lacey Act, which restricts the importation of foreign birds and mammals. Ironically for animal activists, something else falls under the purview of the Lacey Act: preventing animal enterprise "terrorism."

100. Elliot L. Gang, "Down with Down," *Animals Agenda Magazine,* May/June 1998.

101. LA Gustafson, HW Cheng, JP Garner, EA Pajor, and JA Mench, "The Effects of Different Bill-Trimming Methods on the Well-Being of Pekin Ducks," *Poultry Science,* September 2007.

102. TB Rodenburg, MBM Bracke, J. Berk, J. Cooper, JM Faure, D. Guémené, G. Guya, A. Harlander, T. Jones, U. Knierim, K. Kuhnt, H. Pingel, K. Reiter, J. Serviére, and MAW Ruis, "Welfare of Ducks in European Duck Husbandry Systems," *World's Poultry Science Journal,* Volume 61, Issue 4, December 2005.

103. Juliet Gellatley, Clare Druce, and Justin Kerswell, *Ducks Out of Water:*

A report on the UK Duck Industry, Viva! and FAWN, 2006. Also: Juliet Gellatley and Lauren Ornelas, *Ducks Out of Water*, Viva! USA, 2000.

104. Sanjida O'Connell, "Why farmed ducks endure worse conditions than battery hens," *The Independent*, July 6, 2006.

105. Conversation with Lauren Ornelas, April 27, 2011.

106. "Down on the Goose and Duck Farm," *AWI Quarterly*, Volume 58, Number 4, Fall 2009.

107. Heinz Pingel, "Duck and Geese Production around the World," *World Poultry*, Volume 20, Number 8, 2004.

108. Ibid.

109. EFSA Panel on Animal Health and Welfare, "Scientific opinion on the practice of harvesting (collecting) feathers from live geese for down production," *EFSA Journal*, 2010.

110. Per Hermanrud, *Kalla Fakta*, TV4, February 1 and 8, 2009. See www.tv4.se/1.830238/2009/01/29/levande_dun

111. EFSA Panel on Animal Health and Welfare, "Scientific opinion on the practice of harvesting (collecting) feathers from live geese for down production."

112. CBS 5 (San Francisco) *Eyewitness News* report on live plucking, April 30, 2010.

113. M. Zimmerman, "Physiological Mechanisms of Pain and Its Treatment," *Klinische Anäesthesiologische und Intensivtherapie*, Volume 32, 1986.

114. MJ Gentle and LN Hunter, "Physiological and behavioural responses associated with feather removal in *Gallus gallus var. domesticus*," *Research in Veterinary Science*, Volume 50, Issue 1, January 1991.

115. Diane L. Beers, *For the Prevention of Cruelty: The History and Legacy of Animal Rights Activism in the United States*, 84.

116. See *A Gap in Nature: Discovering the World's Extinct Animals* by Tim Flannery and Peter Schouten (New York, NY: Atlantic Monthly Press, 2001).

117. Jessie L. Bonner, "High fashion or bait? Fly ties now hair extensions," *Seattle Times*, June 6, 2011.

118. Michael Mello, "Fullerton fly-fishing shop is center of hair feather

craze," *Orange County Register*, March 7, 2011.

119. From a statement by Thomas Whiting, owner of Whiting Farms, emailed to the author on June 22, 2011.

120. See www.fly-fishing-insider.com/whiting-farms

121. Thomas Whiting, "Whiting Hackle Farms," www.uncleginkscave .com/GC-WhitingHackleFarms.html

122. Michael Mello, "Fullerton fly-fishing shop is center of hair feather craze."

123. International Council of Tanners, www.leathercouncil.org/pers pective.htm

124. A. Severin Johnson, "Packing House Byproducts," Agricultural Marketing Resource Center, Iowa State University, February 2003.

125. Fredrik Wesslau, "The Mania's Over, but Ostrich Products Still Can't Get Off the Ground," *The New York Times*, August 18, 2001.

126. See www.mercyforanimals.org/ohdairy and http://dairycruelty.com .au

127. US Environmental Protection Agency, "Leather Tanning," www. epa.gov/ttnchie1/ap42/ch09/final/c9s15.pdf

128. Dwijendra Narayan Jha, *The Myth of the Holy Cow* (London, UK: Verso, 2002), 37.

129. Peter Popham, "How India's sacred cows are beaten, abused and poisoned to make leather for high street shops," *The Independent*, February 14, 2000.

130. Vijay Singh, "Bullocks end up with broken limbs after 30 hours of truck ride," *Times of India*, February 8, 2011.

131. Mark Magnier, "Where's the beef? Indians don't want to know," *Los Angeles Times*, May 2, 2010.

132. Daniel Pearl, *At Home in the World: Collected Writings from The Wall Street Journal*, edited by Helene Cooper (New York, NY: Simon & Schuster, 2002), 124.

133. Bruce Friedrich, "Why Leather Is a Progressive Issue," *Huffington Post* (www.huffingtonpost.com), May 1, 2007.

134. The slaughter of kangaroos as "pest control" is built on a false premise. Recent studies conducted by THINKK, a nonprofit think tank

based in Sydney, conclude that kangaroos do not destroy crops, nor do they compete with sheep for forage, as the ag industry claims. "Scientific research has refuted the notion that kangaroos need to be killed for pest control or damage mitigation purposes," reads one report by THINKK. "Research suggests that kangaroos only compete with sheep in extreme drought conditions as they eat different food." In other words, the annual killing of 3 million adult kangaroos and 1 million of their joeys for "pest" management is unnecessary and unjustified. See *Shooting our wildlife: An analysis of the law and policy governing the killing of kangaroos*, THINKK, December 2010.

135. Penny Olsen and Tim Low, *Situation Analysis Report: Update on Current State of Scientific Knowledge on Kangaroos in the Environment, Including Ecological and Economic Impact and Effect of Culling*, Kangaroo Management Advisory Panel, March 2006.

136. Ibid.

137. John Kelly, "Kangaroo Industry Strategic Plan, 2005–2010," Australian Government/Rural Industries Research and Development Corporation, August 2005.

138. See *National Code of Practice for the Humane Shooting of Kangaroos and Wallabies for Commercial Purposes* as well as *National Code of Practice for the Humane Shooting of Kangaroos and Wallabies for Non-Commercial Purposes*, both from the Natural Resource Management Ministerial Council, Australia, November 2008.

139. Juliet Gellatley, *Under Fire: A Viva! Report on the Killing of Kangaroos for Meat and Skin*, Vegetarians International Voice for Animals, 2009.

140. www.environment.gov.au/biodiversity/wildlife-trade/wild-harvest/kangaroo/quota/2012.html

141. Dror Ben-Ami, PhD, "A Shot in the Dark: A Report on Kangaroo Harvesting," May 2009.

142. John Frederick Walker, *Ivory's Ghosts: The White Gold of History and the Fate of Elephants* (New York, NY: Grove Press, 2009), 26.

143. Peter Douglas Ward, *The Call of Distant Mammoths: Why the Ice Age Mammals Disappeared* (New York, NY: Copernicus, 1997), 79.

144. Martin Meredith, *Elephant Destiny: Biography of an Endangered Species in*

Africa (New York, NY: PublicAffairs, 2001), 201.

145. Delia and Mark Owens, *The Eye of the Elephant: An Epic Adventure in the African Wilderness* (New York, NY: Houghton Mifflin Co., 1992), 283.

146. Ibid.

147. Sue Armstrong and Fred Bridgland, "Elephants and the Ivory Tower," *New Scientist*, August 26, 1989.

148. Carol Marquis, "'Slaughtered for Their Ivory': Up to 35,000 elephants slain in one year, charity says," *NBC News*, April 30, 2012.

149. Anita Gossmann, "Tusks and Trinkets: An Overview of Illicit Ivory Trafficking in Africa," *African Security Review*, Volume 18, Number 4, December 2009.

150. Conversation with Ken Bernhard, August 31, 2010.

151. Dan Levin, "From Elephants' Mouths, an Illicit Trail to China," *The New York Times*, March 1, 2013.

152. Cain Nunns, "Ivory trade could make Vietnam's elephants extinct within a decade," *Guardian Weekly*, September 21, 2010.

153. Jane Macartney, "Why did the elephant lose his tusks? To beat the poachers," *The Times*, July 18, 2005.

154. Gary Haynes, *Mammoths, Mastodonts, and Elephants: Biology, Behavior, and the Fossil Record* (Cambridge, UK: University of Cambridge Press, 1999), 41.

155. Ian Sample, "Poaching leads to more tuskless elephants," *The Guardian*, July 18, 2005.

156. "Tuskless elephants evolving thanks to poachers," Xinhuanet, July 17, 2005. http://news.xinhuanet.com/english/2005-07/17/content_3229276 .htm

157. Conversation with Dr. Gay Bradshaw, August 8, 2012.

158. "Polar Bear and Walrus Populations in Trouble, Stock Assessment Report Suggests," *Science Daily*, June 19, 2009. www.sciencedaily .com/releases/2009/06/090618195804.htm

159. Jamie Merrill, "Walruses: The friendly, fun-loving, musically talented creatures are under threat from climate change," *The Sunday Independent*, September 11, 2008.

160. US Fish and Wildlife Service, *Hunting and Use of Walrus by Alaska*

Natives, fact sheet, August 2006. For a detailed account of walrus poaching, see *Animal Investigators: How the World's First Wildlife Forensics Lab Is Solving Crimes and Saving Endangered Species* by Laurel Abrams Neme (New York, NY: Scribner, 2009).

161. *Associated Press*, "Alaskan Gets 7 Years for Walrus Killings," *San Francisco Chronicle*, July 13, 2005.

162. Glenn Feldhake, *Hippos: Natural History & Conservation* (Stillwater, MN: Voyageur Press, Inc., 2005), 47.

163. Alexander Gillespie, *Protected Areas and International Environmental Law* (Leiden, The Netherlands: Martinus Nijhoff Publishers, 2007), 226.

164. Correspondence with Emmanuel de Mérode, January 5, 2011.

165. www.iucnredlist.org/apps/redlist/details/10103/0

166. www.wcs.org/saving-wildlife/elephants/hippo.aspx

167. Peter S. Ungar, *Mammal Teeth: Origin, Evolution, and Diversity* (Baltimore, MD: The Johns Hopkins University Press, 2010), 42.

168. Geoffrey Lean, "Unicorns of the Sea: Dying in the depths," *The Independent*, April 8, 2007.

169. Randy Malamud, editor, *A Cultural History of Animals in the Modern Age* (Oxford, UK: Berg Publishers, 2009), 22.

170. William J. Broad, "It's Sensitive. Really," *The New York Times*, December 13, 2005.

171. Arctic Institute of North America, "New Survey Techniques Improve Narwhal Population Estimates," press release, April 2010.

172. Paul Nicklen, "Hunting Narwhals," *National Geographic*, August 2007.

173. Randy Boswell, "Government defends decision to ban narwhal tusk sales," *Vancouver Sun*, December 17, 2010.

174. Peter Douglas Ward, *The Call of Distant Mammoths: Why The Ice Age Mammals Disappeared* (New York, NY: Copernicus, 1997), 81.

175. Samuel T. Turvey, *Holocene Extinctions* (Oxford, UK: Oxford University Press, 2009), 20.

176. Adrian Lister and Paul G. Bahn, *Mammoths: Giants of the Ice Age* (London: Marshall Editions, 2007), 146–147.

177. Esmond Martin and Chryssee Martin, "Russia's mammoth ivory industry expands: what effect on elephants?" *Pachyderm*, No. 47

January–June 2010.

178. Ibid.

179. Martha Gill, "Does mammoth ivory make ethical jewellery?" *The Guardian*, September 27, 2010.

180. Esmond Martin and Chryssee Martin, "Russia's mammoth ivory industry expands: what effect on elephants?"

181. Ibid.

182. Michael McCarthy, "Trade in mammoth ivory 'is fuelling slaughter of African elephants,'" *The Independent*, September 29, 2010.

183. George Frederick Kunz and Charles Hugh Stevenson, *The Book of the Pearl: Its History, Art, Science and Industry* (New York, NY: The Century Co., 1908), 3.

184. Robert R. Stickney, *Aquaculture: An Introductory Text*, second edition (Wallingford, UK: CABI, 2009), 93.

185. Joseph Taylor and Elisabeth Strack, "Pearl Production," from *The Pearl Oyster*, edited by Paul C. Southgate and John S. Lucas (Oxford, UK: Elsevier, 2008), 274.

186. Joseph Taylor and Elisabeth Strack, "Pearl Production," 284.

187. Victoria Finlay, *Jewels: A Secret History* (New York, NY: Random House, 2006), 98.

188. Ibid.

189. Correspondence with Paula Mikkelsen, January 13, 2011.

190. Peter Singer, *Animal Liberation* (New York, NY: HarperCollins, 2002), 174.

191. www.letsgo.com/videos/68265

192. Eugene Newton Anderson and Felix Medina Tzuc, *Animals and the Maya in Southeast Mexico* (Tucson, AZ: University of Arizona Press, 2005), 191.

193. Mary Schoeser, *Silk* (New Haven, CT: Yale University Press, 2007), 17.

194. www.fao.org/es/ess/top/commodity.html?lang=en&item=1185&year=2005

195. See *A Gigantic Mistake: Articles and Essays for Your Intellectual Self-Defense* by Mickey Z. (Rockville, MD: Wildside Press, 2004). For more on worms and endorphins, see "Pain, Suffering, and Anxiety in

Animals and Humans" by David DeGrazia and Andrew Rowan, *Theoretical Medicine and Bioethics*, Volume 12, Number 3, 1991.

196. Correspondence with Thomas Miller, February 11, 2011. Dr. Miller added: "You will find it hard to get sympathy for injuring insects when they are a staple food in many countries around the world."

197. "Study Backs Deep Anesthesia for Babies in Surgery," *The New York Times*, January 2, 1992.

198. Eric A. Wong, "Silkworms Produce Human Type III Procollagen," *ISB News Reports*, March 2003.

199. www.fao.org/es/ess/top/commodity.html?lang=en&item=1185&year =2005

200. Mansur Mirovalev, "Silk's dark side: Uzbek kids made to grow cocoons," *Associated Press*, August 28, 2010.

201. *The Small Hands of Slavery: Bonded Child Labor in India*, Human Rights Watch, January 2003.

202. Jim Stapleton, *Sanctuary Almanac: State of Nature, State of Mind* (Indianapolis, IN: Dog Ear Publishing, 2008), 179.

Chapter 3

Margaret Atwood's quote is from her 1972 novel *Surfacing* (McClelland & Stewart).

1. Ingrid Newkirk, *Free the Animals: The Untold Story of the US Animal Liberation Movement & Its Founder, "Valerie"* (Chicago, IL: The Noble Press, 1992), 281. Incidentally, Ingrid writes that Britches had already acquired his name when he was liberated, a point repeated by other sources. But Keith Mann, former ALF organizer and the author of *From Dusk 'til Dawn: An Insider's View of the Growth of the Animal Liberation Movement* (Warcry Communications, 2009), states that it was the macaque's rescuers, and not UC Riverside researchers, who anointed him "Britches."

2. Deborah Blum, *Love at Goon Park: Harry Harlow and the Science of Affection* (Cambridge, MA: Perseus Publishing, 2002), 204.

3. Ingrid Newkirk, *Free the Animals*, 286.

4. Mike Sager, *Scary Monsters and Super Freaks: Stories of Sex, Drugs, Rock*

'N' Roll and Murder (New York, NY: Thunder's Mouth Press, 2003), 340.

5. www.britches.org.uk/video.asp

6. Ingrid Newkirk, *Free the Animals*, 292.

7. Edna J. Hunter, PhD, "The Vietnam POW Veteran: Immediate and Long-Term Effects of Captivity," from *Stress Disorders Among Vietnam Veterans: Theory, Research and Treatment*, edited by Charles R. Figley, PhD (New York, NY: Brunner-Routledge, 1978), 194.

8. Atul Gawande, "Hellhole," *The New Yorker*, March 30, 2009.

9. Kristine Coleman, "Psychological Enrichment for Animals in Captivity," from *Sourcebook of Models for Biomedical Research*, edited by P. Michael Conn (Totowa, NJ: Humana Press, 2008), 57.

10. Deborah Blum, *The Monkey Wars* (New York, NY: Oxford University Press, 1994), 95. Blum recounts that one of Harlow's doctoral students, Gene Sackett, believes that the modern animal rights movement was fuelled by reports of what was going on inside his professor's infamous lab in the 1960s and '70s.

11. Deborah Blum, *Love at Goon Park: Harry Harlow and the Science of Affection*, 145.

12. Roberto C. Agís-Balboa, Graziano Pinna, Fabio Pibiri, Bashkim Kadriu, Erminio Costa, and Alessandro Guidotti, "Down-regulation of neurosteroid biosynthesis in corticolimbic circuits mediates social isolation-induced behavior in mice," *Proceedings of the National Academy of Sciences*, November 20, 2007.

13. Conversation with Matt Rossell, June 1, 2011.

14. Stephanie Watson, *Animal Testing: Issues and Ethics* (New York, NY: Rosen Publishing Group, Inc., 2009), 11.

15. C. Ray Greek and Jean Swingle Greek, *Sacred Cows and Golden Geese: The Human Cost of Experiments on Animals* (New York, NY: Continuum International Publishing Group, 2000), 23.

16. Roger S. Fouts and Deborah H. Fouts, "Chimpanzees' Use of Sign Language," from *The Great Ape Project: Equality Beyond Humanity*, edited by Paola Cavalieri and Peter Singer (New York, NY: St. Martin's Press, 1993), 30.

17. Margaret A. Boden, *Mind as Machine: A History of Cognitive Science,*

Volume 1 (Oxford, UK: Oxford University Press, 2006), 72.

18. The Cartesian attitude toward animals was not limited to science. The torture of cats seems to have been a particularly gruesome form of entertainment in 17th-century Europe, perhaps best exemplified by a device called the "cat piano." A line of cats were caged into side-by-side boxes arranged by the pitch of their meows. Attached was a keyboard, and when the keys were pressed by a player, a sharp jab was delivered to the cat in the corresponding box. See *The Clockwork Universe: Isaac Newton, the Royal Society and the Birth of the Modern World*, by Edward Dolnick (New York, NY: HarperCollins, 2011).

19. Wallace Shugg, "Humanitarian attitudes in the early animal experiments of the Royal Society," *Annals of Science*, Volume 24, 1968.

20. Stewart Richards, "Anaesthetics, ethics and aesthetics: vivisection in the late nineteenth-century British laboratory," from *Laboratory Revolution in Medicine*, edited by Andrew Cunningham and Perry Williams (Cambridge, UK: Cambridge University Press, 1992), 146.

21. Niall Shanks and C. Ray Greek, *Animal Models in Light of Evolution* (Boca Raton, FL: BrownWalker Press, 2009), 49.

22. Tom Regan, *The Case for Animal Rights* (Berkeley, CA: University of California Press, 2004), 5.

23. Richard Ryder, *Animal Revolution: Changing Attitudes Towards Speciesism* (Oxford, UK: Basil Blackwell Ltd, 1989), 58.

24. Vaughan Monamy, *Animal Experimentation: A Guide to the Issues* (Cambridge, UK: Cambridge University Press, 2000) 16.

25. Wallace Shugg, "Humanitarian attitudes in the early animal experiments of the Royal Society."

26. Gay Bradshaw, PhD, PhD; Theodora Capaldo, EdD; Lorin Lindner, PhD, MPH; and Gloria Grow, "Building an Inner Sanctuary: Complex PTSD in Chimpanzees," *Journal of Trauma & Dissociation*, Volume 9, 2008.

27. Katy Taylor, Nicky Gordon, Gill Langley, and Wendy Higgins, "Estimates for Worldwide Laboratory Animal Use in 2005," *Alternatives to Laboratory Animals*, Volume 36, July 2008.

28. Details about Simba's life at NIRC have been gleaned from

"Chimpanzee research on trial," by Meredith Wadman, *Nature*, Volume 474, June 16, 2011.

29. See http://video.humanesociety.org/video/1016661686001

30. According to the industry trade group Pharmaceutical Research and Manufacturing of America. See www.phrma.org/sites/default/files/159/rd_brochure_022307.pdf

31. FT Bourgeois, KD Mandl, C. Valim, and MW Shannon, "Pediatric adverse drug events in the outpatient setting: an 11-year national analysis," *Pediatrics*, September 28, 2009.

32. John E. Lesch, *The First Miracle Drugs: How the Sulfa Drugs Transformed Medicine* (New York, NY: Oxford University Press, 2007), 179.

33. Carol Ballentine, "Taste of Raspberries, Taste of Death: The 1937 Elixir Sulfanilamide Incident," *FDA Consumer*, June 1981.

34. Jenny Hope, "Arthritis Drug's Death Toll 'Four Times Higher'," *Daily Mail*, January 4, 2005.

35. MAJ McKenna, "Science Watch 'Manhattan Project' for AIDS Q&A with Dr. Mark Feinberg, a Leading AIDS Researcher 'We Need the Human Trials as Well,'" *Atlanta Journal-Constitution*, September 21, 1997.

36. A. Harding, "More compounds failing Phase I. FDA chief warns that high drug attrition rate is pushing up the cost of drug development," *The Scientist*, August 6, 2004.

37. Neal D. Barnard, MD, "Animalistic Methods of Testing," *Washington Times*, July 14, 2002.

38. Jeffrey H. Coben, MD; Stephen M. Davis, MPA, MSW; Paul M. Furbee, MA; Rosanna D. Sikora, MD; Roger D. Tillotson, MD; and Robert M. Bossarte, PhD, "Hospitalizations for Poisoning by Prescription Opioids, Sedatives, and Tranquilizers," *American Journal of Preventive Medicine*, Volume 38, Issue 5, May 6, 2010.

39. C. Ray Greek and Jean Swingle Greek, *Sacred Cows and Golden Geese*, 48.

40. A handout from the Washington, DC-based Foundation for Biomedical Research, for example, states, "[W]hether they are working on human health or animal health studies, scientists place a high priority on 'The

Three Rs' — reduction, replacement and refinement." www.nwabr. org/research/pdfs/FBRFactvsMyth.pdf

41. Kathryn Bayne, Timothy H. Morris, and Malcolm P. France, "Legislation and oversight of the conduct of research using animals: a global overview," from *The UFAW Handbook on the Care and Management of Laboratory and Other Research Animals*, eighth edition, edited by Robert Hubrecht and James Kirkwood (Oxford, UK: Blackwell Publishing Ltd), 108.

42. Stuart Derbyshire, "Time to Abandon the Three Rs," *The Scientist*, February 1, 2006.

43. Jeremy P. Jacobs, "Agencies Hope Robot Can Speed Toxics Evaluations, End Animal Testing," *The New York Times*, May 13, 2011.

44. www.pcrm.org/media/blog/june2011/tox21-robotic-system-could-end-animal-use-in

45. Nick Taylor, "Covance to close Arizona tox site as weak demand continues," Outsourcing-Pharma.com, May 3, 2012.

46. Richard P. Haynes, *Animal Welfare: Competing Conceptions and Their Ethical Implications* (New York, NY: Springer Science + Business Media, 2010), 49.

47. A typical example of this type of cruelty is found at the University of Texas Medical Branch (UTMB), which in 2011 was cited by the USDA for animal abuse after an anonymous UTMB employee tipped off the agency. A more egregious example would be the deaths due to negligence of three primates in 18 months at Harvard University. Finding that the school had violated the Animal Welfare Act, USDA officials cited Harvard in 2012.

48. *Maximum Tolerated Dose*, produced and directed by Karol Orzechowski, Decipher Films, 2012.

49. Scott Plous and Harold Herzog, "Reliability of Protocol Reviews for Animal Research," *Science*, Volume 293, July 27, 2001.

50. Correspondence with Matt Rossell, January 12, 2012.

51. Malin Ideland, "Different views on ethics: how animal ethics is situated in a committee culture," *Journal of Medical Ethics*, Volume 35, 2009.

52. Richard P. Haynes, *Animal Welfare*, 50.

53. Gina Kolata, "Mice Fall Short as Test Subjects for Humans' Deadly Ills," *The New York Times*, February 11, 2013.

54. Chad Gervich, "The Good Doctor," *Orange Coast Magazine*, May 2006.

55. C. Ray Greek and Jean Swingle Greek, *Sacred Cows and Golden Geese*, 18.

56. Steve Woloshin, Lisa M. Schwartz, SL Casella, AT Kennedy, RJ Larson, "Press Releases by Academic Medical Centers: Not So Academic?" *Annals of Internal Medicine*, Volume 150, May 5, 2009.

57. Conversation with Ray Greek, MD, September 22, 2011.

58. Correspondence with Helen Marston, June 23, 2012.

59. Correspondence with Lawrence Hansen, MD, December 14, 2009.

60. http://officeofbudget.od.nih.gov/br.html

61. Harmanjatinder S. Sekhon, Jennifer A. Keller, Neal L. Benowitz, and Eliot R. Spindel, "Prenatal Nicotine Exposure Alters Pulmonary Function in Newborn Rhesus Monkeys," *American Journal of Respiratory and Critical Care Medicine*, Volume 164, Number 6, September 2001.

62. David J. Earnest, PhD; Wei-Jung A. Chen, PhD; and James R. West, PhD, "Developmental Alcohol and Circadian Clock Function," *Alcohol Research & Health*, Volume 25, 2001.

63. Leslie Knowlton, "Nature versus Nurture: How Is Child Psychopathology Developed?" *Psychiatric Times*, July 1, 2005. http://www.psychiatrictimes.com/child-adolescent-psych/content/article/10168/52541?pageNumber=4

64. Donald McNeil, Jr., "Research on Ecstasy Is Clouded by Errors," *The New York Times*, December 2, 2003.

65. Josephine Johnston, "Financial Conflicts of Interest in Biomedical Research," from *Trust and Integrity in Biomedical Research: The Case of Financial Conflicts of Interest*, edited by Thomas H. Murray and Josephine Johnston (Baltimore, MD: The Johns Hopkins University Press, 2010), 7–8.

66. Mriganka Sur, Douglas O. Frost, and Susan Hockfield, "Expression of a Surface-Associated Antigen on Y-Cells in the Cat Lateral Geniculate

Nucleus Is Regulated by Visual Experience," *The Journal of Neuroscience*, Volume 8, March 1988.

67. The US Food, Drug, and Cosmetic Act of 1938 "does not specifically require the use of animals in testing cosmetics for safety, nor does the Act subject cosmetics to FDA premarket approval. However, the agency has consistently advised cosmetic manufacturers to employ whatever testing is appropriate and effective for substantiating the safety of their products." www.fda.gov/Cosmetics/Productand IngredientSafety/ProductTesting/ucm072268.htm

68. Coca-Cola was popular as a nerve tonic when it debuted in 1886, even though each glass contained 8.45 milligrams of cocaine and 80 milligrams of caffeine (which dramatically heightens the effects of cocaine). Bayer, the same company that gave the world aspirin, not only laced its cough syrup with diacetylmorphine, but trademarked the drug as Heroin in 1898.

69. Teresa Riordan, *Inventing Beauty: A History of the Innovations That Have Made Us Beautiful* (New York, NY: Broadway Books, 2004), 21–24.

70. Richard Ryder, *Victims of Science: The Use of Animals in Research* (London: Davis-Poynter, 1975), 36.

71. Mark H. Bernstein, *Without a Tear: Our Tragic Relationship with Animals* (Chicago: University of Illinois Press, 2004), 132.

72. Andrew N. Rowan, *Of Mice, Models, and Men: A Critical Evaluation of Animal Research* (Albany, NY: State University of New York Press, 1984), 204.

73. Nancy Heneson, "American Agencies Denounce LD50 Test," *New Scientist*, November 17, 1983.

74. Silke Bitz, "The botulinum neurotoxin LD50 test—problems and solutions," *Altex*, Volume 27, Number 2, February 2010. In 2011, Botox manufacturer Allergan announced it had developed a method that avoids using animals in testing this product. The company said the new procedure will reduce animal use in Botox testing by 95 percent by 2014 as it secures regulatory approvals outside the United States.

75. Stephen R. Kaufmann and Murray J. Cohen, "The Clinical Relevance of the LD50," *Veterinary and Human Toxicology*, Volume 29, Issue 1,

February 1987.

76. Gerhard Zbinden, *Progress in Toxicology* (Berlin: Springer-Verlag, 1973).

77. Peter Singer, *Ethics Into Action: Henry Spira and the Animal Rights Movement* (Lanham, MD: Rowman & Littlefield Publishers, 1998), 114.

78. Bernard Rollin, "The Moral Status of Animals," from *Pet Loss and Human Bereavement*, edited by Herbert A. Nieburg, William J. Kay, Ross M. Grey, Austin H. Kutscher and Carole E. Fudin (Ames, IA: Iowa State University Press, 1988), 7.

79. Peter Singer, *Animal Liberation* (New York, NY: HarperCollins, 2002), 54.

80. Jordan Curnutt, *Animals and the Law: A Sourcebook* (Santa Barbara, CA: ABC-CLIO, Inc., 2001), 450.

81. Susan E. Davis and Margo DeMello, *Stories Rabbits Tell: A Natural and Cultural History of a Misunderstood Creature* (New York, NY: Lantern Books, 2003), 285.

82. Wanda M. Haschek, Colin G. Rousseaux, and Matthew A. Wallig, *Fundamentals of Toxicologic Pathology*, second edition (Burlington, MA: Academic Press, 2010), 157.

83. R. Roggeband, M. York, M. Pericoi, and W. Braun, "Eye irritation responses in rabbit and man after single applications of equal volumes of undiluted model liquid detergent products," *Food and Chemical Toxicology*, Volume 38, Issue 8, August 2000.

84. Steve Boggan, "Eight million animals face death to test your toothpaste and washing-up liquid," *Daily Mail*, July 29, 2011.

85. Michael K. Robinson, John P. McFadden, and David A. Basketter, "Validity and Ethics of the Human 4-h Patch Test as an Alternative Method to Assess Acute Skin Irritation Potential," *Contact Dermatitis*, Volume 45, Issue 1, July 2001.

86. Investigator's notes, December 3, 2009.

87. Dan Goldberg, "Freak washing machine accident boils lab monkey alive," the *Star-Ledger*, January 18, 2012.

88. Katherine Watkins, "Penn tops Ivy League in animal research violations," *The Daily Pennsylvanian*, September 25, 2011.

89. "Laboratory monkey deaths due to negligence prompt animal activists

to call for crackdown on researchers," *Associated Press*, March 17, 2010.

90. *Associated Press*, "North Carolina: Lab Staff Accused of Animal Abuse," *The New York Times*, July 7, 2011.

91. Ellen Kienzle, Jürgen Zentek, and Helmut Meyer, "Body Composition of Puppies and Young Dogs," *Journal of Nutrition*, Volume 128, Number 12, December 1, 1998.

92. BC Weng, BP Chew, TS Wong, JS Park, HW Kim, and AJ Lepine, "Beta-carotene uptake and changes in ovarian steroids and uterine proteins during the estrous cycle in the canine," *Journal of Animal Sciences*, Volume 78, Issue 5, May 2000.

93. GF Grauer, DS Greco, EN Behrend, MJ Fettman, I. Mani, DM Getzy, and GA Reinhart, "Effects of dietary n-3 fatty acid supplementation versus thromboxane synthetase inhibition on gentamicin-induced nephrotoxicosis in healthy male dogs," *American Journal of Veterinary Research*, Volume 57, Issue 6, June 1996.

94. Merritt Clifton, "Pet food and Procter & Gamble," *Animal People*, June 2001.

95. Katy Brown, "A Nation of Animal Lovers?" (research report), *Ethical Consumer*, March/April 2010.

96. Nancy Kerns, "Pet Food Companies and Animal Research: What Do They Do?" *Whole Dog Journal*, June 2012.

97. Animal Rendering Fact Sheet, Los Angeles County, April 8, 2004, http://animalcare.lacounty.gov/cms1_031226.pdf

98. Michael W. Fox, Elizabeth Hodgkins, and Marion E. Smart, *Not Fit for a Dog! The Truth About Manufactured Cat and Dog Food* (Fresno, CA: Quill Driver Books, 2009), 9.

99. Linda Bren, "Pentobarbital in Dog Food," *FDA Consumer*, May/June 2002.

100. Lynette A. Hart, Mary W. Wood, and Benjamin L. Hart, *Why Dissection? Animal Use in Education* (Westport, CT: Greenwood Press, 2008), 18.

101. Marvin B. Emmons, "Secondary and elementary school use of live and preserved animals," from *Animals in Education: Use of Animals in High School Biology Classes and Science Fairs*, edited by Heather McGiffin and Nanice Brownley (Washington, DC: The Institute for the Study of

Animal Problems, 1980), 43–46.

102. Robert J. Amitrano and Gerard J. Tortora, *Laboratory Exercises in Anatomy and Physiology with Cat Dissections*, 8th edition (Belmont, CA: Thomson Brooks/Cole, 2007), 149.

103. Marcy C. Phipps, RN, CCRN, "The Soul on the Head of a Pin," *American Journal of Nursing*, Volume 110, Issue 5, May 2010.

104. Jonathan Balcombe, PhD, *The Use of Animals in Higher Education: Problems, Alternatives, & Recommendations* (Washington, DC: The Humane Society Press, 2000), 24.

105. Lesley A. King, Cheryl L. Ross, Martin L. Stephens, Andrew N. Rowan, "Biology teachers' attitudes to dissection and alternatives," *Alternatives to Laboratory Animals*, Volume 32, 2004.

106. Heidi Blake, "Schools abandon dissection in Biology lessons over health and safety fears," *Telegraph*, May 3, 2010.

107. Correspondence with Kate Fowler, April 23, 2012.

108. Rian De Villiers and Jaqui Sommerville, "Prospective biology teachers' attitudes toward animal dissection: implications and recommendations for the teaching of biology," *South African Journal of Education*, Volume 25, Issue 4, 2005.

109. Rian De Villiers and Martin Monk, "The First Cut Is the Deepest: Reflections on the State of Animal Dissection in Biology Education," *Journal of Curriculum Studies*, Volume 37, Issue 5, September 2005.

110. Aarti Dhar, "Dissection ban will save 19 million animals every year," *The Hindu*, December 10, 2011.

111. For examples see Paul F. Cunningham, "Animals in Psychology Education and Student Choice," *Society & Animals*, Volume 8, Number 2, 2000, and S. Plous, "Attitudes toward the use of animals in psychological research and education," *American Psychologist*, Volume 51, Number 11, November 1996.

112. Theodora Capaldo, "The Psychological Effects on Students of Using Animals in Ways that They See as Ethically, Morally or Religiously Wrong," *Alternatives to Laboratory Animals*, Volume 32, June 2004.

113. Dorian Solot and Arnold Arluke, "Learning the Scientist's Role: Animal Dissection in Middle School," *Journal of Contemporary*

Ethnography, Volume 26, Number 1, April 1997.

114. Gracia Barr and Harold Herzog, "Fetal Pig: The High School Dissection Experience," *Society & Animals,* Volume 8, Number 1, 2000.

115. Lynda IA Birke, Arnold Arluke, Mike Michael, *The Sacrifice: How Scientific Experiments Transform Animals and People* (West Lafayette, IN: Purdue University Press, 2007), 78.

116. Stephen L. Talbott, "Killing to Understand," *In Context,* Fall 1999.

117. George K. Russell, "The Heart of the Matter," *AV Magazine,* Spring 2005.

118. F. Barbara Orlans, *In the Name of Science: Issues in Responsible Animal Experimentation* (New York, NY: Oxford University Press, 1993), 194.

119. www.the-aps.org/mm/SciencePolicy/About/Policy-Statements /Animals-in-Teaching_1.htm

120. Arnold Arluke and Frederic Hafferty, "From Apprehension to Fascination with 'Dog Lab': The Use of Absolutions by Medical Students," *Journal of Contemporary Ethnography,* Volume 25, July 1996.

121. RW Samsel, GA Schmidt, JB Hall, LDH Wood, SG Shroff, and PT Schumacker, "Cardiovascular physiology teaching: computer simulations versus animal demonstrations," *American Journal of Physiology,* June 1994.

122. Nicholas Bakalar, "Killing Dogs in Training of Doctors Is to End," *The New York Times,* January 1, 2008.

123. Orlans, *In the Name of Science,* 193.

124. Andrew Knight, "Refusing to Quit: Winning the Right to Conscientiously Object at Murdoch University," *Animals Today,* Volume 6, Number 4, March 2002.

125. Correspondence with Andrew Knight, April 27, 2012.

126. For a list of the US schools offering alternatives, see www.animalearn .org/vetSchools.php

127. Nedim C. Buyukmihci, VMD, "Non-violence in surgical training," *Revista Electrónica de Veterinaria,* Volume 8, Number 12B, December 2007.

128. www.neavs.org/alternatives/in-education

129. Andrew Knight BSc., BVMS, *Learning without Killing: A Guide to*

Conscientious Objection (April 2002), 7.

130. Gary L. Francione and Anna E. Charlton, *Vivisection and Dissection in the Classroom: A Guide to Conscientious Objection* (Jenkintown, PA: American Anti-Vivisection Society, 1992), ix.

131. Jonathan Balcombe, *The Use of Animals in Higher Education*, 41–43.

132. www.pcrm.org/pdfs/research/education/ae_costanal.pdf

133. Jonathan Balcombe, "Dissection: The Scientific Case for Alternatives," *Journal of Applied Animal Welfare Science*, Volume 4, Number 2, 2001.

134. Alicia Ault, "Of Mice and Money," *The Scientist*, July 18, 2005.

135. Jonathan Balcombe, *The Use of Animals in Higher Education*, 28–29.

136. Judith Reitman, *Stolen for Profit: The True Story Behind the Disappearance of Millions of America's Beloved Pets* (New York, NY: Kensington Publishing Corp., 1995), 60.

137. Judith Reitman, "From the Leash to the Laboratory," *The Atlantic*, July 2000.

138. Allie Phillips, *Defending the Defenseless: A Guide to Protecting and Advocating for Pets* (Landham, MD: Rowman & Littlefield Publishing Group, Inc., 2011), 57.

139. Correspondence with Allie Phillips, January 24, 2012.

140. Tom Regan, *Empty Cages: Facing the Challenge of Animal Rights* (Lanham, MD: Rowman & Littlefield Publishers, Inc., 2004), 164.

141. Marc Bekoff, *Minding Animals: Awareness, Emotions, and Heart* (New York, NY: Oxford University Press, 2002), 158.

142. Malcolm L. McCallum, "Amphibian Decline or Extinction? Current Declines Dwarf Background Extinction Rate," *Journal of Herpetology*, Volume 41, Number 3, 2007.

143. Michelè Pickover, *Animal Rights in South Africa* (Cape Town, South Africa: Double Storey Books, 2005), 56.

144. The rhesus macaque used to be the most popular species until India implemented a ban on their export.

145. Ardith A. Eudey, "The crab-eating macaque (Macaca fascicularis): widespread and rapidly declining," *Primate Conservation*, Volume 23, 2008.

146. Nada Padayatchy, "Macaca Fascicularis in Mauritius: A Pest Funding

Conservation Projects," from *Monkeys on the Edge: Ecology and Management of Long-Tailed Macaques and their Interface with Humans*, edited by Michael D. Gumert, Agustín Fuentes, and Lisa Jones-Engel (Cambridge, UK: Cambridge University Press, 2011), 238

147. "Mauritius: The trade in primates for research," British Union for the Abolition of Vivisection, September 2010.

148. Crystal Miller-Spiegel, "Primates by the Numbers," *AV Magazine*, Issues 3 & 4, 2011.

149. "Mauritius: The trade in primates for research," September 2010.

150. Correspondence with Karol Orzechowski, April 30, 2012.

151. Conversation with Michelè Pickover, June 20, 2012.

152. Michelè Pickover, *Animals in Laboratories—A South African State of the Nation: Global Lessons and Future Strategy*, a report compiled for Beauty Without Cruelty South Africa, June 2008.

153. Michelè Pickover, *Animals in Laboratories*.

154. Correspondence with Angie Greenaway, December 13, 2011.

155. Chris Kraul, "In Colombia, activist works to preserve monkeys," *Los Angeles Times*, July 10, 2010.

156. Angela M. Maldonado, Vincent Nijman, and Simon K. Bearder, "Trade in night monkeys *Aotus* spp. in the Brazil–Colombia–Peru tri-border area: international wildlife trade regulations are ineffectively enforced," *Endangered Species Research*, Volume 9, August 2009.

157. Peter Bunyard, "Monkey business—A brutal Amazonian trade in Owl Monkeys," *The Ecologist*, March 13, 2008.

158. Francis Bacon, *The Philosophical Works of Francis Bacon* (London, UK: George Routledge and Sons, 1905), 387. See also Brian Luke, *Brutal: Manhood and the Exploitation of Animals* (Champaign, IL: University of Illinois Press, 2007), 132.

159. Lloyd G. Stevenson, "Religious Elements in the Background of the British Anti-Vivisection Movement," *Yale Journal of Biology and Medicine*, Volume 29, 1956. It could be argued that Blundell linked vivisection and animal sacrifice two years earlier, in his 1823 paper on abdominal surgery. Responding to anti-vivisectionists, and referring to his hysterectomy experiments, Blundell asked, "Which will you

sacrifice, your women or your cats?" See *The Development of Gynaecological Surgery and Instruments*, by James Vincent Ricci (San Francisco, CA: Norman Publishing, 1990), 497.

160. Thomas Joseph Pettigrew, *Medical portrait gallery: Biographical memoirs of the most celebrated physicians, surgeons, etc., etc., who have contributed to the advancement of medical science, Vol. 1* (London, UK: Fisher, Son & Co., 1840), 5.

161. Ouida, "The Future of Vivisection," from *The Gentleman's Magazine*, Volume 252, January to June 1882, edited by Sylvanus Urban (London, UK: Chatto & Windus, Piccadilly, 1882), 412.

162. Brian Luke, *Brutal: Manhood and the Exploitation of Animals* (Champaign, IL: University of Illinois Press, 2007), 132. Here Luke is expanding on the work of Michael Lynch, who in 1988 suggested three points of correspondence between vivisection and ritual sacrifice.

163. Joan Dunayer, "In the Name of Science: The Language of Vivisection," *Organization & Environment*, Volume 13, Number 4, December 2000.

164. Correspondence with Dr. John J. Pippin, January 20, 2012.

165. www.politicalanimal.org.uk/area/eu/cloning

166. www.ciwf.org.uk/includes/documents/cm_docs/2010/q/qa_on_cl oning_august_2010.pdf

167. Burcin Ekser, Mohamed Ezzelarab, Hidetaka Hara, Dirk J. van der Windt, Martin Wijkstrom, Rita Bottino, Massimo Trucco, and David KC Cooper, "Clinical xenotransplantation: the next medical revolution?" *The Lancet*, Volume 379, Issue 9816, February 18, 2012.

168. JA Thompson, AM Eades-Perner, M. Ditter, WJ Muller, W. Zimmermann, "Expression of transgenic carcinoembryonic antigen (CEA) in tumor-prone mice: an animal model for CEA-directed tumor immunotherapy," *International Journal of Cancer*, Volume 72, Issue 1, July 3, 1997.

169. www.nap.edu/openbook.php?record_id=10418&page=98

170. See Uncaged's report at www.xenodiaries.org/report.pdf

171. CV Glines, "The Bat Bombers," *Air Force Magazine: Journal of the Air Force Association*, Volume 73, Number 10, October 1990.

172. Jack Couffer, *Bat Bomb: World War II's Other Secret Weapon* (Austin, TX:

University of Texas Press, 1992).

173. Operation Crossroads, Test Able and Test Baker, Joint Task Force One, final report, March 14, 1947.

174. Figures fluctuate from year to year. According to a Department of Defense (DOD) animal care and use report, 488,237 animals were used in DOD research, education, and training in 2007—up from 364,629 animals used in 2006; the number of animals used per year from 1999 to 2006 remained relatively constant, averaging about 354,000 animals. See www.dtic.mil/biosys/docs/au-fy06_07_report.pdf

175. Tom Vanden Brook, "Military Used Pigs in Blasts to Test Armor" *USA Today*, April 6, 2009.

176. Tom Rawstorne, "Is it really right to blow up pigs even if it saves our soldiers' lives?" *Daily Mail*, May 28, 2010.

177. See *The Medical Aspects of Mustard Gas Poisoning* by Aldred Scott Warthin and Carl Vernon Weller (St. Louis, MO: CV Mosby Company, 1919).

178. Tina Wismer, "Chemical Warfare Agents and Risks to Animal Health," from *Handbook of Toxicology of Chemical Warfare Agents*, edited by Ramesh C. Gupta (London, UK: Academic Press, 2009), 722–730.

179. Joseph Barcroft, "The Toxicity of Atmospheres containing Hydrocyanic Acid Gas," *Journal of Hygiene*, Volume 31, Number 1, January 1931.

180. Rob Evans, "The past Porton Down can't hide," *The Guardian*, May 6, 2004.

181. Some critics have argued that the United States government has actually gone beyond defensive measures and has violated the BWC treaty by developing biological warfare agents and stockpiling them at military bases.

182. Judith Reitman, "One Way Ticket to Ground Zero," *AV Magazine*, Spring 2000.

183. Martin Wainwright, "Porton Down's warfare research base staff become insect monitors," *The Guardian*, May 30, 2012.

184. Chandré Gould and Peter I. Folb, *Project Coast: Apartheid's Chemical and Biological Warfare Programme* (New York, NY: United Nations, 2002), 70.

185. Tom Mangold and Jeff Goldberg, *Plague Wars: The Terrifying Reality of*

Biological Warfare (New York, NY: St. Martin's Press, 2000), 243.

186. In 2010, the purchase or use of dogs, cats, marine mammals, and nonhuman primates by the US military for inflicting wounds from any type of weapon to conduct training in surgical or other medical treatment procedures was prohibited.

187. Correspondence with Kathy Guillermo, PETA's vice president of laboratory investigations, June 26, 2012.

188. Don Mann with Ralph Pezzullo, *Inside SEAL Team Six: My Life and Missions with America's Elite Warriors* (New York, NY: Little, Brown and Company, 2011).

189. CJ Chivers, "Tending a Fallen Marine, with Skill, Prayer and Fury," *The New York Times*, November 2, 2006.

190. Katy Taylor, et al., "Estimates for Worldwide Laboratory Animal Use in 2005." The authors estimate that US labs use and kill 17.3 million animals a year, making it the world's leading exploiter in this industry. Japan and Great Britain are numbers 2 and 3, respectively.

191. Gary L. Francione, *Animals, Property, and the Law* (Philadelphia, PA: Temple University Press, 1995), 189.

192. Dale F. Schwindaman, DVM, "The History of the Animal Welfare Act," from *50 Years of Laboratory Animal Science: 1950–2000*, edited by Charles W. McPherson (Memphis, TN: American Association for Laboratory Animal Science, 1999), 147.

193. Gary Francione, *Animals, Property, and the Law*, 189.

194. Daniel Engber, "Where's Pepper?" *Slate*, June 1, 2009. www.slate.com/id/2219224/

195. Coles Phinizy, "The Lost Pets That Stray to the Labs," *Sports Illustrated*, November 29, 1965.

196. *Life*, February 4, 1966.

197. Diane L. Beers, *For the Prevention of Cruelty: The History and Legacy of Animal Rights Activism in the United States* (Athens, OH: Swallow Press, 2006), 177.

198. Tom L. Beauchamp, Rebecca Dresser, John P. Gluck, David B. Morton, F. Barbara Orlans, *The Human Use of Animals: Case Studies in Ethical Choice*, second edition (New York, NY: Oxford University Press, 2008),

290–291.

199. www.aphis.usda.gov/animal_welfare/downloads/awa/awa.pdf

200. Steven Schapiro, *Handbook of Laboratory Animal Science, Volume I: Essential Principles and Practices*, third edition (Boca Raton, FL: CRC Press, 2011), 48.

201. Scott Plous, PhD, and Harold Herzog, Jr., PhD, "Should the AWA Cover Rats, Mice, and Birds? The Results of an IACUC Survey," *Lab Animal*, June 1999.

202. Congressional Record, V. 148, Pt. 1, January 23, 2002, to February 13, 2002, p. 985.

203. For some reason, the USDA has defined rabbits as "poultry," which means these animals are also denied protection under the Humane Methods of Slaughter Act.

204. www.navs.org.uk/about_us/24/0/299/

205. OR Clarke, "Experiments Need Control," *Third Way*, Volume 2, Number 6, March 23, 1978.

206. In their text *Law Relating to Animals* (London, UK: Cavendish Publishing, 1997), Simon Brooman and Debbie Legge explain these prosecutions occurred in 1876, 1881, and 1913. See pages 133–134.

207. See *The Brown Dog Affair: The Story of a Monument That Divided a Nation* by Peter Mason (London, UK: Two Sevens Publishing, 1997).

208. See "The grim truth about that search for your safe cigarette," by Mary Beith, *Sunday People*, January 26, 1975.

209. Dr. Bernard Dixon, "In the Name of Humanity," *New Scientist*, February 20, 1975.

210. Mike Huskisson, *Outfoxed* (London, UK: Michael Huskisson Associates, 1983), 35–36. By some accounts, Mike had removed three dogs from ICI, but his memoir clearly explains he only managed to rescue two. See also Noel Molland, "Thirty Years of Direct Action," from *Terrorists or Freedom Fighters: Reflections on the Liberation of Animals*, edited by Steven Best and Anthony J. Nocella II (New York, NY: Lantern Books, 2004).

211. Harriet Ritvo, "Royal Society for the Prevention of Cruelty to Animals (RSPCA), History," from *Encyclopedia of Animal Rights and Animal*

Welfare, second edition, edited by Marc Bekoff (Santa Barbara, CA: ABC-CLIO, LLC, 2010), 490.

212. Richard Ryder, "Speciesism in the Laboratory," from *In Defense of Animals: The Second Wave*, edited by Peter Singer (Malden, MA: Blackwell Publishing, 2006), 90.

213. Richard Ryder, *Animal Revolution*, 164.

214. Correspondence with Richard Ryder, January 7, 2012.

215. Source: www.biosecurity.govt.nz/files/regs/animal-welfare/pubs/naea c/naeac-ar-10.pdf

216. Michelè Pickover, *Animal Rights in South Africa*, 118.

217. Conversation with Michelè Pickover, June 20, 2012.

218. Michelè Pickover, *Animal Rights in South Africa*, 122.

219. Michelè Pickover, *Animal Rights in South Africa*, 121.

220. Conversation with Ray Greek, September 22, 2011.

Chapter 4

John Efford made this statement on May 4, 1998, before the House of Assembly proceedings when he was the Minister of Canada's Department of Fisheries and Oceans. The full statement is, "Mr. Speaker, I would like to see the six million seals, or whatever number is out there, killed and sold, or destroyed or burned. I do not care what happens to them. The fact is that the markets are not there to sell more seals; 286,000 were hunted and sold. If there was a market for more... seals the commercial sealers would be hunting and selling seals. ... What they wanted was to have the right to go out and kill the seals. They have that right, and the more they kill the better I will love it." That Efford also served as the country's Minister of Natural Resources makes his diatribe all the more chilling. Source: Paul Watson, *Seal Wars: Twenty-five Years on the Front Lines with the Harp Seals* (Buffalo: NY: Firefly Books, 2003), 230.

1. Bile is produced by the liver and stored in the gallbladder. It is a mixture of acids, cholesterol, water, and electrolytes that aids in the digestion of food.

2. Correspondence with Jill Robinson, May 1, 2010.

3.   Yibin Feng, Kayu Siu, Ning Wang, Kwan-Ming Ng, Sai-Wah Tsao, Tadashi Nagamatsu, and Yao Tong, "Bear bile: dilemma of traditional medicinal use and animal protection," *Journal of Ethnobiology and Ethnomedicine*, 5:2, January 2009.

4.   Correspondence with Jill Robinson, May 1, 2010.

5.   Eric Chivian and Aaron Bernstein, *Sustaining Life: How Human Health Depends on Biodiversity* (New York, NY: Oxford University Press, 2008), 227. Ursodeoxycholic acid is also being studied as an aid for heart-attack sufferers.

6.   Yibin Feng, Kayu Siu, Ning Wang, Kwan-Ming Ng, Sai-Wah Tsao, Tadashi Nagamatsu, and Yao Tong, "Bear bile: dilemma of traditional medicinal use and animal protection."

7.   Tom L. Beauchamp, Rebecca Dresser, John P. Gluck, David B. Morton, F. Barbara Orlans, *The Human Use of Animals: Case Studies in Ethical Choice*, second edition (New York, NY: Oxford University Press, 2008), 125.

8.   Richard Ellis, *Tiger Bone & Rhino Horn: The Destruction of Wildlife for Traditional Chinese Medicine* (Washington, DC: Island Press, 2005), 217.

9.   South Korea also has a bear-bile industry, with about 1,000 moon bears held captive in cages, as does Laos, where it's a relatively new trade and numbers of bears have not been recorded.

10. According to CITES, "Appendix I includes species threatened with extinction. Trade in specimens of these species is permitted only in exceptional circumstances." Source: www.cites.org/eng/disc/how.shtml

11. Correspondence with Kelvin Alie, director, Wildlife Trade Program, International Fund for Animal Welfare, May 4, 2010.

12. Correspondence with Bryan Christy, May 6, 2010.

13. G. Tyler Miller and Scott Spoolman, *Sustaining the Earth* (Belmont, CA: Brooks/Cole, 2009), 107.

14. Jeremy Olshan, "Flying 'fur'st class," *New York Post*, May 14, 2011. The defendant in this case, Noor Mahmoodr of the United Arab Emirates, was charged with smuggling endangered species and faced four years in prison but skipped bail and fled Thailand.

15. "Man caught smuggling 18 monkeys in girdle," *Associated Press*, July 20, 2010.

16. Melissa Jenkins, "NSW: Snake Smuggler Gets Prison Term," *AAP General News* (Australia), October 22, 2003.

17. Charles Bergman, "Wildlife Trafficking," *Smithsonian*, December 2009.

18. Ted Williams, "The Pet Offensive," *Audubon*, December 2003.

19. The list of wild "pets" who have behaved violently and paid with their lives is endless. Notable examples include Travis, a chimp who tore the hands and face off his guardian's friend in 2009 and was fatally shot by police; Georgia, a cougar who mauled a 4-year-old girl at a party in 2006 and was subsequently euthanized; a kangaroo who was "put down" after attacking an 80-year-old man in Ohio in 2011; and Teddy, a 350-pound black bear who killed his guardian in 2009 when she entered his 15-by-15-foot steel-and-concrete cage, and was later shot to death by a neighbor. (The bear owner also kept a Bengal tiger and an African lion as pets.)

20. Jim Mason, "A Lion in Every Back Yard," from *A Primer on Animal Rights: Leading Experts Write About Animal Cruelty and Exploitation*, Kim Stallwood, editor (New York, NY: Lantern Books, 2002), 43.

21. Jennifer Yeh, *Endangered Species: Must They Disappear?* (Farmington Hills, MI: Gale Publishing, 2002), 154.

22. Vikram Jit Singh, "Poacher Nabbed with Dead Sambhar," *Times of India*, June 9, 2011.

23. Glenn Feldhake, *Hippos: Natural History & Conservation* (Stillwater, MN: Voyageur Press, Inc., 2005), 48.

24. Nicholas Wadhams, "Poison-Arrow Killings Surge in Africa Elephant Poaching," *National Geographic News*, February 25, 2009.

25. Phillip Muasya, "Poison meat kills poacher in Tsavo East," *Nairobi Star*, June 1, 2011.

26. "WVDNR Makes Arrest in 'Thrill Kill' Deer Poaching Incidents," *The Herald-Dispatch*, April 03, 2010.

27. www.outdoorlife.com/blogs/big-buck-zone/2009/12/are-poachers-ruining-your-season

28. Debra McKinney, "Trap set near home snares, kills dog," *Anchorage*

Daily News, November 30, 2008.

29. Jayanta Kumar Das, "Rapid deforestation causes man-elephant conflict," *Assam Times*, May 7, 2010.

30. Chris Parsons, Patrick Rice, and Laleh Sadeghi, "Awareness of Whale Conservation Status and Whaling Policy in the US—A Preliminary Study on American Youth," *Anthrozoös: A Multidisciplinary Journal of the Interactions of People and Animals*, Volume 23, Number 2, June 2010.

31. Peggy Connolly, David R. Keller, Becky Cox White, Martin G. Leever, *Ethics in Action: A Case-Based Approach* (Malden, MA: Wiley-Blackwell, 2009), 391.

32. The US, Greenland, St. Vincent and the Grenadines, and Russia allow aboriginal hunting of whales for subsistence purposes. In the United States, Inuits are given annual quotas for whales that they are permitted to hunt, and the food products from these whales must not be sold commercially. Norway and Iceland are the only countries that openly hunt whales for commercial purposes (though Japan's "research" program has long been regarded by most observers as a guise to acquire and consume whale meat). Both countries ignore the IWC ban on commercial whaling and undermine international conservation efforts. Since the IWC ban went into effect in 1986, Iceland, Japan, and Norway have killed more than 25,000 whales. (Source: Humane Society International.)

33. To protect the interests of commercial whaling, a treaty called the International Convention for the Regulation of Whaling (ICRW) was signed in 1946 and established the IWC to "provide for the proper conservation of whale stocks and thus make possible the orderly development of the whaling industry." Article VIII of the ICRW, drafted by Birger Bergersen, the first chair of the IWC, exempts any signatory from prohibitions on killing and taking whales as it "thinks fit" for the "purposes of scientific research." Peter H. Sand of the International Fund for Animal Welfare, however, observes that "according to the clear recollection of Professor Lars Walløe (currently head of Norway's delegation in the IWC Scientific Committee), in Bergersen's mind 'the number of whales a country could take for science was less than 10; he

didn't intend for hundreds [let alone thousands] to be killed for this purpose.'" (Peter H. Sand, "Japan's 'Research Whaling' in the Antarctic Southern Ocean and the North Pacific Ocean in the Face of the Endangered Species Convention (CITES)," *Review of European, Comparative & International Environmental Law*, Volume 17, Issue 1, April 7, 2008.)

34. Peggy Connolly, David R. Keller, Becky Cox White, Martin G. Leever, *Ethics in Action: A Case-Based Approach* (Malden, MA: Wiley-Blackwell, 2009), 394–395.

35. *Associated Press*, "Japanese Annual Marine Research Expedition Kills 59 Whales," October 19, 2009.

36. "Japan will never stop whaling: minister," *Brisbane Times*, February 26, 2013. www.brisbanetimes.com.au/environment/whale-watch/japan-will-never-stop-whaling-minister-20130226-2f4jt.html

37. Blaine Harden, "DNA test finds whale meat illegally served in restaurants was from Japan hunt," *Washington Post*, April 15, 2010.

38. Mark Willacy, "Whalers blow whistle on meat racket," Australian Broadcasting Corporation, June 8, 2010.

39. Justin McCurry, "Whistleblower aims to expose dark side of Japanese whaling," *The Guardian*, June 14, 2010.

40. Marlowe Hood, "Whales closer to us than thought, say scientists," Agence France-Presse, June 20, 2010.

41. Nick Gales, Russell Leaper and Vassili Papastavrou, "Is Japan's whaling humane?" *Science Direct*, July 16, 2007.

42. Patrick Ramage, "Local Group Exposes Japanese Whale Hunt," *Cape Cod Today*, January 7, 2006.

43. Justin McCurry, "Japanese whalers blame Sea Shepherd for smallest catch in years," *The Guardian*, April 13, 2010.

44. Interview with Captain Paul Watson, TreeHugger Radio, August 13, 2009.

45. See www.alaskadispatch.com/article/bowhead-whales-see-huge-population-rebound-alaskas-north-slope

46. "Japanese Man Who Smuggled Endangered Butterflies Sentenced to 21 Months in Federal Prison," US Fish and Wildlife Service press

release, April 16, 2007. USFWS is the principal federal agency responsible for conserving, protecting, and enhancing fish, wildlife, and plants and their habitats in the United States. The Service manages the 95-million-acre National Wildlife Refuge System and enforces federal wildlife laws, administers the Endangered Species Act, manages migratory bird populations, restores nationally significant fisheries, conserves and restores wildlife habitat such as wetlands, and helps foreign governments with their conservation efforts.

47. I met Special Agent Ed Newcomer when we were both speakers at an animal-law conference in 2009. He is enormously helpful and was eager to be formally interviewed for this book, but the United States Fish and Wildlife Service denied my request; therefore, unless otherwise noted, Newcomer's comments are from his presentation. For an in-depth profile of Newcomer and his work on behalf of animals, please read Bruce Barcott's "Secret Agent Man," *Backpacker Magazine*, May 2008.

48. Adam Sherwin, "YouTube sensation fuelling trade in an endangered species," *The Independent*, March 22, 2011.

49. Jeffrey Kofman, "Cuteness Curse: Slow Loris YouTube Videos Fuel Illegal Animal Trade," *ABC News*, November 16, 2012.

50. John M. Sellar, "International Illicit Trafficking in Wildlife," *The Police Chief*, June 2007.

51. Steve Bloomfield, "Warlords Turn to Ivory Trade to Fund Slaughter of Humans," *The Independent*, March 17, 2008.

52. Sharon Begley, "Extinction Trade," *Newsweek*, March 1, 2008.

53. Robin McKie, "UN flies to rescue of Congo gorillas," *Observer*, May 9, 2010.

54. Christian Nellemann, Ian Redmond, and Jonhannes Refisch, *The Last Stand of the Gorilla: Environmental Crime and Conflict in the Congo Basin* (UN Environment Programme/Interpol report), March 2010.

55. George Schaller, *The Year of the Gorilla* (Chicago, IL: University of Chicago Press, 1988), xi–xii.

56. George Schaller, *The Year of the Gorilla*, xiii.

57. African Wildlife Foundation, www.awf.org/content/wildlife/detail

/mountaingorilla

58. Elizabeth Weise, "Census finds only 786 mountain gorillas in the world," *USA Today*, December 20, 2010.

59. Michael Hutchins, "The Dilemma of Confiscated Wildlife," from *State of the Wild 2010–2011: A Global Portrait* (Washington, DC: Island Press, 2010), 202.

60. Michael Hutchins, "The Dilemma of Confiscated Wildlife," 200.

61. See "Disposal of Confiscated Live Specimens of Species Included in the Appendices," CITES Conf. 10.7; and *IUCN/SSC Guidelines for Re-Introductions* (1998) and *IUCN Guidelines for the Placement of Confiscated Animals* (2002), both prepared by the SSC Re-Introduction Specialist Group and published by International Union for the Conservation of Nature.

62. Correspondence with Bryan Christy, May 6, 2010.

63. Michelè Pickover, *Animal Rights in South Africa* (Cape Town, South Africa: Double Storey Books, 2005), 54.

64. See "The Coyote: Florida's Newest Predator" at http://edis.ifas.ufl.edu/uw127

65. Correspondence with Camilla Fox, May 21, 2010.

66. Correspondence with Wendy Keefover-Ring, May 21, 2010.

67. Tom Knudson, "The killing agency: Wildlife Services' brutal methods leave a trail of animal death," *The Sacramento Bee*, April 28, 2012.

68. Wendy Keefover-Ring, "War on Wildlife: The US Department of Agriculture's 'Wildlife Services,'" WildEarth Guardians, February 2009.

69. Tom Knudson, "Wildlife Services' deadly force opens Pandora's box of environmental problems," *The Sacramento Bee*, April 30, 2012.

70. Wendy Keefover-Ring, "War on Wildlife: The US Department of Agriculture's 'Wildlife Services.'"

71. In 2007, then-governor Sarah Palin approved an initiative to pay a US$150 bounty to hunters who shot a wolf from an airplane, chopped off the left foreleg, and brought the appendage in as proof. Ruling that the Palin administration didn't have the authority to offer payments, a state judge quickly put a halt to them but not to Alaska's aerial wolf-

slaughter campaign, which persists.

72. Wendy Keefover-Ring, "War on Wildlife: The US Department of Agriculture's 'Wildlife Services.'"

73. Ibid.

74. www.aphis.usda.gov/wildlife_damage/prog_data/prog_data_re port.shtml

75. Ronald Eisler, *Handbook of Chemical Risk Assessment: Health Hazards to Humans, Plants, and Animals*, Volume 2 (Boca Raton, FL: Lewis Publishers, 2000), 1413.

76. Currently, Compound 1080 is registered for use only in 11 states: Idaho, Montana, New Mexico, Ohio (on a case-by-case basis), Pennsylvania, South Dakota, Texas, Utah, Virginia, West Virginia, and Wyoming.

77. François Leydet, *The Coyote: Defiant Songdog of the West* (Norman, OK: University of Oklahoma Press, 1988), 109.

78. Marilyn Greenwald, *Cleveland Amory: Media Curmudgeon & Animal Rights Crusader* (Lebanon, NH: University Press of New England, 2009), 132.

79. "Welfare Implications of Leghold Trap Use in Conservation and Research," American Veterinary Medical Association, Animal Welfare Division, April 30, 2008.

80. Alexandra Paul, "Dog chews through limb to escape leghold trap," *Winnipeg Free Press*, February 21, 2009.

81. USDA brochure, *Wildlife Services: Helping Producers Manage Predation*, Program Aid No. 1722, October 2002.

82. Jessie McQuillan, "The Exterminators," *Missoula Independent*, June 7, 2007.

83. Camilla Fox, "Wildlife advocates condemn Challis coyote killing 'tournament,'" Project Coyote press release, February 18, 2009.

84. Chip Ward, *Canaries on the Rim: Living Downwind in the West* (New York, NY: Verso, 1999), 25.

85. Correspondence with Marc Bekoff, May 3, 2010.

86. www.aphis.usda.gov/lpa/pubs/fsheet_faq_notice/fs_wscoyote.html

87. Wendy Keefover-Ring, "War on Wildlife: The US Department of

Agriculture's 'Wildlife Services.'"

88. Kim Murray Berger, "Carnivore-Livestock Conflicts: Effects of Subsidized Predator Control and Economic Correlates on the Sheep Industry," *Conservation Biology*, June 2006.

89. Ibid.

90. As hunters discuss on the forum board of www.coyotehunter.net

91. Derrick Jensen, *Endgame, Volume I: The Problem of Civilization* (New York, NY: Seven Stories Press, 2006), 279.

92. Walter Kirn, "Reducing Varmints to Mist," *TIME*, August 7, 2000.

93. Fred Durso, Jr., and Jim Motavalli, "Open Season on 'Varmints,'" *E: The Environmental Magazine*, July/August 2004.

94. Correspondence with Lauren McCain of the Prairie Dog Coalition, July 7, 2010. Dr. McCain notes that because there are five species, each with its own level of population loss, 95 percent is an aggregate figure, and it's probably conservative.

95. Ruthanne Johnson, "The Plight of the Prairie Dog," *All Animals*, January/February 2010.

96. Todd Spivak, "Hog Wild," *Houston Press*, August 24, 2006.

97. Hunter Todd Hanson being interviewed by Caro Meldrum-Hanna, "Uproar over pig-dogging 'blood sport,'" *ABC News* (Australia), July 18, 2012.

98. Tim Flannery and Peter Schouten, *A Gap in Nature: Discovering the World's Extinct Animals* (New York, NY: Atlantic Monthly Press, 2001), 167.

99. John EC Flux, AG Duthie, TJ Robinson, and JA Chapman, "Exotic Populations," from *Rabbits, Hares and Pikas: Status Survey and Conservation Action Plan*, edited by Joseph A. Chapman and John EC Flux (Oxford, UK: Information Press, 1990), 147–148.

100. Michael ER Godfrey, *The European Rabbit Problem in New Zealand*, Proceedings of the 6th Vertebrate Pest Conference, University of Nebraska, 1974.

101. The death toll in 2010 was 23,064, while 22,904 rabbits were killed in 2011.

102. Correspondence with Hans Kriek, April 25, 2011.

103. Rosie Manins, "Terminators top in Easter bunny hunt," *Otago Daily Times*, April 13, 2009.

104. Richard Evans, *Disasters That Changed Australia* (Carlton, Australia: Melbourne University Publishing Limited, 2009), 90–91.

105. Thomas Bellows and TW Fisher, *Handbook of Biological Control* (San Diego, CA: Academic Press, 1999), 963.

106. Dr. Tony Peacock, CEO of the Invasive Animal Cooperative Research Centre, from his presentation to the Australian Superfine Wool Growers' Association, October 25, 2009.

107. Thomas Bellows and TW Fisher, *Handbook of Biological Control*, 963–964.

108. Alexandra Kenney, "New York anglers take home big prize money at Long Island shark fishing tournament," *New York Daily News*, June 25, 2010.

109. According to the International Shark Attack File, your odds of being attacked by a shark are 1 in 11.5 million. In one of the US coastal states, you're 80 times more likely to die from a lightning strike than to be killed by a shark.

110. Jason Heller, "Oak Bluffs Monster Shark Tournament, Martha's Vineyard," www.oceansentry.org, August 17, 2008.

111. Joanna Borucinska, Jason Martin, and Gregory Skomal, "Peritonitis and Pericarditis Associated with Gastric Perforation by a Retained Fishing Hook in a Blue Shark," *Journal of Aquatic Animal Health*, Volume 13, Issue 4, December 2001; and J. Borucinska, N. Kohler, L. Natanson, and G. Skomal, "Pathology associated with retained fishing hooks in blue sharks, *Prionace glauca* (L.), with implications for their conservation," *Journal of Fish Diseases*, 2002.

112. Russell Drumm, "A Great White Mistake," *The East Hampton Star*, June 24, 2010.

113. Paul Watson, *Seal Wars: Twenty-Five Years on the Front Lines with the Harp Seals* (Buffalo, NY: Firefly Books, 2003), 13.

114. Krista Mahr, "Kangaroo: It's What's For Dinner, *TIME*, April 30, 2009. Also, an emerging movement Down Under is a group called kangatarians, who eat a plant-based diet and kangaroo meat. (Bonnie Malkin, "'Kangatarians' Emerge in Australia," *Daily Telegraph*,

February 12, 2010.)

115. Correspondence with Glenys Oogjes, June 16, 2010.

116. *National Code of Practice for the Humane Shooting of Kangaroos and Wallabies for Non-Commercial Purposes*, Natural Resource Management Ministerial Council, Australia, November 2008.

117. Dror Ben-Ami, PhD, "A Shot in the Dark: A Report on Kangaroo Harvesting," May 2009.

118. Correspondence with Nikki Sutterby, June 14, 2010.

119. Expert testimony of Desmond Sibraa, former NSW chief food inspector, as detailed in Appendix 1 of "A Shot in the Dark: A Report on Kangaroo Harvesting," compiled by Dror Ben-Ami, PhD.

120. www.dfat.gov.au/facts/kangaroos.html

121. David Nicholls, "The Kangaroo—Falsely Maligned by Tradition," from *Kangaroos: Myths and Realities*, Maryland Wilson and David B. Croft, editors (Melbourne, Victoria: Australian Wildlife Protection Council, 2005), 35–36, 38.

122. www.savethekangaroo.com/background/shooter.shtml

123. John Kelly, "Kangaroo Industry Strategic Plan, 2005–2010," Australian Government/Rural Industries Research and Development Corporation, August 2005.

124. Conversation with Lauren Ornelas, June 13, 2010.

125. Jordan Rau and Nancy Vogel, "Soccer Scores Goal in Senate," *Los Angeles Times*, May 30, 2007.

126. Correspondence with Uta Haas, Social & Environmental Affairs, Adidas Group, June 17, 2010.

127. Dror Ben-Ami, PhD, "A Shot in the Dark: A Report on Kangaroo Harvesting."

128. Nikki Sutterby, "Decimation of an Icon," Australian Society for Kangaroos, October 2008.

129. Constance Casey, "The Deer Wars," *Slate*, January 24, 2006.

130. Deirdre Fleming, "Turns out, there's dollars in scents," *Maine Outdoor Journal*, January 24, 2010.

131. Correspondence with Gayle Reynolds, Leg Up Enterprises, May 4, 2010.

132. Correspondence with Matt Rossell, June 9, 2010.

133. Charles Krebs, *The Ecological World View* (Berkeley, CA: University of California Press, 2008), 480.

134. Correspondence with Dr. Sarah Foster, June 10, 2010.

135. A notable exception is *Poseidon's Steed: The Story of Seahorses, from Myth to Reality* by marine biologist Helen Scales (New York, NY: Gotham Books, 2009).

136. Catherine Wallis, *Seahorses* (Charlestown, MA: Bunker Hill Publishing, 2004), 7.

137. *Essence of Traditional Chinese Medicine*, third edition, (Singapore: Asiapac Books, 2005), 65

138. Rebecca Bowe, "The last roundup? Seahorses struggle for survival," *E: The Environmental Magazine*, September–October 2004.

139. Correspondence with Dr. Sarah Foster, July 23, 2010.

140. Ibid.

141. Rebecca Bowe, "The last roundup? Seahorses struggle for survival."

142. Correspondence with Dr. Sarah Foster, July 23, 2010.

143. "Seahorse Sleuths," KQED-TV, May 19, 2009.

144. www.biologicaldiversity.org/species/fish/dwarf_seahorse/pdfs/Dwarf _Seahorse_Positive_90_day.pdf

145. Peggy Connolly, David R. Keller, Becky Cox White, Martin G. Leever, *Ethics in Action: A Case-Based Approach* (Malden, MA: Wiley-Blackwell, 2009), 179–180.

146. Marc Bekoff, *Animals Matter: A Biologist Explains Why We Should Treat Animals with Compassion and Respect* (Boston, MA: Shambhala Publications, 2007), 126.

147. Kenya Wildlife Service, "Proposal for the Creation of a DNA Forensics Analysis Laboratory at Kenya Wildlife Service Headquarters, Nairobi, Kenya," 2010.

148. Robert Jurmain, Lynn Kilgore, and Wenda Trevathan, *Essentials of Physical Anthropology*, seventh edition (Belmont, CA: Wadsworth, 2009), 127.

149. "Bushmeat smuggling rife in Europe: report," Agence France-Presse, June 17, 2010.

150. Wangari Maathai, *The Challenge for Africa* (New York, NY: Random House, 2009), 264.

151. Chris Tomlinson, "Demand for elephant meat puts Africa's forest herds at risk," *Seattle Times*, June 7, 2007.

152. Stephen Blake, Samantha Strindberg, Patrick Boudjan, Calixte Makombo, Inogwabini Bila-Isia, et al., "Forest Elephant Crisis in the Congo Basin," *PLoS Biology*, Volume 5, Issue 4, April 2007.

153. "Elephant eaters see no shame in jumbo meal," *Bangkok Times*, December 13, 2009.

154. Jerry Hopkins, *Extreme Cuisine: The Weird & Wonderful Foods That People Eat* (North Clarendon, VT: Tuttle Publishing, 2004), 56.

155. Source: World Wildlife Fund.

156. David Bickford, Corey Bradshaw, Navjo Sodhi, and Ian Warkentin, "Eating Frogs to Extinction," *Conservation Biology*, Volume 23, Issue 4, February 2009.

157. Jessica Forster, "Hop It! Campaigners fight frogs' legs sale," *Sunderland Echo*, March 9, 2010.

158. *BBC News*, "A billion frogs on world's plates," January 22, 2009.

159. David Bickford, Corey Bradshaw, Navjo Sodhi, and Ian Warkentin, "Eating Frogs to Extinction."

160. S. Pantel and SY Chin, "Proceedings of the Workshop on Trade and Conservation of Pangolins Native to South and Southeast Asia," TRAFFIC Southeast Asia, 2009.

161. "Anteater meat confiscated at Philippine airport," *Telegraph*, January 4, 2012.

162. Jonathan Watts, "Chinese customs officials seize thousands of dead pangolins," *The Guardian*, July 13, 2010.

163. "Logbooks Seized of Malaysian Pangolin Trade," *Macau Daily Times*, October 29, 2010.

164. David Braun, "Asian Pangolins Being Consumed to Extinction," *National Geographic*, July 13, 2009.

165. Jonathan Watts, "'Noah's Ark' of 5,000 rare animals found floating off the coast of China," *The Guardian*, May 26, 2007.

166. Jim Yardley, "China's Turtles, Emblems of a Crisis," *The New York*

Times, December 5, 2007.

167. Brian Handwerk, "Millions of US Turtles Consumed in China Annually," *National Geographic News,* July 24, 2009.

168. Steve Patterson, "Florida Bans Commercial Harvest of Freshwater Turtles," *Florida Times-Union,* June 17, 2009.

169. Hilary Hylton, "Keeping US Turtles out of China," *TIME,* May 8, 2007.

170. Ted Williams, "The Terrible Turtle Trade," *Audubon,* March 1999.

171. Committee on Sea Turtle Conservation, *Decline of the Sea Turtles: Causes and Prevention* (Washington, DC: National Academy Press, 1990), 72.

172. Jennifer Viegas, "Millions of Sea Turtles Captured, Killed by Fisheries," *Discovery News,* April 6, 2010.

173. Xu Tianran, "Live Fish, Turtle Key Rings Cruel, But Legal," *Global Times,* March 16, 2011.

174. Trevor Corson, *The Story of Sushi: An Unlikely Saga of Raw Fish and Rice* (New York, NY: HarperCollins Publishers, 2008), 280.

175. www.maine.gov/dmr/rm/seaurchin/Urchin%20report%207-04.pdf

176. Clarke Canfield, "Mainers Hope to Save Spiny Sea Urchin Trade," *The Boston Globe,* December 28, 2011.

Chapter 5

Henry David Thoreau is quoted from *A Week on the Concord and Merrimack Rivers* (Boston, MA: James R. Osgood and Company, 1873), 44.

1. Vivian Farrell, "Omak Suicide Race: The Deadliest Horse Race in the World," International Fund for Horses, May 22, 2005, www.defend-horsescanada.org/OmakSuicideRace.html

2. Nick Timiraos, "The Race Where Horses Die," *Wall Street Journal,* August 11, 2007.

3. Michael Wallis, *The Real Wild West: The 101 Ranch and the Creation of the American West* (New York, NY: St. Martin's Press, 1999), 136. A young Ranger named John McMullin came in first place.

4. Joel H. Bernstein, *Wild Ride: The History and Lore of Rodeo* (Layton, UT: Gibbs Smith, 2007), 38.

5. Kristine Fredriksson, *American Rodeo: From Buffalo Bill to Big Business* (College Station, TX: Texas A&M University Press, 1993), 135.

6. You can see the rules, and SHARK's commentary, at www.shark online.org/?P=0000000276

7. See www.youtube.com/watch?v=Eg-9rR-iz1Q

8. See www.all-creatures.org/adow/cam-rod-pic-hb-07.html

9. Martin Griffith, "Illinois Animal Rights Group Targets Reno Rodeo for Horse Abuse," *Huffington Post*, July 6, 2012.

10. www.sharkonline.org/?P=0000000992

11. Elizabeth Atwood Lawrence, *Rodeo: An Anthropologist Looks at the Wild and the Tame* (Chicago, IL: The University of Chicago Press, 1982), 177.

12. Ibid.

13. www.vancouverhumanesociety.bc.ca/media-centre/breaking-news/

14. Rodeo events are not covered by Canadian animal cruelty laws because they are considered "generally accepted practices of animal management" for the treatment of livestock.

15. Carrie Tait and Dawn Walton, "Chuckwagon racers defend their sport," *The Globe and Mail*, July 13, 2012.

16. Valerie Fortney, "A frantic 75-second Chuckwagon race in a quest to be the best," *Calgary Herald*, October 10, 2012.

17. See *The Second Sex* by Simone de Beauvoir (Random House).

18. Marti Kheel, "The Killing Game: An Ecofeminist Critique of Hunting," *Journal of the Philosophy of Sport*, Volume 23, 1996. Marti went on to develop her thesis into the 2008 book *Nature Ethics: An Ecofeminist Perspective* (New York, NY: Rowman & Littlefield Publishers, Inc.).

19. "On Killing," December 7, 2011. http://honest-food.net/2011/12/07/on-killing/

20. Jim Robertson, *Exposing the Big Game: Living Targets of a Dying Sport* (Alresford, UK: Earth Books, 2012), 14.

21. Peter Archer, *The Quotable Intellectual: 1,417 Bon Mots, Ripostes, and Witticisms for Aspiring Academics, Armchair Philosophers... and Anyone Else Who Wants to Sound Really Smart* (Avon, MA: Adams Media, 2010), 187.

22. www.dnr.sc.gov/wildlife/deer/articlegad.html

23. Jim Robertson, *Exposing the Big Game: Living Targets of a Dying Sport*, 15.

24. http://dakotatree.tripod.com/hunting_facts.html

25. M. Andy Pedersen, Seth M. Berry, JC Bossart, "Wounding Rates of White-tailed Deer with Modern Archery Equipment," *Proceedings of the Annual Conference of Southeastern Association of Fish and Wildlife Agencies*, 2008.

26. www.sportsmansguide.com/Outdoors/Subject/SubjectRead.aspx?sid =0&aid=151524&type=A

27. http://gfp.sd.gov/hunting/waterfowl/wounding-losses.aspx

28. www.tovarcerulli.com/2011/03/wounded-animals-uncomfortable-hunters/

29. http://ihea-usa.org/news-and-events/news/incident-reports

30. *Associated Press*, "Family Dog Mistaken for Coyote, Shot and Killed by Hunter," *Bangor Daily News*, December 30, 2011.

31. http://hsa.enviroweb.org/index.php/news/press-releases/392-vicious-attack-on-hunt-saboteur-on-foxhunts-most-prestigious-day

32. Conversation with Kim Stallwood, December 11, 2012.

33. Canned hunts have a long history. In 1902, President Theodore Roosevelt gave the world teddy bears by refusing a canned hunt. After an unproductive outing for black bear in Mississippi, one of the guides ran down a bear with dogs and tied the terrified animal to a willow tree for Roosevelt to shoot. He declined in disgust, and when *The Washington Post* ran a cartoon of the incident, an enterprising maker of stuffed toy animals created "Teddy's Bear."

34. Alfred Lubrano, "'Canned Hunts' Become Target of Controversy: The Quest is Exotic Prey. The Arena–Fenced Preserves, Not the Wild. Foes Include Animal-rights Activists and Many Hunters," *Philly.com*, February 02, 1996. http://articles.philly.com/1996-02-02/news/256 56236_1_boar-pro-hunting-canned-hunt

35. Ted Williams, "The Pet Offensive," *Audubon*, December 2003.

36. www.humanesociety.org/issues/captive_hunts/facts/captive_hunt _fact_sheet.html

37. Ted Williams, "Real Hunters Don't Shoot Pets," *Audubon*, November/December 2010.

38. http://usatoday30.usatoday.com/life/people/2006-11-27-gentry-bear_x.htm

39. Alan Green, *Animal Underworld: Inside America's Black Market for Rare and Exotic Species* (New York, NY: PublicAffairs, 1999), 222–226.

40. www.ohiotrophydeer.com/pricing.html

41. www.youtube.com/watch?v=XSHEeM4icLc&feature=youtu.be

42. P. Lindsey, R. Alexander, G. Balme, N. Midlane, and J. Craig, "Possible relationships between the South African captive-bred lion hunting industry and the hunting and conservation of lions elsewhere in Africa," *South African Journal of Wildlife Research*, Volume 42, Issue 1, April 2012.

43. Gareth Patterson, "Horrors of Canned Lion Hunting," *Mail & Guardian*, May 2, 1997.

44. http://mg.co.za/article/2012-07-04-sa-breeders-embrace-growing-asian-demand-for-lion-bones

45. Here's another way to view the industry's popularity: In South Africa alone, game ranches cover 160,000 square kilometers (61,776 square miles), or 13.1 percent of the country, while 56,000 square kilometers (21,621 square miles)—just 4.6 percent—are occupied by national parks.

46. P. Lindsey, R. Alexander, G. Balme, N. Midlane, and J. Craig, "Possible relationships between the South African captive-bred lion hunting industry and the hunting and conservation of lions elsewhere in Africa."

47. Oliver Harvey, "Come to the World Cup… and shoot a lion," *The Sun*, January 12, 2011.

48. www.voanews.com/content/lion-bone-trade-10aug12/1484066.html

49. Amy Worden, "Witness to a pigeon shoot: Hundreds of birds shot, the wounded pummeled," *Philly.com*, October 11, 2012. www.philly.com/philly/blogs/pets/Witness-to-a-pigeon-shoot-Hundreds-of-birds-shot-the-wounded-pummelled-.html

50. Conversation with Janet Enoch, December 12, 2012.

51. www.dailykos.com/story/2010/03/15/846312/-SHAMELESS-DA-Refuses-to-Prosecute-Animal-Cruelty-Case

52. www.bctv.org/opinion/pigeon-shoots-they-have-them-in-berks-should-be-halted/article_344ba12a-b440-11e1-b8f8-0019bb2963f4.html

53. Per correspondence with Karel Minor, January 17, 2013.

54. RM Schneiderman, "NYC Pigeons Trapped, Kidnapped and Shot for Sport, Group Says," *Wall Street Journal,* May 24, 2010.

55. www.all-creatures.org/aro/nl-19990725-hegins.html

56. Live pigeon shoots made one Olympic appearance, at the 1900 games in Paris, but thereafter were ruled to be cruel.

57. www.huffingtonpost.co.uk/kate-holmes/fox-hunting-the-countrysides-best-kept-secret_b_1016400.html

58. www.spectator.co.uk/columnists/rod-liddle/8834871/the-law-doesnt-change-just-because-youre-on-horseback/

59. Mian Ridge, "English flout hunting ban in foxy style," *Christian Science Monitor,* December 27, 2011.

60. Jonathan Brown, "Threats, car chases and arson: how the hare coursing ban is flouted," *The Independent,* December 26, 2011.

61. Mike Rendle, "Stress and Capture Myopathy in Hares," Irish Hare Initiative, January 2006.

62. www.thejournal.ie/calls-for-an-end-to-inherently-cruel-hare-coursing-444679-May2012/

63. John Fitzgerald, *Bad Hare Days: One Man's Fight Against a Cruel Blood Sport!* (Callan, Ireland: Callan Press, 2011), 225.

64. The 16-percent figure comes from SJ Casselman, "Catch-and-release angling: A review with guidelines for proper fish handling practices," while the 43-percent number is from ER Gilliland, "Evaluation of Procedures to Reduce Delayed Mortality of Black Bass Following Summer Tournaments," Oklahoma Department of Wildlife Conservation, Federal Aid in Sport Fish Restoration, Project F-50-R, Final Report, Oklahoma City, 1997.

65. US Department of the Interior, US Fish and Wildlife Service, and US Department of Commerce, US Census Bureau, "2011 National Survey of Fishing, Hunting, and Wildlife-Associated Recreation," December 2012.

66. KL Pope, GR Wilde, and DW Knabe, "Effect of catch-and-release angling on growth and survival of rainbow trout, *Oncorhynchus mykiss,*" *Nebraska Cooperative Fish & Wildlife Research Unit — Staff*

Publications, January 1, 2007.

67.   Brandon Zimmerman, "Does Catch and Release Hurt Fish?" *Jackson Hole News & Guide*, August 12, 2009.

68.   SJ Casselman, "Catch-and-release angling: A review with guidelines for proper fish handling practices," Fish & Wildlife Branch, Ontario Ministry of Natural Resources, Peterborough, Ontario, July 2005.

69.   Victoria Braithwaite, "Hooked on a myth," *Los Angeles Times*, October 8, 2006.

70.   http://onlinelibrary.wiley.com/doi/10.1111/faf.12010/abstract

71.   For a discussion on this, see www.practicalfishkeeping.co.uk/content.php?sid=5436

72.   Josie Ensor, "Fish cannot feel pain say scientists," *Telegraph*, January 13, 2013.

73.   www.worldfishingnetwork.com/news/team-wins-24-million-at-marlin-fishing-tournament-266595.aspx

74.   Alison Mood, "Worse things happen at sea: the welfare of wild-caught fish," www.fishcount.org.uk, August 2010

75.   Gregory S. Aldrete, *Daily Life in the Roman City: Rome, Pompeii, and Ostia* (Westport, CT: Greenwood Press, 2004), 131.

76.   Lauren E. Cowles, "The Spectacle of Bloodshed in Roman Society," *Constructing the Past*, Volume 12, Issue 1, Article 10, 2011. http://digitalcommons.iwu.edu/constructing/vol12/iss1/10

77.   Doug O'Harra and Natalie Phillips, "Wanted: Healthy, Happy Dogs," *Anchorage Daily News*, February 23, 1997.

78.   www.helpsleddogs.org/remarks-dogdeaths.htm

79.   Julia Rubin, "Dog-Sled Racers Take Heat for Culling Practices," *The Seattle Times*, November 3, 1991.

80.   http://lakotasong.com/48004918-Mass-sled-dog-killing-probed-in-Whistler-B-C.pdf

81.   Lew Freedman, *Father of the Iditarod: The Joe Redington Story* (Kenmore, WA: Epicenter Press, 1999), 5.

82.   Correspondence with Ashley Keith, January 31, 2013.

83.   Dene Stansall and Andrew Tyler, *Bred to Death: How the Racing Industry's Drive for Profit and Glory Is Ruining the Thoroughbred Horse,*

Animal Aid UK, September 2006.

84. Walt Bogdanich, Joe Drape, Dara L. Miles, and Griffin Palmer, "Mangled Horses, Maimed Jockeys," *The New York Times*, March 24, 2012.

85. Dene Stansall and Andrew Tyler, *Bred to Death*.

86. Roger Highfield and Nic Fleming, "Champion Racehorses are Thoroughly Inbred," *Telegraph*, September 6, 2005.

87. Dene Stansall and Andrew Tyler, *Bred to Death*.

88. Bogdanich, Drape, Miles, and Palmer, "Mangled Horses, Maimed Jockeys."

89. http://nbcsports.msnbc.com/id/19468788/

90. Walt Bogdanich and Rebecca R. Ruiz, "Turning to Frogs for Illegal Aid in Horse Races," *The New York Times*, June 19, 2012.

91. Dene Stansall and Andrew Tyler, *Bred to Death*.

92. www.paulickreport.com/news/bloodstock/winstar-announces-2013-stud-fees/

93. Zoe Brennan, "Why healthy foals—some just a day old—are being killed across Britain by a crisis-hit racing industry that is slaughtering adult thoroughbreds in their thousands... to end up as dog food and on French dinner plates," *Daily Mail*, April 9, 2009.

94. Jamie Doward, "'Record' number of thoroughbreds being slaughtered for meat," *Observer*, February 5, 2011.

95. Ray Paulick, "Death of a Derby Winner: Slaughterhouse Likely Fate for Ferdinand," *The Blood-Horse*, July 25, 2003.

96. www.grey2kusa.org/pdf/GREY2K%20USA%20Confinement%20Fact%20Sheet.pdf

97. www.grey2kusa.org/pdf/GREY2K%20USA%204-D%20Meat%20Fact%20Sheet.pdf

98. Ted Jeory, "Dog kennels branded 'disgusting,'" *Sunday Express*, January 22, 2012.

99. www.league.org.uk/uploads/media/17/7354.pdf

100. Erin E. Williams and Margo DeMello, *Why Animals Matter: The Case for Animal Protection* (Amherst, NY: Prometheus Books, 2007), 326.

Chapter 6

Tom Rider is quoted from his June 13, 2000, testimony before the US House Judiciary Committee's Subcommittee on Crime. Rider was speaking in support of the Captive Elephant Accident Prevention Act, which would have outlawed the use of elephants in traveling shows or circuses and for the purpose of offering elephant rides. The bill did not pass.

1. Susan Jacobson, "Trainer Dawn Brancheau decided as child to work with killer whales," *Orlando Sentinel*, February 24, 2010.
2. SeaWorld trainers are taught to not react in such emergencies—to give the animal a neutral response, even smile.
3. Associated Press, "Workers tell of desperate attempt to save trainer attacked by killer whale," *The Guardian*, March 2, 2010.
4. According to the medical examiner's report, Dawn Brancheau also suffered a lacerated liver, a broken sternum, dislocations of her left knee and elbow, and major internal bleeding.
5. See www.huffingtonpost.com/ingrid-newkirk/seaworld-san-diego_b_985566.html
6. Correspondence with Ingrid Newkirk, September 28, 2011.
7. Correspondence with Howard Garrett, September 28, 2011.
8. Correspondence with Lori Marino, October 2, 2011.
9. Leah LeMieux, *Rekindling the Waters: The Truth About Swimming with Dolphins* (Leicester, UK: Matador, 2009), 253.
10. Correspondence with Howard Garrett, September 28, 2011.
11. In 1991, while in captivity at Sealand of the Pacific, a marine park in British Columbia, Tilikum was one of three orcas who killed a part-time trainer, 20-year-old Keltie Byrne, when she fell into the pool. Eight years later, after being sold to SeaWorld Orlando, Tili was found with the body of 27-year-old Daniel Dukes in his mouth. Dukes had either snuck into the park or had remained after closing the night before.
12. Correspondence with Lori Marino, October 2, 2011.
13. Correspondence with Jeff Ventre, September 28, 2011.
14. www.osha.gov/pls/oshaweb/owadisp.show_document?p_table=NE

WS_RELEASES&p_id=18207

15. Correspondence with Dr. Naomi Rose, September 13, 2012.
16. Sally Kestin, "Not a Perfect Picture," *Sun-Sentinel*, May 16, 2004.
17. She died at SeaWorld after six years in captivity.
18. These whales were members of what is known as the Southern Resident community. Since 2005, this whale population has been protected under the Endangered Species Act, but in 1970, capture crews were able to operate with impunity.
19. *Baby Wild Films Presents: The Killer Whale People*, 1999, Baby Wild Films, Michael Harris, producer.
20. Sally Kestin, "Not a Perfect Picture."
21. "SeaWorld Investigation: Secrets Below the Surface," *10News*, May 29, 2007.
22. *Baby Wild Films Presents: The Killer Whale People*.
23. Tim Zimmermann, "The Killer in the Pool," *Outside*, July 30, 2010.
24. The other male, given the name Nandú, and the female, named Samoa, were sold to Acuarama, an aquarium in Brazil. Nandú died there in 1988. The following year, Samoa was sold to SeaWorld in Aurora, Ohio, where she lived until 1990, when she was shipped to SeaWorld in San Antonio, Texas. At the Texas park, Samoa mated and became pregnant, though she and her calf died as she was giving birth in 1992.
25. In 2012, Nakai became the center of a lawsuit filed by PETA when photos of the orca surfaced showing a wound under his mouth so serious it revealed his jawbone. PETA contended Nakai sustained the injury in a fight with two other whales, all of whom are under stress from confinement.
26. http://news.discovery.com/animals/killer-whale-testosterone-surges-documented-by-seaworld.html. In addition to the calves mentioned in the article, Tilikum sired an 18th calf, born at SeaWorld San Diego on February 14, 2013.
27. JK O'Brien and TR Robeck, "The Value of *Ex Situ* Cetacean Populations in Understanding Reproductive Physiology and Developing Assisted Reproductive Technology for *Ex Situ* and *In Situ* Species Management and Conservation Efforts," *International Journal of Comparative*

Psychology, Volume 23, 2010.

28. Correspondence with Dr. Naomi Rose, September 13, 2012.

29. Conversation with Dr. Lori Marino, September 9, 2012.

30. JK O'Brien and TR Robeck, "The Value of *Ex Situ* Cetacean Populations in Understanding Reproductive Physiology and Developing Assisted Reproductive Technology for *Ex Situ* and *In Situ* Species Management and Conservation Efforts."

31. Orcas are in fact members of the marine family *Delphinidae,* which includes such species as the bottlenose dolphin, the Atlantic white-sided dolphin, the Pacific white-sided dolphin, the pilot whale, and the spinner dolphin.

32. www.orcahome.de/orcastat.htm

33. An inventory at www.ceta-base.com/phinventory tries to keep up.

34. Marc Bekoff, "Rewilding Dolphins: Good News for Tom and Misha," PsychologyToday.com, May 12, 2012.

35. Kelly A. Waples and Nicholas J. Gales, "Evaluating and Minimizing Social Stress in the Care of Captive Bottlenose Dolphins (*Tursiops aduncus*)," *Zoo Biology,* Volume 21, Issue 1, March 20, 2002.

36. Tadamichi Morisaka, Shiro Kohshima, Motoi Yoshioka, Miwa Suzuki, and Fumio Nakahara, "Recent studies on captive cetaceans in Japan: Working in tandem with studies on cetaceans in the wild," *International Journal of Comparative Psychology,* Volume 23, 2010.

37. Jean-Michel Cousteau with Daniel Paisner, *My Father, the Captain: My Life with Jacques Cousteau* (Washington, DC: National Geographic Society, 2010), 141.

38. Amanda Cochrane and Karena Callen, *Dolphins and Their Power to Heal* (Rochester, VT: Healing Arts Press, 1992), 144.

39. Conversation with Ric O'Barry, August 24, 2012.

40. http://news.nationalgeographic.com/news/2009/08/090810-cove-movie-dolphins-ngm/ and www.takepart.com/article/2012/08/28/op-ed-return-dolphin-hunts

41. Diana Reiss and Lori Marino, "Mirror self-recognition in the bottlenose dolphin: A case of cognitive convergence," *Proceedings of the National Academy of Sciences,* Volume 98, Number 10, May 8, 2001.

www.pnas.org/content/98/10/5937.full

42. Conversation with Dr. Lori Marino, September 9, 2012.

43. www.wspa-usa.org/wspaswork/marinemammals/USdolphinregs.aspx

44. http://boards.cruisecritic.com/showthread.php?p=35309072

45. Felicity Barringer, "Opposition as Aquarium Seeks Import of Whales," *The New York Times*, October 9, 2012.

46. Amanda Cochrane and Karena Callen, *Dolphins and Their Power to Heal* (Rochester, VT: Healing Arts Press, 1992), 17.

47. Lori Marino and Scott O. Lilienfeld, "Dolphin-Assisted Therapy: More Flawed Data and More Flawed Conclusions," *Anthrozoös*, Volume 20, Issue 3, 2007.

48. Britta L. Fiksdal, Daniel Houlihan, and Aaron C. Barnes, "Dolphin-Assisted Therapy: Claims versus Evidence," *Autism Research and Treatment*, Volume 2012, June 2012.

49. Conversation with Dr. Lori Marino, September 9, 2012.

50. Philippa Brakes and Cathy Williamson, "Dolphin Assisted Therapy: Can you put your faith in DAT?" The Whale and Dolphin Conservation Society, October 2007.

51. Ibid.

52. Mira Micic, "Delfin Gick Till Blodig Attack–Bet Svensk Turist," *Aftonbladet*, November 30, 2012. www.aftonbladet.se/nyheter/article15856746.ab

53. Arelis R. Hernández, "SeaWorld attack: Video captures dolphin biting little girl," *Orlando Sentinel*, December 1, 2012.

54. John W. Stamper, *The Architecture of Roman Temples: The Republic to the Middle Empire* (Cambridge, UK: Cambridge University Press, 2005), 173.

55. Animal Defenders International, *Animals in Traveling Circuses: The Science on Suffering*, July 14, 2008. www.ad-international.org/animals_in_entertainment/go.php?id=1368

56. Correspondence with Hans Kriek, August 8, 2012.

57. Barbara Fitzgerald, "Pachyderm's Personality Not on File," *Sarasota Herald-Tribune*, February 10, 1992.

58. Lynne Bumpus-Hooper, "Mom Describes Terror at Circus," *Orlando*

Sentinel, April 24, 1992.

59.   Louis Sagahun, "Elephants Pose Giant Dangers," *Los Angeles Times*, October 11, 1994.

60.   Gail Laule and Margaret Whittaker, "Protected Contact and Elephant Welfare," from *An Elephant in the Room: The Science and Well-Being of Elephants in Captivity*, edited by Paul F. Waldau, Lisa F. Kane, Debra L. Forthman, and David Hancocks (North Grafton, MA: Tufts University Cummings School of Veterinary Medicine's Center for Animals and Public Policy, 2008), 185.

61.   Complaint filed by the American Society for the Prevention of Cruelty to Animals against Feld Entertainment, Inc., parent company of Ringling Bros., April 24, 2009. In 1998, a year before Benjamin's death, the ex-employees, Glen Ewell and James Stechon, had urged the USDA to exercise its authority under the Animal Welfare Act to confiscate Benjamin and place him in a temporary shelter to protect him from further abuse and mistreatment. www.eswr.com/docs/Ringling/533-1.pdf

62.   http://c206728.r28.cf1.rackcdn.com/Plaintiffs-Will-Call-Exhibit-24.pdf

63.   http://labanimals.awionline.org/wildlife/elephants/Part%205.pdf

64.   http://c206729.r29.cf1.rackcdn.com/03-03-09_Trial.pdf

65.   www.publicbroadcasting.net/wabe/news.newsmain?action=article&ARTICLE_ID=1904626

66.   Roberto J. Manzano, "Ex-Child TV Star Faces Jail for Protest," *Los Angeles Times*, February 2, 2000.

67.   www.carsonbarnescircus.com/caring-elephants/

68.   Roberts received a three-year conditional discharge.

69.   Marc Kaufman, "USDA Investigates Death of Circus Lion," *Washington Post*, August 8, 2004.

70.   *Associated Press*, "Eight Russian circus tigers, lioness die during travel," *USA Today*, December 22, 2009.

71.   Graziella Iossa, Carl Soulsbury, and Stephen Harris, "Are wild animals suited to a travelling circus life?" *Animal Welfare*, Volume 18, Number 2, May 2009.

72.   David Crary, "Groups Try to Stop Circus from Chaining Elephants,"

USA Today, May 21, 2008.

73. Animal Defenders International, *Animals in Traveling Circuses: The Science on Suffering*, July 14, 2008. www.ad-international.org/animals _in_entertainment/go.php?id=1368

74. Graziella Iossa, Carl Soulsbury, and Stephen Harris, "Are wild animals suited to a travelling circus life?" *Animal Welfare*, Volume 18, Number 2, May 2009.

75. www.govtrack.us/congress/bills/112/hr3359/text

76. Vernon N. Kisling, Jr., "Ancient Collections and Menageries," from *Zoo and Aquarium History: Ancient Animal Collections to Zoological Gardens*, edited by Vernon N. Kisling (Boca Raton, FL: CRC Press, LLC, 2001), 11.

77. Laurence Bergreen, *Marco Polo: From Venice to Xanadu* (New York, NY: Random House, 2007), 151.

78. Alexander Sokolowsky, *Observations on the Psyche of the Great Apes* (Frankfurt, Germany: Neuer Frankfurter Verlag, 1908), 17–18.

79. Dale Jamieson, "Against Zoos," from *In Defense of Animals: The Second Wave*, edited by Peter Singer (Malden, MA: Blackwell Publishing Ltd., 2006), 141

80. Matt Walker, "Gorillas and chimps are threatened by human disease," *BBC Nature*, August 29, 2012.

81. KA Terio, L. Marker, and L. Munson, "Evidence for Chronic Stress in Captive But Not Free-Ranging Cheetahs (*Acinonyx jubatus*) Based on Adrenal Morphology and Function," *Journal of Wildlife Diseases*, Volume 40, Number 2, April 2004.

82. Leslie Kaufman, "Date Night at the Zoo, if Rare Species Play Along," *The New York Times*, July 4, 2012.

83. Ros Clubb, Marcus Rowcliffe, Phyllis Lee, Khyne U. Mar, Cynthia Moss, and Georgia J. Mason, "Compromised Survivorship in Zoo Elephants," *Science*, Volume 322, Number 5908, December 2008.

84. Correspondence with Dr. Georgia Mason, September 14, 2012.

85. When Dunda, an African elephant, was transferred from the San Diego Zoo to the San Diego Wild Animal Park in 1988, she was chained, pulled to the ground, and beaten with ax handles for two days. One

witness described the blows as "home run swings." Such abuse may be the norm. "You have to motivate them," said San Francisco zookeeper Paul Hunter of elephants, "and the way you do that is by beating the hell out of them." (Jane Fritsch, "Beatings, Abuse: Elephants in Captivity: a Dark Side," *Los Angeles Times*, October 5, 1988.)

86. Ros Clubb, Marcus Rowcliffe, Phyllis Lee, Khyne U. Mar, Cynthia Moss, and Georgia J. Mason, "Fecundity and population viability in female zoo elephants: problems and possible solutions," *Universities Federation for Animal Welfare*, Volume 18, 2009.

87. According to Rob Laidlaw, chaining elephants at night is happening less and less in US zoos, where it's more common to keep them in stalls at night.

88. http://news.bbc.co.uk/2/hi/6100430.stm

89. Brad Hamilton, "Happy the elephant's sad life alone at the Bronx Zoo," *New York Post*, September 30, 2012.

90. Correspondence with Rob Laidlaw, September 19, 2012.

91. David Hancocks, "Is There a Place in the World for Zoos?" from *The State of the Animals 2001*, edited by Deborah J. Salem and Andrew N. Rowan (Washington, DC: Humane Society Press, 2001), 143.

92. Michael J. Berens, "Elephants Are Dying out in America's Zoos," *The Seattle Times*, December 1, 2012.

93. Ibid.

94. Dale Jamieson, "Against Zoos," from *In Defense of Animals*, 138.

95. Leslie Kaufman, "When Babies Don't Fit Plan, Question for Zoos Is, Now What?" *The New York Times*, August 3, 2012. The article points out that European zoos are allowing some animals to reproduce naturally and raise their young; then officials kill the offspring when they reach maturity.

96. Rhéal Séguin, "Seals' death sentence sparks outcry from animal lovers across Canada," *The Globe and Mail*, September 16, 2012.

97. Although not a "surplus animal," the critically endangered scimitar-horned oryx provides one example. When Texas rancher David Bamberger turned part of his property into a "haven" for this African

antelope in the 1970s, zoos across the US sent him nearly all their remaining oryxes. Bamberger bred the animals, many of whom ended up killed in canned hunts on other Texas ranches, though today oryxes are protected under the Endangered Species Act, thanks in large part to the efforts of Friends of Animals.

98. Dwight Silverman, "Captive Prey: Animals Facing Uncertain Fate in Deals with Hunting Ranches," *Houston Chronicle*, April 5, 1992. In addition, activist Lauren Ornelas has reviewed documents firsthand detailing animals going directly from the San Antonio Zoo to hunting ranches.

99. Amy Wallace, "San Diego Zoo Halts Sales to Breeders Tied to Hunting: Animal Rights: Embarrassed zoo official says the dealers' links to hunting were not known," *Los Angeles Times*, September 18, 1991.

100. Linda Goldston, "Animals once admired at country's major zoos are sold or given away to dealers," *San Jose Mercury News*, February 11, 1999.

101. Christine Lepisto, "Zoo Sells Lions to African Trophy Hunting Park," *Treehugger.com*, May 9, 2010.

102. Erik Jensen, "Hunter buys zoo's endangered antelope, *The Sydney Morning Herald*, August 6, 2009.

103. Animal Defenders International, *Animals in Traveling Circuses: The Science on Suffering*, July 14, 2008. www.ad-international.org/animals_in_entertainment/go.php?id=1368

104. Gay Bradshaw, PhD, PhD; Theodora Capaldo, EdD; Lorin Lindner, PhD, MPH; and Gloria Grow, "Building an Inner Sanctuary: Complex PTSD in Chimpanzees," *Journal of Trauma & Dissociation*, Volume 9, 2008.

105. Maryann Mott, "'Puppy Prozac': Can Animals Benefit From Behavioral Meds?" *National Geographic News*, September 29, 2005.

106. Lucy P. Birkett and Nicholas E. Newton-Fisher, "How Abnormal Is the Behaviour of Captive, Zoo-Living Chimpanzees?" *PLoS ONE*, Volume 6, Issue 6, June 2011. www.plosone.org/article/info:doi/10.1371/journal.pone.0020101

107. VA Langman, TJ Roberts, J. Black, GM Maloiy, NC Heglund, JM Weber,

R. Kram, and CR Taylor, "Moving cheaply: energetics of walking in the African elephant," *Journal of Experimental Biology*, Volume 198, March 1, 1995.

108. Raghunandan S. Chundawat, Neel Gogate, and AJT Johnsingh, "Tigers in Panna: preliminary results from an Indian tropical dry forest," from *Riding the Tiger: Tiger Conservation in Human-Dominated Landscape*, edited by John Seidensticker, Sarah Christie, and Peter Jackson (Cambridge, UK: Cambridge University Press, 1999), 125.

109. Kathleen N. Morgan and Chris T. Tromborg, "Sources of stress in captivity," *Applied Animal Behaviour Science*, Volume 102, February 2007.

110. Graziella Iossa, Carl Soulsbury, and Stephen Harris, "Are wild animals suited to a travelling circus life?" *Animal Welfare*, Volume 18, Number 2, May 2009.

111. Hope R. Ferdowsian, Debra L. Durham, Charles Kimwele, Godelieve Kranendonk, Emily Otali, Timothy Akugizibwe, JB Mulcahy, Lilly Ajarova, and Cassie Meré Johnson, "Signs of Mood and Anxiety Disorders in Chimpanzees," *PLoS ONE*, Volume 6, Issue 6, June 2011. www.plosone.org/article/info:doi%2F10.1371%2Fjournal.pone.001985 5#

112. Honorable John L. Segal, ruling, Superior Court of California, County of Los Angeles, July 23, 2012.

113. www.clearingmagazine.org/archives/767

114. Conversation with Dr. Gay Bradshaw, August 8, 2012.

115. Dale Jamieson, "Against Zoos," 136.

116. Edward G. Ludwig, "A Study of Buffalo Zoo," from *International Journal for the Study of Animal Problems*, edited by Michael Fox, Institute for the Study of Animal Problems, 1981.

117. William Booth, "Naked Ape New Zoo Attraction; Surprise Results From People-Watching Study," *Washington Post*, March 14, 1991.

118. Dale Jamieson, "Against Zoos," from *In Defense of Animals*, 135.

119. www.kimmela.org/wp-content/uploads/2012/10/Testimony-Congress-Marino-04272010.pdf

120. www.kimmela.org/the-georgia-aquarium-plays-the-education-card-

again/

121. www.southernfriedscience.com/?p=4041

122. Stephen R. Kellert, *Kinship to Mastery: Biophilia in Human Evolution and Development* (Washington, DC: Island Press, 1997), 99.

123. Dave McNary, "Studios Back Jackson in 'Hobbit' Animal Flap," *Variety*, November 20, 2012.

124. Errol Flynn, *My Wicked, Wicked Ways: The Autobiography of Errol Flynn* (New York, NY: Cooper Square Press, 2003), 212.

125. Dale Peterson and Jane Goodall, *Visions of Caliban: On Chimpanzees and People* (Athens, GA: University of Georgia Press, 2000), 148.

126. Ibid.

127. Dale Peterson and Jane Goodall, *Visions of Caliban: On Chimpanzees and People*, 145–146.

128. Ian J. Griffiths, "Elephant trainers accused of abusing animal star of *Water for Elephants*," *The Guardian*, May 10, 2011.

129. Richard Verrier, "American Humane Assn. Filing Reveals Payout to Chairman's Partner," *Los Angeles Times*, October 4, 2012.

130. Ralph Frammolino and James Bates, "Questions Raised About Group That Watches Out for Animals in Movies," *Los Angeles Times*, February 9, 2001.

131. www.cbsnews.com/htdocs/pdf/safrica.pdf

132. www.americanhumanefilmtv.org/archives/movies/mr.php?fid=151

133. Richard Verrier, "American Humane Assn. Filing Reveals Payout to Chairman's Partner."

134. Interviewed by Terry Gross on *Fresh Air*, WHYY, January 2, 2013. www.npr.org/2013/01/02/168200139/quentin-tarantino-unchained-and-unruly

135. Aparna Rao, "Peripatetic Peoples and Lifestyles of South Asia," from *Disappearing Peoples? Indigenous Groups and Ethnic Minorities in South and Central Asia*, edited by Barbara Brower and Barbara Rose Johnston (Walnut Creek, CA: Left Coast Press, Inc., 2007), 67.

136. John Joseph, "Bear-Baiting in Pakistan," World Society for the Protection of Animals, February 1997.

137. Maneka Gandhi, "The Shame of Bear-baiting," *SouthAsia Global Affairs*,

October 2010.

138. http://observers.france24.com/content/20110308-pakistani-landlord-idea-fun-pitting-dogs-against-bears-bear-baiting

139. Conversation with Andrew Page, September 28, 2012.

140. www.humanesociety.org/news/news/2010/08/bear_baiting_082310.html

141. "Orangutans Seized in Bangkok Will Be Returned to Indonesia," *Environment News Service*, April 18, 2006. www.ens-news wire.com/ens/apr2006/2006-04-18-01.html

142. http://blog.petaasiapacific.com/animals-in-entertainment/safari-world-takes-a-step-backward

143. Stanley Johnson, "Brutality and the Beasts," *The Sunday Times Magazine*, July 8, 2012.

144. Stanley Johnson, "Brutality and the Beasts."

145. Barry Wigmore, "Horror as Chinese horses are forced to fight to the death," *Daily Mail*, November 30, 2007.

146. Camels spit streams of viscous fluid during fights to demonstrate their prowess.

147. Joe Parkinson, "What's a Bigger Draw Than a Camel Fight? A Camel Beauty Contest, of Course," *Wall Street Journal*, January 22, 2011.

148. Alexander Christie-Miller, "Turkey: Tradition of Camel Wrestling Making a Comeback," Eurasianet.org, January 27, 2011. www.eura sianet.org/node/62784

149. Ali Fuat Aydin, "Camel Wrestling Events in Western Turkey," The Camel Conference, School of Oriental and African Studies, University of London, May 24, 2011.

150. Vedat Çalişkan, "Geography of a hidden cultural heritage: Camel Wrestles in western Anatolia," *Journal of International Social Research*, Volume 2, Number 8, Summer 2009.

151. This description is a construction from news stories, especially reports from Chelsea White, "US 'Aussie' show knocks a kangaroo around for laughs," *Daily Telegraph*, March 6, 2010, and *AAP News* (Australia), "Kraft-sponsored kangaroo boxing cancelled after outcry from PETA activists," March 6, 2010.

152. Herbert E. Gregory, "Lonely Australia: The Unique Continent," *National Geographic*, December 1916. See also *Menageries, Circuses and Theatres* by Edward Henry Bostock (New York: Benjamin Bloom, Inc., 1927). Bostock's memoir contains a long passage explaining how he purchased, trained, and exploited "boxing" kangaroos in the 19th century.

153. www.mediapeta.com/peta/pdf/Universoul-pdf.pdf

154. Mayra Calvani, "The World Society for the Protection of Animals (WSPA) Seeks to End Bullfighting," Blogcritics.org, September 1, 2008.

155. Adam Mark Barwick, *The B/W Bulletpoint Bullfight*, second edition (Madrid, Spain: GWF Publications, 2007), 26.

156. Correspondence with Jose Valle, October 11, 2012.

157. www.bullfightingfreeeurope.org

158. www.parametria.com.mx/DetalleEstudio.php?E=4321

159. www.caracol.com.co/noticias/entretenimiento/el-78-de-los-colombia nos-desaprueba-las-corridas-de-toros-revela-sondeo-de-caracol-radio/20090212/nota/762496.aspx

160. Lindsay Barnett, "Animal activists cry foul over 'bloodless bullfighting' event in Artesia," *Los Angeles Times*, May 26, 2009.

161. Correspondence with Jose Valle, October 23, 2012.

162. Kathleen Kernicky, "Gator wrestlers on ropes," *Sun Sentinel*, May 15, 2007.

163. Allison Glock, "The Gator Wrestlers," gardenandgun.com, November 2008.

164. www.youtube.com/watch?v=6ZhHHVsAnI4

165. Christa Skousen, "Slick and dirty—locals invited to participate in pig wrestling," *Daily Herald*, August 10, 2012.

Chapter 7

Opening quote is from the New International Version of the Bible, 1984.

1. Jim Patten and Yadira Betances, "Woman Charged with Killing a Rooster at a Grave," *The Eagle-Tribune*, May 23, 2009.

2. Crawford H. Toy, "An Early Form of Animal Sacrifice," *Journal of the American Oriental Society*, Volume 26, 1905, 137.

3. JR Hyland, *God's Covenant with Animals: A Biblical Basis for the Humane Treatment of All Creatures* (New York, NY: Lantern Books, 2000), 4.

4. Maria-Zoe Petropoulou, *Animal Sacrifice in Ancient Greek Religion, Judaism, and Christianity, 100 BC to AD 200* (New York, NY: Oxford University Press, 2008), 17.

5. Donald P. Kommers, John E. Finn, Gary J. Jacobsohn, *American Constitutional Law: Essays, Cases, and Comparative Notes* (Lanham, MD: Rowman & Littlefield, 2004), 866.

6. Thomas v. Review Board of Indiana Employment Security Div. (1981).

7. For an in-depth perspective on animal sacrifice in ancient religions of the Near East, see *Understanding Religious Sacrifice: A Reader*, edited by Jeffrey Carter (New York, NY: Continuum International Publishing Group, 2003); Sarah Iles Johnston, *Religions of the Ancient World: A Guide* (Cambridge, MA: Harvard University Press, 2004); and Maria-Zoe Petropoulou, *Animal Sacrifice in Ancient Greek Religion, Judaism, and Christianity, 100 BC to AD 200* (New York, NY: Oxford University Press, 2008).

8. Catherine M. Bell, *Ritual: Perspectives and Dimensions* (New York, NY: Oxford University Press, 1997), 112–113.

9. Stephen M. Wylen, *The Jews in the Time of Jesus: An Introduction* (Mahwah, NJ: Paulist Press, 1995), 55.

10. Some scholars assert the altar was a bit larger than this. Second Chronicles 4:1 of the Hebrew Bible/Old Testament gives the altar dimensions as 20 cubits long, 20 cubits wide and 10 cubits high, but there were actually two lengths of cubit used in ancient construction. The royal cubit is equal to 20.620 inches (52.375 cm) and the standard cubit is equal to 17.674 inches (44.892 cm). Stephen Skinner, author of *Sacred Geometry: Deciphering the Code* (New York, NY: Sterling, 2006), believes Temple craftsmen used the royal cubit, giving the altar dimensions of 17 feet (5.2 meters) high and 34.4 feet (10.2 meters) square.

11. Keith Akers, *The Lost Religion of Jesus: Simple Living and Nonviolence in Early Christianity* (New York, NY: Lantern Books, 2000), 103.

12. James H. Charlesworth, *Jesus and Archaeology* (Grand Rapids, MI: Wm.

B. Eerdmans, 2006), 549.

13. Rynn Berry, *Food for the Gods: Vegetarianism & the World's Religions* (New York, NY: Pythagorean Publishers, 1998), 293.

14. Norm Phelps, *The Dominion of Love: Animal Rights According to the Bible* (New York, NY: Lantern Books, 2002), 88.

15. Stephen H. Webb, *On God and Dogs: A Christian Theology of Compassion for Animals* (New York, NY: Oxford University Press, 1998), 147.

16. Bart D. Ehrman, *Lost Christianities: The Battles for Scripture and the Faiths We Never Knew* (New York, NY: Oxford University Press, 2005), 102. The fragments of the Gospel of the Ebionites were recorded by Epiphanius of Salamis, a church father, in the 4th century CE. This gospel portrays both Jesus and John the Baptist as vegetarians.

17. Bart D. Ehrman, *Lost Scriptures: Books That Did Not Make It into the New Testament* (New York, NY: Oxford University Press, 2003), 12.

18. Richard Bauckham, *Animals on the Agenda: Questions About Animals for Theology and Ethics*, edited by Andrew Linzey and Dorothy Yamamoto (Champaign, IL: University of Illinois Press, 1998), 50.

19. Andrew Linzey, "No More Animal Sacrifices," *The Church of England Newspaper*, August 18, 2000.

20. Matthew Scully, *Dominion: The Power of Man, the Suffering of Animals, and the Call to Mercy* (New York, NY: St. Martin's Griffin, 2002), 96.

21. Some scholars, notably Kenneth Willis Clark in *The Gentile Bias and Other Essays* (Leiden, The Netherlands: EJ Brill, 1980), contend that the Romans did not completely destroy the Temple, and that animal sacrifice actually continued there beyond 70 CE.

22. Abraham Geiger, *Judaism and Its History* (New York, NY: Bloch Publishing Co., 1911), 66.

23. John D. Rayner, *An Understanding of Judaism* (Oxford, UK: Berghahn Books, 1997), 160.

24. Ari L. Goldman, *Being Jewish: The Spiritual and Cultural Practice of Judaism Today* (New York, NY: Simon & Schuster, Inc., 2008), 122.

25. AJ Jacobs, *The Year of Living Biblically: One Man's Humble Quest to Follow the Bible as Literally as Possible* (New York, NY: Simon & Schuster, Inc., 2007), 161.

26. A notable example of Jewish literature that *does* refer to kapparot as sacrifice is the short story "No More Kapores or the Sacrificial Chicken Revolt" by Sholom Aleichem (1859–1916). In Aleichem's fable, chickens stage a violent uprising against their human oppressors just before Yom Kippur, maiming, pecking out eyes, and declaring, "We don't want to be your sacrificial birds!" As with most children's stories, Aleichem's fable ends happily, with the Jewish elders deciding it would be wiser—and safer—to leave the chickens alone. See *A Treasury of Sholom Aleichem Children's Stories*, translated by Aliza Shevrin (Northvale, NJ: Jason Aronson, 1997), 149–156. Aleichem's story is the basis of Erica Silverman's *When the Chickens Went on Strike: A Rosh Hashanah Tale* (New York, NY: Puffin Books, 2003). In trying to discern Aleichem's position on kapparot, I emailed Silverman, who replied, "It's my own belief, based on my reading of his fiction, his autobiographical writings, essays, and letters, that he was very likely opposed to the use of chickens for Kaporos."

27. Abraham P. Bloch, *The Biblical and Historical Background of Jewish Customs and Ceremonies* (Jersey City, NJ: KTAV Publishing House, Inc., 1980), 159. The Torah is comprised of the first five books of the Hebrew Bible (and Old Testament of the Christian Bible)—Genesis, Exodus, Leviticus, Numbers, and Deuteronomy—while the Talmud is the supreme sourcebook of Jewish law, taking the rules listed in the Torah and describing how to apply them.

28. Nosson Scherman, *Yom Kippur—Its Significance, Laws, and Prayers* (Brooklyn, NY: Mesorah Publications, 1989), 105–106.

29. Neta Sela and Roi Mandel, "Rabbis cry 'fowl' on ritual use of chickens," *YNetNews.com*, September 28, 2006, accessed on August 4, 2009.

30. Nathaniel Popper, "Orthodox Call on Sinners to Give Chickens a Fairer Shake," *Forward*, August 27, 2007.

31. Steve Lipman, "Swinging No More: Kaporos and the New Eco-Kosher Movement," *New York Jewish Week*, September 14, 2007.

32. Daniella Cheslow, "Kaparot: Jewish leaders want to end animal killing," *Associated Press*, October 7, 2011.

33. Letter to Rabbi Luzer Weiss, director of the Kosher Law Enforcement Division, New York State Department of Agriculture and Markets, from Philip Schein, Policy Department, People for the Ethical Treatment of Animals, August 22, 2008.

34. Jeremiah Horrigan, "PETA Files Complaint Against Brooklyn Man for Dumping Chickens," *Times Herald-Record*, November 11, 2005. The defendant in this case was Jacob Kalish, who left 307 chickens crammed into wooden crates in a vacant lot in Brooklyn, NY, on or about October 16, 2005. About 35 of the birds had drowned in a rainstorm. Kalish told investigators he wasn't able to find buyers for the birds, who were to be used for the kapparot ceremony. Surviving birds were taken to animal sanctuaries. According to an alert posted on the United Poultry Concerns Website on October 24, the birds were severely dehydrated and encrusted with feces, urine, and blood; some had suffered injured limbs and eyes (see www.upc-online.org/alerts/102405ny.html).

35. Neta Sela and Roi Mandel, "Rabbis cry 'fowl' on ritual use of chickens," *YNetNews.com*, September 28, 2006, accessed on August 4, 2009.

36. Conversation with Karen Davis, July 31, 2009.

37. Karen Davis, *The Holocaust & the Henmaid's Tale: A Case for Comparing Atrocities* (New York, NY: Lantern Books, 2005), xiii.

38. Andrew Strum, "Wheat, Chickens and the Expiation of Sin, or Vegetarian *Kapparot*: The Ancient Origins of an Obscure Egyptian Jewish High Holy Day Custom," from *Eshkolot: Essays in Memory of Rabbi Ronald Lubofsky* (Melbourne: Hybrid Publishers, 2002).

39. Aviva Weintraub, "Poultry in Motion: The Jewish Atonement Ritual of Kapores," from *Jews of Brooklyn*, edited by Ilana Abramovitch and Seán Galvin (Lebanon, NH: University Press of New England, 2001), 212.

40. Fred C. Conybeare, "The Survival of Animal Sacrifices inside the Christian Church," from *American Journal of Theology*, Volume 7, edited by the Divinity School Faculty, University of Chicago (Chicago, IL: University of Chicago Press, 1903), 62.

41. Christine Chaillot, "The Ancient Oriental Churches," from *The Oxford*

History of Christian Worship, edited by Geoffrey Wainwright and Karen Beth Westerfield Tucker (New York, NY: Oxford University Press, 2006), 152.

42. Nerses Manoogian, *From the Pastor's Desk* (Bloomington, IN: AuthorHouse, 2008), 73–74.

43. Correspondence with Father Nerses Manoogian, August 10, 2009.

44. Inigo Gilmore, "Africa's Catholics in Row over Animal Sacrifices," *Sunday Telegraph*, February 27, 2000.

45. Michael Bleby, "Bringing New Blood into the Church," *Church Times*, June 3, 2005.

46. Andrew Linzey, "No More Animal Sacrifices," *The Church of England Newspaper*, August 18, 2000.

47. Christopher Howse, "The Vicars Who Sacrifice Goats," *Daily Telegraph*, July 2, 2005.

48. Rynn Berry, *Food for the Gods: Vegetarianism & the World's Religions*, 294.

49. Gabriel Cousens, *Conscious Eating* (Berkeley, CA: North Atlantic Books, 2000), 377. See also John Davidson, *The Gospel of Jesus: In Search of His Original Teachings* (Bath, England: Clear Books, 2005). Furthermore, in *The Longest Struggle: Animal Advocacy from Pythagoras to PETA* (New York, NY: Lantern Books, 2007), Norm Phelps points out that ancient Christian sources describe a number of the Disciples, including Simon Peter, Matthew, Thomas, and Jesus' brother, James, as following a strict vegan diet.

50. Bruce Lincoln, *Death, War and Sacrifice: Studies in Ideology and Practice* (Chicago, IL: University of Chicago Press, 1991), 204.

51. The legend of Sati and the founding of Kalighat has many variations, but the essence is that parts of Sati's body fell to Earth in a moment of violence as her husband Shiva, stricken with grief upon his wife's death, began a dance that would destroy the world. Lord Vishnu intervened, cutting Sati's body to pieces. Pilgrimage sites, 51 in all, were established wherever a piece of Sati's body landed.

52. Not all Hindus avoid eating meat, but according to "Origin & History of Vegetarianism in India" by Shankar Narayan, president of the Indian Vegan Society, India's vegetarian population is approximately

464 million, or 40 percent of the country. See www.ivu.org/congress/2008/texts/Shankar.doc

53. My thanks to the Visakha SPCA in India (vspca.org) for sharing the report "Data on Animal Sacrifices in AP" with me.

54. GV Ramana Rao, "Mailatheppa: A Bizarre Ritual in the Name of Tradition," *The Hindu*, February 24, 2009.

55. David Kinsley, *Hindu Goddesses: Visions of the Divine Feminine in the Hindu Religious Tradition* (New Delhi: Motilal Banarsidass Publishers, 1998), 112–113.

56. Sanjukta Gupta, "The Domestication of a Goddess," from *Encountering Kālī: In the Margins, at the Center, in the West*, edited by Rachel Fell McDermott and Jeffrey John Kripal (Berkeley, CA: University of California Press, 2003), 73.

57. Richard Ehrlich, "Animal Sacrifice in Nepal," *The Laissez Faire City Times*, Volume 3, Number 36, September 1999.

58. *UPI*, "Goats Sacrificed for Smooth Flying," September 5, 2007.

59. See Norm Phelps, *The Great Compassion: Buddhism & Animal Rights* (New York, NY: Lantern Books, 2004).

60. Bharat Jarghamagar, "Animal Sacrifice Common During Buddha Jayanti," *KantipurOnline.com*, May 20, 2008.

61. Tirtha Bahadur Shrestha, "Scapegoats," *Nepali Times*, October 19, 2007.

62. Correspondence with Maneka Gandhi, August 31, 2009.

63. N. Rahul, "TTD Unlikely to Get Civet Cats," *The Hindu*, August 9, 2008. The reference to whipping the cats to extract the substance and applying it to foreheads comes from Gandhi's article "Animal Sacrifice at the Altar of Religion," *Bihar Times*, November 13, 2007.

64. Bakri Eid literally means "goat feast," and this holiday is known by other names in the Muslim world, including 'Id al-Adha (sacrificial feast) and 'Id al-Kabir (major feast). There are also additional variations in spelling.

65. *Times of India*, "Celebrating Bakri Eid with Fervour," December 8, 2009.

66. See the Qur'an 37:99–109. According to the dominant Muslim tradition, the son nearly sacrificed is Ishmael, 14 years older than his brother Isaac, who is the son Abraham almost sacrificed in the Judeo-Christian

version described in Genesis.

67. Jonah Blank, *Mullahs on the Mainframe: Islam and Modernity among the Daudi Bohras* (Chicago, IL: University of Chicago Press, 2002), 106–107. Blank's description of this dying goat actually seems rather detached for such a sickening scene, and the author admits he eventually became inured to the animals' suffering during the event.

68. Shahid 'Ali Muttaqi, "An Islamic Perspective Against Animal Sacrifice," from www.islamveg.com, accessed on August 20, 2009. Also see: "Animal Experimentation: The Muslim Viewpoint" by Al-Hafiz BA Masri in *Animal Sacrifices: Religious Perspectives on the Use of Animals in Science*, edited by Tom Regan (Philadelphia, PA: Temple University Press, 1987); as well as GC van de Bruinhorst, *Raise Your Voices and Kill Your Animals: Islamic Discourses on the Idd El-Hajj* (Amsterdam, The Netherlands: Amsterdam University Press, 2007).

69. İsmail Büyükçelebi, *Living in the Shade of Islam: A Comprehensive Reference of Theory and Practice* (Somerset, NJ: Tughra Books, 2005), 279.

70. Per Glenys Oogjes, president of Animals Australia. Glenys told me that the official figures for 2008 indicate 4.2 million sheep exported with 35,280 dying during the voyage.

71. 'Ali Muttaqi, "An Islamic Perspective Against Animal Sacrifice," from www.islamveg.com, accessed on August 20, 2009.

72. "Dutch vote to ban ritual animal slaughter, Jews and Muslims unite in protest," *Reuters*, June 28, 2011.

73. "Santería," from *Encyclopedia of Religion in the South*, edited by Samuel S. Hill, Charles H. Lippy, and Charles Reagan Wilson (Macon, GA: Mercer University Press, 2005), 700.

74. Mary Ann Clark, *Santería: Correcting the Myths and Uncovering the Realities of a Growing Religion* (Santa Barbara, CA Greenwood Publishing Group, 2007), 79.

75. George Volsky, "Religion from Cuba Stirs Row in Miami," *The New York Times*, June 29, 1987.

76. Conversation with Bruce Wagman, August 5, 2009. Bruce is also the co-author (with Pamela D. Frasch and Sonia S. Waisman) of *Animal Law: Cases and Materials*, fourth edition (Durham, NC: Carolina

Academic Press, 2009).

77. Linda Stewart Ball, "Court gives Santeria priest OK to sacrifice goats," *Associated Press*, August 1, 2009.

78. Tom L. Beauchamp, Rebecca Dresser, John P. Gluck, David B. Morton, and F. Barbara Orlans, *The Human Use of Animals: Case Studies in Ethical Choice* (New York, NY: Oxford University Press, 1998), 309.

79. 723 F. Supp 1467, Church of Lukumí Babalú Ayé, Inc., and Ernesto Pichardo, Plaintiffs, v. City of Hialeah, Defendant. No. 87-1795-CIV-EPS. United States District Court, S.D. Florida, Miami Division, October 5, 1989.

80. Randi Glatzer, "Mojo Rising," *Vibe*, December 1999/January 2000.

81. Rômulo RN Alves, Sharon E. Brooks, and Nivaldo A. Léo Neto, "From Eshu to Obatala: Animals Used in Sacrificial Rituals at Candomblé 'Terreiros' in Brazil," *Journal of Ethnobiology and Ethnomedicine*, August 26, 2009.

82. Henry Mark Holzer, "Contradictions will out: Animal rights vs. animal sacrifice in the Supreme Court," *Animal Law Review* (Lewis & Clark Law School), Volume 1, 1995. Holzer concluded: "Contradictions will out, as the unfortunate animal victims of the Santerians have learned from the Supreme Court's decision, and as the future victims of other religious practices have yet to learn. Perhaps the day will come when Santerians will be prohibited from sacrificing animals, but it is not likely to arrive until lobsters are no longer boiled alive and eaten in Hialeah."

83. Gary L. Francione, "If Animal Sacrifice Is Wrong, Then Why Is It Okay to Eat Meat?" *OpposingViews.com*, August 2, 2009.

84. Peter Singer, *Ethics Into Action: Henry Spira and the Animal Rights Movement* (Lanham, MD: Rowman & Littlefield, 2000), 52.

85. Matthew Scully, "Fear Factories: The Case for Compassionate Conservatism—for Animals," *The American Conservative*, May 23, 2005.

86. Migene González-Wippler, *Santería: The Religion*, second edition (Woodbury, MN: Llewellyn Worldwide, 1994), xvi–xvii.

87. Henry Mark Holzer, "Contradictions will out: Animal rights vs. animal sacrifice in the Supreme Court," *Animal Law Review* (Lewis & Clark

Law School), Volume 1, 1995.

88. Jane Hamilton-Merritt, *Tragic Mountains: The Hmong, the Americans, and the Secret Wars for Laos, 1942–1992* (Bloomington, IN: Indiana University Press, 1999), xv–xxii.

89. Mark E. Pfeifer, "US Census Releases 2005 American Community Survey data for Southeast Asian Americans," *Asian American Press*, October 28, 2006. The Hmong Population in the US was estimated at 183,265.

90. Anne Fadiman, *The Spirit Catches You and You Fall Down* (New York, NY: Farrar, Straus and Giroux, 1998), 10.

91. Linda L. Barnes and Susan S. Sered, *Religion and Healing in America* (New York, NY: Oxford University Press, 2004), 445.

92. Sue Murphy Mote, *Hmong and American: Stories of Transition to a Strange Land* (Jefferson, NC: McFarland, 2004), 69–70.

93. Christina Pratt, *An Encyclopedia of Shamanism*, Volume 1 (New York, NY: Rosen Publishing, 2007), 206.

94. Nicholas Tapp, *The Hmong of China: Context, Agency, and the Imaginary* (Leiden, The Netherlands: Brill Academic Publishers, 2003), 161.

95. Nicholas Tapp, "Hmong Religion," *Asian Folklore Studies*, Volume 48, Number 1, 1989, 71.

96. Anne Fadiman, *The Spirit Catches You and You Fall Down*, 11.

97. Nicholas Tapp, "Hmong Religion," 83.

98. Brian Bull, "Hmong Funerals," Wisconsin Public Radio, April 13, 2006.

99. Patricia V. Symonds, *Calling in the Soul: Gender and the Cycle of Life in a Hmong Village* (Seattle, WA: University of Washington Press, 2005), 146.

100. Bruce Thowpaou Bliatout, "Hmong Death Customs: Traditional and Acculturated," from *Ethnic Variations in Dying, Death and Grief: Diversity in Universality*, edited by Donald P. Irish, Kathleen F. Lundquist, and Vivian Jenkins Nelsen (London: Taylor & Francis Group, 1993), 90.

101. Nicholas Tapp, "Hmong Religion," 88–89.

102. Nachee Lee, "Sacrificing Animals for the Human Soul," *Dayton's Bluff District Forum*, Volume 18, Number 3, May 2005.

103. Tim Oakes and Patricia L. Price, *The Cultural Geography Reader*

(Florence, KY: Routledge, 2008), 243.

104. Mark Arax, "Hmong's Sacrifice of Puppy Reopens Cultural Wounds," *Los Angeles Times*, December 16, 1995.

105. Alison Dundes Renteln, *The Cultural Defense* (New York, NY: Oxford University Press, 2005), 99.

106. Anne Fadiman, *The Spirit Catches You and You Fall Down*, 108.

107. Nachee Lee, "Sacrificing Animals for the Human Soul."

108. The Cree have a similar legend. The Cree trickster, Wisakedjak, is a spirit in the form of a human. One day he called a meeting of the animals and told them of a time when there would be a race that looked like him, and that they would hunt for their food. The rabbit promised to provide the people with sweet and tender meat, and helpfully explained how he preferred to be killed (by bludgeoning). The bear offered to provide them with warm clothing, as did the buffalo, who added that he was fine with being eaten, that his skin would make excellent shelter, and that his bones and horns could be used for tools. The horse said he would be their slave. Wisakedjak then warned the animals that another race of men would come, and they would kill all the buffalo. See Albert Lightning, "Some Adventures of Wisakedjak," in *Indian Legends of Canada*, edited by Ella Elizabeth Clark (Toronto: McClelland and Stewart, 1960).

109. See Ephesians 6:4–6.

110. Milo Rigaud, *Secrets of Voodoo*, revised edition (San Francisco, CA: City Lights Books, 1985), 94.

111. Heike Owusu, *Voodoo Rituals: A User's Guide* (New York, NY: Sterling Publishing Co., 2003), 16–17

112. Lucinda Mosher, *Praying: The Rituals of Faith* (Harrisburg, PA: Church Publishing, Inc., 2005), 135.

113. Carl Olson, *The Many Colors of Hinduism: A Thematic-Historical Introduction* (Piscataway, NJ: Rutgers University Press, 2007), 54.

114. Wendy Doniger, *The Hindus: An Alternative History* (New York, NY: The Penguin Press, 2009), 149.

115. Source: National Turkey Federation—www.eatturkey.com.

116. Conversation with Brian Luke, August 10, 2009.

117. Karen Davis, *More Than a Meal: The Turkey in History, Myth, Ritual, and Reality* (New York, NY: Lantern Books, 2001), 92.

118. Conversation with Karen Davis, July 31, 2009.

119. Karen Davis, *More Than a Meal*, 69–70.

120. See Genesis 22:1–19.

121. In *More Than a Meal*, Karen Davis debunks the often-cited myth that President Harry S. Truman began the practice of "pardoning" a turkey just before Thanksgiving. Davis asserts President George HW Bush made this tradition official in 1989, though his predecessors Kennedy, Nixon, and Reagan all displayed their own compassionate moments by "sparing" the lives of turkeys presented to them.

122. Conversation with Brian Luke, August 10, 2009.

123. Brian Luke, *Brutal: Manhood and the Exploitation of Animals* (Champaign, IL: University of Illinois Press, 2007), 131.

124. Bruce Lincoln, *Death, War and Sacrifice: Studies in Ideology and Practice* (Chicago, IL: University of Chicago Press, 1991), 204.

125. Walter Burkert, *Homo Necans: The Anthropology of Ancient Greek Sacrificial Ritual and Myth*, translated by Peter Bing (Berkeley, CA: University of California Press, 1983), 35–47. Not all historians agree with Burkert; religious scholar Burton Mack, for example, argues there is scant evidence that Paleolithic humans hunted animals, while there is plenty to suggest they engaged in ritual sacrifice.

126. Author and feminist Barbara Ehrenreich observes that war is a form of ritual sacrifice, leading Brain Luke to postulate that animal sacrifice has fallen from favor in the world only because people have returned to sacrificing human beings through modern warfare. See Brian Luke, *Brutal: Manhood and the Exploitation of Animals* (Champaign, IL: University of Illinois Press, 2007), 129.

127. Conversation with Karen Davis, July 31, 2009.

Chapter 8

Booker T. Washington quote from *The Booker T. Washington Papers, Volume 4: 1895–98*, Louis H. Harlan, editor (Champaign, IL: University of Illinois Press, 1975), 212.

1. Peter Conrad, "I have to admit it: I was wrong about Hirst," *Observer*, September 14, 2008.

2. Fiachra Gibbons, "Hirst accused of sadism over butterfly collage," *The Guardian*, August 15, 2003.

3. Roya Nikkhah, "Damien Hirst condemned for killing 9,000 butterflies in Tate show," *Telegraph*, October 4, 2012.

4. Statement given to the author by Jenny Woods, PETA media manager, February 3, 2009.

5. ACLU, "Freedom of Expression in the Arts and Entertainment," February 27, 2002.

6. *One and Three Chairs*, a work by Joseph Kosuth.

7. That's not to say that conceptual artists in the '60s didn't indulge their desire to destroy life. In 1967, Ralph Ortiz was famous for a piece he called *The Life and Death of Henny Penny*, in which he swung a live chicken over the audience and cut off her head with shears. Then he beat the animal's body against a flamenco guitar. He repeated the performance later that year with another chicken and a piano. He explained that he'd grown up slaughtering chickens on a farm, so this sort of gratuitous violence was no big deal.

8. Thaindian News, "New Techniques Confirm Blood of Animal Sacrifices on Ancient African Sculptures," December 2, 2007.

9. Alex deMarban, "Board OKs Art Use of Animal Parts," *Anchorage Daily News*, May 21, 2006.

10. "Liquidising Goldfish 'Not a Crime,'" *BBC News*, May 19, 2003.

11. Roya Nikkhah and Julie Henry, "Fish killed in conceptual artist's exhibition at Tate Modern," *Daily Telegraph*, February 14, 2009.

12. This is according to two sources: HondurasThisWeek.com, November 13, 2008; and Lora Adomeit of the World Society for the Protection of Animals, who told me in a January 8, 2009, email: "As far as we know there were no live animals used in the biennial, as the rules of participation prohibited it."

13. Gerard Couzens, "Outrage at 'starvation' of a stray dog for art," *Observer*, March 30, 2008.

14. Writing in *The Drogheda Independent*, Christine Doherty explains that:

"As well as having toys, water and a bed inside the cages, the abandoned dogs will be fed and walked twice a day." ("Dog Exhibition Row," February 25, 2009.) A publicity shot on the Droichead Arts Centre's website, however, shows the two dogs in barren metal pens.

15. "If Art Could Save Your Life—Exhibition/New work by Artist Seamus Nolan," www.droicheadartscentre.com/whats-on/index.php?id=2#e _289

16. Correspondence with John Carmody, February 27–29, 2009.

17. Ian O'Doherty, "You Call This Art?" *Irish Independent*, February 25, 2009.

18. Elaine Keogh, "Controversial stray dog exhibition opens," *Irish Independent*, February 27, 2009.

19. Alison Comyn, "Every Dog Has Its Day," *The Drogheda Independent*, March 4, 2009.

20. www.brooklyneagle.com/categories/category.php?category_id=27 &id=19895

21. Otterness' film was a lengthy piece that details the artist adopting the dog, caring for the dog over a period of time, and finally executing the dog. In 2011, San Francisco—a town with more dogs than children— became the latest flashpoint in the controversy surrounding Otterness after the city awarded him two commissions, resulting in a public outcry and calls that the contracts be rescinded.

22. According to numerous sources, Abdessemed filmed these scenes at a slaughterhouse in Mexico. In *The Boston Globe*, art critic Sebastian Smee wrote: "The animals whose deaths [Abdessemed] filmed were, in the words of San Francisco Art Institute president Chris Bratton, 'part of an already existing circuit of food production in rural Mexico.' But the manner of their killing was undoubtedly brutal. Certainly, it involved none of the factory-style mechanization that characterizes slaughterhouses in the United States, and that for unaccountable reasons we seem to find more acceptable." "An in-your-face provocateur," October 19, 2008.

23. Joshua Sabatini, "Art Institute Stands Behind Violent Exhibit," *San*

Francisco Examiner, March 24, 2008.

24. San Francisco SPCA press release, March 27, 2008.

25. Conversation with Val Mizuhara, January 8, 2009.

26. Correspondence with Kalista Barter, January 16, 2009.

27. Jerry Saltz, "Adel Abdessemed's Fighting-Animal Video Sparks Art-World Uproar," *The New York Times Magazine*, May 4, 2009.

28. Peter Archer, *The Quotable Intellectual: 1,417 Bon Mots, Ripostes, and Witticisms for Aspiring Academics, Armchair Philosophers... and Anyone Else Who Wants to Sound Really Smart* (Avon, MA: Adams Media, 2010), 185.

29. "Animal Killer Artist Unrepentant," *Sunday Times Australia*, December 13, 2003.

30. Ibid.

31. Correspondence with Andrew Butler, April 13, 2007.

32. Irina Meleshkevich, "In the Gloomy Forest of Modern Photography," *Herald of Europe*, June 2005.

33. Correspondence with Aimée Baldwin, November 5, 2012.

34. Lydia Martin, "From toast of art world to guest of federal pen," *Miami Herald*, May 20, 2012.

35. David Goligorsky, "Wim Delvoye–Belgian Artist," *Perpenduum*, July 31, 2008. http://perpenduum.com/2008/07/wim-delvoye-belgian-artist/

36. James Graff, "Mediums with a Message," *TIME Europe*, 2003.

37. Paul Laster, "Bringing Home the Bacon: Wim Delvoye," *ArtAsiaPacific*, September/October 2007.

38. My thanks to Margo DeMello, author of *Bodies of Inscription: A Cultural History of the Modern Tattoo Community* (Duke University Press, 2000), for educating me on how tattoos are made.

39. Trying to determine the sensitivity of a pig's skin, I consulted Dr. Tim Blackwell, a veterinary scientist specializing in swine at the Ontario Ministry of Agriculture, Food and Rural Affairs in Canada. Dr. Blackwell told me: "I know of no studies directly comparing the sensitivity of pigs' skin to that of humans. I assume there is variation between breeds, between individuals, and between areas of skin on the body. I think most animals have pain receptors on the outside of their

bodies to alert them to any noxious stimuli they may come in contact with. Probably the more critical question and unfortunately the one that is more difficult to answer is how much pain and for how long?"

40. Paul Laster, "Bringing Home the Bacon: Wim Delvoye," *ArtAsiaPacific*, September/October 2007.

41. Lissette Olivares, "Wim Delvoye's Art Farm," *NY Arts Magazine*, November/December 2005.

42. Robert Enright, "Vim and Vigour: An Interview with Wim Delvoye," *Border Crossings*, November 2005.

43. "Exhibitions—Wim Delvoye," *The Moscow News*, March 10, 2008.

44. Peter Beudert and Susan Crabtree, *Scenic Art for the Theatre: History, Tools, and Techniques* (Woburn, MA: Focal Press, 1998), 127.

45. Conversation with Kathleen Myers, April 3, 2010.

46. Correspondence with Rebecca Doyle, product consultant with US-based paintbrush manufacturer Dick Blick Art Materials, March 3, 2009.

47. NA Balakirev and EA Tinaeva, "Fur Farming in Russia: The Current Situation and the Prospects," *Scientifur* (Volume 25, Number 1, 2001), 8.

48. John F. Richards, *The Unending Frontier: An Environmental History of the Early Modern World* (Berkeley, CA: University of California Press, 2006), 533.

49. Devdutt Pattanaik, *Indian Mythology: Tales, Symbols, and Rituals from the Heart of the Subcontinent* (Rochester, VT: Inner Traditions International, Limited, 2003), 128.

50. Maneka Gandhi, "Painting Death with Mongoose Hair," Heads & Tails, February 26, 2008.

51. Malini Shankar, "Winning the battle against poaching," *India Together*, November 4, 2008.

52. "'Don't Buy Trouble' Warns Traffic India's New Film on Illegal Wildlife Trade," World Wildlife Fund press release, August 26, 2008.

53. Correspondence with Samir Sinha, March 5, 2009.

54. Correspondence with Ashok Kumar, March 5, 2009.

55. Prasanna Yonzon, "Mongoose Trade in Nepal," *Tiger Paper* (Regional

Quarterly Bulletin on Wildlife and National Parks Management, Volume 32, Number 2), April–June 2005.

56. I asked paintbrush manufacturers in China, India, the UK, and the US why animal-hair brushes are in such demand. Laura Hamilton, sales coordinator for Cottam Brush in the UK, told me that tradition plays a major role. "Paintbrushes have been filled with [animal-hair] bristle for many years and has been considered the best-quality filament for a long time." She also said price is a factor. "High-quality synthetic fibers are very expensive and are therefore not very retail-friendly."

57. Correspondence with Sue Coe, March 31, 2009.

58. Ibid.

59. Candace Jackson, "Downtown Art Show Sends Meat Packing," *Wall Street Journal*, May 8, 2010.

60. Quoted from the artist's statement about his work, www.nyartbeat.com, May 9, 2010.

61. Dan Piraro, *Bizarro and Other Strange Manifestations of the Art of Dan Piraro* (New York, NY: Harry N. Abrams, 2006), 86.

62. Correspondence with Peter Hamilton, February 6, 2009.

63. CBC (Canadian Broadcasting Corp.) television news report, January 6, 1990.

64. Ibid.

65. Ibid.

66. Correspondence with Peter Hamilton, February 6, 2009.

Chapter 9

The opening quote is from the article "Jungle Traffic: Investigating the Live Elephant Trade," by Michael Timmons. www.rattlethecage.org/elephant_traffic.htm

1. See *Nietzsche in Turin: An Intimate Biography*, by Lesley Chamberlain (St. Martin's Press, 1996).

2. "Prof. Nietzsche Dead," *The New York Times*, August 26, 1900.

3. An early animal rights book, Anna Sewell's 1877 novel *Black Beauty*, told the story of an abused horse and the cruelties he endured as a puller of London taxicabs. The American Humane Education Society

gave away more than 2 million copies of the book with the hope that it "shall have as widespread and powerful influence in abolishing cruelty to horse as *Uncle Tom's Cabin* had on the abolition of human slavery." (See "The Story of Black Beauty," by Guy Richardson, from *National Magazine*, April 1910, p. 595.)

4. Jared M. Diamond, *Guns, Germs, and Steel: The Fates of Human Societies* (New York, NY: WW Norton & Company, Inc., 1999), 159.

5. Diane L. Beers, *For the Prevention of Cruelty: The History and Legacy of Animal Rights Activism in the United States* (Athens, OH: Swallow Press, 2006), 64–66.

6. Gerald Carson, *Men, Beasts, and Gods: A History of Cruelty and Kindness to Animals* (New York, NY: Charles Scribner's Sons, 1972), 93.

7. www.thedailybeast.com/newsweek/2007/09/24/tradition-or-cruelty.html

8. www2.nycbar.org/pdf/report/uploads/20072178-ReportonA.7748-S.5013whichwouldprohibittheoperationofhorsedrawncarriagesinNewYorkCitySeptember2011.pdf

9. Conversation with Sally Eckhoff, February 8, 2013.

10. www.banhdc.org/archives/ch-fact-20060511.html

11. Correspondence with Holly Cheever, February 8, 2013.

12. Fernanda Santos, "Manhattan: Carriage Driver Remains in Critical Condition," *The New York Times*, January 4, 2006.

13. Kerry Burke and Michael White, "Carriage horse dies after tree crash near Central Park," *New York Daily News*, September 15, 2007.

14. Correspondence with Donny Moss, February 9, 2013

15. Correspondence with Elizabeth Forel, February 11, 2013.

16. Correspondence with Donny Moss, February 9, 2013. Donny adds: "The one thing we don't know is why Christine Quinn is supportive of the carriage industry in the first place. What I have been told by political consultants is that the Queens Democratic Party, which has the ability to influence city-wide elections, supports the horse-drawn carriage industry and has asked Quinn to protect it. To date, protecting the industry has been more politically expedient for her than banning it. The fact that the Teamsters have made protection of

the carriage trade a signature issue must also contribute to her support of the industry."

17. For a partial list of incidents worldwide, see www.all-creatures.org /articles/act-c-shdc-acc.html

18. Correspondence with Holly Cheever, February 8, 2013.

19. Kevin Belmonte, *Hero for Humanity: A Biography of William Wilberforce* (Colorado Springs, CO: Nav Publishing Group, 2002), 269–270.

20. *Saving the Slumdog Donkeys*, directed by Andrew Barron and produced by Angela Vos, 2011. Available to view on www.cultureunplugged .com/play/6679

21. Children are typically bonded laborers, with parents working to pay off debts. Children's guardians are provided one month salary for each child taken to a kiln. See www.animalnepal.org/documents/donkey/ DonkeyAppeal.pdf

22. www.fao.org/ag/AGA/AGAP/FRG/Draught/chap141/chap141.pdf

23. Shahabat Khan, "Donkey Management and Utilization in Peshawar, Pakistan," from *Donkeys, People and Development: A Resource Book of the Animal Traction Network for Eastern and Southern Africa*, edited by Paul Starkey and Denis Fielding (Technical Centre for Agricultural and Rural Cooperation, 2004), 236.

24. www.sparelives.org/index.pl/donkeys

25. "Brick by Brick: Supporting Working Kids & Donkeys at Lalitpur Brick Kilns," Animal Nepal, January 29, 2009.

26. Colleen Patrick-Goudreau, *Vegan's Daily Companion: 365 Days of Inspiration for Cooking, Eating, and Living Compassionately* (Beverly, MA: Quarry Books, 2011), 224.

27. www.elephantconservationcenter.com/index.php/en/ecperience-conservation/condition-elephants-laos

28. www.dailytimes.com.pk/default.asp?page=2008%5C02%5C20%5C story_20-2-2008_pg4_17

29. Gay A. Bradshaw, *Elephants on the Edge: What Animals Teach Us about Humanity* (New Haven, CT: Yale University Press, 2009), 63.

30. Charles Begley, "A Report on the Elephant Situation in Burma," funded by EleAid, October 2006.

31. Charles Begley, "A Report on the Elephant Situation in Burma."

32. Gay A. Bradshaw, *Elephants on the Edge: What Animals Teach Us about Humanity* (New Haven, CT: Yale University Press, 2009), 187.

33. John Brecher, "Baby elephant tortured into submission before illegal smuggling from Burma to Thailand," nbcnews.com, March 3, 2011.

34. Zaw Min Oo, "The Training Methods Used in Myanmar Timber Enterprise," *Gajah*, Volume 33, 2010.

35. www.eleaid.com/index.php?page=elephantsinthailand

36. Correspondence with Lek Chailert, March 28, 2011.

37. William Gasperini, "Uncle Sam's Dolphins," *Smithsonian*, September 2003.

38. John Kistler, *Animals in the Military: From Hannibal's Elephants to the Dolphins of the US Navy* (Santa Barbara, CA: ABC-CLIO, LLC, 2011), 323.

39. http://news.bbc.co.uk/2/hi/world/middle_east/670551.stm

40. Richard O'Barry with Keith Coulbourn, *Behind the Dolphin Smile: One Man's Campaign to Protect the World's Dolphins* (San Rafael, CA: Earth Aware Editions, 2012), 274.

41. David Helvarg, "Whales, Sea Lions, Dolphins Used as 'Spies' by US Navy," *The Ottawa Citizen*, May 30, 1985.

42. Richard O'Barry with Keith Coulbourn, *Behind the Dolphin Smile*, 275.

43. www.pbs.org/wgbh/pages/frontline/shows/whales/interviews/obarry1.html

44. http://dolphinproject.org/blog/post/the-navy-should-stop-using-captive-dolphins

     For the full story, see *To Free a Dolphin* by Richard O'Barry and Keith Coulbourn (Los Angeles, CA: Renaissance Books, 2000).

45. Jeanette Steel, "Navy dolphins, sea lions losing out to robots," *San Diego Union-Tribune*, November 30, 2012. www.utsandiego.com/news/2012/nov/30/navy-dolphins-losing-out-to-robots

Chapter 10

1. Scott Glover, "9th Circuit's chief judge posted sexually explicit matter on his website," *Los Angeles Times*, June 11, 2008.

2. http://definitions.uslegal.com/a/animal-sexual-abuse/

3. Correspondence with Carol Adams, August 26, 2012.

4. JR Rosenberger, *Bestiality* (Los Angeles, CA: Medco Books, 1968).

5. Debra Hassig, *The Mark of the Beast: The Medieval Bestiary in Art, Life, and Literature* (Oxford, UK: Routledge, 1999), 72.

6. Hani Miletski, *Understanding Bestiality and Zoophila* (East-West Publishing, LLC, 2002), 14.

7. EP Evans, *The Criminal Prosecution and Capital Punishment of Animals* (London, UK: William Heinemann, 1906), 147.

8. John M. Murrin, "'Things Fearful to Name': Bestiality in Colonial America," from *Pennsylvania History*, Volume 65, (Penn State University Press, 1998), 24.

9. John M. Murrin, "'Things Fearful to Name': Bestiality in Colonial America," from *Pennsylvania History*, Volume 65, 25.

10. Bestiality remained a hanging offense in England until 1861, when the death penalty was retained only for those convicted of murder, piracy, arson in the Royal Dockyards, and high treason. The punishment for bestiality was reduced to life in prison—a sentence still in effect.

11. www.pet-abuse.com/cases/10483/AZ/US/

12. www.utilitarian.net/singer/by/2001——.htm

13. *William Crawley Meets...*, BBC One, March 20, 2007. www.youtube.com/watch?v=gAhAlbsAbLM&feature=relmfu

14. Gordon R. Preece, *Rethinking Peter Singer: A Christian Critique* (Downers Grove, IL: InterVarsity Press, 2002), 25.

15. AC Kinsey, WB Pomeroy, and CE Martin, "Sexual Behavior in the Human Male," 1948, and AC Kinsey, WB Pomeroy, CE Martin, and PH Gebhard, "Sexual Behavior in the Human Female," 1953.

16. Morton Hunt, "Sexual Behavior in the 1970s," Playboy Press, 1974.

17. Thomas Francis, "Those Who Practice Bestiality Say They're Part of the Next Sexual Rights Movement," *New Times Broward-Palm Beach*, August 20, 2009.

18. Correspondence with Dr. Hani Miletski, July 22, 2012.

19. www.academia.edu/422242/The_Natural_Order_of_Disorder_Paedophilia_Incest_and_the_Normalising_Family

20. Keith Fraser, "Bestiality: Vancouver man pleads guilty, handed suspended sentence," *The Province*, October 2, 2012.

21. Josef Massen, *Zoophilie—Die sexuelle Liebe zu Tieren/Zoophilia—The Sexual Love of/for Animals* (Cologne, Germany: Pinto-Press 1994).

22. Humans have been known to suffer, as well. In an infamous 2005 case, for instance, a Seattle man died after fornicating with an Arabian stallion, who perforated his colon.

23. Helen MC Munro, "Animal sexual abuse: A veterinary taboo?" *Veterinary Journal*, Volume 172, 2006.

24. Melinda D. Merck and Doris M. Miller, "Sexual Abuse," from *Veterinary Forensics: Animal Cruelty Investigations*, second edition, edited by Melinda D. Merck (Ames, IA: John Wiley & Sons, Inc., 2013), 233.

25. Melinda D. Merck and Doris M. Miller, "Sexual Abuse," from *Veterinary Forensics*, 235.

26. PO Peretti and M. Rowan, "Zoophilia: Factors related to its sustained practice," *Panminerva Medica*, Volume 25, Issue 2, April–June, 1983.

27. www.bbc.co.uk/news/world-europe-20523950

28. Rebecca Cassidy, "Zoosex and Other Relationships with Animals," from *Transgressive Sex: Subversion and Control in Erotic Encounters*, edited by Hastings Donnan and Fiona Magowan (Oxford, UK: Berghahn Books, 2009), 108–109.

29. Sue Cross, "The Sexual Abuse of Animals is Deeply Shocking: A Case for the Vegan Option Continued," *Huffington Post*, September 19, 2012. www.huffingtonpost.co.uk/sue-cross/the-sexual-abuse-of-anima_b_1898449.html

30. Researcher Harry Harlow, whose disturbing experiments were addressed in Chapter 3, forced reluctant female monkeys to reproduce by tying them to a device he also called "the rape rack."

31. http://james-mcwilliams.com/?tag=rape-rack

32. www.vivo.colostate.edu/hbooks/pathphys/reprod/semeneval/collection.html

33. Kevin J. Stafford, "Electroejaculation: a welfare issue?" *Surveillance*, Volume 22, Number 2, January 1, 1995. See also JP Damian and R.

Ungerfeld, "The Stress Response of Frequently Electroejaculated Rams to Electroejaculation: Hormonal, Physiological, Biochemical, Haematological and Behavioural Parameters," *Reproduction in Domestic Animals*, Volume 46, Number 4, August 2011.

34. The beautiful, iridescent colors you see enlivening the feathers of wild turkeys have also been bred away by the turkey industry, because feather buds (the pinfeathers) are less noticeable under the skin of a plucked bird if they are white.

35. Peter Singer and Jim Mason, *The Way We Eat: Why Our Food Choices Matter* (Emmaus, PA: Rodale Press, 2006), 28–29.

36. Marquis de Sade, *Juliette* (New York, NY: Grove Press, 1968), 189.

37. Andrea M. Beetz, "Bestiality and Zoophilia: A Discussion of Sexual Contact with Animals," from *The International Handbook of Animal Abuse and Cruelty: Theory, Research, and Application*, edited by Frank R. Ascione (West Lafayette, IN: Purdue University Press, 2008), 204.

38. Jamie Doward and Mark Hudson, "Riddle of the horse rippers," *Observer*, July 3, 2004.

39. Alexandra Schedel-Stupperich, "Criminal Acts Against Horses: Phenomenology and Psychosocial Construct," *Dtsch Tierarztl Wochenschr*, Volume 109, Issue 3, March 2002.

40. John Robbins, *Diet for a New America: How Your Food Choices Affect Your Health, Happiness and the Future of Life on Earth* (Walpole, NH: Stillpoint Publishing, 1987), 349.

41. Hani Miletski, *Understanding Bestiality and Zoophilia*, 188–189. It is unclear if Isaac ever received the aid of a mental health professional.

42. American Psychiatric Association, *Diagnostic and Statistical Manual of Mental Disorders*, third edition, revised (Washington, DC, 1987), 405.

43. After he was caught and confessed to shooting 13 people, killing six of them, Berkowitz claimed he'd been acting under the orders of his neighbor's possessed dog.

44. Jack Levin and Arnold Arluke, "Reducing the Link's False Positive Problem," from *The Link Between Animal Abuse and Human Violence*, edited by Andrew Linzey (Eastbourne, UK: Sussex Academic Press, 2009), 165–166.

45. Lenore EA Walker, *The Battered Woman Syndrome* (New York, NY: Springer Publishing Company, 1984).

46. Carol J. Adams, "Woman-Battering and Harm to Animals," from *Animals and Women: Feminist Theoretical Explorations*, edited by Carol J. Adams and Josephine Donovan (Durham, NC: Duke University Press, 1999), 66–68.

47. Clifton P. Flynn, "Battered Women and Their Animal Companions: Symbolic Interaction Between Human and Nonhuman Animals," *Society & Animals*, Volume 8, Number 2, 2000.

48. For more information on this issue, please see *Animals and Society: An Introduction to Human-Animal Studies*, by Margo DeMello (New York, NY: Columbia University Press, 2012).

49. Clifton P. Flynn, "Women-Battering, Pet Abuse, and Human–Animal Relations," from *The Link Between Animal Abuse and Human Violence*, edited by Andrew Linzey (Eastbourne, UK: Sussex Academic Press, 2009), 117.

50. www.pandys.org/articles/sexual_assault_involving_animals.pdf

51. Adam M. Roberts, "Crush Videos," from *A Primer on Animal Rights: Leading Experts Write About Animal Cruelty and Exploitation*, edited by Kim W. Stallwood (New York, NY: Lantern Books, 2002), 148.

52. Carol J. Adams, *The Pornography of Meat* (New York, NY: The Continuum International Publishing Group, Inc., 2004), 142.

53. Nick Pisa, "Mother of three, 40, who got sexual kicks from crushing animals in her stilettos escapes jail sentence," *Daily Mail*, April 24, 2012.

54. Hearing before the Senate Judiciary Committee: "Prohibiting Obscene Animal Crush Videos in the Wake of United States v. Stevens," September 15, 2010.

55. Hearing before the Subcommittee on Crime of the Committee on the Judiciary House of Representatives, 106th Congress, First Session on HR1887 and HR1349, September 30, 1999.

56. In 1999, foot and crush video fetishist Bryan Loudermilk was spotted by friends pinned beneath the left rear tire of his parked Honda Passport. With a board and pillow positioned for comfort, it appeared

Loudermilk was a willing participant in a human crush experiment. Nevertheless, his friends called 911, and rescue workers took him to the hospital, where he died.

57. http://judiciary.house.gov/legacy/cree0930.htm

58. People v. Thomason, Case Number B139424, California Court of Appeal, 2nd District, October 30, 2000.

59. Opponents to HR 1887 said the bill would intrude on 1st Amendment guarantees of freedom of expression, constitute an unnecessary federal intrusion into state affairs, and divert prosecutors from more serious offenses. In response, Gallegly amended the bill to exempt depictions if they have "serious religious, political, scientific, educational, journalistic, historical, or artistic value."

60. www.huffingtonpost.com/geoffrey-r-stone/dog-fighting-and-the-firs_b _551138.html

61. Correspondence with Matthew Liebman, December 11, 2012.

62. Helen MC Munro, "The Battered Pet: Signs and Symptoms," from *Child Abuse, Domestic Violence, and Animal Abuse: Linking the Circles of Compassion*, edited by Frank R. Ascione and Phil Arkow (West Lafayette, IN: Purdue University Press, 1999), 200.

63. Ibid.

Index

4-D meat, 50, 159, 291
4-H (ag program), 55, 66
4-h (patch test), 155, 159
30 Rock, 427

Abbas, Fakhar, 346
Abdessemed, Adel, 406–410
Abraham 361, 377, 393
Adams, Carol, 445, 460, 462,
    471–473, 479–480, 483–484,
    486–488, 491–492, 494–495
Adams, John, 280
Adidas, 250–251
Adomeit, Lora, 590n
aerial gunning, 233–234
Afghanistan, 84, 431,
Akash Bhairab, 374
Akers, Keith, 361
Alaska, 108, 222, 232, 234, 286–287,
    401
alcoholic beverages, 51–52
Alex the camel, 350
'Ali Muttaqi, Shahid, 378–379
alligators, 99, 353–354, 389,
America's Next Top Model, 79, 114
American Animal Hospital
    Association, 236
American Anti-Vivisection Society,
    197
American Civil Liberties Union, 400
American Council of the Blind, 125

American Federation of Television
    and Radio Artists (AFTRA),
    342–343
American Humane Association
    (AHA), 340–344
American Medical Association, 11,
    194
American Museum of Natural
    History, 482
American Physiological Society, 167
*American Rodeo: From Buffalo Bill to
    Big Business*, 267
American Veterinary Medical
    Association, 20, 170, 236, 469
Amory, Cleveland, 236
Animal Aid, 62, 162, 288, 292, 356
Animal Behavior Society, 472
Animal Concern, 36
Animal Consultants International,
    170
Animal Crush Video Prohibition
    Act, 467
Animal Defenders International
    (ADI), 180, 320, 325, 343
Animal Legal Defense Fund
    (ALDF), 197, 357, 467
Animal Liberation, 6, 449, 484
Animal Liberation Front (ALF), 197,
    199
Animal Liberation NSW, 248
Animal Manifesto, The, 472, 482, 485

Animal Nepal, 431, 432, 442

Animal Protection Act, 204

Animal Revolution, 472

Animal Rights Action Network (ARAN), 405–406

Animal Rights Africa, 231

Animal Rights International, 482

Animal Rights in South Africa, 179, 204

Animal Welfare Act (AWA), 138, 158, 174, 175, 195, 196, 198

Animal Welfare Institute, 232

Animals Asia, 214, 216, 262

Animals (Scientific Procedures) Act 1986, 200, 201

Animals Australia, 54, 92, 202, 247, 264, 292, 356

Andhra Pradesh, 372, 377

Animal Place, 66

animal sacrifice, 181, 182, 359–397

animal testing, 124–212

Annals of Internal Medicine, 146

Anne the elephant, 325–326

antelope, 74, 92, 277, 334, 413

antibiotics, 10–13, 17, 21, 25, 32, 135

Any Which Way You Can, 343

aquaculture, 30–36, 159

Aquarium des Îles-de-la-Madeleine, 333

Arauz, Randall, 40

Arctic Institute of North America, 109

Arluke, Arnold, 165

arsenic, 12–13, 24, 25

artificial insemination, 4, 18, 309–311, 454–455

astaxanthin, 35

Atwood, Margaret, 124

Atwood Lawrence, Elizabeth, 270

Australian Conservation Foundation, 251

Australian Society for Kangaroos, 248

Aviagen, 15

Avisodomy, 456

baboons, 148, 179, 180, 185, 187, 191, 197

Baby Fae, 185–186

Babylon, 328, 361

Bacon, Francis, 181

Bad Hare Days, 282

Bakri Eid, 377–378

Baldwin, Aimée, 413

Baldwin, Alec, 427

balut eggs, 22–23

Band of Mercy, 199

Bannon, Marcella, 406

Barbarosa the goat, 192–193

Barker, Bob, 342–343

Barker, Nigel, 79–80

Barter, Kalista, 409

bats, 187, 243

Bauckham, Richard, 364

Baur, Gene, 7, 20

bear baiting, 345–347

bear bile, 4, 214–216, 262

Becky the elephant, 325

beetles, 51, 114

Begley, Charles, 434

Bekoff, Marc, 58, 238, 472, 474–475, 481–482, 485, 489, 494, 497

Belinda the dog, 460

Bella the dog, 75

Belle the elephant, 331

Belloni, Francis, 168

Beltsville pigs, 186

Benjamin the elephant, 298, 323

Berger, Kim, 238

Berkowitz, David, 459

Bernhard, Ken, 106

Berry, Thomas, 489

Bert, Theresa, 32

Best Friends Animal Society, 219

bestiality, 444–469

Bexell, Sarah M., 489

Bill and Lou the oxen, 58

Billy the elephant, 337

Biological Weapons Convention, 190

biomedical research, 126, 129–132, 137, 177, 178, 206

Bioresource Research Centre, 346

Birke, Lynda, 165

Bittman, Mark, 487

Blank, Jonah, 37

Blinders: The Truth Behind the Tradition, 429

Blundell, James, 182

Bobby Roberts Super Circus, 326

bobcat, 75, 251

Bonita the horse, 48

Book of the Pearl: Its History, Art,

Science and Industry, The, 112

Botswana, 106, 122

Bottomfeeder: How to Eat Ethically in a World of Vanishing Seafood, 34

bovine spongiform encephalopathy (BSE), 24–26

Boyle, Robert, 131

Bradshaw, Corey, 258

Bradshaw, Gay, 107, 338

Braithwaite, Victoria, 284

Brancheau, Dawn, 298–304

Brandeis, Louis, 8

Bratton, Chris, 409

Bravo Packing, 49–51

Brazil, 18, 41, 180, 254

breaking hens, 17–18, 456

Brenner, Malcolm, 451

Brewer, Sarina, 412

brick kilns, 431–432

Britches the monkey, 124–126

British Union for the Abolition of Vivisection (BUAV), 133, 178, 206

Broderick, Matthew, 342

Bronx Zoo, 330

Brown Dog Affair, 198

Brown, John, 496

Brush, Erik, 39

Brutal: Manhood and the Exploitation of Animals, 182

Buck and Luther the dolphins, 439–440

Budd Inlet, 308

Buddha the orangutan, 343

buffaloes, 62, 99, 375, 376

bull riding, 266, 268, 269

bullfighting, 1, 351–353

bullhook, 320, 322–326, 343

bunchers, 175

Burch, Rex, 138

Burkert, Walter, 394

Burkholder, JoAnn, 28

Burma, 403, 434, 436

Burton, John, 63

Busch Gardens Reproductive
Research Center, 310

Bush, George W., 198

Bushmeat Project, The, 257

Butler, Andrew, 411

butterflies, 227, 399

Buyukmihci, Ned, 20, 142

Bwindi Impenetrable National Park,
230

calf induction, 59–60

Calgary Stampede, 271

California State University Channel
Islands, 463

California Students' Rights Law, 166

Çalişkan, Vedat, 350

Cambodia, 106, 259, 436

camels, 328, 349, 350, 357, 426

Canadian Council on Animal Care,
202

Candomblé, 382

canned hunts, 276–279

canthaxanthin, 35

Care for the Wild, 71, 111

Carmody, John, 405

Carolina Biological Supply
Company, 174

Carr, Dawn, 29–30, 399

Carson & Barnes Circus, 324

Cassidy, Rebecca, 453

Castro, Fidel, 380

Catholicism, 369, 380, 382

cats (domesticated and feral), 2, 9,
73, 73, 76–77, 131, 134, 149, 154,
156–159, 161, 162, 164, 172,
174–177, 185, 188, 195, 196, 199,
219, 232, 275, 283, 300, 384, 395,
404, 409–412, 417, 418, 447, 448,
458, 459, 475, 482, 484

Catskill Game Farm, 333

Center of Applied Biodiversity
Informatics, 255

Central Park Zoo, 335

Cetacean Society International, 437

Chaffin, Diane, 465

Chailert, Sangduen "Lek," 436

Chapouthier, Georges, 225

Charge of the Light Brigade, The, 341

chariot races, 286, 319

Charles River Laboratories, 157, 174

Charlton, Anna, 171, 382

charreadas, 267

Check Mate the horse, 269

cheetahs, 329, 339

Cheever, Holly, 428, 430

Cheney, Dick, 275

Cheyenne Frontier Days Rodeo, 269

chickens, 3, 8–16, 20, 21, 22, 24–27,
31, 32, 55–58, 63, 96, 99, 198, 221,

283, 341, 366–368, 374, 380, 381, 386, 387, 396, 410, 421, 456, 458, 483

China, 38, 39, 41, 47, 49, 70–72, 76, 77, 96, 101, 105, 106, 107, 111,115, 190, 191, 213, 215, 216, 217, 227, 229, 237, 254, 256, 259–261, 278, 317, 321, 328, 346–349, 385, 386, 415–416, 418, 430, 446, 464, 484, 486

chiru, 92–94, 118

Christianity, 181, 359, 364, 368–371, 393, 446, 447

Christy, Bryan, 217, 231

chuckwagon racing, 271, 286

circuses, 196, 276, 318–327, 332, 334, 336, 343, 351, 356

civet cats, 377

Claire the horse, 341

Class B dealers, 174–176, 292

clams, 113

Clinton, Bill, 466

Clyde the lion, 326

Coalition to Abolish the Draize Test, 482

Coalition to Ban Horse-Drawn Carriages, 429, 442

Cochran, Thad, 197

cockroaches, 114, 169

Code of Practice for the Care and Use of Animals for Scientific Purposes, 201

Códice Gallery, 403–404

Coe, Sue, 420–421

Cole Brothers Circus, 325

Colgate-Palmolive, 158, 207

Colombia, 42, 180, 352

Common Farming Exemptions, 7–8

Compound 1080, 235–236, 244

Conrad, Peter, 398

Convention on International Trade in Endangered Species of Wild Fauna and Flora (CITES), 81, 93, 105, 106, 108, 109, 111, 177–180, 216, 229, 231, 254, 259

Copenhagen Zoo, 333

Cousteau, Jacques, 312

Cousteau, Jean-Michel, 312, 340

Couto, Richard, 48–49

Covance, 141

Cove, The, 43–44, 46, 65, 313

cows, 10, 21, 24–27, 32, 47, 52, 55, 56, 59–63, 84, 99–102, 104, 185, 232, 240, 267, 268, 283, 289, 387, 444, 447, 454, 473, 487, 492

coyotes, 75, 232–240, 251, 263, 275, 413

Creede, Susan, 464–465

Creekstone Farms Premium Beef, 26

crocodiles, 345, 353–355, 389

Cross, Sue, 454

Crowe, John, 306

Cruelty to Animals Act 1876, 198, 200, 201

crush videos, 462–467

CSI: Crime Scene Investigation, 446

Cuba, 352, 380

Cubby the bear, 277

Cutteridge, Brian, 451–452

Dahmer, Jeffrey, 459
Daily Telegraph, 370
Dakshinkali Temple, 374–375
dancing bears, 345
Darwin, Charles, 491
Datta, Sreeradha, 102
Davis, Karen, 4, 22, 56–58, 367, 368, 391, 392, 395
de Mérode, Emmanuel, 108–109
De Molina, Enrique Gomez, 413–414
de Sade, Marquis, 456
De Villiers, Rian, 163
de Vries, Lucia, 432–433
debeaking, 94, 95
deer, 74, 99, 221, 222, 234, 239, 251, 273, 274, 275, 277, 328, 333, 377, 407, 413, 417
Delvoye, Wim, 414–416
DeMello, Margo, 292
Democratic Republic of the Congo, 108, 229
denning, 233
Depictions of Animal Cruelty Act (HR 1887), 465
Derbyshire, Stuart, 138–139
DeSalvo, Albert, 459
Descartes, René, 130, 181, 448
Désir, Dowoti, 389–390
detoeing, 16, 17
Dharmananda, Subhuti, 254
Diagnostic and Statistical Manual of Mental Disorders, The, 458, 459

Diamond, Jared, 426
Directive 2010/63, 201
Do Fish Feel Pain?, 284
Dr. Hadwen Trust for Humane Research, 133
dog racing, 290–292, 296
dog sled racing, 286–288, 292, 294–295
dogs, 2, 9, 65, 72–78, 99, 127, 129–131, 143, 145, 151–154, 156–159, 161, 167–168, 170, 171, 173–176, 182–185, 188–189, 192, 194–196, 198, 199, 205, 219, 222, 227, 232, 235, 241–242, 247, 251, 274, 275, 279, 281–283, 286–288, 290–292, 294, 296, 300, 324, 337, 341, 345–347, 351, 357, 382, 384, 386, 388, 403–406, 409, 410, 411, 426, 431, 446, 447–449, 451, 458–461, 465, 466, 473, 475, 484
Dolly the sheep, 184–185
dolphin-assisted therapy (DAT), 316–318
Dolphin Discovery, 318
Dolphin Project, The, 313, 357, 443
dolphins, 2, 3, 4, 41–46, 65, 300, 305, 311–318, 339, 340, 356, 426, 436–440, 443, 451
donkeys, 67, 426, 431–432, 441, 442, 446
Donovan, Josephine, 472
Douglass, Frederick, 496
Dove, Rick, 28
down, 94–97

Doyle, Blayne, 320–321

Draize, John H., 154

Draize tests, 151, 153–155, 482

Droichead Arts Centre, 404–406

ducks, 22, 23, 55, 61, 94–96, 273, 275, 374

Dunayer, Joan, 182, 183

Duncan, Ian, 16

Durgä, 373–374

Dzangha-Sangha National Park, 257

East International, 71

Easter, 88, 243, 244, 370

Eating Animals, 6

Ebionites, 363

Edenmont, Nathalia, 410–412

education, use of animals in, 58, 126, 160–173, 208–210

Efford, John, 213

Ehrlich, Richard, 374

Eight Belles, 288–289

Einstein, Albert, 205, 422

EleAid, 434

electroejaculation, 455

Elephant Nature Park, 436, 443

elephants, 1, 3, 99, 104–108, 110–112, 122, 220, 221, 222, 228, 257, 262, 273, 298, 314, 315, 319–332, 334, 336–338, 343, 345, 425–426, 433–436, 441, 443

Elixir Sulfanilamide, 135–136

Elizabeth I, Queen, 190

Elizabeth II, Queen, 80

Elvira the horse, 269

Emory University, 300

Empty Cages: Facing the Challenge of Animal Rights, 176

Endangered Species Act of 1973, 331

Engel Jr., Mylan, 472, 475–479, 482–483, 485–486, 489–491, 497–499

Enoch, Janet, 279

Equal Rights Amendment, 492

Ethologists for the Ethical Treatment of Animals, 472

Ettlin, Rex, 338

Eukanuba, 158, 207

European Food Safety Authority, 96

Evans, Chris, 9

Evaristti, Marco, 401–402

Everglades Alligator Farm, 345

Fadiman, Anne, 386, 388

Farm Sanctuary, 64, 66, 407

Farm Sanctuary: Changing Hearts and Minds About Animals and Food, 7, 20

Fast Food Nation, 6

Fauna Foundation, 132

Fawcett, Robert, 287

FDA, 12, 13, 25, 26, 135–137, 141, 154

Fear Factor, 22

feathers, 4, 32, 94–100, 262, 377, 412

Feld Entertainment, 323

Feld, Kenneth, 324

Feminist Care Tradition in Animal Ethics, The, 472

Ferdin, Pamelyn, 324

Ferdinand the horse, 290

FFA, 55–56, 58, 59, 66

Finlay, Victoria, 112–113

fish, 2, 27–38, 41, 42, 49, 51, 81, 82, 134, 151, 169, 188, 198, 200, 224, 253, 254, 262, 265, 283–285, 316, 384, 401–403, 475

fishing, 29, 30, 40–42, 81, 82, 94, 98, 224, 246, 254, 255, 261, 283–285, 307, 383

Fitzgerald, James, 439

Fitzgerald, John, 282

Flicka, 342

Flipper, 45, 312, 315, 316, 438

Flosint, 137

Flynn, Clifton, 460–461

Flynn, Errol, 341

Foer, Jonathan Safran, 6

Food Animal Concerns Trust (FACT), 25–26

Food, Drug, and Cosmetic Act of 1938, 135

Food Empowerment Project (foodis-power.org), 65, 264, 397

Food Inc., 6

Forel, Elizabeth, 429

Forks Over Knives, 6

Forward, 366

Fossey, Dian, 230

Foster, Sarah, 254

Fowler, Kate, 162

Fox, Camilla, 232

Fox, Michael, 382

foxes, 68, 70, 72, 86, 233, 241, 249, 251, 252, 253, 274, 281, 282

Fracastoro, Girolamo, 446

Francione, Gary, 171, 383, 494, 499

Franklin, H. Bruce, 38

Fredriksson, Kristine, 267

Free Willy, 305

Friedlander, Lester, 45

Friedrich, Bruce, 102

Friends of Animals, 333

Frisco, Tim, 320–322, 324–325

Frog Girl: The Jenifer Graham Story, 166

frogs, 126, 161, 162, 165, 166, 172–174, 177, 258, 289, 410

fur, 68–89, 116–120, 250, 252, 262, 273, 382, 383, 401, 417–418, 420, 489, 490

Fur Council of Canada, 85

Gabon, 134

Gadhimai Jatra Mela, 375

Gadhimai temple, 375

Gallegly, Elton, 465, 467

Gandhi, Maneka, 101, 376, 377, 418

Garrett, Howard, 300, 302

Garrison, William Lloyd, 496

Gatorland, 354

Gawthorpe, Richard, 5

Geiger, Abraham, 364

Gentle Jungle, 343

Gentry, Troy, 277

Germany, 82, 144, 317, 334, 352, 453, 457

Gibson, Rick, 422–423

Gillard, Julia, 91

Goat Lab, 192

goats, 47, 55, 61, 63, 99, 129, 134,
185, 188, 192, 221, 232, 235, 328,
341, 359, 370–374, 376–379, 381,
389, 406, 417, 446, 447, 458

Gold, Jared, 114

Goldsberry, Don, 306–308

Golu Mian the goat, 377

González-Wippler, Migene, 384

Goobers the baboon, 185–186

Goodall, Jane, 472

gorillas, 134, 137, 228–230, 256, 328,
329

Gourmet, 28

Graham, Bill, 252

Graham, Jenifer, 166

Graham, Mark, 384

Granger, Thomas, 447

Great American Circus, 320

Great Ape Project, The, 449,

Great Ape Protection and Cost
Savings Act, 137

Great Easter Bunny Hunt, 243–244

Greek, Jean Swingle, 137, 145

Greek, Ray, 137, 145, 146, 148, 149,
183, 205

Green Mountain College, 57–58

Greenaway, Angie, 180

Greenland, 79, 109

Greger, Michael, 25, 27

Grescoe, Taras, 34

Griffin, Ted, 305–307

Grizzly the dog, 222

guinea pigs, 134, 151, 154, 169, 174,
188, 196, 462

Gujarat, 101, 372

Guns, Germs, and Steel, 426

Gupta, Sanjukta, 373

Gus the bear, 335

Hajj, 378–379

Hamilton, Healy, 255

Hamilton, Peter, 422–423

Hancocks, David, 331

Hannibal, 426

Hansen, Lawrence, 147

Happy the elephant, 330

Harden, Chad, 271

Harned, Pat, 323

hare coursing, 281–282, 295

hares, 281–283, 295, 388

Harlow, Harry, 124, 127

Harnell, Boyd, 43

Hart, Gale, 420

Have Trunk Will Travel, 343

Hays, Jack, 267

Heifer International, 61

Helms, Jesse, 197

Herzog, Harold, 143, 471, 473–474,
480, 484, 493, 495

Hillside Animal Sanctuary, 47, 64

Himal the mule, 433

Hinduism, 101, 102, 360, 371–377,
390, 418

hippopotamus, 108, 109, 220, 333,
345, 413

Hirsch, Meir, 367

Hirst, Damien, 398–401, 412

Hmong, 385-388, 394

Hobbit, The, 340, 341

hog dogging, 242

Holmes, Kate, 281

Holzer, Henry Mark, 383, 384

Homo Necans, 394

Honker the reindeer, 277

Hooke, Robert, 130–131

Horowitz, Jonathan, 421–422

horse bucking, 266–269

horse-drawn carriages, 1, 427–431

horse racing, 65, 288–290, 295, 342, 454

horse ripping, 457

horses, 45, 47–51, 65–67, 99, 104, 134, 185, 189, 196, 240, 265–271, 277, 281, 286, 288–290, 295, 296, 324, 334, 341, 342, 344, 348, 349, 352, 406, 408, 417, 425–432, 441, 442, 447, 454, 457, 458

Hot Shot, 268, 269

House Rabbit Society, 211

How Shelter Pets are Brokered for Experimentation: Understanding Pound Seizure, 176

Howse, Christopher, 370

Hugo the orca, 309

Hugo, François, 81–83

Human Rights Watch, 116

Humane Methods of Slaughter Act, 8, 45, 198

humane myth, 21

Humane Research Australia, 147, 209

Humane Society International (HSI), 25, 65, 76, 251, 263, 304, 358

Humane Society of Berks County, 280

Humane Society of the United States, The (HSUS), 14, 34, 76, 77, 84, 134, 197, 277, 278, 347, 357, 382, 404

Humane Society University, 472

Hungary, 96

Hunt, Helen, 342

Hunt, Morton, 450

hunting, 1, 40, 44, 73, 93, 108, 109, 218, 223, 239–252, 256, 260, 272–282, 293, 333, 334, 383, 394, 467

Hunting Act 2004, 281

Huntingdon Life Sciences, 187

Huskisson, Mike, 199

Hutchins, Michael, 230

Iams, 158, 207

Iceland, 223, 298, 305, 308

Iditarod, 286–287, 294

Igualdad Animal (Animal Equity), 352, 358

Imperial Chemical Industries, 199

In Defense of Animals, 407

India, 18, 62, 67, 92, 93, 101–102, 105, 115, 116, 118, 163, 190, 205, 220, 345, 360, 371–373, 375, 376, 390, 402, 416, 418–420, 430, 431, 433,

436, 441, 446, 447, 484, 485

Indonesia, 228, 254, 258, 260, 348, 403, 413, 436

Inside Edition, 49

Inside SEAL Team Six: My Life and Missions with America's Elite Warriors, 192

Institute for Cetacean Research (ICR), 224

Institutional Animal Care and Use Committee (IACUC), 141–144, 196

International Fund for Animal Welfare (IFAW), 217, 225, 229, 263

International Hunter Education Association, 275

International Union for Conservation of Nature (IUCN), 109

International Whaling Commission (IWC), 223

Iosca, Paolo, 463

Iraq, 105, 193, 437

Irish Independent, 405

Islam, 346, 377–379

Israel, 41, 150, 163, 191, 317, 362, 366, 396, 431,

Italian Anti-Vivisection League, 463

Italy, 49, 118, 119, 187, 352, 425, 430, 446, 463, 464

ivory, 104–112, 122, 220, 227, 262, 377

Jackson, Peter, 341

Jacobs, Arnold, 365

Jamieson, Dale, 332, 338, 339

Janet the elephant, 320–322

Japan, 26, 36, 42–46, 49, 105, 106, 112, 174, 187, 217, 223–226, 228, 251, 254, 261, 290, 311, 313, 314, 317, 346, 438

Jaws, 245, 246, 318

Jean, Michaëlle, 80

Jeannie the chimpanzee, 132

Jerusalem Society for the Prevention of Cruelty to Animals, 367

Jesse James, 341

Jesus, 362–364, 368–371, 488

Jewel the elephant, 337

Jewels: A Secret History, 112

Jewish Museum, 368

Jiménez, Guillermo Vargas ("Habacuc"), 403–404

Johns Hopkins University, 148

Johnson, Ken, 410

Johnson, Lyndon, 195

Johnson, Severin, 100

Johnson, Stanley, 349

Jones, Hardy, 44

Jones, Mark, 111

Jones, Pattrice, 58

Judaism, 360–368, 370

Just Food: Where Locavores Get It Wrong and How We Can Truly Eat Responsibly, 472

Kafka, Franz, 490

Kali, 371–374

Kalighat Temple, 371–372

Kangaroo Industry Association of Australia (KIAA), 247, 251

Kangaroo Management Program, New South Wales Department of Environment and Conservation, 251

kangaroos, 102–104, 122, 219, 247–251, 263, 264, 277, 339, 351

kapparot (kapores), 365–368, 394, 396

karakul lambs, 83–84, 118

Kariv, Gilad, 366

Karyn the cat, 176

Karzai, Hamid, 83

Kathy the dolphin, 312–313

Katina the orca, 304

Keefover-Ring, Wendy, 234

Keiko the orca, 305

Keith, Ashley, 287

Kellert, Stephen, 340

Kennedy, Anthony, 360, 381

Kentucky Derby, 288, 290

Kenya, 105, 106, 220

Khan, Kareem, 377

Kheel, Marti, 272

Killer Whale People, The, 306

killing tournaments, 239–247

King Kong, 446

Kinsey, Alfred, 450

Kinship to Mastery, 340

Kinsley, David, 373

Kiok, Michael, 453

Kipling, Rudyard, 325

Kirby, Dustin, 193

Kirkman, Stephen, 81

Knight, Andrew, 168–170

Kojima, Hisayoshi, 226–227

Kokamenko, Omer, 257

Kozinski, Alex, 444–445

Krungsee the elephant, 435

Kumar, Ashok, 419

Kunstraum Dornbirn Gallery, 402

Kunz, George Frederick, 112

Kürten, Peter, 459

Laboratory Animal Welfare Act of 1966, 195

Laboratory for Experimental Medicine and Surgery in Primates, 132

Ladakh, 92, 93

Laidlaw, Rob, 330

Lakshmana Temple, 447

Laos, 106, 179, 259, 385, 387, 388, 433, 434, 436

Larry the lamb, 5–6

Larson, Gary, 410

Lash Lure, 150

Laule, Gail, 322

Lavigne, David, 81

Lawler, Kathy, 320

Lawson, Peggy, 270

LD50 test, 151–153, 200, 205

League Against Cruel Sports, 291, 293

Learning without Killing: A Guide to Conscientious Objection, 170

leather, 2, 99–104, 121

Lee, Nachee, 387

leopards, 218, 220, 222, 227, 277, 328, 329, 345, 389

Levi, Edward H., 467

Lewin, Brent, 434–436

Li, Zhang, 107

Liddle, Rod, 281

Liebman, Matthew, 467

Lifeforce Foundation, 422

Lincoln, Bruce, 371, 394

Linzey, Andrew, 362, 364, 370, 371

lions, 233, 273, 277–279, 319, 326, 328, 333, 334, 339, 345, 389, 444

Lipman, Steve, 366

live export, 52–54, 66, 90, 92, 117, 421

live plucking, 95–97

Living Among Meat Eaters, 471, 487

Lizard King, The, 217, 231

lobsters, 28–29, 34, 51, 262, 384

Lolita the orca, 309

Los Angeles Zoo, 337

Lower, Richard, 131

Luck, 342

Ludwig, Edward, 338

Luke, Brian, 182, 391–394

Lukumí Babalú Ayé, Church of the, 380–382

Lulu the elephant, 1

M-44 device, 235

macaques, 124, 125, 178, 179, 218

Mack, Grant, 125

madagh, 369

Madison, James, 495

Madonna, 83

Magat, Margaret, 23

Maggie the elephant, 1

Mahabharata, The, 418

Mailatheppa, 372–373

Mallinson, Brian, 5–6

mammoths, 110–111

Mann, Don, 192–193

Manoogian, Nerses, 369

maquech (makech), 114

Mara the elephant, 1

Marcellini, Dale, 339

Marine Mammal Program, 436, 438, 439

Marine Mammal Protection Act of 1972, 307, 339

Marineland, 45, 312, 314

Marino, Lori, 300, 302, 310, 314, 315, 317, 339, 437

Mars (food company), 158, 208

Marston, Helen, 147

Martin, Chryssee, 111

Martin, Esmond, 111

Martínez, Javier, 351

Mason, Georgia, 329

Mason, Jim, 17, 219, 455, 456

Massen, Josef, 452

Masson, Jeffrey, 32

maternal deprivation, 124, 127

Mathews, Dan, 70

Mauritius, 178

McBean Galleries, 408

McCartney, Stella, 83

McClanahan, Rue, 482

McCollum, Bill, 464

McHugh-Smith, Jan, 407

McWilliams, James, 14, 58, 471, 474, 480–481, 484–485, 488–489, 493–494, 495–497

Meireles, Cildo, 402–403

Meleshkevich, Irina, 412

menhaden, 36–38

Merced, Jose, 381

Merck & Co., 136

Merck, Melinda, 453

Mercy For Animals (MFA), 20, 22, 30

Meyer, Peter, 402

Miami Seaquarium, 45, 309, 313

mice, 2, 127, 134, 136, 142, 145, 146, 148, 151, 152, 154, 174, 185, 186, 188, 197, 198, 200, 232, 410, 411, 463, 465

Michael, Mike, 165

Mikkelsen, Paula, 113

Miletski, Hani, 451, 457, 458

Milgram, Stanley, 476–477, 479

Miller, Doris, 453

Miller, Thomas, 115–116

Million Years Stone Park & Pattaya Crocodile Farm, 354

Millman, Suzanne, 15

Ministry of Defense, 188

mink, 69, 70, 72, 77, 86, 88, 417, 418

Minor, Karel, 280

Misha and Tom the dolphins, 311

Mizuhara, Val, 408

Modern Savage, The, 472, 484

Modular Immune In vitro Construct, 140

Mogadishu, 106

mongooses, 417–420

Monk, Martin, 163

Monster Shark Tournament, 245

More Than a Meal: The Turkey in History, Myth, Ritual, and Reality, 392

Morris, Desmond, 74

Moss, Donny, 429

Most Important Fish in the Sea: Menhaden and America, The, 38

Moua, Chia Thai, 387–388

Mowat, Farley, 79

mules, 185, 189, 431–433, 441, 442

mulesing, 16, 90–92, 117

Mullahs on the Mainframe, 377

Munro, Helen, 452

Munro, Ralph, 308

Murdoch University, 168–170

Museum of National Identity, 404

MV *Cormo Express*, 52

Myanmar Timber Enterprise, 434

Myers, Kathleen, 417

Nakai the orca, 309

Nalani the orca, 304

Namibia, 78, 80–83, 84, 106, 122

narwhals, 109–110

Nash, Ellen-Cathryn, 49–50

Nathanson, David, 317

National Animal Ethics Advisory Committee, 203

National Anti-Vivisection Society, 198, 209

National Bio and Agro-Defense Facility (NBAF), 190–191

National Cattlemen's Beef Association, 26

National Center for Prosecution of Animal Abuse, 176

National Institute of Environmental Health Sciences, 141

National Institutes of Health, 143, 147, 206

National Primate Research Center, 128

National Resource Council, 140

National Science Foundation, 143, 161

National Zoo, 339

Nebuchadnezzar II, King, 328

Nietzsche, Friedrich, 425, 426

Nepal, 92, 374–376, 420, 431–432, 442

Nestlé, 158, 207, 208

Netherlands, The, 72, 82, 163, 187, 321, 352

Network for Animals, 349

New Iberia Research Center, 133

New York Aquarium, 312, 315

New York Jewish Week, 366

New York Medical College, 168

New York Times, The, 288, 289, 316, 384, 410, 425, 466

Newcomer, Ed, 227–228

Newkirk, Ingrid, 91, 299

Nicholls, David, 249–250

Nicklen, Paul, 110

night monkeys (owl monkeys), 180–181

Nixon, Richard, 235

Nolan, Seamus, 404–406

NozBonz, 15

O'Barry, Richard "Ric," 44–45, 65, 312–314, 356, 438–440

O'Doherty, Ian, 405

O'Meara, Edmund, 131

O'Neill, Brendan, 68

Observer, 398

Occupational Safety and Health Administration (OSHA), 303, 304

Omak Stampede, 265

Omak Suicide Race, 265–266

Oogjes, Glenys, 54, 92, 247

Operation Crossroads, 188

Opren, 137

orangutans, 134, 137, 256, 343, 347–348, 357

Orca Network, 300

orcas (killer whales), 298–311, 313,

Ornelas, Lauren, 95, 250

Orwell, George, 471

Orzechowski, Karol, 179

Otterness, Tom, 406

Ouida (Maria Louise Ramé), 182

Oxfam, 67

Oxford University, 329,

Oyagak, Herman A., 108

oysters, 33, 34, 112–113, 122

Pace, Henry, 5

Packy the elephant, 331

Page, Andrew, 347

Pakistan, 92, 345, 347, 431, 441

Palin, Sarah, 234

pangolins, 258–259

Papastavrou, Vassili, 225

Parker, Elizabeth, 26

Patarroyo, Manuel Elkin, 180–181

Patrick-Goudreau, Colleen, 49, 397, 433

Patterson, Gareth, 278

Payne, Nicole, 251

Payne, Steven, 324

Paz, Octavio, 444

pearls, 112–114, 122

Penn Cove, 306–307, 309

People for Animals (PFA), 101, 118, 376, 395, 418, 420, 441

People for the Ethical Treatment of Animals (PETA), 29, 55, 66, 69, 70, 71, 76, 77, 91–92, 102, 156–158, 174, 192, 196, 258, 299, 324, 351, 357, 367, 376, 395, 399, 407, 411

Performing Animals Welfare Society, 1, 357,

Pepper the dog, 194–195

pet food, 37, 50, 81, 103, 157–160, 207, 208, 290, 291, 306

Pfiesteria piscicida, 27–28

Phalana, Victor, 370

Phelps, Norm, 182, 363

Philippines, The, 22, 348, 349, 464

Phillips, Allie, 176

Physicians Committee for Responsible Medicine (PCRM), 167, 173, 184

Pickover, Michelè, 179, 204, 231

pig dogging, 242

pigeon shoots, 279–281

pigs, 1, 10, 12, 13, 15–16, 26, 32, 49, 55, 58, 59, 61, 63, 99, 104, 129, 134, 151, 154, 161, 163–165, 169, 171, 172, 185, 186, 187, 188, 192, 193, 241–243, 283, 289, 355, 357, 384, 385–387, 407, 414–416, 417, 447, 448, 454, 466, 477–478, 492

Pippin, John, 183–184

Piraro, Dan, 420, 422

Plous, Scott, 143, 197

Poland, 96, 192

Pollan, Michael, 487

Politics of the Pasture: How Two Oxen Sparked a National Discussion about Eating Animals, The, 472

Polo, Marco, 328

Pornography of Meat, The, 445, 462

Portland Zoo, 331

Porton Down, 188, 191

Portugal, 353

post-traumatic stress disorder (PTSD), 287, 336

pound seizure, 175–177

Prairie Dog Coalition, 241

prairie dogs, 240–241, 247

Pretoma (Programa Restauración de Tortugas Marinas), 40, 65

Prevention of Cruelty to Animals

Act, 372

Principles of Humane Experimental Technique, The, 138

Proceedings of the National Academy of Sciences, 145

Procter & Gamble, 158, 207

product testing, 126, 149–160, 201, 207–208

Professional Laboratory Research Services, 156–157

Professional Rodeo Cowboys Association (PRCA), 267–269

Project Coyote, 232, 263

Project Seahorse, 254, 264

Project X, 342

Psihoyos, Louie, 43, 46, 313

Qalandar, 345–346

Quinn, Christine, 429

rabbits, 52, 54, 55, 61, 70, 74, 77, 88–89, 134, 151, 153–156, 164, 171, 174, 175, 185, 188, 189, 196, 205, 208, 211, 232, 239, 243–245, 251, 282, 283, 410, 411, 412, 417, 448, 456, 458, 463, 482

Rajdevi Panchawati Temple, 374

Rainbow the pony, 341

Ramirez, Richard, 459

Randall, Dick, 74

rape rack, 55, 454

Rashi, 368

rats, 3, 134, 136, 145, 148, 151, 153, 154, 161, 169, 171, 172, 173, 174,

185, 188, 197, 198, 422, 465

Rayner, John, 365

Redington, Joe, 287

Reino Aventura, 305

Reiss, Diana, 315

Rider, Tom, 298

Riesterer, Elke, 435

Rembrandt, 446

Replace, Reduce, Refine, 138–141, 203

Resnick, Joseph, 195

Ricaurte, George, 148

Rieder, Arnold, 236

Ringling Brothers and Barnum & Bailey Circus, 323, 324, 326

Rise of the Planet of the Apes, 344

Roach, Steve, 25

Roberts, Bobby, 326

Roberts, Moira, 326

Robertson, Jim, 274

Robbins, John, 457

Robins, John, 36

Robinson, Jill, 213–215

Rocky the kangaroo, 351

rodeos, 196, 265, 266–271, 286, 292, 293, 342

Rollin, Bernard, 153

Roodeplaat Research Laboratories (RRL), 191

Rose, Naomi, 304, 310

Rossell, Matt, 128, 143, 252, 253

Rossiter, William, 437

Royal College of Veterinary Surgeons, 469

Royal Society for the Prevention of
  Cruelty to Animals (RSPCA), 199,
  200, 403, 430
Royal Society of London, 130
Roxarsone, 13
Runkle, Nathan, 22
Running Free, 344
Running W, 341, 344
Russell, George, 165
Russell, WMS, 138
Russia, 70, 72, 74, 78, 83, 109, 110,
  112, 190, 191, 237, 317, 417, 418,
  437, 485
Rutgers Animal Rights Law Center,
  382
Ryder, Richard, 150, 183, 199, 200,
  472, 479, 483, 486, 491, 494, 499

sable, 69, 70, 88
*Sacred Cows and Golden Geese: The
  Human Cost of Experiments on
  Animals*
*Sacrifice: How Scientific Experiments
  Transform Animals and People, The*,
  145
Sædyrasafnid Aquarium, 308
Safari Club International, 277
Safari World, 347–348
Sainath, Palagummi, 61–62
St. Augustine Alligator Farm, 354
salmon, 31–35
San Antonio Zoo, 333
San Diego Zoo, 333, 339
San Francisco Art Institute (SFAI),

  406–407
San Jose Mercury News, 334
*Sanctuary Almanac: State of Nature,
  State of Mind*, 117
Santería, 360, 379–382, 384, 394
Santería: The Religion, 384
Save Animals From Exploitation
  (SAFE), 60, 244, 293, 321, 357
SaveABunny, 211
Schaller, George, 93, 230
Schiltz, Patric, 145
Schlosser, Eric, 6
Schwab, Kellogg, 12–13
Screen Actors Guild (SAG), 342, 343
Scully, Matthew, 364, 384
sea lions, 81, 298, 327, 339, 436, 437,
  440
Sea Shepherd Conservation Society,
  224, 263
sea urchins, 261–262
seahorses, 253–255, 262, 264
Sealand of the Pacific, 302, 308
seals, 35, 36, 78–83, 213, 247, 250,
  306, 327, 333
Seattle Public Aquarium, 305
Seattle Times, The, 332
SeaWorld, 45, 298–304, 306–310, 318
SeaWorld vs. OSHA, 304
Seeton, Johnna, 279
Segal, John L., 337
Sellar, John M., 228–229
Serengeti Park, 334
shahtoosh, 92–94, 118
Shamu the orca, 306

Shanghai Contemporary Art Fair, 416

Shapiro, Paul, 14

SHARK (Showing Animals Respect and Kindness), 267, 269, 279, 280, 293

shark finning, 38–41, 64–65

sharks, 42, 46, 99, 161, 245–247, 253, 262, 398

Shaw, Hank, 272–273

Shawcross, Arthur, 459

Shedd Aquarium, 316

sheep, 6, 16, 24, 26, 32, 47, 52–55, 63, 66, 74, 84, 85, 89–92, 99, 103, 134, 169, 184, 185, 188, 232, 234, 235, 237, 238, 247, 277, 283, 341, 361, 362, 363, 379, 381, 389, 399, 407, 417, 420, 421, 446, 447, 454, 458, 459

shokushu goukan (tentacle porn), 446

Shrestha, Tirtha Bahadur, 375

silk, 115–116, 123

silkworm, 115–116

Simba the chimpanzee, 133–134

Singer, Peter, 6, 113, 448–449, 455–456, 484

Sinha, Samir, 419

Siperstein-Cook, Laurie, 96

Sixth Extinction, The, 39

slow lorises, 228

Smith, Betsy, 317

Smith, Gregory H., 87

Smithers, Bart, 83

Smoothie the horse, 429

snakes, 49, 99, 191, 218, 314, 318, 339, 389, 410, 418, 446

Sniffy the rat, 422–423

Society for the Protection of Animal Rights in Egypt, 432, 442

Society for the Study of Ethics and Animals, 472

Sokolowsky, Alexander, 328

Solomon, King, 361

Some We Love, Some We Hate, Some We Eat: Why It's So Hard to Think Straight About Animals, 471

Sorvino, Amanda, 49–50

Sorvino, Paul, 49

South Africa, 74, 80, 82, 100, 106, 122, 162, 179, 180, 190, 191, 204, 237, 266, 278–279, 291, 334, 369

Southern Ocean Whale Sanctuary, 223

Spain, 1, 137, 187, 237, 266, 267, 351, 358, 485

speciesism, 199, 472, 491, 494

Spencer, George, 448

Spindel, Eliot, 143

Spira, Henry, 153, 384, 482

Spirit Catches You and You Fall Down, The, 386

Spotty the horse, 429

Stallwood, Kim, 276

Stanton, Elizabeth Cady, 491

Stapleton, Jim, 117

steer roping, 270

stereotypies, 15, 89, 127, 216,

335–337

Sterling-Krank, Lindsey, 241

Stewart, Jimmy, 274

Strader, Gary, 233–234

Strawberry Fudge the horse, 269

Stevens, Robert, 466

Stevenson, Charles Hugh, 112

Stowe, Harriet Beecher, 496

sulfanilamide, 135–136

Supreme Court, 8, 360, 380–381, 383, 466–467

surplus animals, 331–334

Sutterby, Nikki, 248

Swain, Rick, 84–85

Sweet and Sour the horse, 269

Swimmer Nullification Program, 439

Swiss Animal Protection, 71

Switzerland, 163

Tai the elephant, 343

Taiji, 4, 42–44, 313–315, 438

Taku the orca, 304, 309

Tanzania, 105

Tapp, Nicholas, 387

Tarantino, Quentin, 344

Taronga Western Plains Zoo, 334

Tate Modern, 399, 402

Taylor, Michael, 169–170

Temple of King Solomon, 361

Texas State University–San Marcos, 471

Thailand, 1, 218, 330, 347, 348, 354, 403, 435, 436, 443,

Thanksgiving, 391–393, 397

Thieme, Marianne, 379

Thomason, Gary, 465

Thoreau, Henry David, 265

Tibet, 92–93

Tier 1 Group, 192

Tilikum the orca, 298–304, 308, 309, 320

Tina the elephant, 337

Tintle, Jodie Ann, 299

Tlhagale, Buti, 369–370

Tongkum the elephant, 436

Tox21, 141

traditional Chinese medicine, 213, 215–216, 254

TRAFFIC India, 419

Transgressive Sex: Subversion and Control in Erotic Encounters, 453

Trapholt Art Museum, 401–402

trapping, 73–76, 85–88, 94, 117, 126, 178–180, 220–222, 235–238, 244, 251, 263, 280, 308, 345, 417, 459

Traveling Exotic Animal Protection Act (HR 3359), 327, 356

Trevan, JW, 152

Tyler, Andrew, 62, 63

Tyler, Steven, 98

Tufts University Cummings School of Veterinary Medicine, 170

tuna, 34, 36–37, 41–42, 262, 285

Turkey, 82, 317, 349

turkeys, 16–18, 24, 58, 239, 277, 391–395, 447, 454, 455–456

turtles, 40, 42, 161, 177, 259–261, 381, 473

Udall, Mark, 234

Ufuk the camel, 350

Uganda, 105, 230, 336

Uncaged, 158, 187

Understanding Bestiality and Zoophilia, 451

United Poultry Concerns, 4, 22, 56, 57, 64, 367, 395

United States Department of Agriculture (USDA), 46, 47, 158, 174, 175, 186, 192, 195, 197, 232, 233, 234, 237, 238, 323

United States v. Stevens, 466

University of California–Davis, 21

University of California–Riverside, 115, 124–125

University of California–San Diego, 147

University of California–San Francisco, 148

University of Chicago, 467

University of Colorado–Boulder, 238, 472

University of Guelph, 15, 16

University of Illinois College of Veterinary Medicine, 170–171

University of Kent, 335

University of London, 198

University of Wisconsin–Madison, 127

US Army Medical Research Institute of Infectious Diseases (USAMRIID), 190

US Department of Defense, 193

US Navy, 436, 440

Uzbekistan, 84, 116

Valle, Jose, 352–353

Vanderbrook, Chedva, 367

Vegfam, 67

Ventre, Jeff, 302–303

vervet monkeys, 179

Veterinary Journal, The, 452, 472

Vick, Michael, 410

Victims of Science, 199

VINE Sanctuary, 58, 64

Vioxx, 136

Virunga National Park, 108

Visakha Society for Protection and Care of Animals, 376

Visser, Margaret, 393

Viva!, 95, 250

Viva! USA, 94, 95, 97

Volkan, Kevin, 463

Voodoo, 389–390

Wagman, Bruce, 380–381

Wallace, David Foster, 28–29, 34

walruses, 108, 437

Walter and McBean Galleries, 408

Ward, Chip, 237–238

Warner Bros., 305

Washington, Booker T., 398

Water for Elephants, 343

Way We Eat: Why Our Food Choices Matter, The, 455

Watson, Paul, 266, 247

Webb, Stephen, 363

Weinreb, Tzvi Hersh, 366
Weintraub, Aviva, 368
Weir, Johnny, 68, 69
Wetterling, Björn, 410–411
Whale and Dolphin Conservation
   Society, 311
Whiting Farms, 98–99
Whittaker, Margaret, 322
Why Animals Matter, 56, 292
Wickens, Jim, 83
Wilberforce, William, 430
WildAid, 93
WildEarth Guardians, 234, 235
Wildlife Conservation Nepal, 420
Wildlife Conservation Society, 109
Wildlife Services, 233–239, 413
Wildlife Society, The, 230
Wildlife Trust of India (WTI), 419
Williams, Erin, 55–56, 292
Winnebago, 388
wolves, 234, 235, 251
Wonder Dust, 324
Woods, Jenny, 399
wool, 52, 66, 84, 89–94, 117–118
Worden, Amy, 279
World Conservation Union, 107
World Land Trust, 63
World Society for the Protection of
   Animals (WSPA), 404

World Wildlife Fund (WWF), 31,
   118, 294, 419
wound labs, 191–193, 205

xenotransplantation, 185–187

Yale University, 340
Year of Living Biblically, The, 365
Yebron, Dino, 349
Yoruba, 379–380
Young, Peter, 72
Yukon Quest, 286, 295

Zaikowski, Carolyn, 454
Zambia, 105
Zbinden, Gerhard, 153
Zelda the cow, 56
Zimbabwe, 106, 122
Zimmerman, M., 97
Zoocheck, 330, 357
zoophilia, 450–453
zoos (bestiality), 450, 451
zoos (animal prisons), 1, 32, 44, 49,
   50, 51, 54, 177, 196, 217, 218, 231,
   252, 276, 307, 311, 314, 315, 319,
   321, 322, 327–340, 347, 348, 354,
   356
zoosadism, 456–458

About the Author

Mark Hawthorne is the author of *Striking at the Roots: A Practical Guide to Animal Activism* (Changemakers Books), which empowers people around the world to get active for animals. He gave up eating meat after an encounter with one of India's many cows in 1992 and became an ethical vegan a decade later. His writing has been featured in *Vegan's Daily Companion* (Quarry Books) and in the anthologies *Stories to Live By: Wisdom to Help You Make the Most of Every Day* and *The Best Travel Writing 2005: True Stories from Around the World* (both from Travelers' Tales). Mark is a frequent contributor to *VegNews* magazine. He and his wife Lauren live in California. You'll find him tweeting @markhawthorne.

MarkHawthorne.com